CONTEMPORARY SOCIAL PROBLEMS

CONTEMPORARY SOCIAL PROBLEMS

VINCENT N. PARRILLO
JOHN STIMSON
WILLIAM PATERSON COLLEGE OF
NEW JERSEY

ARDYTH STIMSON
KEAN COLLEGE OF NEW JERSEY

John Wiley & Sons
New York   Chicester   Brisbane
Toronto   Singapore

Text and cover design: Karin Gerdes Kincheloe
Cover illustration: Karin Sullivan

Library of Congress Cataloging in Publication Data:

Parrillo, Vincent N.
    Contemporary social problems.

    Includes index.
    1. Sociology. 2. Social problems. I. Stimson, John.
II. Stimson, Ardyth. III. Title.
HM51.P33 1985   361.1   84-26938
ISBN 0-471-86280-0

Printed in the United States of America

10 9 8 7 6 5 4 3 2

To our spouses—Beth, Ardyth, and John—without whose support this book would not have been possible

We wrote this book because we wanted to create a lively and readable text providing students with more than a dry, depressing recitation of statistics and description. We involve students by smoothly integrating sociological theory and current knowledge, punctuated with boxed inserts exemplifying or augmenting the topics under consideration. In addition, we emphasize how the social definitions of problems impact upon perceived causes and attempted cures. Another important aspect of the book is our use of plausible, alternative future scenarios, giving readers an understanding of the possibilities for social change.

Chapters 1 and 2 establish the knowledge base for the sociological study of social problems. Chapter 1 examines impediments to studying social problems, the roles of the social scientist, the elements of a social problem, some misdirected "common sense" responses, and four major sociological orientations. These orientations are used in each chapter to describe the variety of theoretical contributions available to sociology. Chapter 2 departs from other social problems books in that it analyzes the impact of society on the individual, including problems of alienation and anomie, together with the search for meaningful identities. Here we show how people's expectations and the social conditions generating their concepts about the quality of life affect their individual assessment of social problems and their solutions.

Following this grounding in the sociological perspective, the remaining chapters each focus upon specific social problems. Organized in thematic units of increasingly broader social categories, these 15 chapters are grouped in units about challenges to individuals, society, social institutions, and the quality of life. Significantly, each thematic section begins with an introduction to that grouping of chapters, providing a unifying direction of study. Throughout the book we employ an eclectic approach to show how the varying theoretical analyses (deviance, functionalist, conflict, and interactionist) each provide a different "lens" for examining a particular social problem.

Our colleague, Mary Lou Mayo, is the author of Chapter 11 on the family, and we thank her for her fine contribution. Yvonne Chilik offered invaluable research assistance, making our task a much lighter one. At John Wiley and Sons, we were fortunate to work with a creative and knowledgeable editorial and production staff. Specifically, we express our appreciation to Carol L. Luitjens and Irving L. Cooper for their faith and support in the project, to Karin Kincheloe for an attractive book

PREFACE

design, to Patricia Connolly and Michele Millon for their most helpful copy editing, to Elyse Rieder for her photo research, and to Harold Vaughn for his careful supervision over the book's production. Finally, we thank the administration at both William Paterson College and Kean College for their encouragement and allowances, enabling us to devote our energies more fully to writing this book.

Vincent N. Parrillo
John Stimson
Ardyth Stimson

PART ONE

SOCIOLOGY OF SOCIAL PROBLEMS   2

CHAPTER 1

Definitions and Perspectives   5

Impediments to Defining Social Problems   6
What We Feel We Can Do   6
Societal Problems   6
The Fallacy of Inevitability   7

The Role of the Social Scientist   7
Value Judgments   7
The Limits of Observation   8
Objectivity and Theory   12

The Four Elements of a Social Problem   13
The Persistence of Social Problems   14
Individual or Social Damage   16
Offense to a Powerful Group's Standards   18

False Causes and Misdirected Interventions   19
Cultural Lags: Myth of the Undeserving   19
Quasi-Theories   21
The Myth of the Invisible Hand   22

Sociological Orientations to Social Problems   22
Introduction: Four Views of Social Order   22
Individual Faults and Deviant Behavior Emphasis   23
Institutional Faults and System Disorganization Emphasis   27

CONTENTS

Inequality and Inevitable Conflict Emphasis   29
Interaction and Social Interpretation Emphasis   30

The Future of Social Problems   32
Rules for the Future   32
Methods for Studying the Future of Social Problems   33

Summary   34
Suggested Readings   35
Glossary   36

CHAPTER 2

The Individual in Modern Society: Alienation and Anomie   39

The Quality of Individuals' Lives   40
Types of Life Satisfactions   40

The Impact of Society on the Individual   41
Shyness: A Cultural Fact   44
Embedded and Enmeshed in Society   44

Anomie: Disorganization, Separation, and Meaninglessness   49
The Loss of Community   49
Anomic Conditions   50
The Rust of Progress: Functionalists' Concerns   51
Vagueness and Specialization   53
Secularization and Search for Meaning   53
New Cults   54

Alienation: Powerlessness and Self-Estrangement   56
Powerlessness   56
False Values and Self-Estrangement   57
The Human Commodity   58

Searching for Meaningful Identities   60
Individual Negotiation and Social Change   60

The Future   62
Pessimistic Scenario   62
Optimistic Scenario   64

Suggested Readings   66
Glossary   67

PART TWO
CHALLENGES TO INDIVIDUAL WELL-BEING   68

CHAPTER 3
Alcohol and Drug Abuse   71

What is a Drug?   72
    Alcohol   72
    Amphetamines   76
    Caffeine   76
    Cocaine   77
    Depressants   79
    Marijuana   79
    Narcotics   83
    Tobacco   84

Understanding Drug Attitudes   86
    Individual Faults and Deviant Behavior   86
    Institutional Faults and System Disorganization   88
    Inequality and Inevitable Conflict   89
    Interaction and Social Interpretation   91

Social Consequences of Drug Use   93
    Crime   93
    Automobile Accidents   94
    Health   96
    Economic Losses   97
    Professional Sports   99

Social Control and Solution Attempts   100
    Preventive Programs   101
    Treatment Programs   102
    Corrective Efforts   104
    The British Approach   104

The Future   105
    Pessimistic Scenario   105
    Optimistic Scenario   106

Summary   107
Suggested Readings   108
Glossary   109

CHAPTER 4

Sexual Expression 111

Sexual Conformity and Deviance 112
The Cross-Cultural Context 112
Homosexuality: Deviation or Variation? 113
Definitions of Homosexuality: Past and Present 114

Homosexuality in America: Stigma, Sanctions, and Gay Reactions 115
Differential Treatment of Homosexual Men and Women 115
The Nature of the Homosexual Relationship 118

The Gay Subculture 118
Female Homosexuality 118
Impersonal Sex: A Gay Male Phenomenon 119

Other Variations 120
Transsexualism 120
Transvestism Defined 123

Rape 124
The Crime of Rape Defined 124
The Plight of the Rape Victim 125
Preventing Rape 126

Commercial Exploitative Sex 128
Pornography 129

Prostitution 130
The Sexual Career of a Prostitute 130
Professional Prostitutes 131

Sociological Perspectives 132
Individual Faults and Deviant Behavior 132
Institutional Faults and System Disorganization 134
Inequality and Inevitable Conflict 134
Interaction and Social Interpretation 134

The Future 135
Pessimistic Scenario 135
Optimistic Scenario 137

Summary 138
Suggested Readings 139
Glossary 140

CHAPTER 5

Deviance and Crime   143

Deviance and Crime Defined   144
Crime and Punishment in Historical Perspective   145
Crime, Laws, and Prosecution   146

Reported Crime   147
Measuring the Extent of Crime   147

Crime That Is Not Systematically Monitored   152
White-Collar Crime   152
Computer Crime: A Rapidly Growing Threat   157
Unique Problems Associated with Combatting Computer Crime   157
Juvenile Delinquency   159

Explaining Crime and Delinquency   162
Discredited Physical Explanations   162
Psychological Explanations   163
Sociological Explanations   163

The Criminal Justice System   167
The Police   167
The Prisons   167

Solutions Past, Present, and Future   171
Solutions Aimed at the Offender and Potential Offender   171
Solutions Aimed at the Criminal Justice System   172

The Future   174
Pessimistic Scenario   174
Optimistic Scenario   175

Summary   176
Suggested Readings   178
Glossary   180

CHAPTER 6

Violence, Terrorism, and War   183

Vigilantism in American History   184
Violence as a Social Problem   185
Three Common Justifications of Violence   186

Criminal Violence   186
Criminal Violence in the United States   187

Homicide 189
   Murderers and Their Victims 190
   Rape Is Violence 191

Terrorism 192
   Terrorism Past and Present 192
   Societal Reaction to the Terrorist 194
   Political Terrorism 194
   How Effective Is Terrorism? 194
   International Terrorism 196
   Nuclear Terrorism 197

War 197
   Reasons for War 198
   War in America's Past and Present 198
   The Special Case of Nuclear War 199

Sociological Perspectives 203
   Individual Faults and Deviant Behavior 203
   Institutional Faults and System Disorganization 203
   Inequality and Inevitable Conflict 204
   Interaction and Social Interpretation 204

The Future 205
   Pessimistic Scenario 206
   Optimistic Scenario 207

Summary 208
Suggested Readings 209
Glossary 210

PART THREE

CHALLENGES TO SOCIAL EQUALITY 213

CHAPTER 7

Aging in a Youth-Oriented Society 215

The Graying of America 216
   Demographic Factors 216
   Values About Age 218

Myths and Stereotypes 222
   Mental Capacities 222
   Sexuality 223
   Negative Attitudes 224

Problems of the Elderly   224
Retirement   225
Economic Problems   227
Housing   232
Health Care   232
Exploiting the Elderly   237

Sociological Perspectives   239
Individual Faults and Deviant Behavior   239
Institutional Faults and System Disorganization   240
Inequality and Inevitable Conflict   242
Interaction and Social Interpretation   242

The Future   243
Pessimistic Scenario   243
Optimistic Scenario   244
Conclusion   245

Summary   246
Suggested Readings   247
Glossary   248

CHAPTER 8

Race and Ethnic Relations   251

Institutionalized Discrimination   252
Education   253
Employment   258
Housing   261
Legal Justice   263

Specific Problem Areas   264
Native Americans   264
Black Americans   268
Hispanics   269
Migrant Workers   269
Illegal Aliens   270

Sociological Perspectives   271
Individual Faults and Deviant Behavior   272
Institutional Faults and System Disorganization   275
Inequality and Inevitable Conflict   275
Interaction and Social Interpretation   276

The Future   277
Pessimistic Scenario   277
Optimistic Scenario   278

Summary 279
Suggested Readings 280
Glossary 282

CHAPTER 9

Poverty 285

The Nature of Poverty 286
Absolute Deprivation 287
Relative Deprivation 288

Who Are The Poor? 290
Minority Status 291
Family Structure 291
Age 293
Locale 296

The Impact of Poverty 297
Health 297
Housing 298
Family Life 298
Psychological Scars 299
Education 299
Work 299

Who Is To Blame For Poverty? 300
Individual Faults and Deviant Behavior 300
Institutional Faults and System Disorganization 303
Inequality and Inevitable Conflict 305
Interaction and Social Interpretation 306

Work and Welfare 308
The Nonworking Poor 308
The Welfare Poor 309
The Welfare Rich 313

Eliminating Poverty 315
The "Trickle-Down" Approach 315
The "Robin-Hood" Approach 316
The Interventionist Approach 316

The Future 317
Pessimistic Scenario 317
Optimistic Scenario 318

Summary 319
Suggested Readings 320
Glossary 321

CHAPTER 10

 Sexism 323

Biological Justifications for Sexism 324
Weakness of the Biological Argument 324

Socialization and Sexism 325
Values and Goals 325
Internalization of Roles 326

Effects of Sexism 328
Women as a Minority Group 328
Biological Limitations and Deformations 328
Powerlessness in Interaction 331
Sexual Harassment 333

Arenas of Change 335
Education 335
Working for Less 336
Political and Legal System Sexism 339

Sociological Perspectives 341
Individual Faults 341
Institutional Faults 342
Inequality and Inevitable Conflict 343
Interaction and Social Interpretation 344

The Future 347
Pessimistic Scenario 348
Optimistic Scenario 349

Summary 349
Suggested Readings 350
Glossary 352

PART FOUR

CHALLENGES TO SOCIAL INSTITUTIONS 354

CHAPTER 11

The Family 357

Contemporary Families in Transition 358
Social Change or Social Problem? 359

Divorce 361
Factors Contributing to the High Rate of Divorce 361

The Impact of Divorce on Adults   362
The Impact of Divorce on Children   364

Single-Parent Families   365
Families Headed by Women   366
Nonmarital Births   367

Violence and Abuse   367
Incidence of Family Violence   369
Social Factors Linked to Violence   371
Runaways   373

Sexual Violence and Victimization in the Family   373
Marital Rape   373
Incest   374

Violence and Victimization: The Need for Societal Intervention   375
Services for Battered Wives   375
Intervention in Child Abuse   375
The Police   375
Prevention of Family Violence   376

Why Are Families In Trouble?   377
Individual Faults and Deviant Behavior   377
Institutional Faults and System Disorganization   378
Inequality and Inevitable Conflict   379
Interaction and Social Interpretation   380

What Can Be Done To Help Families?   381

The Future   383
Pessimistic Scenario   383
Optimistic Scenario   384

Summary   385
Suggested Readings   386
Glossary   388

CHAPTER 12

Problems in Education   391

Characteristics and Contradictions   392
Compulsory and Universal Education   392
Community Control   393

The School as a Bureaucracy   394
Conformity and Obedience   394
Hierarchy of Authority   394

Education and Social Class   395
Dominance of Middle-Class Values   395
Ability Grouping   397

Integration and the Quality of Education   400
Busing   403
School Funding   403

The Declining Quality of Education   405
What's Wrong With Our Schools?   405
Subject Matter   407
Academic Standards   408

Sociological Perspectives   409
Individual Faults and Deviant Behavior   409
Institutional Faults and System Disorganization   410
Inequality and Inevitable Conflict   412
Interaction and Social Interpretation   413

How Can We Improve Education?   414
Equitable School Districts   414
Better Teachers   418

The Future   420
Pessimistic Scenario   420
Optimistic Scenario   421

Summary   422
Suggested Readings   423
Glossary   425

CHAPTER 13

The Concentration of Economic and Political Power   427

Corporate America   428
Who Owns The Corporations?   429
Engulf and Devour   430
The Irrelevance of Evil   431

Government-Corporate Alliances   434
Financial Benefits   435
The Military-Industrial Complex   436

Multinational Corporations   440
International Impact   441
Abuse of Power   442

Contents

Who Really Runs America? 443
The Power Elite Model 443
The Pluralist Model 444
Comparison of the Two Models 445

Sociological Perspectives 447
Individual Faults and Deviant Behavior 447
Institutional Faults and System Disorganization 448
Inequality and Inevitable Conflict 449
Interaction and Social Interpretation 450

Power to the People 451
Regulatory Agencies 451
Citizen Groups 452

The Future 453
Pessimistic Scenario 454
Optimistic Scenario 454

Summary 455
Suggested Readings 456
Glossary 458

CHAPTER 14

Health Care 461

Physical Health 462
The Medicalization of Life 463
Changes in the Health Care System 463
Dominance of Modern Medicine 464
The Social Organization of Health Care 465
The AMA and the Business of Medicine 465
The Hospital Industry 468
Doctors and Nurses 471
Medical Insurance 473
Rise of the Private Sector 475

Bioethics: Life and Death Decisions 477
Abortion 477
Keeping the Dying Alive 479

Mental Health 479
The Nature of Mental Disorders 482
The Medical Model 482
Socioeconomic Factors 484

Sociological Perspectives 486
Individual Faults and Deviant Behavior 487

Institutional Faults and System Disorganization   487
Inequality and Inevitable Conflict   489
Interaction and Social Interpretation   490

The Future   492
   Pessimistic Scenario   492
   Optimistic Scenario   493

Summary   494
Suggested Readings   495
Glossary   496

PART FIVE

CHALLENGES TO THE QUALITY OF LIFE   498

CHAPTER 15

Urban Decline and Growth   501

Changing Urban America   502
   Urban Sprawl   502

Housing Problems   503
   Redlining and Abandonment   503
   Urban Renewal   504
   Public Housing   504
   Housing Subsidies   505
   Defensible Space: A Successful Concept   505
   Gentrification   508

Transportation Problems   511

Can Snowbelt Cities Compete With Sunbelt Cities?   513
   Northeast Resurgence   514
   A New Economic Function for the City   515

Political Fragmentation   519

Hope From Past Policy Failures   520
   Self-Help Rehabilitation   520
   Collaborative Planning   520
   Unplanning Streets and Sidewalks   521
   Social Utilities Not Social "Services"   521

Sociological Perspectives   522
   Individual Faults and Deviant Behavior   522
   Institutional Faults and System Disorganization   523

Inequality and Inevitable Conflict   523
Interaction and Social Interpretation   526

The Future   527
Pessimistic Scenario   527
Optimistic Scenario   528
Conclusion   528

Summary   529
Suggested Readings   530
Glossary   531

CHAPTER 16

Population and Ecology   533

The Scope of the Problem: Images of the World System   534
Malthusian Pessimism   534
Earth as a System: The Limits to Growth Study   535
The Earth as a Lifeboat   535
Demographic Transition Theory   536

Population Pressure on the World   537
Continuing Growth   538
Resource Depletion: The Scarcity of Cropland   540
Hunger in Developing Nations   541
Extinction of Species   542
Transformation of Natural Processes: Acid Rain   544

Ecosystem Problems   544
Ecosystem Thinking   544
Current Ecosystem Problems   546
Dangerous Practices and Regulation Difficulties   547
What Can Be Done About Pollution?: New Jersey's Program   550

The Persistence of Ecological and Population Problems   550
Positions That Deny the Need for Action   551
Cultural Supports for Population Growth and Resource Depletion   552

Sociological Orientations and Solutions   554
The Individual Faults Emphasis: Excess/Unwanted Fertility   554
System Disorganization Emphasis: Changing Institutions   554
Inequality and Inevitable Conflict Emphasis   555
Social Interaction: Interpretation Emphasis   556

Population Policy and the Control Dilemma   558
Beyond Family Planning   558
Policy Proposals for Population Reduction   559

The Future   562
Pessimistic Scenario   562
Optimistic Scenario   563

Summary   565
Suggested Readings   566
Glossary   567

CHAPTER 17

Work and Occupational Trends   569

Occupational Trends   570
Rise of the Service Sector   570
The Impact of Automation   572

Unemployment Problems   575
Who Is Unemployed?   575
Effects of Long-term Unemployment   579

Job Satisfaction   582
Measuring Workers' Satisfaction   582
Attributes of Job Satisfaction   586

Sociological Perspectives   588
Individual Faults and Deviant Behavior   588
Institutional Faults and System Disorganization   589
Inequality and Inevitable Conflict   591
Interaction and Social Interpretation   592

Occupational Health and Safety   594
Government Intervention   594
Health Hazard Occupations   595

The Future   598
Pessimistic Scenario   598
Optimistic Scenario   599

Summary   600
Suggested Readings   600
Glossary   602

Notes   603
Photo Credits   635
Index   637

CONTEMPORARY SOCIAL PROBLEMS

Social problems affect everyone, regardless of age, sex, race, or economic level. At some point in our lives societal problems ensnare all of us, perhaps in the realms of old age, health care, or work and leisure. Because of race, religion, gender, or low income, some of us encounter daily problems of unequal treatment and opportunity. Others experience instability in their lives from chemical dependency, family dissolution and disorganization, technological change, or declining neighborhoods. Crime and violence affect many directly, while others live fearfully in their shadow, threatened further by the possibility of nuclear war.

Whatever the problem—real or imagined, experienced or dreaded—most individuals respond only to situations affecting them or seen as likely to do so. This individualistic attitude generally results in a tendency toward indifference to social conditions seen as having no direct personal impact. Even reactions to recognized problems depend on value judgments and social interpretations.

How accurate are the decisions we make about solving social problems? Do we act with sufficient understanding? Knowing specific data about the incidence of a problem is not enough; we need to probe beyond our assumptions of causes and effects to determine scientifically the underlying causes and social costs of remedy. Reporting about social problems is journalism, speculating over what to do about them is philosophy, but scientifically investigating and analyzing them is sociology—the "stuff" of this book.

In this section we shall set a conceptual framework for the objective study of various social problems discussed in subsequent chapters.

Chapter 1 provides insights about the nature of social problems and how our subjectivity often leads us to false conclusions and misdirected efforts at solutions. To study this subject more objectively, you will learn about four major sociological perspectives for examining our social order. Think of them as different lenses, each offering a unique portrait of the same reality. A wide-angle lens, for example, reveals more in scope than a regular camera lens, while a telephoto lens offers greater detail. Yet all focus on the same subject and accurately depict the scene.

Is it possible for life itself to be a social problem? Does modern society create alienation, a loss of community, and sense of meaninglessness? Do we feel lost, disenchanted, or overwhelmed by the complexities of our secular world? Before we examine specific problems, we must first understand the impact of society on individual expectations about the quality of life. In Chapter 2 we look at these concerns, with particular emphasis upon society's power in shaping roles, relationships, and expectations. If we can grasp the contradiction of our disillusionment with modern life and our simultaneous discarding of the past, we will have valuable insight into people's reality perceptions about those life conditions called social problems.

ONE
SOCIOLOGY OF SOCIAL PROBLEMS

1
DEFINITIONS AND PERSPECTIVES

IMPEDIMENTS TO DEFINING SOCIAL PROBLEMS

In the next section we will define the four elements of a social problem. But first we must discuss why we need a special definition. Why are our problems not clear to all of us? Why are so many dangerous or discriminatory social conditions never really fully recognized by society? Also, why do many problems that we agree should be alleviated never receive attention? The answers to these questions are usually ascribed to subjective or emotional factors: we do not care enough, or the individual is not concerned with anyone else's welfare. There are, however, other powerful cultural factors operating. Our society precludes many attempts at change and problem amelioration because it teaches us that ''some things are just natural and inevitable,'' and that it would be useless or wrong to attempt to change them.

What We Feel We Can Do

The first quality that a social condition must have in order to be regarded as a social problem is that some segment of society feels it is morally offensive, harmful, or dangerously inefficient. But an additional sentiment must be present before we accept something as a social problem: we must feel able to change it. People fear events such as blizzards or hurricanes, but they spend almost no time thinking about their causes. Weather is seen as natural, that is, beyond human control. We adapt to it and ''live with it.''

Societal Problems

A society's theories about what can and cannot be understood or solved are as much a part of its culture and are as constantly changing as are the rules about what is right and wrong. Furthermore, these ideas of why things happen, and what it would take to correct damage, are sometimes no more rational or scientific than the morals and mores of that society. (Mores are rules of social living that are felt to be crucial for the survival of the society and whose violation brings forth strong sanctions.) The quickest way to demonstrate that our everyday culture sometimes provides contradictory and irrational suggestions about how things should be done is to quote common American proverbs:

> ''Look before you leap.'' . . . . ''He who hesitates is lost!''
> ''Out of sight, out of mind,'' . . . ''Absence makes the heart grow fonder.''

Which piece of advice should you follow? Neither! You should come to a conclusion by examining the specific facts of the case. But very few of us do. We make our decisions using guesses based on inadequate data and the prevalent cultural assumptions about why things happen. Because of this reliance on nonscientific assumptions many important problems are ignored, misunderstood, or felt to be normal parts of existence. Sometimes, even though we feel we should change conditions, we accept value-laden traditional notions that make us think society is fixed in its present pattern. Let's examine a few outstanding examples.

The Fallacy of Inevitability

The scientific study of social problems is new because until recently, people did not feel any need for it. They had other traditional or religious explanations for the conditions around them. For example, the problem of who should have power or privilege in society was solved by the notion of the "divine right of kings." A small group related by "royal blood" was felt to have the natural, god-given right to the power of life and death over all other society members.

Similarly, in the area of health problems, a very high death rate during medical treatment was accepted as natural. The doctor was seen as "doing the best he could." The first doctor who suggested that surgeons wash their hands before operating was severely persecuted and ostracized for his unnatural ideas (See Box 1.1). Mental illness provides even more flagrant evidence of an irrational theory preventing factual inquiry. Possession by demons was all the explanation needed for hundreds of years, and people did not feel the need to study the real causes of illness, or ways to cure it, because they thought they already had the answers. This all began to change, however, when examples of breakthroughs in science and engineering began to show that a better life was attainable.

THE ROLE OF THE SOCIAL SCIENTIST

Our views of social problems are often intertwined with our personal prejudices, politics, and values. Here are some important considerations complicating the difficult task of being objective in a value-laden social world.

Value Judgments

Value judgments are real; that is, they have real effects, a real impact on what individuals and society decide to do. They are not just emotional responses or irrational traditions. The decisions about which problem is most serious, or which should receive highest priority for solution, must be based on people's moral decisions. There is no scientific way to decide whether a high crime rate is "worse" than a high divorce rate, or robbery is "worse" than alcoholism.

But these policy decisions should be based on objective evidence, that is, accurate statistics measuring the real extent of the problem, and estimates of the consequences of trying to help a given problem. It should be the scientists' job to deal in what is, and what will occur, if a particular policy is made. The traditional view says that scientists' contributions lie in choosing the means to achieve solutions, not in

BOX 1.1

A TRULY MODERN HERO

Information seems to be getting in the way all the time. Human beings have had to guess about almost everything for the past million years or so. Our most enthralling and sometimes terrifying guessers are the leading characters in our history books. . . .

Persuasive guessing has been at the core of leadership for so long, for all of human experience so far, that it is wholly unsurprising that most of the leaders on this planet, in spite of all the solid information that is suddenly ours, want the guessing to go on. It is now their turn to guess and guess and be listened to.

You know why I think research funds in this country have been so severely curtailed? (We now spend less on research than any other industrialized nation.) It isn't in order to balance the stupid budget. It is in order to keep new truths from getting in the way of politicians all the time. It is intolerable to politicians, so melodious with their guesses, that ordinary citizens, having been to a public library, can say, with absolute authority, "You're wrong." . . .

What good is an education? The boisterous guessers are still in charge, the haters of information. And the guessers are almost all highly educated people! Think of that.

If you make use of the vast fund of knowledge now available to educated persons, you are going to be lonesome as hell. The guessers outnumber you—and now *I* have to guess—about 10 to one.

What I can give you to cling to is a poor thing, actually—not much better than nothing, maybe worse than nothing. It is the idea of a truly modern hero. It is the bare bones of the life of Ignaz Semmelweis.

My hero is Ignaz Semmelweis. He was born in Budapest in 1818, and he lived for 47 years. He became an obstetrician, which should make him modern hero enough. He devoted his life to the health of babies and mothers. We could use more heroes like that. There is damn little caring for mothers or babies or old people or anybody physically or economically weak these days.

I have told you how new all this information we have is. It is so new that Louis Pasteur's idea that many diseases are caused by germs is only about 120 years old.

choosing which problems should be attacked. But often they must also act as advocates in order to bring attention to the facts.

The Limits of Observation

The most important component of the scientific approach is the observation of facts. But human powers of observation are limited, and are strongly guided by our prejudgments (see Box 1.2). Unless people are trained, and facts are used in a controlled way, biased impressions will be gathered instead of "facts." Katzer, Cook, and Crouch explain three complications that demonstrate that "seeing is *not* believing."[1]

Ignaz Semmelweis also believed that germs could cause disease. He was horrified when he went to work for a maternity hospital in Vienna to find that one mother in 10 was dying of childbed fever there. They were poor people. Rich people still had their babies at home.

Semmelweis observed hospital routines and began to suspect that doctors were bringing the infection to the patients. He noticed that the doctors often went directly from dissecting corpses in the morgue to examining mothers in the maternity ward. He suggested, as an experiment, that the doctors wash their hands before touching the mothers. What could be more insulting? How dare he make such a suggestion to his social superiors? He was a nobody, you realize.

But all that dying went on and on and Semmelweis, having so far less sense about how to get along with others in this world than you and I would have, kept asking colleagues to wash their hands. They at last agreed to do it, in a spirit of lampoonery, of satire, of scorn. How they must have lathered and lathered and scrubbed and scrubbed.

The dying stopped.

Imagine that: the dying stopped. He saved all those lives. Subsequently, it might be said that he has saved millions of lives—including quite possibly, yours and mine.

What thanks did Semmelweis get from the leaders of his profession and Viennese society—guessers all? He was forced out of the hospital and out of Austria itself, whose people he had served so well. He finished his career in a provincial hospital in Hungary. There he gave up on humanity and on knowledge, and on himself. One day in the dissecting room, he took the blade of a scalpel with which he had been cutting up a corpse, and he stuck it on purpose into the palm of his hand. He died, as he knew he would, of blood poisoning soon afterward.

The guessers had had all the power. They had won again. Germs indeed!

The guessers revealed something else about themselves, too, which we should duly note: they aren't really interested in saving lives. What matters to them is being listened to, as, however ignorantly, their guessing goes on and on.

You Couldn't See It All If You Wanted to

Our senses and powers of attention are limited. The flow of events is much too full of details for us to comprehend. Eyewitness accounts of even outstanding events like violent crimes very seldom agree. Experiments have shown that people miss about 40 percent of the main facts in any situation.

You Interpret Everything You See

The images that come before your eyes have all been previously defined and explained to you during your socialization, creating **internalized norms** within you.

BOX 1.2

GRAPHIC GULLDUGGERY
In the event you haven't guessed, gull-duggery combines the meanings of the verb *gull* ("to cheat," "trick," "dupe") and the noun *skullduggery* ("mean trickery," "craftiness"). Why did I coin it? Well, for one thing, I like alliteration. More importantly, graphs are often used to trick or dupe the reader in a mean and crafty manner.

THE RUBBER BAND BOUNDARY

What makes the *rubber-band boundary chart* particularly insidious is that it is generally used to present important data and commonly appears in serious publications (I have seen them repeatedly in the most highly respected newspapers as well as in weekly news magazines). The rubber-band-boundary chart is really the progeny of graphic anarchy. By this I mean that there are no universally agreed-upon methods of representing the relative lengths of the vertical and horizontal axes. Therefore, these axes are like rubber bands, ready to expand or contract on demand of the user.

Let us say that the user is a sales manager of a department in a large discount store. He has kept a careful record of the sales figures of all the personnel working under him, and he wants to use these figures to put a burr under the saddle of salespeople who, he feels, are not giving their all to the dear old shop. What does he do? He draws bar graphs representing the weekly dollar volume for each salesperson, but he stretches the vertical axis and contracts the horizontal axis. He states, "Ms. Dee, you are obviously not holding up your end of the workload. The rest of the department is carrying you. If you don't believe me, look at the sales chart." (See figure a.)

But Ms. Dee has not been caught off guard. Without her manager knowing it, she has been taking prolonged coffee breaks each afternoon while preparing the hors d'oeuvre shown in figure b. She replies, "It's strange to hear you say that. As you can see, I'm doing about as well as anybody. A few sales, one way or the other, and I would be the top in the department."

When a person suddenly gains sight after a long period of blindness, he or she must learn to see. Reality doesn't just jump out at us because our culture selects what we pay attention to, and ignore, and how we evaluate each element. For example, the "halo effect" is the tendency for us to evaluate everything about a person, all their characteristics, as either good or bad. If the societal opinion of a type of person (say, a medical doctor), is good we usually perceive all of that individual's acts as fine and efficient. This process also works the other way. Stop and think. You can probably remember some ethnic or social group that you were told to see as "people who could do nothing right."

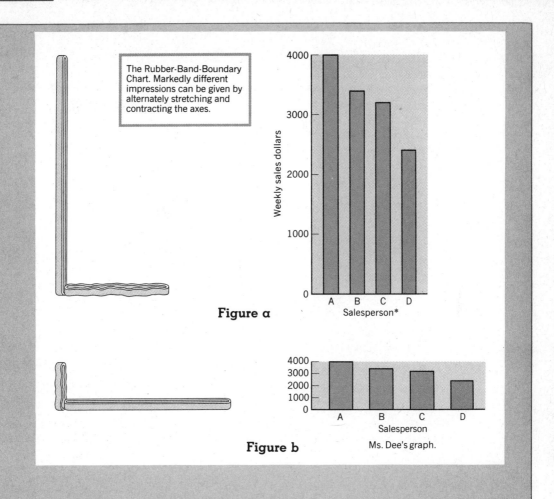

The Rubber-Band-Boundary Chart. Markedly different impressions can be given by alternately stretching and contracting the axes.

Figure a

Weekly sales dollars

Salesperson*

Figure b

Salesperson

Ms. Dee's graph.

SOURCE: Richard P. Runyon, *How Numbers Lie: A Consumer Guide to Numerical Deception*, Lexington, Mass.: Lewis Publishing, 1981, pp. 36–38. Reprinted by permission.

You Produce Some of What You See

This is because your presence changes the situation. People usually try to find out what you want them to say, or at least they avoid saying what might offend you. People try to fulfill each others' expectations. You must also guard against your own expectations. "People have a tendency to see what they expect to see. Or, 'seek and ye shall find, whether it is there or not.'" For example, many studies have shown that when elementary school teachers are fooled into thinking that some of their students are "late bloomers" who are about to blossom forth, these teachers treat them differently, and the "chosen" students do in fact "bloom" above their classmates.

These women are approximately the same height. Some psychologists who understand the cues we use to make judgments have deliberately constructed a room that distorts reality. Our perceptions of the world are filtered through physiological habits and culturally learned interpretations which may be a distortion of the actual reality.

Objectivity and Theory

Sociologists believe that people can learn to control their biases, at least during the time they are engaged in professional activities. But sociologists do not leave this to trust. There are specific steps and rules involved in doing research, and they are all designed so that scientists can watch each other and independently assess results and possible biases. This is why every research report has a detailed section on methods of research. It may seem boring and unnecessary to the lay reader, but it is there so that another scientist can repeat the study if he or she does not trust the results.

Value judgments are not trustworthy ways to understand or interpret the observations you make. Sociologists substitute theoretical orientations as ways of organizing the data they collect (see Box 1.3). As we have seen, observation of social life needs some focus because there is so much going on that we cannot see it all. Sociologists,

BOX 1.3

THEORY

While one could conceivably label any description of reality a "theory," the term is generally used more rigorously. When a statement that links together two or more concepts is widely agreed upon, it is given the status of a *proposition*. A *theory* consists of a set of propositions which are systematically interrelated and which purport to explain some phenomenon.

Probably most research is conducted in an effort to test propositions. The research begins with a theory and uses empirical evidence to find out how well that description actually fits reality. If amenable to observation, either the basic propositions or deduced propositions may be tested against empirical data. In testing theory, the goal is not merely to find support for one theory, but also to eliminate less likely theories. Thus, Durkheim began his study of suicide by attempting to show that previous theories of suicide could not be true. Durkheim first tried to show that suicide is not a result of mental illness or psychopathic states by showing that rates of suicide and insanity are not related. In the same manner he attempted to discredit theories which attributed the causes of suicide to race, heredity, climate, seasonal temperatures, and imitation before defending his theory of suicide in terms of social forces.

Research also has the dual role of both *specifying* and *generalizing* the domain of the theory. For example, a theory about social power may state that power underlies all organizational relationships. A more specific theoretical statement could be that while people at all organizational levels hold certain kinds of power, those in higher-status positions always have more power than those in lower-status positions. One might also attempt to expand the relationship between power and organizational hierarchies to include other social hierarchies. In this case it might be stated that lawyers have more power than clients or that doctors have more power than patients. Naturally, specification and generalization of theory are major concerns because we strive to explain as many phenomena as possible.

SOURCE: Susan Gustavus Philliber, Mary R. Schwab, and G. Sam Sloss, *Social Research* (Itasca, Ill.: F. E. Peacock, 1980), pp. 14, 15. Reproduced by permission of the publisher, F. E. Peacock Publishers, Inc., Itasca, IL.

as scientists, are only allowed to use tentative hypothetical models based on the evidence gathered so far. Theories only begin to take firm shape as knowledge begins to mount up behind one model or another.

THE FOUR ELEMENTS OF A SOCIAL PROBLEM

Most of us feel we could quickly name the two most important social problems, but if you pause now and try it, you will be surprised how difficult it is. Could any of us take the responsibility of choosing the one problem that needs all our society's immediate attention? To make such decisions, we must be very clear about our definition of a social problem. The definition of what is a social problem must be broken down into four main components. Most recognized social problems have:

1. Persisted for a period of time.
2. Been perceived as having caused physical or mental damage to individuals or society.
3. Offended the values or standards of some powerful segment of society.
4. Generated competing proposed solutions, each being evaluated differently by groups who are in different social positions within society. Disagreements delay the formation of a consensus on how to attack the problem.

The Persistence of Social Problems

It seems that a new social problem surfaces every day: a new form of crime or pollution, or some new threat to the moral order of life. It is true that there are some new problems (for example, computer crime is a new form of theft) but the majority are old problems that keep returning in forms that seem brand new. The scenes of adolescent boy and girl prostitutes in New York or Hollywood that shock us on the evening news are, after all, just a variation on the oldest profession, which has been viewed quite differently from time to time and place to place. Why have some social problems persisted for so long? We can isolate three forces acting to sustain problems.

Persistence Due to a Desire for Quick Cures

When John D. Rockefeller decided to put some of his many millions into major philanthropic works, he did it with his characteristic demand for an immediate profit. Rockefeller called together leading doctors and said he would put up the money if they could come up with a disease that could be totally wiped out, immediately. By a rare chance, it just happened that pellagra, a disease that had caused much suffering in the southern United States, had been under study for many years and a cure had just been found. The doctors could therefore fulfill Rockefeller's demand for immediate results, but only because there had been years of prior study.[2] Rockefeller's demand was not unusual; his attitude is a common one: the desire for quick cures. We often give up if solutions are not immediate.

Persistence Due to Interconnectivity

When a social problem has persisted for as long as, say, prostitution, it appears that it may be built into society, almost as a natural part of everyday life. Some sociologists have said that prostitution serves positive functions for society, for example, as an outlet valve for sexual energies that might lead to other more damaging forms of behavior. These functional theorists feel that there is a high degree of **interconnectivity** between societal institutions, and that the parts support each other; to change any one element you must examine and change many others. Other sociologists feel that prostitution is a form of exploitation of women and is related to other institutions and social inequalities. For example, if you wish to eradicate prostitution, you must first examine the society's forms of dating and marriage, its sex roles and views of women, as well as its often macho sexism of seeing people only as sexual objects.

The "oldest profession" is an outstanding example of a persistent social problem. It has recently been more openly practiced and controversial. Is prostitution a necessary part of society? Is it due solely to the exploitation of women? Why hasn't this problem been solved?

Persistence Because Someone Is Profiting

One social group's loss can be another group's gain. Resistance to antipollution regulations is often due to factory owners' or workers' desires to avoid reducing profits or jobs. The gains from resisting new policies are not always monetary, though. Many solutions are resisted because they threaten to upset society's traditional authority structure. The resistance to women in managerial authority is a recent example. The threat does not have to be direct, or powerful, or even real in order to cause a reaction. Change will be resisted if it upsets how we think things should be. Every society's power structure of vested interest groups is justified by an ideology that seems to explain why some members "deserve" more power or privilege. A solution that contradicts the ideological structure is frequently rejected as nonsensical or too radical unless there is strong enough proof and support to overcome the ideology.

Individual or Social Damage

City dwellers are often cynical about obtaining services from City Hall. One expression of this attitude is the saying, "the only way to get a street light installed at your busy intersection is to have a child hit by a car." Unfortunately, this is not always an unfounded attitude; government tends to respond only *after* significant damage has occurred.

Incidence, Prevalence, and Trend

It is not just government officials who need this prod of evidence of significant damage. We all know that air pollution is hurting us, but it has not caught our attention and become the center of a powerful social movement because we don't yet have clear-cut measures of the damage it causes.

Sorting out the real damage that should get our attention from the transitory, sensational, but not fully substantiated incidents we see everyday on television, demands scientific objectivity and precise definitions. Sociologists assess the severity of a social problem by three measurements: rates of incidence, prevalence, and the direction of its trend.

Incidence measures the occurrence of new cases. For example, in 1982 in New York City alone, about 20 cases per week of a penicillin-resistant strain of gonorrhea were being reported. There had been no known cases five years earlier. This statistic is alarming, even though there were only 20 people involved, because it demonstrates an "outbreak" of a new problem. The rapid incidence of Acquired Immune Deficiency Syndrome (AIDS) is, of course, more frightening because no cure is known.

The **prevalence** rate of a given condition depends on how widespread it is and how many members of the population are affected. This is what is usually meant when we say "there is a high rate of crime, or disease, etc." The crime prevalence rate for a given neighborhood is calculated: "Of all the households, how many were burglarized last month?" Of all the people who possibly could have suffered this problem, what proportion actually did?

A problem may also be considered important because the rate for this year is significantly higher than last year's rate. We become aware that some new force for change might be operating. It takes a number of time periods of movement in one direction for us to begin to believe that a **trend** is really under way. Too often, sensational interpretations of only one change can cause panic. In actuality, it may be only a limited, chance occurrence that will disappear as rapidly as it appeared. Economists, for example, will consider the economy "in trouble" only after our Gross National Product (GNP) has declined for three quarters in a row.

The most serious problem, of course, would be one that has all three characteristics increasing: a high incidence of new cases, a widespread prevalence, and a rapidly growing trend. All these measurements are relatively easy to calculate and will be illustrated using real data in later sections.

Cost/Benefit Analyses

As you read through the following chapters, you will discover that one of the most important jobs of the sociologist is to estimate the future importance of some as yet unrecognized problem. This is usually done by trying to assess the future cost if the problem were to be left unattended and comparing it to the benefit from various possible interventions. Cost benefit analysts working with social problems usually use either of two perspectives: individual costs or social costs.

When looking at the damage to individuals that a problem causes, we must consider both present suffering and the loss of future opportunities. Ethnic or sexual discrimination, for example, hurts immediately through embarrassment, frustration, and lost income. But the ultimate damage is much higher. Exclusion from education and early job opportunities changes the course of entire lives. These hidden costs must be carefully calculated when deciding which are the most damaging problems.

When social costs are considered, sociological analysis becomes important. Some problems that seem threatening begin to look relatively unimportant, and others are shown to have far-reaching effects. The cost of violent crime in a city neighborhood is usually thought of in terms of, say, the number of older people who are mugged. This is certainly reason enough to be concerned. But when we step back and sociologically analyze the overall effects, we find that there may be an even greater injury from the fear of assault. Older people don't leave their homes, they become lonely and isolated, and their community forgets they are there, so less help and protection are available, and their problems multiply.

When we look at a problem from the social cost perspective, we almost always find that it is more expensive than we at first expected. The social interconnections of the problem are discovered by thinking in terms of the possible causal chains of events; for example, ethnic discrimination causes poor education, which could lead to less opportunity in the job market, which leads to unemployment, which might strain the marriages of the unemployed, which leads to a less than happy emotional atmosphere for the children, which might drive them into the streets, and so on. This series of events does not always happen, and it might take different branchings at any link in the chain. For example, unemployment might make illegal activities more attractive to the individual, and thereby raise the crime rate.

Many of these "spindle-boys" got so tired on their 12 hour shifts that they fell into the machine and died. Child labor abuses forced recognition of the costs of progress and the need to control the free growth of industrialization.

Offense to a Powerful Group's Standards

There is a subjective, moral-outrage component of all social problem definitions. Frequently nothing is done until a significant group recognizes the problem and feels that it is obnoxious.

Stratification and Problem Definitions

All known societies are stratified into layers with varying degrees of power and prestige. Sometimes religion is the basis of prestige and privilege and the clergy hold positions of power, as in fundamentalist Muslim countries like Iran. Today, as in the past, the warrior class seizes the government, as in the frequent army takeovers in less developed nations. Stratification is based on economic classes that are closely related to occupational prestige and the accumulation of wealth.

When Americans have been presented with a list of all existing occupations, in study after study they report about the same set of prestige ratings. Doctors and other professionals are rated highest while blue-collar workers, no matter how skilled, are rated lower than most white-collar workers.

When subgroups of society come together and recognize their common economic or political interests and begin to act or think together, they are called social classes.

Members of a social class begin to see the entire society from their point of view, and form a set of moral and life-style definitions about themselves and others that is unique. This is a complicated process, discussed in detail in Chapter 9 on Poverty. What is relevant here is that what one group sees as a problem (e.g., welfare, or social security, or tax loopholes), another may not see as a valuable part of the society. People in positions of power tend to value stability and social order and the preservation of the present privilege structure. Those trying to gain power to promote changes are very interested in new ideas and innovative policies. Sometimes these differences in perspective are also associated with age. Those in power happen to be older and are trying to maintain the structure that nurtured them, while those who are beginning their careers see many ways to improve the system.

FALSE CAUSES AND MISDIRECTED INTERVENTIONS

Much neglect and damage have been caused by having the wrong causal theory. We often hold on most strongly to false beliefs in areas that threaten or disturb us the most. Because we feel we need to know so badly, we settle for plausible sounding traditional myths.

Before we study social problems we should bring some false cultural traditions and half-baked theories out into the open. This is very similar to beginning to get to know someone from another country or of another race. You should first examine and reject the false prejudices that might cloud your judgment and block the acceptance of the things you are about to learn.

Cultural Lags: Myth of the Undeserving

Our beliefs about why things happen, or how things operate, often lag behind historical developments. This is called **cultural lag,** and happens most frequently when technological inventions restructure the world and our tried-and-true ways of doing things don't have time to catch up. *Survivals* are ideas or practices that live on after their original utility has past. Bows and arrows survive as children's toys, or exotic hunting-hobby weapons. But many survivals are dysfunctional.

Using herbs or roots instead of medicines could be harmful. Making decisions using only star signs and omens is dangerously inadequate. In developing countries, the desire for very large families survives and causes dangerously rapid population growth even after the agricultural life-style that supported them has faded.

The survival attitude that most frequently keeps us from understanding social problems is the habit of attributing the cause of a problem to the "bad character" of the individuals caught up in them. Nineteenth-century views of social problems were dominated by the notion that people in trouble had somehow brought it on themselves. Even the sick or mentally ill were felt to have been responsible because they must have had some weakness that allowed their conditions to develop. This was often expressed in such phrases as "lack of moral fiber," or "defective development."

The use of phrenology, the estimation of a person's future from the bumps on the head, and the reading of palms or horoscopes still survive. Each of these techniques was popular in a past age. Even outlandish cultural solutions tend to persist. Our acceptance of modern solutions of human problems often lags behind our scientific knowledge.

F. L. Cook demonstrates the erroneous nature of the overconfidence in this belief in the early days of social work:

> One of the earliest distinctions in the history of public assistance was that between "the deserving" and the "undeserving." This was one of the major concepts in the Elizabethan Poor Law of 1601, and it continues to be used in decisions about who gets helps today. . . . The assumption as to whether or not the individual *caused his own plight*. . . . In fact, the first question that Charity Organization Society workers asked themselves in the late 1800's and early twentieth century to determine who should be helped was: "What is the cause of the distress?" And if the person *caused* his/her own plight, he or she was considered undeserving and denied aid.[3]

This **character-flaw** fallacy is still used more than it should be. Cloward and Piven, two well-known critics of social work, warn against thinking of the client's personality development or family relationships as the source of his or her poverty or emotional problems. They say that this misplaced theoretical emphasis on blaming the victim keeps the client, and the social worker, from looking to the social system and the surrounding institutions when attributing blame. It amounts to "throwing sand in the eyes of the client"; making them believe that they themselves, or their families, are to blame.[4]

Quasi-theories

Every society develops ways of quickly smoothing things over, ways of explaining away disturbances so that people can get on with life's business. Sometimes these explanations are totally false; but their truth or falsity doesn't really matter in most situations. Their function is not to make us really understand what's going on, but to calm down the social situation, to dissolve the fear, upset, or conflict that the problem caused. This is very apparent in small social groups. If someone says something harshly critical about another, a third friend will immediately jump in to explain that "she's just like that," or "he's in a mood." In other words: "I know the simple cause for the harsh words, but it's trivial, or will go away soon, so let's not examine it, let's get on with our conversation." This type of quick cure is also apparent in political life.[5] Real differences, and sometimes open conflicts, between groups are explained away by the quasi-theory of inadequate communication. "If people would just sit down quietly and discuss their differences, they would see that we are all basically the same." The problem is not real, this quasi-theory states, it is just a symptom of a failure to communicate. Sometimes this might be true; but frequently, groups that are in conflict are divided by contradictory interests, or the competition for power.

Quasi-theories are damaging because they smooth over, neutralize, and de-emotionalize conflicts that could really be cured, and not just be temporarily patched over. Two of these dangerous quasi-theories are the sweet mystery of life and the Panglossian quasi-theories:

The sweet-mystery-of-life quasi-theory says that love, birth, and death are areas of life that we will *never* understand. They are in the control of mysterious forces beyond our awareness. Therefore, it is said, social scientists are probably wasting their time. And yet, divorce rates are skyrocketing, America has an inordinately high infant mortality rate, and if you are poor, or a minority group member, you are going to die earlier than the majority group members. These disruptions do exist, and we are making progress in understanding them.

Panglossian quasi-theories are based on the notion that "time will heal all wounds."[6] They usually run like this: We are living in a very complicated society, with major changes underway; it is the best of all possible societies, but the problems will take a little while to work themselves out. The implications are that we should not do anything to interfere with the forces of urbanization, migration, assimilation, or economic cycles. We should just "grin and bear" their consequences.

The Myth of the Invisible Hand

We tend to hope that everything will work itself out, that the system will "heal" itself. We want to believe that outside intervention is needed in only very special cases. When we hear a proposal for government support or social benefits, we say, "Why is this problem so special that we should break our normal rule of letting things take their natural course?" But, this is *not* our normal rule. Our social system is already a very complex web of social programs that control or alleviate social problems.[7] They are carried out by government, industry, and private voluntary agencies, and billions of dollars are given to individuals, businesses, and communities. See Box 1.4 for examples from just the area of social welfare, of the many types of assistance that are built into our system.

SOCIOLOGICAL ORIENTATIONS TO SOCIAL PROBLEMS

Sociologists approach social problems in four main ways. Here, we deal only with the main emphases of each of the orientations. Detailed explanations of each orientation's specializations will be fully presented and applied in the appropriate chapters.

Introduction: Four Views of Social Order

The phenomenon of social conformity, the orderliness of societal life, is a good example with which to introduce the four emphases. When we look around us in society, we see a good deal of confusion and many people who break rules, but we also see an overwhelming amount of conformity. Most people obey the rules almost all the time. Most people feel guilty if they think about committing a crime. This is a great marvel of social life, that human animals live together without even more conflict and confusion! How is this accomplished? Here are answers illustrating the four sociological orientations or emphases:

1. *Individual Faults and Deviant Behavioral Emphasis.* Individuals are socialized by their families so that the rules of society become integral parts of their personalities; the rules are internalized. Most of us end up wanting to be law-abiding members of society. When this training doesn't "take," individuals become deviants or nonconformists.

2. *Institutional Faults and System Disorganization Emphasis.* The institutions of society have been developed over time in order to provide the answers to all of our significant problems by fulfilling all our necessary human and social functions. For example, the rules and methods for training the young are handled by the educational institution and the family. When there is a social problem, for example, juvenile delinquency, it must be because one of these institutionalized parts of the social system has broken down. Individuals who are left without adequate guidelines and supervision will inevitably deviate and cause problems. They are, in effect, being socialized into deviance.

3. *Inequality and Inevitable Conflict Emphasis.* Conformity and orderliness are shams. They appear to be the natural way of social life only because the powerful people and the organizations of social control have a vested interest in maintaining the status quo without disruptions. The have-nots don't see life as peaceful or orderly. The real fact of social life is inevitable conflict between groups that have unequal status and privileges. What the other orientations often call "deviation" is really a normal part of the change and struggle of social life.

4. *Interaction and Social Interpretation Emphasis.* Orderliness is not the result of monolithic institutions, nor the product of large-scale class conflicts. Orderliness is a day-by-day accomplishment created by individuals who interact face to face and interpret and reinterpret the traditional ways of doing things in society. The way to understand social problems is to see how the people who are actually involved see them and to examine how problems impact on the everyday lives of individuals.

Now we present the emphases in full. Please notice that each orientation directs us toward a different area in which to look for the causes of social problems.

Individual Faults and Deviant Behavior Emphasis

Nineteenth-century sociologists made the mistake, prevalent in their time, of seeing all people suffering from problems as sick and in need of curing. This pathology perspective relied on a medical model, treating all "different" behaviors as due to some form of social illness. The modern version, says that "the failure of people to cope"[8] is the cause of their problems. Earlier notions about "character flaws," "defective makeup," and ideas that problems such as poverty or crime were perpetuated by the in-breeding of the "dependent" and "delinquent" classes[9] have mostly disappeared. But even today, there still exists the "assumption that it is necessary to

BOX 1.4

POLICY NOMENCLATURE—
CLARIFYING
THE CHOICES   . . . what kinds of social policy are most desirable? Should,

for example, all groups benefit in similar or equal ways from social policy? Only
some groups? How does one decide who gets what in our society and in what
proportions? Of course, this is basically a normative question, and it will not be
answered conclusively here. However, there is a real need to have a way of an-
swering these normative questions, and the *first* task is to exemplify through the use
of a framework and a common language what the choices of social policy are. The
intent is to help clarify what the choices are in social policy by making sure a clear-
cut and agreed-upon way of talking about the range of these choices is available.
The table presented here illustrates how the matrix of choices available can be
portrayed in a skeletal way. A useful exercise would be to see how many policy
examples could be fitted into the cells of the table.

A couple of general points about the matrix will show why common nomenclature is so central to the field of social policy. We must stretch, clarify, probe,
analyze, and ultimately decide what kinds of social policy are most desirable. A
way to begin to do that is to focus on three simple concepts: the direct beneficiaries
of policy, the sector to be used for developing policy, and the coverage of policy.
First, should policy be designed to *directly* impact on individuals or groups, communities or geographic areas, or business or governments? There are many indirect
beneficiaries of policy, but at a minimum who are the intended and direct beneficiaries? *Second,* should it, could it, and will it be done through either the public or
private sector, or both? This allows us to examine, in any policy area, whether
public policy is the core and private policy supplemental or vice versa. This helps to
clarify what balance is intended and ultimately most desirable. *Third,* ''coverage
of policy'' refers to whether it should be highly targeted and available only to a
selected and restricted collectivity, or broadly available in society or the community. The coverage of policy is really a continuum that runs from highly selective to
universal. Illustrations of programs that fall into this matrix are presented in the
table. There may be some debate over which program fits where—and that should
happen—but the point here is to make sure that a clear way of portraying the
choices is available. It might be significant if it were possible to add up accurately
the amount of money spent in each of these areas. Perhaps it would sharpen the
debate over who gets what, but more important is who *should* get what, and why?
*The first issue in the field of social policy is the inadequacy of the nomenclature
used.* A definition of social policy and a matrix for clarifying choices is offered as a
way of thinking about the issue.

Matrix of Choice for Social Policy

Coverage of Policy	Direct Beneficiaries of Policy		
	Individuals or Groups	Community or Geographic Area	Business and Governmental Organizations
Selective			
Public	Aid to Families with Dependent Children (AFDC)	Model Cities	Antirecession financial assistance to governments
	Medicaid	Urban renewal	Countercyclical revenue sharing
	Title XX (Social Services)	Economic developmental assistance	Loan guarantees for New York City
	Comprehensive Employment and Training Programs (CETA)	Area redevelopment assistance	Loan guarantees for Chrysler Corp.
	Headstart Programs	Community action programs	Disaster relief loans for business
		Community development block grants	Small Business loans
Private	Employee benefits	Voluntary and cooperative economic assistance to distressed areas	Flexible credit and mortgage policies for both business and government
	Paid maternity leave		
	Day-care on job site		
	United Way funded programs	United Way funded programs	
	Other nonprofit social welfare programs	Other nonprofit social welfare programs	
Universal			
Public	Children's allowance	Hospital construction	General revenue sharing
	Child welfare services	Airport construction	Tax credits to business
	Social Security	Federal highway programs for primary and secondary systems	
	Hot lunch program		
	Energy tax credits	Sewage treatment plants	
	Tuition tax credits		
	Vocational education		
	Nutrition program for elderly		
Private	Employee benefits	Voluntary and cooperative economic planning (Chambers of Commerce)	Flexible credit and low interest rates
	Vacations		
	Sick leave		
	Health		
	Pensions	Some United Way and other nonprofit social welfare programs	
	Some United Way and other nonprofit social welfare programs		

SOURCE: Milan J. Dluhy, "Introduction: The Changing Face of Social Policy" in John E. Tropman, Milan J. Dluhy, and Roger M. Lind (eds.) *New Strategic Perspective on Social Policy* (New York: Pergamon Press, 1981), pp. xviii–xx.

change people before they can take adequate advantage of the institutional opportunities available to them in society."[10]

David Matza calls this the correctional perspective: "The goal is ridding ourselves of the deviant phenomenon."[11] People with any problem are considered morally base and separated out of society in prisons or institutions. Resocialization is the only solution. The system, with its rules, is seen as the only correct alternative, and individuals must be made to fit into the roles it provides.

Appreciation of Deviance

In the twentieth century this correctional emphasis was replaced by an **appreciative orientation** to deviance.[12] Instead of blaming the victims of problems, sociologists began to study and to appreciate why these people were different, how they were *forced* to adopt what we now call alternative or sometimes deviant life-styles. The

Being isolated and alone is often not an individual's own choice. Our cultural idea that being different is the person's own fault, and something that can and should be changed as soon as possible, causes us to make outcasts of many people.

scientific term *deviance* was coined specifically to do away with the moralistic overtones attached to words like sick, criminal, defective, and so on. A *deviant is anyone who does not follow the accepted ways of their group.* This is supposed to be a neutral statement. The deviant is someone who does not do what is expected at that time, in that place. All of us have been ''deviant'' at some time or other. We have broken some rule or violated some expectation, and sometimes broken the law.

Illegitimate Means to Shared Goals

Using this perspective, we find that the questions for scientific study now are: Why do some laws get violated more than others? Why do some types of people violate rules more than others? And, most importantly, what is it about society that creates nonconformists and deviants? Robert Merton's theory of differential access to the means of achievement is the most influential example of a societal fault that leads to individual deviance.[13] Merton assumes that all members of American society value achievement leading to success. Most of us take the approved road of educational and occupational striving. Some Americans, however, do not have access to these means because of discrimination against their ethnic or class backgrounds. They are discouraged from taking the legitimate paths of preparation for success. They, therefore, are forced to invent and take illegitimate means. That is why the jails are disproportionately occupied by the ''lower classes.'' It is not their ''characters''; it is the combination of the discriminatory environment and the socialization of strong success motivations forced on them by the majority culture.

One of the weaknesses of the deviant behavior orientation is that it provides very little scientific evidence about why one form of deviance rather than another receives the outrage and punishment of society. No explanation of society's rules or society's strong punishment reactions, is provided. We are told that deviance is a violation of the value consensus of the majority society. But, ''no reason for such mass agreement is given beyond that of a spontaneous growth of homogeneous public morality.[14]

We now move to orientations that place even more emphasis on the society's faults as the root causes of social problems. They help us understand that society's rules are transitory and promote an understanding of how they sometimes develop or change in ways that create, rather than control, individual deviance.

Institutional Faults and System Disorganization Emphasis

What we usually call ''the system'' is really a structure of rules, norms, and traditional ways of doing things. It is made up of the values of a society (competition, honesty, success, etc.); the status positions (occupational, class-structure, gender roles); and society's **institutions** (the family, the justice system, religion, governmental bureaucracy). They seem to make up a fixed, all-powerful superstructure that is too stable to change. But ''the system'' is really in constant change and each norm or rule should be thought of as only our best possible solution, so far, for the problem of holding that party of society together as a functioning unit.

The Functionalist Emphasis

The main concern of system theorists, and functionalist sociologists, is the balance of society's institutions. It is assumed that if it can be kept in dynamic equilibrium, that is, changing but not disrupted, society's smooth functioning will benefit all individuals. System theorists, as well as social pathology theorists, compare society to the human organism. This prompted the adoption of the sometimes questionable medical model of social problem analysis. For every type of malfunction or disease of the body, there is a corresponding "social ailment." This is called using the **organismic analogy,** and remember that we are really comparing two systems that are only vaguely similar, and by no means congruent. Many sociologists entirely reject the comparison; they feel that society is far more changeable and less threatened by new elements, or conflicts, than is the human body. For example, few would agree that the protests of the 1960s were comparable to psychiatric disorders. Change or deviance should not be treated as "disease" or "malfunction." This would be socially stagnating because it fosters the conviction that the status quo should be maintained at all costs.

Many of today's problems can be traced to system changes that have been underway for over a century. As Western society changed from a small-scale agrarian folk society into a technologically dependent urbanized mass society, most traditional social structures and roles were dislocated. This has created disillusionment and confusion among individuals caught up in the process of system breakdown and reorganization. Two types of system changes caused major social problems: disorganization and structural specialization.

Disorganization of traditional cultural standards is most apparent among people drawn to the city by the need for work because their agricultural way of life is rapidly disappearing. Most Americans' ancestors went through this painful transition in which traditions had to be given up in order to grasp the "opportunity for a better life." Today, we see this continuing among the Mexicans who enter the Southwest and the Appalachian Whites who move north hoping for industrial jobs. Intense confusion develops as the old definitions of values as basic as "manhood" or "family-centeredness" are threatened by the new expectations of industrial life. This confusion is one example of anomie due to disorganization; the feeling of rulelessness, of not knowing what is correct; the rootlessness of not being able to go back home, or go forward, when all goals seem cloudy or unattainable. As you can imagine, such a feeling can be a powerful stimulant of individual and social problems. Many sociologists see anomie as the underlying cause of much of our crime, divorce, and intergroup violence.

Structural specialization and differentiation also weaken the order and rules of society. Only a few hundred years ago, when most of our ancestors lived in small farming communities, there were basically only four occupations; serf, landowner, soldier, and priest. Each had its own very definite rights and privileges. Although few of us would claim that this was the best of all possible worlds, it had the virtue of being simple and orderly. People knew who they were and what they were "allowed" to do. Industrialization, scientific and social invention, and political revolution have transformed society so that it is almost impossible to count the number of occupations, and it is probably impossible to determine all the separate subgroups that exist in modern society. Some will find themselves in coalition, uniting to achieve the same values or goals, but many will find themselves competing for social or economic opportunities. For example, who has the most important social problem: the farmers who have remained on the land but are in danger of losing their farms, or the ex-farmers, who have already been forced off the land and can't find jobs in the cities? The people involved are quite similar in background, but their newly different statuses have them in direct contention for society's help and support.

In addition to economic or interest group competition, special groups are divided by conflicting traditional values. The value conflict orientation sees most social problems as group differences and maintains that the more specialized we become through differentiation, the more disagreements there will be. A problem arises when one group feels that its values or expectations are being violated. The solution can be found by either the reestablishment of consensus through compromise, or by one group exercising its power to change the system to fit its own design. In a society as differentiated as America, there will necessarily be many value disagreements; abortion, prayer in the schools, and the sexual revolution are obvious examples.

Inequality and Inevitable Conflict Emphasis

The central fact of social life, and therefore of social problems, is that society is structured so that some individuals have more power and privileges than others. They control the unequal distribution of scarce economic resources and rewards and the power associated with them. Those who have more attempt to maintain their advantages and to pass them on to future generations; those who have less attempt to equalize the structure. For conflict theorists, until the unequal social structure is changed, problems such as crime, poverty, pollution, poor health care, and economic depressions, will be impossible to eradicate.

False Values

Conflict theorists see the other theoretical emphases as little more than apologies for the present system. They only deflect our attention and blame away from the existence of a controlling, established group of elites, by blaming the cause of problems on either the victims or the "bureaucrats." For example, conflict theorists say that it is neither value conflicts nor inadequate socialization that creates problems; it is the dominant importance of the system's competition–success values. That is, the common values that the other sociological emphases call the societal consensus and the basis of our cherished togetherness, conflict theorists see as the underlying destructive force. Crime is stimulated by the "lust for property" that is central in American values. Violent crime is legitimated when people see violence and naked power used as instruments of social control to maintain the privilege structure.

Because of these false values, people become alienated. Alienation is a product of the way in which society is structured and, therefore, can only be overcome by progress toward a new society that allows true equality and individual dignity. Therefore, conflict theorists are generally positive about social changes or new lifestyles. These are not conceived of as "deviance" in need of social control, or "nonconformity" in need of resocialization, but as attempts to protest against, or to reorganize the faulty system. For example, many crimes are seen as natural acts that follow from people being oppressed.

Whose Problems? Whose Profit?

Even if you do not accept the somewhat radical version of conflict orientation just presented, the conflict emphasis still offers practical guidelines for the analysis of social problems. One of the first questions we should ask is "Whose problem is it?" That is, who is being hurt, or deprived? Each problem is identified with some special group, or layer of society. Knowing the relative power of social status of the problem-sufferers will help us to understand the type of social action that may or may not be able to aid them. The next question is: "Could some group be profiting from the problem?" Illegal immigration, for example, is certainly not discouraged by factory owners who are able to hire the "illegals" at poverty wages. Finally, if one problem group is to be helped, what other groups might be deprived in the competition for scarce resources or limited power?

Interaction and Social Interpretation Emphasis

This social psychological emphasis concentrates on the ways in which people perceive and define the events that influence their lives. Symbolic Interaction, which provides the theoretical background for the approach, deemphasizes the idea that society is an overpowering, consensual structure of rules and values. Instead, it emphasizes the image of society as the sum total of individuals' interrelationships in everyday life. Society's operating rules are not seen as a fixed set of commandments, but as millions of separate interpretations that are made as individuals face problems together. The individuals on the scene, experiencing and interpreting the events, apply the general societal norms. This cooperative interpretation is what determines what is really going on. For example, sociologists who study crime using this emphasis might concentrate on the thought processes of the police officer who first arrives on the scene of a disturbance. How does he or she choose to see it? Is the man with a gun in his hand a murderer leaving the scene of a crime? Is he a neighbor trying to protect his home? Is he just distraught, or very dangerous? Persons' entire lives could be changed by the way the officer defines that one moment.

Two areas in which sociologists use this approach are: (1) the labeling theory description of how people come to be called mentally ill, or juveniles become defined as delinquents; and (2) **negotiated meanings** resulting from a process that takes place whenever society considers attacking a social problem.

Labeling theory states that it is frequently not the individual's own behavior that gets him or her treated as a "deviant," "delinquent," or "crazy." Instead, it is being "noticed" by society, and being defined as a "deviant" by others, that may begin the causal process of changing a "normal" person into a person who willingly thinks of him or herself as "deviant." A delinquent career is developed through a long social process. Many of us participate in some form of rulebreaking or even lawbreaking when we are young. Something serious begins to happen only if we are caught and singled out through a process of official "tagging, defining, identifying, segregating,

Policework exemplifies the importance of each individual's definition of the social situation. What is the officer thinking, right now? If he decides that the man in the car is a dangerous killer, the situation could suddenly become explosive. What we anticipate and expect of others often strongly influences the outcome of social situations.

describing, and emphasizing."[15] If the labeling experience is powerful enough, the individual may come to accept the definition that society has forced upon him or her. Society's reaction may convince these individuals that they are "that type of person." A grammar-school student may be inattentive or distracted for any number of reasons (problems at home, poor teaching, hunger, etc.). If the school authorities take notice and define him or her as a "bad student," it can lead to a self-definition as one of "those bad kids" who is just waiting to be old enough to leave school. Labeling theorists, therefore, do not study deviants, but the ways in which society makes people into deviants. Why do some and not others get singled out? How can we interrupt that process of definition as a delinquent? Or, how can we undo it, once society has destroyed a person's self-image?

Social Change through Reinterpretation
The main element of the interpretive approach is the idea that the process of social change is inherent in our day-to-day activities; we constantly change our ideas and the ways we look at things. Some ideas are traditionally valued and are therefore harder to change than others, but change is constantly occurring.

THE FUTURE OF SOCIAL PROBLEMS

Sociological orientations help us understand the origins of social problems and the social forces that reinforce their persistence. They also help us judge which problems will be most damaging in the future. The 1960s and 1970s were times of experimentation and protest in American social life. A great deal of hope motivated the attempts to "make war on poverty" and give "power directly to the people." But we did not know enough about how to anticipate the results of our actions. In the 1980s we know that a lot more time and study must be given to a policy before it is inaugurated. Anticipation of possible alternative futures is the main element of planning.

There are many critical choices to be made: environmental pollution, poverty, welfare, political domination by elites, minority groups without justice, the increasing complexity of social life, entire industries endangered by foreign competition, crime and violence, nuclear power, migration, dying cities, family breakdown, nuclear war, and so on.[16] In short, we have begun to doubt the inevitability of progress. We must make choices, and they all depend on our ability to estimate what will probably happen in the near future.

Rules for the Future

We Can't Always Predict the Future
But We Do Invent It

Today's decisions are tomorrow's realities. We are living out the decisions of the last generation. For example, our commitment of billions of tax dollars for the creation of a massive highway system subsidized the automobile and trucking industries. This decision helped to make us dependent on gasoline, significantly increased pollution, and promoted suburbanization.

What You Don't Know Can Hurt You:
Latent Effects

One of the sociologist's roles is to try to isolate *all* the possible consequences of a proposed social change. As you read this book you will become aware that you have been supporting policies and attitudes that have had some very nasty side effects. Government policies subsidizing highway construction and gasoline companies have promoted pollution. Sexist attitudes not only create psychological anguish, but also damage the economy by discriminating against useful workers and managers.

Robert Merton's distinction between manifest and latent effects is a basic tool for anticipating consequences. Manifest effects are those that are obvious, and expected. We intend to help immigrants when we tell them to assimilate, drop their old-country ways, and participate in the American dream. But we do not intend to destroy their ethnic identity and hurt them by leaving them between heritages. Looking for all the alternative futures means paying special attention to those **latent consequences** that are hidden inside the developing problem, or the proposed solution.

"Plan or Be Planned for"

This is a motto found on the wall of a grass-roots community organization in the heart of a western Philadelphia ghetto area.[17] There is no question that our society is a planned society, and will remain so. All too frequently the official planners have acted as the "soft cops" of society[18] by choosing programs that would maintain orderliness and the status quo. One of the sociologists' jobs is to keep official planners thinking of innovative alternative solutions, to get them to act rather than react.

Our society usually gets estimates of what will happen in the future by seeking out an authority, what is called a "genius forecaster," and listening to him or her just as the early Greeks listened to an oracle. There are, however, much more scientific methods. We can all learn to be our own experts for the important problems that will determine our lives.

Examine the Taken-for-Granted

Willard Waller warned us that our thinking about social policy tends to stay within the boundaries of our taken-for-granted assumptions.[19] We hardly ever look at all the alternatives, only at the ones that do not disturb our current values or ideas of what is correct. It took Americans many generations to act against monopolies and robber barons because the idea of free competition was so much a part of our view of economic life. Real criticism of present society can only be done with the mind wide open, looking for all possible future solutions. We may have to upset traditional values, or adapt accepted social institutions to solve our problems. The tools and working attitudes of Futurism can help us. By systematically considering scenarios depicting alternative futures, we can learn to shed our socially conditioned inflexibilities.

Methods for Studying the Future of Social Problems

In addition to the tools of sociological analysis, this book will use three futurists' methods: (1) *trend impact analysis,* looking for a pattern in the problem's development that we can use to predict its future; (2) *cross-impact analysis,* looking at all the social forces associated with a problem in order to find side effects and interrelationships; and (3) *scenarios,* formulating two alternative *futures* for each problem that has sufficient data, the optimistic future and the pessimistic future.

Trend extrapolation, is the easiest and most common form of guessing what will happen; it is also the most faulty. For example, we have continued to believe that because there has always been growth in the American economy, and we have always been the world leader in technology, we could expect it to continue. We now know that even this firmly established trend has suddenly become very unstable.

Cross-impacts are the effects that one problem might have on another. What would be the effect on urban crime if unemployment were to increase, or decrease? Will the awareness of energy limitations substantially affect people's life-style attitudes and make them want to be more self-sufficient? This is where the sociological theories we have reviewed will be most helpful. We can use them to find clues, to find the important social interconnections between problems and society's structure.

Scenarios are used by all of us in everyday life. They usually begin, "What if . . . ," or "Suppose I . . ."; "If I took that job in Hawaii . . ."; "If I married Bobbie next year instead of next month. . . ." What we are doing is laying out alternative futures, like a pile of different movie scripts, in order to allow us to choose future roles we want to play, or avoid. The most interesting are the provocative, "surprise sensitive" forecasts. "If I married a millionaire," or, "inherited all the money in the world," or, "became President," "what would be the first thing I would do?" The daydreams and speculations often have a useful purpose; we get to "play with" deciding what we really want out of life. Sociologists and futurists also compose scenarios for large-scale societal alternatives. We will present, in each chapter, two alternatives in the form of descriptions of what it might be like to live in: (1) the world that could happen if attitudes, inventions, or policies, are developed that improve our chances; and (2) the negative side; if trends take a turn for the worse, and problems start to develop and accelerate.

SUMMARY

1. The definition of dangerous conditions as social problems is often impeded by our feeling that we are unable to do anything about them. Believing in inevitable evolution and individual responsibility for successful competition are two other strong, however, inaccurate, impediments.

2. The social scientists' contribution is to remain objective by avoiding value judgments and studying problems using the scientific method. They replace emotional reactions and cultural biases by developing sociological theories of social problems.

3. Most recognized social problems have four attributes: they (a) have persisted; (b) caused significant damage; (c) offended the values of some powerful segment of society; and (d) have a number of proposed solutions.

4. Problems persist due to a lack of knowledge; interconnectedness with other problems or cherished institutions; or because someone is profiting.

5. Scientists attempt to provide accurate damage estimates based on quantitative indices of incidence, prevalence, and trend of the problem's development. They attempt to calculate both the individual and social costs of problems.

6. Values and standards of judgment of problems' severity can change markedly over time. People also tend to evaluate problems from within the ideology of their own social class positions. Politics and group interest have strong influences on problems' definitions.

7. The recognition of social problems is confused by cultural lags such as the myth of the undeserving, and quasi-theories such as "inadequate communication" and "the sweet-mystery of life."

8. Individual Faults/Deviant Behavior is the first of the four sociological orientations to problems. It emphasizes the medical model, or seeing deviant individuals as sick and in need of retraining by society.

9. The Institutional Faults/System Disorganization model emphasizes the breakdown of the "organism" of society. Structural differentiation and change have de-

stroyed the functional balance of society, and individuals cannot find secure social positions.

10. The Inequality/Inevitable Conflict emphasis concentrates on the alienation caused by false beliefs in the profit motive and the unequal power structure.

11. The Interaction/Social Interpretation orientation tells us that problems are often distorted, or even created, by the way we socially define them. Labeling of individuals as deviants is a complex and often inaccurate process.

12. Understanding the future can be facilitated by practicing the "art of anticipation." This involves realizing we invent our future; examining our taken-for-granted assumptions about possible solutions to problems; searching out latent effects of inventions before implementing them; and not allowing others to plan our lives for us.

SUGGESTED READINGS

Berger, Peter. *Invitation to Sociology*. New York: Doubleday, 1963. The classic description of "Sociology as a Form of Consciousness" is very helpful in seeing through apparent problems and recognizing real social problems and their causes.

Collins, Randall. *Sociological Insight: An Introduction to Non-Obvious Sociology*. New York: Oxford University Press, 1982. The social importance of nonrationality and unanticipated interrelationships is demonstrated during analyses of religion, power, love, crime, and property.

Douglas, Jack. *Investigative Social Research: Individual and Team Field Research*. Beverly Hills: Sage, 1976. How to infiltrate, examine taken-for-granted feelings, overcome self-deceptions, and get at the truth in social groups.

Katzer, Jeffrey, Kenneth Cook, and Wayne Crouch. *Evaluating Information, A Guide for Users of Social Science Research*. Reading, Mass.: Addison-Wesley, 1982. How to read and understand research reports and to judge how much belief you can safely invest in them. Excellent sections on assumptions, bias, noise, and rival explanations in research.

Komarovsky, Mirra (ed.). *Sociology and Public Policy: The Case of Presidential Commissions*. New York: Elsevier, 1975. Case histories of four famous commissions (Obscenity and Pornography; Population Growth; Violence; and Law Enforcement) and analyses of how they could have more effectively faced their problems.

Tanur, Judith et al. (eds.). *Statistics: A Guide to Political and Social Issues*. San Francisco: Holden-Day, 1977. Studies specially collected to introduce the policy importance of statistics to "beginners."

Terkel, Studs. *American Dreams: Lost and Found*. New York: Ballantine, 1980. Interviews with hundreds of people describe our problems and dissatisfactions from all possible social perspectives.

Wilson, John. *Social Theory*. Englewood Cliffs, N.J.: Prentice-Hall, 1983. Brief but very well-organized descriptions of the sociological perspectives, in comparison, and in an historical context.

GLOSSARY

Appreciative orientation   Looking at people from different groups with a curious interest in order to find out the ways in which you or they differ.

Cultural lag   The gap occurring when technology and knowledge change faster than our social norms or attitudes.

Incidence   Measurement of the seriousness of a problem by the number of new cases within a given time period.

Institution   An organized set of rules for doing things, centering on a particular societal activity, such as education, family, government, and so on.

Interconnectivity   Joined or interrelated parts of a system, societal or ecological, wherein what happens to one part often affects many others.

Internalized norms   Rules of society that become part of individuals' beliefs and attitudes.

Latent consequences   The hidden, unexpected effects of a social change, not manifestly obvious when the change was planned.

Negotiated meanings   A central concept of interactionist theory stating that what we think something means is often based on social arguments and agreements rather than any exact scientific study or definition.

Organismic analogy   The belief that a biological organism, such as the human body, is a good model for understanding the needs and functioning of human societies.

Prevalence   Measurement of the seriousness of a problem by assessing how widespread it is.

Scenario   An organized story about a possible future, exemplifying current trends and expectations and showing their impact on life in the future.

Trend   Measurement of the seriousness of a problem in its pattern of increase or decrease over time.

2

THE INDIVIDUAL IN MODERN SOCIETY: ALIENATION AND ANOMIE

Before we discuss the variety of social problems confronting our society, another topic warrants our consideration. Since, as we discussed in Chapter 1, reality perceptions and value judgments influence attitudes and actions regarding social problems, we need some understanding about people's expectations and the social conditions generating their concepts about the quality of life. Do people expect too much today? Are they too easily dissatisfied? Does modern society create a sense of meaninglessness, lack of community, and alienation? Do we desperately seek meaning in our lives? Or do we tend to detach ourselves from situations, playing out societal roles without any personal commitment, while drifting aimlessly through an overwhelming series of demands and responsibilities? Answers to these questions will help us to understand better how individuals assess social problems and their solutions.

THE QUALITY OF INDIVIDUALS' LIVES

Recent concern about the quality of life marks a turning point in the way we evaluate and understand life in society. In the past, we judged how well society was *providing* for its members; we were concerned only with the quantities of necessities or luxuries available. This new trend toward concern with quality alerts us to the need for understanding and improving the full range of noneconomic societal institutions, each capable of limiting or lowering our health, freedom, or happiness.

Overconcern with material productivity had narrowed policymakers' views of social life. For decades, federal taxes financed the collection of data on thousands of economic indicators, but the study of the social indicators related to individuals' levels of satisfaction or happiness has only recently begun. Sociologists contribute to this new understanding of the power of society to affect individuals' lives in the following ways:

1. What appear to be microlevel individual problems often result from macrostructured societal problems. Sociologists emphasize society causes many of our day-to-day difficulties in relating to each other (anomie) and confusions in our definitions and feelings about ourselves (alienation).

2. Sociologists demonstrate the side effects, or latent functions, of society's cherished values. By placing modern life in a historical context, we can see that our overemphasis on materialism is not the sole cause of our value confusions. Our valued goals of individualism, rationalism, and technological progress contribute heavily to our modern problems.

Types of Life Satisfactions

Basically, individuals expect from society three types of life satisfactions: having, relating, being. As we shall now discuss, these three categories of need fulfillment determine people's judgment of their life quality.

Having

Only this type involves material resources, though it receives the most attention. Yet in a nationwide survey of people's levels of satisfaction, Campbell found that we overemphasize the relationship between financial situation and happiness. Setting aside the obvious and extreme case of poverty and its misery, Campbell found "people of every degree of happiness and satisfaction at every point on the income scale."[1] Social values and a range of social group participations, not just material success, affect life satisfaction. Even what would seem to be clear-cut measures of success—income and possessions—lose their meaning unless society provides unambiguous standards for choosing between values. Even increased "having" can bring confusion rather than satisfaction.

Relating

Enormous changes in our ways of relating to each other began with industrialization and urbanization. They are still underway and accelerating. Traditional forms of interrelationships have been replaced, or just discarded. Families are smaller; we now tend to live as separate couples, or even by ourselves rather than in large extended family groups. Also, our social relationships are filtered through governments and bureaucracies, and are much less personal than before.

We call the negative effects of these changes **anomie,** the breakdown of the traditional laws, rules, and values that help to hold society together. The word *normlessness* names the confusion we feel when we don't know what to expect from others' behavior. In its extreme form, normlessness becomes social disorganization and true lawlessness. People who "don't want to get involved" forget the obligations and responsibilities all society members must follow in support of each other (see Box 2.1).

Being

Satisfaction with who we are, or have become, is the third element involved in judging whether we are leading a quality life. Campbell found that satisfaction with oneself was not related to the usual social categories of education, income, or age. Instead, it was related to feeling that one has control over one's life, as opposed to feeling that one's life is being controlled by outside forces.[2] Sociologists use the term **alienation** to describe individuals' feelings that their lives lack meanings and direction. Some call this feeling inauthenticity, the meaninglessness felt, for example, when you are performing at school or on the job only because of outside pressure and not because the task provides any personal satisfaction or has any relationship to what is essential in your life.

THE IMPACT OF SOCIETY ON THE INDIVIDUAL

Emile Durkheim's *Suicide* became the classic sociological research study because it demonstrated that social forces contributed to even the most personal, and seemingly psychological, decision: whether or not to take one's own life. Through careful

BOX 2.1

TEENAGE SUICIDE IN THE
SUNBELT

Plano is not a perfect city, but it may well be quintessential—of its kind. It is groaning under a population explosion—from 17,000 in the early '70s to 72,000 by 1980, nearly 90,000 in 1983. And it is nagged by the boredom and restlessness typical of a community with a largely transplanted and homogeneous middle-class citizenry. For the past three years Plano's divorce level has stood at about 1,000 a year—a reflection, perhaps, of lingering affinities with Dallas, which has the country's third highest divorce rate. Even so, it does not seem capable of nurturing the sort of terminal despair that has surfaced recently among its young people.

This year there have also been 16 apparently unrelated suicide attempts by Plano adolescents. According to police reports, 11 females and 5 males ranging in age from 13 to 24 years old have tried to kill themselves using any available means, including overdoses of Valium, Alka-Seltzer, Anacin, Tylenol, Sominex and an assortment of unidentified potions. One 18-year-old girl carved up her chest with a pair of scissors. A 19-year-old boy slashed his left index finger with a razor blade. Another tried to hang himself with his own shirt. The methods seemed halfhearted (the classic cry for help, perhaps), yet the willingness of so many young people to flirt with death in order to call attention to their problems is profoundly disturbing in itself.

The teen suicide profile in Plano accords roughly with the national pattern. Every year approximately 5,000 teenagers kill themselves, and as many as half a million more make attempts. Three times as many girls try to kill themselves, but boys tend to use more decisive methods—and succeed four times more often. The national totals have remained essentially unchanged for the past five years, but they represent an alarming 300 percent increase in adolescent suicides since 1955. The 13-to-14-year-old age group, moreover, is the only segment of the population whose death rate has increased (by 13 percent) in recent years, and among 15-to-19-year-olds, suicide is now the second leading cause of death, after traffic accidents—many of which, in fact, are suspected suicides.

Experts have advanced dozens of reasons for the teen-suicide phenomenon, among them the decline of religion, the breakup of the nuclear family and competitiveness at school and in the shrinking job market. Teenagers are generally said to be more pessimistic about the future, less fortified by altruistic beliefs than their older brothers and sisters were. And there is the fact that only 38 percent of the country's young people now live with both natural parents. "This creates enormous stresses on some of them," says Charlotte Ross, executive director of the pioneering San Mateo (Calif.) Suicide Prevention and Crisis Center. "There is less and less of a strong and stable support system for many of these kids." On the whole, today's teens would seem vulnerable to what the 19th-century French sociologist Emile Durkheim called "anomic" suicide, which tends to appear, he wrote, in the presence of social disruption and personal loss.

NEWCOMERS

Plano, despite its middle-class comforts, has an abundance of both disruption and loss. It is afflicted by the rootlessness and isolation characteristic of a place where nearly everything and everyone is new. A 1979 survey showed that 82 percent of Plano's citizens had lived there less than 10 years, 59 percent for 4 years or less. "The kids who have the hardest time are the ones from small towns who have never moved before," says 16-year-old Dee-Dee Heppner, herself a seasoned veteran of six moves around the Southwest. "You can spot them in class or at lunch because they sit by themselves and don't talk to anyone."

IDENTITY

There is fierce pressure to "make it" in a new place where the parents are high achievers and demand much of the children. . . . Says Dr. Philip K. Armour, a University of Texas sociologist who is completing a study of suicide in the sun belt: "They're dealing with establishing an identity in a place where there aren't any extended families or reference groups. In this kind of community, a peer-group attachment is a validation of yourself. When that is lost, you cease to exist—you die psychologically and socially."

SUFFERING

Suicide is sometimes called the ultimate self-indulgence, but adolescence, as Haim observes, "is a multiple bereavement." These children are mourning the "lost paradise" of childhood; their pain is real enough. In any event, the suicide statistics for 15-to-24-year-olds continue to inch up. And in the anomic new communities of the sun belt, the problem seems epidemic. Phoenix has the highest adolescent suicide rate in the country, Dallas the second highest.

SOURCE: David Gelman, "Teenage Suicide in the Sun Belt," *Newsweek* (August 15, 1983), pp. 70–71.
Copyright © 1983, by Newsweek, Inc. All Rights Reserved. Reprinted by permission.

empirical study, Durkheim ruled out poverty, the natural environment, and other popular theories of the causes of suicide. He demonstrated that social rhythms were highly correlated with changes in the suicide rates. Durkheim's important theoretical contribution was the concept of anomie: the condition in which weakened social bonds and a lack of rules contribute to an increase in suicides.[3] His major finding was that change, not misery or even severe poverty, prompted suicides to increase. For example, rapid economic change, whether boom or bust, caused social disruption and more individuals to turn to suicide.

Durkheim isolated egoism as the second major social influence on increased suicide rates. Where a nation's values were strongly centered on group organization, as in Ireland where the Catholic Church wielded influence, even terrible economic deprivation did not increase the suicide rate. In Protestant Germany, where individuals were supposed to work out their own relationships with God, suicides were relatively frequent, even during times of comparative economic plenty. Durkheim attributed this to the egoistic-individualistic values of Protestantism, which made the individual feel alone and unsupported by society.

Shyness, A Cultural Fact

If you find it surprising that such personal events as suicide are socially influenced, you are not alone. Philip G. Zimbardo found that even professionals mistakenly think of isolation and shyness as personal problems.[4] When he discovered that about 5 percent of the student body at a college went to the campus clinic complaining of loneliness, he asked what was being done about it. Zimbardo learned that each patient was given some personalized treatment. Zimbardo then asked, "Suppose all 500 came to the clinic at the same time? . . . What would the diagnosis be, and where would the therapist look for its causes?" The clinician readily replied that the clinic would call the dormitory office to find out what had caused such a mass reaction. Zimbardo points out that just because the students presented themselves one at a time, there was no reason to continue to ask each of them "What's wrong with *you*?" instead of "What's wrong out there?" We pass sentence on individuals rather than on social situations (see Box 2.2).

Embedded and Enmeshed in Society

You can be justifiably skeptical when a sociologist tells you of society's overwhelming power. The process of socialization is so efficient that we do not feel society's power. However, a list of some of the social structures that control and organize your life will make society's power clearer.

Institutions

In traditional societies, when areas of life are considered by society to be central because they deal with basic human needs such as family, education, politics, defense, or economics, then what are merely traditional solutions come to be seen as sacred. They become institutionalized when sets of interlocking social roles become established as the proper ways to behave in important situations. The individual

The girl on the left seems separated from the situation, in a world of her own. Our culture is contradictory. It places value on belonging, but, at the same time, it has rules against appearing overly friendly that make us shy and hesitant.

automatically fits himself or herself into the preestablished obligations and responsibilities. Tradition establishes more than the norms of behavior; it also provides the desirable goals for each of life's situations. For example, competitive success, procreative marriage, and then retirement to a life of leisure were traditional goals almost unquestioned until recently.

   Institutions' powerful effects go unnoticed. It is only when they become inadequate that we are forced to think about the "proper" way to form a social arrangement. For example, the institution of romance and marriage is presently disorganized and each individual is now forced to decide among alternative ways of finding

BOX 2.2

CULTURAL PROGRAMMING

In which hand do you hold your fork while eating? In the left when you are cutting your food, and in the right when you eat it? Probably so, *if* you are an American; Europeans always keep a fork in their left hand. Do you bow when meeting a friend on the street? Americans probably don't, but it would be rude for Japanese not to. Would you be more willing to help a foreigner or a compatriot? Depends on the way your cultural background defines ingroup and outgroup. For Greeks, ingroup includes family, friends, and tourists, but not other Greeks who are strangers. This is not so with Parisians or Bostonians, both of whom, as a group, have been shown to be more ready to grant help to compatriots than foreigners.

To an extent we often fail to appreciate, our culture conditions our perception of reality while programming the structure of our thoughts, feelings, and actions. Even so fundamental a reality as pain has been shown to elicit very different reactions depending on one's cultural background. Italians are very sensitive to pain and exaggerate its intensity. Jews also react strongly to pain, but are more concerned than Italian patients about its implications for their future health. Anglo-Saxon Protestants display emotional reactions to pain only in private. In contrast, Irish patients "bite the bullet" and silently endure pain without complaint or showing their suffering, even in private.

How do cultural values and practices program people to be shy? You might frame an answer to this question by designing the shy society you would develop if you were minister of the interior. On your list of ten ways to promote shyness, you'd probably want to mention:

and keeping a mate, or is it a partner, or is it a companion? (See Box 2.3 which describes the popularity of Personal Ads. When an old institution fails, new, organized, ritualized social forms begin to take its place.)

Careers and Timetables

Institutions provide the daily rituals ordering our lives. We can proceed from one situation to the next without concern, knowing what role to slip into and which to leave behind. The high-school student leaving the family breakfast table to join her friends on the way to school has no trouble facing a sharp change in expectations.

But everyday life would be intolerable if it consisted of merely passing from one ritual to another.[5] We need a density to our lives, a sense that we are going along in some direction, a way to judge if things are going as expected. We usually accomplish this by constructing a number of careers inside our lives. We judge our sexual

1. Valuing rugged individualism (making it on one's own, going it alone, doing it my way).

2. Promoting a cult of the ego (narcissistic introspection, self-absorption, and self-consciousness).

3. Prizing individual success and making failure a source of personal shame in a highly competitive system.

4. Setting limitless aspirations and ambiguous criteria for success, while not teaching ways of coping with failure.

5. Discouraging expression of emotions and open sharing of feelings and anxieties.

6. Providing little opportunity for intimate relations between the sexes and strict taboos on most forms of sexual expression.

7. Making acceptance and love contingent on fluctuating and critical social standards of performance.

8. Denying the significance of an individual's present experience by making comparisons to the unmatchable glories of past times and the demands of future goals.

9. Fostering social instability through mobility, divorce, economic uncertainty, and any other way possible.

10. Destroying faith in common societal goals and pride in belonging to the group.

Consider whether this prescription of a shyness-generating society has already been filled for you. Don't many of these values exist in your work, school, and everyday life? I believe that in any society where shyness is a prevalent, undesirable problem we will also find variants of these ten elements.

SOURCE: Philip G. Zimbardo, *Shyness*, © 1977, Addison-Wesley, Reading, Massachusetts, pp. 211–212. Reprinted with permission.

or marital career in much the same way as our occupational timetable. Have we progressed far enough fast enough? Is there room for growth and advancement? Similarly, we give our leisure, economic, social, and other interests meaning by locating them in larger timetables. The sum of these compartments is our life plan. This is how we organize the realm of being that we discussed earlier. But accurate self-evaluation is difficult because we are measuring ourselves by so many timetables simultaneously.

Multiple Realities

Careers structure pathways aiming toward one of the desirable states described for us in our cultural values. Therefore, they should simplify our lives and give them meaning. But we also have **role overabundance.** In our stratified and highly diversified society, we actually encounter several realities, several views of what is desirable.

BOX 2.3

ADS SEEK VALENTINES ALL YEAR

She is slim, smart, funny, spontaneous, spiritual, into films, and a Brooke Shields look-alike. He is athletic, brainy, humorous, creative, caring, into Mozart, and a Tom Selleck look-alike. And like thousands of others, they are swimming upstream in an alphabet soup of SWF's, DBM's and such, looking for love in the classifieds. This is becoming a very respectable, middle-class thing to do.

Fifteen years ago, few publications carried personals columns and anyone who used them was considered a loser or whatever the term was in those days. Since then, there has been a steady proliferation of such columns in newspapers and magazines and in publications that cater to a special audience, such as tennis players or rock music fans. High-tech personals for computer buffs appear on electronic billboards.

"My own mother took out an ad in *New York Magazine* after my stepfather died," a woman in her 20's said. "I said, 'Mother, you're 52 years old! I can't believe you're doing this.' The upshot was that she met one or two very lovely men and now she wants to help me write an ad. I may take her up on the offer."

. . . For those who aren't do-it-yourself types, there are personals writers who promise to deliver winning copy for a fee. . . . [psychotherapist Jane Klenberg] and other professionals warn that the motivation behind such ads is always an unknown and an element of danger may be present. They recommend that the first date be held in a public place. . . .

Although [*The Village Voice* in New York's Greenwich Village] has been printing personals for 23 years, [publisher] John Evans believes the column is more valued

> Persons at different points in society, possessing more or less power, prestige, status, and wealth, have very different images of the world. . . . Also, the several ethnic, racial, and religious groups . . . give different meanings to their life-worlds.[6]

We also find a number of different meaning systems in society at any given time. Mills explained the many interpretations we might apply to each other's behavior, calling them vocabularies of motive.[7] Contradictory explanations occur every day in our society. For example, the Marxian vocabulary attributes peoples' behavior to an economic struggle or profit-greed; businesspeople's meanings are similar, but they see behavior in terms of rational competition for gain; Freudian explanations see us as unconsciously driven by elemental needs that emerge in unexpected, sometimes uncontrollable, actions; the oldest and most traditional explanation is the moral vocabulary, categorizing behavior as "right" or "wrong," with these labels leading to acceptance or condemnation; hedonistic meanings center on the calculation of the pleasure or pain involved in each situation. Mills showed us that each of these vocabularies was the dominant explanation of people's behaviors in some recent

by readers today, because it is harder to meet people in New York. "You don't pick people up on the bus here," he said. "You try to get home to your safe little apartment without being killed."

Citing the results of a recent survey of personals column advertisers, the publisher said that ads placed by women drew an average of 49 replies, while men's ads drew only 15 replies. The same pattern has appeared in surveys by other publications. . . .

The *Voice* mails out 200,000 replies a year, Mr. Evans said: "We think of these letters as the modern version of valentines. Years ago a valentine wasn't something you bought from Hallmark. It was a letter written, often anonymously, to impress someone."

. . . On the other hand, Raymond Shapiro thinks of the personals as sociology. . . . In tracking the personals over the past 15 years, Mr. Shapiro has observed that the ads reflect profound social changes as well as passing fads and vogues. Among the more fundamental changes he cited were: "the drifting away from pure hedonism to the desire for family life and children," "the emergence of homosexuality as something to be presented in a very positive way" and "a moderation and maturing of feminism."

Feminists' ads in the late 60's through early 70's tended to be "militant in tone," he said. Then, in the mid-70's an ad appeared that, in Mr. Shapiro's view, exemplified a watershed in the women's movement: "FEMINIST, 33, Now allowing men to buy her drinks."

Today, he speculated, the same woman would probably be advertising for a "nurturing man willing to share housework and child care."

SOURCE: Georgia Dullea, "Ads Seek Valentines All Year," *The New York Times* (February 13, 1984), p. A18. Copyright © *The New York Times*. Reprinted with permission.

historical period. They all still exist, side by side, and it is often difficult to avoid confusion when attempting to choose between them.

In summary, society provides institutional roles and expectations, daily rituals, evaluations of various career accomplishments, and ways of explaining each other's actions so that they are meaningful. But modern society does not do any of these things in a clear-cut or simple way. Multiple competing goals and explanations provide more confusion than guidance.

ANOMIE: DISORGANIZATION, SEPARATION, AND MEANINGLESSNESS

The Loss of Community

Sociologist Ferdinand Tönnies, in 1887, made an important distinction between the traditional, all-encompassing, emotionally supportive **community** (Gemeinschaft) and the modern efficiency-based society (Gesellschaft). At the time, many were extolling the freedom and wealth that would be available in the coming age, but Tönnies was anticipating its social-psychological costs. His description of the horrors of Gesellschaft, "which for Tönnies meant the whole complex of impersonal, abstract, and anonymous relationships which characterized capitalism, nationalism, and all the forces of individualism, bureaucratization, and secularism which he could see eating away at the social fabric," was profoundly influential.[8]

The Great Emptiness
Tönnies's distinction found its most influential expression in the Chicago School of Sociology's view of modern urban life as inherently undesirable and pathogenic. This assumption of the superiority of stable small communities was shared by many sociologists and social critics and is best exemplified by Robert MacIver's description of the "great emptiness":

> Back in the days when unremitting toil was the lot of all but the very few and leisure still a hopeless yearning, hard and painful as life was, it still felt real. People were in *rapport* with the small bit of reality allotted to them, the sense of the earth, the tang of the changing seasons, the consciousness of the eternal on-going of birth and death. Now, when so many have leisure, they become detached from themselves, not merely from the earth. From all the widened horizons of our greater world a thousand voices call us to come near, to understand, and to enjoy, but our ears are not trained to hear them. The leisure is ours but not the skill to use it. So leisure becomes a void, and from the ensuing restlessness men take refuge in delusive excitations or fictitious visions, returning to their own earth no more.[9]

Romantic Nostalgia
As you will see in Chapter 15 on urban problems, the assumption that cities necessarily destroy warm or orderly social relations has been proven to be false. Tönnies and his interpreters were incorrect in believing that a community could only exist in the small agrarian villages of the past. They were correct, however, in seeing some form of social-emotional integration as basic for a satisfactory social life. Community has had a difficult time reemerging in the inhospitable surroundings of a city or bureaucracy, changing in the process out of necessity.

Anomic Conditions

Anomie is not an unfamiliar idea; people frequently discuss it using other names. We say that modern society is aimless, goalless, disorganized, fragmented, or in the process of dissolution. We hear that people are rootless, frustrated, and feel empty. We will examine the historical roots of these feelings; but first let us see some examples of how societal changes are related to these feelings.

Separation into Individuals
Not so long ago we thought of ourselves as part of some larger unit, and only a few of us were alone. Currently almost 25 percent of the population lives alone, more than ever before. Many are under 40, choosing not to marry for a variety of reasons.

"Women in this group are often the first women in their families to live alone."[10]

Transitions

Significant changes in status cause emotional disruptions and necessitate difficult adaptations. Individuals must now face twice as many significant transitions as in the recent past. The traditional phases of life used to be childhood, marriage, childbirth, childrearing, and finally, the dissolution of the marriage. The Census Bureau reports that you will also probably face: a period of living away from your family before marriage; a longer time in which to be single; and a high divorce or separation rate, often leading to a high second marriage rate (about 83 percent of men remarry, 75 percent of women), in turn leading to a redivorce rate slightly higher than the first-marriage divorce rate.[11] Each of these transitions is potentially disorienting, and the effects of this turbulence of social relationships on children is just beginning to be studied. Startling facts demonstrating these changes surface every day. In Westchester, New York, you can make your child support payments with your credit card!

The Rust of Progress: Functionalists' Concerns

For more than a century, functionalists have been warning us that material progress cannot provide the structure and meanings that humans need.[12] Individuals, they maintain, are not strong enough to achieve progress, or manage it, without social controls, which is why system disorganization is so serious. Durkheim said it this way:

> to achieve any result, the passions first must be limited. Only then can they be harmonized with the faculties and satisfied. But since the individual has no way of limiting them, this must be done by some force exterior to him.[13]

Today material progress provides longer and more comfortable lives, but many believe it provides no limits or sense of direction.

Modern functionalists are also concerned with the disproportionate emphasis placed on success. All Americans want it but cannot define what it is. Do we want to "make a million" or is that no longer enough? We are uncertain and indefinite about our goals and expectations. Many Americans feel that striving for success is "meaningless not because they lack the capacity or opportunity to achieve what is wanted but because they lack a clear definition of what is desirable."[14]

The Game of Competition

Functionalists say we have lost our normative standards during our all-out pursuit of this diffuse, undefinable goal of success. As long as fair competition was the highest value, most followed the rules of the game, trying to outdo others using accepted norms of behavior. We now place too much stress on results, thereby encouraging achievement of success by any means. Institutionalized standards therefore become irrelevant in decisions about success, and society becomes progressively more unstable.

Learning to compete is a long and sometimes dangerous process involving physical and psychological injuries. The value on competition is passed from generation to generation, and the losers are urged to keep on trying.

Vagueness and Specialization

Sociologist William I. Thomas characterized modern life as the constant effort to define the vague: the inability to get a complete grip on a situation or the best way out of it. Premodern individuals did not constantly ask themselves, "why do I do this, and why do I do this the way I do it?"[15] Instead of experiencing the past and its traditions as essential and useful parts of present decisions, we see them as inadequate and necessarily in need of improvement.

Disenchantment

Modern life disillusions us, yet we have no patience with traditional solutions unless they work quickly. We modernize instead of valuing past explanations and techniques. In the process, we also discard those meaning systems, spiritual or sacred justifications, or enchanting notions that made premodern life meaningful and orderly. Traditional solutions literally come to mean nothing.

This is usually called the Weberian Paradox. German sociologist Max Weber made us aware that scientific efficiency demystifies our lives and threatens the very roots of our personalities. "Rationalization spreads at the cost of 'love, hatred, and all purely personal, irrational, and emotional elements which escape calculation.'"[16]

Secularization and the Search for Meaning

In the past, religion was a powerful and pervasive society-wide institution. It regulated both thought and action. "The world as defined by the religious institution . . . *was the world*. . . . To step outside the world as religiously defined was to step into a chaotic darkness, into anomie, possibly into madness."[17]

Secularization is the process removing both social-structural and symbolic elements of individuals' lives from religious control. We have had not only a separation of church and state, but also a secularization of consciousness. As sociologist Peter Berger observes, "The modern West has produced an increasing number of individuals who look upon the world and their own lives without the benefit of religious interpretations."[18]

Berger notes that sometimes we do not notice the completeness of this shift; culture lag exists between secularization of the economy and the family and state. Religious symbols survive in the statehouse and in politicians' rhetoric, and they remain part of the meanings attached to family formation. However, religious meaning no longer permeates the everyday life of the individual, especially the economic activities and their related evaluations of self-worth. The plausibility of the religious definition of reality has collapsed for many people, taking with it the one common standard previously used to judge activities as legitimate. Individuals now face a wide variety of explanations, none with the power to coerce nor the traditional foundation to convince fully.

Berger holds out little hope for a return to monopolistic religion. Once pluralism has taken hold, it becomes impossible for one religion to unite all members of society in a common "plausibility structure." It is impossible to keep the members of even one small "religious world" separate and together, away from the many competing systems. But this does not mean that individuals have given up the search for meaning.

New Cults

Religious dissent and the creation of new religious forms is an original foundation of American values. We have many churches, sects, denominations, and cults, but the recent growth in new cults has been extraordinary even by American standards. Since 1965 at least 1,300 new religious groups have been formed in the United States.[19] If we add the large number of personal growth groups and counterculture groups, we cannot help but be overwhelmed by the thousands of people who are willing to join groups seen by most people as either radically new, or overly strict. Many of these groups attempt to return to traditional forms of Christianity, and many are adaptations of Eastern mysticism. They are influential enough for one futurist to feel they may be the basis of two of the three possible religious futures of the United States.

Fundamentalism

How do we explain the resurgence of fundamentalism in America? Many social observers see it as a reaction against an alienating modern society. Horowitz views this religious trend as part of a worldwide reaction to advancing modernity.[20] In the Middle East, especially in Iran, we are witnessing a powerful and dominating response to the industrial/scientific values of development. Widespread returns to fundamentalist Catholic, Protestant, or Islamic sects have occurred elsewhere in both capitalist and socialist systems.

Will religious revivalism become a stable element in American society or merely a "cyclical event" or reactionary movement? Only time will tell, but Horowitz cautions it would be a miscalculation to regard it as nothing more than another phase like "hanging loose" or "environmentalism."

> What we are witnessing is not simply a challenge to modernity but an assault upon complexity, especially against scientific findings and formulas. The religious mood of exaltation and fervor, even if it remains confined to a statistical minority, is a relatively painless way to knowledge. In place of many books is The Good Book; in place of relativism is moral certainty; in place of a series of questions begetting more questions is a series of answers stimulated by the rhetoric of certainty.[21]

Some see American fundamentalism as a specific reaction to traditional Protestantism's concentration on "future-oriented instrumentalism."[22] Often called the Protestant Ethic, this emphasis was on individual achievement through present denial and future planning. In terms of the life-satisfaction categories discussed earlier, too much concentration on *having* and too little on *being* or *relating* have sparked the return to unquestioned basic tenets. Fundamentalism apparently satisfies a yearning for immediate experience, for mind-altering insights, for the mysticism that negates utilitarian individualism and glorifies harmony with nature.

Altruistic Escape

A cult is the simplest and usually most temporary organizational form that a group of adherents can take, often emerging from larger established organizations. A splinter group will organize around a new specific way of worshipping or a charismatic personality. Cults also form around musicians, artists, or movie stars, described as having a "cult following." Such cults are usually strikingly different, provoking strong positive and negative reactions.

The Jesus Movement is a fundamentalist cult, supplying meaning for thousands of young people who previously felt empty or alienated. Though declining somewhat in influence, it remains a source of group solidarity and security through adherence to strict religious principles. Other fundamentalist and mystical cults are more extreme, requiring new members to surrender their "outside" personalities, their possessions, and all connections to the outside world. Although some cases of deception and brainwashing occurred in the growth of some cults, they usually do not depend on such recruitment methods.

Many people are willing to surrender to what nonbelievers see as harsh discipline in order to be part of what appears to be a rigid but meaningful order. The joiners do seem drawn from a special group of people constantly searching for a place in the world. One study found that 90 percent of the members of a well-known cult had previously been in similar groups.[23]

To understand this phenomenon of willingness to give oneself fully to a group, we must once again call on Durkheim's analysis of the interrelationship between social integration and suicide. He described very tightly knit groups as promoting altruistic suicide whenever the group's welfare took over primary importance in each member's mind. We frequently find this orientation in its extreme form in militaristic cultures. Kamikaze pilots sacrificed themselves by the thousands in an attempt to delay the invasion of the Japanese homeland. A Prussian army officer might commit suicide to avoid bringing disgrace to his unit or family. Entire units of the army of the nineteenth-century African King Chaka would march over a cliff at his command rather than show disobedience.

These are only a few historical examples of groups causing individuals to devalue and even give up their individual selves. What is strange about the current situation is that the push to surrender does not come from a monolithic, overly integrated society overwhelming the individual, but from social change and the disintegration of traditional values driving lost individuals to seek out new, small groups in which to submerge themselves.

One common characteristic setting apart the new authoritarian cults is intolerance of doubt or deviation. One specialist even defines a cult as "any group that equates doubt with guilt."[24] These cults usually form around one strong, charismatic leader, who often assumes the role of paternalistic superfather, or even the role of a divine representative.

The People's Temple

The extreme case of allegiance and surrender of self occurred in 1978, when 900 followers of Jim Jones joined him in suicide in their retreat in Guyana. To understand this tragedy, we need to use a combination of the ideas we have been discussing.

First, the members came from groups badly treated by society with reason to be anomic: they were poor and most were black. Second, they had often been sensitized as previous members of other altruistically oriented sects promoting total ecstatic surrender to belief. Finally, Jones was a diabolically able charismatic leader who encouraged total allegiance. He had previously used mock suicide as a ritual performance to unite the group.[25]

The Awareness Trap

The social problem of lost or anomic individuals goes beyond the cult's subjugation of a relatively few people. Schur alerted us to our preoccupation with individual happiness and growth, and the danger of it exaggerating many of our social problems.[26] In our search for our "real" selves and "meaningful relationships," we lose sight of the structured, institutionalized sources of inequality and disintegration in the larger society.[27] This reminds us of the original theme of this chapter, that we tend to blame ourselves and each other for problems solvable only by changing the social structure providing our values and constraints. This is also a central point of the next section, the conflict perspective.

ALIENATION: POWERLESSNESS AND SELF-ESTRANGEMENT

Freedom for self-actualization is the central concept of Marx's view of the individual in society. True humanity can be found only after release from the domination of "things." To liberate themselves, to develop all capacities inherent in their generic essence, people must be able to exercise conscious, rational control over their natural environment and over their own lives.[28]

Powerlessness

Work plays a central role in the Marxist view of self-fulfillment. The ideal situation allows work to be art; each "job" grows naturally into its best result. No standardization, and certainly no assembly line, exists. Industrialization and capitalism, however, force the production of "things" with no personal connection to the worker. With labor disconnected from product identification, the process is too abstract to be personally satisfying.[29] This is the psychological import of the famous Marxian phrase, the "loss of the tools of production." According to Marxists, capitalism demands that people become workers to be moved from factory to factory as money markets shift.

Meaninglessness of Commodities

Disagreeing with Functionalists, conflict theorists reject disintegration or system breakdown as the cause of meaninglessness. Instead, they insist, the system itself warps individual lives. Loss of control, choice, and self-expression certainly is destructive, but not as important as another type of powerlessness: the inability to define or evaluate oneself.[30] Sennet and Cobb found the most prevalent fear among workers was of the people above them in the bureaucratic hierarchy who have little

Imagine sorting raspberries, eight hours a day, five days a week. You know the feeling if you have had a boring repetitive job. When work gives us nothing but a paycheck, we are alienated from a source of achievement and self-satisfaction.

understanding of the workers' lives or jobs, and who make arbitrary judgments about them.[31]

White-Collar Powerlessness

Several sociologists have noted how few of us work on assembly lines, perhaps only 2 percent.[32] Most people are white-collar workers, who like factory workers, are also in jeopardy of alienation as a result of meaningless jobs. Their "paper-pushing" work becomes just as routine and abstractly meaningless.

> To get a white-collar job you must stay in school. Schooling is supposed to develop your internal powers, make you as a person more powerful in relation to the productive order of the society. The move into white-collar work is in this way a consequence of your having become a more developed human being. Yet most of those flowing into white-collar work find the reality quite different—the content of the work in fact requires very little mind at all.[33]

False Values and Self-Estrangement

When people believe in the false commodity-based system, the final step in alienation occurs. Once we produce something, it tends to dominate us. We reify, or give a particular reality to, cars, other status symbols, and social arrangements such as

Isolation and alienation are not limited to the blue-collar world of the production line. Paper-shuffling is also often a meaningless and powerless occupation that cuts individuals off from one another giving them little sense of personal satisfaction.

status structures and governments. We then become dependent on them for our evaluations of our own and others' achievement, or status, in the community. Our products and institutions become more real than our basic needs.

Conflict theorists believe the rich manage the economy for their own benefit. Those with privilege often deliberately create false values through obfuscation and rationalization to maintain their powerful positions. These theorists become suspicious when they hear a business executive explaining the nonnecessity of government regulation, that the mysterious workings of the "invisible hand" somehow balances out all our individual competitions. Even non-Marxists suspect use of this doctrine of competition that encourages people to work as hard as possible, competing with each other to increase productivity.

The Human Commodity

Two coincidental changes in the societal role of individuals, forced by the maturing of industrial capitalism, created even greater self-estrangement: the change from producer to consumer, and from entrepreneur to **commodity-self**, evaluation of oneself in terms of salability to others.

Consumption
In early factory-based capitalism, individuals were simply workers producing as much as possible, as cheaply and as quickly as possible. Producers soon realized an economy based on mass production could not continue to grow without an endless demand for new goods. A plan to "civilize" the masses replaced the earlier goal of satisfying basic material needs. Advertising began an "uninterrupted fabrication of

pseudo-needs'' to educate the ''masses into an unappeasable appetite not only for goods but for new experiences and personal fulfillment.''[34] Conflict theorists treat this personal growth through stimulation of consumption as one of the most suspicious and distracting of our false values.

Competitive Personalities

C. Wright Mills alerted us to the personal dangers in the change from small-business competition to the age of corporate bureaucracies.[35] Our competition is no longer producing a more salable product. Now we sell our own personalities. We compete through our abilities to shape ourselves into the most attractive and effective of tools for pleasing superiors in the system. Keyes says this promotes the **stewardess syndrome**: we smile warmly at strangers we have just met as if sharing some deep intimacy.[36] Even these commodity-emotions are not our own ideas. We are creating them in a conscious repackaging of the self into an ''organization person.''

Narcissism

Lasch warns us that competition and the cold-blooded sale of our remade personalities have spread from the economic marketplace and now pervade our personal-emotional interactions. He says we have already left the time of passive conformity.

We are taught to package ourselves as if we were commodities on the open market. We can lose the ability to form real identities during the process of creating a pleasing appearance and playing social roles that are calculated to not offend others.

We no longer just give up our individualities to the organization; we are now active predators, using our outer selves to attract opportunities to score against each other. This overriding **narcissism** is the ultimate alienation nightmare. False consumption values make us compete, using voluntarily created false selves, and we are unable to see ourselves, or others, as real or valuable.

SEARCHING FOR MEANINGFUL IDENTITIES

Symbolic interaction, our fourth and final sociological viewpoint, does not see individuals as controlled or dominated by the social structure. Interactionists acknowledge the need for stable reference standards so everything need not be freshly created, but also see our interpersonal rules as constantly changing adaptations to new situations. This is an optimistic view. Inside even the most oppressive social structure, the possibility exists of forming new agreements on how to live together within it or of planning how to modify it. The self can survive.

The second disagreement that symbolic interaction has with the previous outlooks concerns "phoniness" or pre-arranged role-playing. Acting is constant and typical. Almost all of us preplan and present the best appearance and nicest personality we can. Most of us manage information and cover up what we consider to be our weaknesses. This is a normal adjustment to others' expectations and not a recent development caused by a particular societal situation. Interactionists acknowledge our problems, but suggest they are less overwhelmingly monolithic than other sociological orientations would have us believe. Our individual problems are exaggerations of the normal interpersonal processes, and can be modified without changing the entire social structure.

Individual Negotiation and Social Change

Interactionists concentrate on the ways we make our specific selections from the cultural rules around us, and how we continuously redefine those rules. We tend to adapt or modify norms in three main ways: transformation, role distance, and impression management.

Transformation

Society is fragile and based on the accumulation of our mutual expectations. Unless these are reconfirmed constantly, they quickly become confused and fall away. Sociologist Peter Berger says even slavery, the most oppressive of situations, is so fragile it can only be maintained by quick, violent reactions to any new idea.[37] In a freer situation, such as a romantic relationship, the changes in definition from "date" to "boyfriend" or "girlfriend" and then to "fiancé(e)" can each cause a tumult of confusion, and possible dissolution of the relationship if the partners' definitions are even slightly incongruent.

Drawing by Henry Martin © 1971 The New Yorker Magazine, Inc.

"Hi, there, the me nobody knows!"

This man has spent a lifetime acting out identities that fit others' expectations. He thinks he still has a self that is separate and valuable. What do you think? The sad part of the joke is that he talks to "himself" using a standard, conventionally pleasing, greeting.

Role Distance

Detachment from the current situation need not be the total escape found in cults or in Eastern mysticism. We all sometimes feel "outside" the roles we play.[38] We want to feel that we are above certain roles and we often want others to know we feel that way. The business executive who dresses like a college teacher (and vice versa) is making an overt statement, distancing himself or herself from the situation. The classic example is the mother who punishes a child and says, "I'm only doing this for your own good." In effect she is saying that she, as an individual, is not doing the spanking, it is the mother role that forces her to punish.

Impression Management

We often play social roles from a distance, without any personal commitment. This fact has two very different implications. The first is optimistic: we do not necessarily have to fit ourselves in the roles the structure forces upon us. We can reflect on them and avoid some of the worst restrictions or obligations. When we adopt a new status, such as a job or parenthood, we might find ourselves unable to feel everything we should. Supposedly, we "grow into" the role, eventually feeling the emotions people expect us to feel. This means that insincere interaction allows for smooth operation of the system and that individuals have the ability to hide from the system while trying to change it.

The second implication is pessimistic: honesty is not a requirement of an effective role performance. Insincere interaction is frequent and manipulative, as illustrated with three false poses commonly occurring in romantic relationships. In one pose, one partner frequently "plays hard to get" by managing to look uninterested when he or she actually is attracted to the other.[39] In another, many females feel forced to "play dumb" and hide their intelligence or capabilities in order to fit stereotypical expectations.[40] But Karp and Yoels illustrate the dirtiest trick of all:

> a cynical lover could quite consciously behave ineptly in order to convince the woman he is trying to seduce that he is inexperienced and she is the first he has ever loved. A sincere lover might really be inexperienced and, therefore, behaves ineptly. The two individuals have put on identical acts—they have both performed ineptly as lovers—yet one would be cynical and the other a sincere performance.[41]

THE FUTURE

The "American century" of world industrial leadership only lasted about 50 years.[42] Questioning and disruption have replaced confidence. Our factories no longer are the most efficient in the world, and now represent our past.

Today the new emphases are technology, large managerial organizations, and the Information Society. It will take many chapters in this book to describe all the implications of this shift. Our concern in this chapter is the effect it has on the average individual's image of society, relationships, and happiness.

The next 20 years will continue to be dominated by wasteful adaptations, described by Alvin Toffler as reactions to future shock[43] (see Box 2.4). After these reactions have run their course, real change will begin. It could go well or badly. The new technologies could make us freer and allow more sociability and interaction, or they could be used to monitor, control, and separate us. For example, computer-communication technology gives us the ability to have private lives, living and working in our "electronic cottages." This could allow us leisure and freedom, or it could cut us off from each other even more completely. Here are two scenarios that present extreme possibilities. The real future probably lies somewhere in between.

Pessimistic Scenario

Having

Technology is the major force in the year 2025, but controlled by an integrated network of megacorporations. Distinguishing between the government and the private sector is difficult. What the optimistic forecasters forgot was that the technologists never were in control of the economy or its change. Back in the 1980s, for example, only 4 percent of those in *Who's Who* had technological occupations. The rest were financiers, lawyers, and other managers. The computer-information revolution has now become just another way to control output. In fact, the computer is more accurate than any human manager at counting exactly how many letters are typed, or sales are made, or outputs are produced in a day.

Individuals' attitudes are still competitive and advancement in the system is still the challenge. This is especially evident in the widespread "hurried baby syndrome." Beginning at age 2, children are carefully graded and categorized by their "system poténtial." Having determined each child's level of competition, adults segregate bright children from the less able. Thereafter, the children's education and socialization reflect that categorizing at age 2.

Relating

Because of the new communication techniques, the visual media are people's constant companions. Much like Ray Bradbury's description of "The Family" in *Farenheit 451,* all four walls of the average home are surround-o-vision. A continuous, realistic soap-opera family involves everyone, all day long. These characters are more real than life. With everything available on the screen, no need exists to shop or leave one's home computer station. Even the annual visit with the family is much more convenient by surround-o-vision's two-way hookup. Privacy is just as outmoded as face-to-face interaction. Continuous records, if only for consumer buying studies, monitor everything purchased and everyone contacted.

Part of the reason that the media are so attractive is that interpersonal and romantic relationships have become so manipulative. Individuals are interested in satisfying their own needs by obtaining a quick release of tension so they can return to competition. Even the more serious are interested in fulfilling their emotional potential and sharing has become unimportant.

Being

Government-controlled education uses tracking segregation to insure that people are always competing against others of equal skill and talent. Therefore, from the earliest ages there is high stress and only the most competitive avoid demotion to a lower level. For the many who can't or won't accept the lifelong pressure, there are few alternatives. They can drop out into one of the hundreds of quasi-religious sects, or they can move to one of the special cities set aside for alternative life-styles. But even these alternatives have become institutionalized, run by stable business-oriented organizations. Like the major corporations, they have leadership hierarchies with positions inherited from parents or relatives.

Three types of escape exist for the unconnected. Fantasy has become big business; very elaborate "adventures" can be recreated, using drugs and electronic effects. Second, scientists have isolated the brain's pleasure center and perfected the way to continuously stimulate it. Millions of people devote their lives to earning enough to afford a "hookup," and their only dream is to earn enough never to be unhooked again. Finally, suicide is no longer a crime. In fact, it is encouraged, and surviving family members receive cash rewards.

BOX 2.4

VICTIMS OF FUTURE
SHOCK
When we combine the effects of decisional stress with sensory and cognitive overload, we produce several common forms of individual maladaptation. For example, one widespread response to high-speed change is outright denial. The Denier's strategy is to "block out" unwelcome reality. When the demand for decisions reaches crescendo, he flatly refuses to take in new information. . . .

An unknowing victim of future shock, The Denier sets himself up for personal catastrophe. His strategy for coping increases the likelihood that when he finally is forced to adapt, his encounter with change will come in the form of a single massive life crisis, rather than a sequence of manageable problems.

A second strategy of the future shock victim is specialism. The Specialist doesn't block out *all* novel ideas or information. Instead, he energetically attempts to keep pace with change—but only in a specific narrow sector of life. . . .

Superficially, he copes well. But he, too, is running the odds against himself. He may awake one morning to find his specialty obsolete or else transformed beyond recognition by events exploding outside his field of vision.

A third common response to future shock is obsessive reversion to previously successful adaptive routines that are now irrelevant and inappropriate. The Reversionist sticks to his previously programmed decisions and habits with dogmatic desperation. The more change threatens from without, the more meticulously he repeats past modes of action. His social outlook is regressive. Shocked by the arrival of the future, he offers hysterical support for the not-so-status quo, or he demands, in one masked form or another, a return to the glories of yesteryear. . . .

If the older reversionist dreams of reinstating a small-town past, the youthful, left-wing reversionist dreams of reviving an even older social system. This ac-

Optimistic Scenario

Having

By 2025 factories have been automated and people freed from repetitive assembly lines and paper pushing. Increased leisure is a direct benefit, creating a redefinition of what is good in life. Instead of "having" commodities, the highest value is now placed on "doing" things with others sharing similar interests. Individuals who in the industrial past could only find a creative outlet through their work now have additional ways to achieve success and a feeling of authenticity. But work has also been remarkably freed. The instruments of production have been taken away from the control and the life-style of large corporations. People are primarily employed in providing services for each other or in handling information and making decisions.

The work force approximates the original guild model. Specialists and experts are able to move on to new employment if conditions ever become oppressive, and therefore can choose their own life-styles.

counts for some of the fascination with rural communes, the bucolic romanticism that fills the posters and poetry of the hippie and post-hippie subcultures. . . .

Finally, we have the Super-Simplifier. With old heroes and institutions toppling, with strikes, riots, and demonstrations stabbing at his consciousness, he seeks a single neat equation that will explain all the complex novelties threatening to engulf him. Grasping erratically at this idea or that, he becomes a temporary true believer.

This helps account for the rampant intellectual faddism that already threatens to outpace the rate of turnover in fashion. . . .

The Super-Simplifier, groping desperately, invests every idea he comes across with universal relevance—often to the embarrassment of its author. Alas, no idea, not even mine or thine, is omni-insightful. But for the Super-Simplifier nothing less than total relevance suffices. . . .

Most of us can quickly spot these patterns of behavior in others—even in ourselves—without, at the same time, understanding their causes. Yet information scientists will instantly recognize denial, specialization, reversion and super-simplification as classical techniques for coping with overload.

All of them dangerously evade the rich complexity of reality. They generate distorted images of reality. The more the individual denies, the more he specializes at the expense of wider interests, the more mechanically he reverts to past habits and policies, the more desperately he super-simplifies, the more inept his responses to the novelty and choices flooding into his life. The more he relies on these strategies, the more his behavior exhibits wild and erratic swings and general instability.

SOURCE: Alvin Toffler, *Future Shock*. (N.Y.: Bantam, 1970), pp. 358–62. Copyright © 1970 by Alvin Toffler. Reprinted by permission of Random House, Inc.

Relating

The advent of economically free individuals destroyed the need for rationalistic overorganized corporate bureaucracies. Computer voting has made interactive democracy possible. "Weekly inputs" from the whole nation through home terminals now decide each major issue. With government automated, people feel they can control its direction. Individuals now come together through the discovery of mutual interests and talents, rather than fitting into the same system slot. Privatization is the major direction of change. Individuals are free from the necessity of searching for a sense of success in the mass society due to a sense of belonging in the local interest or work group.

Being

Rigid role-playing and manipulation faded when private life was divorced from the need for a job in a bureaucracy. Abandonment of the denials of change has substantially reduced alienation and meaninglessness. People's acceptance of the need to keep up with change by constantly modifying goals has made learning, flexibility, and acceptance of individual differences the highest human values. The proliferation of so many different interest groups and subcultures has allowed almost everyone to find a group with whom to share a meaningful and acceptable, preferred life-style.

SUGGESTED READINGS

Berger, Peter, Brigette Berger, and Hansfried Kellner. *The Homeless Mind*. New York: Vintage, 1973. A description of the effects of modernization on the individual's consciousness, and the limits of attempts at demodernization.

Cohen, Stanley, and Laurie Taylor. *Escape Attempts: The Theory and Practice of Resistance to Everyday Life*. Baltimore, Md. Penguin, 1978. How we get through our days by mental management, identity shifts, and transformation of the banal, trivial, and repetitious.

Goffman, Erving. *Interaction Ritual: Essays on Face-to-Face Behavior*. Garden City, N.Y.: Doubleday/Anchor, 1967. Individual problems traced in detail within their determining social fabrics. The sections Alienation From Interaction, and Embarrassment and Social Organization, are pertinent classics.

Hawken, Paul, James Ogilvy, and Peter Schwartz. *Seven Tomorrows: Seven Scenarios for the Eighties and Nineties*. New York: Bantam, 1982. Interesting integration of three value orientations (frugal, survival, and achievement values) as bases for alternative futures.

Huxley, Aldous. *Brave New World Revisited*. New York: Harper & Row/Perennial, 1965. The creator of one of the most famous fictional futures prophetically describes our current troubles with propaganda, the arts of selling, chemical persuasion, and overorganization.

Josephson, Eric, and Mary Josephson. *Man Alone: Alienation in Modern Society*. New York: Dell, 1962. Compilation of social scientific, fictional, and political statements on isolation, work, identity, integration, and rebellion.

Lasch, Christopher. *The Culture of Narcissism*. New York: Warner, 1979. A provocative description of the postconformity generation. The competition of all against all has moved beyond the marketplace and now also controls our leisure and intimacies.

Pawley, Martin. *The Private Future*. New York: Pocket Books, 1977. The causes and consequences of community collapse in the Western world. The inevitable retreat to secondary, created, private reality, and the triumph of "sensation divorced from action."

Smith, Adam. *Powers of Mind*. New York: Ballantine, 1975. "Every mind trip under the sun" is interestingly described. All the alternative escapes and self-improvement-movements of the 1970s explained in a popular discussion.

Eakins Press Edition. *The Bitch-Goddess Success: Variations on an American Theme*. New York: Eakins, 1968. Excerpts from throughout American history, and from all its sectors demonstrating that "success is our national disease."

GLOSSARY

Alienation   Disconnection from meaningful or authentic social participation, resulting from loss of control of one's life or being forced to do senseless work.

Altruistic escape   When the social group places more value on the group and its beliefs than on individual life, people more easily give up their individuality, or even their lives when confronted with adversity.

Anomie   A feeling of confusion and loss of direction resulting from rapid change or breakdown of social norms and values.

Commodity-self   When an individual evaluates himself or herself only in terms of what will be salable to others; what pleases society.

Community   A neighborhood or other group in which individuals feel emotionally connected and willing to support each other.

Narcissism   Excessive concentration on yourself, your appearance, pleasure, and "scoring" in social competition.

Quality of life   Measuring and judging the worth of our lives not just by the quantity of things we have or produce, but by our health and happiness.

Role overabundance   Having too many different roles to play, with their conflicting demands often causing confusion or anguish.

Secularization   The long-term trend of the lessening power of established religion in social life, and the increasing power of science, technology, and rationality.

While prevailing societal values, attitudes, and beliefs set the framework of understanding for social interaction, not everyone accepts the dominant cultural precepts. Nor does everyone follow similar life-styles and behavior patterns in their pursuit of happiness. Remembering our discussion in Chapter 1 about the importance of social definitions, we must now ask at what point do such differences of self-expression become social problems? Is snorting cocaine or being homosexual, for example, a private or public matter?

In this section we shall examine several aspects of concern about the maintenance of social stability in people's lives. Part of our attention will be on the choices people make about their life-style and recreational activities, and how those choices may pose problems for the individuals themselves or for society in general. Society's response, as you will see, is to label these as deviant behaviors, in an attempt to repress them. Another consideration in this section will be those disruptive patterns within society creating fear, harm, or potential harm, all of which undermine our sense of security and well-being. Throughout all four chapters, you should note the importance of shared values and attitudes in shaping reactions to the social situation.

Specifically, Chapter 3 focuses on the physical and social consequences of alcohol and drug abuse, both for the user and society. Why are some forms of recreational drug use acceptable but not others? How widespread is the problem? In what ways does drug use harm the rest of society? What forms of social control and solution attempts are effective?

In Chapter 4 our subjects are those that often provoke moral outrage in others: varying forms of sexual expression and behavior. Some see pornography, prostitution, homosexuality, and nonmarital births as not only immoral but also as corruptive manifestations of a degenerating society. Others view the situation quite differently. Part of our concern will be how society defines these matters and enacts policies to deal with them.

The many dimensions of crime and the workings of the criminal justice system comprise Chapter 5. Just as values have shifted about drug use and sexual behavior, so too have they changed about what constitutes a crime. Certainly crime receives much public attention, but as you will discover, many inconsistencies exist in preventive and corrective efforts. Why? And why do we seem unable to control crime?

Chapter 6 deals with violence, an unfortunate constant in modern life. Fear of becoming a victim of violent crime, whether perpetrated by criminals or terrorists, haunts many of us, as does the threat of nuclear war. Does our fear distort the reality? Are we living in more violent times? How do we explain all the violence? More importantly, how do we stop it?

TWO
CHALLENGES TO INDIVIDUAL WELL-BEING

FACTS ABOUT ALCOHOL AND DRUGS

One out of two Americans will be involved in an alcohol-related auto accident sometime in their lifetime.

One-half of all traffic fatalities involve alcohol and 20 percent, or 5,000, of these fatalities are teenagers.

Drug use costs the American economy at least $26 billion annually.

Cocaine use among high-school students quadrupled between 1972 and 1982.

Two-thirds of all Americans have smoked marijuana.

Heroin is the least used drug in the United States.

About 37 percent of all Americans smoke even though it reduces life expectancy and causes 340,000 deaths annually.

3
ALCOHOL AND DRUG ABUSE

Throughout history, public acceptance or rejection of a particular drug may change. Coffee, containing the drug stimulant caffeine, was under attack in seventeenth-century England. In 1674, for example, a pamphlet called ''The Women's Petition Against Coffee'' claimed men were becoming less sexually active because they were forsaking ''good old'' ale to drink ''base, black, thick, nasty, bitter, stinking, nauseous'' coffee.[1] Yet by the eighteenth century, English coffee houses were a respectable social institution. Smoking cigarettes was then considered more offensive, but not so in the twentieth century, until public awareness of its health hazards occasioned another shift in public attitude toward cigarette advertising and smoking in public areas.

What are acceptable practices in one culture may not be in another. Possession of marijuana is still a criminal offense in most states, but it is acceptable in most of the Middle East and North Africa. Drinking is an institutionalized practice in the United States but forbidden by the Koran in Islamic countries. In India the nation's constitution prohibits alcohol consumption, but opium is openly sold in the marketplace. Cocaine use or possession draws severe penalties in a great many countries, while South American Indians, particularly those in the Andes mountains, use it almost universally.

Cultural values and group norms thus determine what forms of drug use are socially acceptable and what forms constitute a social problem. Definitions of drug use and abuse may change through historical periods or vary from one setting to another. Moreover, legal definitions may be at variance with public mores, as during Prohibition. Also, legal and public definitions may be inconsistent within a society, as were recent state differences in the minimum drinking age and the legality of marijuana use.

WHAT IS A DRUG?

From a scientific and sociolegal perspective, a drug is any substance which chemically alters the functioning of the brain or nervous system.[2] The term **psychoactive drug** refers to a chemical substance which affects consciousness, mood, or perception. Still, society tends to view some psychoactive drugs as problematic but not others. For example, despite the scientific proof of their harmful qualities and habit-forming nature, society does not classify alcohol and tobacco as harmful drugs. In this section we shall examine the characteristics and dangers of all commonly used drugs, regardless of their social definition.[3]

Alcohol

Taken in moderation, alcohol is rather harmless and is even beneficial in relieving feelings of stress. As a mild sedative at the end of the workday or as a moderate sociable activity, drinking alcoholic beverages is both fashionable and fairly safe. The problem, of course, is excessive drinking. Alcohol abuse creates staggering social problems: traffic accidents and fatalities, broken marriages, disorderly behavior, crime, ruined careers, poverty, and physical debilitation. Virtually all social scientists and medical experts agree that alcohol abuse is the most serious drug problem in our society today.

Effects

Alcohol is a **depressant** on the central nervous system. Its effects vary with the amount consumed, its speed of consumption, and the tolerance level of each individual. It can reduce tension, loosen inhibitions, and therefore make one feel relaxed and happy. It can also impair memory, judgment, coordination, stimulus response time, and motor skills (speech, walking, hand and arm movements). Excessive drinking may produce a stupor, deep sleep, coma, or death (see Table 3.1).

Dangers

Drinkers can become psychologically dependent on alcohol, needing it to be at ease among people or to cope with a difficult situation. They may further become physically dependent, unable to abstain without experiencing severe withdrawal symptoms (rapid heartbeat, sweating, nausea, and tremors). Alcohol withdrawal also has a greater probability of being fatal than narcotics withdrawal. Potentially deadly as well is the combination of alcohol and other drugs, particularly barbituates.

TABLE 3.1 The Effects of Alcohol

Amount of Distilled Spirits Consumed in 2 Hours, ml (fl oz)	Percent of Alcohol in Blood	Typical Effects
89 (3)	0.05	Loosening of judgment, thought, and restraint; release of tension; carefree sensation
133 (4.5)	0.08	Tensions and inhibitions of everyday life lessened
177 (6)	0.10	Voluntary motor action affected; hand and arm movements, walking, and speech clumsy
296 (10)	0.20	Severe motor impairment; staggering; loud, incoherent speech; emotional instability (extreme drunkenness); 100 times greater traffic risk
414 (14)	0.30	Deeper areas of brain affected. Parts affecting stimulus response and understanding confused, stuporous
532 (18)	0.40	Deep sleep; inability to take voluntary action (equivalent of surgical anesthesia)
651 (22)	0.50	Coma; anesthesia of centers controlling breathing and heartbeat; death

SOURCE: *The New York Times* (December 21, 1977), p. C11 (adapted from information furnished by the National Clearing House for Alcohol Information in Morris Chatetz, M.D., *Why Drinking Can Be Good for You,* Briarclitt Manor, N.Y.: Stein and Day, 1976).

Alcohol can irreversibly damage the liver (cirrhosis of the liver is the fourth major cause of death among those age 25 to 50), brain cells, and other body tissue. Drinkers also run a much higher risk than nondrinkers of cancer of the mouth or throat, and a 15 times greater risk if they both smoke and drink. Alcoholics usually suffer from malnutrition, and in addition to cancer, are also more susceptible to heart disease.

Use

Most Americans are light to moderate drinkers. Amount of alcoholic consumption is greatest among young adults 18 to 25, of whom 67.9 percent are current users of the drug.[4] Steady drinking is fairly common among adults over 26, but the percentage of 56.7 is not as great as the younger age group. Almost twice the percentage of college-educated people drink compared to those with only a high-school education. The affluent consume more alcohol than the poor, and more males than females, Whites than Blacks, urban than rural residents have heavier drinking habits. Alcohol consumption per capita is greatest in the Northeast, followed by the West coast.[5]

Teenage drinking has increased significantly in recent years. The National Institute of Alcohol Abuse and Alcoholism, in a random sampling of high school stu-

Alcohol is a commonly used drug, its moderate use commonplace at social gatherings. Middle-class adults consume more alcohol than the poor and are more likely to serve hard liquor at parties and social events than working-class or low-income adults. College-educated people also tend to drink more than others.

dents, found that 30 percent had been "pretty drunk" at least once within the past month and 7 percent get drunk every week.[6] The number of drinkers and those with drinking problems increases each successive year, from seventh grade through high-school graduation (see Figure 3.1). Current estimates place the number of teenagers with a drinking problem at 3.3 million, and the number of adult problem drinkers at 10 million. Most alcoholics are between the ages of 35 and 50, and approximately 70 percent are male, though the underreporting of female alcoholics may lessen the accuracy of this statistic.

FIGURE 3.1 Drinking and Problem Drinking among Junior and Senior High School Students

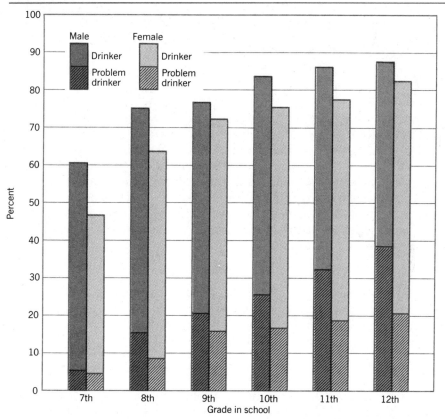

Problem drinking was defined as being drunk at least six times during the past year or experiencing complications from drinking at least twice during the past year in at least three of the following five situations: (1) getting into trouble with teachers or the principal; (2) getting into difficulty with friends; (3) driving after having a "good bit" to drink; (4) being criticized by someone the student was dating; or (5) getting into trouble with the police. (*Donovan and Jessor 1978, as contained in Noble 1978.*)

Amphetamines

A group of synthetic drugs, amphetamines are **stimulants** ("uppers"), legal through prescription use, and safe if patients follow directions. They increase the activity of the central nervous system, producing alertness and energy, and a euphoric state in higher doses. Most common as "pep pills" for athletes, truck drivers, "cramming" students, and dieters are Benzedrine and Dexedrine. These small-dosage users take the amphetamine for a practical purpose and are not likely to abuse the substance use. The second form of amphetamine use involves taking a deliberately higher dose to achieve a "rush" or intense high. Another means is by injection of the liquid methedine ("speed").

Effects

Amphetamines are often used to overcome fatigue and sleepiness because they increase the heart rate, raise the blood pressure, and cause excitement and restlessness. They depress the appetite, dilate eye pupils, dry out the mouth, and cause headaches, dehydration, diarrhea, and paleness. They can also cause anxiety, mood swings, panic, paranoia, hallucinations, convulsions, and coma.

Dangers

Amphetamines do not cause a physical dependence, but the body does build up a **tolerance,** making increasingly larger doses necessary. Heavy users are likely to lose hair and teeth, become underweight and suffer brain damage that impairs speech and thought. Since amphetamines remain in the body for some time, frequent use of even small amounts may cause psychosis, paranoia, and bizarre behavior. A real danger of psychological dependence exists, since using "uppers" to "keep going" can become a compulsion. Injected overdoses can kill and use of unsterilized needles can cause serious infection. Abrupt withdrawal can create depression, apathy, and sleeplessness.

Use

About 20 million Americans have used amphetamines, with women accounting for 60 percent of that number. Amphetamine use has lessened significantly since 1970 with the decline of the "hippie" movement, tough new federal restrictions on prescriptions, and reluctance of physicians to prescribe them.[7]

Caffeine

Even though it does not have the public identification as a drug, caffeine is nonetheless a psychoactive drug that affects the body system. As a natural substance, caffeine is found in coffee, tea, cola drinks, cocoa, and chocolate candy. It is also chemically added to various commercial products, such as No-Doze and Excedrin.

Effects

Caffeine is a mild stimulant of the central nervous system. It alleviates fatigue, producing increased alertness, mental, and motor activity. Morning coffee and the English pot of tea at four in the afternoon—a low ebb period of alertness for many people—are institutionalized "pick-me-up" practices. Caffeine also causes restlessness and insomnia. Drinking five or more cups a day can cause irritability, stomach cramps, or chest pains.

Dangers

While probably the safest of the psychoactive drugs, caffeine can result in **addiction.** Heavy coffee drinkers who stop consumption experience such **withdrawal** symptoms as depression, agitation, nervousness, or a jittery feeling. An extremely heavy dose (10 or more grams) can be fatal. Many people develop a psychological dependence on caffeine, unable either to function until they have their morning coffee or to continue functioning until after their coffee or tea break.

Use

Caffeine is the most widely used stimulant in American society. Millions of young people drink cola daily. About 91 percent of all Americans drink either coffee or tea regularly, over 180 billion cups each year. Because caffeine is a legal drug, its cost is low in comparison to the illegal drugs and no negative labeling or deviant subculture exists for caffeine consumers.[8]

Cocaine

A stimulant drug extracted from the leaves of the South American coca plant, cocaine was used medically as a very effective local anesthetic and to reduce bleeding in nose and throat surgery. In the late nineteenth century cocaine became quite respectable as a social drug. A French chemist, Angelo Marini, received a medal of appreciation from the Pope for introducing a highly popular new wine with cocaine as an ingredient.[9] Psychoanalyst Sigmund Freud frequently took cocaine and urged his friends and colleagues to try it as a remedy for fatigue, depression, and indigestion. Many physicians recommended it for tubercular patients.[10] If you are a Sherlock Holmes fan, you will recall Sir Arthur Conan Doyle depicted his sleuth regularly injecting himself with cocaine. Today's Coca-Cola no longer contains the cocaine from which it took its name, but until 1903 it did and was touted for its "pick-me-up" qualities. This early enthusiasm for cocaine waned as it became associated with crime and violence, leading to its ban in 1914 with the Harrison Act.[11] In recent years it has become popular among affluent young adults able to afford its cost ($100 a gram or $2,800 an ounce).

Effects

Snorting this crystalline powder produces feelings of pleasure, confidence, and competence within minutes, the high lasting up to an hour. Another form of cocaine is called "freebase," which can be smoked. It produces a more euphoric effect but it fades within minutes and depression often follows. Claims that the drug increases sexual ability and pleasure, as well as creativity, have not been substantiated. Most likely these effects take place only as a result of psychological benefits for those believing they exist, augmented by the exuberance and stimulation a cocaine high produces.

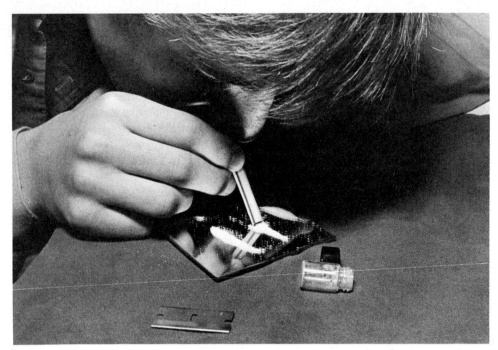

Snorting cocaine is more popular among affluent young adults, partly because of its high cost. About 10 million Americans are regular users, and another 5 million—including about 15 percent of all high school seniors—have tried cocaine at least once. Males are more likely to use this stimulant drug than females.

Dangers

Cocaine is relatively safe compared to other drugs but its extensive use does cause problems. Continuous sniffing can cause inflammation or ulcers in the nasal mucous membrane. Smoking or injecting is far more hazardous, its prolonged use possibly resulting in dangerous increases in heart rate and blood pressure, extreme depression, paranoia, agitation, and even psychosis. Hepatitis and other infections have occurred because of unsterile needles. This drug does not cause physical addiction but the powerful compulsion to reuse it—especially when smoked—can easily create a serious psychological dependence on it (see Box 3.1).

Use

Its high cost makes cocaine primarily a drug of the middle and upper classes. According to the National Institute on Drug Abuse, cocaine use has quadrupled between 1972 and 1982.[12] Cocaine sales are big business though, generating over $30 billion income annually, less than only seven major corporations listed in the Fortune 500.[13] Cocaine users generally have first used other drugs, usually stimulants, barbituates, and hallucinagens. Most cocaine users are also multidrug users, particularly of alcohol, marijuana, and amphetamines.

Depressants

A great many drugs are **sedative-hypnotics** ("downers"), legally used by prescription as tranquilizers and sleeping pills, but easily overused by people under stress or anxiety. Included are benzodiazepine (Valium, Librium) and meprobamate (Miltown, Equanil). Also well known are the barbituates, especially the fast-acting pentobarbital (Nembutal), secobarbital (Seconal), and amobarbital (Amytal). More recently, a chemically different drug with similar effects—methaqualone (Quaalude)—has become fashionable among young people.

Effects

All of these drugs produce effects similar to alcohol. In normal medical doses they lower blood pressure and slow down breathing, heart rate, and muscle reactions. Taken moderately, sedatives do remove inhibitions somewhat, but other personality changes vary in individual users. Some become calm and relaxed, yet others become lively and even aggressive. In abuse doses, the drugs result in slurred speech, staggering, and stuporous confusion. Quaaludes are reputed to be a "love drug," because they supposedly make the user more desirous for sex and enhance sexual pleasure. In reality, the drug is a depressant on the central nervous system and serves only to lessen inhibitions, much like alcohol and barbituates.

Dangers

All of these drugs are dangerous because they can cause physical dependence. Many drug experts believe they are more highly addictive and resistant to treatment or cure than heroin. These drugs can kill, since they produce mental confusion and loss of memory, thereby making an accidental overdose quite possible as users take an additional dose. Moreover, the mixing of sedative-hypnotics with alcohol can be toxic, causing convulsions, coma, or death. Combined use with amphetamines (together or in alternative stages), if continued, causes serious physical and psychological deterioration.

Use

Pharmaceutical firms manufacture more than 300 tons or 3.5 billion doses of barbituates in the United States every year. In an average year about 11 percent of all Americans use barbituates, either legally or illegally. Prescriptions for both barbituates (18 million annually) and tranquilizers (90 million annually) are actually lower than 10 years ago, as physicians became more aware of their dangers. Still, their use and abuse are so widespread that they have been called America's "hidden drug problem."[14]

Marijuana

The dried leaves of the hemp plant *cannabis sativa* is marijuana and its dried resin is the six times more powerful hashish. Marijuana is the most widely misunderstood drug, despite extensive study by researchers and national commissions in Canada, Great Britain, and the United States. In 1972 Canada eliminated marijuana use from

BOX 3.1

"DOING" COCAINE: A VICTIM'S ROAD TO RUIN

. . . The first time I did cocaine was in Aspen, Colo. I was in the restroom of a nice restaurant and a girl dipped her fingernail in a vial and shoved it up my nose. I didn't know what was going on. I was with friends, and I remember them telling me it was an aphrodisiac.

After dinner, our group's host was doing it. He would take a snort and go, "Ooh, ahh." I wondered what he was "oohing" about, because it didn't do a thing for me. I spent the next decade investigating.

Every time that I heard someone had cocaine for sale, I would buy. Eventually I had two safety-deposit boxes full of it.

I had so much of the stuff that I used to keep a cookie jar filled with it for my friends. Of course, I know now that I was manipulated by those people. When I started running low, my friends quit coming around.

TELL-TALE TRUNK

Then I got busted. A friend had put some in my trunk, and I didn't know about it when I waved down a cop to change a flat tire. He arrested me for possession.

The charge was expunged, though. The attorney general owed my lawyer a favor, and the case was delayed and delayed. To get off, part of the deal was that I go to a hospital in Connecticut for three months.

But by then I was really obsessive about cocaine, addicted to it. It wasn't a secret to anybody because I stuttered, didn't eat, never slept. I had to snort probably every 10 minutes. One time I was in Hawaii when I ran out of coke, and I left in the middle of my vacation to come back and get more.

Then I met this guy who used a needle and I started "shooting" cocaine. It was totally different, an instant rush. It makes you crazy. You go on three and four-day binges. I was cooking up "hits" every 30 minutes, putting a little rock in a spoon, adding water and drawing it up through a cotton ball with a syringe.

However much coke you have, you use it, no holds barred. On one binge, I took too big a hit. I closed by eyes and was drifting off. When I opened my eyes, this guy I was with looked scared. He said I'd been having a seizure. I didn't believe it until I saw my blood all over the wall where I had spit up.

It got so I wouldn't buy coke unless I had Quaaludes to keep me from getting too crazy. Then bootleg Quaaludes came out. They make you even crazier.

I was beat up by this guy who was desperate to get more drugs.

When I didn't give him money, he knocked his fist through the wall, pulled the phones out of the wall, ripped a door off the hinge, dragged me across the floor by my hair, beating me. He was crazed, driving the car all over the yard. I crawled out of my kitchen, too weak to get up, and a girl who lived behind me called the police when she saw I was bleeding all over.

They say I kicked the door off the ambulance when they took me away. I woke up in the hospital with my mother and other people around who thought I was dying.

Even after all that, I just couldn't wait to get back to cocaine. It got to the point where I sold my furniture, some pieces several times before the first buyers could pick them up. I sold the jewelry I inherited from my grandmother. I sold my car, my stereo. In the last year I spent $100,000 on drugs—$80,000 in six months. As for the eight years before that, I can't even guess how much I spent.

Two years ago I weighed 80 pounds, and I'm 5 foot 4½. I was a skeleton. Then I got beat up again by this guy who said he was so concerned that I was trying to kill myself doing drugs. He broke my nose, gave me a black eye. Of course, he did drugs, too. Crazy.

My mother took one look at me and took me bodily to a drug-treatment center in Arizona. I was so crazy when walking through the airport that I tried to get a policeman's gun so I could go through the machine that sets off the alarm. Every chance I got, I lay down in the corridor. My mother dragged me onto the airplane, into first class.

RETURN TRIP

At the drug center, we had lectures and group therapy. I had bad withdrawal, the shakes. I didn't sleep for eight days.

They started getting me in touch with my feelings, feelings I'm not sure I ever felt before. I was at the point that I couldn't have given you one word for any feeling, whether it was pain, guilt, remorse, anything. I did a lot of justifying, anything but being honest with myself. But they force you to be honest.

That's made me well—or made me want to be well.

I haven't done coke now for 18 months. I don't think I have to fight the cocaine, but I haven't been around it, and I'm not associating with any people who do it, so it's hard to say. I know I wouldn't snort again, because after using a needle, snorting is like learning to read a book backwards.

I don't have cravings, but I sure would be scared to be around coke. I think that if it were right here with a syringe, I'd do it. I know I would.

My plans are just to take it one day at a time. I'm not making any plans.

its list of criminal narcotics offenses and shortly thereafter reduced penalties for its possession. In the same year the U.S. National Commission on Marijuana and Drug Use recommended similar action. Eleven states now have mild penalties, but possessing marijuana in other states remains a criminal offense with possible stiff jail sentences. Two-thirds of all Americans over 18 still think the drug should remain illegal, as do about three out of five teenagers today.[15] Yet marijuana smoking is increasing and is now widespread, with one-third of the total American population age 12 or older now having tried it.[16]

Effects

First-time users often experience few, if any, sensations, and sometimes the drug subdues or depresses, producing drowsiness. The most common effects, however, are a relaxed state of euphoria, talkativeness, giddiness, and loud laughing, increased appetite, and increased sensory sensations, with the feeling one is "floating"and that time has slowed down. The drug produces reddened eyes, dryness in the mouth and throat, and a slight increase in heart rate.

Dangers

Claims that marijuana causes brain or chromosome damage, disruption of cell metabolism, or reduction of the male sex hormone, testosterone, and infertility have not so far been supported by careful research. It can, however, cause lung damage like any form of smoking and impair motor coordination, thereby increasing the risk of automobile accidents. The "amotivational syndrome" or lack of concentration on life-goal motivation among heavy marijuana users does exist, but we do not know for certain if such other variables as personality and family environment are possible causative factors. Marijuana is not addictive, has no withdrawal symptoms, does not develop tolerance, does not dilate pupils or cause death, and does not lead to the use of other drugs. Peer pressure is the greatest cause of multidrug use and so far as marijuana is concerned, the two most likely additional drugs are alcohol and tobacco. No causal relationship exists between marijuana use and subsequent heroin use, as once feared.[17]

Use

In 1962, only 4 percent of adults aged 18 to 25 had ever smoked pot, but by 1982 that figure had risen to 64 percent. A total of 57 million out of 182.5 million Americans age 12 or older—31.3 percent—have tried marijuana,[18] the fourth most commonly used drug, after caffeine, alcohol, and tobacco. One out of every two high-school seniors and two out of every three college students nationwide have smoked marijuana at least once, and about 17 percent of the high-school seniors and 35 percent of the college students do so at least once a month.[19] Americans now spend more than $6 billion a year on marijuana, more than the combined total spent on ice cream, hot dogs, and apple pie.[20] Its use is increasing among all social groupings, whether of age, gender, race, or socioeconomic status.[21] Physicians also prescribe marijuana for glaucoma and it has promising potential for treating asthma, multiple sclerosis, tumors, and negative side effects of chemotherapy.[22]

TABLE 3.2 Drug Use, by Type of Drug and by Age Group: 1979
(Current users are those who used drugs at least once within month prior to this study. Based on national samples of 2,165 youths, 2,004 young adults, and 3,015 older adults. Subject to sampling variability; see source)

Type of Drug	Percent of Youths (12–17 yr.)		Percent of Young Adults (18–25 yr.)		Percent of Adults (26 yr. and older)	
	Ever Used	Current User	Ever Used	Current User	Ever Used	Current User
Marijuana	30.9	16.7	68.2	35.4	19.6	6.0
Inhalants	9.8	2.0	16.5	1.2	3.9	.5
Hallucinogens	7.1	2.2	25.1	4.4	4.5	(z)
Cocaine	5.4	1.4	27.5	9.3	4.3	.9
Heroin	.5	(z)	3.5	(z)	1.0	(z)
Analgesics	3.2	.6	11.8	1.0	2.7	(z)
Stimulants*	3.4	1.2	18.2	3.5	5.8	.5
Sedatives*	3.2	1.1	17.0	2.8	3.5	(z)
Tranquilizers*	4.1	.6	15.8	2.1	3.1	(z)
Alcohol	70.3	37.2	95.3	75.9	91.5	61.3
Cigarettes	54.1	12.1	82.8	42.6	83.0	36.9

z = Less than 0.5 percent.
 * Prescription drugs.
SOURCE: U.S. Bureau of the Census, *Statistical Abstract of the United States, 1984*, Table 195, p. 126 (Washington, D.C.: U.S. Government Printing Office, 1984).

Narcotics

Narcotics are opiates, either natural (codeine, morphine, and opium) or synthetic (heroin, meperidine, [Demerol], and methadone). All have pain-killing properties and are very important to modern medicine. Before they realized their highly addictive qualities, physicians once indiscriminately prescribed morphine and later heroin, unintentionally creating patient addicts. Methadone is commonly used to treat heroin addicts, but is itself addictive and has become a street drug as well. Codeine is normally found in cough medicines; morphine, heroin, and meperidine have indispensable uses in medicine and surgery, as they relieve physical pain and psychological distress.

Effects
The initial effect of a shot of narcotic is a pleasant relaxation followed by listlessness and drowsiness. Opiates are powerful depressants, which slow down the body organs, curbing hunger, thirst, and the sex drive. Users develop a tolerance for the drug and require increasingly larger doses for relief and the avoidance of withdrawal symptoms, which vary according to the degree of drug dependence. About 4 to 6 hours after injection, withdrawal symptoms begin. Full-blown symptoms start about 12 to 16 hours after a shot. They may include shaking, sweating, chills, abdominal pains, vomiting, diarrhea, muscle aches, runny eyes and nose.

Dangers

Narcotics are highly addictive but less deadly than alcohol, barbituates, and tobacco which directly or indirectly cause the deaths of thousands of people each year compared to a few hundred deaths annually from heroin overdose. Heroin withdrawal is less harsh than withdrawal for alcoholics or barbituate addicts, which unlike heroin withdrawal can be fatal. Alcohol and tobacco are far more damaging physically, so a narcotics addict with a steady supply of the drug who avoids excess doses can continue for decades without signs of physical ill effects or body deterioration. Using an unsterile needle or contamination of other paraphernalia can cause infection; liver damage from hepatitis is common among heroin users.

Use

Although many Americans consider narcotics use our most serious drug problem, its rate of use is the lowest of all drugs mentioned in this chapter. Only 0.8 percent of adults over age 35, 3.6 percent of young adults age 18 to 25, and 1.1 percent youth age 12 to 17 have ever tried heroin, and the percentage of regular users is far lower.[23] About half a million people are heroin addicts in the United States.[24] Most addicts are males living in large cities—particularly New York, Los Angeles, San Francisco, and Chicago. Most addicts are under 30, poorly educated, and from a low-income background. More Blacks tend to become addicted than Whites, but heroin use has spread among the white middle class.

Tobacco

Smokers develop a greater tolerance for nicotine, a highly addictive drug, rather quickly and so tend to increase their daily consumption. Most smokers consume 15 or more cigarettes a day, or an average of at least one for every waking hour.[25] Dependence on tobacco becomes so strong that breaking the smoking habit is extremely difficult. Studies have shown that more than 80 percent of the people who make sincere efforts to stop smoking, even through special clinics, fail to do so.[26]

The well-publicized harmful effects of cigarette smoking did result in mandatory warnings on all packs and a ban on radio and television tobacco advertising. Still, many young people and adult women begin smoking, mostly because of peer pressure and the image successfully generated by the tobacco industry that smoking makes one mature, sophisticated, and sexually attractive. Many people also hold a cavalier attitude that the health hazards are not immediate but distant, and that they can quit at any time.

Effects

Nicotine is a stimulant raising blood pressure, accelerating the heart rate, yet intensifying one's alertness and dulling the appetite. Some smokers claim that smoking relaxes them. However, that sensation is either due to the false belief that it does, thereby psychologically causing that result, or else by "lighting up" one overcomes withdrawal symptoms that occur if one has overextended smoking intervals. Withdrawal symptoms include nervousness, excitability, anxiety, irritability, headaches, drowsiness, and a loss of energy.

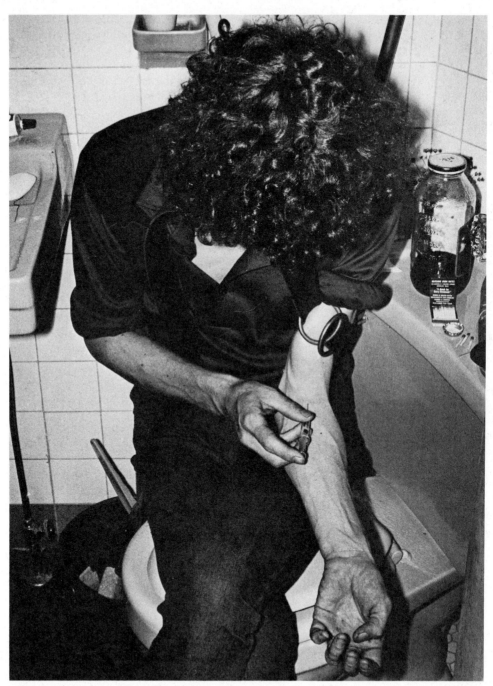

When considering serious drug problems, most Americans think of people "shooting up" with narcotics, but reality is different than the perception. Only a half million people are regular users, making narcotics use the lowest of all drugs. Alcohol, barbituates, and tobacco directly or indirectly cause far more deaths.

Dangers

Tobacco is probably the most physically harmful of all drugs Americans use. Smokers inhale nicotine, coal tars, nitrogen dioxide, formaldehyde, and other substances that continually assault the body. Chances of emphysema, bronchitis, throat and lung cancer significantly increase, as do the probability of heart disease and stroke, especially among women using birth control pills. The surgeon general estimates that smoking causes about 340,000 deaths annually, with 129,000 of 430,000 cancer deaths associated with smoking. Cigarette smoking reduces life expectancy: someone smoking less than half a pack a day has a 4-year shorter life expectancy while someone smoking two or more packs a day has 8 fewer years.[27] Pregnant women smokers double the probability of a miscarriage or premature birth, and are likely to have a child born underweight. About 75 percent of all fires in homes, apartments, and hotels are the result of careless smoking, and accidental death by fire smoking in bed is fairly frequent.[28]

Use

About 52 million Americans smoke, or 32.6 percent of the adult population. More adult males than females smoke, but among teenagers smoking is equally likely for either sex. Since nicotine is addictive, consumption increases with age, and as three-fourths of today's adult smokers began before age 21, we can expect a greater sexual balance among adult smokers in the near future.[29] The greatest rate of smokers is in the 25 to 44 age grouping, in which about 37 percent smoke. About 31 percent of those aged 17–21 are smokers.[30]

UNDERSTANDING DRUG ATTITUDES

Drug use is so widespread in American society that it is part of the daily life of almost every person. From birth through life's ailments to death, drugs ease our pain and suffering. For many, drugs serve such utilitarian purposes as keeping us awake, helping us sleep, or eliminating our stress. Recreational drugs increase our pleasure or sociability at festive or informal gatherings. We take other drugs routinely without thinking of them as drugs, such as when we smoke cigarettes or drink caffeinated beverages.

Since all drugs, alter mind, mood, and physical functioning, their varying social definitions and social significance are at least as important to our understanding as their physiological capabilities. Why are some drugs legal or respectable and others not? What causes value conflicts within a society about certain drugs? What occasions hostile social reaction to certain drugs, in particular? If we consider our four theoretical perspectives as different lenses to view the same problem, we can gain many valuable insights.

Individual Faults and Deviant Behavior

The deviance approach does not offer answers to the above questions because it focuses upon those failing to internalize society's drug-use norms. Violating these norms can take several forms: administering an illegal drug, abuse or overconsuming a legal drug, or taking drugs such as peyote that are permitted only for certain groups (in this case by Native American Church). This perspective is quite limited, since it fails to address the concerns of social definition of drugs and varying reactions, either over time periods or to the different drugs. Instead, the deviance approach looks to physiological or personality explanations as to why individuals abuse drugs.

Physiological Explanations

One popular belief is that drugs produce physiological changes in the body, thus creating an irresistible desire for more. Vincent Dole and Marie Nyswander, the founders of the methadone treatment program for heroin addicts, suggest people have different levels of susceptibility.[31] For those highly susceptible individuals, taking drugs develops in them a "drug hunger," continuing even if no physical dependence exists. The inner craving or drug hunger is likened to an individual's craving for sweets, but on a more habitual basis.

Another physiological approach, particularly with alcoholism, is that drug abuse is an inherited predisposition, passed from one generation to the next. The genetic theories either propose the transmission of a nutritional deficiency offset by alcohol or drug consumption, or an inherited fondness for the chemical properties of the drug. Proponents of these beliefs theorize that both alcoholism and drug use often occur in families, with children of addicts becoming addicted themselves.[32]

Abundant evidence suggests that physiology alone cannot explain alcoholism or drug addiction. Not all alcoholics are the children of alcoholics nor do the children of alcoholics necessarily become alcoholics themselves.[33] Medical addicts today usually discontinue drug use after discharge from a hospital while others who thought they were addicted to a drug (which in fact could not produce physical dependence) nevertheless continued to behave as addicts.[34] Although physiological effects on the body in taking the drug and the withdrawal discomfort discourage its discontinuance, biological explanations are only partially helpful at best. Psychological and environmental factors are also important considerations.

Psychological Explanations

The first of two major psychological theories as to why people abuse drugs centers on personality weaknesses. Concentrating on the role played by early childhood experiences in shaping adult personalities, psychologists note that lack of sufficient love and affection impairs a child's personality development, causing an emotionally insecure person for whom drugs offer solace, self-satisfaction, or escape from reality. Extensive studies of addicts have resulted in a composite portrait wherein researchers identify them as hostile, immature, dependent, maladjusted, manipulative, and narcissistic.[35]

A second approach is that of the behaviorists, maintaining that continued drug use occurs through a process of association and reinforcement. This stimulus-response conditioning begins with the positive reinforcement the pleasure user associates with the drug. Continuance rests upon negative reinforcement, that is, avoidance of unpleasant withdrawal symptoms. Thus tense individuals may turn to alcohol, barbituates, or tranquilizers to relieve stress. In finding the pleasant outcome satisfyingly relaxing, a pattern of continued use may emerge wherein heavier use and addiction result. What initially begins as a pleasant alternative now continues as a physical addiction.

Both personality and social learning or behavioral theory are important to our understanding of drug use and abuse. However, no one type of personality is more likely to lead to drug abuse; many different behavioral patterns can occur in promoting drug use. Moreover, none of these perspectives help us to understand shifting values and value conflicts in a society over drug use.

Institutional Faults and System Disorganization

Functionalist theory focuses upon the social norms and conditions that foster drug use in a society, rather than upon the particular reasons why individuals would use drugs. As you have seen, the use of some drugs is socially acceptable: alcohol, amphetamines, caffeine, cocaine, depressants, marijuana, narcotics, and tobacco are condoned by society for moderate use for either medical, recreational, or therapeutic use. Prescription drugs, particularly, are highly functional for medical practitioners and their patients. One notable example is how the number of patients confined to mental hospitals has dropped by more than two-thirds, from about 560,000 in 1956 to less than 160,000 today, through drug therapy—the use of mood-altering psychopharmaceuticals.[36] That some have become homeless city dwellers lacking social competency is a dysfunction requiring corrective action.

Drugs are a multibillion dollar industry in this country, providing a living for the tens of thousands involved in providing drugs through growing, processing or manufacturing, distributing, and selling. The alcohol, pharmaceutical, and tobacco industries prosper, as does the highly profitable illegal drug market. The abuse and misuse of drugs also provides jobs for those enforcing drug laws or helping those addicted to drugs.

Anomie

Rapid social change—high technology, shifts in occupational patterns, lack of urban jobs for low-skilled minorities concentrated in cities, disappearing rural work opportunities—help create social problems: poverty, alienation, greater social class disparities. The outside pressures of school, work, and everyday life also place great stress upon individual and family well-being. For many people enmeshed in feelings of confusion, their societal role threatened by occupational dislocation or changing traditions, drugs offer an escape from unpleasant or difficult situations. Prevailing social norms about drug use do not necessarily influence such individuals, since they either do not think themselves an integral part of the society or they are caught up among many social demands and seek drugs as a refuge. The dysfunctions of alienation, confusion, rootlessness, stress, anxiety, and unattainable goals occasioned by the social system can create in some individuals a sense of normlessness regarding drugs. Despite societal remonstrances, drugs are a tempting alternative.

Value Conflict

Our widespread diversity in occupations and specialization has brought about significant structural differentiation, with the existence of countless subgroups or subcultures. Consequently, achieving a value consensus about drug use is difficult to achieve. What is acceptable to one group often is not to another. The failure of Prohibition offered a notable illustration of a clash of values, in which widespread public deviance ended an unpopular law which had originally enjoyed sufficient support to be passed in the first place as a constitutional amendment.

Present-day value conflicts abound. Antismoking groups have succeeded in having laws passed restricting smoking in public areas and forbidding television advertising, but the federal government continues subsidies to the tobacco industry, despite the surgeon general's warnings of the dangers inherent in tobacco use. Marijuana and cocaine enjoy widespread and growing use, often at socially fashionable gatherings, yet if caught the user faces felony charges in most states. In the sixties, marijuana use was a deliberate means of expressing rejection of middle-class values by the hippies. Young people today often view illegal drug use as a way of asserting their independence from the older generation's values.

Inequality and Inevitable Conflict

Conflict theorists also emphasize value conflicts in analyzing the drug problem, but their focus centers on how and why those with power and influence react to various forms of drug use. If a drug becomes identified with a group whose social characteristics are disreputable or considered threatening to the society, it is likely to be declared illegal. The powerful, in this view, act to protect themselves from a potential threat rather than responding to health hazards posed by that form of drug use. A related point is that the dominant group attempts to force its morality on others, especially if a subgroup has a "subversive" life-style (e.g., the hippie counterculture of grass, LSD, free love, communal living, nonmaterialism).

Drugs and Social Class

We have numerous instances of changing values when previously legal drugs become associated with a low status group. For example, excessive drinking has existed since Puritan times and was called an "addiction" as early as 1785 by Dr. Benjamin Rush, surgeon general of the United States. However, not until native-born Americans associated alcohol with the swelling numbers of poor Irish Catholic immigrants did the all-out Prohibition movement begin. By 1855, the height of Irish migration, 13 of the 31 states had prohibition laws. Although most repealed or modified the laws by 1863, the advent of the Women's Christian Temperance Union (WCTU) directed its antiliquor campaign in the late nineteenth century primarily at the Blacks or Catholic and Jewish immigrants living in poverty in the cities. During the World War I era, the Anti-Saloon League argued that the major beer breweries were all German-American owned and were destroying American character and productivity.[37] With anti-German feeling still high after the war, Prohibition was adopted nationwide in 1919.

Similarly, growing opium poppies, manufacturing and selling opiates were all legal in the nineteenth century. You could buy opiates in pharmacies, grocery and general stores, as well as by mail order, for teething, coughs, diarrhea, dysentery, consumption, pain, "woman's trouble," or any other purpose. Hundreds of patent medicines containing opium or morphine were easily accessible. Only when anti-Chinese sentiment flared up in the 1870s during economic hard times and Whites agitated against Chinese cheap labor, did antiopium laws pass. Even then, the laws were aimed at the Chinese coolies (Chinese import of opium, opium dens), not at opium use itself.[38]

Cocaine was at first a respectable drug until newspapers around the turn of the century linked it with Blacks, criminals, and violence. Media sensationalism initiated a public belief that "Blacks plus cocaine equals raped white women" and the drug became illegal in 1914.[39] Heroin receives greater attention than more widely used dangerous drugs because it is frequently associated with poor non-Whites and criminals. Marijuana, as mentioned earlier, became synonymous with antiestablishment subcultures, but now that many "normal" affluent Whites use it, marijuana laws are becoming liberalized in many states.

Interest Groups

Powerful corporate interests spend hundreds of millions of dollars each year to influence public opinion and legislators. Tobacco, for example, is a major crop in several states, generating income opportunities for manufacturers, wholesalers, transporters, advertising agencies, vending machine companies, and retailers. Through the industry's advocate, the Tobacco Institute, they conduct intensive lobbying to fight and discredit the efforts of the American Cancer Society and citizen groups to enact antismoking legislation. Despite current estimates holding tobacco responsible for one death in the United States every 90 seconds, the tobacco industry has been very successful in preventing any action to restrict tobacco use.

Another highly effective group in protecting its self-interest is the pharmaceutical industry. Each year it manufactures billions of amphetamines—enough for a month's supply for every infant, child, or adult in this country.[40] No medical justification exists for such overproduction of a drug proven to be potentially dangerous to the user. Yet when Congress passed the Comprehensive Drug Abuse Prevention and Control Act in 1970, the industry succeeded in preventing the inclusion of amphetamines in the dangerous drug category. In that bill possessing marijuana, a less dangerous substance, was declared a serious crime, but there was no mention of amphetamines at all.

Drugs band together an unlikely alliance of special interest groups. Religious groups seeking prohibition or severe restriction of drugs for moral reasons are supported by organized crime, for whom illegal substances offer enormous profits on the black market. Law enforcement agencies also join them in advocating a tougher drug policy since that will mean higher department budgets, better pay, more personnel, and job security. Perhaps the most notable example is how Harry J. Anslinger, head of the Narcotics Bureau from 1931 to 1962, waged an effective propaganda campaign against marijuana. With his budget and staff cut back 4 consecutive years from 1933 to 1936, he launched a media attack on marijuana, calling it an assassin of youth that led to heroin addiction. He offered the newspapers stories about "dope fiends"

BOX 3.2

FOR U.S.—A DUBIOUS
DISTINCTION

Americans may flinch when they hear the United States described as a drug-happy society, but the facts are indisputable: Illicit-drug use per capita in the U.S. exceeds that of any other industrial nation.

Among European nations, West Germany has the most serious heroin problem. Still, the situation is worse in America, which has 450,000 to 500,000 addicts.

The Soviet Union has negligible drug problems, although it suffers heavily from alcoholism.

Japan, America's keenest economic competitor, fought off amphetamine and heroin epidemics after World War II with stringent laws. It took the same approach with marijuana. Foreigners caught with pot are arrested and deported. Japan now has the lowest illegal-drug consumption of any developed nation.

Dr. Gabriel Nahas of Columbia University, an expert on drug use here and abroad, says the U.S. in 1980 became "the world's largest consumer of marijuana, ahead of countries where it has been used for centuries—India, Pakistan, Afghanistan, Iran and Egypt."

Nahas notes that Egypt, a nation long dominated by hashish—the Arabic word for marijuana—imposed harsh penalties to reduce drug use in the 1950s and 1960s. At that time, its per capita consumption of hashish was only one tenth that of the U.S.

The United States does not lead the world in heroin addiction. That distinction belongs to Iran, with up to 1 million heroin and opium junkies. At least two other Third World countries—Pakistan and Malaysia—also have higher heroin-use rates than the U.S., experts say.

SOURCE: Reprinted from *U.S. News & World Report*, May 16, 1983. Copyright, 1983, U.S. News & World Report, Inc.

who committed "marijuana atrocities." The bureau sponsored a commercial movie, *Reefer Madness,* which showed movie-house audiences how hopelessly hooked marijuana users would stop at nothing to get the "killer weed." Anslinger's crusade culminated with passage of the Marijuana Tax Act of 1937, designed to eliminate use of the drug. Needless to say, the Narcotics Bureau received increased funding to fight this "evil."[41]

Interaction and Social Interpretation

Users may view drugs as an adventure, an escape, a necessity, or a religious experience. What is a patient aid to the medical profession can be evil to moralists if used nonmedically. The underworld finds it a lucrative trade while law enforcement personnel see it as the center of criminal activity. Drugs become redefined from time to time and their symbolic meaning as an evil, a social problem, or an acceptable practice is the basis upon which interactionist theorists build their analyses.

Societal Norms

Although some people may have maladjusted personalities or other psychological characteristics influencing their drug experimentation, sociologists find such individualized explanations inadequate since drug use does not occur in isolation from society. Interactionists look upon drug use as a behavior pattern that is learned through the socialization and resocialization occurring through group interaction. Because drinking alcohol is an acceptable social practice, for example, children grow up learning a favorable definition and attitude about its use. As they grow older, they are more likely to drink also. Similarly, a maturing individual will be strongly influenced by adults' habitual use of tobacco, caffeine, stimulants, or sedatives.

Cultural Factors

The prevalence of norms among certain ethnic groups about alcohol consumption illustrates the differences in learned behavior patterns. Orthodox Jews restrict drinking to special occasions among relatives and close friends, consider excessive drinking a bad reflection on their culture and more the behavior of non-Jews. Having learned norms on moderation in childhood, even adult Jews who have drifted away from orthodoxy continue their restraint in drinking.[42] Italian-American children grow up in households where wine drinking is an integral part of eating, and again, moderate consumption is the norm. Neither Italians nor Jews tend to drink to relieve stress, since they have not defined drinking as an acceptable means of relieving problems, but as a part of family life.[43] Irish-Americans, on the other hand, have traditionally associated drinking with any social gathering, and it is used to create a good time. Traditional Irish values do not hold public drunkenness as disgraceful as do Jews and Italians, unless it results in income or property loss. Consequently, excessive drinking at these gatherings is not uncommon. A relatively high rate of alcoholism exists among Irish-American males but is rare among Italians and Jews.[44]

Drug Subcultures

Almost all learning occurs within primary groups, a small number of people who personally and directly interact with each other over a period of time. Peer groups are the major agent of socialization for drug-taking. New users of any drug—alcohol, amphetamines, cocaine, marijuana, or others—are usually introduced to the use and effects of the drug through their friends. If the dominant culture has a negative attitude about particular drug use, an individual is more likely to use it anyway when in the presence of a group of friends who approve its use. Since drugs are most commonly taken within the social context of a group where reassurances make drug use more desirable, the longer and more intense a person's association with a drug subculture is, the more likely that group's norms will outweigh those of the dominant society.

Once an individual begins using these drugs, the shared experience draws that person closer to the group and its norms. For many, the comradery within the group is just as important as the effect of the drug, and they use it to retain group acceptance. Others, often called "mellow dudes" within the subculture, devote their free time to a life of parties, music, and sex, augmented by marijuana, cocaine, and Quaaludes, with occasional use of amphetamines and hallucinogens. "Turning on" others is a common act of friendship in their view.[45]

Among drug addicts a more intensive subculture exists. Labeled as deviants by a society and its laws, the drug addict experiences disapproval, rejection, and exclusion from conventional groups. Forced to interact with others sharing the need for a regular drug supply, a closer bond develops among addicts as they struggle to survive and find sources for drugs. Isolated from the rest of society, they gradually assume a deviant identity and their behavior centers around continued drug use, reinforced by the ideology they now share with the only group that does not condemn them.[46]

SOCIAL CONSEQUENCES OF DRUG USE

At first glance the misuse of drugs would simply seem an act of self-abuse or potential self-destruction. Actually though, drug abuse creates many social and economic dysfunctions in a society, and both innocent victims and society as a whole suffer. While some of these social problems are generated by society's own norms, the fact remains that the consequences of drug misuse and abuse can be devastating upon the entire community. Some of these problems are obvious and quantifiable, but others lie hidden and their cost to society is less easy to measure.

Crime

The popular belief that drug use causes crime is inaccurate, although a strong correlation exists between violent crime and certain drugs. Up to 86 percent of all murders and 72 percent of all rapes, for example, have been committed by people who drank alcohol immediately beforehand.[47] Amphetamine users, reacting to the drug's powerful effects, have been disproportionately represented in violent crimes, particularly assault and robbery. Significant evidence exists, in fact, to show that those using alcohol, amphetamines, or barbiturates are far more likely to commit murder, rape, and assault than narcotics addicts.[48]

Heroin addiction has a strong correlation with nonviolent crime, as addicts often steal, burglarize, sell drugs, or prostitute themselves to support their habit, which may cost them as much as $150 a day. Drug laws, while enacted to protect society from harmful drug use and crime, actually have the reverse effect and produce other unintended negative consequences as well. They drive up the price causing addicts to take desperate measures to feed their habit.[49]

In making certain drugs illegal, society creates a black market enormously profitable to organized crime. Thus underworld monopoly, combined with the risk of producing, transporting, or selling the illegal drugs, drives the price up far beyond its actual cost. Most addicts are unable to afford such high costs and are forced to resort to criminal activity, spending much of their time in this capacity instead of any normally productive function within the society. Besides securing money for the drug at other's expense, these addict criminals endanger their health and life by the varying strength and impurity of the available dope. On the other hand, affluent addicts including physicians (one estimate places the number of physician addicts at 1 in 100),[50] are able to get an adequate supply without financial strain and undistinguishably continue to function otherwise normally for decades without noticeable health impairment.

What becomes apparent, then, is that narcotics addiction itself does not cause crime but rather its illegality. Because addiction is labeled an act of criminal deviance instead of a sickness, the punitive laws cost society millions of dollars each year in enforcement costs and severely strain our judicial and prison systems. Organized crime prospers from selling drugs, addicts commit crimes to buy drugs, and the criminal drug laws continue to produce crime and criminals.

Disrespect for the law is another consequence of these unenforceable drug laws, much like Prohibition was; the irrational and arbitrary nature of the drug laws (alcohol and tobacco are legal but marijuana is not, for example) appears hypocritical to many. Two-thirds of all American young adults between 18 and 25 have tried marijuana, meaning most have broken the law. Hundreds of thousands of Americans have been caught possessing marijuana and have thus acquired criminal records. Yet the evidence is substantial that a nonaddictive, calming drug does not lead the user to commit any crime other than to use it or sell it. Such widespread use of a drug declared illegal serves only to engender negative attitudes toward the legal justice system.

Automobile Accidents

One out of every two Americans will be involved in an alcohol-related auto accident, one way or another, sometime in their lifetime. In recent years, traffic fatalities from alcohol have numbered about 25,000 a year, half of the annual total. In a 2-year period the figure exceeds the total number of American deaths in the Vietnam war over a 10-year period. One-fifth or 5,000 of those killed each year in alcohol-related automobile accidents are teenagers.[51] In addition, alcohol use is responsible for over a half-million serious personal injuries and many millions of dollars of property damage every year. The total annual cost of all medical expenses and property damage resulting from alcohol-induced automobile accidents exceeds $1 billion (see Table 3.3).

The role of other drugs in auto accidents is becoming an additional cause for concern. The National Institute on Drug Abuse reported in 1977 that marijuana was a factor in about 15 percent of all auto accidents.[52] Whether they are stimulants or depressants, drugs impair one's judgment and diminish driving skills. The result can either be acts of recklessness or reduced capacity to stay alert and react quickly to a situation.

Alcohol remains by far the most serious cause of auto accidents because of its widespread use, particularly among drivers aged 22–34 (see Tables 3.3 and 3.4). In recent years several states have begun countermeasures. In 1984, twenty-three states had set the minimum legal drinking age at 21, others at 20, reversing a trend that had previously seen the legal age set at 18 or 19 in almost all states. Beginning

TABLE 3.3 Summary of Alcohol Related Accidents, 1979–80

	Proportion Alcohol Related %		Total Accidents		Persons Affected
	Intoxicated (BAC ≥ .10)	Alcohol Involved (BAC ≥ .01)	Reported Accidents	Unreported Accidents	Number Alcohol Related
Fatal	47–50	55	45,000	0	24,000–27,500 fatally injured persons
Injury	18	18–25	2,500,000	390,000	708,000 injured persons
Property damage only	5	8	4,300,000	11,000,000	1,224,000 property damage accidents involving alcohol
All accidents	11	11	6,845,000	11,390,000	2,000,000 motor vehicle accidents of all kinds that involve alcohol

SOURCE: National Safety Council.

TABLE 3.4 Driver Age and Alcohol Involvement in Accidents (Nass 1979–80)

Driver Age	Percent of Driver License Population*	Percent of Vehicle Miles Traveled†	Percent of All Accident Drivers	Percent in Age Group with Alcohol Involvement	Percent of All Alcohol Involved Accident Drivers
16–17	3.2	1.95	7.9	4.6	4.8
18	2.2	1.97	4.8	6.7	4.9
19	2.4	2.31	4.6	7.9	5.5
20	2.5	2.74	3.9	8.7	5.1
21	2.6	2.31	4.2	9.1	5.8
22–24	7.0	8.38	10.0	10.6	16.3
25–34	25.0	27.40	23.5	6.6	24.0
35–44	17.1	19.48	12.6	5.9	11.4
45–54	12.8	17.53	9.7	8.9	13.2
55–64	12.4	10.72	6.5	4.8	4.8
65+	10.6	5.10	5.5	2.8	2.4
	100%	100%	100%		100%

SOURCE: * *Highway Statistics 1980* (FHWA).
         † 1977 NPTS tapes (comparable with FHWA statistics from their publication *Characteristics of Licensed Drivers and Their Travel*, October 1980).

Alcohol-related accidents, such as this one, cause about 25,000 deaths and 500,000 serious personal injuries each year. At some point in their lives, one out of two Americans will be involved in an alcohol-related auto accident. Federal legislation now obliges states to get tougher with motorists driving while intoxicated.

October 1, 1986, any state with a minimum drinking age under 21 will lose 5 percent of their federal highway-construction funds; by October 1987 they will lose 10 percent, as the federal government acts to reduce traffic fatalities among young people.

Health

Drug dependence exacts a heavy toll on the personal health and mental well-being of the users and quite often their families as well. Alcoholics, for example, can expect to live 10 to 12 years less than nonalcoholics. The death among alcoholics is about three times greater than that of the total population. About 33,000 a year die from cirrhosis of the liver, the sixth most common cause of death in the United States.[53] Continuous heavy drinking also leads to malnutrition and weakened body resistance to infectious diseases, contributes to many types of heart ailments and possibly to cancer. A third of all suicides each year are by alcoholics. Incidents of family violence, child and spouse abuse, are fairly common among problem drinkers, as are above average rates of emotional illness among family members brought on by stress, coping with unpredictable behavior, and finanical worries.

Alcohol is the third major cause of birth defects in this country. About one in every 350 to 500 infants born have birth defects because their mothers drank alcohol during pregnancy.[54] Because a human fetus is unable to metabolize alcohol, its blood alcohol level becomes about 10 times greater than that of the mother. Children born to alcoholic mothers are themselves addicted and are likely to have **fetal alcohol syndrome,** which comprises many congenital problems including mental deficiency, heart problems, and deformities. Similarly, narcotic addict mothers have babies who are addicted at birth, suffering from the **fetal narcotic syndrome,** or withdrawal symptoms. Newborns whose mothers frequently took barbituates or other sedatives also display these symptoms at birth, and all infants, regardless of the drug involved, gain weight with much difficulty.

Smoking also affects people's health significantly. The surgeon general estimates that 340,000 people die each year from coronary heart disease, lung disease, or cancer resulting from smoking. It is also responsible for many respiratory problems, particularly emphysema, which can progress until breathing requires intermittent pure oxygen; early death is still inevitable. Blood circulation problems can also result from smoking. The surgeon general places the annual cost in health care expenses and lost production and earnings from smoking illnesses at $28 billion.

Another dimension to health problems caused by drug abuse is the deaths, comas, and other bodily dysfunctions brought on by mixing alcohol with other drugs or overdosing. About 50,000 people each year are treated in emergency rooms, almost all from the combination of alcohol with other drugs, from which 2,500 die each year, compared to 1,000 from heroin.

Economic Losses

From airline hangers and construction sites to chemical plants, nuclear plants, and offices, taking illegal drugs on the job has become a serious problem for American business. Experts now admit drug use has spread to virtually every occupation, and its cost to the economy is staggering. One authoritative study put the total annual cost at nearly $26 billion, including $16.6 billion in lost productivity due to absenteeism and other factors (see Box 3.3). Roger Smith, chairman of General Motors, has said absenteeism due to alcohol and drug abuse costs the corporation a billion dollars a year.[55]

Most of the workers are not addicts. They could be secretaries or blue-collar workers who smoke a joint at lunchtime; high-tech employees or Wall Street traders who snort their lines of coke at work; night-shift workers who take amphetamines to keep up their energy level. The result is often damaged or contaminated products, shoddy repairs, an increase in minor injuries and absenteeism, and a decrease in output. Employees taking drugs on the job are absent far more often than straight workers, three times more likely to be injured, and one-third less productive.[56]

U.S. industry has been suffering from many problems in recent years, and drug abuse is clearly a contributing factor. Between 1967 and 1981, America's manufacturing output increased 39 percent, far behind other nations with a far less serious drug problem. For example, Great Britain increased its productivity by 57 percent in the same time period, West Germany by 90 percent, and Japan an impressive 209 percent.[57] The United States has a greater illicit-drug use per capita than any other

BOX 3.3

DRUG ABUSE: THE COST
TO THE ECONOMY
A government-sponsored study by the Research Tri-
angle Institute shows the staggering economic toll of drug use. Its 1977 findings
have been adjusted for inflation to reflect the costs in 1983 dollars.

LOST PRODUCTIVITY

Absenteeism, slowdowns, mistakes and sick leave	$4.9 billion
Drug-related deaths	1.3 billion
Imprisonment	2.1 billion
Leaving jobs for criminal careers to support habits	8.3 billion

MEDICAL EXPENSES

Treatment in rehabilitation centers, in hospitals and by doctors	$1.9 billion
Administration of treatment programs, research and training	367 million

CRIME

Federal, state and local expenditures for courts, police and prisons	$5.2 billion
Alarm systems, locks and other preventive steps for businesses and individuals	1.6 billion
Property destroyed during criminal acts	113 million
Total	$25.8 billion

SOURCE: *Newsweek*, August 22, 1983, p. 55. Reprinted by permission.

industrial nation; Japan has the lowest. After World War II, Japan had very serious amphetamine and heroin problems, but overcame them with stringent laws. Similarly, Japan is severe on marijuana users.

American business has begun to address the problem. Many companies hire drug consultants to run educational seminars for management and other employees. More than 4,500 companies, including almost all the 500 biggest, have employee-assistance programs for drug and alcohol abusers. Companies use drug-sniffing dogs in employees' parking lots or conduct undercover operations to find the contraband and its users. One drug consulting firm said it finds illegal drugs on one of every eight employees it searches.[58] Companies utilizing investigations and treatment ap-

Two auto workers share a marijuana cigarette during their lunch break at the Chevrolet manufacturing complex in Flint, Michigan. Workers using illicit drugs cost American business $26 billion annually in economic losses due to absenteeism, lowered productivity, inferior products and repairs, and injuries.

proaches usually report a decrease in theft and absenteeism and improved productivity.[59]

Professional Sports

Until 1982, we paid little attention to alcohol and drug abuse among professional athletes. All that changed, however, with the arrest and conviction of several National Football League (NFL) players on charges of possession of cocaine or conspiracy to distribute it. Suspensions followed. In baseball, one player was fined $54,000 after he required treatment twice in eight months for cocaine dependency. These turned out not to be isolated cases. All teams in all competitive sports have players with drug problems. The National Basketball Association (NBA) now has a confidential telephone hot line for its players to seek counseling and medical help. All baseball and football teams have arrangements with drug rehabilitation centers for those seeking help. In the 1983 off-season, the NFL reported that 43 players received treatment for alcohol and drug abuse. Many more, however, are believed dependent on drugs, particularly cocaine.[60]

The life-style of professional athletes—coddling; lots of money; long hours to spend traveling and staying temporarily at many places; pressures; and lack of job security—produce both temptations and inducements to use drugs. Once athletes become hooked, their stamina and skills deteriorate, as numerous ex-athletes and their coaches have confirmed. The social consequences are not limited to shortened

BOX 3.4

WHEN THE NAVY DECREED "ZERO TOLERANCE" OF DRUGS

As bleak as the drug picture is nationally, in the U.S. armed forces the news is upbeat. Results of an extensive survey, to be announced soon, are expected to show big declines in drug use in the military since 1980.

That was the year the Pentagon discovered that nearly half of its junior enlisted personnel had smoked pot in the previous 12 months and more than a third had lit up in the previous month.

Penalties were stiffened, and new programs were devised to strip drugs of their glamour. The Navy tried extra hard. Not only had it found 48 percent of its sailors were smoking pot at two major bases in 1980, but in May, 1981, it suffered a second blow.

During a training exercise, a jet crashed into the U.S.S. *Nimitz,* killing 14 and injuring 42. Drugs did not cause the crash, the Pentagon ruled later. But six of the dead flight-deck crewman had traces of marijuana in their bodies. That showed drug use aboard ship, and it raised questions of whether those crewmen might have lived had they abstained.

Adm. Thomas B. Hayward, then chief of naval operations, ordered "zero tolerance" of drug abuse. His words, which reverberated throughout the Navy: "Not on my watch, not in my division, not in my Navy."

Now, says a Navy spokesman, "We're using all the tools we can"—mandatory urinalyses, drug-detecting dogs, warrant officers with antidrug training and expanded remedial-education programs for drug users. As a result, pot smoking has been cut in half.

SOURCE: Reprinted from *U.S. News & World Report,* May 16, 1983. Copyright, 1983, U.S. News & World Report, Inc.

careers for the athletes. Both the integrity and popularity of sports can be undermined by questions of on-field performances. The all-American image of our athletes—the respect youngsters have for them—erodes. Even worse, these athletes offer improper role models for impressionable young people.

SOCIAL CONTROL AND SOLUTION ATTEMPTS

The early 1900s had marked a change in the social definition of drug addiction. The Harrison Narcotics Act of 1914 made the manufacture, sale, and use of cocaine and opiates a federal offense except for "legitimate medical uses." This law, following passage of state antinarcotics legislation, made certain drug use a criminal activity instead of a health problem, while other drugs like alcohol and tobacco were not negatively reclassified, even as health hazards.

Identification of certain drugs as a social problem constituting criminal activity was, as we have seen, the result of their perceived association with lower-class minorities and crime. Efforts at resolving the drug problem in America have primarily focused on repressive measures—arrest and punishment. Although the federal government established a few hospitals in the 1930s to treat addicts, it has only been in the past two decades—with the spread of illicit drug use to the middle and upper classes—that increased preventive and treatment programs have grown along with corrective actions.

Preventive Programs

Attempts to educate people about the dangers of drug use have had varying results, partly because of the approach taken. Generally, drug education programs have either employed scare tactics, incorporating a great many distortions and inaccuracies, or a more scientific and accurate presentation.

Scare Tactics

Drug education programs which use scare tactics, emphasizing all the possible terrible consequences, have a long history of dismal failure. Not only do such alarmist approaches arouse youthful curiosity instead, they also contradict the facts gained from firsthand experience or from friends. Because many young people know of the positive aspects of drug taking and typically have a cavalier belief in their own invulnerability to risk, these emotional and often misinformed appeals lose credibility.

One false belief, a part of the mythology concerning drugs, is the "stepping-stone" theory, that "soft" drug users become "hard" drug users. In 1973 the National Commission reported that its survey of the nation's population found that 70 percent believed marijuana users eventually want to try something stronger like heroin.[61] This belief has been extensively promoted by law enforcement agencies, particularly the Federal Narcotics Bureau, with severe actions taken against all drug users to prevent their escalation to heroin. This belief is based on the premise that most heroin users began with marijuana. In fact, no causal relationship exists between marijuana use and subsequent heroin use, and almost all marijuana users do not progress to hard drugs.[62] If we were to be consistent in this logic of outlawing marijuana because heroin addicts once used it, we should also outlaw aspirin, coffee, cigarettes, and antacids, since addicts used them as well.

Balanced Approaches

In the past 10 years a more rational approach to drug education has occurred, based upon more accurate information. Through funded teacher preparation programs, curriculum guides, texts, and audiovisual materials aimed at various grade levels, more and more schools are now giving more realistic presentations. Their success will be dependent upon including complete information, both positive and negative, no matter whether the drug is legal or illegal. If marijuana, for example, is safer in having few negative effects, that needs to be said; if it does prove to have negative effects, that information needs to be included. One fact, nonetheless, appears certain: the value of drug education programs lies not in their deterring drug use, but in their influence in reducing indiscriminate drug abuse.[63]

Treatment Programs

Different methods have been tried to deal with alcohol and drug abuse as a medical and psychological problem rather than an act of criminal deviance. Through professional assistance in either self-help addict communities or in health clinics, rehabilitation efforts have met with limited success. Some combine a detoxification effort with a building of self-confidence and willpower to avoid a relapse into drug taking, while others offer a substitute maintenance program or therapeutic sessions to combat the problems fostering drug dependency.

Alcoholics Anonymous (AA)

Perhaps the best-known organization, its numbers tripling since 1968 from 170,000 to 586,000 members, including many women, young people, and polydrug users, Alcoholics Anonymous offers a mutual support system and sense of security to its members. Instead of trained therapists or treatment programs, AA utilizes small group dynamics among alcoholics to share their drinking histories, confirm the need for total abstinence, take the challenge one day at a time, meet together frequently to reinforce their resolve, and call one another when the temptation to drink becomes strong. An emphasis on spiritual beliefs and help from God, together with a positive reinforcement of self-image, is an important part of this interdependent member effort. Precise information about the effectiveness of AA is hard to document because of the organization's insistence upon maintaining the anonymity of its members. From what we do know, however, it would appear that the success rate is about 50 percent, considerably better than other drug addiction programs.[64]

Methadone Clinics

If a person has been a heroin addict for at least one year and failed in at least two other attempts at treatment, acceptance into a **methadone-maintenance** program is possible. Volunteers accepted first enter the clinic to become gradually stabilized on a regular dosage of methadone instead of heroin. Methadone is a synthetic narcotic, also addictive, that prevents any withdrawal symptoms but satisfies physical cravings. Taken orally, usually mixed with fruit juice, it does not produce a high, allows a person to function normally, and its effects last about 24 hours, four times longer than heroin. Once stabilized, the person is discharged but must return to the clinic each day for an additional dose.

Methadone is simply substituting an illegal form of drug addiction for a legal form of drug addiction. Its cost—about $2 a week compared to possibly $100 a day for heroin—makes it, however, an acceptable alternative to many addicts. An estimated 85,000 persons are now treated with methadone, most under federally funded programs. Many methadone users qualify for welfare and are part of the "street people" found in cities, often drinking from a wine bottle in a paper bag and panhandling.[65] Methadone is also popular on the black market as a temporary street alternative to heroin. Although an overdose of methadone can be fatal, the death rate among users is far less than that of heroin addicts, and significantly, the crime rate is 20 times less. However, methadone clinics meet considerable opposition from neighborhood residents who fear the presence of addicts in their community.

Therapeutic Communities

These programs are a total immersion effort in which the volunteer lives for over a year in a treatment center where strict discipline, monitored daily routines, continuous antidrug indoctrination, and intensive encounter-group sessions dominate. Beginning with Synanon in California in 1959 as the prototype, other therapeutic communities—Phoenix House, Daytop Village, and others—came in existence and together they treat about 10,000 people. Staffed by both professionals and former addicts, their efforts to resocialize addicts have been rather unsuccessful. More than three-fourths of the addicts drop out and many of those who complete the program return to drug use.[66]

Antagonistic Drugs

Another attempt at behavior modification has been through negative reinforcement—using **antagonistic drugs** to negate any benefit from renewed taking of the drug to which one is addicted. For alcoholics, the drug Antabuse creates such

Therapeutic communities employ total immersion and resocialization efforts to instill self-confidence and a secure sense of identity in addicts seeking control of their lives. Intensive encounter-group sessions, like this one at Daytop Village, force individuals to strip away their masks and excuses to face reality.

violent nausea if the person then drinks alcohol that there is a powerful motivation not to drink again. Two narcotic antagonists—Cyclazocine and Naloxone—each prevent the euphoria usually produced by heroin and other opiates. However, the success of these drugs is contingent upon whether addicts take them long enough to overcome the psychological dependency on the drug. Not all addicts are willing to take the antagonistic drug regularly, and many lapse back into alcoholism or narcotics addiction a year or more later because they are unable to cope with some current problem.

Corrective Efforts

The criminalization of drugs has been totally counterproductive. The failure of Prohibition clearly demonstrated that legislation and law-enforcement efforts do not eliminate a drug problem. Similarly, the laws against cocaine, heroin, marijuana, and other drugs have failed to reduce their use. Instead they have created a drug subculture and even worse social problems by providing a lucrative source of income for organized crime, and they have increased individual criminal acts and prostitution by addicts needing money to pay for the expensive drugs.

Efforts at preventing the drugs from reaching consumers have also been counterproductive. Occasional drug busts and seizures of contraband command headlines, but law-enforcement officials are the first to admit that is only the tip of the iceberg compared to what safely reaches its destinations for distribution. Eliminating one supply simply generates another source, whether it be the country (opium and marijuana can be harvested in many locales) or the arrest of a dealer. Both in Mexico and in the United States, the government has supported heavy spraying of marijuana fields with the deadly weed-killer paraquat. When these harvested crops reached U.S. markets anyway, about a third of the total U.S. marijuana supply was contaminated, producing a far greater health hazard than before it was sprayed.

The British Approach

In sharp contrast to the American classification of drug addicts as criminals for whom punishment in the form of imprisonment and the ending of their supply are considered appropriate, the British have long viewed addiction as a sickness to be treated. This social definition has merited quite different government policies and legal practices.

Under the British program, physicians must register all narcotics-addicted patients with the government. When a patient cannot achieve complete withdrawal, but can function satisfactorily with a controlled dosage to prevent withdrawal symptoms (though not achieve a "high"), that patient may continue on a heroin maintenance program. Thereafter the addict receives a steady but strictly regulated supply of the drug either at a nominal charge if he or she is able to afford it, or free of charge, if not. The government requires strict accountability to prevent physician overprescribing or any illegal use of the drug.

Anyone found with heroin who is not a registered patient, or with a supply other than that allowed, is criminally prosecuted. Physicians face imprisonment and loss of license if they violate the laws governing usage of the drug. As a result, narcotics abuse is far less in Britain than in the United States, as is drug-related crime, since addicts need not steal to get the drug. Because it is of uniform strength and purity as a prescription drug, deaths from overdose or contaminated supplies are virtually nonexistent.[67]

THE FUTURE

We appear headed in two directions simultaneously concerning the drug program. The government spends tens of millions of dollars on antismoking campaigns while spending tens of millions of dollars on tobacco subsidies. Some states are decriminalizing individual marijuana use, while other states refuse to do so and the federal government launches countermeasures of field burnings and sprayings, arrests, seizures of contraband, and prosecution. Alcohol consumption is increasing among young people, as is the use of various other drugs. Use of marijuana and hallucinogens has declined among the young, but use of cocaine and abusive use of other stimulants or depressants has increased. We are a drug-taking society, but where are these somewhat contradictory trends taking us?

Pessimistic Scenario

Despite extensive government efforts, by the year 2025 drugs had sapped the nation's strength to such an extent that it was now a second-rate world economic power. A generation of Americans—exposed to alcohol, marijuana, cocaine, and other drugs at an early age—had grown up and taken its life-style with it into the work place. Coked-up, stoned, or strung-out employees had cost American industry so many billions of dollars in slowed productivity, absenteeism, lateness, and irrational decisions that its high product cost and poor delivery record weakened, which made the United States fall behind all other industrialized nations in output.

Relentless police crackdowns continued to result in the seizure and destruction of record amounts of contraband, but the overall supply kept growing. The dope supply was now so pervasive that finding coke, pot, or pills was no more difficult than getting a drink somewhere after the bars close. Prisons were overcrowded with people who had been convicted of various drug offenses, including mandatory jailing of those convicted of drunken driving. Still the drug epidemic was so great that most people scoffed at the authorities' futile attempts to stem the tide.

Drug-related crime continued to plague the nation. Heroin was still an expensive habit to maintain and most addicts had to steal or prostitute themselves to pay for it. Reduced productivity had reverberations throughout the society as large segments of low-income urbanites found themselves unemployed with little chance of ever getting work. They had fallen victim not only to harsh economic realities but also to the temptations of escapist reality that heroin first offered. Alarmed by the increase in heroin addicts, greater repressive measures of arrests and convictions only worsened the matter. Street crime and suburban car theft and burglaries had skyrocketed, drug-related deaths and killings were frequent, and organized crime flourished at a cost of billions of dollars to the economy each year.

If a nation's strength lies in its people, then the United States was clearly in trouble. The youth in 2025 had an even stronger drug-use role model than their parents had when they were young. Alcoholism and drug dependency were rampant in the schools as well as at work. A great many people only went through the motions of the day's activity until the moment when they "could get a buzz on." As a result, the curiosity, determination, perseverance, and concentrated activity that had led to so many discoveries, inventions, and technological achievements were anachronistic behaviors of the past. We were no longer moving forward as a civilization and some thought we never would again.

Optimistic Scenario

The United States was still a drug-taking society in 2025, with even more types of synthetic drugs on the market. The key difference was that a major revision of our drug laws had eliminated drug abuse as a social problem for society. A blue-ribbon national commission had made sweeping recommendations that legislators and the voting public—themselves more knowledgeable about drug use than they had once been—had accepted.

In some cases, tighter restrictions were enacted. Physicians had to keep detailed records of all drugs prescribed. Pharmaceutical firms were limited in the quantity of drugs they could manufacture. A mandatory reduction in alcohol content in liquor allowed people to drink more with less effect. Computerized mental alertness ignition systems had effectively eliminated drunk drivers from the roads.

Most significant was the change in official policy about any form of drug use. Preventive informational programs in the schools and media were designed to eliminate drug abuse and addiction, but taking psychoactive drugs was now recognized as a matter of individual choice. Legal recreational drug centers functioned much like bars, allowing moderate use, ensured by required machine body scans for maximum chemical substances allowed. Tobacco was still legal, but the government had removed its subsidies, offering instead lucrative subsidies to the farmers to grow other crops for export to the burgeoning world population. Marijuana was now legal and sold commercially over the counter.

An enlightened and informed public used drugs moderately and the number of alcoholics and drug addicts had dropped significantly. Addicts were defined as "sick" and treated. Incurable heroin addicts reported to heroin maintenance clinics, modeled after the old twentieth-century British system. Since drugs were legal, quality-controlled, and inexpensive, no profit in illegal sales existed. Organized crime lost one of its major bankroll sources; drug-related crime nosedived. Law enforcement personnel were able to concentrate their energies on other criminal activities, which in turn brought about a reduction in those areas as well. All of this also eliminated the drug subculture which had existed in response to previous stigmatizing and persecution.

Through licensing, taxation, regulation, abuse prevention programs, and redefinition of drug users, the nation had stopped creating social problems by its drug policies, as well as the problems engendered by drug misuse and abuse.

SUMMARY

1. Alcohol and other drugs have long been an institutionalized part of many different cultures throughout world history. What is of sociological interest is not only how cultural values about their acceptability vary from one society to another, but also how social definitions about their use change within one society over a period of time.

2. Psychoactive drugs are chemical substances affecting consciousness, mood, or perception. Some of the more harmful ones, such as alcohol, tobacco, and barbiturates, do not carry the same societal criticism as do less harmful drugs like cocaine and marijuana. All, however, can produce harmful effects, including life endangerment, if used excessively.

3. Drug use is widespread in American society, but American values consider some drugs respectable and others a social problem. The deviance approach does not explain the variance in the social definition of drugs but focuses instead on those failing to internalize the society's drug-use norms. Physiological cravings, either inherited or produced from taking drugs, cannot alone explain addiction. Explanations about personality weaknesses or psychological conditioning are helpful, but since different personality types use drugs and different behavioral patterns occur in promoting drug use, they do not provide a complete answer.

4. Functionalist analysis examines the benefits of moderate drug use for medical, recreational, or therapeutic reasons and the dysfunctions resulting from value conflicts and waste of human potential. Conflict analysis examines the clash of dominant-minority moral values and special-interest groups with self-serving motivations. Interactionist analysis stresses socialization, resocialization, and peer group norms.

5. Many serious problems result from drug use: a profitable black market for organized crime, personal health problems, ruined careers, severe economic losses to individuals and businesses, and the harsh reality of thousands of deaths, millions of serious personal injuries, and billions of dollars of property damage from drug-related accidents.

6. Drug dependence takes a heavy toll on our personal and mental health. Drug abuse shortens one's life, causing various health problems and often violence, in the case of excessive drinking. Newborns often suffer birth defects or addiction because of the mother's use of alcohol or narcotics. Drug abuse has infiltrated both professional sports, shortening players' careers, and American business, costing nearly $26 billion annually in economic losses.

7. Attempts at solution have included both preventive and treatment efforts. Rehabilitation efforts, whether by self-help therapeutic communities or health clinics, have had limited success. Employing antagonistic drugs or corrective efforts has not been very effective. The British model of treating drug addiction as a medical not a criminal problem offers a workable alternative approach.

SUGGESTED READINGS

Cohen, Sidney. *The Substance Abuse Problems*. New York: Haworth Press. 1981. Excellent, easily understandable book about each of the commonly abused drugs, reasons for abuse, effects, and possible remedies.

Duncan, David, and Robert Gold. *Drugs and the Whole Person*. New York: John Wiley, 1982. Offers broad overview of drug use, prevention, treatment, and personal responsibilities, with separate chapters on drugs and sex, drugs and the law.

Goode, Erich. *Drugs in American Society,* 2nd ed. New York: Knopf, 1984. A definitive sociological introduction to drug use and abuse, including an interactionist view of attitudes toward various drugs.

Haskins, Jim. *Teenage Alcoholism*. New York: Hawthorn Books, 1976. Provocative examination of development and treatment of this increasingly serious problem, with illustrative case studies.

Inglis, Brian. *The Forbidden Game*. New York: Charles Scribner's Sons, 1975. A comprehensive, historical account of drugs, drug use, drug laws, and suppressive efforts throughout the Western world.

Phillips, Joel L., and Ronald W. Wynne. *The Mystique and the Reality*. New York: Avon, 1980. Penetrating look at the allure cocaine has for users, probable reasons for its spreading use, and the physiological effects on the body.

Sandmaier, Marian. *The Invisible Alcoholics: Women and Alcohol Abuse in America*. New York: McGraw-Hill, 1980. Revealing portrait of an often ignored dimension of alcoholism, the problem drinking of women of all ages and backgrounds.

GLOSSARY

Addiction A state of habitual drug use to such an extent that cessation causes severe physical and/or psychological trauma.

Antagonistic drug A counteractive drug causing either nauseousness from alcoholic drinking or prevention of euphoria if a narcotic is taken.

Depressant A sedative–hypnotic drug intended to relieve stress or anxiety, but often overused or abused.

Fetal alcohol syndrome Addiction and congenital problems suffered by infants born to alcoholic mothers.

Fetal narcotic syndrome Addiction and withdrawal symptoms suffered by infants born to narcotic addict mothers.

Methadone maintenance A means of treating heroin addiction through stabilization by substituting daily dosages of methadone, a synthetic opiate.

Narcotic A drug having both a sedative and pain-relieving action, whether natural opiates (codeine, morphine, opium) or synthetic (heroin, methadone, meperidine, or Demerol).

Psychoactive drug Any chemical substance affecting consciousness, mood, or perception in an individual.

Sedative-hypnotic A term describing depressant drugs such as barbituates, Quaaludes, tranquilizers, and sleeping pills.

Stimulant Any drug, often amphetamines, that raises blood pressure, reduces fatigue, and elevates mood and alertness.

Tolerance In terms of drug use, the physiological adaption to chemical substances, thereby requiring greater amounts to achieve the same "high."

Withdrawal The physical and/or psychological trauma experienced by an addict ceasing to take a particular drug.

FACTS ABOUT SEXUAL EXPRESSION

80 percent of college students "totally approve" of premarital coitus for people who love each other, but only 20 percent approve of sex between casual acquaintances.

In 78 percent of forcible rapes the attacker had a knife or gun.

U.S. homosexuals number at least 11 to 14 million people.

In a study of AIDS victims, the median number of lifetime male homosexual partners was 1,100 and some reported as many as 20,000.

30 percent of college women reported that a man had used some physical force to make them kiss or pet when they did not want to, and 8 percent reported submitting to intercourse because of force.

4
SEXUAL EXPRESSION

The sexual expression of human beings is greatly varied. Cultural norms have always focused and modified the human sex drive. All societies regulate the choice of sex objects—those people who can be legitimately desired. In no society is either the number or type of sex objects, or the sexual activity engaged in, left entirely up to the individual. There are always types of sexual behavior that are forbidden, often by law, and people with whom the individual is forbidden sexual contact.

SEXUAL CONFORMITY AND DEVIANCE

The Cross-Cultural Context

Sexual Variations

The actual content of the norms governing acceptable sexual expression vary enormously over time and place. For example, in Western civilization we tend to think that kissing and touching the breasts of the female are natural forms of sexual expression. In many cultures, however, the breasts have no erotic meaning and kissing is viewed as disgusting.

Sexual norms in the United States can in part be traced back to the Old Testament, which placed severe restrictions on any sexual contact outside of **heterosexual** marriage. At one point we defined the only "normal" sexual expression as that between a male and a female, lying down face to face, with the male on top. People in many societies found this practice strange: Pacific Islanders, presumably after observing the behavior of visiting missionaries, thought it remarkable enough to call such behavior "sex in the missionary position."[1]

Even those acts considered by our society as the most deviant are, or have been, viewed as normal forms of sexual expression in other places and times. For example, in some societies rape is the way in which all women are first taken.[2] Among the Yanomamo Indians, a woman from another tribe who is captured in battle will be gang-raped, first by those who captured her, and then by those men waiting in the village for the return of the War Party.[3] These acts are not considered war crimes nor are they even defined as deviant acts of brutality.

Even incest, the most universally condemned of all sexual practices, is regarded as perfectly natural for the gods of many different peoples. Japanese mythology tells the story of Izanagi and Izanami, a brother and sister who as creators of the world invented many things, including sexual intercourse.[4] Among ancient Egyptians, not only the gods but also members of the royal family were expected to marry a sibling.[5]

In most societies, including our own, rules exist not only for governing sexual behavior but even "for breaking the rules." Married couples are expected to be sexually monogamous, but if they are not, some infidelities are more serious and disloyal than others.

Social Control of Coitus

We have said that all societies regulate the sexual activities of their members. In virtually all societies, marital coitus accounts for most of the sexual activity engaged in by adults.[6] Of the preliterate societies that have been studied, roughly two-fifths to

In our society, the kiss expresses both affection and sexual interest. We see this young couple as behaving "normally." For those who were not socialized into our Western civilization, this scene would be strange and even disgusting. The definitions of acceptable sexual expressions vary enormously over time and place.

one-half allowed females to have premarital coitus. This percentage rises to about 70 percent if we include societies that do not consider premarital coitus to be an important deviation. In almost all societies males are allowed more freedom in this area than females.[7]

In all societies, once a marriage has taken place, different **sanctions,** or rules, apply. These may be so strict and so well enforced that sexual activity with anyone other than the spouse is punishable by execution, as in many Arab countries. A society may forbid extramarital coitus in general, but may allow such coitus at certain ceremonies or festivals. For example, wife lending, among certain specified individuals may even be part of the marriage ceremony. Almost universally, the restrictions on extramarital coitus are more severe for wives than for husbands.[8]

Homosexuality: Deviation or Variation?

Even though the norm and the ideal in our society is to choose a sexual partner from among members of the opposite sex, some are attracted to their own sex. The only figures considered reliable on the extent of male and female homosexuality are provided by the Alfred C. Kinsey Institute for Sex Research. According to its most current estimates, compiled in the late 1960s, 4 percent of the total adult population are male homosexuals and 1 to 2 percent are female homosexuals. Most experts consider these figures to be conservative. If these figures are applied to the 1980 Census, the country has a homosexual population of between 11 and 14 million.[9]

If numbers are our criteria, it appears that homosexuality is a sexual variation, not a deviation. The distinction between normal and deviant sexual behavior is not always clear. One way to approach this distinction is to examine the degree of stigma and/or the number of formal and informal sanctions associated with homosexuality. These have varied over time and among different groups.

Definitions of Homosexuality: Past and Present

Distinguishing among Homosexuals, Transsexuals, and Transvestites

Most of our knowledge of the sexual behaviors and norms of any given period of history before the Kinsey studies of 1948, can only be inferred from the literature and public writings of the times. We do not really know how most people were behaving.

The term **homosexual** simply refers to a person's sexual preference for someone of the same sex. It tells us nothing about life-style or manner of dress. Transsexuals truly feel they are trapped in the body of the wrong sex. A **transsexual** born biologically male feels that "she" is truly a woman trapped by some horrible mistake in the body of a man. A **transvestite** chooses to dress as if he or she were a member of the opposite sex. It is possible for an individual to be homosexual, transsexual, and a transvestite. Though there is no clear agreement among psychiatrists and psychologists as to the exact boundaries of each of these behavior patterns, they are generally seen as separate and will be treated separately here.

Homosexuality in Ancient Greece

Homosexuality has existed and been described throughout recorded history. When a homosexual looks at the history of homosexuality he or she is likely to say, "Freud had to teach the West what it had once known but then forgot—that man is naturally bisexual. Homosexuality was practiced by the ancient Babylonians and Egyptians, the first civilized men. Among the Greeks it was not only accepted as a natural expression of sexual instinct but praised as being even more genuine and tender than heterosexual love."[10] The word *pederasty* literally means the love of boys, and most homosexuality in ancient Greece was between men and adolescents, not adult males. "To the Greeks, a boy was someone between puberty and close to 20."[11] Homosexuality in ancient Greece was primarily between a well-born teacher or mentor and his student or apprentice. Homosexuality among people other than the aristocracy is not so well documented. About the only evidence we have is the mention of freeborn male prostitutes.

The role and position of women and marriage was very different from how it is today. Marriages were arranged, and a woman remained under the authority of her father, never really becoming part of her husband's family. Women received no schooling and were basically isolated from the world. Very little companionship between the sexes was possible.

"To the bisexual Greek, women and boys were both defined as submissive non-males. Many non-Western societies have similar attitudes and behavior patterns, and one finds this in highly diluted form in much of the Mediterranean world today.

A man can have boys as well as women as long as he takes a clearly dominant role and 'womanizes' partners of both genders.''[12] Humphries found this to be true in his famous study of impersonal sex in public restrooms. When questioned later about their self-definitions, those who defined themselves as nonhomosexuals justified their sexual identity by saying they merely allowed men to "service" them.

Homosexuality in Western Europe
In Europe throughout the Middle Ages and the Renaissance, homosexuality as well as heterosexual sodomy were considered sins and crimes. "Both continued to be punishable by death in most of Europe, from Italy to Sweden to England. . . . A former provost of the University of Paris was burned in 1586 for injuring a boy in the act of anal rape. In Venice in 1492 a nobleman and a priest were publicly beheaded and burned for committing homosexual acts."[13] These events tell us the stance of the Church and the society toward homosexuality, but not how prevalent it was.

Prevalence of Homosexuality in Preliterate Societies
Exclusive homosexual relationships are not common in preliterate societies. Homosexual activity may be accepted or even encouraged on specific occasions or at a particular point in the life cycle, but it is extremely rare for two adults of the same sex to have an enduring sexual relationship. The sexual activity that is permitted in two-thirds of known preliterate societies most often takes the form of contact between adolescent boys and adult men.[14]

The most complete study done of patterns of sexual behavior in other societies shows that female homosexuality occurs less frequently. Of 76 societies studied, female homosexuality existed in only 17.[15]

HOMOSEXUALITY IN AMERICA: STIGMA, SANCTIONS, AND GAY REACTIONS

Until recently homosexuality was clearly labeled as deviant sexual behavior. For example, in the 1950s being discovered or even suspected of homosexuality could have severely disrupted a person's life. Being fired was quite possible; being taunted was probable. Going into areas known to be frequented by male homosexuals and beating them up was a popular teenage sport, as was beating up lesbians to see how tough they really were. To most homosexuals, "passing," or carrying out their lives in such a way as to appear heterosexual, was crucial.

Differential Treatment of Homosexual Men and Women

U.S. laws, though not as harsh as the British laws (until 1861 in Britian anal intercourse was punishable by death), have been very harsh toward male homosexuals. Until recently many of the sexual acts commonly practiced in America; for example, oral-genital sex and anal sex, were considered to be "crimes against nature" and were against the law. These laws, usually lumped under sodomy statutes, have been used primarily against male homosexuals.

The Beginnings of Gay Pride

Even during the 1950s and 1960s, small groups of men and women refused to conceal their sexual preferences. They did not label themselves as sick and did not wish to be cured. They felt they deserved the same social and legal rights as everyone else. These homosexuals, male and female, referred to themselves as **gay,** a self-selected term that indicated their preference for sexual partners of the same sex.

As the groups of self-admitted gays grew larger and as more heterosexuals became sympathetic to their goals, discriminatory laws began to change. For example, those sex acts commonly practiced by male homosexuals were decriminalized in a few states during the late 1960s.[16] Sodomy between consenting adults was no longer illegal in those states.

Today these Gay Rights groups have grown in size, visibility, and effectiveness. Many heterosexuals now feel that sexual preference is not grounds for any type of social or legal discrimination. Nevertheless, as more and more homosexuals came "out of the closet," backlash responses grew. Such reactions seem to come in response to an advance in a minority group's status. Visible gains by a group previously the victim of social and legal discrimination provoke hostile responses from the movement's opponents. For example, in the late 1970s Anita Bryant, a singer and ex-Miss America, led a drive against homosexuals in Dade County, Florida, that led to the repeal of that county's homosexual rights ordinance. "Bumper stickers bearing the slogan, 'Kill a Queer for Christ' appeared on some Dade County cars."[17]

Despite such sporadic incidents, by 1978 legal measures to protect the rights of homosexuals had been enacted in more than 40 cities and counties and were being considered in many others.[18] Today, the law is being used as a tool to prevent discrimination against gays rather than as a tool to punish them. Yet the reluctance to accept homosexuality as merely an alternative choice of sex partner still exists, particularly among older people.

Gay Activist Groups on Campus

A growing number of college students now live openly as homosexuals. At several large universities they have formed a supportive subculture. For example, at the University of Wisconsin at Madison, a 4-year-old gay organization has 150 members.[19] The numbers for this and similar organizations are small, but the school's open recognition of homosexuality is a sign of far greater acceptance than previously existed. Smith College lists its lesbian organization between junior ushers and lifeguards in the college directory.

On coed campuses, separate organizations often represent gay men and gay women because some lesbians believe that gay men are not sensitive to the concerns of gay women. They say gay men are still able to enjoy societal privileges not yet open to women.

Increasingly, both male and female homosexuals are demanding that society recognize their right to choose a same-sex person as the focus of their sexual desires. Gay rights groups have grown in size, visibility, and effectiveness. Many people, both homosexual and heterosexual, feel that sexual preference should not be grounds for any social or legal discrimination.

The Nature of the Homosexual Relationship

As with members of any group defined as deviant, many homosexuals remain invisible. Since we have no real knowledge of the whole spectrum of homosexual relationships, we can make no conclusive statements about the typical homosexual relationship. Nevertheless, one of the most comprehensive studies of homosexuals carried out so far does provide some clues (see Table 4.1).

Among male homosexuals only 14 percent reported being involved in a closed couple relationship in which the couple is basically monogamous and considers their relationship to be stable. This type of relationship is the one most similar to the traditional heterosexual ideal. However, among female homosexuals, 38 percent are involved in this type of relationship. Among both men and women, about 25 percent are involved in a relationship with one person that is not sexually exclusive.

The Functionals are extremely sexually active and not attached to any sort of relationship. Approximately 25 percent of the male sample reported having had sex with more than 1,000 partners. There are more men than women in this category; "active" men are far more active than "active" women. The dysfunctionals are just as active sexually but are unhappy about their sexual experiences and their lives in general. The asexuals report that they deal with their unhappiness about their sexual pattern by withdrawing from most sexual activity.

THE GAY SUBCULTURE

Female Homosexuality

Female homosexuals usually refer to themselves as lesbians or simply as gay females. The term **lesbian** comes from Lesbos, the birthplace of the female poet Sappho who first wrote of the love between women.[21] The term lesbian has been used to define a type of sexual behavior, and emotional preference, or self-identity.

Background Characteristics

The question of what factors make someone more likely to have a homosexual orientation rather than a heterosexual one has no definitive answer. Some social scientists say the second-class status of women makes it common for girls to go

TABLE 4.1 Types of Homosexual Relationships Found among 1,000 Men and Women, by Percent

	Men	Women
Closed couple	14	38
Open couple	25	24
Functionals ("Swinging Singles")	21	14
Dysfunctionals	18	8
Asexuals	23	16

SOURCE: Alan P. Bell and Martin Weisberg, *Homosexualities: A Study of Human Diversity* (New York: Simon & Schuster, 1978).

through a "tomboy" stage. But boys have no comparable pattern. At no time in the life of a young male is it socially rewarding to act more feminine. "In a study based on a nationwide sampling of lesbians, less than half of whom had been in psychotherapy, 78 percent said they had been 'tomboys' compared with only 48 percent of a control group. In adult life many of these same women had taken on the traditional female role but had not found it to be satisfying."[22]

Sex and Romance

An important difference in the behavior of gay women from that of gay men seems to come from basic differences in the sexual socialization in our society. Boys begin by being interested in sex, and as they mature become more interested in love and intimacy as part of the sexual relationship. Girls begin with feelings of romance and then find themselves sexually involved.[23]

Gay women "come out," that is, have a sexual experience with another woman, much later than gay men. "Lesbians, committed to romance before sex, may be drawn to women for years before engaging in homosexual acts."[24] Lesbians have fewer sexual partners than do male homosexuals, and are more likely to form stable, lasting relationships. "Long" is a relative term, and a relationship that lasts as long as 3 years is pointed to with pride.[25]

Roles and Status

Both male and female homosexuals insist that the roles in a homosexual relationship are often not sharply defined. Different status is given to the male and female roles among homosexuals of both sexes. The traditional female role does not have a high status in either group. In the lesbian subculture, just as in much of our society, the male role has more prestige: the aggressiveness and ability to control is most admired.[26] This admiration for aggressiveness can lead to a paradoxical way of status raising among lesbians. A "fish" (femme) can raise her status to that of a "stud" (butch) by seducing as many women as possible. A "fish" who has slept around could lose the "slut" stigma by switching to the sexually aggressive masculine role and thereby get a new start in gay life. In the male gay world, the more admired role is also that of the "butch" who may be hypermasculine in manner.[27]

Since data are lacking, we really don't know what attitudes or behaviors are typical among gay females. Many studies have involved either people who were in therapy, belonged to gay activist groups, or went to popular gay meeting places. Their responses to interviews and questionnaires may or may not accurately reflect gay life.

Impersonal Sex: A Gay Male Phenomenon

Recently a particularly frightening disease has been found to afflict homosexual men. Acquired Immune Deficiency Syndrome (AIDS) at this point is incurable and often fatal, and strikes promiscuous homosexual men more often than any other group. "In a 1982 study of 50 AIDS victims . . . the Centers for Disease Control in Atlanta found that the median number of lifetime sexual partners for these men was 1,100, with a few of the men reporting as many as 20,000. The median number of different partners for a homosexual control group without the disease was 550."[28]

As was shown in Table 4.1, there are a variety of life-styles among homosexuals. But only those who view sex as an impersonal transaction were mentioned during arguments with the American Psychiatric Association's decision in 1975 to remove homosexuality from its list of disorders.[29] The homosexual subculture provides many settings for sex without any personal involvement, such as gay baths, massage parlors, doorways, and public restrooms called tearooms.[30] An extreme example of how impersonal this type of sex actually is can be seen in the use of the "glory hole"—"a circular cut-out in bathroom-like stalls that allows one to have oral sex with a neighbor in the next stall without introductions or small talk."[31]

A variety of explanations have been made for the existence of such sexual activity. The two mentioned most often are that the social and even physical danger involved in being identified as a homosexual necessitates anonymity, and that the prevalence of self-hatred among homosexuals makes impersonal sex more acceptable.

The threat of AIDS seems to be causing a change and a reexamination of this sexual pattern. Those who once considered themselves to be celebrating "gay liberation" when they went to places like the gay baths have become frightened of the possible physical consequences.[32]

OTHER VARIATIONS

Transsexualism

Transsexualism is sometimes confused with homosexuality. A transsexual feels that he or she is trapped in the wrong body. A female transsexual feels she is really a man who by a mistake of nature ended up in the body of a woman. Unlike homosexuality, choice of sex object has nothing to do with transsexuality. Often the sexual preferences of the transsexual are oriented toward members of the same biological sex, but most do not identify with the homosexual community and may in fact be hostile to it.[33] Since his own biological sex is seen as a mistake, a transsexual man involved sexually with another man does not define the relationship as homosexual but as a conventional one involving a woman (himself) and a man.

During the 1920s and 1930s, clumsy attempts were made at sex-change surgery. Occasionally scientific literature would mention a man who had castrated himself because of his desperate desire to be a woman. In general, these people were considered to be at the extreme end of the homosexual continuum. Transsexualism as a distinctive syndrome was first described in 1949 by Dr. David Cauldwell. At the same time, a team of surgeons and an endocrinologist in Denmark started to combine surgery and hormones to change a person's sex. In 1962 the well-publicized transformation of George Jorgensen, an American ex-G.I., into Miss Christine Jorgensen brought a flood of letters to the surgeons in Denmark.[34] The press coverage of this first sex-change operation brought hope to many unhappy transsexuals.

The one thing all transsexuals share is a desperate, determined desire not to continue to live in the wrong body. The risks or pain of surgery, or of hormonal treatments, and the ridicule to which they are often exposed are seen as trivial

When George Jorgensen became Christine Jorgensen, the idea of a "sex-change operation" received a great deal of public attention. Growing up as George, Christine felt she was actually a woman who had somehow been given the "wrong" body. She did not define the operation as bringing about a change, but rather as correcting a mistake so that she could live as she was meant to.

BOX 4.1

SUSAN F. (NEE WALTER FAW) CANNON '46

This memorial to Susan—known to us in college years as Walter—Cannon is out of the normal pattern. All our lives have happiness and sadness, accomplishments and defeats, aspirations and discouragements. Walter had more than most of all of these things.

He was a courtly southern gentleman. He was soft-spoken and intelligent, one of the few authentic geniuses in our class. He was to many of us a drinking companion, a sympathetic listener, a friend.

Professionally, he did well. He had a severe stuttering problem, so he became a world-class debater at Princeton. He earned a physics degree. Don Hegstrom convinced him that physics, in this context, was dull and that he should maybe go for his Ph.D. in the history of science at Harvard. He did.

Walter was a scholar, and a certified intellectual (a label he wore with modesty and grace), a voracious reader, a creative thinker, a historian of national note, a teacher, a poet, an author, an editor (''The Smithsonian Journal of History''), and a curator of the Smithsonian Institution.

Walter Faw Cannon was also Susan Faye Cannon, a fact that she did not recognize until several years ago. Several years ago, Walter publicly proclaimed that he was a female in a male body. And just last year, he had a surgical sex change against the advice of his doctors. Three months before she died, she called and told a classmate that it had been demonstrated conclusively that genetically he had always been a woman. She was very glad, because she had always suspected it and, in more recent years, known it to be a fact.

Walter/Susie, you were a person with guts. You did what you had to do. We're truly sorry you didn't make it to our 35th Reunion. You wanted to. But you suffered in your last year with hospital stays and deteriorating health.

But, we've known you, admired you and loved you as both a man and a woman and a friend. Bon voyage, Walter, and so long, Susie.

The Class of 1946

SOURCE: Reprinted by permission of the Sterling Lord Agency Inc. Originally in *Psychology Today*, October 1982. Copyright © 1982 by Aaron Latham and Andrea Grenadier.

compared to the relief at finally becoming the right sex. The case of Susan Faye Cannon, born Walter Faw Cannon, is typical of the misery felt by transsexuals. The following obituary (see Box 4.1) provides a summary of the life experiences of such a person.

Transvestism Defined

Transvestism literally means cross-dressing or putting on the garments of the opposite sex.[35] Taken in the literal sense, many heterosexual women on any given weekend may be involved in transvestism when they wear the shirts of their fathers, husbands, or boyfriends. Heterosexual men are less likely to borrow the clothes of their mothers, wives, or sisters. Our society often defines a female as looking "cute" in male attire; no such approval is given to men wearing female attire. People cross-dress for many reasons, some that have little or no sexual connection.

Sexually Related Cross-Dressing: The Fetishist and the Transvestite

There are two main classifications of sexually related cross-dressing: the fetishist and the transvestite. Fetishist cross-dressing means putting on specific items of clothing belonging to the opposite sex for the specific purpose of becoming sexually aroused. This type of **fetishism** has never been documented among women; it seems to be a male phenomenon.[36] For example, a man would be a fetishist if he found it sexually

These homosexual men are not really trying to "pass" as women. No attempts have been made to hide their obviously male moustaches. They are "in drag." Their costumes are meant to be caricatures of the opposite sex. These bartenders, at a gay "after the prom" graduation party, look exactly as they wish to: like gay men "in drag."

exciting to wear a pair of lace panties under his usual male attire, or could only make love while wearing his wife's nightgown. Several studies have shown that most men in this category are primarily heterosexual, married, and have children. They live in a conventional male manner except for the fetishist cross-dressing.[37]

The true transvestite dresses and acts as much as possible as if he or she actually were a member of the opposite sex. "Passing" and being accepted as a member of the opposite sex is a source of great satisfaction. "The (male) transvestite's obsessive interest in feminine garb and role shows in a letter written to Transvestia, a magazine published in Los Angeles 'by, for, and about transvestites.' . . . One letter describes an exciting venture of shopping at a tall girls' dress shop. Another discusses if it is fittingly feminine for a transvestite to wear slacks, as some women do. . . . Another letter describes the woman within and the 'exquisite joy of being able to be Dorothy for the evening, manicuring and painting my nails and feeling that everything that I'm wearing is just right'."[38]

The heterosexual transvestite often marries and may keep his deviation secret. Often the transvestite avoids the gay world because he does not want homosexual love making, only to "pass" as a woman.

Drag versus Passing

When homosexuals cross-dress on occasion it is called being in **"drag."** The goal is not really to pass as a member of the opposite sex, and the costumes are more like caricatures. Among males, female makeup and gestures will be exaggerated and elegant. "A minority of female homosexuals dress always, or in their leisure hours, as men; unlike male drag queens, their male attire mimics the blue-collar, jean-clad male rather than the elegant male."[39]

RAPE

The Crime of Rape Defined

Rape is a crime of violence. Forcible rape is an act of aggression, not the expression of sexual desire. "Instructions supplied by the Federal Bureau of Investigation request that an offense should be classified as forcible rape or attempted forcible rape if it involved actual or attempted sexual intercourse with a female forcibly and

TABLE 4.2   Facts on Forcible Rape

1. Forty percent of all rapists were known to the victim to some extent.

2. In 78 percent of all cases, the attacker had a knife or gun.

3. Thirty-one percent of all rapes occurred in the victim's home.

4. Seventy-seven percent of all rapes involve victims and rapists of the same race.

SOURCE: Andrew Hacker, *U.S.: A Statistical Portrait of the American People* (New York: Viking Press, 1982), p. 94.

against her will. This definition excludes specifically male rape victims, especially in institutions, and cases of statutory rape, where no force was used and the victim was legally incapacitated from agreeing to participate in the act.''[40] How local police departments apply and use these instructions is unknown, so the actual number of forcible rapes is extremely hard to estimate. It is estimated that at least 50 percent of all rapes remain unreported.

Current Rape Laws

Many people feel that rape will remain a major social problem until and unless there is a change in the traditional attitudes and assumptions reflected in and reinforced by existing laws. These assumptions include:

1. The victim is guilty until she proves her innocence.
2. An unarmed man cannot rape a healthy woman unless she cooperates.
3. Women lie about being raped to get back at a man.
4. Once a woman has given consent, the act must be completed.
5. The victim's sexual past determines the validity of her accusation.[41]

Facts on Forcible Rape

Rape is not a crime that only occurs between strangers (see Table 4.2). But it definitely involves force: almost 80 percent of all rapists are armed.

The Plight of the Rape Victim

Proving Nonprovocation

Despite some changes in the way rape cases are processed by the police, the average victim, when reporting the crime, must prove herself worthy of belief, act in a way that produces trust in the listener, and prove she is of good character. If the victim has delayed reporting the crime by even one day she is often not believed. As Table 4.3 shows, many rapes are never reported. "Many victims report that they were asked very personal questions by the police, justified as necessary to ascertain if the

TABLE 4.3 Reasons Given by Women Who Did Not Report Rape

	(%)
It was a private personal matter	34
Nothing could be done	16
Fear of reprisal	16
Not important enough	14
Reported it to someone other than police	12

SOURCE: "192,000 Women Who Said They Had Been Victims of Rape," *U.S. Bureau of the Census*, In Andrew Hacker, *U.S.: A Statistical Portrait of the American People* (New York: Viking Press, 1982), p. 94.

case would hold up for the prosecution. Doubts have been expressed, however, that such legal requirements can explain questions such as "Aw, come on, didn't you really enjoy it?' and 'How many orgasms did you have?"[42]

Rape in Marriage

Is it possible for a man to rape his wife? Is it only rape if the wife was physically overpowered and severely beaten? Both society and the law are at last beginning to grapple with this problem.

By most states' legal codes, a husband cannot rape his wife. "The 'legal fiction' as judges sometimes call it, is that the wife consents at the time of marriage to all future sex with her husband."[43] People are beginning to question this assumption. Studies of forced sex in marriage reveal that it is both more common, and traumatic, for the wife than had previously been recognized. One study which used a very conservative definition of forced sex, that is, demanding evidence that force was used, estimated that 14 percent of married women had had their husbands attempt or complete at least one act of rape with them.[44]

Preventing Rape

As can be seen from Table 4.4, rape prevention is extremely complex. The first and most obvious strategy involves teaching individual women to avoid rape. Teaching workshops that instruct women in tactics of self-defense and other rape avoidance techniques are being given throughout the country. What the specific tactics should be is still open to debate, and will remain so until the question of the relationship between resistance and the chance of physical injury is resolved. The important issue is the recognition that women should and must find the most effective ways to resist. Fear of rape is the constant companion of a woman alone. Even in her car she may be the target of a bumper-rapist (see Box 4.2).

TABLE 4.4 Prevention of Rape: Immediate Strategies

	Time of Intervention	
	Before Rape	*After Rape*
Individual level	Teach individual women to avoid rape	Rehabilitate individual rapists after conviction
Institutional level	Change socialization patterns for male and female children	Improve criminal justice system to facilitate prosecution of rapists and remove them from the community
	Improve criminal justice system for its symbolic and deterrent effect	

SOURCE: Lynda L. Holmstrom and A.W. Burgess, "Rape and everyday Life," *Society*, 20 (July/August 1983), p. 38.

BOX 4.2

'BUMPER-RAPISTS'

As the incidence of rape increases throughout the country, it's just a question of time before the enterprising insurance industry begins offering rape coverage.

Two companies—American Bankers Life Assurance of Florida and RLI Insurance of Peoria, Ill.—already offer policies insuring the victims of criminal violence. But to date these policies have not caught on. Their benefits are relatively modest, and in some cases, crime victims are reimbursed by a state agency.

Women who drive vehicles, however, should be aware of what some officials call a "new, vicious, well-planned and malignantly calculated" method of rape. Men who practice it are called "bumper-rapists."

A "bumper-rapist" is a man who spots a woman driving alone and bumps his vehicle (usually stolen) into hers. When the frightened woman emerges from her car to inspect the damage and exchange licenses, he threatens her with a knife or gun. He forces her into his car, drives off, rapes and robs her.

In a recent California case, "bumper-rapist" Rudolph Perkins, 33, was sentenced to 151 years in prison for assaulting more than two dozen women in a 30-month period. Jacqueline Connor, the deputy district attorney in Los Angeles who prosecuted in the case against Perkins, has this advice for women drivers involved in car bumper or fender accidents: "Never stop your car in a dark area. If you do, never roll down your window to converse with the man whose vehicle has hit yours. If your car can move, drive to a police station, a filling station, or some lighted area where there are people. Don't get out of your car on a highway. Put on your emergency lights if your car is stalled."

SOURCE: *Parade* (March 14, 1982), p. 11.

Changing Our Socialization Patterns

Closely related to the issue of resistance by individual women are our socialization patterns for male and female children. For example, in a study previously discussed, 21 percent of the women had agreed to have intercourse, even though they didn't want to, merely because the man had insisted. In other words, they had acknowledged the man's right to determine when sexual activity should occur. From this perspective, rape is the extreme end of a continuum of the association of male sexuality and aggressiveness. This means that rape, like all other behaviors, must be understood in terms of its sociocultural context.

Improving the Criminal Justice System

The criminal justice system must be improved in rape cases. Some steps toward reform are already being made, including:

1. The establishment of rape crisis centers that victims can call to find out what to expect from medical, police, and court procedures. [Loss of funding has caused some of these centers to close.]

2. The assignment of policewomen to the questioning of rape victims in some police departments.

3. Changes in the requirements for the amount of evidence of physical injury necessary before rape can be charged.[45]

These changes are by no means typical of all rape investigations. The court system is still geared toward preventing an "unwarranted" accusation of rape. For example, some laws require corroboration, and imply that a woman with a "reputation" is less likely to resist sexual assault.[46] "Corroboration of the victim's word is not required by law in order to convict an offender of any other crime; therefore, any distinction between an uncorroborated charge of kidnapping, assault, or robbery, and an uncorroborated charge of rape should be abolished.[47] It is also argued that a person's general pattern of sexual behavior is irrelevant in rape investigations. Only when the institutional response to victims is improved will the rate of reporting increase.

Identifying and Rehabilitating the Rapist

Since an estimated 80 percent of all rapes are never reported to the police, any description of the typical rapist is highly suspect. We can only say that the majority of convicted forcible rapists are between the ages of 15 and 25 and come from a lower-class background, which in fact seems to be far more related to the frequency of conviction than of the propensity to rape. More than 40 percent of rapists are married and about half have previous arrests records for rape and other crimes.[48]

Five basic treatment patterns have been tried in the rehabilitation of sex offenders: group therapy, behavior modification, self-help groups, individual psychodynamic therapy, and drug therapy. There are no clear-cut findings on the relative effectiveness of any of these treatments. However, the increased interest in the treatment and rehabilitation of the sex offender indicates an awareness that the rapist will probably rape again.

COMMERCIAL-EXPLOITIVE SEX

The sex industry in our society is extremely profitable. A great deal of money is spent on sexually explicit material and the purchase of the sexual services of men and women. In the mid-1980s, a new form a commercial sex emerged—"Dial-a-Partner." Lines are leased from the telephone company, a respectable name is adopted, and advertisements are placed in sexually explicit magazines. The wording of these ads indicates to those "in the know" that sexually explicit conversations can be purchased by dialing the telephone number advertised. Since these businesses have disguised names, the calls can be charged to a credit card (see Box 4.3).

Box 4.3

TELEPHONE SEX

Recently the Federal Communications Commission asked for public comment on the sex services known generically as ''Dial-a-Porn.'' They received more than 25,000 responses almost all with the same message: ''Do not try to regulate 'Dial-a-Porn' services: ban them.'' A typical letter said:

> ''We were dismayed to see charges on our phone bill to the ''Dial-a-Porn'' number in New York. Upon questioning we discovered that our children had gotten the number from friends who had gotten it from other friends, and called it without our knowledge. We are appalled that such a thing would be allowed to continue.

Despite such public outcry telephone sex services are continuing to exist and to be very profitable.

SOURCE: *The New York Times,* (February 19, 1984), p. 3.

Pornography

The definition of **pornography** varies according to time and place. We cannot say that any written, visual, or spoken presentation of sexual interaction or genitals is pornographic. ''Some of the artifacts from historic and prehistoric cultures that depict sexual interaction, such as the bas-reliefs that adorn some Indian temples, have a religious basis, celebrating life and fertility.''[49]

The courts have not been able to come up with an acceptable definition of pornography. ''Court definitions of obscenity, the legal term for pornography, have ranged from material which on the whole appeals to prurient interests and has no redeeming social value, to a reluctance to define obscenity and a delegation of that task to local communities.''[50] We propose the following working definition: Pornographic material depicts both normal and abnormal sexual behavior in a way designed to stimulate the consumer and induces violent disrespect for and degradation of the subject.

Pornography and the Degradation of Women

Susan Brownmiller has summed up the attitude of many women toward pornography by saying: ''The gut distaste that a majority of women feel when we look at pornography . . . comes, I think from the gut knowledge that we and our bodies are being stripped, exposed, and contorted for the purpose of ridicule to bolster that 'masculine esteem' which gets its kick and sense of power from viewing females as anonymous, panting playthings, adult toys, dehumanized objects to be used, abused, broken and discarded.''[51]

Exposure to pornographic material in the United States is widespread: a recent study with a representative sample of adults found that 84 percent of men and 69

Defining what is pornographic is very difficult. Not all presentations of sexual interaction are pornographic. The courts have not yet come up with a definition that is acceptable to everyone. A theater such as this might be closed in one community but allowed to exist in another.

percent of women had been exposed to written or pictorial depictions of explicit sexual activities.

PROSTITUTION

The Sexual Career of a Prostitute

Becoming a professional **prostitute** involves more than just a decision to suspend morality and "do what comes naturally" for money. Rules and techniques must be learned through a process known as "being **turned-out**." It has been suggested that a prostitute's sexual career goes through three stages before the final professionalization is complete.

Stage I: Drifting from casual sex to the first act of prostitution. This stage is often characterized by a pattern of "pick-up" sex. Often the pattern is reinforced by peer group expectations of the way to get excitement and male attention. When the "kicks" these experiences provide fade, the idea of adding the incentive of money develops. Doing it for profit instead of giving it away lends new appeal to the activity.

Stage II: Transitional deviance. During this stage the individual usually engages in prostitution as a part-time activity. Self-definition remains partially in the conventional world. The person may continue to work at a conventional job and maintain social ties with the straight world. It is during this transitional period that the person finds out if he or she (1) is willing to satisfy a broad range of client requests, including some that seem very odd; (2) can learn to adapt to police surveillance and entrapment procedures; (3) can handle clients who are unable to pay; and (4) can substitute a business ethic for previous motivations.[70] If the person cannot adjust to all these conditions, his or her identity may remain that of an occasional or part-time prostitute.

Stage III: The acquisition of the deviant identity of the professional prostitute. The individual now fully accepts identification of self with that of a prostitute.[52]

Professional Prostitutes

Within the general category of prostitute are many distinctions. The lowest rung is occupied by the street-walker—an individual who approaches men on the street and indicates a willingness to exchange sexual activity for money. The approach must be made carefully in case the man is a police officer who could make an arrest for soliciting. Both male and female prostitutes consider the street hustler to be at the very bottom of the scale.

The middle rank in the status hierarchy is occupied by the house prostitute. House prostitution is a growing industry.[53] Such houses are legal in Nevada, and Oregon has enacted legislation that legalizes them, although in a disguised form. Since January 1977, these houses have been licensed as "relaxation treatment businesses" to allow the state to exercise some control without unconstitutional interference. Salaries in these houses in Oregon are barely competitive with other female occupations. Sex workers receive about 20 percent of the clients' fees; usually netting a base take-home pay of $50 per week. Other income is of course received in tips and extras for specific sex acts.

Such houses are far from new, nor are they limited to heterosexuals. For example, during the eighteenth century, a male homosexual club called the "Mollies" gathered to dress in women's clothes, drink, and party. Houses of homosexual prostitution were known as "molly houses." One of the most famous, located in a popular English resort, was run by Margaret Clap, known as Mother Clap.[54] Her name survives today in the slang term for a form of sexually transmitted disease.

Today, those who run such houses prefer to employ professional prostitutes who have learned the skills and accepted the values that make for success. Barbara Heyl studied a house specifically devoted to the training of new prostitutes. The training took from two to three months and included three main areas of "study":

1. Strategies for managing clients, including the skills to be used with older men and how to handle "kinky" tricks.

2. The verbal skills that comprise "hustling," the sexual rap that encourages clients to purchase the more expensive services. Teaching the novice prostitutes to talk about sex was the most difficult part of the trainers' job.

In our society, women have been conditioned to not talk about sex and a successful prostitute must be verbally aggressive.

3. "Racket" or prostitution values, such as the encouragement to take a new name to symbolize a new identity. The dangers of maintaining contacts in the straight world were stressed.

Those prostitutes who operate from a client list either through personal referrals or as part of an escort service occupy the highest status position. Though there are males who operate similarly, the majority of such prostitutes are females known as "call-girls." These women are expected to be personable and to accompany clients to a variety of functions.

SOCIOLOGICAL PERSPECTIVES

The study of deviations and variations in human sexuality suffers from a lack of empirical evidence and theoretical development. Information is lacking because there is no list of homosexuals, rapists, prostitutes and their customers, or consumers and producers of pornography available for the researcher. We can only interview those who either volunteer or who have been arrested. We have no reason to assume this gives us the whole picture or even an accurate one. Without a good empirical foundation it is very difficult to build or test theories. We can, however, describe the main perspectives that have been used.

Individual Faults and Deviant Behavior

Depending on time and place, most types of sexual activity have been defined as at best unhealthy. Those who indulged in too much sex were seen as either ill or risking illness. For example, physicians in the eighteenth century defined "the sexual act for both males and females as involving a loss of bodily fluids that would have to be replaced by bodily inputs. If sexuality were excessively indulged in, the body would be drained of energy."[55] They believed that overindulgence in sex could lead to tuberculosis, jaundice, cancer, and even death.

By the nineteenth century it was the sexually "different" person who was the focus of study. Until today, Freud's explanations of sexual differences and individual pathology have dominated. Freud said sexual distortions occur when the flow of the libido or sexual energy is disturbed. Sexual abnormality comes from the inability to transfer libido energy to outside objects. Homosexuality was seen as an inability to focus on an appropriate partner of the opposite sex. Therapy attempted to redo the person's development so that this transfer could be made.

Those who hold this perspective feel that sexual deviations can be best explained by finding the traumas a person has experienced or the defects of his or her personality. In this view, the rapist is unable to relate to women in a normal way, the prostitute is a lesbian who is "getting back at" men, and pornography is used by people to compensate for their sexual inabilities or perhaps as an outlet for their sexual perversions.

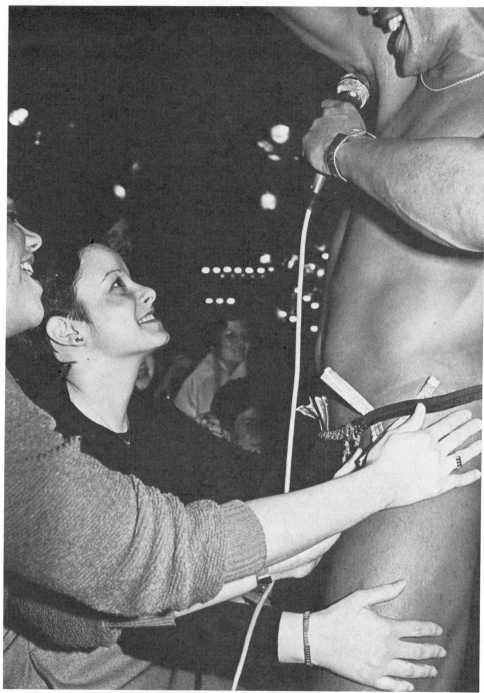

There is an increasing demand for men to become paid sex objects. More and more nightclubs feature male belly dancers. Women come to these "females only" clubs just as men have traditionally gone to girlie shows and do so for many of the same reasons.

Institutional Faults and System Disorganization

This view sees deviation as a symptom of social disorganization and the breakdown of society's institutions. The family is the crucial source of appropriate or inappropriate sexual lessons. Family disorganization leads to disrupted role relationships which in turn leads to deviant sexuality. For example, either the absence of a father or a poor relationship with him predisposes a male to homosexuality. There is insufficient empirical evidence to prove or disprove this theory.

The breakdown of social norms and controls is seen as being related to the spread of prostitution and pornography. If sexual norms were operating properly these industries could not flourish since there would be no sellers or buyers. The increase in rape is seen as partially rooted in an inefficient legal system where rapists are not caught, jailed, or properly rehabilitated.

Inequality and Inevitable Conflict

In the areas of sexual deviations discussed in this chapter, the conflict approach is actually a conflict/feminist approach. Homosexuality, rape, prostitution, and pornography are all seen as being rooted in the basic subjugation of women in our society. Rape is the extreme example of the dominance of men in initiating sexual activity. Until our basic socialization patterns change and men and women are truly defined as equal, men will use sex aggressively and women will submit.

Susan Brownmiller, a particularly eloquent proponent of this perspective, has said:

> Hardcore pornography is not a celebration of sexual freedom; it is a cynical exploitation of female sexual activity through the device of making all such activity and consequently all females "dirty."
>
> . . . Rape is not a crime of irrational, impulsive, uncontrollable lust, but is a deliberate, hostile, violent act of degradation and possession on the part of a would-be conqueror, designed to intimidate and inspire fear.[56]

For some feminists, lesbianism is the only response to men's would-be domination. Healthy relationships between men and women, sexual or otherwise, are seen as impossible until the male domination of our society has been eliminated.

Interaction and Social Interpretation

For the symbolic interactionist, sexual deviance can best be understood in terms of the concepts that apply to any deviant behavior.

Deviant Careers

The concept of "career" is used by sociologists to mean any continuing role or activity in a person's life. Any sort of deviance can be examined from this point of view. If a young person engages in a homosexual act (if we accept the Kinsey data we are referring to more than one-third of all males), the act per se does not mean the beginning of a career as a sexual deviant. For the career to begin, the person committing the act must be labeled as a deviant: he or she must be stigmatized and rejected by society, forcing the search for another reference group, in this case, the homosexual subculture. Identifying with and eventually joining the homosexual subculture begins the deviant career.

Sexual Scripts
"Many sociologists now draw heavily on the idea of socially determined 'scripts' for explaining both heterosexual and homosexual development and deviance. It has become an axiom that heterosexuality, like homosexuality, must be socially learned. This view is often tied to any attempt to normalize homosexuals, with the claim that as a group they differ from heterosexuals only in the gender of their sexual partners."[57]

Labeling Theory: Primary, Secondary, and Tertiary Deviance
Once a label has been applied, a process may begin that changes the original deviance from primary deviance, a random, isolated piece of behavior from a person who is a conformist in the rest of his or her life, to secondary deviance, a persistent pattern of behavior that leads to deviant status and eventually membership in a deviant subculture with its own norms and patterns.[58]

"Tertiary deviance exists when previously stigmatized individuals reject the negative views others hold of them, create a new in-group ethic which affirms their worth as equal members of society, and hence reject accommodative strategies of stigma management."[59] The concept of tertiary deviance was introduced by Kitsuse, who defined it as "the deviant's confrontation, assessment, and rejection of the negative identity embedded in secondary deviation, and the transformation of that identity into a positive and viable self conception."[60]

The positive aspects of homosexual identity are often found in the group's most prestigious publications. A content analysis of articles and stories published in the *Ladder,* a well-known lesbian publication, shows a change from secondary to tertiary deviance. For example, during its early years, the *Ladder* advocated an accommodative stance. Lesbians were urged to fit in as well as possible, to conceal any outward differences between themselves and straight women. The change to tertiary deviance began when the *Ladder* changed from a lesbian periodical to a feminist magazine openly supportive of lesbians. Increasingly, lesbianism was defined as a choice made by women in response to a sexist society. It was defined as a sensible choice, and a radical political statement, not a deviation for which a person was labeled and rejected. "With tertiary deviance, self-worth is based on self-evaluation."[61]

THE FUTURE

Pessimistic Scenario

Today in the year 2025 sexual expression is rigidly defined and controlled. The government spends a great deal of its time and money enforcing what the Sexual Outlaws scathingly describe as the "Three Rs:" sex with the Right person (your spouse); sex for the Right reason (to have children); and sex in the Right position (the "missionary position").[62]

Despite vigorous governmental attempts at control, there are many Sexual Outlaws. The immense profits that can be made by running a House of Prostitution or by selling sexually explicit materials of any kind more than cover the protection money that must be paid. Gang wars over the control of the highly profitable sex industry dominate the news.

How did this state of sexual prohibition develop? Scholars speaking on the illegal Sex Broadcasting Network say it all began during the late twentieth century. Most say there were four highly publicized trends that brought about the extreme backlash of repressive legislation:

> 1. An epidemic of sexually transmitted diseases called attention to how far people actually had strayed from the "Three Rs of Sex." The amount and diversity of human sexual activity was generally acknowledged for the first time.
>
> 2. Just as legal persecution of homosexuals was ending, a killer disease, AIDS, struck a small percentage of homosexual men. Since most of the victims of this disease were homosexual, people became afraid. Society-wide fear of the disease and publicity given to the possible causes and cures of this disease brought a great deal of attention to the most promiscuous segments of the homosexual community. Pressure groups demanded repeal of antidiscrimination laws. In the existing climate of fear and shock they prevailed.
>
> 3. The increase in the rate of pregnancy among unmarried teenagers was blamed on an "epidemic of permissiveness."
>
> 4. Cable television brought sexually explicit films into homes all over the country. People who did not wish to see such films found them on their sets, accessible to their children. This wide exposure to material considered pornographic by several dissimilar groups prompted attempts to ban Cable TV, and when this proved impossible, to regulate it.

Experts say it was the coming together of these trends that brought us to our current state.

Once attempts to legally define what was "normal" and "acceptable" began, many groups demanded their particular standards be reflected in the law. The final decision of the *Commission to Define What Is Right and Normal in Sexual Behavior* decreed that any behavior outside of what has now been nicknamed the "Three Rs" was abnormal. To make sure their recommendations were followed, all sexual activity except that between married couples who wanted children was prohibited by law. People who either engaged in or wished to engage in any other form of sexual activity were treated as deviants and criminals.

Sexual prohibition seems to have created the same underworld as that created by the prohibition of alcohol. Society has not really accepted the limitations that have been legally placed on sexual expression. It is not unusual for a wealthy family to hire an entire Sex House for a son's or daughter's sixteenth birthday. Finding sexual outlets is risky and expensive, and freedom of sexual expression is for the rich. Restriction of legal outlets has led to a sex industry of a size, cost, and scope not dreamed of in the twentieth century. The broad base of support for this industry comes from all segments of the society. A small, piece of gold wire twisted in the shape of a D, symbolizing the underground motto "We Are All Deviant" is worn under the lapels of married heterosexuals, single homosexuals, rapists, those who have many sexual partners, and those who have none. Since all have been labeled deviant, it becomes harder to distinguish what society finds truly acceptable.

Optimistic Scenario

In the year 2025, human sexual behavior is governed by the principle of Freedom with Responsibility. When reading about the middle and late twentieth century, people are surprised to see how sexual expression was once defined as "sex," a separate and isolated part of human activity. During those years, so many people had been branded as different and strange that a form of surrender had occurred. No distinction was made between a loving homosexual relationship and the compulsive pursuit of hundreds of anonymous homosexual partners, between the portrayal of the erotic relationship of a loving couple and the sexual subjugation of an unwilling victim. Sexual variations and deviations blurred together. Many types of sexual expression practiced by many people were defined as falling outside the rules governing other human relationships. For example, sex for recreation demanded no recognition of the needs or values of another person. In those days pursuit of individual physical pleasure became almost a duty, one that people did not even enjoy.

With the recognition of the diversity of human sexual expression came acceptance and the redefinition of the meaning and place of sexual expression. Laws that reflected neither true morals nor actual behavior were repealed. No longer was any act of oral sex punishable in New York by a year in jail or a $1,000 fine. Even New Jersey repealed its law that had demanded a penalty of 20 years in jail and a $50,000 fine.[63]

Today we recognize that sexual expression must be governed by the same values that govern all relationships. The exact physical nature of the expression is considered much less important than whether it contributes to the partners' well-being. Looking back, the beginnings of this trend can be seen in such acts as the issuance by the United Presbyterian Church of the following statement endorsing "those sexual (erotic and genital) expressions which build up communion between persons, establish a hopeful outlook on the future, minister in a healing way to the fears, hurts, and anxieties of persons, and confirm to them the fact that they are truly loved, (these) are actions which confirm the covenant Jesus announced."[64] Similar statements were issued by many religious groups. All urged the adoption of "loving concern" as a standard. Being open with your sexual partner and knowing that partner in a meaningful way became very important.

Today permissiveness with affection is a guiding principle. Those who have chosen the alternate life-style of homosexuality accept the same principles as do heterosexuals. Cruel, uncaring homosexuals and heterosexuals are considered deviant by the society.

Men and women are equal partners in all parts of life, including sexual expression. Beginning with the efforts of feminist groups against rape came a recognition that our previous patterns of sexual socialization had led to an unhealthy "male-the-sexual-initiator" syndrome that was harmful to men and women. Initiating sexual activity is now considered appropriate for both men and women. The behavior is judged in terms of whether or not there are mutually agreed upon goals such as communication, pleasure, friendship, love, and mutual growth.

With the recognition that women were not sexual objects came a decline in the pornography industry as a destructive force. No longer are the only erotic films and books available those which contain violence toward and the exploitation of women. For those who enjoy erotic films and books, there is a wide selection depicting loving relationships. The pornography industry still exists, but serves a small market considered pathological by most of society. There are still those who are sexually aroused by force and cruelty but they are a smaller and smaller segment of society.

There are no legal restrictions on sexual activity between consenting adults. There are, however, stronger moral and value restrictions than existed in the twentieth century.

SUMMARY

1. The sexual expression of human beings varies greatly. Cultural norms have always focused and modified the human sex drive. The actual content of the norms governing acceptable sexual expressions vary enormously over time and place.

2. It has been estimated that there are between 11 and 14 million homosexual adults living in the United States. If numbers are our criteria, it appears that homosexuality is a sexual variation and not a deviation. Nevertheless, being homosexual in our society means facing both formal and informal sanctions.

3. Today, the law is being used as a tool to prevent discrimination against gays rather than as a tool to punish them. There are now Gay Activist groups throughout the country including college campuses.

4. Rape is a crime of violence. Forcible rape is an act of aggression, not the expression of sexual desire. The law and public opinion must be changed to fully reflect this. In no other crime is the victim forced to prove nonprovocation.

5. The sex industry in our society is extremely profitable. A great deal of money is spent on sexually explicit material and the purchases of the sexual services of men and women.

6. What is defined as pornographic varies according to time and place. We propose the following working definition: Pornographic material depicts both normal and abnormal sexual behavior in a way designed to stimulate the consumer and induces violent disrespect and degradation of the subject.

7. Becoming a professional prostitute involves more than just a decision to suspend morality and "do what comes naturally" for money. Rules, techniques, and values must be learned through a process known as "being turned-out."

8. Four main perspectives have been used to explain human sexuality. Those who focused on individual faults feel that sexual deviations can be best explained by finding a trauma a person has experienced or the defects in his or her personality. The system disorganization emphasis sees deviation as a symptom of social disorganization and the breakdown of society's institutions. The conflict/feminist approach sees homosexuality, rape, prostitution, and pornography as being rooted in the basic subjugation of women in our society. For the symbolic interactionist, sexual deviance can best be understood in terms of the concepts that apply to any deviant behavior, deviant careers, sexual scripts, and labeling theory.

SUGGESTED READINGS

Bell, Alan, and Martin Weinberg. *Homosexualities: A Study of Diversity Among Men and Women.* New York: Simon and Schuster, 1978. Survey results of a study of San Francisco homosexuals. Reactions to today's problems and life-styles.

Brownmiller, Susan. *Against Our Will: Men, Women, and Rape.* New York: Bantam, 1975. Challenging presentation of the historical dimensions of sexual violence and rape and their roots in the male-female relationship.

Crisp, Quentin. *The Naked Civil Servant.* New York Signet, 1968. Autobiographical description of "coming out" in England in 1931 as an exhibitionist homosexual. Personal, legal, and social problems interwoven in a dramatic account.

Henslin, James, and Edward Sagarin (eds.). *The Sociology of Sex.* New York: Schocken, 1978. An introductory reader covering all socially interesting sexual arenas from abortion to visual sex.

Karlen, Arno. *Sexuality and Homosexuality: A New View.* New York: W.W. Norton, 1971. The total compendium of sexual behaviors through the ages and the morals and attitudes that have tried to categorize and control them.

Marshall, Donald, and Robert Suggs (eds.). *Human Sexual Behavior: Variations in the Ethnographic Spectrum.* Englewood Cliffs, N.J.: Prentice-Hall, 1971. A cross-cultural context is provided by both descriptions of sex's place in interesting cultures and summary statements by anthropologists on sex and human social life.

Nichols, Jack. *Men's Liberation: A New Definition of Masculinity.* Baltimore, Md.: Penguin, 1976. The chapters on sexual definitions of maleness, for example, "Size and Status: the Bigger-Than-Thou Penis Syndrome," provide important insights into sexual problems.

Peplau, Letitia Anne, and Constance Hammen (eds.). "Sexual Behavior: Social Psychological Issues." *Journal of Social Issues,* Vol. 33, No. 2, 1977. Papers on premarital sex, dating intimacy, arousal, and aggression, and values exemplify the scientific study of sex and its problems.

GLOSSARY

Drag   Dressing in a way that imitates or mocks the way members of the opposite sex dress.

Fetishism   Becoming sexually aroused only under conditions not sexually arousing to most people, such as one with a foot fetish finding feet the most erotic part of the body.

Gay vs. Straight   Terms used in the homosexual subculture to designate whether one is homosexual (gay) or heterosexual (straight).

Heterosexual   An individual who is sexually attracted to the opposite sex.

Homosexual   An individual who prefers to have sexual activity with a person of the same sex.

Lesbian   A female homosexual.

Pornography   Any written or visual material produced deliberately to be sold to those seeking sexual stimulation.

Prostitute   A person who sells sexual favors.

Rape   Sexual activity with an unwilling person, involving the use of force or threat of harm.

Sanctions   Positive (rewards) or negative (punishments) controls applied to shape people's behavior.

Transsexual   A person who feels he or she is actually a member of the opposite sex, sometimes undergoing surgery to become physically what one feels psychologically.

Transvestite   An individual who habitually dresses in the clothes of the opposite sex; can be bisexual, homosexual, or heterosexual.

"Turn-out"   To train a person to become a professional prostitute.

FACTS ABOUT CRIME

Every two seconds a serious crime is committed in the United States.

More than one-third of the nation's households were victimized in 1980.

Only 14 percent of burglaries are ever followed by an arrest.

Shoplifting costs Americans $24 billion per year.

No federal law specifically prohibits computer crime.

In New York City the 17 judges assigned to Manhattan Criminal Court were assigned 85,512 cases.

Eighty-five percent of the people in the United States favor more and longer prison sentences. But, it would cost $10 billion to build the facilities needed to do this.

More than 23,000 neighborhood groups have been organized and they are reducing crime.

5
DEVIANCE AND CRIME

If our behavior violates the norms of our group, we will be punished in some way. In every situation, we have expectations about how people should act. These expectations are not so rigid that we must all act like robots. All norms allow for a range of acceptable behavior. As long as we stay within this range, diversity is tolerated. Once our behavior goes beyond this range of tolerance, we will be punished, our behavior defined as deviant, and appropriate sanctions (rewards and punishments) will be applied to us.

Deviant behaviors are the variations that are not acceptable, and are regulated and controlled by society.[1] For example, sanctions may be applied to the parent who is abusing his or her child, either formally or informally. For instance, friends and relatives and/or neighbors may tell the person how offended they are by the way the child is being treated. In other cases, they may refuse to speak to the abuser or even threaten to go to the "proper authorities." Should the proper authorities be involved and the behavior defined as a crime, then the formal machinery of sanctions would begin to operate.

Deviance and Crime

If the parents' abuse of the child takes a form that is specifically prohibited by law, then the behavior is a crime. Crime is a legal category. "What is a crime in one country is not a crime in another; what is a crime at one time, is no crime at another. The law is forever changing, adding new crimes to the catalogue and cancelling former ones."[2] All crime is defined as **deviance,** but not all deviance is defined as being a crime. For example, our society defines homosexuality as being outside of the range of acceptable sexual diversity for "most people." However, our society does not define homosexuals as criminals. There are though, sex acts that are prohibited by law which include such crimes as rape or molesting or having sex with a child. These laws, however, apply to both homosexual and heterosexual acts; anyone breaking these laws is a criminal. In contrast, in other societies, some forms of homosexual behavior are not even considered to be deviant while in still others, just being homosexual is considered to be a crime.

Crime Is Relative

What you are freely doing today may have been a crime in the past, or perhaps may be a crime in the future. As the groups with power and influence change, the laws change. For example, today there are groups that would like to decriminalize certain drugs and as a consequence some drug laws have been modified. This appears to be a mellowing on the part of society, unless you are old enough to remember when the "life" in cola drinks came from cocaine. The move to again raise the legal age of alcohol consumption to 21 appears to be a toughening of the attitude toward alcohol, unless you are old enough to remember when it was a crime for anyone to drink an alcoholic beverage.

For behavior to be defined as criminal, three conditions must be present: (1) The label of crime must have been officially imposed; (2) by authorized persons and agencies who are operating as agent of; (3) a politically organized society.[3] The key terms here are *officially, authorized,* and *politically organized.* In our society a group of people cannot suddenly decide that a type of behavior is so offensive to them that it must be treated as a crime and punished. For example, your neighbor may be playing his stereo so loudly that you, and everyone living nearby, think that grabbing it and throwing it out the window would be the appropriate punishment for his crime. If your group carries out this plan you will be the criminals. Unless there is a law that prohibits the loud playing of music during the specific hours that you are being annoyed, there is nothing you can do. Even if there is such a law that officially labels the act a crime, you and your neighbors are not the authorized persons and agencies allowed to enforce it. You can only report the offender to those authorities so that the penalties developed by the politically organized society can be administered.

Crime and Punishment in Historical Perspective

Medieval punishments that now seem obscene and inhuman to us were at one time commonplace and fully supported by the mores. For example, torture was an accepted part of imprisonment. It was also expected and accepted that jailers and even chaplains would extort fees from prisoners for such "services" as enough food to avoid starvation.[4] Nor did the law really protect the average person. For example, one law supported by the society provided for the confiscation of all the property of any man who had been designated as a criminal. If a man had no property, his wife would be sexually violated by a public official as a substitute penalty.

Settlers in Massachusetts Bay Colony felt they were following God's will when they made the following crimes punishable by death: idolatry, witchcraft, blasphemy, adultery, rape, and the stubbornness or rebelliousness on the part of a son against his parents.[5] In other words, it is quite possible that, if you were a male who had disobeyed your parents, you would have committed a crime that would have made you subject to the death penalty if you had lived in old New England. Women were not mentioned in this law, either because no one could conceive of their rebelling, or because their rebellion was not considered to be important.

Being accused of being a witch was not just a crime in old New England. In Europe, between the fifteenth and seventeenth centuries, 500,000 people were convicted of witchcraft and burned to death. Their specific crimes included: a pact with the devil, journeys through the air over vast distances mounted on broomsticks, kissing the devil under the tail, and copulation with *incubi* (male devils equipped with ice-cold penises).[6] You could also be convicted of being a witch if you were accused of causing hailstorms or ruining crops. How did you become vulnerable to such an awful fate? Merely through the accusation of another person. Once accused, torture was applied until a confession was obtained. If you confessed immediately, you might be spared torture and be "mercifully" strangled before you were burned. Actually, at that time, some of the people so accused really believed they were witches and had flown through the air or had intercourse with the devil.[7] Today we would define such persons as being mentally ill and try to provide treatment for them.

Not all crimes of the past were so frightening. For example, at one time in colonial New Jersey, a man could be fined for kissing his wife on Sunday. This fine did not apply to kissing during the week, though. Nor were all punishments so extreme. For example, disorderly drunks were placed in "stocks," a wooden contraption that provided a seat for the offender and holes into which his or her arms and legs fit. While the offender was so confined, friends and neighbors would gather around and sneer. If they were especially tired of the offender's behavior, they sometimes took this opportunity to throw things at the confined person. Adultery was another punishable crime. For example, in 1692, if a man ran away with another man's wife, both runaways got 10 lashes at the stake.[8]

Crime, Laws, and Prosecution

Is everyone equal under the law? The **law** as a type of formal social control comprises: (1) explicit rules of conduct; (2) planned use of sanctions to support the rules; and (3) designated officials to interpret and enforce the rules.[9] The goal of having these formally prescribed patterns is to ensure that every person is treated equally; that when a rule is violated, only the nature of the violation matters, not the identity of the violator. In actual practice, the values and norms of the groups in power play a role in determining which laws are enforced and which offenders are arrested. In addition, the law allows for great variation in the length and severity of the sanctions actually imposed for the violation of the same rule.

Laws and Norms of the Society
The study of crime is often based on the assumption that criminal law accurately reflects the social norms of most of the members of society. In practice, in a complex society such as ours, this is not always true. Many diverse groups must live together despite their having different values and norms. Therefore, there are many people holding cherished values that are not reflected in the law and many laws that go against the cherished values of some people.

For example, the segregation laws that once existed in some states were contrary to the deep moral conviction, held by much of the society, that all people are equal. Labeling a public facility "for Whites only" was an outrage to many people, yet these laws once existed and were enforced because the people then in power did not share the view that all members of the human race were equal.

Differential Enforcement of Laws
Just because a law exists does not ensure that violators will be treated as criminals. An act is only a crime if it is treated as a crime. In many states, most forms of gambling are against the law. For example, if you are running a weekly poker game, where the players bet real money and the winners keep their winnings, you are violating a law. Will you ever be arrested and prosecuted? That depends. Are you a middle-class person, well established in your community? Are the other players like you? Do you have a place where this game can take place "privately," away from the eyes of others? If this is true, it is unlikely that you will ever be defined as engaging in a criminal activity. But if you are a "street kid" organizing the same type of game, with the only difference being that you must use an accessible place where

people are able to see you, you may very well be arrested and treated as a law violator. Differential arrest patterns are a problem in our society. "If you are a poor black ghetto dweller, then the odds are about one out of five or six that you will be arrested during the next twelve months."[10] Quite possibly it will be for an activity that a wealthy white person also pursues completely unpenalized.

At times, the consequences of not enforcing a law are terrible. For example, after it was established that eating paint containing lead could cause brain damage or death in young children, landlords were forbidden to use such paint and told to repaint places where it had been used. This seems like an especially clear-cut case of a law that everyone would want enforced. Yet it has not always been enforced. For example, New Haven, Connecticut, has the highest number of reported deaths of young children from eating paint containing lead. Yet, even in this city, there are several cases where landlords have failed to eliminate the hazardous paint and have had repeated poisoning in buildings they own.[11] Contrary to what we might expect, the citizens of New Haven have *not* risen up in anger. Instead, as is so often the case, the reaction of many to hearing about this was to say, "Well, parents shouldn't let their children eat paint." In a sense, they blamed the victim.

It is often convenient to blame the victim. Blaming the victim gives us the comfort of an explanation, and relieves us of the responsibility for social action. If we say that the woman who was raped shouldn't have gone on such a dark street, that the poor person who was "ripped-off" when making a purchase shouldn't have gone into that store, or, that the person who was robbed should have had better locks, then we can conveniently get off the hook and divert blame, instead of feeling there is something we must correct.

REPORTED CRIME

Measuring the Extent of Crime

Index Crimes and the Uniform Crime Report

There are two major approaches taken to determine the extent of crime. One perspective is provided by the FBI through its Uniform Crime Reporting Program and its published *Uniform Crime Report* (UCR). The FBI bases this report on the monthly and annual reports it receives from law enforcement agencies throughout the country. Each month city police, sheriffs, and state police file reports on crimes that are known to them. These offenses are grouped within the following categories:

1. *Murder and Nonnegligent Manslaughter.* Includes willful felonious homicides and excludes attempts to kill, suicides, accidental deaths, and justifiable homicides.
2. *Forcible Rape.* Includes forcible rapes and attempts to rape.
3. *Burglary.* Includes any unlawful entry to commit a felony or a theft and includes attempts to commit a felony or theft.

4. *Robbery*. Includes stealing or taking anything of value by using force or threat of force, and includes attempts to do so.

5. *Aggravated Assault*. Includes assault with intent to kill.

6. *Larceny*. Includes theft of property or articles of value without the use of force, violence, or fraud.

7. *Motor Vehicle Theft*. Includes all cases where vehicles are driven away and abandoned but excludes vehicles taken for temporary use and returned by the taker.

These are known as the **Index crimes.** Figure 5.1 shows us that an Index crime was committed every two seconds within the United States in 1982. The UCR also contains data on crimes cleared by arrest (see Figure 5.2), and on persons arrested

FIGURE 5.1   Crime Block 1982

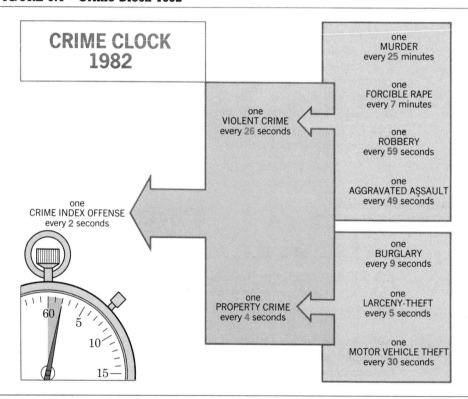

The crime clock should be viewed with care. Being the most aggregate representation of UCR data, it is designed to convey the annual reported crime experience by showing the relative frequency of occurrence of the Index Offenses. This mode of display should not be taken to imply a regularity in the commission of the Part I Offenses; rather, it represents the annual ratio of crime to fixed time intervals.

SOURCE: *Crime in the United States Uniform Crime Reports*. Washington, D.C.: U.S. Department of Justice, Federal Bureau of Investigation, September 11, 1983.

FIGURE 5.2   Crimes Cleared by Arrest 1980

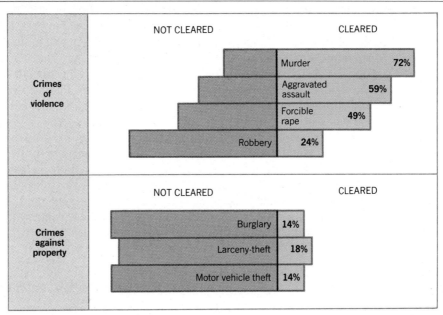

SOURCE: *Crime in the United States Uniform Crime Reports,* (Washington, D.C.: U.S. Department of Justice, Federal Bureau of Investigation, September 10, 1981).

for all criminal offenses by sex and race of offender.[12] To ''clear'' by arrest means that the reported crime has been investigated, and an arrest has been made.

Victimization Reports
A second perspective on the extent of crime is supplied by the Bureau of Justice Statistics through its *National Crime Survey* (NCS), sometimes referred to as Victimization Reports, and conducted by the Bureau of Census. This survey, based on a representative sample of households, is designed to find out who has been the victim of a crime, and the nature of that crime. The survey is conducted nationally on a continuous basis. Since it focuses on crime victims, we learn such things as characteristics of victims, victim-offender relationships, (stranger-nonstranger), and whether or not the police were notified about the incident. Since not all crimes are reported to the police, these victimization reports help us get a clearer picture of crimes that are not known to the police.

Critics point out that these victimization reports are often quite inaccurate since they are based on what people chose to tell the interviewer. For example, in one study of people who were known to have reported being victimized to the police, only 47 percent told a follow-up interviewer that they had been victimized.[13]

Nevertheless, these two sets of data reported are the best sources we have for estimating the extent of known crime in our society.

How Much Crime Really Exists?

If by crime we mean every violation of the law, we have no accurate idea. If we make our question more specific and ask, "How many households in the United States have been touched by a known serious crime?" then we do have an answer. Judging from the years 1975–1980, the answer is approximately one in three (see Table 5.1). More than 24 million households, one-third of the nation's households, were victimized in 1980. The *Index of Households touched by crime* was developed because a crime touches not just one victim, but entire families. Families suffer with the specific victim, sharing the pain, hardship, sense of violation, and aftermath of fear that crime can cause.

What about arrest data? If we relied on arrest data in deciding how much crime existed, we would make a severe underestimate, especially for property crimes (see Figure 5.1). Most crimes are never cleared by arrest. For example, only 14 percent of all burglaries are ever cleared by arrest. This is not too surprising since in a burglary the victim never sees the person who commits the theft. If there is contact, the act is classified as a robbery. The clearance rate for robbery is a little higher (24 percent), perhaps because the victim can supply a description of the offender.

Why Aren't All "Crimes" Reported?

There seem to be eight basic reasons why crimes are not reported:

1. *Many "crimes" are known only to the offender.* For example, have you ever driven while under the influence of an intoxicating substance? In the legal sense you are guilty of a crime: "Driving while Impaired."

2. *The offender may be a friend or relative whom the victim does not want to harm or embarrass.* For example, much known "theft from

TABLE 5.1 Households Touched by Crime, 1975–80:

	Number and Percent Distribution by Type of Crime					
	1975	*1976*	*1977*	*1978*	*1979*	*1980*
Percent of households touched by:						
All crimes	32.0	31.5	31.3	31.3	31.3	30.0
Rape	0.2	0.2	0.2	0.2	0.2	0.2
Robbery	1.4	1.2	1.2	1.1	1.2	1.2
Assault	4.5	4.4	4.7	4.6	4.8	4.4
Personal larceny	16.4	16.2	16.3	16.2	15.4	14.2
Burglary	7.7	7.4	7.2	7.2	7.1	7.0
Household larceny	10.2	10.3	10.2	9.9	10.8	10.4
Motor vehicle theft	1.8	1.6	1.5	1.7	1.6	1.6
Households touched by crime (thousands)*	23,377	23,504	23,741	24,277	24,730	24,222
Households in U.S. (thousands)	73,123	74,528	75,904	77,578	78,964	80,622

NOTE: Detail does not add to total because of overlap in households touched by different crimes.
* These figures may not complete to percents shown because of rounding.
SOURCE: "The Prevalence of Crime," Washington, D.C.: Bureau of Justice Statistics (March 1981). NCJ-75905.

households'' has been shown to be committed by a person who has a right to be there, that is, a baby-sitter, domestic, or relative.[14] We can only imagine how much more there may be that is never reported. Another type of crime where the attacker is known to the victim is aggravated assault. Again, we can assume there are many more assaults we know nothing about.

3. *The offense may be potentially embarrassing to the victim.* The injured party may feel that discovery of his or her hidden behavior might be more harmful than the offense itself. For example, if a person is being black-mailed, it might be preferable to ''pay'' rather than report the blackmailer. The risk that the victim's hidden act (e.g., adultery, certain sex practices, noncriminal abortion) might be made public is more fearsome than being victimized by a blackmailer. Unfortunately, many women also feel this way about the crime of rape. They are so afraid of being marked as ''soiled'' that many rapes are never reported.

4. *Often people fear reprisals from their assailants.* This is particularly true of older people who have been systematically robbed by young neigh-bors. Over and over, the same sad story is told. Usually only after the

Studies have shown that almost everyone has, at one time or another, taken something from a store without paying for it. Most shoplifters steal less than $30 worth of goods at a time, yet it has been estimated that in 1980, shoplifting cost Americans about $24 billion.

victim has been harmed so seriously that others have become aware of the problem is the crime discovered. Even if the assailant is unknown, the feeling that you will be "gotten" if you report the crime seems to be a strong deterrent.

5. *The "crime" seems too trivial to justify the time and effort it would take to report it.* Many acts of vandalism and petty theft don't seem worth the effort. A broken window, a slashed tire, a stolen garden hose may not be considered important enough to report. Crimes such as these, on a society-wide basis, add up to significant inconvenience and financial loss, but are not significantly harmful to any given victim.

6. *A "what's the use" attitude is developing on the part of citizens, especially in the larger cities.* The media constantly report on our "revolving door" criminal justice system. People begin to feel that even if the offender is picked up, no charge may be made; even if a charge *is* made, no conviction and sentencing may ever take place; even if there is sentencing, the offender may spend no time in prison. It sometimes seems futile to report an incident to the police, and perhaps testify in court, knowing that the reported offender may receive no punishment.

7. *There is often no desire on the part of segments of the public to enforce certain laws.* This had been traditionally true in the area of "substance abuse." During the 1920s and early 1930s, even though drinking any alcohol was against the law, very few people would think of reporting someone for buying or selling alcohol. Today similarly, some people would not report someone for selling certain drugs to willing adult consumers. There would have to be more to the "offense," such as trying to interest very young people in drugs considered to be dangerous, or selling "bad" drugs. The gambling laws are often treated in the same way. We, as a public, seem to have no great interest in enforcing them.

8. *The victim may be reluctant to have any contact with the police at all.* This may come from the victim's fear that his or her own illegal activities might be revealed. Those operating outside the law constantly victimize each other. The reluctance may also come from previous contact with the police in which the victim was unfairly or harshly treated.

CRIME THAT IS NOT SYSTEMATICALLY MONITORED

White-Collar Crime

The concept of white-collar crime was first introduced by Edwin H. Sutherland in 1939.[15] He originally defined it as a violation of the criminal law by a person of the upper socioeconomic class, committed in the course of his occupational activities.[16]

He felt we needed this concept for two reasons. First, criminologists tended to concentrate on what we now call the Index Crime, or those acts of theft or violence for which persons from lower socioeconomic backgrounds are most apt to be arrested. Since the easiest group for the criminologist to study is the convicted criminal, that is, the person who has come to the attention of some agency of society, many theories of crime would then *and* now focus on the psychological problems and "personal pathology" of these convicts. Sutherland wanted to make the point that criminality existed in many places where an explanation based on individual pathology made no sense. As he put it. "General Motors does not have an inferiority complex. U.S. Steel does not suffer from an unresolved Oedipus problem, and the DuPonts do not desire to return to the womb".[17] His point was that all three of these groups engaged in illegal practices, doing things that directly or indirectly harmed people. Corporations steal, and deceive, and produce harmful products. We must, therefore, look for explanations that consider this type of behavior when we try to "explain" crime. Sutherland's primary contribution was to shift our attention to a broader range of acts that must be considered when we talk about crime.

How Is the Concept of White-Collar Crime Used Today?

Though some people call all immoral and/or illegal acts committed by members of the middle or upper classes "White-collar Crimes," it is more useful to divide these acts into three categories: (1) crimes committed by corporations or other large organizations; (2) the immoral and often illegal acts built into the informal code of many occupations; and (3) property offenses committed by employees with the employer as the victim. The personal and social costs of these crimes are enormous. Let us examine each in detail.

1. *Crimes committed by corporations or other large organizations.* Included here are acts that are presently illegal and acts that many people feel *should* be illegal. For example, false advertising, dangerous design shortcuts, unfair elimination of competition, and pocketing profits are condemned but ongoing practices.

False advertising is prevalent. Despite various "truth in advertising" laws, we are regularly and often deliberately deceived. For example, while studying the effectiveness of several commercials for a hair-coloring product, one of the authors found that all the actresses used in the commercials had one thing in common; none had ever used a hair-coloring product. The manufacturers insisted on this, since they knew nothing could compete with "natural" hair, especially not their product. This was a rather subtle form of deception. There are, unfortunately, far greater abuses. Dangerous and ineffective products are regularly advertised as safe and effective.

Dangerous design shortcuts have done severe and irreparable harm. For example, a few years ago it was discovered that one of the popular subcompact cars would "blowup" and burn, if hit from the rear. Several people were subsequently killed and a great public outcry arose. Yet, even though company memos were discovered proving that company officials were more or less aware of the design "flaw" that made blowing up likely, and even though it appeared that these officials had decided that the "cost-effectiveness" of this design nevertheless made it the most desirable, no one was sent to jail. Whether companies produce defective and dangerous products, because of ignorance, incompetence, or in a cynical attempt to save money, they are, in any case, certainly stealing from us. Yet, the unfortunate reality is that that type of prosecution rarely leads to what most people would consider to be appropriate punishment.

2. *The immoral and often illegal acts built into the informal codes of many professions.* Socialization into any profession involves inducting the recruits into both the formal and the informal structure. The informal structure often contains elements that "outsiders" consider to be immoral. It may even contain elements that are illegal. By profession, we mean a relatively homogeneous group of workers whose members share identity, values, and a common definition of their role and interests.

A particularly interesting example is given by Stoddard who has proposed that the informal "code" operating in many police departments supports behavior that is actually illegal.[18]

The "code" contains "offenses" reflecting two levels of seriousness; first is mooching, chiseling, favoritism, and prejudice. Mooching and chiseling, that is, not paying full price, and expecting free coffee and cigarettes or liquor from local merchants, is explained by participants as being "deserved" compensation. They feel they deserve these things since they provide protection despite their poor pay and difficult working conditions. Outsiders do not agree and see this behavior in terms of people being forced to pay up. Favoritism and prejudice are opposite sides of the same issues. It is accepted that those with influence will be treated as special, given "courtesy cards" or free parking stickers; and those without influence, often members of minority groups, will be ignored or even abused. Stoddard proposes that it is not just "bad" cops who do these things, but rather that these behaviors are an accepted part of the shared role definitions in many police departments.

The second level of the "code" includes acceptance of what Stoddard calls shopping, shakedowns, extortion, and bribery; all of these are profit crimes that are particularly easy and tempting for the police to carry out. The police are usually given entry to any building where a robbery has occurred, so there is ample opportunity for them to pick up things. Shopping refers to taking little things, and shakedown refers to taking expensive items for personal use and blaming it on "a criminal." Extortion and bribery include demands for financial rewards, based on the mutual understanding between giver and taker that future assistance will be given by the police officer or that current prosecution will be avoided.[19]

Stoddard makes no claims that this code operates everywhere, but he does document that this code is actually operating in the "midcity" police department he studied.

3. *Property offenses committed by employees with the employer as the victim*. Experts say that white-collar crime causes 20 to 30 percent of all bankruptcies. It has been estimated that for every dollar's worth of merchandise lost to shoplifters, company employees steal $15 dollars worth. The typical corporate thief has been working for the company for 9 years and began stealing after about 6 years. Even though 85 percent of all thefts are committed by lower-rung employees, such as warehouse, delivery, clerical, or sales personnel, executives commit fewer but much larger thefts and are responsible for 80 percent of the dollar loss. Government experts placed the cost of this type of white-collar crime at over $40 billion in 1979.[20]

Why do people, who would probably insist they are "honest," do this? Part of the answer is that many people see acts of theft committed against large, impersonal, bureaucratic organizations as being less wrong than acts of theft against a person.

If there is no answer to the question "Whom am I hurting?" these acts are much easier to accept. Studies have found that "taking things" like tools, or supplies, from a factory is not seen as stealing.[21]

It is estimated that, in the United States, one in four fires is intentionally set. Arson for profit has become big business. In our big cities, arson for revenge is an increasing and frightening trend. Fires caused twice the damage in 1982 than in 1973.

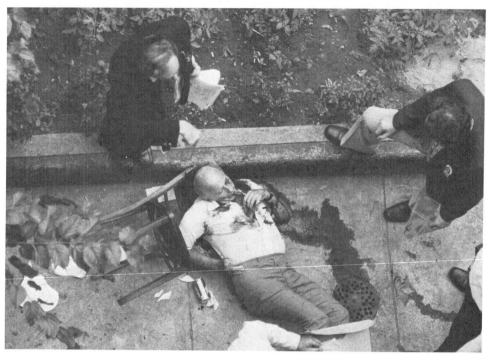

Gangster movies and real-life gangster slayings, such as this one in July 1979 of Mafia chieftain Carmine Galante in Brooklyn, focus public attention on the actions of organized crime. While such occurrences are real and a social problem, they divert us from such other illegal activities as computer and white-collar crime.

Why Is So Little White-Collar Crime Detected and Prosecuted?

The reasons for the lack of detection and prosecution of white-collar crimes can be summarized as follows:

1. The courts are very lenient toward the middle-class people, and these are the people most often accused of such crimes.

2. No effective way of dealing with offending corporations has yet been devised.

3. Efforts to make criminal laws more effective in cases involving corporations have been blocked by business interests.

4. Special boards and commissions are widely relied upon to protect society; that is, lawyers regulate lawyers, doctors regulate doctors, so standards and practices are controlled *within* industries with these groups often protecting only their own members and interests.[22]

In short, those who commit some white-collar crimes are relatively immune from prosecution because of the class bias of the courts and the power of the upper classes to influence which laws will be implemented. In addition, we must sometimes rely upon boards and commissions for the regulation of some professions and corporations because it is often very difficult for any outsider to know when laws are being broken. However, a result of this freedom to self-monitor is that these groups tend to protect their members and interests rather than society.

Computer Crime: A Rapidly Growing Threat

The rapid growth of computer use, in all parts of our society from the grocery store to the development of missiles, coupled with increased computer usage skills among large segments of our society, has spawned a potentially dangerous type of crime. **Computer-related crime** can be defined as any illegal act in which knowledge of computer technology plays a role. Computer-related crimes are difficult to detect and solve. Often finding the crime takes just as much, or more, expertise as committing it did. Potential victims include all organizations and persons who use or are affected by computer and data communications systems. For example, at this moment your academic record is stored in your college's data files. If you had a rival, who was applying to the same company or graduate school you were, and this rival had skills and access to these files, your As could be changed to Bs or even Cs. Since some schools forward transcripts directly, without the student ever seeing them, you might not become aware that you had been a victim of a crime until it was too late.

Computer-related crimes have generated a new jargon to describe the various types of automated criminal methods. For example, (1) *data diddling* involves changing the information that goes into the computer. Was your checking account really credited with the full amount? Was your A really recorded on your transcript? Probably, if these things were not accurately done, the fault lay with human error. But there are circumstances where changing the "input" could be to someone's advantage. (2) *Trojan Horses* involves putting secret instructions into computer programs. Some programs are so complex that no one person is aware of all the components. To take an extreme example, many weapons are computer controlled. Putting in secret instructions so that the target became a "friend" instead of an "enemy" could have catastrophic consequences. (3) *Salami techniques* involve taking small amounts from a large number of accounts. The possibilities for this type of theft are endless. For example, much of our money is now "electronic" or "plastic" money. The person in charge of any accounting system where such money is "stored" could very easily set up his or her own false account and then feed into it very small, barely noticed amounts, from all the other accounts. This "false account" would soon grow quite large and many people would not even notice that they were being robbed, since the discrepancy between the sum they thought they had and the two or three dollars less the computer listed them as having was so small.[23]

Unique Problems Associated with Combatting Computer Crime

Three factors make it particularly difficult for the FBI to deal with computer crime: (1) There is no federal law that specifically prohibits computer crime; (2) agents must have special training in how computers operate so that they can learn how to find evidence of a crime; and (3) it is estimated that three-quarters of computer "break-ins" are done by juveniles who cannot be prosecuted to the full extent of the law.[24]

Since the FBI has only recently begun to keep statistics on computer crime, we cannot officially say whether computer-related crime is going up or down or staying the same.

The Hackers

The term hacker is used to describe a person who is extremely skilled in using computer systems and uses these skills to break into various computer systems. For a true hacker the goal is not profit or "real" destruction. The hacker is seeking the intellectual challenge of overcoming the security systems that prevent outsiders from

"I know I don't have to wear a mask. I just can't pull a heist without one."

Even though it doesn't always seem like a real crime, tampering with computer files is a growing problem in our society. The perpetrators are often well-educated, middle or upper middle class, and able to steal millions of dollars by such techniques as "shifting" small amounts of money from many different bank accounts into their own accounts.

gaining access to the information stored in the computers of businesses, hospitals, universities, and government agencies. As innocent as this may seem on the surface, hackers can and have done great damage to such records. For example, it is quite easy to delete files and scramble nonclassified medical records at the Sloan-Kettering center for cancer treatment. The computer has easy access for doctors and researchers and contains no classified material. ''Yet a doctor could kill a patient by prescribing a medicine or performing surgery based on incorrect records—computer records that have been tampered with.''[25]

Damage such as this has caused some hackers to offer their skills to the FBI in order to stop the unthinking damage being caused by hacker networks.

Software Piracy

This refers to the illegal copying of expensive copyrighted material. Even though software piracy can be very profitable, often hacker networks break into protection systems just to prove they can. Whatever their original goals, once the code is broken, others often step in to make huge profits. It has been estimated that piracy of software costs $100 million dollars a year.

Juvenile Delinquency

Societies have always decried the ''rampant misconduct of youth.'' For example, in seventeenth-century France, teachers were frequently beaten by pupils. Writers in America in the 1800s decried the fact that no decent man could safely walk the streets of San Francisco. The term hoodlum was coined during that time to describe members of teenage gangs.[26] For long periods of history, children in most societies were treated as miniature adults. Slowly, the notion that childhood was a special time, a time when the child should be protected, nurtured, and disciplined in specific ways was developed. The concept of juvenile delinquency is a reflection of the decision that a crime committed by a ''child'' is not and should not be viewed in the same way as the same crime committed by an adult.

What Is Juvenile Delinquency?

Juvenile delinquency is a *legal* category. A young person committing a violation of the **Juvenile Justice Code** comes under the jurisdiction of a court structure set up specifically to deal with young offenders. The maximum age of juvenile court jurisdiction may vary from state to state and be different for boys and girls within the same state; 16 is the usual dividing line.

Juvenile courts were first developed in the early 1900s. Their stated purpose was to save the children. Before these special courts, young offenders came to court along with adults and were treated in basically the same ways. Only children under 7 were completely exempted from responsibility for their acts, since they were defined as unable to have criminal intent. If the offenders were between 7 and 14, sometimes circumstances surrounding the act were taken into account. After 14, a person was legally an adult and would be sentenced in the same way as any other adult.[27] These early child savers were very concerned with controlling children.[28] At that time, children were defined as being naturally inclined to being bad, and therefore the job of society was to force obedience. Subsequently, a wide range of activities was defined as special juvenile "crimes" that required court intervention. These became what we now call **status offenses.** They include offenses such as cutting school, running away, disobeying parents, or being generally uncontrollable.

Reclassifying Status Offenses

Since adults can only come under the control of the court for specific law violations, many people feel the rights of young people are being violated when they are placed at risk of being sent to state facilities or reformatories for nonspecific "misbehavior." There is, therefore, a movement to "decriminalize" status offenses: to remove them from the jurisdiction of the Juvenile Court System. In 1962, New York separated PINS (persons in need of supervision); that is, those who have engaged in noncriminal misbehavior, from other offenders, and they are therefore not labeled or incarcerated as delinquents. They are sent instead to treatment agencies. In 1965, Illinois similarly separated MINS (minors in need of supervision) from other young offenders. In 1967, Florida also developed the category CHINS (child in need of supervision), thus distinguishing this category from other juvenile offenders. By the early 1970s, about 40 states had separated juvenile status offenses from their former delinquency classification.[29]

The stated goal of the juvenile justice system is to "treat" not "punish" the offender. Far too often, there are neither the facilities nor programs needed to accomplish this goal. Young people find themselves in detention centers so underfinanced and poorly staffed that their problems are only increased.

Juvenile Delinquency and the Medical Model

The focus in juvenile court has traditionally been the offender, not the offense. Diagnosis of the child's problems, and the psychological and social factors that may have contributed to those problems, were stressed. Since in the past, many of the young people appearing in court were status offenders, this approach seemed appropriate. Under such circumstances, it would appear reasonable that the juvenile justice system should not, when handling such cases, be an adversarial system with the court being against the child, but a tolerant, advocacy agency interested in finding the best "treatment," not punishment.[30] However, with status offenders not diverted to family court or other agencies and more and more young people being involved in serious crimes, this model is currently being challenged.

Who Are the Delinquents?

As in all types of crime, our information comes in large part from arrest figures and reported crime. Modest estimates reflect that about 25 percent of all people arrested are under 18.

Arrest figures show us:

1. Many more boys are arrested than girls.
2. Arrest rates for juveniles are highest in the largest cities, next highest in the suburbs, and lowest in rural areas. This same pattern exists for all crimes.
3. Arrest rates are highest among children from broken homes and very large families.
4. Those arrested have usually done badly in school, have dropped out of school entirely, or are behind in grade level achieved.
5. Those arrested usually live in areas marked by economic and social deprivation. (Where you live is more important than the status of your own family in terms of your risk of being arrested.)

Many people feel these official rates reflect police practices and court attitudes, rather than reflecting a true picture of the extent and nature of juvenile crime. For example, it has been found that once the police and the residents have defined an area as being high in delinquency, higher police activity leads to higher surveillance and more arrests.[31]

In the United States, we have had an historical societal tendency to see poverty and "inadequacy" as somehow related, and this mistake has led to a tendency to see delinquency as a lower-class problem.

Almost everyone agrees that this is not true. Many studies have attempted to test how much official figures underestimate middle- and upper-class delinquency and overestimate lower-class delinquency. Unfortunately, the different ways people have chosen to measure social class and delinquency have led to mixed findings. Questions measuring "delinquency" have ranged from "Have you ever taken something that didn't belong to you?" to "How many times have you been arrested?"

One thing is clear: when we move away from official figures to self-reports, juvenile delinquency exists in all social classes. For example, Travis Hirschi found that, based on self-reports, sons of professional men and executives committed the fewest delinquent acts, though otherwise there were no differences associated with social class.[32] Voss found that middle-class youths actually reported a higher amount of delinquency behavior than did lower-class youths.[33] Many other researchers have found no significant differences in self-reported delinquency along class line. If the relationship exists at all, it is very complex.

EXPLAINING CRIME AND DELINQUENCY

Discredited Physical Explanations

Most of the early attempts to explain crime emphasized the faults and inadequacies of the criminals themselves. They left people with little hope that the criminal could be rehabilitated or changed, since "criminality" was part of his or her personality.

One of the first theories to be widely accepted was proposed during the nineteenth century by an Italian medical doctor, Ceasare Lombroso. Basing his opinions on autopsies of convicted criminals, he concluded that some people were born to be criminals. They were "bestial" in appearance, and so we could all recognize them immediately. Evolutionary theories were very popular at that time, and Lombroso concluded that these people represented a lower stage of development.[34] They were an earlier form of man, *homo delinquens,* from which modern man, *homo sapiens,* evolved. They could be recognized by their big ears, long arms, and other unattractive physical characteristics.[35]

Though this sounds ridiculous to us, this was a popular theory for quite some time. It was appealing because it was so clear-cut and simple. Even today there is evidence that some people respond to the notion of being able to tell a criminal by his or her "looks." One of the authors worked closely with a student who was attending class on a release program while an inmate of a state prison. This student was convinced that if he could only afford to have his hairline changed, he would be hassled less by the police. (Lombroso had said that a "low forehead" was one of the characteristics of the "born criminal.") Guards and fellow inmates had often told this student that he "just looked like a criminal." Since he was picked up for questioning over and over, even in areas where no one had ever seen him before, it seems hard to deny that there may be many people who are influenced by attitudes like those of Lombroso.

The "physical type" theory was given more support, for a little while, during the 1940s and 1950s by the work of a husband-wife research team, Sheldon and Eleanor Glueck. Their findings seemed to indicate that muscular, solidly built boys, the *mesomorphs,* were more likely to be delinquent than either the tall, slender, small-boned *ectomorphs,* or the soft, plump *endomorphs.* They claimed no causality, only association.[36]

Psychological Explanations

After the collapse of the "physical theories" of Lombroso, Freud's explanation was very popular until the 1930s. He believed that crime was an outgrowth of the repressed, unconscious, emotional traumas of childhood.[37]

Many psychologists continue to search for the personality disorders that are associated with criminal behavior. They do this by giving tests such as The California Psychological Inventory or the Minnesota Multiphasic Personality Inventory to both criminals and noncriminals. These tests contain questions about the habits, feelings, and attitudes of the individual. They hope to be able to distinguish between criminal and noncriminal personality "traits." No distinguishing personality type has, as yet, been isolated.[38] Though psychological explanations may help in the treatment of individual cases, increasingly, criminologists have turned to societal forces for their explanations.

Sociological Explanations

Crime and delinquency are explained in basically the same way. More attention has been given to the young criminal or "delinquent" because most criminal careers begin early in the life cycle.

Though there are several theories of perspectives used to guide the study of crime, they are actually complementary, not contradictory. Each of the following approaches emphasizes a different part of the process of becoming a criminal. Depending on what question you are asking, one or the other might prove more useful. Some questions are so basic that all these theories have tried to answer them. For example, if you wonder, as most people do, why one person rather than another becomes a criminal, all five will give you a possible answer. The Societal Reaction Theorists (the Interactionists) will say it is because of the way his or her early misbehavior was treated. The Strain and Opportunity theorists will say it is because it was the only way that person could achieve the success we are taught to want in our society. The Subcultural and Differential Association theorists will say that it is because the person was taught that criminal activity was the way to get what you wanted. Those who focus on Bonding, Control, and Drift will say that some people don't really become part of our conventional moral order. Respect for, and commitment to, being a good citizen never develop. If the opportunity presents itself, these people will commit criminal acts. Conflict theorists will say a "criminal" is whomever those in power wish to define as a criminal.

As we look at each perspective in more detail, it will become evident that the first emphasizes social interaction while the others all have an institutional emphasis.

Individual Faults and Deviant Behavior

Criminal behavior is learned in exactly the same way noncriminal behavior is learned. If an individual grows up in a social environment where people hold ideas that the larger society defines as "deviant," that individual will be a deviant. For example, if a young person who associates with criminals wants their approval and admires them, a criminal career becomes "normal." This is the same process that operates when a young person living in an environment stressing honesty, hard work, and social service grows up to be a model citizen.

This sounds a bit simplistic to us now. At the time the theory first appeared, it was very important because it stated that: (1) criminality is not inherent; (2) criminality is not the result of a flawed personality; and (3) criminality is not the result of being brought up incorrectly. To become a criminal, a person must be taught the necessary attitudes, values, and skills. How the people around you view legal codes in general, or specific laws, is very important. If you are taught that these laws are the product of values you don't share, you will be much more willing to violate them. For example, in a supportive college environment, the law that requires registration for the draft may be considered wrong. Violating such a law wouldn't seem "criminal" to the people doing the violation. There are many laws that various subcultural groups see as meaningless, or merely imposed on them by groups within the society who have more power.

Institutional Faults and System Disorganization

Robert Merton, an extremely important American sociologist, strongly refuted individual explanations of deviant and criminal behavior.[41] He pointed out that the way our society is organized produces conditions that can lead to a great deal of deviance and criminal behavior. Our culture places great emphasis on success. We want material possessions; we want to be important and respected, and we want to *win*. We are also taught that there are certain acceptable ways we can go about getting all these things we so badly want. What causes deviant behavior is the unequal distribution of the resources needed to follow the acceptable ways to success. Your socioeconomic position, how people of your race or ethnic group are treated by your society, your age, your sex, and many other less visible variables determine if you will be able or even allowed to legitimately pursue certain desirable goals. In a heterogeneous society like ours, there are many norms, and not all are equally valued by all groups. When such a state of norm confusion exists, we say that a state of anomie exists. When a society is both anomic and contains people who are blocked from achieving their goals by legitimate means, the odds are higher that many will try to achieve their goals by illegitimate means.

Richard A. Cloward developed Merton's "means-ends" theory further by pointing out that people don't just vary in terms of their opportunities to use legitimate means, but also in their opportunities and access to illegitimate means. You cannot become a drug dealer unless you have someone from whom to obtain the drugs as well as customers willing to buy them. It is hard to become a prosperous thief if you cannot find anyone to buy what you have stolen. This helps us to understand both the development of criminal behavior in some people and not others and the particular form this behavior takes. For example, a person living on a poor isolated farm does not have as much chance to engage in as many forms of illegal activity as does a person in a heterogeneous city.[42]

Working with Lloyd Ohlin, Cloward applied this theory of "opportunity" to explaining juvenile delinquency.[43] Lower-class youths, especially those living in urban areas, had the same commitment to material success as did middle- and upper-class youths. However, the lower-class youths either had no access to the needed schooling or felt they couldn't possibly succeed in school and therefore turned to the readily available illegitimate means.

Another approach involves the bonding, control, and drift theories. These are the theories that see crimes as caused by a weakened relationship between the conventional moral order and the criminal. This weakened bonding can come about either because the agencies of social control in the society have become weak or disorganized, or because the individual is unaffected, for some reason, by the control these agencies try to exert. By agencies of social control we mean informal groups (family, neighborhood, and friends), and formal organizations (the churches, schools, and criminal justice system).

Hirschi's Social Control Theory states that conformity is achieved when the socialization process forms an important bond between the individual and the society. This bond is made up of four major elements. (1) *Attachments,* especially to the family. The parents should serve as important role models. (2) *Commitment* to the acceptable goals of the society. An example would be wanting a good education and trying hard to get it, so that a good paying job will be available in the future. A person with this commitment would not risk the future by participating in criminal behavior. (3) *Involvement* in the society, participation in conventional activities which can lead to socially valued success and higher status. (4) *Believing* in the rules of society, and accepting the moral values of the society.[44]

When all elements of the bond are strong, the individual is insulated from the temptation to commit criminal acts. A similar notion is put forth by Reckless when he states, "the assumption is that there is a containing external social structure that holds individuals in line, and that there is also an internal buffer which protects people against deviation from the legal and social norms."[45] This containment theory also stresses the relationship of the larger "moral society and the bond of the individual to that society." Delinquency expert David Matza concentrates on explaining how this bond is sometimes weakened. Peer-group interaction occasionally creates temporary permission to engage in delinquent behavior. There is not total attitude change, but only the development of "reasons" to explain why the general rules don't apply to this particular situation. Most of our rules of conduct contain exceptions. For example, you should not steal, unless you or someone else would starve if you didn't. Matza has analyzed and extended these "good reasons" used by young people to justify why under these circumstances their behavior was not really wrong. For example, a common "technique of Neutralization" is "Denial of the Victim." An example of this "neutralization" would be, "It was all right to vandalize that store because the owner is a mean man who had treated us badly."[46]

Inequality and Inevitable Conflict

According to most conflict theorists, especially those who are also Marxists, capitalism itself is the cause of crime. Crime will remain a problem as long as a society has capitalism as its economic system. Criminologists should concentrate on changing society, not the criminals. Most crime is a rational, unavoidable protest against an oppressive and exploitive society.

For example, criminologist Willem Bonger, writing from the perspective of Marxist socialism, argued that "violations of the criminal law are encouraged in a capitalistic society by the unrestrained competition for monetary gain."[47] Bonger feels that the crime problem would be solved under the ideal socialist system, since everyone's needs would be satisfied. Without the sharp class distinctions and privilege distinctions we now have, there would be no motivations for anyone to commit crimes.

The conflict perspective concentrates attention on the class struggle, the defects of capitalism, and the inequalities of the administration of criminal justice.[48]

Therefore the most important question for the conflict theorist would be: Why are some acts that deprive people of property seen as crimes while others, just as damaging or even more damaging, are not treated as crimes? For example, snatching a woman's purse is seen as a crime and punished as a crime. If, however, the landlord of the apartment where that same woman has been living for 20 years decides to evict her so that he can convert his building to a condominium, and make a high personal profit, he is called a smart businessperson, not a criminal. The answer given by the conflict theorists would be that the purse snatcher belongs to a powerless exploited group while the landlord belongs to the privileged capitalist class. Most laws have been specifically developed to protect the interests of that class.

Interaction and Social Interpretation

The focus in these theories is on the responses of society to certain behaviors. Society labels certain people criminal or delinquent. This labeling sometimes occurs for reasons other than their behavior: it may be that such people are politically threatening, or members of a despised group, or just unluckily arrested because the police have a quota to fill.[39] In other words the actual breaking of rules means very little in and of itself. For example, if a young person is repeatedly stealing from the local store, and no one knows about it, and no sanctions (punishments) have ever been given because of this behavior, the person is not labeled a "criminal." Furthermore, he or she may or may not continue to steal, and this stealing may or may not affect any other part of his or her life.

For the labeling theorist, then, this is not deviant behavior since deviance is "that behavior that has been so labeled."[40] Once a person is caught and labeled though, an entirely different pattern would be predicted. The "offender," once in the hands of law-enforcement officials, would be branded and made an outcast. Once the label has been applied, a process is begun that may change the original primary deviance to secondary deviance. *Primary deviance* is a random, isolated instance of behavior by a person who is law-abiding in the rest of his or her life. *Secondary deviance* is a persistent pattern of behavior that often leads to the status of repeater/criminal. Membership in a deviant subculture with norms and standards that support law-breaking may be the final step in the process.

The interactionists remind us that we must look at the sequence of acts that lead to becoming a true deviant. Once a child has been labeled as "bad" and treated this way by parents and teachers, perhaps being isolated and rejected by the "good" kids, he or she is more likely to adopt the social role of being a delinquent and look for others occupying that same role.

THE CRIMINAL JUSTICE SYSTEM

The Police

The first contact a suspected offender usually has with the criminal justice system is the police. The public has always regarded their police with a mixture of appreciation and resentment: appreciation because the police can be called upon to help in all kinds of emergencies, and resentment because they aren't always willing or able to help. Additional anger has come from what the public sometimes perceives to be hostility and lack of regard in the way some categories of people are treated whenever they have contact with the police. At times it appears that the police "hassle" and persecute people who fall into certain "social types." Is this the result of bias or prejudice on the part of individual police officers? Sometimes this is the case. However, as conflict theorist Jerome Skolnick points out, to understand police behavior, we must realize that the nature of their work requires that they must be constantly alert to potential danger. This has led many members of the police to develop "a perceptual shorthand to" identify certain kinds of people as *symbolic assailants,* that is, "as persons who use gestures, language and attire that the policeman has come to recognize as a prelude to violence."[49]

The symbolic assailant may or may not actually pose a threat; in either case it is the appearance that generates the hostile police behavior. For example, the way a young man is dressed, or even the way he is walking, may trigger a negative reaction because these things have been associated with trouble in the past. Police personnel are specifically trained to be suspicious, and to be particularly suspicious of "them." Who "they" are varies from area to area. The following list has been proposed as a description of "them" (see Box 5.1).

The Prisons

There has been a backlash against what the public has seen as the inconsistency and leniency of the courts. Current studies have shown that up to 85 percent of the people in the United States favor more and longer prison sentences.[50]

The criminal justice system is responding, and a larger percentage of convictions are leading to prison sentences. For example, in 1976 in California, 27 percent of those convicted of a serious crime went to prison; now 35 percent do. The jump is even sharper in New York City; in 1970, 24 percent of those convicted of a serious crime spent time in prison; in 1980, 54 percent did.[51]

Prisons Are Badly Overcrowded

There are three factors that are currently leading toward overcrowded prisons: (1) public demand for harsher sentencing; (2) public reluctance to pay for building more prisons; and (3) public refusal to let a prison be built in *their* town. If the present trend of sending more and more convicted criminals to prison continues, it would cost $10 billion to build the facilities needed to hold them.[52] Even when there is

BOX 5.1

HOW POLICE ARE TRAINED TO SELECT SUBJECTS FOR FIELD INTERROGATION

A. Be suspicious. This is a healthy police attitude, but it should be controlled and not too obvious.

B. Look for the unusual.
   1. Persons who do not "belong" where they are observed.
   2. Automobiles which do not "look right."
   3. Businesses opened at odd hours, or not according to routine or custom.

C. Subjects who should be subjected to field interrogations.
   1. Suspicious persons known to the officer from previous arrests, field interrogations, and observations.
   2. Emaciated-appearing alcoholics and narcotics users who invariably turn to crime to pay for cost of habit.
   3. Person who fits description of wanted suspect as described by radio, teletype, daily bulletins.
   4. Any person observed in the immediate vicinity of a crime very recently committed or reported as "in progress."
   5. Known trouble-makers near large gatherings.
   6. Persons who attempt to avoid or evade the officer.
   7. Exaggerated unconcern over contact with the officer.
   8. Visibly "rattled" when near the policeman.
   9. Unescorted women or young girls in public places, particularly at night in such places as cafés, bars, bus and train depots, or street corners.
   10. "Lovers" in an industrial area (make good lookouts).
   11. Persons who loiter about places where children play.
   12. Solicitors or peddlers in a residential neighborhood.
   13. Loiterers around public rest rooms.
   14. Lone male sitting in car adjacent to school ground with newspaper or book in his lap.
   15. Lone male sitting in car near shopping center who pays unusual amount of attention to women, sometimes continuously manipulating rearview mirror to avoid direct eye contact.
   16. Hitchhikers.
   17. Person wearing coat on hot days.
   18. Car with mismatched hub caps, or dirty car with clean license plate (or vice versa).
   19. Uniformed "deliverymen" with no merchandise or truck.

SOURCE: Jerome H. Skolnick, "The Policeman's Personality," *Justice Without Trial* (New York: John Wiley, 1966), pp. 42–62.

money available, citizen groups fight the idea of the prison being located in their own town or city. For example, recently in Florida, community groups successfully prevented authorities from choosing each of 50 proposed sites.[53] Both raising the money and finding a place to build a prison takes a great deal of time, and as this time passes, conditions within our prisons grow worse and worse.

The 350,000 persons presently in state and federal prisons are housed mostly in antiquated, crowded buildings. In some areas of the United States, the prison population has grown so rapidly that prisoners are housed in tents or hastily built or prefabricated buildings.[54] Sixty-six percent of the prison population is housed in cells that measure approximately 6 × 10 feet. This means there are people spending most of their day in an area that is about the size of the average small bathroom. There is no privacy, since often two or more persons are in cells designed to hold only one.

Overcrowding contributes to another serious problem: lack of the professional staff needed to provide counseling or job training services. Only 1 in 10 inmates receives any job training at all. Nor are there enough guards to protect inmates from each other. Violence and drugs proliferate, opportunities for rehabilitation are skimpy, and exchange of tips on criminal techniques is a major pastime. As one inmate said, ''Many of us come in here ignorant, and we won't come out able to cope with society any better because we can't even deal with our own problems.''[55]

Consequences of Overcrowding

All these factors: too small spaces of confinement; no counseling or training; and no protection from other inmates help to create tinderbox prisons. Prisons today are filled with rage and frustration. For example, in 1981, in a maximum security state prison in New Mexico, convicts seized control for 36 hours. What happened during those 36 hours tells us something of the total horror of prison life:

> Armed with knives, clubs, acetylene torches, a group of prisoners seized 12 guards. They stripped their hostages naked, beat them, slashed them, and sexually assaulted some of them. 'But the worst was reserved for fellow prisoners, especially suspected informers and other outcasts of prison life, such as the mentally disturbed or retarded. Gangs raped them repeatedly, blow-torched their eyes and genitals, threw men from tiers, decapitated (cut off their heads) them or fired tear-gas canisters point blank into their faces.' Thirty-three were killed, 90 hurt.[56]

Another indicator of how intolerable prison is for some inmates is the suicide rate in prison, which is 16 times higher than that of the general population.[57] Since the majority of those who kill themselves had been originally arrested on drug or alcohol charges, and therefore are people we would expect to sorely need social services, this too seems to be worsened by the understaffing now existing in our prisons.

Our prisons are old, crowded, and totally inadequate. Even though the public is demanding harsher sentencing for criminals, there is great reluctance to build more prisons. In addition, no one wants a prison built in their town. Severe overcrowding is the result.

SOLUTIONS PAST, PRESENT, AND FUTURE

Solutions Aimed at the Offender and Potential Offender

The programs stemming from explanations focusing on individual characteristics have, for the most part, been very disappointing. The techniques that have been used, including casework, individual psychotherapy, group counseling, special education programs, and behavior modification programs have not produced the hoped-for results. One of the most famous examples of this type of program was the Cambridge-Somerville study. It began with the selection of a large group of young persons considered to be at risk of becoming delinquent. Half of the group were given extensive treatment by caseworkers. This was the **experimental group**. The other half served as the **control group**. As in all properly conducted experiments, these groups were identical except for the fact that the experimental group was given treatment and the control group was not. This means that the investigators could monitor *both* groups over time: see how many in each group became delinquent, how serious this delinquency was, and how, in general, the lives of these youths turned out. If the experimental group had done much better, then it would have meant that the treatment "worked"; that is, it had prevented young people from becoming criminals. But in this case, the treatment did not work. All the efforts of caseworkers to establish strong bonds with the youths made no significant difference at all.

Is it possible that the benefits of the program would show up later? Here the results seem even more disappointing. A follow-up study 30 years later indicated that the treated group, now in their late forties, had many more problems than average.[58]

In 1978, Romig did a systematic evaluation of 170 programs that both focused on individual characteristics and used one of the approaches previously mentioned (casework, psychotherapy, etc.). He concluded that these programs have not worked; they did not reduce the likelihood that youths will eventually get into trouble.[59] This is a particularly strong and interesting finding because he only reviewed studies that had used "relatively sound" research methodology.

Some programs focusing on changing social interaction patterns have actually had the effect of increasing the problem they were trying to solve. Such programs have included: (1) direct intervention into youth gangs; (2) the creation of temporary groups for therapeutic purposes such as raising the self-esteem of the members; or (3) training teachers, police, parents, and others who have regular contact with young persons in the techniques of effective interaction. The most ineffective of these programs have been the ones that increased or strengthened the existing ties the members already had with deviant groups. One example of this type of approach is the detached workers programs. These were very popular in the late 1960s and early 1970s. Each youth gang was assigned its own worker. The goal was to encourage the gang to substitute "constructive" activities for their previous destructive activities such as gang wars, thefts, and harassment of neighborhood residents. Unfortunately, the actual result of this intervention was to increase the frequency and intensity of the interaction within the gang. This in turn seemed to increase both intergang violence and collective predatory activities.[60] The gang became more important than ever and the rest of society and the conventional world seemed further away.

Programs based on strengthening individual ties to the conventional moral rules seem to show the most promise. In these programs, the actual treatment may still focus on the individual, but since the cause of the problem is seen as coming from flaws in the social system, these programs also take into account the individual's relationship with that social system. It has been found that lawbreakers and potential lawbreakers often feel as if they have "nothing to lose," that there is no point in abiding by the rules of conventional society since they can't succeed anyway. The goal of the programs that try to combat this feeling of anomie is to increase the bonding between the individual and the conventional society. There is, however, substantial evidence that simply consuming a young person's time by providing constructive activity will not reduce delinquent behavior. As Hirschi has pointed out, being a delinquent is not a full-time job.[61] To achieve the goal of giving a person motivation to obey the conventional rules, a program must provide "something to lose." The programs that have worked all give the participants a real stake in the society: either real job opportunities, jobs the participants themselves defined as jobs with possibilities for advancement, or specific skills that the participants felt would eventually lead to such a job.[62] We must, in other words, improve people's access to the legitimate means of success. We cannot just say "you must do it the right way," without providing the possibility that they *can* do it the right way.

In the Future Programs Must Also Focus on the Society

It is not enough to say that it "works" to give the individuals a "stake in the society." The flaws in the society must also be addressed and changed. For example, the point of entry into the society, for most people, is through the schools. If the schools reject and ignore the needs of all but the already motivated middle-class students, they will be depriving many young people of their chance to succeed. We must modify the way certain early assignments are made into ability groupings. This premature labeling often has negative effects. If you are labeled a "dummy," you are hardly likely to value the organization that so labeled you, or develop the confidence and self-esteem necessary for personal growth and success. There must also be programs that eliminate the assignment of undesirable traits to persons having certain socioeconomic, racial, and ethnic backgrounds. Job-training programs for both youths and adults must be just that: actual training that will allow them to earn a real place in the conventional society.

Solutions Aimed at the Criminal Justice System

Americans are joining forces to protect their own communities. Faced with high crime rates and overworked, understaffed police forces, people are forming their own anticrime surveillance units. This is a movement that cuts across geographical divisions and social class lines. For example, one rapidly growing national program is Neighborhood Watch. Its format is simple, but extremely effective. If persons who do not seem to belong, or who are acting suspiciously, are spotted in a neighborhood, someone calls the police. Since most of us know the people on our own street, and the types of visitors usually expected, and how these visitors behave, we are extremely effective "watchers." Instead of saying: "The fact that that car has circled my block three times is none of my business," people are saying "something is odd on my block; it should be checked out." This program now has over 23,000 organized groups, and it is estimated that 10 million individuals are participating.[63] And it seems to work. For example, in Connecticut, the year after Neighborhood Watch began, residential burglaries decreased by nearly 25 percent. Similarly, in New York City, 13,000 public housing tenants formed their own "Watch" groups. The crime rate in 764 buildings involved went down. In some cases, the crime rate was cut merely by stationing female volunteers in lobbies to screen strangers and alert the police. It is not just in crime-ridden urban areas that such programs are operating. In Tarlington, Texas, an extremely affluent neighborhood comprising 421 homes, volunteers patrolling in golf carts have cut the burglary rate to zero.[64]

Incentives to Encourage People to Give Information to the Police

For example, Crime Stoppers in Rockford, Illinois, makes it profitable to give useful leads to the police. Reward money comes from donations from businesses, individuals, and civic groups. Every week, the "crime of the week," an unsolved felony, is described in detail on television and in the local newspapers. If you call with information, you are given a code number, so your anonymity is completely protected. A review board comprising both police and private citizens reviews your information to see if it is truly helpful in solving the case. If it is, you set up a meeting, at a place of your choice, and two board members bring you your reward, which usually ranges between $100 and $1000. In 1983, over 212 felonies were solved using this system. There are many problems with using such a system. (1) The incentive of money may cause greedy people to try to "turn in" a likely person even if that person is innocent. (2) Instead of defining cooperation with the police as part of being a good citizen, this program is another indication that if the formal agents of social control cannot reduce the crime problems, the informal and perhaps even more effective agent, the neighborhood, will at least try to take over.

There Is More Community Concern for the Victims of Crimes

In California in 1982, this concern took the form of a referendum to consider an extreme Bill of Rights for crime victims. Fifty-six percent of the voters were in favor of the measure. It requires convicted criminals to make restitution to those they harmed. It also contains the controversial provision providing the victims with an input into the assailant's sentencing. The idea frightens many people for several reasons. If the assailant has already severely harmed the victim during the commission of a crime, then the restitution provision may actually place fewer restraints on the violent criminal.[65] For example, fears that the victim will demand large sums of money for compensation, and demand a severe penalty for retribution, may provide a greater motivation to kill the victim and perhaps escape detection entirely.

Provide Work for Prisoners

Chief Justice Warren Berger proposed that we transform our prisons from "warehouses" into factories with fences around them."[66] This would help in two ways:

1. The prisoners could develop useful job skills. At the present time, less than 1 prisoner in 10 does any work at all. The vast majority of those that do work are not doing anything they could use on the outside. For example, many are making license plates, a job only prisoners are allowed to do.

2. The work of prisoners could help pay the great cost of keeping a person in prison. (This is estimated to be as high as $25,000 per year.)

Work programs for prisoners must be designed carefully; otherwise they could be a way to harass or exploit the prisoners. For example, in Australia, instead of working at something that could be useful on the outside, "work" has often meant rock-splitting. Since the "work" was considered to be part of the sentence, prisoners were even being placed in irons or given a reduced diet, as a punishment for being idle.[67] Nevertheless, some programs show promise. In Finland, for example, first offenders and selected repeaters are assigned to labor colonies, where "normalization" of life is the primary goal. The prisoners work for union wages in a free atmosphere. This seems to help in the adjustment process. Even more serious offenders, serving longer sentences, enter such institutions for the last six months of their sentence and are trained and paid.[68] If we devise a system that trained prisoners and paid them, we could perhaps overcome the actual and emotional helplessness with which they face the outside world upon release. We would be giving them "the something to lose" that appears to be the most promising of all solutions.

Maintaining Family Ties while in Prison

Part of keeping prisoners attached to the conventional social order is to remind them that they have identities other than that of "prisoners." For example, a prisoner who is a spouse or a parent is constantly reminded of the larger society. There is some supporting evidence that programs that provide for conjugal visits help to cut the recidivism rate. Prisoners under this system have a 5 percent recidivism rate, contrasted with the overall recidivism rate of 30 percent. A conjugal visit means the prisoner is allowed to spend time *alone* with his or her spouse, and/or other family members. The prison provides a place for this visit. Keeping alive these sexual and personal ties with family members seems to aid both prison adjustment and adjustment after release.[69]

THE FUTURE

Pessimistic Scenario

By the year 2025 the years of neglect and avoidance of the crime problem have caught up with us. Citizens are trapped in their own neighborhoods. Those fortunate enough to be able to afford a "protected community" have some feeling of safety as long as they remain within its limits. If they venture out, vigilante groups from other communities who might mistake them for "intruders" are as much a threat as are the roving criminal bands that have come to be known as "pirates."

For a short period during the late twentieth century it seemed as if the crime surge was over. The population was aging and the number of young people, who were most often blamed for the serious crimes such as robbery, burglary, and auto theft, was shrinking. However, new dangerous trends were being established and they were ignored. Our bipolar criminal justice system was allowing some people to escape being sentenced, usually those committing the so-called white-collar crimes. The system was also erratically sentencing other types of criminals. The court system was referred to bitterly as a lottery. An attitude of "why not go for what I want" became prevalent. This attitude was present among the young, the poor, the old, the rich, the powerful, and the powerless. Bankers with computer skill tampered with accounts and desperate young illegal aliens took what they felt they needed from anywhere they could.

In 2025 there is little we can count on as being "safe." Each day is a battle. Even being a student is more stressful because of the widespread practice of "grade tampering." Since competition for success is ruthless because only a high income will permit a person to live in a Protected Community and buy the computer equipment that will allow work to be done while remaining in that area. Grade tampering is, therefore, widespread. To achieve success, a person must first be admitted to the appropriate high school. Since admittance is based on a combination of social factors and power and influence, the system is known to be "crooked" and it encourages cheating and "dealing." Since a combination of the poor economy and the artificial shrinking of institutions of higher education mandated in the late twentieth century has led to a much smaller pool of available colleges, only 20 percent of the students will be able to go on to college. Being in the top of your class is so important that tampering with both one's own records and the records of competitors is common and sophisticated.

A large proportion of society is completely excluded from even trying to achieve success through "legitimate" means. Those without skills take what they can in whatever way they can. Those with computer skills are forced to hire themselves out to whoever will pay and almost every field has developed an illegal computer underground. Doctors anxious to appear successful change the results of their treatments and experiments. Investment counselors siphon off accounts from their customers. No computerized record can be trusted and the large powerful corporations have ceased to use them.

Optimistic Scenario

By the year 2025 the crime waves of the twentieth century are no longer a major social problem. The interaction of many factors brought about this change.

When crime reached such a level that it was part of the daily lives of people of all ages and of all socioeconomic positions, society finally fought back.

They realized that combatting crime was not just the problem of law-enforcement officials. Crime could not be controlled; it had to be prevented. Neighborhood Watch groups were formed everywhere, and they cooperated with each other. These groups not only immediately reported criminal activity in their neighborhoods, but also became the centers for mobilization of resources and of a new sense of community. Feelings of responsibility for the neighborhood extended beyond watching for crime and came to include feelings of mutual respect and interdependence among people. This led to increased concern for the general well-being of others. Young people felt responsible to and for their older neighbors. Vandalism and malicious mischief disappeared. When a youngster did show signs of destructive behavior the community was immediately aware of it, disturbed by it, and took steps to find out what problems were causing the behavior.

Therefore, early detection and treatment of criminal behavior led to a sharply reduced career criminal population. Improvements in education and the economy, and stronger antidiscrimination laws have almost eliminated the pool of deprived people who were kept from achieving material success through hard work. Intelligent changes in the enforcement of immigration laws cut the flood of exploitable immigrants that had further increased our pool of people for whom criminal activity seemed the only way to survive. Those who do enter the country are helped in their adjustment by both a sponsoring family and social service agencies.

Those people who do commit a crime are sure of two things: (1) they will be caught and (2) they will be sentenced. The advances in technology have linked together all agencies of law enforcement. Within a short time after a crime has been committed a complete description of the act is simultaneously broadcast to all agencies. There is no place to hide. Perhaps more important, citizens cooperate with the police. The emphasis on community and "quality of life" that has replaced the overly materialistic values of the twentieth century encouraged every citizen to cooperate. Now that crime has been sharply reduced, all cases come to quick trial. Sentencing is clear-cut, based on the nature of the crime and the previous record of the offender. Only violent criminals are removed from society. If a person is not a danger to either self or others, intensive rehabilitation is begun.

Since computer literacy exists throughout the society, the "menace" of the late twentieth century, computer crime, no longer exists. Any tampering with any system is immediately detectable. In addition, the truly creative "hackers" take pride in protecting, rather than destroying, the systems that are so valuable to society.

Crime still exists, but it no longer is seen as an overwhelming or unstoppable part of every citizen's life. It is defined as a handleable social problem and society has made the investment to stop it.

SUMMARY

1. Deviant behaviors are variations that are not acceptable and that are regulated and controlled by society. When these deviant behaviors are specifically prohibited by law they are defined as crimes.

2. Crime is a relative concept. What you are freely doing today may have been a crime in the past, or perhaps may be a crime in the future.

3. The study of crime is often based on the assumption that criminal law accurately reflects the social norms of most of the members of society. In practice, in a complex society such as ours, this is not always true. Often the law does not reflect the cherished values of many people and may even go against strongly held values of others.

4. We can only study those crimes that are reported. When we talk about the extent of serious crime, the source is usually the FBI Crime Index. Seven serious crimes comprise this Index; murder and nonnegligent manslaughter, forcible rape, burglary, robbery, aggravated assault, larceny, and motor vehicle theft.

5. There are eight basic reasons why many crimes are not reported: (a) many crimes are known only to the offender; (b) the victim does not want to identify the offender; (c) the crime may be potentially embarrassing to the victim; (d) the victim fears reprisal from the assailant; (e) the crime seems too trivial to justify the time and effort it would take to report it; (f) citizens feel nothing would come of reporting the crime; (g) the public has no desire to enforce some laws; and (h) the victim is reluctant to have any contact with the police.

6. The concept of white-collar crime was first introduced by E. W. Sutherland in 1939. His primary contribution was to focus our attention on immoral and/or illegal acts committed by members of the middle and upper classes. These acts are divided into three categories: (a) crimes committed by corporations or other large organizations; (b) the immoral and often illegal acts built into the informal code of many occupations; and (c) property offenses committed by employees with the employer as the victim.

7. Computer crime is a growing problem. Computer-related crime can be defined as any illegal act in which knowledge of computer technology plays a role. Computer-related crimes are difficult to detect and solve. Often finding the crime takes just as much expertise as committing it did. In addition there is no federal law that specifically prohibits computer crime. Even if there were, it is estimated that three-quarters of computer break-ins are done by juveniles who cannot be prosecuted to the full extent of the law.

8. Juvenile delinquency is a legal category. A young person committing a violation of the Juvenile Justice Code comes under the jurisdiction of a court structure set up specifically to deal with young offenders. The maximum age of juvenile court jurisdiction varies from state to state. The age of 16 is the usual dividing line.

9. Though there are four sociological perspectives that guide the study of crime, they are actually complementary, not contradictory. For example, if you wonder, as most people do why one person rather than another becomes a criminal, all four will give you a possible answer. The Social Reaction Theorists will say it is because of the way his or her early misbehavior was treated. The Strain and Opportunity Theorists will say it is because crime is the only way that person could achieve the success we are taught to want in our society.

The Subcultural and Differential Association theorists will say that it was because the person was taught that criminal activity was the way to get what you wanted. The Conflict Theorist will say that a "criminal" is whomever those in power wish to define as a criminal.

10. Despite problems, our court system tries to function according to three principles: (a) all people are equal in the eyes of the law and will be judged in exactly the same way; (b) an individual is to be considered innocent until proven guilty; and (c) everyone deserves a speedy trial.

11. Currently prisons are badly overcrowded. Three factors have caused this condition; (a) public demand for harsher sentencing; (b) public reluctance to pay for building more prisons; and (c) public refusal to let a prison be built in their town.

12. The future of crime will be influenced by the following factors. (a) The declining proportion of young people in the society (the group that currently commits the largest proportion of serious crimes); (b) the rapid advance of our technology, particularly in the area of computerization and cable TV—these advances provide greater opportunities, both for the commission of crime and the apprehension of criminals; (c) the flood of immigration, both legal and illegal, that is creating larger and larger groups of deprived people who cannot achieve the "good life"; (d) the resources available to strengthen our courts and improve our prison system.

SUGGESTED READINGS

Braly, Malcolm. *On the Yard*. Baltimore, Md.: Penguin, 1967. Slightly fictionalized account of a prisoner's experiences, reactions, and insights into why he kept going back to prison.

Ianni Francis, A. J. *A Family Business: Kinship and Social Control in Organized Crime*. New York: Mentor, 1972. The inside workings of the "the family." Ianni contends they are not superefficient bureaucrats, but relatives who disagree.

Matza, David. *Becoming Deviant*. Englewood Cliffs, N.J.: Prentice-Hall, 1969. An excellent review of the weaknesses of the "pathology" and "correction" perspectives, and a theoretical reorientation of the delinquency field.

Niederhoffer, Arthur. *Behind the Shield: The Police in Urban Society*. New York: Doubleday, 1967. The early and now classic statement of the personal problems of police officers' cynicism and anomie on the job.

Quinney, Richard. *The Problem of Crime*. New York: Dodd, Mead & Co., 1974. Comprehensive review of the history of American crime and the development of the many views that make up American criminology.

Rogers, Joseph W. *Why Are You NOT a Criminal?* Englewood Cliffs, N.J.: Prentice-Hall, 1977. Personal accounts by people who considered crime but chose the straight life are analyzed sociologically.

Sanders, William B. *The Sociologist as Detective*. New York: Praeger, 1974. A collection of basic research projects on crime and police. How data are collected, and what facts you should trust.

Schur, Edwin M. *Radical Non-Intervention: Rethinking the Delinquency Problem*. Englewood Cliffs, N.J.: Prentice-Hall, 1973. Provocative suggestion for accommodating diversity instead of forcing young people to adjust or be labeled.

Thomas, Piri. *Down These Mean Streets*. New York: Vintage, 1967. Still the best autobiographical account of the lure and pressures of "the life" of violence and drugs on a ghetto youth.

Thompson, Hunter. *Hell's Angels*. New York: Ballantine, 1967. Thompson takes us on a ride with the wildest deviant organization of our era, explaining everything he can.

GLOSSARY

Computer-related crimes Crimes requiring knowledge of and access to computer systems.

Control group The group in the classical experimental design whose scores are compared to those of the experimental group to see what would have happened without treatment.

Deviance The violation of social norms beyond the allowed zone of tolerance.

Experimental group The group in the classical experimental design receiving the treatment.

Index crimes The seven most serious crimes tracked monthly by the FBI: murder, forcible rape, burglary, robbery, aggravated assault, larceny, and motor vehicle theft.

Juvenile Justice Code The laws and court structure set up specifically to deal with persons under 16.

Law Institutionalized, codified rules for behavior carrying with them specified punishments.

Medical model The assumption that a form of sickness has caused the young offender to commit crimes, and seeking the best treatment for him or her.

Status offenses A wide range of activities once defined as crimes for those 16 and under, such as running away, cutting school, or being uncontrollable.

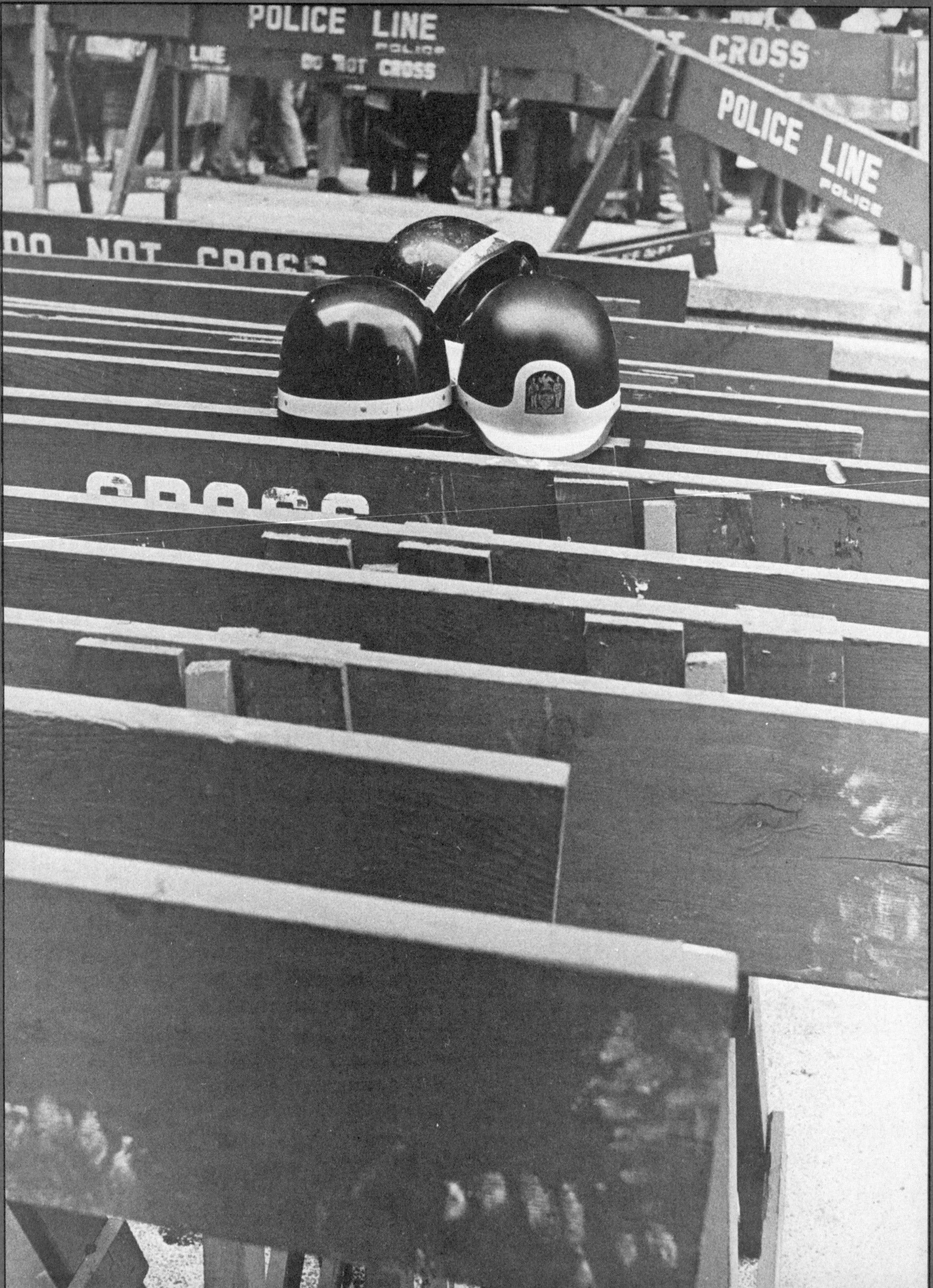
POLICE LINE
CROSS
NOT CROSS
POLICE LINE
POLICE

FACTS ABOUT VIOLENCE

Where the sex of both victim and murderer were known, 63 percent of murders were one male by another, in 21 percent males killed females, and in only 2 percent of cases did a female kill another female.

In 34.1 percent of robberies, the persons victimized said they were also injured.

Three times as many women as men say they fear they will be victims of personal attacks.

Two thirds of murder victims are killed by acquaintances or relatives.

Past political terrorists restricted their violence to only their enemies; now most acts are against the general public.

In the anti-Draft riots of 1863 in New York City, at least 50,000 people joined the mobs and 1300 were killed.

6
VIOLENCE, TERRORISM, AND WAR

Few aspects of society are more confusing to outsiders than our attitude toward violence. We deplore violent crime, enter war with great reluctance, and find violent solutions to be least satisfactory in all situations. Yet ritualized gunplay makes the Western one of the most popular types of film. In the 1920s and 1930s the Western hero was pure and innocent and only interested in his horse and justice. He dedicated his life to the elimination of "bad" guys, usually shooting them cleanly and accurately.

Today's Western hero lives a more complicated life. He has relationships with both good and bad women; he sometimes wears a suit and lives in the city. He nevertheless is still eliminating the bad guys quickly, efficiently, and usually violently. This hero skips the time-consuming and sometimes futile process of bringing the enemy to justice in societally approved ways. The character "Dirty Harry," created by Clint Eastwood in the early 1970s, shoots, beats, tortures, and tricks criminals in the name of justice. "Dirty Harry" movies always make a huge profit, so we can conclude that at a minimum, people find him interesting, if not admirable.

It is difficult to find the exact reason for our often contradictory fascination with and horror of violence, but part of the answer can be found in our own history.

VIGILANTISM IN AMERICAN HISTORY

Vigilantism, the use of violent force to protect community values, is very much a part of American history. Organized groups taking the law into their own hands are known as vigilante groups, whose extralegal (not sanctioned by law) violence reinforces shared values. From 1767 to about 1900, vigilante activity was an almost constant factor in American life.[1] The groups were not just the well-known lynch mobs of the West or the Ku Klux Klan of the South. Vigilantism in the eastern half of the United States occurred as much, if not more, as in the western half. Vigilantism was justified as a response to the absence of effective law and order in many newly settled regions. When the foundations of an orderly stable life (churches, schools, cohesive communities, and effective systems of law and order) were absent, groups of citizens banded together to create or preserve the way of life they felt was right.

> A Vigilante roundup of ne'er-do-wells and outlaws, followed by flogging, expulsion or killing, not only solved the problem of disorder but had crucial symbolic value as well. Vigilante action was a clear warning to disorderly inhabitants that the newness of the settlement would provide no opportunity for eroding the established values of civilization.[2]

Many cruel and ugly acts have been committed against innocent people in the name of preserving community values. Vigilantism may appear in the beginning to be the only solution to the absence of a legal system of social control, but it easily turns into a reign of terror by any group with the means to enforce its will violently. For example, the Ku Klux Klan even today commits despicable, violent acts in the name of its value of White Supremacy, a value totally rejected by most of our society.

Are the Guardian Angels modern vigilantes? This controversial group voluntarily patrols areas that they think are unsafe. Are they a group of bullies committing illegal acts in the name of protecting the community? The police say that they are part of the problem, not its solution.

Violence as a Social Problem

People define violence as a social problem only when it is directed against an innocent target and is carried out by an unauthorized agent. As long as we are talking about violent crime, urban riots, assassinations, terrorism, or child and spouse abuse, a consensus exists that violence is a problem in our society. Once we move to the need for defending our country or having the police carry and use weapons, a consensus is no longer absolute.

In dealing with violence we must recognize that the description of the act does not give us the evaluation of the act. If we are told that one person has violently beaten another, we may automatically disapprove to some extent because of a general feeling that violence is never the best solution. But our reaction will probably change when we are told more about the persons involved. For example, if we find out that the attacker was a large male and the victim his wife, we will condemn and deplore the act. If we also learn that he had just found out that his wife had been unfaithful and had been taunting him, we will probably still deplore his behavior but we will understand it better. If, however, we find out that the attacker was a mother who had come upon someone harming her child, we would probably say her violence was justified and feel a certain pleasure that the attacker had been appropriately punished. In other words, we tend to evaluate any violent act in a particular context. Similarly, those committing violent acts often feel they are justified.

Three Common Justifications of Violence

The three most common types of justifications given for acts of violence are neither mutually exclusive nor exhaustive. In other words, more than one can be used to explain an event and still others may be unique to particular situations.[3]

Necessary Violence

One justification is that violence is the only way to achieve a desired end. In other words, the value of the end or goal is so compelling, so "right," that any means used to achieve it are acceptable. These ends may be religious salvation (as was the case with the Jesuits); the security and survival of a people (as in the case of Mideast terrorism); or even profit (as with sociopathic criminals).

Duty and Obedience

Throughout history, obedience to the commands of a supernatural being or a person in authority has been employed as a justification for violence. The responsibility for making certain ends mandatory or desirable is attributed to forces beyond the person's control.[4] This is the most common justification given for violent acts committed during a war. It is a soldier's duty to obey, no matter what the command. For example, during the Nuremberg War Crimes trials, most admitted to but claimed no responsibility for concentration camp atrocities because they were following orders.

Extenuating Circumstances

The argument here is that the violent act was a unique and unusual event caused by strange forces. These may include fear, exhaustion, temporary insanity, demonic possession, influence of drugs or alcohol, or anything that emphasizes the loss of personal control over behavior.

CRIMINAL VIOLENCE

Few things are as terrifying as the idea that one might be the victim of a **violent crime.** The fear of being mugged, robbed, assaulted, raped, or even murdered is part of the lives of almost all Americans. It affects the woman driving alone at night through a neighborhood she feels is dangerous. It affects the plans of the worker choosing between two jobs, one located in a "safe" area, one in a "dangerous" area. Even if the job located in the "dangerous" area offers more money or greater chances for advancement, the lure of the "safe" area will probably prove to be stronger. Such fears about being the victim of a violent attack are so powerful that a person's satisfaction with living in an urban area is directly related to the strength of that fear. Fearing crime has an even stronger effect on one's satisfaction with city living than actually having been the victim of a crime.[5]

Fear of violent crime has ruined the quality of life for many of us. Almost half of the people living in communities with more than 50,000 residents feel that there is an area within a mile of their homes where they would be afraid to walk at night.

Criminal Violence in the United States

From about 1960 through the early 1970s, crime of all types increased steadily and finally peaked in 1974. The crime rate held at this high point until the early 1980s and then began to drop off.[6] In 1982 reported violent crime dropped significantly. According to data provided by the FBI's *Uniform Crime Reports* (UCR), violent crimes such as armed robbery, forcible rape, and murder dropped by approximately 6 percent. Remember, FBI figures reflect only reported crimes, about a third of all offenses actually committed.[7] Nevertheless, data from many sources indicate the rate of crimes of personal victimization are dropping (see Figure 6.1). The rate, however, remains high: a violent crime is committed every 25 seconds. Nor is the decline evenly distributed. Even though there is a decline in the nation as a whole, dramatic increases have occurred in some areas. For example, in 1981–1982 reported crimes rose by more than 20 percent in Houston, but declined by 5 percent in New York City.[8]

Why is the rate declining? To answer this question we must look at who commits most of the violent crimes. Juveniles, those under 18, commit about a quarter of the violent crimes against people.[9] Half of all reported violent crimes are committed by males age 15 to 24. This age group constitutes a declining percentage of our total population, resulting in the crime rate decline, which may drop further since projections show an even smaller percentage of the population in that age category in the future. But, since many other factors (quality of law enforcement, community

FIGURE 6.1 Lawbreaking Takes Another Dip

	Where violent crime fell in 1982		Where violent crime rose in 1982	
		Change From 1981		Change From 1982
	Cleveland	−24.5%	Charlotte	+29.5%
	Boston	−22.0%	San Antonio	+27.0%
	Columbus, Ohio	−17.6%	Houston	+20.2%
	Phoenix	−14.1%	El Paso	+11.7%
	Newark	−13.1%	Honolulu	+ 9.5%
	Kansas City, Mo.	−12.8%	Minneapolis	+ 9.4%
	Birmingham	−12.4%	Memphis	+ 7.8%
	San Jose	−12.3%	New Orleans	+ 5.9%
	Toledo	−11.6%	Nashville	+ 5.2%
	San Diego	−11.5%	Milwaukee	+ 4.9%

A report from the Federal Bureau of Investigation on September 11 shows the biggest decline in crime in five years and may signal more decreases ahead.

That's because the 4.2 percent dip in the crime rate in 1982 is credited to two trends expected to continue: Longer prison terms for lawbreakers and a drop in that part of the population that is most crime prone—persons age 18 to 25.

Still, the level of crime remains high, as these figures show—

SOURCE: *U.S. News & World Report* (September 19, 1983), p. 12.

TABLE 6.1 Murder Victims, by Weapons Used or Cause: 1970 to 1981

		Weapons Used or Cause of Death							
	Murder Victims,	*Guns*		*Cutting or Stabbing*		*Blunt*[a]	*Strangu-lations,*		*All*[b]
Year	*Total*	*Total*	*Percent*	*Total*	*Percent*	*Object*	*Beatings*	*Arson*	*Other*
1970	13,649	9,039	66.2	2,424	17.8	604	1,031	353	198
1972	15,832	10,379	65.6	2,974	18.8	672	1,291	331	185
1973	17,123	11,249	65.7	2,985	17.4	848	1,445	173	423
1974	18,632	12,474	67.9	3,228	17.3	976	1,417	153	384
1975	18,642	12,061	65.8	3,245	17.4	1,001	1,646	193	496
1976	16,605	10,592	63.8	2,956	17.8	806	1,330	227	694
1977	18,033	11,274	62.5	3,440	19.1	849	1,431	252	787
1978	18,714	11,910	63.6	3,526	18.8	896	1,422	255	705
1979	20,591	13,040	63.3	3,954	19.2	997	1,557	276	767
1980	21,860	13,650	62.4	4,212	19.3	1,094	1,666	291	947
1981	20,053	12,523	62.4	3,886	19.4	1,038	1,469	258	879
1982	19,485	11,721	60.2	4,065	21.0	957	1,657	279	806

NOTE: Based solely on police investigation.

SOURCE: U.S. Bureau of the Census, *Statistical Abstract of the United States: 1984*, Table 296, p. 181.

[a] Refers to club, hammer, etc.

[b] Includes poison, drownings, and unknown.

actions, local social programs, social conditions, and economic conditions) are involved, this decline might not necessarily continue or be homogeneously distributed throughout the country.

HOMICIDE

There is no typical murderer or typical murder victim. In 1982 over 19,000 people were murdered, a murder occurring every 25 minutes. If the 1981-82 dip is only temporary and we return to the previous pattern of steady increases, then over the course of a normal life span more than 1 in every 200 of us may be murdered (see Table 6.1).[11]

The media are more likely to cover either murder sprees or the murder of people during a crime of profit. Such stories involve and frighten us: it is extremely easy for each of us to picture ourselves being in the wrong place at the wrong time.

The story in Box 6.1 is typical. The story of three ordinary people being drawn together by blind chance makes what happens relevant and immediate to all of us. These types of killing do occur, but media overcoverage tends to give us the idea that they are the norm. This is not the case.

The odds are that this person was murdered by someone he knew. Two-thirds of all homicide victims were killed by a relative, friend, or acquaintance. We fear being killed by a stranger, but this type of murder is relatively infrequent. The most common murder weapon used is a gun, then a knife, and a blunt instrument.

BOX 6.1

RENDEZVOUS WITH A KILLER

It was just past 9 o'clock on the languid Sunday evening of April 20, 1980, and Patrolman James Hartley was standing outside a Texas Star convenience store, questioning a sorely frightened black man named Israel Nedd. It had been a bad spring in Port Arthur if you worked nights behind a grocery counter as Nedd's wife did, an outlaw time of robbery and random shooting, and Nedd had been keeping her company against the dark. He had stepped out for a minute to get a pack of cigarettes from his car and was fishing for them in the glove compartment, he said, when these two white dudes came careening out an alley toward the store. Next thing he knew, he was looking at a .38 and bullets were coming straight at him, tearing up the front end of his car. Wild West time, man; it could have been Frank and Jesse James for all Nedd knew, but he didn't take names or ask the dudes what they had against him. He hit the floorboards until the slugs quit flying.

Officer Hartley was cleaning up the last details when, at 9:06, a fresh urban Mayday came crackling over his patrol-car radio: Shooting at 7-Eleven store, Ninth Avenue and Lewis. Hartley knew the place; it was really a Sak-n-Pak, not a 7-Eleven, but all convenience stores were called 7-Elevens in the language of the street. This one was three minutes away, and he had a hunch that the same two gunmen were involved. "I'll take it," he radioed back and headed east, siren howling. He pulled up in the parking lot, in the glow of the big white-lit Sak-n-Pak sign on the roof, and walked in to a blood-drenched nightmare—the worst he had witnessed in eight years on the job.

The first thing he saw, elbowing through a knot of 10 or a dozen people, was the barely conscious form of Athanasios Svarnas lying belly up on the oily asphalt with

Murderers and Their Victims

One-third of all murder victims are related to their killers: jealous spouses kill each other, fathers kill their sons, mothers kill young children, and older children kill their younger siblings. These ugly and shocking events are often related to drinking, depression, frustration, and rage.[12]

Another one-third of all murder victims are killed by friends or acquaintances, often as the result of fighting accompanied by heavy drinking. In most murders of this type, both attacker and victim are men. One study found that 7 out of every 100 victims were killed after a lover's quarrel. In cases where victim and murderer knew each other, the victim often goaded the killer shortly before the murder.

The final third are killed by strangers, usually during the commission of another felony. Of these, 50 percent are killed during a robbery, 15 percent during a rape or other sexual offense, 5 percent during a narcotics offense, and the rest during other types of offenses.

the right side of his jaw blown open; he was alive, but he was sliding deep into a coma and turning a livid purple. "We've got one down," Hartley radioed headquarters. Then he pushed through the door into the store. Shirley Drouet was sitting on a case of Similac powdered milk behind the sales counter, her head pitched forward, the blood dribbling from a hole between her eyes into her lap and onto the floor; she was wheezing and gurgling mechanically, but you didn't need to be a doctor to tell she was dying. In the narrow space before her lay Joe Broussard, his head on her feet with a telephone receiver loosely cradled between his dead hands. He had been wounded in the chin and the neck. The blood streaked his face and was puddling on the front of his shirt.

They had been, as Broussard's brother, Ernie, would reflect long afterward, "like planets that line up once in a lifetime"—three ordinary people drawn together by blind fortune and placed in the way of a fourth carrying a .38-caliber revolver and a heavy load of intoxicants and rage. Shirley Drouet, 43, was there because she had to be, working nights at $3.45 an hour to pay for her groceries, her one-room flat and her independence. Joe Broussard, also 43, had stopped by on a neighborhood errand after a weekend away in Baton Rouge. Tommy Svarnas, 27, was a crewman on a Greek freighter anchored in port for a few days and had hitched a ride with Broussard, heading for the Port Arthur Seamen's Center. They were chance players in a bad dream; their separate paths had converged at the Sak-n-Pak when J. D. Autry walked in out of the night and reduced all of their lives to rubble. . . . Shirley Drouet died from her wounds, as did Joe Broussard. Tommy Svarnas was left, in his brother's words, "A baby again in a man's body." [J. D. Autry was caught, convicted, and executed.]

SOURCE: "Rendezvous with a Killer," *Newsweek* (October 17, 1983), pp. 50 ff. Copyright 1983, by Newsweek, Inc. Reprinted by permission.

Characteristics of Murderers

Half of all murderers are under 30, while only 10 percent are over 50. Men commit about 75 percent of all murders. When women do kill, they are most likely to kill members of their own families.[13]

Murder Weapons

The most systematic record we have of murder weapons is provided by data from police investigations of homicides (see Table 6.1). This does not give us the whole picture, since not all homicides are investigated. We do know, however, that in known homicides, guns are used in about 60 percent of such homicides, knives in about 21 percent, followed by blunt objects as the third most common weapon.

Rape is Violence

Rape is sometimes misclassified as a sex crime or a crime of passion. The rapist does not desire or like women. As discussed more fully in Chapter 4, rape is an assaultive crime based on anger, frustration, and other complex social-psychological disturbances. It has been said that in the twentieth century rape has become the fastest growing, most underreported, and least punished crime in the United States.

As in many crimes of violence, in almost 50 percent of all reported rapes, the assailant is not a stranger.[14] The rapist and victim are usually of the same race, age group, neighborhood, and status in life.

The characteristics of the rapist can only be described for those who are caught and convicted. Of this group most:

1. Are not found to be mentally ill.
2. Tend to have a deep-seated dislike of women.
3. Tend to have feelings of powerlessness.
4. Tend toward other violent behavior.
5. Tend to be young.

Since many rapes go unreported, this remains a crime we must be cautious in interpreting. A societal tendency to wonder what the victim did to bring about the assault still exists, and until this is corrected, many rapes may remain unreported.

TERRORISM

Terrorism is the use of intimidation, coercion, threats, and violent attacks to achieve the objectives of an individual or of a group. Terrorism always implies violence and destruction or the threat of violence and destruction. Terrorist acts physically harm individuals and destroy property.

Governments sometimes use terrorist tactics to control their citizens. For example, during the 1970s and 1980s, certain South American dictators used death squads to round up "enemies of the government" and secretly execute them. Many people simply disappeared. This is called **repressive terrorism.** When the same tactics are used by groups who are not in power, the acts are called **revolutionary terrorism.** Criminals may also use terrorist tactics such as taking hostages and blowing up or threatening to blow up buildings to force society to give in to their demands. Usually if the stated goal is profit for the person making the threat, the act is not labeled as **criminal terrorism** but rather as another form of crime. Sometimes those committing the act define it as "justified revolutionary terrorism" while the majority of society defines it as violent crime. In short, how terrorist tactics are defined and treated depends upon the situation in which they occur.

Terrorism Past and Present

In about 1535 a group called the Anabaptists, located in Switzerland, Germany, and the Low Countries (Holland and Belgium), believed that government was evil because it stood between man and God. They felt therefore that "the existing society had to be destroyed so that the new order could be established, with its laws revealed by the inner light of the prophet or leader."[15] This was the first time that anarchical philosophy embraced the total leadership of an inspired individual. In the name of their cause, they burned cities, destroyed property, and killed those considered to be their enemies. They were guided by the same beliefs found in many terrorist groups today: belief in the healing properties of violent destruction, the importance of violence as an end in itself, and the dream of building an entirely new social order on the ruins of the old. Anabaptist terror led to the destruction of their society and the deaths of their leaders because their terrorist tactics were countered by more powerful counterterror.

Social analyst Ovid Demaris believes another religious group, the Jesuits, provides the closest parallel to today's concept of a terrorist group.[16] Organized by Ignatius Loyola in 1533 to combat the Reformation and spread the Roman Catholic faith among the "heathen," their principles and the nature of their secret society caused them to be damned and feared by both Protestants and Catholics. The Jesuits were famous for the way they solved specific cases of right or wrong by complex, subtle, and often misleading logic. For example, once the principle of "the end justifies the means" is accepted, nothing is wrong as long as it is done for the right reasons. For the Jesuits, **assassination** or killing a ruler who had turned away from the church was a sacred duty, not a crime.

> . . . The Jesuit assassin was prepared in a ceremony called the Blessing of the Dagger. . . . A Casket (container) covered with hieroglyphics and bearing the representation of a lamb (symbolic of Christ) on its lid was placed on the table. . . . When he opened the casket he found the dagger wrapped in a linen cloth . . . (the dagger was blessed by the deacon) and hung around the neck of the chosen one.[17]

If the deed was carried out successfully, it was defined as a noble act. Both the Anabaptists and the Jesuits used their own definitions to separate guilt and innocence. The tactics and justifications of these groups were the same as those used by some groups today: killings were defined as necessary assassinations.

Modern Terrorism: There Are No Innocents.

Starting at midafternoon, bombs aimed only at civilian targets began going off in the heart of Belfast. Thirteen persons died in 20 explosions in an hour and a half, and 130 more were rushed to hospitals, among them more than 20 children and two 72-year-old women. The provisional Irish Republican Army (IRA) claimed credit for this day's work as it had for many others.[18]

Until the middle of the twentieth century, terrorism was similar to the politics of assassination, following a code roughly parallel to the rules and laws governing war. Even though the terrorists were usually self-appointed judges and juries, and their evidence often satisfied no one but themselves, some attempt was made to distinguish between the guilty and the innocent. Today's terrorists claim the right to kill anyone or everyone. There are no innocent people.

The Just Assassin

Camus tells the story of a young revolutionary chosen to throw a bomb into the carriage of a corrupt political official. When the time actually comes, the young revolutionary sees two small children sitting on the official's lap and does not throw the bomb. When he tells his comrades of his decision, they agree there are limits to what can be justified.[19] Today there are no limits.

Societal Reaction to the Terrorist

Societal reaction to any act of terrorism depends on definitions of terrorists and terrorism, with three broad categories existing. Paranoid terrorists act out of sickness and delusion, criminal terrorists act for personal profit, and political terrorists act from a desire to bring about a change in society.

Negotiators dealing with the paranoid terrorist generally will make any promise requested. This terrorist is seen as sick and unable to understand what he or she is doing; therefore, these promises do not need to be kept once the danger to self or others has passed. During acts of criminal terrorism, concern is almost entirely focused on the victims and potential victims. Since the criminal is acting neither out of delusions nor from political concern, but rather, for profit, his or her welfare is seen as a secondary consideration.

Dealing with the political terrorist is the most difficult. The first decision that must be made is whether any bargaining should take place. Some governments will not negotiate with terrorists, believing it would only encourage more groups to try such tactics. Other governments, usually those who place a great value on individual human life, say that in any and all situations, protecting innocent people from harm is the most important consideration. Terrorism is an extremely rare event in Communist countries because terrorists know these governments are unlikely to make concessions to them.[20] International terrorism is particularly difficult to control since governments with different values must reach a common agreement.

Political Terrorism

When we hear that a building has been bombed and innocent men, women, and children killed, we are horrified. When we then hear that several political terrorist groups have proudly claimed credit, most of us are even more shocked. What values could possibly justify such an act of violence? According to Gurr, two main types of justifications are usually given: *normative justifications,* the attitudes and beliefs men hold about the intrinsic desirability of taking or threatening violent action, and *utilitarian justifications,* the beliefs men hold about the extent to which the threat or use of violence will enhance their power and the power of the community or group with which they identify.[21]

In 1983 a particularly dangerous group of terrorists emerged in the Mideast. They called themselves Hezbellah, which means "Party of God." This Shiite Moslem group has claimed credit for countless terrorist bombings that have killed hundreds of innocent men, women, and children.[22] Such acts are deeply rooted in their religious/political traditions, and their entire value system is based on normative and utilitarian justifications for such acts. Because of their beliefs and tactics, they have come to be known as the "suicide bombers."

How Effective Is Terrorism?

To answer this question we must look first at what most terrorists are trying to accomplish. Terrorist activity usually attempts to accomplish one or more of the following goals:

1. To call attention to the existence, importance, and power of the group.
2. To discredit the ability of the regime currently in power to protect the people.
3. To force the government in power to use such repressive measures in retaliation that individual freedom will be curtailed and the people will rebel.

Even here in the United States, where individual freedom is an extremely important value, some people see signs of such actions. For example, in 1983 several members of the U.S. House of Representatives suggested a successor to the House Un-American Activities Committee (which carried out what many have called the ''witchhunt'' for Communists during the 1950s). The creation of a Subcommittee on Security and Terrorism is not necessarily a threat to individual freedom, but if the FBI is given too much leeway to investigate such groups, individual freedom may be threatened.

The effectiveness of an act of terrorism depends entirely upon the reaction to the act. It seems that terrorist acts have been most effective in calling attention to the group. Terrorism has, in fact, been called primarily an ''advertising'' activity. Pyotr

Beirut was once a prosperous city, but terrorist attacks, and the wars they caused, have reduced it to rubble. No one has been spared—innocent men, women, and children have been maimed and killed. Terrorism destroys everyone in its path. If the terrorists call attention to their cause, their goal has been achieved.

Alekseevitch Kropotkin, an ardent advocate of terrorism, stressed the "conversion" effects of such acts. "Through the terrorist deeds which attract general attention, a new idea insinuates itself into people's heads and makes converts. Such an act does more propagandizing in a few days than do thousands of pamphlets."[23]

Does this actually happen? We in the United States are aware of causes, issues, and groups whose actual political settings are thousands of miles away. We also have come to identify as "political" the acts of small groups of self-appointed political terrorists. When Patty Hearst was kidnapped by a group calling itself the Symbionese Liberation Army, some believed the group was fighting oppression; others saw it as a criminal kidnapping. In this country, the second goal has been a failure; no converts have been won through violence, nor has the government itself been discredited through acts of terrorism against it.

International Terrorism

According to the U.S. State Department, national governments conducted 140 terrorist incidents between 1972 and 1982.[24] In 1983 terrorism killed more people than in any year in recent history.

The effectiveness of terrorist attacks against military targets is becoming so great that it was labeled "Warfare on the Cheap" by the *New York Times*.[25] State-sponsored terrorism was defined in 1983 by the Department of Defense as "the unlawful use or threatened use of force or violence by a revolutionary organization against individuals or property with the intention of coercing or intimidating governments or societies, for political or ideological purposes."[26]

Some believe worldwide terrorism is in fact beginning to weaken the confidence of people in other nations that the United States or other Western nations can maintain an orderly society.[27] If terrorist groups continue to unite behind this purpose, these feelings of insecurity may continue to grow. It is to the terrorists' advantage to appear to be a worldwide network. When a crowd was machine-gunned at Israel's Lod airport in 1972, a great deal of publicity was given to the fact that the killers were a Japanese Red Army contingent trained in Mideast terror camps.[28] Such publicity is one of the major goals of the terrorists.

Combatting International Terrorism

As terrorism has increasingly become a worldwide phenomenon, counterterrorism programs have also developed. Elite units have been formed to battle terrorism. In West Germany, the Federal Criminal Office has built a computerized collection of 10 million bits of information about radical groups. This data bank has proven to be very useful in locating and arresting terrorists.[29] The system keeps track of such information as the complete description of the weapons and types of explosives used in terrorist attacks, personal data such as fingerprints, voice and handwriting characteristics, and descriptions of bullets and tools. When an incident occurs, all these factors can be analyzed and specific probable suspects can be located. For example, if a phone call is made saying that a bomb has been planted in a certain location, it might be possible to identify the voice, whose type of operation it most resembled, and to track down the people making the threat.

It has been suggested that the only way to discourage terrorists from operating on an international scale is to establish a firm international agreement that no nation would knowingly shelter terrorists. Given the current state of world affairs, it is unlikely that this will happen. As we have said, the acts of violence that are called terrorism are often viewed quite differently by different groups. Only total agreement that nothing justifies the killing and maiming of innocent people would be really effective.

It has also been suggested that worldwide agreement to refuse to even bargain with terrorists would cut down on their activity. This would not solve the problem, since in many incidents terrorists make no demands. Rather, their goal is to call attention to the terrorist group and its cause. This is why after an event such as a bombing, many groups wish to claim credit.

Perhaps if greater attention were paid to the many legitimate grievances existing in the world today, less terrorist activity would occur. If repressed and unjustly treated groups had a true forum to at least express their pain, then those groups still resorting to violence would be generally condemned. Today, while almost everyone deplores the violence used, many people are sympathetic to the cause some terrorists are representing.

Nuclear Terrorism

One of the most serious problems to emerge during the past few years has been the very real threat of nuclear terrorism. The combination of increased technological knowledge and the increasingly international nature of terror networks leads to the potential of the following hypothetical news story:

> On December 24 the White House received a letter stating that unless
> its demands are met, a terrorist group will explode a nuclear device in
> a major Eastern city.

What could we do? An entire nation could be held captive by a group that may or may not be able to carry out its threat.

Israel is in particular danger of nuclear terrorism. Already a prime target of Arab and other allied terrorist groups, Israel would be in grave danger if the leaders of a country such as Libya develop nuclear capability.

Almost every country in the world has ideological and ethnic groups unhappy with the government in power. While the United States does not have as many internal problems as other countries, it has assumed the leadership of the world's democracies, and it could therefore easily become a target of any group.[30]

WAR

It is becoming increasingly difficult to distinguish between war and terrorism. Often those engaged in terrorist activities define themselves as being "at war." Gwynn Nettler defines **war** as "an organized struggle among groups of individuals who recognize themselves as politically independent and morally justified in asserting their will violently."[31] This definition could include most terrorist activities. We will use the term *war* to refer to violent conflict between organized and independent nations.

Reasons for War

War was once a profitable and almost exciting activity. Such wars were fought by gentlemen soldiers in limited areas, for limited and realizable goals. About 190 years ago war tactics changed. "The advent of the French Revolution and the subsequent renovation of armies by Napolean initiated a process whereby war between nations became total involving not just the defeat of fielded armies, but complete destruction of the opponent's war-making potential."[32] Today, war includes the prospect of total destruction of civilization. We have seen the suffering of innocent men, women, and children continuing in the aftermath of even limited war.

War in America's Past and Present

It has been said that we are a nation that constantly flirts with the idea of war as a way of achieving our desired goals. "As a nation with a Minuteman tradition, a history of successful aggressive wars, and a love affair with weapons in general, the United States has enjoyed the added bonus of never suffering the invasion by a foreign power."[33]

Since 1775 the United States has been involved in nine major wars: the Revolution, the War of 1812, the Mexican War, the Civil War, the Spanish-American War, World Wars I and II, the Korean War, and the Vietnam War.[34] Despite domestic opposition to several of these wars, no widespread antiwar violence in the United States has occurred, although many isolated incidents connected with each of these wars have happened.

Americans' Reactions to Their Wars

Before the official outbreak of the Revolutionary War there were numerous violent outbreaks: the Boston Massacre and the mobbing of Stamp Act collectors are the best known. Most of these incidents were actually the acts of people taking sides in a civil war by defining themselves as Tories (wishing to remain part of the British Empire) or as Rebels (wishing to become an independent nation). They were not, therefore, true antiwar protests.

The Civil War sparked a great deal of domestic violence rooted in both antiwar sentiments and the taking of sides. Opposition to the draft was the major source of antiwar violence in both the North and South. The **conscription system** was extremely unfair. For example, in the North, if you had $300, you could buy your way out of serving in the Army. Public opposition to this practice exploded into violence in the New York City Draft Riot of 1863. No violent protest, before or since, matches this riot in size or destruction. Mobs with as many as 50,000 people fought with police, militia, and federal troops. As many as 1,300 people were killed.[35] Mobs not only turned against the government, but also viciously attacked Blacks, blaming them for the cause of Emancipation, which was the rallying cry for the North.

During World War I almost every case of violence occurred when patriotic mobs attacked opponents of the war. World War II was an entirely different situation. After the surprise attack by Japan, no opposition occurred as resources were mobilized to fight the war. Though there was a lack of consensus about our participation in the Korean War, little public opposition took place.

Our least accepted war was fought in Vietnam. As the war continued, fewer and fewer people believed in its legitimacy. After 1967 there were more and more acts of violence protesting the war. Antiwar demonstrators destroyed the property of those providing war supplies, and police turned increasingly violent in their suppression of protest.[36] Unlike all previous wars, with the exception of the antidraft riots of the Civil War, the war in Vietnam was accompanied by strong and violent protest, especially among young people. This action was without historical parallel, since young people in the United States had previously been a major source of patriotic sentiments.

The Special Case of Nuclear War

We have said that over time, war has changed from limited conflicts between armies of professional soldiers, who at least in part desired to defend the honor of their group or bring profit to it. As technology developed and the ambitions of nations grew, wars increased in scope and in human and material costs. Wars killed soldiers and civilians alike. Nations and peoples were devastated and destroyed. But "safe" areas have continued, countries and areas that have never been invaded by a foreign power. The United States is one of these places. Today with nuclear weapons, we face for the first time the prospect of a war having no safe places, a war that could totally destroy the world. Many nations already have nuclear capability and many more are on the brink of acquiring this deadly force (see Table 6.2).

TABLE 6.2 Widening Availability of Nuclear Devices

Countries That Have Built and Tested Nuclear Devices	Countries Believed Capable of Building a Nuclear Bomb	Countries That Could Have a Nuclear Bomb within Six Years
United States	Argentina	Australia
Soviet Union	Canada	Austria
Britain	West Germany	Belgium
France	Israel	Brazil
China	Italy	Denmark
India	Japan	Iraq
	Pakistan	South Korea
	South Africa	Netherlands
	Sweden	Norway
	Switzerland	Spain
		Taiwan

SOURCE: *Newsweek* (December 5, 1983), p. 56.

During the Vietnam war, antiwar protests took place throughout America. Even soldiers who had fought in Vietnam joined in protest marches. Fewer and fewer people accepted the war's legitimacy. Many groups considered it unpatriotic to be for the war, a situation without precedent in American history.

The survivors of a nuclear conflict will find a foreign environment: natural resources would be destroyed, the skilled operators and even raw materials needed to run society's complex machinery might be gone, and some regions might be uninhabitable due to high radiation levels. The society would suffer from an enormous psychological shock.

Surviving Nuclear War

Whether or not a strong civil defense program could effectively increase the chances of surviving nuclear war has been hotly debated. The argument has taken three approaches:

1. *The Scientific and Technological Level.* Those who feel civil defense is worthless argue that civilization would be totally destroyed by nuclear war and that nothing could protect against this disaster. Those who advocate a strong civil defense system say any attack would have varying levels of survivability and that we could increase the survival rate by building enough proper shelters for everyone.
2. *The Moral and Ethical Level.* The critics brand civil defense plans as dangerous since they indicate a war readiness that could provoke an attack. Advocates claim a responsible government must provide such protection for its citizens and that such preparedness would even deter an attack.
3. *The Strategic and Utilitarian Level.* Anticivil defense activists say no plan can work. Procivil defense activists maintain a workable plan can be found.[37]

Disagreement on these issues exists within and between nations. The Soviet Union, China, Switzerland, and Sweden have built extensive shelter systems; the United States has not.[38] Critics say the lack of shelters in the United States leaves the population more vulnerable since enemies know of the lack of protection.

Preventing Nuclear War

Peace movements have formed throughout the world. Many of these groups propose unilateral disarmament by their country. In other words, they propose that their country stop preparing nuclear weapons and destroy whatever weapons have already been developed. These groups argue that they only have influence in their country. If people in all nations pushed for unilateral actions, no nation would continue to prepare for war.

In sharp contrast are the groups arguing war can only be prevented by making their country so strong that no one would dare attack. They wish to increase defense spending and stockpile as many weapons as possible. Proponents of this school say that what deters nuclear war is not simply more weapons but a "protected strategic force that can strike back even if it is attacked first. Such a force removes that temptation to strike first."[39]

These group members argue that man has never succeeded in abolishing a human invention. The use of biological and chemical weapons has been restricted, but even these were used in Southeast Asia and Afghanistan.

The spectre of this fireball haunts us all today. The characteristic shape of the nuclear blast is familiar to even the youngest child. Since it is almost impossible to picture a "limited" nuclear war, the very word "war" implies the possible destruction of our world.

SOCIOLOGICAL PERSPECTIVES

We have examined the many forms of violence that both fascinate and horrify us. We have seen how tightly violence is interwoven into the social fabric. Why do husbands kill their wives? Why do terrorist groups bomb houses and department stores, kill and maim innocent men, women, and children? In trying to explain the prevalence of violence, sociologists use one of the four following orientations.

Individual Faults and Deviant Behavior

This approach defines all who commit acts of violence as being defective in some way. In other words, the assumption is that some people would commit a violent act and some would not. The ''just deserts'' model of criminologist Andrew Von Hirsch is based in part on the idea of predicting who is likely to commit a violent act. If an offender is considered likely to repeat that crime, a longer sentence results. One judgment a mental health professional is constantly asked to make is whether an individual is likely to be violent. Many therapists resent this attempt to make them agents of social control.[40]

Focus on an individual's potential for violence has led to the examination of the following questions:

1. What are the person's relevant demographic characteristics?
   a. Age (violence is greatest in the late teens).
   b. Sex (men tend to commit more violence than women).
   c. Social class (the lower the social class is, the more likely ''street violence'' is to occur).
   d. History of drug or alcohol abuse (such behavior seems to be associated with acts of violence).[41]
2. What is the person's history of violent behavior?
3. What are the current sources of stress in the person's environment?

These and similar questions are used to predict a person's future behavior. They are all based on the assumption that particular forces existing in the person's background and current situation might provoke deviant behavior, such as violence.

Those following this perspective would look at a terrorist's background to see how the behavior pattern developed: why he or she was drawn to violence.

Institutional Faults and System Disorganization

Sociologists working from this general perspective look at forces in the larger social system to explain violence. Their area of greatest interest is collective violence, or violence arising from conflicts among social groups such as Blacks and Whites, government and its citizens, or between any recognized groups. For example, the problem of violent crime in the streets would be approached by looking at the social conditions that have fostered it. In other words, violent street crime is provoked by social changes leaving our cities with large groups of unemployed citizens who do not recognize the police as legitimate agents of social control.

Violence, according to this view, primarily reflects underlying social maladies. These theorists assert that if the family, neighborhood, and criminal justice system were working properly, there would be no violent personal attacks. Agents of social control would prevent them.

Functionalists look at all social events in terms of their functional or dysfunctional consequences. For example, war has two positive functions: to create new nations by enlarging and solidifying borders; and to build solidarity within the society by uniting against a common enemy. The causes of war are, therefore, found in forces such as population pressures or the scarcity of resources forcing society to seek land to fulfill its needs. For the functionalist, social events are to be evaluated in terms of whether or not they fulfill some need of the social system.

Inequality and Inevitable Conflict

For the conflict theorist, violence is the natural and inevitable consequence of inequality and repression in society. Individual, national, and international violence can only be dealt with by eliminating oppression. People are forced into violent crime by the unfair distribution of resources and opportunities within society. The resultant stress and despair leads to violent acts. Violence is merely an extreme form of resolving social conflict. To understand violence, one must understand the distribution of power and how that power is exercised within the society.

Conflict theorists feel that society and most sociologists focus too narrowly on individual and criminal violence. This is both misguided and has dangerous effects. They think we frequently use our concerns about violence as excuses for repression and for the maintenance of overly powerful police and military establishments. How can we justify nonviolent solutions, they argue, when the government uses execution as a punishment, and extends its international influence through covert and overt uses of force?

Society's values and institutions encourage individual violence. The strong value on competition, profit, and winning at any cost, all promote the adoption of violent solutions. We are inconsistent in our definition of violent actions; only when carried out by an enemy, do actions become defined as violent.

Interaction and Social Interpretation

A key concept in symbolic interaction is that what people do depends on how they define the situations in which they are involved.

An extremely popular explanation for violent behavior has been the violence subculture hypothesis. In other words, a person behaves violently because he or she was taught proviolent values and attitudes. Proponents of this theory say this **subculture of violence** is worldwide and exists within many cultures. In this subculture, violence is the only appropriate response to a perceived challenge or insult. To react in any other way is to lose all respect for oneself. This hypothesis has not been empirically verified. In one study of inmates of a Michigan prison, no value differences were found when violent and nonviolent offenders were compared. In a study of violence in the sport of hockey, however, players who fought more, and received more major penalties, did have more proviolent value-attitude patterns than nonviolent players.

What people perceive is a selective process. We learn value orientations toward all objects in our environment. The member of the terrorist group is not attacking "innocent victims," but striking a blow at members of the oppressor group in the name of freedom or religion. In conflicts of all kinds, combatants form **contrast conceptions** of each other. For example, during the depression years following World War I, many insecure Germans constructed a negative image of Jews by attributing to them many of the traits they feared and condemned in themselves.[42] An extreme case of this contrast conception can be seen in times of war. "We" are strong, courageous, honest, and self-sacrificing, fighting only to preserve lives and freedom. "They" are cruel, aggressive, and unfeeling, fighting out of cruelty. It is often a shock to realize that as many Germans as Americans believed "God was on our side."

Definitions of others as "enemies" makes feasible atrocities that would not otherwise be tolerated. "Offing a pig" is seen as quite different from brutally murdering a young man who is in the process of performing his job. "Keeping society safe" is quite different from coldly beating an antiwar protester. Symbolic interactionists thus believe we cannot understand and explain any violent act without understanding how the act was defined by the aggressor.

The idea of contrast conceptions helps us understand violence that has occurred between lawbreakers and the police, labor and management, Blacks and Whites, or between nations. In each case, both sides defined the other as an "evil" that had to be controlled. Once such intergroup violence has begun, participants are swept along.

> Because men have fought so often only to discover afterward that
> their adversaries were not actually what they had thought, the question
> arises as to why we have not learned to act more intelligently. Bertrand
> Russell once noted that the one lesson we learn from history is that
> men do not learn from history.[43]

Our interpretation of what other world powers are doing and are capable of doing underlies our own preparations for war. Symbols and interpretations are central to human behavior. It we interpret information coming from the Soviet Union to mean they are building a new type of weapons systems, we may go ahead and build such a system ourselves. If they, in fact, had not planned to build such a system, our action might bring about action on their part that had not been previously planned.

THE FUTURE

Although the violent crime rate has declined slightly, the average American runs a higher risk of being the victim of a violent crime than of being hurt in an auto accident.[44] Nevertheless, crime continues to plague society. The urban violent crime rate is nearly twice that of suburban areas, and more than three times that of rural areas. Contrary to popular belief, the poor and the young, rather than the aged, are the most frequent victims of violent assaults. Though they are more fearful, women are half as likely to be assaulted as men.

Since the group committing the most criminal violence—males age 17 to 24—is becoming a smaller and smaller part of our population, we can look forward to further decreases in violent crime in the future.

Pessimistic Scenario

By the year 2025, random physical destruction and danger had become a daily part of life. The word ''violence'' had disappeared from common usage in about the year 2000 since it no longer symbolized an act all agreed was wrong. A few elderly people would try to describe the ''old days,'' when anyone who harmed anyone else or destroyed anyone else's property, or even threatened to, was called a ''terrorist'' or a ''violent criminal.'' They would tell of the days when society put such people in very expensive institutions called prisons, before it was recognized that any act could only be evaluated in relative terms: who did it and why.

Once society decided that ''eliminating'' disruptive people was the best solution to crime, prisons were abolished, saving a great deal of money. This money was instead used to build a total shelter system that could protect 70 percent of the population from nuclear attack. After years of debate as to how this shelter space should be allocated, a complex system was developed to assign each man, woman, and child in the United States a ''priority'' number. A person with a number above 30 would be allowed into a shelter in the event of a nuclear attack. The criteria used in the selection were physical health, intelligence as measured by standardized tests, and estimates of future contributions to society. More women were allowed in than men to ensure the continuation of the species. The ratio decided upon was one man for every three women. When the ratings were assigned, the Great Shelter Riot broke out, creating unprecedented waves of death and destruction throughout the nation.

Most of the larger cities have been eliminated. Decentralization was necessary because of the increase in what used to be called bombings by international terrorists. People were unwilling to enter large public buildings such as stores, restaurants, or even offices since these were often targets. The increase in terrorist attacks coupled with the increase in violent street crime caused most large businesses to seek more protective settings. Since the number of ''suicide'' terrorist squads is still increasing, even our ''fortresslike'' buildings with extremely limited access may not protect us much longer.

For years now Americans have recognized that physical force is a constant reality and would always be used by those who could. A panel of recognized experts devised guidelines for the ''Use of Force to Preserve a Healthy Society.'' It was decided that the phrase *Direct Physical Action* (DPA) should be substituted for the old term ''violence'' which had such negative connotations.

It was time for the United States, and indeed the world, to openly admit that talk did not always solve problems, that DPA was often called for. Forms of DPA were defined as:

1. *Heroic DPA*. Any act during a time of war that destroys an enemy or any resource needed by the enemy, resolving the longstanding debate as to what was heroism and what was a war crime.

2. *Strategic DPA*. Any act aimed at weakening a potential enemy's strength. This replaced the more negative, less accurate term of international terrorism.

3. *Official DPA*. Any act needed to subdue a person who is breaking the law.

4. *Protective DPA*. The execution of those considered dangerous.

5. *Spirited DPA*. Those acts needed to win a sporting event.

6. *Inventive DPA*. Those acts needed to make movies and television more entertaining.

7. *Criminal DPA*. Any act aimed at personal profit that does not benefit the nation or local government.

Optimistic Scenario

In 1983 the world began to recognize dangerous trends: the killing of Christmas shoppers in London by a group of terrorists is usually cited as the catalyst of this growing fear. All over the world, innocent people were being killed. Violence was becoming an increasing part of life, and fear was becoming a constant companion.

In 1990 came the first act of nuclear terrorism. Nuclear devices were placed in Washington, D.C., London, and Berlin. Fortunately they were disarmed before they exploded by excellent antiterrorist agencies developed by these three countries. This act, however, marked the turning point in definitions of the proper uses of violence. Recognition finally came that the dangerous concept of "the end justifies the means" could result in death and destruction for all. World leaders met and condemned *all* acts of violence and terrorism. The distinction among a "freedom fighter," "soldier," "terrorist," and "violent criminal" was eliminated. All acts of violence, for whatever reason, were officially pronounced criminal acts and any country assisting, sheltering, or not apprehending such persons was guilty of aiding in the commission of a crime.

Nations have cooperated in unprecedented numbers, and incidents of terrorism have been almost eliminated. The widely publicized pleas, discussions, and statements of so many world leaders condemning violence led to the reexamination of violence in every part of life. Although there will probably always be sociopaths and psychopaths who have no regard for their own or others' lives, violence against another person is never justified. Nothing is worth harming another person.

Enormous amounts of money have been spent not just on understanding the causes of violent behavior, but also in publicizing the reality of its aftermath.

Three factors led to the reduction of violent crime. The first was demographic and the other two were the result of improved interventions into social problems.

The population continued to age as the birthrate decreased. Fewer young males were available for the job market, and therefore fewer were left unemployed and subject to the pressures that might turn them to violent crime.

At the level of individual intervention, the accumulating knowledge on the cyclical nature of family violence led to techniques for interrupting its development. As family violence and the many forms of intrafamilial abuse were recognized as treatable social problems, people voluntarily sought therapy, as they now do for depression. This also drastically reduced the number of teenagers spreading violence from the home into the streets.

The educational institution also changed in its definition of violence and those who commit it. Instead of trying to ignore or suppress violence, these institutions now have taken on the role of identifying and referring children and their families for counseling. The violent children are no longer labeled and segregated into a separate track; they are helped.

SUMMARY

1. Americans hold ambivalent attitudes toward violence. We deplore violence while at the same time glorifying those who use it "in the name of the law."

2. The use of violent force to protect community values is part of American history. Organized groups taking the law into their own hands are known as vigilante groups. Although in the beginning it may appear to be the only solution to the absence of a legal system of social control, vigilantism can easily turn into a reign of terror.

3. Violence usually becomes a social problem only when it is directed against an innocent target and is carried out by an unauthorized agent.

4. From about 1960 through the early 1970s, crime of all types increased steadily until the highest point was reached in 1974. The crime rate held at this high point until the early 1980s and then began to drop off.

5. Two-thirds of all murderers know their victims. One-third of all murder victims are related to their killers, and the other third are killed by friends or acquaintances.

6. The relationship between possession of guns and crime is not clear-cut. We do know, however, that there is an increased use of handguns in homicides.

7. As in many crimes of violence, in almost 50 percent of all reported rapes, the assailant is not a stranger. The rapist and victim are usually of the same race, age group, neighborhood, and socioeconomic status.

8. Terrorism is the use of intimidation, coercion, threat, and violent attacks to achieve the objectives of an individual or of a group. Terrorism is becoming a greater and greater threat. As terrorism has increasingly become a worldwide phenomenon, counterterrorism programs have also developed.

9. Since 1775 the United States has been involved in nine major wars. Despite this, the United States has never been invaded by a foreign power. We have been one of the "safe" areas of the world. With the threat of nuclear war, we face for the first time the prospect of no "safe" areas.

10. The Individual Faults and Deviant Behavior emphasis defines all who commit acts of violence as being defective in some way. Those who follow this perspective examine the individual's characteristics and background in order to find the source of the violent behavior.

11. Functionalists look at all social events in terms of their functional or dysfunctional consequences. War is seen as having two positive functions: to create new nations by enlarging and solidifying borders and to build solidarity within the society by uniting against a common enemy.

12. For the conflict theorist, violence is the natural and inevitable consequence of inequality and repression in society.

13. A key concept in symbolic interaction is that what people do depends on how they define the situation in which they are involved. Symbolic interactionists feel we cannot understand or explain any violent act without understanding how the act was defined by the aggressor.

SUGGESTED READINGS

Barnet, Richard J. *Real Security: Restoring Power in a Dangerous Decade*. New York: Simon and Schuster, 1981. A comprehensive argument that national security cannot be thought of as merely a military problem, but one affecting all of society's institutions.

DeMaris, Ovid. *Brothers in Blood: The International Terrorist Network*. New York: Charles Scribner's Sons, 1977. Accounts of contemporary terrorist groups' organization, goals, and violent acts.

Elliott, John, and Leslie Gibson (eds). *Contemporary Terrorism: Selected Readings*. Gaithersburg, Md.: International Association of Chiefs of Police, 1978. Discussions of current terrorist threats and how best to combat them.

Goldstein, Jeffrey, H. *Aggression and Crimes of Violence*. New York: Oxford University Press, 1975. Discussion of the relationship between the human tendency for aggression and ways to reduce contemporary violence.

Harris, Marvin. *Cows, Pigs, Wars, and Witches*. New York: Vintage, 1974. Anthropological speculations on the origins of societal violence.

Rose, Thomas, and Paul Jacobs (eds). *Violence in America: A Historical and Contemporary Reader*. New York: Vintage, 1969. An historical context for current discussions by examining America's past and the violence of the 1960s.

Short, James F., and Marvin Wolfgang (eds). *Collective Violence*. Chicago: Aldine-Atherton, 1972. Excellent papers on the theory of violence, comparative perspectives, and the varieties of violence in America.

GLOSSARY

Assassination   The murder of a political enemy.

Conscription system   The way in which people are chosen to join the armed forces.

Contrast conceptions   Often done in war, the assignment of all good traits to one's own group and all bad traits to the enemy group.

Criminal terrorism   Use of the tactics of terrorism for personal gain.

Repressive terrorism   Use of the tactics of terrorism by the group in power.

Revolutionary terrorism   Use of the tactics of terrorism by a group hoping to gain power.

Subculture of violence   The concept of a worldwide subculture that teaches pro-violent values and attitudes, defining violence as the only appropriate response to a perceived challenge or insult.

Terrorism   The use of intimidation, coercion, threat, and violent attacks to achieve the objectives of an individual or group.

Vigilantism   The use of violent force to protect community values, justified by saying no other way exists to preserve that way of life; many cruel and ugly acts against innocent people have been committed in the name of preserving community values.

Violent crime   Crimes of violence such as robbery, rape, assault, and homicide.

War   An organized struggle among groups of individuals who recognize themselves as politically independent and morally justified in asserting their will violently.

Americans have always firmly believed in the abstract ideal of equality. From the stirring words in the Declaration of Independence affirming the self-evident truth that all of us are created equal, to the political rhetoric of today, we find abundant testimony to this fundamental value in our culture. Yet past and present realities offer not only contradictions to this stated ideal, but continuing patterns of inequality as well. How can this be? If our way of life is rooted in the concept of equality, why do extensive problems of unequal treatment and opportunity occur?

Social scientists offer varying theories and explanations for this divergence between the ideal and the real, and we shall discuss them in the following chapters. Whatever the reason, the presence of any form of inequality emerges as a social problem when the public becomes aware of the need to correct the social conditions exasperating people's expectations or denying them equal life opportunities. Until then, a rationalized consensus or ideology—a generalized set of beliefs—serves to justify the existing order, providing societal members with a comforting defense against the unpleasant realities refuting proclaimed statements about equality.

Chapter 7 examines the problems of growing old in a youth-oriented society. Greater longevity, social change, and emphasis on youth, beauty, and usefulness have combined to make old age a less venerated time of life than in past generations.

In Chapter 8 we discuss the more commonly recognized area of inequality: racial and ethnic minorities. Here we shall look at how the unequal treatment of minority groups pervades our social customs and our economic, educational, legal, and political institutions.

The problem of poverty draws our attention in Chapter 9, a topic often linked with minority groups. As with other social problems, we shall study its causes, impact, societal perceptions, and solution efforts.

Sexism, the topic in Chapter 10, is one of the most recently defined social problem areas. Our concern here will be with the growth of the feminist movement and the gender inequalities existing in today's society.

In reading the next four chapters you should look for elements common to the various topics discussed, such as widely shared public misconceptions, stereotyping, discriminatory actions, exploitation, and efforts to combat the problem. Note also how much of the difficulty lies in societal value orientations, not in inherent weaknesses of the victims.

THREE
CHALLENGES TO SOCIAL EQUALITY

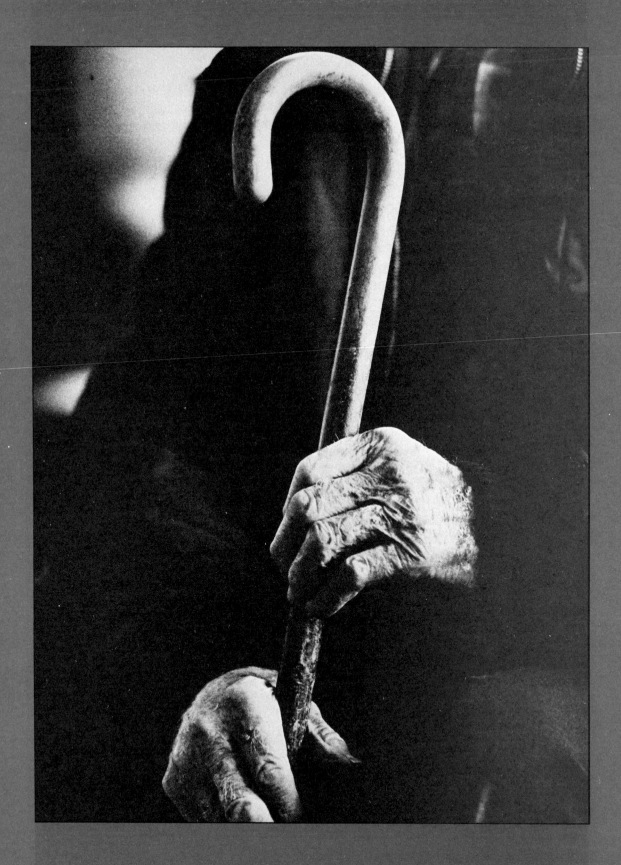

FACTS ABOUT AGING

Every day another 5,000 Americans reach the age of 65.

In 1980, 11 percent of the American population was 65 or older; within 50 years it will be 20 percent.

Mental health problems, including senility, affect only 15 percent of the elderly.

About 25 percent of the elderly live in poverty, but one-third Hispanic and almost one-half Black elderly are poor.

The elderly personally pay twice as much in health costs as do people under 65.

About 25 percent of the patients in nursing homes do not have to be there.

About 80 percent of all Americans die in an institution, away from family and familiar surroundings.

7
AGING IN A YOUTH-ORIENTED SOCIETY

Value systems about old age vary from culture to culture. The peasants of Abkhasia in the Georgian republic of the Soviet Union, and the peasants of Vilcabamba in southern Ecuador, both live long, healthy, and productive lives, the apparent result of their diet and high degree of integration at all age levels.[1] The West African Ibo elderly experience no psychosenility, indolence, or isolation, remaining important and productive members of their society throughout their lives.[2] The Confucian ideal of filial piety among many Asian peoples places their elderly in high social esteem. In Scandinavia extensive health care and social services have virtually eliminated social problems among the aged, although general feelings about their low status and obsolescence remain.[3] In contrast, the elderly in the United States often experience both lower status and greater deprivation, the result of modernization and cultural orientations.

Long a neglected segment of American society, problems of senior citizens have drawn increased public attention in recent years. Several factors explain this heightened awareness, including demographic changes in the population composition, increased group cohesiveness, and political clout among older citizens. In addition, more people now recognize the increased victimization of the elderly due to various social and economic factors, such as health-care costs, inflation, unemployment, urban decay, rising crime, and consumer exploitation.

THE GRAYING OF AMERICA

The U.S. Bureau of the Census has identified those 65 and over as the fastest growing group in the country. In 1900, 3 million persons (4 percent of the total population) were 65 or older; in 1980, this age group numbered 25 million (11 percent of the total). The number of senior citizens will increase even more dramatically in the future, as the "baby boom" generation of this century becomes the "senior boom" of the next. About 55 million people (20 percent of the total) will be 65 or older by 2030 (see Figure 7.1).[4]

Every day another 5,000 Americans reach the age of 65. Three-fourths of the population reaching that age live on the average for another 16 years to age 81. Because of the increasing proportion of older citizens in our society, social scientists now utilize two subcategories: those 65–74 and those 75 or older. In 1980, the 65–74 age group numbered about 16 million and the 75 or older age group numbered about 9 million. By the end of the century, 45 percent of the elderly will be 75 or older, and well over half of this group will be over 80.[5]

Demographic Factors

Three major reasons for the larger proportion of older people are increasing **life expectancy** (average number of years a newborn can expect to live), increasing **life span** (the maximum length of life possible), and declining birthrate. Reductions in infant mortality, improved nutrition, and advances in health care have significantly increased life expectancy. Boys born today can expect to live to be 73, and girls to be

FIGURE 7.1 Growth of the Older Population of the U.S.: 1900–2030

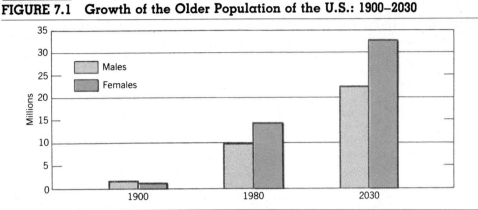

SOURCE: U.S. Bureau of the Census, reported in *America's Elderly: Policy Implications* (Washington, D.C.: Population Reference Bureau, 1984).

81, although the increased participation of women in the labor force may lessen this differential. Increased life expectancy has emerged through the medical profession's success in reducing major causes of death for those over 55 (open-heart surgery, coronary bypass operations, kidney transplants, etc.).

Since industrialization began in the nineteenth century, America's birthrate has been dropping, interrupted only in the 1940s and 1950s by the baby boom. Since 1972, we have experienced a 2.1 or lower birthrate which, if sustained over time, will result in **zero population growth**—a stable population size. This means a continued rise in the median age of the population, with fewer young people and a greater proportion of older people. In 1980, for example, the number of people over 60 exceeded the number of children up to age 10, as well as youths aged 11 to 19.[6] The median age has risen from 22.9 in 1900 to 30 in 1980, and it is projected to be 37 by 2030 (see Figure 7.2).

Some states—like Florida, Arizona, Nevada, New Mexico, and Hawaii—are rapidly increasing their proportion of senior citizens, who are attracted by the climate and recreational opportunities. However, fewer than 5 percent of the retired elderly move away to such locales, either because they cannot afford to do so or because they prefer to remain near family and friends. Sixty-three percent of Americans 65 or older actually live in metropolitan areas. Senior citizens also constitute the highest proportion of small town and rural populations and are least represented in suburbs. Many of the snowbelt states have the greatest percentages of the nation's older and poorer senior citizens, which places even greater demand in these economically depressed areas for economic, health, and social assistance for the aged.[7]

The dramatic changes in the nation's population structure affect all of us, both now and later when we ourselves are old. Some view the growing numbers of elderly as a burden to society, particularly in terms of cost of support services. Social security payments and other taxes increase for the nonelderly, while the elderly

FIGURE 7.2   Median Age of Americans, 1970–2030

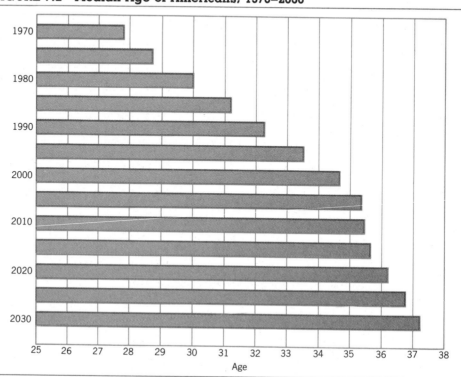

SOURCE: U.S. Bureau of the Census, reported in *America's Elderly: Policy Implications* (Washington, D.C.: Population Reference Bureau, 1984).

demand more of society's resources. Others see the increasing median age of the American people as a good sign that older people will achieve more power and a more respected status in society. In the meantime, we are experiencing a period of transition in which many aged, despite their growing numbers, often suffer negative attitudes, neglect, isolation, deprivation, and despair, as we shall discuss.

Values About Age

We can better understand the position of the aged in American society if we examine how the social construction of reality affects the perception of old people, as well as their own self-perceptions. The American people are products of a youth-oriented culture in which physical attraction, productivity, sexuality, usefulness, and worth are rarely attributed to the old. So pervasive is this orientation that it has resulted in **ageism**, the manifestation of prejudice, aversion, or even hatred toward the old.[8] Like the ideologies of racism and sexism, this generalized set of beliefs abounds in negative stereotypes, ignores individual differences, and assumes the subordinate status of the aged lies in a biological, rather than social explanation (see Box 7.1).

BOX 7.1

MYTH OF HELPLESSNESS

Who will speak for older people? Most effectively, older people themselves. "If I am not for myself," asked the Hebrew sage, Rabbi Hillel, "who is for me?"

And that would appear to be at least part of the problem. Many aging men and women do not appear to be for themselves. They have accepted stereotyping; they have accepted old age as a "condition of loss, a time to quit, a mandate to withdraw" (the quotation is from Dieter Hessel, editor of *Maggie Kuhn on Aging*). If ageism begins with lack of understanding, a negative perception of all those over a certain age, then to change that perception, people over a certain age have to have good and positive feelings about themselves, a positive self-image.

Ageism may not manifest itself in contempt. It may appear as kindness—professionals, family, friends of older people, all of them overprotective and overhelpful, making decisions for "grandma" or "grandpa" and thereby confirming their feelings of inadequacy, dependency, helplessness. The myth of helplessness and uselessness may feed on itself. . . .

One of the most destructive shibboleths about aging, most sociologists feel, is embodied in the concept of "appropriate behavior"—what kind of activities to attempt, how to enjoy leisure, even what colors to wear "at that age."

Prescribed behavior ignores differences and eliminates options. "At that age" the prescription may call for slippers and the rocking chair; but what if you'd rather go dancing? Or do what a group of over-65s in Chicago did: Though none had ever performed anywhere before, they formed an acting troupe to show audiences all over the country, in the words of one trouper, that "creative energy knows no barrier."

Or the 4,000 students over 60 (the oldest was 104) who enrolled in the Institute of Study for Older Adults financed by the New York City Department of Aging: "The most motivated people I've ever worked with," the Institute's director called them.

As for love and marriage and sex, at least one recent study has indicated that one of every four men and women over 75 remains sexually active. By conscious or unconscious ageist standards, however, it is indecent for "senior citizens" to be interested in sex, and ludicrous to think of love and marriage.

SOURCE: Irving R. Dickman, *Ageism—Discrimination Against Older People* (New York: Public Affairs Committee, 1979), pp. 20–22. Copyright © 1979 by Public Affairs Committee, Inc. Used with permission.

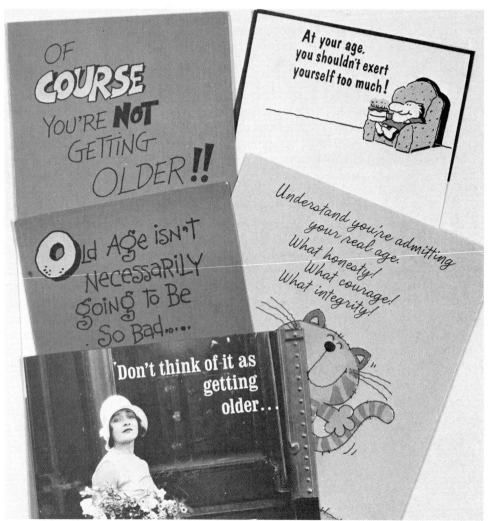

Humorous birthday cards may joke about losing physical or sexual prowess, but they touch on very real fears. Growing older in a youth-centered society often generates emotional crises for many adults. Some avoid the issue, others become depressed or seek to recapture their lost youth, while a few accept aging positively.

Changing Values

Rapid social change in industrial societies generated a shift in value orientations toward the aged. Preindustrial societies (including colonial America), rooted in tradition, had usually looked to old people as the source of wisdom and experience, deferring to their judgment on any problems facing the family or community. With a large **extended family** (two or more kinship families sharing economic and social responsibilities) and with property ownership generally passed on to the oldest male (primogeniture), older people were typically the more powerful and affluent. Industrialization and technology revolutionized the existing social order, bringing about the **nuclear family,** a unit of parents and their children living apart from other relatives. Land ownership was no longer the only main source of wealth. Increased mobility was possible, and one had to keep abreast constantly of new discoveries and developments to remain competitive.

Before the industrial age, the aged still worked, had clearly defined roles, were held in high esteem, and continued to make valuable contributions to the family and community. In an industrial society where one's work determines one's status or worth, people tend to view the aged as outmoded or obsolete, no longer productive, necessary, or important. The "Detroit Syndrome" whereby people, like cars, are assigned a limited useful life to be replaced by newer models (younger workers), is an unfortunate by-product of an industrial society coming to believe that "new" means "better."[9] As a result, age prejudice has been institutionalized in our society in laws, employment practices, advertising, media portrayals, and intergenerational interaction.[10]

Personal Fears

Our emphasis upon youth and our attitude toward the old play upon our own fears of growing old. When we are young we look forward to birthdays because they signify important milestones, such as beginning or ending a certain school level, getting a driver's license, or reaching the legal drinking age. Adults, in contrast, view birthdays less grandly and some often present a personal crisis. Becoming 30, 40, or 50 are difficult ages for many people to reach without some emotional distress. Most humorous birthday cards joke about being over the hill of physical and sexual prowess, and so help bring some degree of fear to birthdays.

In her highly popular book *Passages*, Gail Sheehy commented on the so-called midlife crisis between the ages of 35 and 45 that most of us experience:

> The middle of the thirties is literally the midpoint of life. The half-way
> mark. No gong rings, of course, but twinges begin. Deep down a
> change begins to register in those gut-level perceptions of safety and
> danger, time and no time, aliveness and stagnation, self and others. It
> starts with a vague feeling. . . .
>   *I have reached some sort of meridian in my life. I had better take a*
> *survey, reexamine where I have been, and reevaluate how I am going*
> *to spend my resources from now on. Why am I doing all this? What do*
> *I really believe in?*
>   Underneath this vague feeling is the fact, as yet unacknowledged,
> that there is a down side of life, a back of the mountain and *I have*
> *only so much time before the dark to find my own truth.*[11]

Advertising

Advertisers, in order to sell their products, continually reinforce people's uneasiness about growing older. Cosmetics, lotions, creams, baby oil, and even dishwashing liquid are marketed as products to smooth and soften skin and keep mothers looking as young as their teenage daughters. The "secret" of Oil of Olay, the "miracle" of

Porcelana, and the "magic" of Grecian Formula can help all of us be part of the "Pepsi Generation." When we are "past our prime," the commercials alert us to the apparent preoccupations of old age: constipation, irregularity, hemorrhoids, loose dentures, baldness, and "tired" blood.

Avoidance Responses

With apprehension and unspoken fears, many of us enjoy avoidance responses to cope with our growing older. We use euphemisms for old age ("senior citizens," "golden-agers") or death ("passed away," "resting," "reward"). We avoid contact with the dying as much as possible, even if we are doctors or nurses in a hospital.[12] Many of us also limit greatly our interaction with the elderly, perhaps because they are living testimony to a part of the life cycle we don't want to think about. As a result, age segregation is the fastest growing form of segregation in the United States today.[13] Singles, young married couples, older married couples, and senior citizens each tend to live near similar life-cycle cohorts. Consequently, people at different age levels interact with each other less and less frequently.

MYTHS AND STEREOTYPES

Closely interrelated to the prevalence of ageism in our society are the myths and stereotypes that are all too commonly believed. Because a society tends to address a social problem in terms of the generally accepted definition of the situation, examining both the false and accurate portrayals of the American elderly is important.

Mental Capacities

One of the most commonly held beliefs, and in large measure, responsible for much ageist prejudice and discrimination, is that advancing age occasions a decline in one's mental faculties. Intelligence, memory, and learning ability are thought to be less than they were in earlier years. "You can't teach an old dog new tricks" is the traditional folk saying. Old people are often thought of as senile, childlike, and out of touch with reality.[14] Such beliefs often result in discriminatory practices in hiring or promotions, or in a reluctance to train or educate older people in new areas.

Despite such popular notions, research studies—including longitudinal studies of the same persons over many years—show little overall decline in mental ability with age. Certain physiological changes may occur in one's outward appearance, and reflexes and responses may slow down a little, but intellectual capabilities remain constant or increase with age even into and past the seventies. Verbal comprehension, numerical skills, inductive reasoning, and the ability to organize and process visual materials are intellectual areas where older people develop increased capacities.[15] Other studies have revealed the elderly to be just as capable of learning as younger people, although the process may take a little bit longer.

The view that many seniors are senile and/or childlike is just not true. Mental health, primarily organic psychoses, is a problem for perhaps 15 percent of those over 65, but very few aged are senile. Those showing overt signs of senility can often be helped by treatment.

Sexuality

Another misconception about older people is that they are sexually inactive because of a lack of interest and/or ability. When an old couple marry, many people find it quaint or amusing and attribute the motivation to a need for companionship but not sexual fulfillment. Considering our youth-oriented society, it is not surprising that people mistakenly view the aged as asexual. Romance is for the young, sexual attraction means good-looking bodies, and having sex is a young person's "thing." Old people should "act their age," and if they don't, they're "dirty old men" or "sex-crazed old women." All forms of media reinforce this thinking through emphasis on young people in love. Older people, either because of their more conservative sexual values or societal disapproval, tend to avoid public displays of sexual interest in another person.

Recent research findings present a very different reality about sexual interest and capacity among old people. Masters and Johnson observed that men and women well into their eighties and beyond were physiologically capable of having a pleasurable

Enjoying love and companionship in one's later years is a commonly cherished goal. However, many incorrectly think sexuality among the aged is nonexistent. Studies have shown sexual fulfillment can continue well into one's eighties. Attitude, not physiology, is the major determinant of sexual activity.

sex life.[16] Other studies have also found no end point in sexual fulfillment for people in good general health in their later years.[17] The Duke University studies, begun in 1954 and still continuing, found much variability in sexual behavior among old people, depending in part on their marital status. Fifteen percent increased their sexual interest and activity as they aged, but unmarried women were almost totally inactive sexually. Approximately 50 percent of both sexes had sexual interest when they were in their eighties and nineties, with about 20 percent still sexually active.[18]

Sexuality among the aged is more a matter of attitude than of physiology. Those accepting their body changes due to the aging process can continue to enjoy sexual activity. Society allows men to age more gracefully than women, who are harshly judged as they experience a "humiliating (aging) process of gradual sexual disqualification."[19] As a result, sexuality remains an important component of the older man's self-esteem and self-organization, but when the older woman no longer feels attractive, her feelings of self-worth are diminished.[20]

Negative Attitudes

Research on young people's attitudes toward the aged generally indicate a negative tendency and the prevalence of stereotypes. Most children have few contacts with the elderly outside of their own families, and so their generalized perceptions of older people rest on the one-dimensional characters of old people and witches in fairy tales and children's stories. Studies of children up through sixth grade usually show this presence of stereotypical thinking. Children typically assign such positive traits as friendly, good, kind, and trusting and negative characteristics of sick, ugly, mean, and sad.[21]

Adolescents demonstrate almost totally negative values and attitudes toward the aged.[22] One study of high-school students, however, did show a majority holding positive attitudes about the elderly.[23] Generally though, adolescents hold negative views, which gerontologists continually find equally pervasive among adults as well.[24] It would appear various socializing influences shape one's attitudes toward the elderly more negatively as one grows older.

Not all people, of course, hold negative stereotypes. Various experiences during childhood and adolescence may form positive attitudes. What is important for our consideration is the frequency of the appearance of negative ones, and how these contribute to the lower esteem of older citizens. Moreover, such negative stereotypes may influence policymakers into selecting an inappropriate solution to an improperly perceived problem.

PROBLEMS OF THE ELDERLY

Being old in America does not necessarily have to mean facing many problems, and for a fortunate few this is the case. For the majority of older people, however, the prevailing negative stereotypes severely limit their life chances and create a variety of problems. Although chronic and debilitating illnesses eventually affect most old people, the major problems are actually economic and social in nature. A few of

Retirement parties serve as a "rite of passage" from an occupational to a leisure role in society. Some lose their sense of self-worth, having immersed their identities in their work, while others eagerly await the chance to enjoy their free time. Career and economic security are key factors affecting attitude.

these problems emerge from the personal adjustments needed in the transition to this later stage of the life cycle, but most result from societal attitudes and practices.

Retirement

Only the last two generations of Americans have faced the promise or problem of retirement. Earlier workers, with shorter life spans and performing mostly manual labor, worked until they died. Scientific advances, technology, and education have generated greater longevity as well as a changed labor force. About 80 percent of workers are now in tertiary occupations—the white-collar or service jobs—and only about 20 percent are self-employed. These changes mean different attitudes about a lifetime of work by both employers and employees.

Certain occupations—firefighters, police, and military personnel, for example—partially attract people by their 20 or 30 years and out policy. Some people—especially professionals, managers, and specialists—tend to prefer later retirement, perhaps because of greater intrinsic satisfaction in their work. Still other workers, mostly blue collar, tend to retire before the mandatory retirement age. Retirement clearly has many meanings to potential retirees: an end of self-worth, a new beginning, a well-deserved rest and opportunity to enjoy life, a change of careers, two paychecks, or a chance to do what one really wants to do.

Present and Future Retirees

Since the 1950s, labor force activity among older persons in the United States has declined significantly (see Table 7.1). Early retirement has caught on rapidly for males, but females have gone against this trend. Since 1947 the number of women aged 55 to 64 in the labor force has doubled to over 42 percent.[25] This pattern probably reflects changing attitudes about women working, allowing both widows and mothers of grown children to seek jobs with employers eager to hire them. Employers can also downgrade jobs, hiring women at lower wages.

Retirees age 65 and over today have a median educational attainment of only 9 years, and only 15 percent have attended college.[26] Workers with such educational backgrounds tend to retire early because their jobs usually hold little intrinsic satisfaction for them. Moreover, they worked in a era of far less leisure time and face a more difficult adjustment to using their free time, particularly since they are less likely to enjoy reading or self-improvement learning activities.

The next generation of retirees will be better educated, in better jobs, and accustomed to shorter work weeks and more leisure time. They will probably adjust more easily to retirement and enjoy it more, but will also be more likely to postpone retirement. The question of mandatory retirement may thus become an even more important issue than at present, since many older workers presently retire early or willingly at age 65.[27]

Mandatory Retirement

Proponents of mandatory retirement argue that it opens up jobs and promotion opportunities for younger people, minorities, and women. Companies maintain it enables them to employ people with new perspectives while simultaneously humanely removing deadwood. Opponents maintain this act of expulsion is ego shattering and socially dislocating for individuals whose identities and friendships are dependent on their work activities.

TABLE 7.1 Labor Force Participation Rates of Older Workers by Sex, Annual Averages, Selected Years, 1950–1979

| | Men | | Women | |
Years	Age 60–64	Age 65 Plus	Age 60–64	Age 65 Plus
1950	—	45.8	—	9.7
1955	82.5	39.6	29.0	10.6
1960	81.1	33.1	31.4	10.8
1965	78.0	27.9	34.0	10.0
1970	75.0	26.8	36.1	9.7
1975	65.7	21.7	33.3	8.3
1979	61.8	20.0	33.9	8.3

SOURCE: U.S. Department of Labor, Bureau of Labor Statistics, *Monthly Labor Review,* November 1980.

Is mandatory retirement a serious and extensive problem? Many think so and call forced retirement at a certain age arbitrary and discriminatory. Many jobs, people argue, can be performed until a very advanced age. Such indiscriminate action toward all old people, regardless of their physical and mental abilities, is unfair, often reduces their standard of living, and further strains the social security system. In response to these concerns, Congress passed the 1978 amendments to the Age Discrimination in Employment Act, raising the allowable age for mandatory retirement, in most cases, to 70, and completely eliminating an age maximum for federal employees.

What impact this legislation will have is uncertain. Prior to its passage, studies using several data sources (National Council on Aging, Louis Harris 1974 Survey, National Longitudinal Study, Retirement History Survey, and Social Security Surveys of new beneficiaries) indicated that only 5 to 10 percent of retired workers were forced to retire.[28] A Department of Labor study in 1979 revealed only about 1 in 35 retired men (and an even smaller proportion of women) age 60 and over said they wanted work.[29] In contrast, a 1979 Harris survey identified nearly half the retirees questioned saying they preferred to be working, and more than half said they would have preferred to keep working rather than retire.[30] Part of the difference in the findings can be attributed to the type of questions asked about realistic and hypothetical work options available. Few job modification opportunities (part-time phased retirement) are available and the types of jobs available are likely to be dissatisfying low-skill, low-paying ones. Many choose retirement because they do not wish to remain in the same dissatisfying jobs, but unable to find more satisfying employment, they retire.[31]

Retirement presents more of a problem for some people than for others. Psychologists have identified it as one of the 10 most stressful life events for individuals.[32] Differences in individuals and life circumstances will heavily influence the ease or difficulty in adjustment. Those adapting to the loss of a major role by finding workable substitutes in personal relationships, leisure activities, and self-fulfillment will fare better.[33] Another difficulty with retirement is reduced income either dropping people into or near the poverty level, or else making it difficult for them to cope with inflation and meet expenses on a fixed income. One study found about a third of retirees have difficulty adjusting to retirement, mostly for the two reasons just mentioned.[34]

Economic Problems

Most people over 65 experience a drop of one-third to one-half in income, sending many into poverty for the first time. Unfortunately, their reduced income is not offset by fewer expenditures. No longer working means less clothing and transportation expenses, but the elderly pay a greater proportion of their fixed income for food, housing, and health care than younger people. Those who own their own home usually have the mortgage paid off, but taxes, energy, and maintenance costs place heavy demands upon many elderly with limited incomes. Renters, especially older women living alone, may pay as much as 35 percent of their income for housing.[35]

Employment

Even before retirement age, older workers are often victims of job discrimination. Companies prefer to hire people under 40, and unemployed workers above that age experience great difficulty finding new jobs. The 1967 Age Discrimination in Employment Act was intended to protect workers aged 40 to 65, making it illegal to advertise positions with age restrictions or to deny employment for reasons of age. In practice, however, employers can easily circumvent the law by stating older workers are "overqualified" because of their extensive experience or "underqualified" because of their educational background.

Most of the 2 million senior citizen males and the 1.1 million females still in the labor force are working in low-paying, white-collar and service jobs. More seniors would work part-time to supplement their income if they could, but available job opportunities do not match their needs. In addition, social security recipients under age 72 who work have their benefits reduced by 50 cents for every dollar earned in excess of $230 a month. The purpose of this economic penalty is supposedly to discourage work competition between pensioners and younger workers, but it also serves to keep many within or near the poverty level.

Poverty

About 25 percent of all elderly live near or below the poverty level, and the elderly are disproportionately represented among all poor households. Not unexpectedly, women and minorities are heavily overrepresented among the elderly poor. Almost half the aged Blacks, including 60 percent of the aged black women, are among the poorer population segments. The older Hispanic population has one-third its number living in poverty.

Generally speaking, the economic position of the nation's elderly has improved somewhat. In 1970 one out of four elderly persons was living below the poverty line, but improvements in social security benefits reduced the number of elderly poor. Today 15 percent live in poverty compared to the national poverty rate of 12 percent.[36] Another 60 percent of the elderly—or 35 million—would fall below that line without social security. In a 1981 Harris survey, 17 percent of the elderly regarded lack of money as a "very serious problem."

Social Security

Although intended to provide only the base of retirement income, social security has become the sole source of financial support for millions of Americans (see Figure 7.3). Approximately 50 percent of all income the elderly receive comes from social security; 10 percent comes from private pensions, and 10 percent from interest on retirement savings. Thirty percent of the elderly depending almost exclusively on social security benefits have incomes below the poverty line.[37]

Despite dramatic increases in private pensions over the last 30 years, these cover only 20 percent of the elderly, and usually offer very low benefits. Social security accounts for more than 75 percent of the $9.1 billion in retirement benefits paid monthly in this country. In 1982 the average retired worker received a monthly social security check of $419—not very much to live on.[38]

FIGURE 7.3 Income of the Elderly

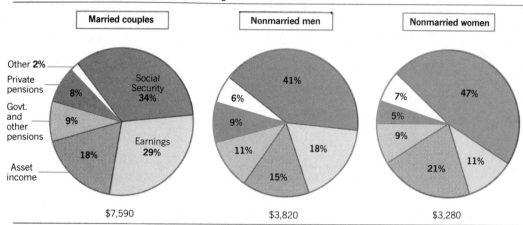

NOTE: Median income 1978. Other includes public assistance and other income sources.
SOURCE: U.S. Department of Health and Human Services, Social Security Administration *Income of the Population, 55 and Older* (Washington, D.C.: U.S. Government Printing Office, 1979).

Social security presents several problems. Besides offering inadequate benefits in its unintended role as sole source of income for one-half of the elderly, the amount of benefits vary according to the worker's past earnings. Those working poor, particularly minority workers who often earned less because of job discrimination, also thereby receive less than others when they retire. Another inequality of benefits is that many working married women receive no more in benefits than if they had never contributed to the system, because of what is known as the "dual entitlement" rule (full benefits to the head of the household and less to the dependent spouse).

Contributors to social security are also penalized if they are lower paid workers. Because the deduction is a fixed amount (6.7 percent of the first $34,500 of salary in 1984), low and moderate income workers pay a larger proportion of their annual income in social security tax than high income workers. In fact, about half of all Americans pay more in social security taxes than they pay in income taxes.

Another very serious problem confronting social security is that the ratio of retired to active workers (the **dependency ratio**) is increasing. This places greater pressure on the whole system, as the social burden for providing adequate retirement income falls upon a decreasing number of active workers. At present, three workers pay social security taxes for each retiree, compared to 35 in the late 1940s. The future ratio depends heavily upon the age at which workers retire in the years ahead. As Figure 7.4 shows, the dependency ratio changes significantly as the typical retirement age increases. If 65 remains the typical retirement age, then the dependency ratio will change from about 26 percent in 2000 to about 42 percent in 2050. However, if increased longevity, inflation, and the changes in the mandatory retirement age encourage most people to retire later in life, then the dependency ratio will remain relatively stable at about 27 percent with a typical retirement age of 70.

FIGURE 7.4   Projected Dependency Ratios

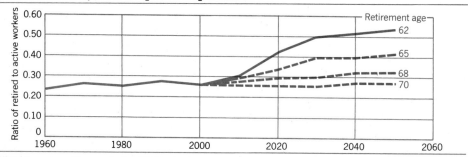

NOTE: Based on Census Series III Projections.
SOURCE: U.S. Office of Management and Budget, *Monthly Labor Review,* November 1980.

Social security is an excellent example of how policymakers have created an illusory solution and then defined the problem in terms of that solution. As supplemental income, elderly welfare, or insurance against unexpected income loss (disability, death of a spouse), social security fills a critical need. However, it is not a pension plan. Pension plans pay high returns for the money invested because they are advance-funded with money set aside, earning interest, instead of the social security pay-as-you-go system. Since older people presently receive far more benefits than they pay in and today's college-educated workers will most likely receive far less than they pay in, social security is in reality an income transfer and welfare system.

Disillusionment about social security is becoming more widespread with repeated federal efforts to restore its stability. Only in 1984 did the federal legislators who repeatedly voted the payroll tax increases, and the bureaucrats in the Social Security Administration who run the program, become paying contributors to social security themselves. Until then they had instead belonged to a federal retirement pension program.

Other Government Support

Since 1974 the Supplemental Security Income (SSI) program has brought some limited financial help to about 8 percent of the elderly not covered by social security. These public assistance monthly payments offer a maximum of only $208 a month for an individual and $312 for a couple with no other income. This amount is far below the national poverty line, but does prevent total destitution for these elderly.

Some elderly people, perhaps out of pride, refuse such public welfare assistance, while others are unaware of or unable to claim benefits. The Population Reference Bureau identifies one-tenth of today's elderly as functionally illiterate and two-thirds without a high-school diploma. This lack of education is often a handicap to learning about benefits and overcoming the paperwork and bureaucratic hurdles built into many assistance programs.

The Gray Panthers give vivid testimony that old people are not useless. The combined efforts of its members have wielded considerable political clout, helping shape legislation favorable to their needs. Recently they widened their activism, such as in this antinuke rally in New York's Times Square.

Housing

As you would expect, the housing accommodations of the elderly are closely inter-twined with their economic situation. For at least 30 percent of the elderly, reported a U.S. Senate Committee on Aging, housing is "substandard, deteriorating, or dilapidated" because that is all they can afford. Yet government housing for the elderly, begun just in the mid-1950s, now provides housing for only 3 percent of the aged. Another 25 percent live with one of their children, but the remainder live alone or with a spouse, most commonly in decaying urban neighborhoods or in isolated rural regions.[39]

The elderly tend to remain at home more, to be less mobile and therefore more dependent upon others for services and transportation. Adequate housing, therefore, means not only the physical comforts of one's home, but its location in a safe environment with sufficient nearby medical services, as well as recreational, shopping, and other social opportunities. For most elderly, unfortunately, such a residential situation is not theirs to enjoy.

Concentrated primarily in the north central and southern regions, the rural elderly (almost 30 percent of the total elderly population) experience perhaps the greatest deprivation.[40] They most likely lack health services and live in older substandard, poorly insulated, poorly heated dwellings. Because of low population density, the rural elderly also tend to live isolated, lonely, and limited lives.

Sixty-three percent of Americans 65 and older live in metropolitan areas.[41] Although far more facilities and services are available than in rural areas, the elderly do not necessarily live in neighborhoods near to them. Their reduced income and mobility, and also their vulnerability to street crime, make them less likely to enjoy available urban opportunities. Often living in deteriorating neighborhoods, urban life for many elderly is a combination of insecurity and subsistence. For the 7.8 percent suburban elderly, housing problems usually center on meeting rising property taxes, fire insurance rates, and maintenance costs, as well as getting around, since many do not drive and public transportation is quite limited in the suburbs.[42]

Health Care

A primary concern of the elderly is health care, since they experience greater health problems than other age groups. Although a substantial majority of people over 65 are in reasonably good health, the Public Health Service reports that 86 percent had chronic illnesses. However, these chronic conditions—including visual impairment, heart conditions, diabetes, arthritis, asthma, and hypertension—usually have little or no interference with their mobility or activities. Only 5 percent of the elderly population is institutionalized, with about another 10 percent too sick to care for themselves.[43]

Using chronological age is a convenient means of categorizing, but wide variations exist in the aging process among individuals and in their self-concept of being "old." Sixty-five is an arbitrary age used to define socially the beginning of old age, but one's body does not begin to fall apart because a person reaches that age. Most people 65–74 are healthy, active, and have a positive self-image. Serious physical decline and illness becomes a greater reality from age 75 onwards. Thus, the degenerative processes of aging result in more days of incapacitation, trips to the doctor's office, or stays in hospitals.

Stress, most people agree, definitely ages people and it has been shown to cause various illnesses, including coronary heart disease and stroke. Through use of a rating scale for measuring stress within a year's time period, researchers have found that the most serious life crises had the most serious effects on health.[44] Some of the life-crisis events requiring the greatest amount of coping and social readjustment are ones more likely to occur among the elderly: death of spouse, death of close family member, personal injury or illness, retirement, change in family member's health, change in financial status, death of close friend. Apparently, older people become more susceptible to serious illness, at least in part, because of the toll exacted upon their body systems from the more frequent high-stress life changes they experience.

Medical Expenses

Although at present they comprise 11 percent of the total U.S. population, the elderly represent one-third of the hospital population and use one-fourth of the prescribed drugs. Their medical expenses are three times greater than those of middle-aged adults and six times greater than for young adults, yet the income of the elderly is usually far less than that of young and middle-aged adults. Medicare and Medicaid programs have greatly reduced the personal health costs to the elderly, but since they do not cover all expenses, the elderly average twice the personal health costs of those under 65.[45] We should also note as well older people disproportionately fall victim to medical quackery.

With increased age, older people also become less mobile, driving themselves less because of high automobile costs, including insurance, fuel, and maintenance as well as the infirmities of old age. Many therefore become more dependent upon others to travel to clinics, doctor's offices, and hospitals. Physicians tend to take less interest in treating elderly patients because of ageist biases, their preference for more challenging cases with dramatic cure possibilities, and their lack of preparation in geriatrics. Many physicians never had a course in geriatrics in medical school; the number of geriatrics specialists on medical school staffs today is minute.[46] Few in the medical profession are oriented or prepared to treat elderly patients, nor are they likely to be in the near future, despite the growing numbers of elderly and the fact that they presently comprise one-third the hospital patients.

Nursing Homes

Considerable controversy exists over using nursing homes and the quality of care that patients receive within them. People from cultures where age is venerated and the extended family still commonplace—such as among Asians, Native Americans, Cubans, and other Latin Americans—are dismayed at the tendency of many native-born Americans, particularly middle-class Whites, to place the elderly in nursing homes instead of caring for them at home. American societal values, however, stress the nuclear family (parents and dependent children) living apart from other family members. In addition, the growing egalitarianism within families and the high cost of living have resulted in many women working nowadays and thus unable to stay at home caring for aged relatives.

BOX 7.2

A LITANY OF ABUSES IN NURSING HOMES

Of all the hearings before state and federal bodies since about 1972, perhaps the greatest impact on public consciousness—and conscience—came from the 1974 revelations of the Subcommittee on Long-Term Care of the U.S. Senate Special Committee on Aging. The Subcommittee compiled a shocking "litany of abuses" nationwide, a record "replete with examples of cruelty, negligence, danger from fires, food poisoning, virulent infections, lack of human dignity, callousness and unnecessary regimentation, and kickbacks to nursing home operators from suppliers." The variety of wrongdoing is numbing: "gang visits" by doctors to multiple patients, sometimes seeing only the medical records, not the person; failure of physicians to respond to emergencies; widespread abuse of tranquilizers; insufficient or tainted food; excessive use of physical or drug restraints; theft of residents' funds; untrained, inadequate, and sometimes sadistic staff; the lack of activities, the lack of privacy, and—most important—the lack of human dignity.

A few specific illustrations:

Food figured frequently in testimony. At a Minnesota home, when insects were found in the cereal, the head nurse ordered it fed to the patients anyway. At a Chicago home, one patient's uneaten food was transferred to a second (and sometimes to a third) patient's plate; a Chicago home that spent 54 cents per patient per day on food was topped by another that spent only 37 cents.

A Florida witness reported physical restraints such as ropes and chains being used on people in nursing homes. Chemical restraints are used even more fre-

Still, the question remains: Are nursing homes a necessity or a dumping ground? Numerous studies have shown that at least 25 percent of the nursing home patients do not need to be there.[47] Some observers see this fact as illustrative of ageism in our society as we put out of sight and out of mind those uncomfortably reminding us of our own future decline.[48] When we institutionalize people, the prolonged exposure to the same stimulus results in a systematic reduction in their alertness and attentiveness as well as in other detrimental effects.[49] When Americans place the elderly in nursing homes as an action of early resort and not last resort, they are most likely accelerating their aging process and mental decline.

Another important concern is the quality of care in nursing homes. While thousands of the nation's 23,000 nursing homes have fairly good, patient-oriented services, it is also true that greed, negligence, and widespread abuses exist in a great many others. Understaffing is a serious problem, resulting in most patient care rendered by poorly prepared and poorly paid aides and orderlies, whose turnover rate is high. Indiscriminate drugging to keep patients docile, physical abuse, inattentiveness to patient needs (washing, assistance in eating, laundering, incontinence or

quently: a Minnesota nurse, according to testimony, deliberately increased sedative doses (sometimes by stealing sedatives from other patients) to quiet rambunctious patients.

In a sampling of 75 homes (average age of residents, 79), 40 percent of the residents had not been seen by a doctor for more than three months. Most medications were prescribed over the phone: the fact is that 80 to 90 percent of all medical care and supervision in these homes were provided by untrained aides and orderlies. Many of these workers were literally hired right off the street and paid the minimum wage. Turnover: 75 percent.

Perhaps the worse abuse reported was lack of any activity at all. "On warm days," a member of the Ralph Nader Task Force on Nursing Homes reported, "the patients were wheeled up to the front porch . . . to watch the cars rush by. . . . A few watched an unfocused television, while others . . . stared absently at the opening and shutting of the elevator door."

The New Jersey Nursing Home Commission's three-year study, released in September 1978, cited patients left sitting on toilets hours at a time, and some even fed lunch there . . . a patient "restrained" by being tied to a towel rack . . . a meal at which 16 slices of cheese were to be divided among 21 patients . . . roaches in a bedside cabinet . . . male and female patients nude and exposed. Perhaps worst of all, operators were permitted to continue running homes for years after such abuses were reported.

SOURCE: Irving R. Dickman, *Nursing Homes: Strategy for Reform* (New York: Public Affairs Committee, 1979), pp. 2–4. Copyright © 1979 by Public Affairs Committee, Inc. Used with permission.

aid in going to the bathroom), unnecessary use of physical restraints (being tied to a chair for hours) are, unfortunately, quite common (see Box 7.2).

According to the Senate Special Committee on Aging, a large portion of American nursing homes have major deficiencies in sanitary conditions and fire safety.[50] In 1978 the House Committee on Aging reported widespread kickbacks of nursing homes with physicians, pharmacies, and medical suppliers to defraud the government and patients, as well as the presence of organized crime in the ownership or operation of many nursing homes. Mary Mendelson, one of the leading critics of nursing homes, has reported that some spend as little as 78 cents a day to feed each patient.[51] Poor diet, neglect, lack of stimulation and human interaction, and inadequate care combine to bring about physical decline, depression, injury, and a prison-like, waiting-room-for-death atmosphere.

Many of the nursing home abuses are the product of an ill-conceived social policy and ineffective government regulation. Since 1965, Medicare and Medicaid payments have covered almost all nursing home expenses. With little accountability and virtually no state enforcement of minimum standards, nursing home owners and

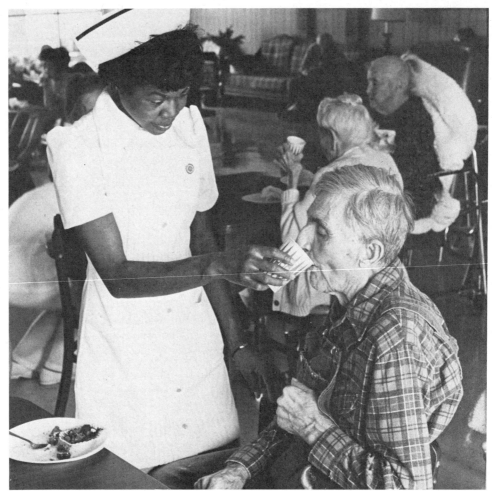

Quality of care in the nation's 23,000 nursing homes varies greatly. Many, such as this one in Charlotte, Tennessee, provide good, patient-oriented services. Others accelerate the aging process through depressing atmospheres, neglect, lack of stimulating activities, poor diet, and indiscriminate drugging.

operators—with little or no knowledge of gerontology or health care—can make huge profits through padded bills, hidden charges, and cut corners on expenses (food, heat, staff, etc.). The number of nursing homes has mushroomed since 1965 as the government-guaranteed payments have created an industry apparently more interested in profiteering than in care and concern for the elderly. Those facilities are neither "homes" nor do they offer much that could be called "nursing."

Public indifference toward these abuses probably stems in part from a desire simply not to know about an aspect of life we would rather not face ourselves. Secondly, the oft-quoted figure of only 5 percent of the elderly in nursing homes misleads us into thinking such a fate really awaits only an unfortunate few. However, studies have shown that while only 4–5 percent of the elderly may be in a nursing home at any one time, about three-fourths of all old people die in one.[52] If we live long enough to reach old age, we are far more likely to spend the last part of our lives in a nursing home. Awareness of that reality may spur the nonelderly into corrective measures before they too are trapped in a noncaring nursing home.

Death and Dying

In the youth-oriented culture of American society, death has become a subject to be avoided in thought, word, or interaction with a dying person. We put the dying elderly in a bureaucratic care institution away from us with the rationale their death will therefore be more dignified and painless. Instead dying is usually more stressful for both patient and family. Numerous studies have shown doctors and nurses avoid normal contact with dying patients as much as possible; they offer them little emotional support, and treat them as less than full human beings.[53] Four out of five people today die in some type of institution away from family and familiar surroundings, often feeling lonely and rejected. (see Box 7.3)[54]

In the presence of a dying person, visitors frequently feel embarrassed and pretend that death will not occur. Hospital staff and relatives often conspire to maintain a **closed-awareness** context, in which patients do not learn of their impending death, in contrast to an **open-awareness** context in which they are told the truth. Much research has shown that the great majority of terminally ill patients prefer the open-awareness context and that they benefit from it by being able to approach death with peace of mind instead of depression and worry.[55]

In recent years **hospices** have become an increasingly popular means of allowing terminally ill patients to die at home with family and friends. This institutionalized program—through which hospitals offer outpatient services of nurses, physicians, and counselors in home–health care—is actually a return to the practice of just two generations ago when the dying passed away in their beds at home amidst their loved ones. Facing death as a natural consequence in this way offers "death with dignity" to the individual and enables family members to accept the death more easily. Dying at home allows the patient to remain an individual, with some sense of place and meaning, instead of experiencing depersonalized treatment and possible neglect in a health-care institution.

Exploiting the Elderly

Age, physical weakness, and dependency upon meager fixed incomes result in the vulnerability of many elderly to exploitation by family or strangers. Most older people do live relatively stable and secure lives, but others nevertheless suffer abuse, constant fear, and victimization.

Child abuse and wife beating have become recognizable social problems, and Americans are now becoming more aware of the problem of battered aged. Beneath the façade of a loving family and home environment lies the reality that the depen-

BOX 7.3

SUICIDE IN THE LATER
YEARS

Recently in Toronto an elderly suicide victim was discovered. Not unusual, you say. Perhaps, but he had lain dead in his own house for sixteen months before anyone thought to investigate. While normal services continued—the mail was delivered, the lawn was mowed—he lay in his house beside his unread suicide note, a silent witness to isolation and indifference about his person.

The fact that research interest in suicidal behavior infrequently focuses on the elderly in our society bespeaks a similar attitude of indifference. Though public attention is often pointed to the increase in youthful suicides, it is still true that in general suicide rates are higher among older age groups. Those over 65 years of age, though they represent only 8.7% of the population, account for 10.6% of all suicides (Statistics Canada, 1976; 1978). In Canada in 1976 the annual suicide rate for men aged 65 and over was 73% higher than the general population. Between 1976 and 1978 the number of reported suicides increased 34.1% among older persons. These data acquire added significance with the projection that by the year 2001, 12% of the Canadian population will be 65 years of age and over, and their number will have risen to 3.3 million from the present 1.8 million (Schwenger, 1977).

These prospects, based of official statistics, are disturbing enough but they significantly underestimate the true magnitude of the problem of self-destruction among the elderly. While, as Jack Douglas (1967) and others have emphasized, the validity and reliability of official suicide statistics generally leave much to be desired, officially reported suicide rates among the elderly present special problems of underreporting. Because officials resist the certification of a death as "suicide" when alternate causes are plausible, older people, suffering from potentially fatal health problems, are more often incorrectly certified when death occurs by suicide. Furthermore, in recent years, the increased proportion of older persons who reside in institutional settings may contribute to greater underreporting. Those responsible for the care of the elderly in such institutions, both staff and attending physicians, may be understandably hesitant to report self-inflicted deaths that occur under their care. Further, given the high rates of morbidity and death from natural causes, there would be greater opportunity to conceal evidence that points to suicide.

SOURCE: George K. Jarvis and Menno Bolt, "Suicide in the Later Years," *Essence 4* (1980): 145–148. Reprinted with permission.

dent elderly adult may be a source of emotional, physical, and financial stress to their children.

> Much of this battering takes the form of benign neglect—inadequate knowledge about caring for the elderly which results in harm. Tying an elderly kin, who needs constant watching, into a bed or chair in order to complete housekeeping or shopping; or the excessive use of sleeping medication or alcohol to "ease" their discomfort or make them more manageable are common forms of this abuse. Other documented abuse is, however, lacking any such benign neglect. The reported battering of parents with fists and objects to "make them mind" or to change their mind about wills, their financial management, or signing of other papers, is, unfortunately, a growing phenomenon.[56]

Urban elderly are potential crime victims, especially those living in decaying neighborhoods. They are often unable to move away because of limited income and emotional ties to the area in which they have long lived. Their physical inability to repel attackers, intimidation by bullies, poor eyesight, failing health, reluctance to testify, and the relative ease with which they can be confused on the witness stand, encourage the criminal element to take advantage of them. Still, despite extensive publicity about urban elderly crime victims, they are actually less often victimized than other age groups.[57] Nevertheless, they often live in constant fear of becoming a victim.

Both urban and suburban elderly often fall victim to various flim-flam activities regarding medical cures, health aids, home repair, and swindle schemes. Their naïveté about these age-old con games, their susceptibility to the apparent friendliness of strangers as they live primarily in a world of social isolation, and their gullibility about "get-rich-quick" schemes because of their meager incomes all contribute to their vulnerability.[58] The elderly are easy marks for the con artists because the old are too trusting of people who seem to bring a welcome respite to their lonely lives.

SOCIOLOGICAL PERSPECTIVES

Instead of simply examining the statistics and data about the aged and the problems they face, social scientists attempt to formulate a theoretical framework in which to understand the causes and possible solutions to the social situation. Our four theoretical viewpoints once again offer different approaches to these insights.

Individual Faults and Deviant Behavior

Ageism, like the other prejudicial ideologies of racism and sexism, identifies a group as inferior to others in society. Once a generalized belief exists that older people are inherently less than others in usefulness and ability, a society tends to behave in a fashion to make that belief a social reality. It becomes easy for others then to blame old people for their problems. For example, how often have you heard someone say,

"What else do you expect from someone that old?" Such comments reinforce the notion that aberrant behavior is normal among older people. If a younger person is in a cross mood, one expects it to be temporary; when an old person is in a cross mood, many attribute it to old people being typically "crotchety."

Bad moods are perhaps the least important faults assigned to old people. As you have read, many people blame old age for a variety of things: diminished intellectual capability and flexibility, loss of beauty, of sexual desire, and of effectiveness. Because old people do not function as the nonold, their perceived lessened abilities are deviant from the "contributing" members of society. Through this view the problems with old people result from their inability to function in the mainstream of human behavior. They have worn out their value to society.

When society blames other victims for social problems—the poor, minorities, criminals, cities, and so on—corrective measures are still attempted even if they are misdirected. Old age, on the other hand, cannot be reversed or corrected. No value changes in the elderly or job preparation or behavior modification will be the solution if others believe diminished mental and physical ability is part of being old. Better to "put them out to pasture" than endure their "incompetence" and "intransigence." This perspective ignores the many accomplishments of people in their golden years: political leaders, Supreme Court justices, artists, musicians, philosophers, inventors. The list of creative, energetic, and active people who have made significant contributions in their later years is practically endless. Another problem with this view is that it ignores individual differences, creating a negative generalization about old people and grouping them as a subnormal entity. Most important, this perspective fails to consider how a socially defined reality creates many of the problems old people face.

Institutional Faults and System Disorganization

The functionalist view emphasizes the tendency of a society to maintain stability. Lack of equilibrium is then the basis for understanding the elderly's problems. Rapid social change has created social disorganization and dysfunctions in society concerning the elderly. The lower birthrate and longer life span have resulted in a greater proportion of older people than ever before, but they have fewer functions to perform in an industrial society. Gone are their respected roles as senior members of the extended family, and as we have seen, societal attitudes and social policy have built in an obsolescence to their occupational roles. Within this context we may consider two major conflicting theories in social gerontology: activity and disengagement.

Activity Theory

This dominant theoretical perspective holds that people of all ages require adequate levels of social activity to remain well adjusted. In the 1940s the writings of Ernest Burgess, one of the first social gerontologists, identified a lack of social functions as the reason for the needless exclusion of the aged from socially meaningful activity, resulting in their having a "roleless role."[59] Activity theorists maintain that if new activities replace those an aging individual is forced to give up, that person is more likely to be better adjusted mentally, physically, and socially.[60] Such newfound

Finding meaningful roles for the elderly enhances their self-esteem and life experience. The volunteer work of this surrogate grandmother at a day care center in Berkeley, California, gives her a sense of satisfaction while simultaneously providing a valuable service to a young working mother.

roles, suggested Arnold Rose, might be found through the creation of a subculture of older persons.[61] Such a group cohesiveness could lead to mutually supporting roles and activities.

Disengagement Theory

In contrast, this school of thought argues that the usual and even inevitable pattern is for people to become more passive and decrease their activity as they reach old age.[62] To maintain optimal functioning, a modern society requires persons with new skills and energy. So a mutual withdrawal occurs, its times and form dependent on the individual. Social interaction and social ties weaken as society seeks out "new blood" and aging individuals recognize their own diminishing capacity and seek escape from the stress of daily life encounters.

The disengagement theory has been heavily criticized.[63] This controversy has stimulated much research, some of which supports the theory while most does not. Some aged do disengage, but studies have demonstrated that disengagement is not inevitable with old age.[64] Society is more likely to withdraw roles from the aged than they themselves are likely to relinquish them. Perhaps Robert Atchley most effectively made this point in his comment, "Disengagement is not what most older people want. It is, however, what older people get."[65]

Inequality and Inevitable Conflict

Conflict theorists focus upon the elderly as a disadvantaged minority group, suffering at the hands of the rest of society. The social stratification hierarchy is comprised of various age groupings competing with each other for limited social resources. For example, younger people benefit from new job or promotion opportunities because of mandatory retirement practices. Government assistance in financial aid for college students, low-cost day-care centers, restraints on property taxes, or improvements in Medicaid or social security benefits are each of more importance to different age groups.

In industrial societies middle-aged people dominate the control of the social resources, holding a disproportionate share for themselves. This age inequality results in discrimination against the elderly similar to that against other minorities. A false ideology (ageism) justifies this structured social inequality for biological reasons (mental and/or physical inability of old people to perform meaningful economic or social roles). Consequently, the elderly are victims of negative stereotypes, unequal opportunity, job discrimination, criminal actions, and disproportionate high rates of poverty.[66]

From this victimization and tension, conflict theorists suggest, come organized social movements and political action to challenge and correct the inequality. For more than a quarter of a century, the elderly have formed organizations, hired lobbyists, and attempted to use political clout upon elected officials. Their political actions in 1981, for example, dealt President Reagan his only major legislative defeat in his first year in office, forcing him to withdraw his plan to reduce social security benefits.

Interaction and Social Interpretation

People learn social behavior in interaction with other people and through this interaction they form self-concepts. In old age, however, individuals experience a lack of reference groups, role loss, and vague or inappropriate information about acceptable actions. These social conditions deprive the elderly of feedback concerning their identity, roles, behavior, and the general value to their social world.[67]

Western society stigmatizes old people largely because of the persistence of the work ethic and the measurement of personal worth in terms of social utility. Older people, suggest behavioral scientists J. A. Kuypers and Vern L. Bengston, develop an increased dependence on current external cues because of diminished ego strength, uncertain identity, lack of role models, and specific norms. Told directly they are incompetent or obsolete, they internalize these negative societal attitudes and adopt the obsolete role assigned to them. In this role they learn new appropriate behaviors and skills, which means weakening their previous work and social skills. This negative cycle of events then intensifies as the elderly become even more susceptible to feelings of uselessness, which society or even other family members help reinforce (see Figure 7.5).

FIGURE 7.5 Social Breakdown Syndrome Model

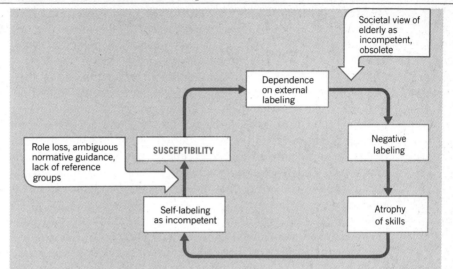

SOURCE: J. A. Kuypers and Vern L. Bengston, "Social Breakdown and Competence: A Model of Normal Aging," *Human Development* 16 (1973): 181–201. Reproduced by permission of Albert J. Phiebig, Inc., White Plains, New York.

This model is known as the **social breakdown syndrome;** it shows how societal definition of the situation results in the social reconstruction of reality, causing negative changes in the individual's self-concept. To break this cycle of events, Kuypers and Bengston believe that intervention needs to be focused on changing societal attitudes, especially in terms of work determining personal worth. Another possibility is helping the elderly develop greater self-confidence and coping mechanisms through their own self-determination. Improving the conditions of aging (health care, housing, and financial security) would also improve self-perception.

THE FUTURE

What kind of old age awaits the readers of this book some 40 or 50 years from now? Just as life is dramatically different now from your grandparents' prime years, so too will it be changed when you are one of the elderly. Let us once again make some projections of present-day tendencies through different manipulations of some of the variables affecting social problems of today's elderly.

Pessimistic Scenario

By 2025 the position of the elderly had deteriorated into a far more serious social problem than in the late twentieth century. A number of factors had contributed to this situation, but one of the most significant was the rebellion years earlier of young and middle-aged adults against the costly social programs for the aged. The increasing dependency ratio of retired people to workers made the costs of social security, Medicaid, Medicare, and other support programs too prohibitive. A taxpayers' revolt and government cutbacks because of budget crises, coupled with increased demands due to the growing elderly population, resulted in a grossly inadequate support system for the elderly.

Affirmative Action and other civil rights legislation had finally occasioned gainful employment and a decent standard of living for all racial and ethnic groups. However, the rapid social change—including the continuing knowledge explosion, technological advances, and full-blown effects of the computer age—only accelerated human obsolescence in the labor market. What jobs had not been assumed by computers required people with better reflexes or alertness than the elderly were thought to possess. Consequently, if the elderly were able to find work at all, and most did not, it was in such low-paying, low-status jobs as domestic servants, custodians, or sales clerks.

Segregated housing for the elderly was commonplace. The fortunate few lived clustered together in condominiums or retirement villages but most eked out an existence in decaying urban neighborhoods, which were the only low-rent areas they could afford. The stigma attached to living in such undesirable, high-crime areas further reinforced the prevailing ageist stereotypes. The nonelderly could not understand how people would want to live that way. They avoided going to these depressing areas of society's nonproductive element, and hoped they themselves did not live to see the day they became so uscless and uncaring about their own lives and environment.

Like many minority slum dwellers of the twentieth century, the twenty-first-century elderly living in urban ghettos led lives of apathy and despair. With little hope for improvement, shunned by the rest of society, and struggling to survive from day to day, the nation's elderly kept mostly to themselves and endured the unsympathetic attitude of the rest of society. Resources were becoming too scarce, medical expenses too high, and the cost of living too high to ''waste'' the allocation of limited goods and services on those who had already ''lived a full life.''

Life expectancy was not so long as it had been in the late twentieth century. The suicide rate was now much higher among both the elderly and those approaching old age. Reduced health care had also resulted in an increase in the mortality rate among the elderly, as did the inadequate diets among the large population of elderly poor. Government funding cutbacks had decreased the number of nursing homes; most of those which remained were places to be dreaded, not anticipated. To be old in America was a fate worse than death, so many preferred the latter.

Optimistic Scenario

Delayed retirement until 70 or even later had stabilized both the labor market and the costs of social benefit programs for the elderly by 2025. Zero population growth had been attained and the ratio of retired people to workers was now holding constant. With so many occupational tasks accomplished through computer terminals in one's home, the elderly—who had spent most of their adult lives working with computers—continued working in this capacity without having to travel back and forth to a separate place of work. For those fully retired, company pension plans and individual retirement plans like IRA or Keogh had brought financial security to most of the nation's elderly.

Later retirement kept many older Americans in important decision-making positions in both government and business. Political action groups such as the Gray Panthers and American Association of Retired Persons had succeeded in getting legislation passed that provided increased benefits and protection for the aged. Organized and active in civic matters, the elderly exerted considerable political power.

Medical advances had eliminated many of the debilitating aspects of old age, such as arthritis and rheumatism. Old people now most often died peacefully of natural causes without being incapacitated for prolonged periods. As a consequence, they remained far more mobile throughout their lives, socially interacting on a regular basis with friends and relatives. Videophones, electronic communications systems for shopping, information, counseling and outside contacts, as well as home entertainment systems, all brought the world to one's door. Social isolation was no longer a significant problem.

Operating fully in the mainstream of society, the elderly in their later years enjoyed economic, political, and social power. As had previously happened to many of the nation's minority groups when they assimilated, the elderly no longer suffered from negative stereotyping and discrimination. In fact, their secure position and retention of power brought about a shift in value orientations. The elderly once again held high status, as in preindustrial societies, and others admired them for their accumulated wisdom. Their counsel was eagerly sought and their advice heeded, as were their decisions obeyed.

Their economic security enabled the elderly to live in dispersed residential patterns, if they chose, interacting fully with other age segments. Some did live in senior citizen communities, but most preferred to remain away from such segregated facilities. Death in a nursing home was now a rarity, since the veneration of age and the status the elderly enjoyed no longer allowed shutting them away in a depersonalized institution. The hospice movement had grown to such an extent that dying in familiar surroundings with loved ones around was the usual occurrence.

The golden years of life had truly become golden. One could reflect upon the life experience with greater satisfaction than in earlier generations and enjoy the present as the end of life approached. Death was no longer a welcome respite from harsh reality, nor something to be feared. Death was, as Kübler-Ross had said two generations ago, simply the final stage of growth.

Conclusion

Both scenarios are possible, of course, or some midground between them. Social problems of age may continue much as they are today, worsen considerably, or be eliminated. Faith in the evolutionary process of social improvement, or in technology to solve these problems, is not enough. The degree to which the social problems discussed in this chapter will be resolved rests far more heavily upon the recognition by the nonelderly that these problems also affect them and are ultimately their own problems. Values, attitudes, and social policy will set in motion the real future of the elderly in America.

SUMMARY

1. A declining birthrate and increased life expectancy are steadily raising the median age of the U.S. population. Only 4 percent of the population was 65 or older in 1900, but the figure was 11 percent in 1980 and will reach 20 percent in 50 years. Whether this continuing increase of old people will be a burden to society or a gain in their status and power is unclear.

2. Our youth-oriented culture has resulted in ageism, the manifestation of prejudice, aversion, and discrimination against older people. Industrialization helped bring about a value shift from high esteem for older people to a "Detroit Syndrome" mentality, in which people now tend to view older people as outmoded or obsolete.

3. One consequence about our value orientations about age is our own increasing fear of getting older. Advertisers play upon this fear to sell their products, intensifying the conception that age means loss of beauty and acceptance. Many of us, including medical professionals, even avoid contact with the dying. Most also minimize their interaction with older people, making age segregation the fastest growing form of segregation today.

4. Studies have consistently proven false the popular belief that advancing age means lessened intellectual and sexual capability. Very little mental decline actually occurs, and senility is the exception, not the norm. Sexuality is more a matter of attitude than physiology. People in their eighties can remain sexually active, although marital status and self-esteem are important variables. Studies also show the increasing prevalence of negative age stereotypes from young children to adolescents, which shows the effects of social conditioning.

5. Retirement presents a stressful life experience for many people in terms of self-identity and reduced income. Some label mandatory retirement arbitrary and discriminatory, while others argue its advantages in opening job and promotion opportunities for others and pumping "new blood" into organizations.

6. Workers over 40 often experience job discrimination despite legislation against such practices. Those over 65 suffer a drop of one-third to one-half in income, sending many into poverty for the first time. About one-fourth of all older people live in or near poverty, with women and minorities disproportionately represented.

7. Social security provides about half of all income for the elderly, and for 50 percent it is their only income source. Never intended as a sole income source, social security is an inadequate retirement income. Additionally, its funding is in jeopardy because of its pay-as-you-go system and the increasing dependency ratio of retired beneficiaries to taxpaying active workers.

8. Rural elderly are most likely to live in poorly heated, poorly insulated, substandard dwellings. Urban elderly often live in decaying neighborhoods, vulnerable to

street crime. Suburban elderly encounter problems of property taxes, maintenance costs, and mobility.

9. More subject to health problems as they age, seniors personally pay twice the medical expenses compared to those under 65. Considerable evidence shows nursing homes are often dumping grounds, with at least 25 percent of the patients unnecessarily placed there. Serious problems of abuse and neglect exist in many of these nursing homes, which are highly profitable enterprises with their government-guaranteed payments.

10. The hospice movement offers a promising alternative to the current practice of four out of five people dying in an institution, away from family and familiar surroundings. Maintaining a closed-awareness context to a dying person is usual, even though an open-awareness context is more beneficial for everyone.

11. Some people have a tendency to blame old people for their situation in that they have outlived their usefulness. Functionalists view the imbalance as resulting from the rapid increase in large numbers of old people, and shifts in occupational role needs; activity theory emphasizes the need for new roles to replace old ones, while disengagement theory holds that both society and the individual mutually withdraw activity interactions. Conflict theorists believe the old are an oppressed minority, while interactionists stress the susceptibility of the aged to societal labeling.

SUGGESTED READINGS

Atchley, Robert C. *The Social Forces in Later Life,* 3d ed. Belmont, Calif.: Wadsworth, 1980. An excellent introduction to social gerontology, providing a solid understanding of the social aspects of aging.

Barrow, Georgia M., and Patricia A. Smith. *Aging, Ageism, and Society.* San Francisco: West Publishing Company, 1979. A highly readable and comprehensive look at the impact of values and beliefs on policy and practice toward the aged.

Butler, Robert N. *Why Survive? Being Old in America.* New York: Harper and Row, 1975. A clear, compelling, well-written account of the problems of old people by an expert advocate of social policy for the aged.

Kübler-Ross, Elizabeth. *On Death and Dying.* New York: Macmillan, 1969. A classic work by one of the most influential writers in the field, this is essential reading for anyone interested in aging or death.

Mendelson, Mary A. *Tender Loving Greed.* New York: Knopf, 1974. A devastating exposé of the fraud and exploitation of old people by nursing homes, with vivid examples of the abuses by profiteers.

Sheehy, Gail. *Passages.* New York: Dutton, 1976. An intriguing, eye-opening study of the characteristics and crises at different stages of the life cycle that most of us experience.

GLOSSARY

Ageism   The manifestation of prejudice, aversion, or even hatred toward the old.

Closed awareness   Not informing a patient of impending death.

Dependency ratio   The proportion of retired workers to active workers.

Extended family   Two or more kinship families sharing economic and social responsibilities.

Hospice   Institutionalized outpatient care and counseling, allowing terminally ill patients to die at home with family and friends.

Life expectancy   The average number of years a newborn can expect to live.

Life span   The maximum length of life possible.

Nuclear family   A unit of parents and their children living apart from other relatives.

Open awareness   Informing a patient truthfully about impending death.

Social breakdown syndrome   A negative cycle of events wherein ageist labeling leads to obsolete self-definitions and adoption of that role.

Zero population growth   A stabilized population in which the number of annual births equals the number of annual deaths.

FACTS ABOUT RACE AND ETHNIC RELATIONS

Eighty three percent of white students graduate from high school, compared to 72 percent of Blacks, and 55 percent of Native Americans and Hispanics.

About 700 bilingual programs in 68 languages are now taught in schools.

Illinois, Michigan, New York, and New Jersey have the most intensely segregated schools.

Black unemployment has been twice that of Whites for 25 years.

Native Americans have a suicide rate twice the national average and a death rate from alcoholism seven times greater.

In 1982, 35.6 percent Blacks lived in poverty compared to 12 percent Whites.

Over 80,000 illegal aliens are caught monthly, which is only one in three.

8
RACE AND ETHNIC RELATIONS

The United States is the greatest receiving nation in the world. It has accepted over 50 million immigrants since 1820, and presently accepts over 400,000 new immigrants annually. Because of such a continuous influx of diverse peoples, race and ethnicity have long been significant factors in American culture concerning identity and social acceptance. All minority groups have experienced some degree of prejudice and **discrimination,** but some have been less successful than others in overcoming these barriers.

Why do some groups "succeed" while others do not? Why are some groups able to climb the socioeconomic ladder more quickly than others? What prevents other groups from getting ahead? There has never been a shortage of answers to these questions over the years, though most of these answers have been too simplistic or lacking in objectivity. In this chapter we shall examine various patterns of intergroup relations in an effort to understand both the complexity and irony of the minority experience in the United States.

INSTITUTIONALIZED DISCRIMINATION

One of the most difficult problems in race and ethnic relations is **institutionalized discrimination.** This term refers to differential and unequal treatment of a group or groups deeply pervading the social customs and institutions (economic, educational, legal, and political).

This differential treatment is often not motivated by prejudice, but instead flows from dominant group assumptions about the abilities and role of a minority group in the society. Because such practices are built into the structure of a society, the discrimination is subtle and informal, and therefore less obvious to the societal members. The actions are neither deliberate nor caused by hatred, so they are not as easily recognized for the discriminatory acts they really are. It all seems so normal and "natural."

For instance, a white child growing up in the South in the first half of the twentieth century did not have to be taught prejudice against the Blacks. All that was necessary was to observe the situation. Blacks could not use the same parks, playgrounds, drinking fountains, restrooms, restaurants, waiting rooms, or railroad cars. They rode in the back of the bus only, attended different schools, and usually dropped out of school early. They lived in shanties, tenements, or substandard housing on the back streets. They were found only in low-status, low-paying jobs, and frequently were arrested for drunkenness, brawling, or more serious crimes. To that white child who grew into an adult, it seemed rather apparent that the Blacks were an "inferior" group. Few then realized that the social problems regarding the Southern Blacks were the results of patterns of discrimination, not from weakness within the Black minority.

The preceding capsule portrait—with certain variations—could just as easily be drawn of many other minority groups in America, both past and present. The people and times may change, but the patterns continue and the blame usually falls on the victim rather than the society which unintentionally caused the situation. We shall now look at four specific areas of institutionalized discrimination: education, employment, housing, and legal justice, as they affect some of today's minorities. Other areas of inequality—ageism, sexism, and health care—are discussed in Chapters 7, 10, and 14, respectively.

Education

From the time Thomas Jefferson first advocated mass education for an enlightened citizenry to the present, America's approach toward education has been different from that of the rest of the world. Instead of a quality education for only the economically and/or intellectually elite, this country's orientation has been to provide a full education for everyone, though it has not been completely successful in doing so. Still, deeply ingrained in American culture is the faith in education as the route to upward mobility and better socioeconomic status than one's parents.

As a major societal institution, however, the education system has not been impartial in the kind of education offered all children. Social class and cultural biases are built into the schools. Middle-class values of order, discipline, self-control, and deferred gratification place at a disadvantage the lower-class child whose family environment usually encourages freer emotional expression, less self-restraint, and immediate gratification. Most schools no longer deliberately attempt to strip away ethnic identity as was common practice just two generations ago, but cultural biases in textbooks, language, examples, and even time do exist.

This bilingual class in Dallas looks peaceful enough, but such programs generate considerable controversy. Opponents argue that the programs, staffed by poorly trained people who are themselves deficient in verbal skills, are too costly and hamper assimilation. Supporters insist that such programs ease adjustment and accelerate learning.

For some, the schools are an alien world, and they feel self-conscious and inadequate. If sensitive teachers do not take corrective action, the alienation of these students leads to their dropping out (see Figure 8.1). Those remaining in school often do not achieve as well as other students, partly because of environmental influences and partly because their teachers' low expectations for them offer little motivation to do better. Concerted efforts have brought about increased enrollment of racial and ethnic minorities in colleges in recent years, but as indicated in Figure 8.2, these groups still trail behind Whites at all levels of educational attainment.

Desegregation and Busing

Mixed results in achieving desegregation have occurred since the 1954 Supreme Court ruling struck down desegregated schools. In January 1983, the Joint Center for Political Studies in Washington, D.C. sent a requested report to Congress, citing significant progress against desegregation in the South. The number of Blacks attending "intensely segregated" schools with over 90 percent minority students had dropped from 68 percent in 1963 to 33 percent. Atlanta and Washington, D.C., in contrast, continued to have the fewest white students among the nation's 50 largest urban school districts. In contrast, Illinois, Michigan, New York, and New Jersey have the highest percentage of Blacks in schools with over 90 percent minority students. The report also identified the worst segregation problems to be in most northern and western urban centers, notably Newark, New York City, Chicago, Philadelphia, Washington, D.C., Detroit, and Los Angeles. The greatest percentage drop from 1968 to 1980 of white students attending schools with Blacks occurred in Sacramento and Anaheim, California. The report found school busing did not contribute to white flight from city schools, but that instead the changes reflected socio-economic factors and value orientations about suburban living.

Part of the difficulty of achieving less segregated schools has been residential patterning. Many Whites have moved from cities into the suburbs, leaving large concentrations of Blacks and Hispanics in urban neighborhood clusters. One desegregation effort—use of "magnet schools" offering intensive instruction in specific

FIGURE 8.1 High-school Dropout Rates, 1980

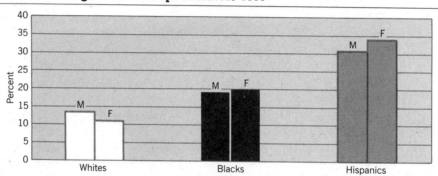

SOURCE: U.S. Department of Education.

FIGURE 8.2 The Education Pipeline for Minority-Group Students

Graduate from high school		
Whites		83%
Blacks		72%
Chicanos		55%
Puerto Ricans		55%
American Indians		55%

Enter college		
Whites		38%
Blacks		29%
Chicanos		22%
Puerto Ricans		25%
American Indians		17%

Complete college		
Whites		23%
Blacks		12%
Chicanos		7%
Puerto Ricans		7%
American Indians		6%

Enter graduate or professional school		
Whites		14%
Blacks		8%
Chicanos		4%
Puerto Ricans		4%
American Indians		4%

Complete graduate or professional school		
Whites		8%
Blacks		4%
Chicanos		2%
Puerto Ricans		2%
American Indians		2%

Percent of Cohorts

SOURCE: Ford Foundation reported in *Chronicle of Higher Education* (February 3, 1982), p. 11.

areas like science or fine arts, attracting students from all school districts within a school system—has been somewhat successful in cities such as Buffalo, Los Angeles, and Milwaukee. Another approach, redrawing school district boundaries to achieve a better racial balance in the schools, has also had limited success, since it is constrained by geographic and demographic realities. The lines can only be changed so much within a given territory, and the population composition already there may not alleviate the situation too much.

Busing has been the most utilized solution to ending segregated schools. In many cases, this was a voluntary and even cooperative effort—as in Cleveland—and desegregation through busing was achieved with little difficulty. However, busing efforts in some areas, whether a local decision or court ordered, have resulted in

Americans have long believed in education as the best means to upward mobility and improved living standards. Although minority children have been victims of cultural and social class biases in the schools, today we see positive signs of greater educational achievement among all minority groups, although problems remain.

considerable controversy, intense resentment in affected neighborhoods, and even violence. While not the only community to experience such negative reactions, South Boston emerged as representative of the backlash to forced busing. A court-mandated busing plan in 1974 became a volatile issue as Whites feared both a lowering of academic standards and loss of community control and neighborhood identity. The result was massive and sometimes angry demonstrations and occasional violence and stoning of buses, requiring police escorts to protect the busloads of black children coming into the white neighborhood schools. Today about half the district's 57,000 students are bused, but white enrollment in the public schools has dropped in 10 years from 70 percent to 33 percent. More Whites are now enrolled in private schools than in public schools.[1]

Mixed Results

Integration has worked best in areas where the school systems are regionalized. In school districts where city and suburban schools are combined into a county educational system—such as Nashville and Charlotte, North Carolina—busing has been very successful because affluent Whites were unable to leave the school system. In some other areas where the school district ends with the city's boundaries, busing has been discontinued because so few Whites were left. Also, opposition to busing has increased. A 1979 Harris poll reported 43 percent of Blacks oppose busing for racial integration, as do 85 percent of Whites, the latter figure up 10 percent from a similar survey in 1975. The Justice Department under the Reagan administration, as well as several federal judges who had originally ordered busing, have in recent years refused to push mandatory transportation as a remedy for segregation.

The original thrust behind busing had been to improve the quality of education and achievement of minority youngsters, who were thought to be at a disadvantage because they lacked peer role models and a "middle-class" school environment. Such considerations emerged from a major study headed by sociologist James S. Coleman in 1966, which found that differences in educational achievement of Blacks and Whites were not caused by differences in school or teacher resources but in social-class backgrounds. The Coleman Report implied that integration of lower-class minority students in middle-class majority schools would result in higher achievement without any negative impact on majority student achievement. This report profoundly influenced educational policy and provided the stimulus for desegregation through busing. Coleman has now changed his views, believing that court-ordered desegregation has not improved race relations but worsened them, as evidenced by angry responses and white flight from urban areas.

Utilizing busing to end segregated schools resulting from residential patterning has sometimes intensified intergroup hostilities. Organized protests, such as this 1974 rally at Boston Commons, or even violence have marred such efforts. In other cities, like Cleveland, Ohio, and White Plains, New York, busing worked peacefully.

Employment

In previous generations, minority workers could find employment in many low-skill jobs, even with little command of English, and gradually improve their occupational status. Technological change has significantly changed the entry-level jobs now available in the labor market, making education even more important in securing decent-paying jobs (see Figure 8.3). Sweatshops, a remnant of the past, continue to exist, however (see Box 8.1).

Only 31 percent of the labor force is now in a blue-collar occupation.[2] As a postindustrial society for a quarter of a century now, the United States offers work opportunities mostly in professional, health care, and other service occupations. Most of these fields require at least a college degree, and since low-income families usually have low-education levels, such job opportunities for them are unlikely. Minority representation in white-collar jobs is improving, however. In 1972 they comprised 6.6 percent of all white-collar employees but increased to 9.1 percent by 1980. The difficulty with this figure is that "white collar" is a very broad term and the level and types of positions held can still be low-level, low-paying ones.

Unions and Hiring

Two generations ago the southern, central, and eastern European–American minority workers were able to secure their piece of the American Dream through the union movement, which gave them better pay, better working conditions, shorter hours, and many fringe benefits. Black and Hispanic workers today have frequently met with fierce resistance from the trade unions in their efforts to gain entry through apprenticeship positions.[3] However, in some areas—notably the unions for carpenters, electricians, steel and auto workers, state and municipal employees—the proportion of Blacks equals or exceeds their 12 percent proportion of the total population.[4] Other unions and blue-collar occupations remain tough to crack. Hard economic times also affect newly unionized minority workers more because the union seniority system means they would be the first to be laid off.

Affirmative Action programs have been an area of intense controversy ever since the Civil Rights Act of 1964 mandated "equal rights" in hiring. If the percentage of

FIGURE 8.3   Percent Unemployment, 1980

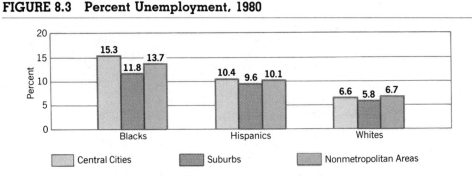

SOURCE: U.S. Department of Labor.

BOX 8.1

SWEATSHOPS ARE BACK
AND THEY'RE THRIVING
After nearly being wiped out a decade ago, thousands of new garment-industry sweatshops have sprung up in New York and other cities in the last few years, using a growing supply of illegal immigrants as a prime source of labor. Average hourly pay is $2, versus the $8.97 manufacturing production workers typically earn. No benefits come with the jobs, and wages, usually paid in cash, are kept off the employers' books. . . . Rooting out the illegal activity, however, often proves difficult because many employers . . . conduct business in clandestine settings.

In the Corona section of Queens in New York, workers at one 40-employee shop do their jobs in a dirt-floored basement beneath a barbershop. Nearby, a store with a meat-market sign never raises its gates; inside, ceiling-mounted fluorescent lights illuminate rows of sewing machines. Workers at a sweatshop next to a Queens post office enter through a karate-school facade.

Even shops with relatively good working conditions try to stay hidden from public view. One in the New York provides a clean, well-lit environment that is warm in winter and air-conditioned in summer. Nevertheless, it operates without outside signs. Like most, it dispenses with the legal formality of time clocks and employee bulletin boards. In the event of a raid, workers can scurry through a back door to a delicatessan owned by the sweatshop proprietor.

Although conditions vary, the common ingredients among such operations are low wages and lack of benefits—paid vacations, sick days, health and life insurance, pensions, disability pay, social security, and worker's compensation.

Some sweatshops charge workers for the "privilege" of being paid in cash, others say they're taking out for taxes and Social Security and just pocket the money for themselves. . . . If the worker ever tries to collect from the government later, they find there's no record of their ever having worked.

Most, however, never contact the government, officials say. The reason: as many as 75 percent of sweatshop employees are undocumented aliens afraid of being caught and expelled from the country. They prefer to work in anonymity, away from contact with immigration, Social Security, labor and Internal Revenue Service authorities. . . . The best that many of these workers can hope for, say experts, is to find better jobs.

SOURCE: Reprinted from *U.S. News & World Report*, January 16, 1984. Copyright, 1984, U.S. News & World Report, Inc.

their minority employees is significantly lower than that in the labor force, employers must take steps to correct the imbalance in future hirings. Critics, such as black economist Thomas Sowell, complain that the ''numbers game'' or quota system was not the intent of the civil rights legislation.[5] This interpretation of preferential treatment for certain minority groups, instead of ensuring equal rights in hiring, they argue, discriminates against white males and breaks society into warring fragments.

This question of reverse discrimination has not yet been completely resolved. The question at issue is this: At what point do the efforts to secure equal opportunities in life for one group infringe upon the rights of other groups? Enforcing laws against job discrimination appears possible only through accountability for those hired. Yet using specific group membership as a criterion for employment is discriminatory and generates social tensions in society. In January 1984, the U.S. Civil Rights Commission decided it would no longer seek the utilization of quota systems to correct the imbalance. Just how the imbalance will be redressed then remains with us.

Social Indicators

Two social indicators of the employment inequality for minorities are unemployment and income. Historically, Blacks have been disproportionately represented among the unemployed. By December 1982, jobless rates had reached post–World War II

Employment of minority workers is often a challenging problem. Affirmative Action programs help ensure fairer hiring practices but provoke charges of reverse discrimination. Economic downturns usually affect minority workers more heavily, throwing them into the ranks of the unemployed faster and longer.

record high levels of 20.8 percent for Blacks, 15.3 for Hispanics, and 9.7 percent for Whites. Among the Hispanic-origin population, the unemployment rates were 11.2 percent for Cubans, 13.9 percent for Mexicans, and 17.6 percent for Puerto Ricans.[6]

Since then, unemployment has eased somewhat, but at the time of this writing, the recovery has been weaker for Blacks and Hispanics than for Whites. The 2 : 1 unemployment ratio between Blacks and Whites has been fairly constant for the past 25 years. An alarming increase in black teenage unemployment has occurred, however. In 1954 about 55 percent were employed, often in the public sector, but in 1983 only 20 percent were working, the result of the recession and government cutbacks.[7]

Median black family income has always been substantially below that of white families. As shown in Table 8.1, during the 1950s and 1960s Blacks earned about 55 percent the income level of Whites. By 1975 the percentage improved to slightly more than 65 percent, but since then some slippage has occurred. Because of inflation, the actual income gap in dollars has greatly widened.

Another reflection of the employment and income picture for minorities is the poverty rate (see Figure 8.4). Here too both improvement and slight regression have occurred due to the recent recession. In 1959, 55.1 percent of the black population lived below the poverty level set by the federal government. By 1975, that figure had dropped to 31.3 percent, but increased to 35.6 percent in 1982. For Whites the unemployment percentages were 18.1 in 1959, 9.7 in 1975, and 12.0 in 1982. The 3 : 1 ratio of black and white poverty rates has been consistent for the past several decades.

Housing

As we have discussed, the problem of segregated schools is closely related to that of housing segregation. For the most part, American minorities remain highly concentrated, often isolated, in specific regions, neighborhoods or blocks. Blacks and Hispanics often live in the cities and Whites live increasingly in the suburbs. The 1980

TABLE 8.1 Median Income of Families

Year	White ($)	Black ($)	Black Income as a Percent of White Income	Actual Income Gap ($)
1950	3,445	1,869	54.3	1,576
1955	4,605	2,549	55.4	2,056
1960	5,835	3,233	55.4	2,602
1965	7,251	3,994	55.1	3,257
1970	10,236	6,516	63.7	3,720
1975	14,268	9,321	65.3	4,947
1980	21,904	13,843	63.2	8,061
1981	23,517	14,598	62.1	8,919
1982	24,603	13,598	55.3	10,995

SOURCE: U.S: Bureau of the Census, *Statistical Abstract of the United States, 1984,* Table 762, p. 463.

FIGURE 8.4   Percent Persons Below Poverty Level, 1982

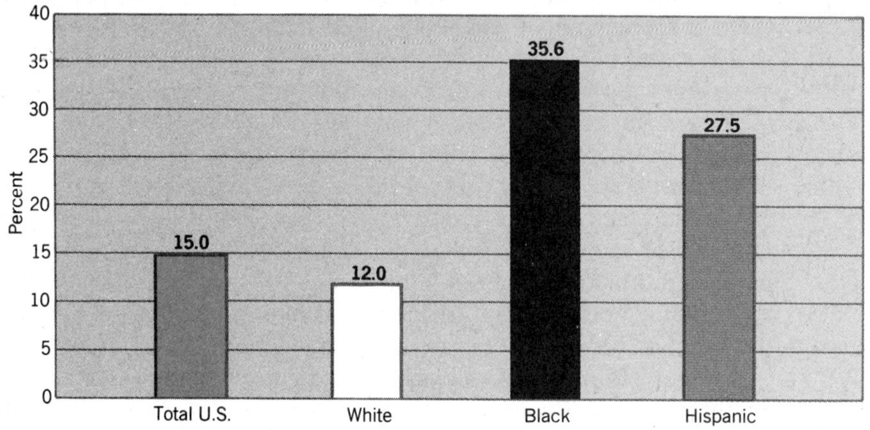

SOURCE: U.S. Bureau of the Census, Statistical Abstract of the United States: 1984 (Washington, D.C.: U.S. Government Printing Office, 1984), pp. 471–475.

Census revealed that Blacks, for example, comprise only 5 percent of the suburban population, but almost 80 percent live in urban areas. What is happening in America is an increasing residential segregation pattern of dark-skinned minority peoples confined to the decaying urban core, surrounded by the white ring of suburbia. With the growth of suburban office and industrial parks, shopping malls—as well as social, cultural, and recreational facilities—fewer white suburbanites are even venturing into the central cities. Racial isolation is becoming even more a reality than before.

Yesterday's Policies: Today's Problems

While housing discrimination reflects racist attitudes and actions to some degree, many of today's problems are an outgrowth of federal government legislation and policy decisions made almost 40 years ago. A serious housing crisis confronted the nation in the post–World War II era, caused by returning GIs, the baby boom, migration to the cities, and the lack of new housing built during the Depression and war years. Passage of the Housing Act of 1949 placed emphasis on building on vacant land, not rebuilding on already developed land (see Chapter 15). With government supporting private builders and providing low-cost mortgages to buyers, suburbia sprang into existence, setting in motion the movement of stores, hospitals, churches, offices, industries, and other support services that shortly followed. In the 1950s, the results were impressive: the housing crisis evaporated and one out of every two Americans could afford to own a home.

Simultaneously, however, the guidelines of the Federal Housing Authority (FHA) and Veterans Administration (VA) for mortgage guarantees virtually eliminated any chance for minority people to buy a house even if they could afford it. Federal policy was based on the goal of keeping social stability by retaining neighborhood homogeneity. As Eunice Grier and George Grier point out:

> . . . the Power of the national government was explicitly used to prevent integrated housing. . . . Thus, the Underwriting Manual of the Federal Housing Administration . . . warned that "if a neighborhood is to retain stability, it is necessary that properties shall continue to be occupied by the same social and racial group." It advised appraisers to lower their valuation of properties in mixed neighborhoods, "often to the point of rejection." FHA actually drove out of business some developers who insisted upon open policies.[8]

This officially sanctioned practice, which had begun earlier in the mid-1930s, was not reversed until 1962, when President John F. Kennedy signed an executive order creating an integrationist federal housing policy. For almost 30 years though, federal housing agencies effectively established segregated residential patterns which became even more pronounced after President Kennedy's action.

Legal Justice

Another form of institutionalized discrimination is found in the justice system. The blindfolded symbol of Justice holding the balanced scales represents the American ideal of equal treatment for all under the law. In reality, the system is flawed, because it is comprised of human beings whose biases reflect those of the society. The police officer as the gatekeeper into the legal system, the judge who sets bail for the accused and the sentence for the guilty, and the jury who decide a defendant's fate, all attempt to be objective, but as many studies have shown, are actually influenced by subjective factors.[9]

Throughout American history, the minority groups at the bottom of the socioeconomic ladder have been disproportionately represented in arrests, convictions, and imprisonment. Irish, Chinese, Italians, Poles, Slovaks, Blacks, Native Americans, and Hispanics, among others—each have been or presently are caught in this inequality of administering justice. Reasons suggested for the disparities include:

1. The tendency of police to arrest minority group members more often, even in discretionary cases.

2. The tendency of judges to set high bail, using it punitively to detain defendants.

3. The difficulty for the poor to afford bail, thereby keeping them in jail for months, up to a year, before their trial.

4. The lack of a jury of peers, since juries tend to be overrepresented by people of a higher social class and different racial and ethnic background.

5. The poor quality of court-appointed legal defense.

6. The disparities in sentences between minority and dominant group members for the same crimes.

Like other social institutions, the justice system reflects the Anglo middle-class cultural biases of those in control. It has been fairly common for police, prosecutors, judges, and juries to believe low-income minority groups have an inherent tendency to commit crimes. For example, in the early twentieth century, one sociologist lamented the presence of so many Greek immigrants because of their "racial characteristic [of] lack of reverence for law."[10] For the Greeks of 70 years ago or the Blacks and Hispanics today, this pervasive attitude of their disregard for the law becomes a self-fulfilling prophecy. Negative stereotyping and suspicion leads to tighter surveillance, more frequent arrests, and a greater tendency to convict and impose harsher punishment. As shown in Table 8.2, Blacks receive much more severe sentences than Whites and are disproportionately represented in prisons. Comprising just 12 percent of the population, they total 42 percent of the jail population. In past generations, other minorities were so disproportionately represented even though then, as now, almost all members of that minority group were decent, hard-working people struggling to survive.

A greater public awareness exists about the prevailing prejudices and discriminatory practices in the legal system, thanks to studies by lawyers, social scientists, presidential task forces, and the U.S. Commission of Civil Rights. At the moment, however, awareness has not translated into remedies. The problems continue. Perhaps this form of institutionalized discrimination cannot be overcome until those of education, employment, and housing are first resolved.

SPECIFIC PROBLEM AREAS

Until now we have been looking at problems in race and ethnic relations with a focus on the inequalities in our social institutions. In this section we shall first look at specific minority groups and then at present concerns about legal and illegal immigration.

Native Americans

In past years much has been said about the exploitation of Native Americans, but surprisingly few Americans are aware of the extent of their suffering today. More than half of the 1.4 million Native Americans live on or near the 261 reservations situated on 52 million acres of land held in trust by the federal government. Over 625,000 live in urban areas, especially in Los Angeles, Boston, New York City, Chicago, Dallas, Denver, Seattle, San Francisco, and San Diego. The urban Indians usually blend in with the rest of the urban poor rather than clustering in recognizable Indian neighborhoods, so their ethnic identity is less known and their problems generalized among the other urban poor.

The reservations, whose desolation has sent thousands of Native Americans to the cities in search of jobs and a better life, present as bleak a picture of poverty and despair today as they did 100 years ago. Reservations were never meant to be successful or self-sufficient; they were places to put people. Today these open-air slums have no real economy. Pacific Northwest Indians have an average 61 percent unemployment rate, with some local tribes exceeding 75 percent. Such figures are also common in the Southwest. On reservations with oil, natural gas, coal, or uranium reserves, the mineral royalties bring each tribal member only slightly over $400 a year.[11]

TABLE 8.2 **Federal Prisoners under Sentence, by Offense and Race: 1981[a]**

Offense	Total	White Num-ber	White Aver-age Sen-tence (mo.)	Other Races Num-ber	Other Races Aver-age Sen-tence (mo.)	Offense	Total	White Num-ber	White Aver-age Sen-tence (mo.)	Other Races Num-ber	Other Races Aver-age Sen-tence (mo.)
Total[b]	20,358	12,758	102.4	7,600	144.2	Securities violations[c]	102	73	79.3	29	71.5
Drug laws	5,387	4,030	75.8	1,357	104.5	Counterfeiting	389	310	59.5	79	48.0
Robbery	4,312	2,152	178.3	2,160	178.3	Fraud	739	597	50.3	142	37.8
Larceny/theft	2,225	1,345	60.5	881	49.2	Kidnaping	416	476	373.7	140	400.2
Firearms	804	603	59.1	201	52.4	Juvenile delinquency	9	4	14.5	5	68.4
Immigration	954	934	15.3	20	15.0	Burglary	70	41	94.8	29	112.9
Forgery	539	229	55.1	310	48.8	Government[d]	2,342	592	298.3	1,732	213.4

[a] These data pertain only to the federal offender population housed in federal institutions during or on the last day of the fiscal year ending **Sept. 30.** Represents more than 89 percent of the sentenced federal prisoner population.

[b] Includes offenses not shown separately.

[c] Transporting false or forged securities

[d] Includes offenses committed on government reservations, the high seas, territories, and the District of Columbia.

SOURCE: U.S. Bureau of Prisons, *Statistical Report*, annual, in *Statistical Abstract of the United States, 1982–83*, Table 33, p. 192.

Demographic statistics testify to the harshness and deprivation of reservation life. Native Americans have a life expectancy of about 10 years less than the national average. Their suicide rate is twice the national average, three times greater among young Native Americans, and seven times greater among Northwest Indians, according to the Association of American Indian and Alaska Native Social Workers. Deaths from alcoholism in 1979 (latest available data) were 57.3 per 100,000 compared to 7.4 nationally. Other age-adjusted death rates are shown in Table 8.3. From

TABLE 8.3 **Indians and Health: Age-Adjusted Death Rates per 100,000 Population in 1979**

	Indians and Alaskan Natives	All Races
Motor-vehicle accidents	79.3	23.7
All other accidents	61.4	20.0
Alcoholism	57.3	7.4
Homicide	25.5	10.4
Pneumonia, influenza	23.1	11.4
Diabetes	22.8	10.0
Suicide	21.8	11.9
Tuberculosis	4.4	0.7

SOURCE: Indian Health Service, Centers for Disease Control.

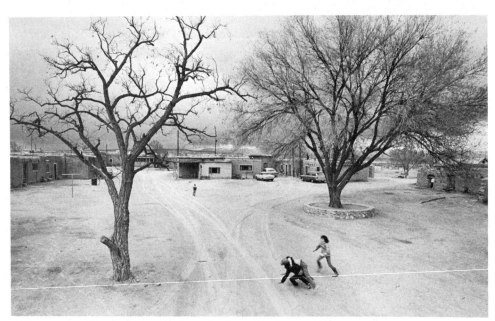

Indian reservations remain desolate locales of high unemployment and little hope for improvement over 100 years after their establishment. Unlike this San Juan, New Mexico, reservation, others lack adequate housing, electricity, and indoor plumbing. Reservations are frequently little more than open-air slums.

50 to 60 percent of young Native Americans drop out of school before completing the 12th grade, compared to the national average of 23 percent.[12] The 1980 Census also revealed that about one-third of Indian housing lacked indoor plumbing and almost one-half the housing units had no bathroom.

In recent years Indians have taken legal action to recover land or seek compensation for lands illegally seized in the past. In 1977 the Passamaquoddy and Penobscot in Maine, with the support of the U.S. Justice Department, reached an out-of-court settlement with the state for $25 million, while the Indians in the Pacific Northwest regained their privileged fishing rights to the steelhead and salmon.

The sharpest conflict remains in the Southwest over water rights, a region where water is a precious commodity. Urban sprawl, irrigation and reclamation projects, as well as deep wells sunk all around the edge of reservations, have diverted water from the Indians to farms and communities of Whites. In October 1983 President Reagan approved a water system for the Papago in Arizona, due for completion in 1992 (see Box 8.2). The Ak-Chin in the state, whose 11,000 acres of cultivated land in the mid-1970s shrunk to less than 5,000 acres from reduced water supply, face the bleak prospect of a complete loss of water within 5 years, with no prospects of a water system for them.[13] Insufficient water throughout the West means not all needs—Indians, agriculture, mining, development—can be met. Who gets what, though, is unresolved. Most of the water fights end up in the courts, where they linger but seldom die. Over 50 lawsuits—from Arizona to Montana to California—await a decision.

BOX 8.2

HUMAN RIGHTS IN AMERICA

"In over the 207 years that we have had a government, in well over a hundred years of our relationship with our Indians, we have never, I repeat, never, lived up to the moral obligations that we owe these people. . . .

"I think we pay far more attention to the human rights of people living in the countries of South Africa, or Central America, or you name it, than we pay to the human rights of Indians living within our states. . . .

"The Papago Indian tribe, with 13,000 members and a reservation spread over 5,000 square miles has only one hospital. A number of years ago, this hospital burned down, and believe it or not, it took (the government) 10 years to reconstruct it. . . .

"The Hopi Indians have only one hospital and it's been reduced to being open only three days a week. They lack adequate communications and transportation systems to reach patients with what medical aid is available. The Hopis also have no high school, even though there is money in the jobs bill to at least start a high school. . . .

"The vast Navajo Reservation, the largest that we have, and the largest population of any Indian tribe, does not need any detailed description by me as to their lack of health and education facilities, decent roads running north and south, communications and on down the list. These people have the highest unemployment rate in the United States and suffer along with the other Indians. . . .

"Our Senate Select Committee has been informally advised that the Department of Health and Human Services no longer intends to engage in the construction of hospitals serving Indian people. As a matter of fact, the Indian Health Service has refused to release funds appropriated by the Congress in fiscal years 1982 and 1983 for the planning and design of hospitals. . . . As a member of the United States Senate, as an American citizen, who has lived most of his life with these Indians. I'm just plain fed up, sick and tired of the neglect of these people. . . . Please, Mr. President, let's establish something in our own back yard that we can begin to be proud of before we wander around this earth trying to teach other people how to live and how to act toward each other. Let's act toward each other in this country like we really meant what we talk about."

SOURCE: 1983 Letter from Senator Barry Goldwater of Arizona to President Ronald Reagan. Shortly thereafter, President Reagan approved a multimillion dollar water project for the Papago.

Black Americans

Numbering 26.5 million or 11.4 percent of the population, Black Americans are the largest minority group in America. Following the civil rights legislation and urban riots of the 1960s, Blacks were able to make significant advances in education and employment though, as we have discussed, problems still remain. In the mid-1980s we now find a contradictory blend of progress and stagnation. Improved educational levels and opened job opportunities have enabled about one-third of the black population to enter the middle class. At the same time almost the same number now constitute a "permanent poor underclass," mired in urban ghettos and habitually unemployed or underemployed.[14]

In 1960, 11 percent of all employed Blacks were in professional, technical, and craft jobs, but their representation almost doubled to 21 percent by 1980. The number of black men in professional positions grew at a slightly faster pace than that of white males during the 1970s but by 1980, 16 percent of all white men were employed as professional workers, twice the black male proportion.[15] Blacks increased their numbers in high-paying job categories by a considerable margin, but it was usually from a small base. For example, in 1970, there were 446 black female lawyers but 4,272 by 1980; black female psychologists increased from 501 in 1970 to 4,551 a decade later, black male psychologists from 461 to 2,414.[16] The number of Blacks in professional and managerial positions now exceed 1.8 million, more than two-and-a-half times the 728,000 in 1965.[17]

While these gains occurred, poor Black Americans, heavily concentrated in the central cities, have experienced a worsening of their economic situation due to government cutbacks and further erosion of low-skill job opportunities. Of particular concern is increasing black youth and young adult joblessness. Their catastrophic proportions of long-term unemployment creates a multigenerational poor, blocked from any opportunity for upward mobility.

> If the evidence presented in recent longitudinal research is correct, then black youth joblessness will have a long-term harmful effect on their chances in the labor market. . . . [A] significant segment of the black population is in danger of being permanently locked out of the mainstream of the American occupational systems. It cannot be over-emphasized that the increasing black youth joblessness is a problem primarily experienced by lower-income Blacks; for example, 67 percent of unemployed black teenagers living at home in 1977 were from families with incomes of less than $10,000. And among those unemployed teenagers living at home and not enrolled in school, 75 percent were from families with less than $10,000 incomes and 41 percent were from families with less than $5000 income.[18]

Unemployed men are more likely to abandon their families than employed men.[19] The rising percentage of female-headed black families is a symptom of their deteriorating economic condition, not its cause.[20] Affirmative Action programs are of no value in low-wage industries where labor supply exceeds demand. Inner-city unemployment rates are twice the national average because the weak educational backgrounds of those residents do not meet the prerequisites for the specialized white-collar jobs mostly available in central cities. Some argue that only economic reform aimed at improving the job prospects of these black poor, with day-care centers so those female heads of households can work, will break the cycle of perpetual poverty among the urban black poor.

Hispanics

High immigration and fertility rates are producing a burgeoning Hispanic American population, growing by 61 percent during the 1970s to 14.6 million by 1980. Hispanics or Latinos fall into four major categories: the 8.7 million of Mexican origin, 2 million Puerto Rican, 803,226 Cuban, and 3 million from the Caribbean and Central and South America. Although they all share a common Spanish heritage in language and culture and are mostly poor and Catholic, considerable diversity exists among them.

Four out of five Mexican Americans live in the Southwest, but they include the old-family Spanish Americans in northern New Mexico and southern Colorado, the rural poor and the urban poor living in barrios, the assimilated second- or third-generation Mexican Americans living in southern California, and illegal aliens working wherever they can. About one-fourth of all Mexican Americans or Chicanos live in poverty, possessing limited education and job skills. Through the efforts of some Chicano leaders like Cesar Chavez (United Farm Workers), Reies Tijerina (Alianza), Rodolfo Gonzales (La Raza Unida), and David Sanchez (Brown Berets), Chicanos have gained national attention and scored some successes in improving conditions. At present though, about 80 percent of the Mexican-American population lives in urban areas, often in overcrowded, substandard housing.

One in three Puerto Ricans lives in poverty, the worst ratio of all Hispanic groups. Unlike their island where race is subordinate to social class, dark-skinned Puerto Ricans find the Anglos' perception of them as ''Black,'' restricts them more than fair-skinned Puerto Ricans. Puerto Ricans themselves continue to stress their ethnicity alone, maintaining a single ethnic community. Encountering continual problems of unemployment, poverty, racism, and crime has prompted many to return to Puerto Rico. Others have put down roots on the mainland, though, and more cohesive ethnic neighborhoods have developed.

Most of the Cubans who have come to the United States since 1959 have been light-skinned, middle-class political refugees. Well-educated and possessing occupational and entrepreneural skills, they settled primarily in the Miami and New York regions, often in blighted urban neighborhoods. Within a short time these areas became stable and revitalized, as the Cubans prospered from their investments and enterprises. More recent arrivals, particularly among the 125,000 Mariel boatlift in 1980, have been of limited education and job skills, with 20 percent of them dark skinned.[21] Among Cubans, crime, unemployment, and poverty have now become a problem that heretofore had not been of concern.

Migrant Workers

Migrant farm laborers number from 1.5 to 2 million and are a mixture of several racial and ethnic groups. About half are Black Americans, one-third are Haitians, Mexicans, or Puerto Ricans, and the rest are native-born Whites. Some reside year-round in Florida or the Southwest, seeking employment daily from the crew leaders who have contracted with the farmers and growers to harvest their crops. Others follow the harvest season northward, winding up in Washington, Michigan, or upstate New York, before returning south to repeat the cycle.

Many thousands of these migrants are held in economic bondage by unscrupulous crew leaders who themselves can earn over $100,000 a year. Strict discipline, including threats, beatings, and terrorizing with guns, chains, and dogs have been reported.[22] Crew leaders gather the migrant workers, transport them to the camps or fields, pay them, and sell—at inflated prices—food, alcohol, cigarettes, toilet articles, even clothing. Living in unbelievably deplorable dwellings with rancid smells, cockroaches, lack of toilets or indoor plumbing, these people work themselves to exhaustion, barely earning enough to pull themselves out of this enslaving system. A migrant family of six, with the children usually picking the fruits and vegetables also, earned a median family income in 1982 of $3,900, less than half the government's official family poverty income level of $9,287.[23]

Despite television and print media exposés since 1960, the plight of the migrant workers remains relatively unchanged. Their life expectancy is only 49 years. Several hundred die each year from pesticide poisoning, working among the newly dusted or sprayed crops without a place to wash their hands. Diarrhea, TB, and parasitic diseases are quite common, given the poor living conditions, primitive sanitation, and bad food. Excluded from the minimum wage law, collective bargaining, or overtime provisions, they benefit little, if at all, from unemployment benefits, workmen's compensation, social security, or child labor laws. Children, in fact, usually begin working at age 8. About 86 percent never complete high school because of their traveling and needed help in the fields.

Farmers believe they have been unfairly cast as the villains. Burdened by heavy costs, they try to save what they can, and cannot afford additional costs to provide for the migrant workers. The Department of Labor is understaffed and encounters much resistance from the farm lobby. As transients, the workers are unknown in a given locality, poorly educated, and unorganized. Many have a limited command of English and are unable to overcome their exploitation. So a self-perpetuating system, unknown to most Americans, has changed little over the decades and continues to entrap the next generation in its web.

Illegal Aliens

A major cause for concern among political and civic leaders is the growing number of illegal aliens in the United States, for which estimates range from 5 to 12 million. The Border Patrol apprehends over 80,000 illegal aliens each month, but estimates it only catches 1 in 3. Slipping across the 1,933-mile border is easy, many doing so in broad daylight after reaching a border town by bus (see Box 8.3).

Mexicans overwhelmingly comprise the illegal alien population, about four out of every five. Other major sources of illegal aliens are Colombia, Dominican Republic, El Salvador, Guatemala, Haiti, and Jamaica. In 1977, immigration officials apprehended 480 illegal aliens in Atlanta from 71 different countries, while in Dallas they captured illegal aliens from 59 countries.[24] Poverty and population pressures in their own countries are luring a great many different nationalities to enter the "land of opportunity" any way they can.

The popular view of undocumented aliens working mostly on farms is partially correct, but many also head for the cities. Some work for low wages in sweat shops and others bring blue-collar skills, earning good money in construction and factory jobs. Since the 1970s, a significant increase in the number of undocumented Mexicans has occurred in midwestern cities, and of Caribbean and South Americans in the northeastern cities.[25] Significant concentrations of these workers are in service and light industry, especially in New York and Boston.[26] Only 7 percent of employed Mexicans were farmworkers in 1980, compared to more than 75 percent of the males in blue-collar work, including 21 percent in the well-paid craft occupations.[27]

Considerable debate exists about the impact of illegal aliens upon American society. The most frequent complaints are that they depress the wage scale, displace low-skilled American workers who are often minority group members themselves, thereby increasing the cost of assistance and social service programs. Others dismiss the charges, claiming the illegals are taking jobs no one else wants and their consumerism actually helps the economy. Except for those illegally in the country for criminal purposes (drug trafficking, theft, robbery), crime is not a serious problem since undocumented aliens must walk a narrow line to remain unknown to the authorities. To what extent the illegal aliens are thus victims of unreported crimes is unknown.

With the number of illegal aliens continuing to skyrocket, a loud clamor arose for the United States to regain control of its borders. The 1984 Simpson-Mazzoli bill granted amnesty for those already here, required employers to verify the legal status of job applicants, and set penalties for employers who hire illegal aliens. The measure generated intense controversy, raised Hispanic fears of job discrimination, and alarmed local officials about increased tax dollars for social services to newly qualified aliens. At this writing no compromise bill of the House and Senate versions has been agreed upon.

Compounding reaction against illegal aliens was a June 1982 ruling by the U.S. Supreme Court, which held that Texas must provide free education for children who have entered the country illegally. This 5-4 decision was based upon the 14th Amendment, saying in part ". . . nor shall any state . . . deny to any person within its jurisdiction the equal protection of the laws." Critics claim the Constitution's definition of "Person" does not include noncitizens arriving in a state against the law by their own determination, without accepting the jurisdiction.[28] In addition to requiring public funding for the schooling of children, state officials worry about the extension of such a ruling into unemployment and welfare benefits, health services, and free college education.

SOCIOLOGICAL PERSPECTIVES

Sociologists have long sought to understand the causes of prejudice and discrimination. Extensive study on the subject has enhanced our understanding, but considerable disagreement remains. In the area of race and ethnic relations, the first perspec-

BOX 8.3

INVASION FROM MEXICO
The dilemma of a developing nation living next door to one of the world's richest countries comes to life in places such as El Paso, across the Rio Grande from a mean Juarez slum known as Arroyo Colorado. Gaunt and raggedly dressed people carrying a few belongings in sacks poise for a dash to American soil. Found there at any hour of day or night, they wait only for the right moment to make their run for what they hope is a decent, if not prosperous, life.

Pressure Points:
Areas of Most Illegal Entries Into U.S.

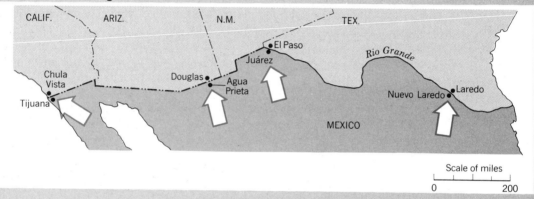

On one cold, bright February morning, some 100 young men and women stood silently on the Mexican side intently watching—and being watched by—a handful of green-uniformed Border Patrolmen. After a 45-minute standoff, most of the officers departed to attend to other parts of the so-called tortilla curtain separating

tive of finding fault among individuals is a very common one. The functionalist and conflict views provide analyses of societal factors causing the problems in intergroup relations. The interactionist approach examines the consequences of social interpretations of others who are different. Each perspective in its own way offers a focus for understanding more about the complexities of intergroup relations.

Individual Faults and Deviant Behavior

This perspective attempts to understand why people become prejudiced and discriminate against others. One controversial research finding was that people with an **authoritarian personality** also had a high level of intolerance and prejudice toward

El Paso from Juarez. It was then that the patient Mexicans split up and began quickly crossing up and down the river.

Some are caught by the Border Patrol's rear guard as they sprint through nearby freight yards. Others are arrested crossing a highway leading west toward the Florida Mountains and New Mexico. But for each arrest, others make it to south El Paso's crowded and anonymous barriers. . . .

The Border Patrol's main problem is that it is outmanned. While it has 2,300 agents on the border—covered by an 111-million-dollar budget—no more than 300 are on duty at a time because of rotating shifts and vacations. With a force smaller than the Baltimore Police Department, the El Paso station's 380 agents must cover 85,000 square miles of desert and mountains. . . .

The agency tries to compensate with advanced technology. In Chula Vista, Calif., for instance, hillsides and canyons are mined with magnetic and seismic sensors that signal the presence of man or machine. When a sensor picks up footsteps, an alert is bleeped to a computer at sector headquarters atop a hill overlooking the border. The computer automatically prints out the sensor number, type, location and number of aliens traversing the area.

New infrared scopes used at Chula Vista can home in on body warmth in pitch-darkness. Four-wheel-drive trucks, all-terrain vehicles and trail bikes extend the patrol's reach into rugged canyons. Even so, officials believe twice as many agents would be needed to seal off the border. . . .

No one really knows how much aliens cost taxpayers, but some experts believe the figure runs into hundreds of millions of dollars, perhaps billions. . . . Texas spends more than 85 million dollars each year to educate 61,000 children of illegal aliens. . . . Los Angeles 415 million dollars. . . . Los Angeles spent 76 million dollars last year on health care for undocumented aliens. . . . New York up to 12 million.

SOURCE: Reprinted from *U.S. News & World Report,* March 7, 1983. Copyright, 1983, U.S. News & World Report, Inc.

minority groups.[29] The studies indicated these prejudiced individuals were characterized by rigidity of view, dislike for ambiguity, strict obedience to authority figures, a high regard for conventional behavior, and an intolerance of weakness in anyone, including themselves. While understanding about a relationship between personality and prejudice is helpful, this does not necessarily mean it is a cause-effect one. The sequence could be the other way around or both might reflect yet some other factor.[30] Though critics have attacked the methodology, analysis, and anticonservative bias of the researchers, interest in authoritarianism as a factor remains significant.

A second approach, **frustration-aggression,** suggests that when people become frustrated, feelings, of anger and aggression manifest themselves.[31] Frequently one is unable to strike out against the source of the frustration, either because it is unknown

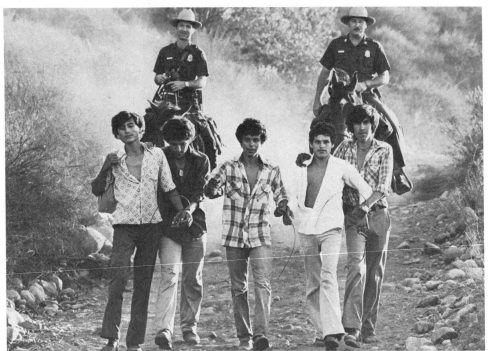

These five Mexican young adults, being marched by border patrol agents to a holding center shortly after their apprehension, represent only a minute fraction of the illegal-alien problem. The 80,000 illegal aliens caught each month probably account for only one-third the actual number that slips across the border to find work.

or too powerful. In such instances, the result may be displaced or free-floating aggression directed against a more visible, vulnerable, and perhaps even socially sanctioned target, one unable to strike back. A number of studies have confirmed this tendency.[32] In one such study, the researchers found prejudicial attitudes increased against certain minority groups among young men after they were obliged to take a long, difficult test and denied an opportunity to see a movie at a local theater.[33]

Scapegoating, blaming another for one's problems, is one form of defense projection. Another is simply blaming the victim for the problem. This action allows those possessing adequate resources to absolve themselves of any responsibility by attributing inherent character flaws to those suffering deprivation. Flinging negative epithets like "lazy" or "naturally dishonest" or "lacking self-respect" about an entire group conveniently blurs the social reality.

Sometimes people denigrate others to justify maltreatment of them. To reassure ourselves that the things we do and the lives we lead are proper, we rationalize our actions. We can feel justified in discriminating, subjugating, enslaving, or even killing others, if we are able to convince ourselves that the other group is inferior, immoral, or less than human. History is filled with examples of people who thought this way. As defenders of the true faith, the Crusaders killed men, women, and children who were "infidels" (Muslims) or "Christ-killers" (Jews). American soldiers massacred "gooks" in a Vietnamese village even though some were infants and frail, elderly people. A milder form of **self-justification** is use of a prestige hierarchy, ranking various racial and ethnic groups by status and associating only with those of equal or higher status.

Institutional Faults and System Disorganization

Functionalist analysis begins with the premise that the ideal structure of a social system is one in which all its parts interact smoothly with each other. The social cement binding a society together is its normative integration, the mutual sharing of values and attitudes, allowing people to live together equally and harmoniously. System disorganization occurs when a society fails to adjust to the arrival of large numbers of immigrants. Even the continued presence of partially assimilated minority groups presents problems. Both minority groups—the new and the old—retain enough differences to reduce the unity and cohesiveness of the society.

Unsuccessful efforts at integration or **pluralism**—accompanied by prejudice and resentment—generate discrimination and hostilities. This situation is dysfunctional to society because it wastes human resources by denying people full opportunities to make their contributions. This system disorganization, if not corrected, becomes entrenched, resulting in some groups denied equal opportunity from one generation to the next. As a tradition of restricted opportunities and participation continues, problems of poor education, income, unemployment, housing, health and longevity, crime and delinquency become a burden to society and the minority people who endure them. The dysfunctions of discrimination to society are its cost—in terms of lost productivity and welfare assistance—as well as remaining a continuous source of social unrest and reciprocal antagonism.

Functionalists stress that the most effective method of resolving these problems is to put the social system back into balance. Effective reform to eliminate discrimination must occur, eliminating the barriers to full social, political, and economic opportunities. If we make these adjustments and reorganize our social institutions, we shall build new relationships among people and begin to foster mutual respect and cooperation. A fully integrated society would probably produce the fewest conflicts, but can also attain unity in a pluralistic society if all groups accept and respect the rights and subculture of each other. As long as a common core exists with allegiance to American society, differences need not be divisive if all work together in peaceful coexistence and cooperation.

Inequality and Inevitable Conflict

Because people tend to become more hostile when their security is threatened, social scientists have examined closely how economic competition and conflict breed prejudice. Throughout American history we find many examples of rising ethnic antagonism in times of high unemployment and intense job competition. This pattern has held true for many different minority groups in the late nineteenth century and early twentieth century for Asians on the West Coast, Germans and Italians in the South, and for southern, central, and eastern Europeans in the industrial Northeast and

North Central states; and since the 1960s for Blacks and Hispanics in many parts of the country.

Economic exploitation is a key reason for inequality. Employers have often hired cheaper minority workers at the expense of other nonminority wage earners. When the labor market splits this way along ethnic lines, ethnic prejudice, racism, and hostility arise and dominate the labor conflict.[34] A few of the numerous examples are the efforts of Samuel Gompers and the American Federation of Labor in the late nineteenth century to bar Chinese workers from coming to America, the killings of Hungarian and Slavic miners in Pennsylvania in the 1890s, or the race riots in many American cities in 1919 brought about by returning war veterans seeking jobs in competition with Blacks migrating to the North.

Factory sweatshops still exist and still exploit minority workers, whose limited English, lack of resources, or illegal alien status make it impossible for them to object to their low wages or poor working conditions. Whether in factories or on farms, the illegal and legal alien workers also accept wages low by American standards because they are still better than what they have previously known. This can depress the wage scale in that region, displace American workers, and set the stage for antagonism and confrontation. When manufacturers find labor cost rising because of the collective bargaining process, they often relocate to nonunion areas in the South or to Hong Kong, South Korea, or Taiwan, thereby generating ethnic prejudices in the affected workers against those who have replaced them.

Conflict theorists examine both past and present minority problems by asking, "Who benefits?" Members of a society who occupy privileged positions strive to maintain their status and allow only a small number to enter their circle. Acting in their own self-interest, they exploit those with little power and create an ideology and value system to reinforce their dominance. As this belief system pervades the society, a false consciousness evolves that deceives people into thinking that what they see is the "normal" state of affairs.

Interaction and Social Interpretation

Interactionists concentrate on the daily encounters between members of different groups. When the dominant and minority groups are similar in their values, appearance, and life-style, the interrelationship will more likely be harmonious and assimilation will occur. The greater and more visible the cultural differences, the probability of conflict increases and assimilation, if desired, becomes more difficult.[35] This perspective emphasizes ethnocentric factors resulting in a definition of the situation, which can lead to misunderstandings and problems between members of unlike groups.

Alfred Schutz, an early interactionist and immigrant to the United States, pointed out that part of the problem for immigrants is their lack of "intersubjective understanding."[36] What he meant was that we live in a shared world with a reciprocity of perspectives. For the native, every social situation is more than just a coming together of identities and roles; it is also shared realities—the intersubjective structure of consciousness. People live out each day in a familiar world, responding to the familiar routine without reflection or questioning. What is taken for granted by the native, however, is problematic to the stranger. To the newcomers, or "greenhorns" as immigrants were once called, every situation is new and so experienced as a crisis. As they struggle to cope with the language and customs, they may well become the comical butt of jokes or the objects of scorn, derision, and prejudice because they are "different."

Religion is often a basis for cultural conflict, as found among otherwise ethnically similar Protestants and Catholics in Northern Ireland, Christians and Muslims in Lebanon, Muslims and Jews in the Middle East, and Hindus and Muslims in India. In the United States Catholics, Jews, Mormons, and Quakers have each experienced prejudice and discrimination because of their faith. Other cultural attributes may invite negative reactions as well. The Chinese language, clothing, food, eating utensils, queue or pigtail hairstyle have all prompted nativist derision; so have the Sikh turbans or saris respectively worn by some Asian Indian males and females. Ethnic foods and cooking aromas, certain leisure activities (Hispanic cockfights, for example), life-cycle events (Irish wakes, Polish weddings), or other forms of behavior (Asians bowing when greeting someone, Native American silence in unfamiliar situations)—while not necessarily practiced by all members of those respective groups—are nevertheless common enough to foster possible ethnocentric reaction.

THE FUTURE

Scars from past treatment of Blacks and Native Americans still mar American society, but not the descendants of past waves of European immigrants. Those previously maltreated white ethnic groups are mostly now well-integrated, even though their retention of Catholicism or Judaism and certain other cultural attributes made the nation a more pluralistic one. Today's immigrants—many of them Asians or Hispanics—come to a far different America, raising concerns whether past **assimilation** patterns are reliable indicators for the newcomers. Let us project some future possibilities based on current trends, understanding though that unforeseen events may dramatically alter the picture in unexpected ways.

Pessimistic Scenario

By 2025, the population composition of American society had dramatically changed. The black population now comprised about 17 percent of the total, Hispanics about 33 percent, and Asians about 25 percent, for a combined total of 75 percent. Whites, alarmed by their shrinking numbers, still held political power because of occupational status and accumulated wealth, and they tried desperately to preserve their power base in a manner reminiscent of the outnumbered Whites in South Africa in the 1980s.

The United States had become a far more pluralistic and multiracial society than ever before, but the question had arisen as to how much longer the country would remain united. Buoyed by the independence of Quebec, serious separatist movements were underway among Mexicans in the Southwest and among the Cubans in Florida. In both areas, the Hispanics were so concentrated that virtually no other ethnic groups lived there. With these regions torn by violence and terrorist bombings, with their congressional representatives causing much agitation and legislative roadblocks on Capitol Hill, and with their extremely high poverty rate and subsequent welfare and social service costs draining the economy, many white leaders were giving serious consideration to the advantages and practicality of allowing the separatism to occur.

Blacks were also highly segregated, living mostly in the older central cities that the Whites had all but abandoned. Poverty and unemployment still remained a serious problem, but the Blacks had at least achieved structural assimilation within these urban areas. They were now in major policy-making positions in all social institutions within these cities—including civic, economic, education, and legal. Because of continuing outmigration, no national corporations were headquartered in these cities any longer, having moved to other cities or suburban campus settings.

Many companies had established all-Black offices, franchises, or manufacturing plants within the cities that—in addition to the privately owned black stores, restaurants, and service establishments, civil service, and municipal jobs—provided employment opportunities. In effect, these two dozen major black cities had become mini-nations within the United States, self-contained in their work, leisure, and residence for the inhabitants, but heavily dependent upon the ''import'' of foodstuffs and other items from white America. Federal block grants and domestic aid programs helped support these metropolitan racial enclaves.

The country was torn apart by dissension. It had lost its national identity and sense of community. Cultural integration had been replaced by cultural separatism. The greatest receiving nation had sealed its borders in an attempt to regain its sense of self. Legal and illegal immigration had been severely curtailed. All were required to carry identification papers on them at all times; papers were cross-checked in a master computer file for job hiring and payment. Clashes between Blacks and Hispanics were frequent because of the fierce economic competition for jobs. Sometimes their anger was directed instead against the Whites, who themselves thought the Asian Americans were behind the unrest in order to make a power grab for themselves. The Asians, who completely dominated California, were also heavily represented elsewhere on the West Coast and East Coast. Mostly middle class, they were the second most powerful group in the country, had developed close economic and political ties with the Far Eastern countries, and were more influential than ever in shaping foreign and domestic policy. Native Americans still remained poverty stricken on their reservations. America's pluralism was now a realization of the nativists' worst fears.

Optimistic Scenario

Recovery from economic hard times and successful conversion of business and industry to the advanced computer age had brought a period of growth to the United States. The country was more diversified than ever before. Instead of a land of three major faiths—Catholicism, Judaism, and Protestantism—it was a land of many major faiths, including Buddhism, Hinduism, and Islam. Because of the large Hispanic-American population, Catholicism had replaced Protestantism as the predominant religion of the land. Religious diversity existed, as it always had, but it was not a source of friction, since equal educational opportunity and economic security for all had brought about a culturally integrated society.

Government policymakers had years earlier focused their energies on economic self-sufficiency for all its citizens as the most effective approach to build cultural bridges and reduce intergroup prejudices and tensions. State and regional planning and controls had superseded municipal, making local control an obsolete concept. This enabled large-scale planned integration of low-, middle-, and high-income housing with business and industry, bringing all types of people into contact with each other. The successful integration of education, employment, and housing had resulted in mainstreaming of minorities and the elimination of generalized negative stereotypes. The criminal justice system reflected this intergroup harmony in having no minority group more represented than any other.

Emphasis on economics as the key to intergroup harmony had extended to the Caribbean basin and Latin America, as well as to Indian reservations and central cities of the United States. Improved economic conditions in the countries to the nation's south had been more effective than any other measure to stem the tide of legal and illegal immigration. Although Latinos still migrated to the United States, their numbers were much more manageable, as improving economic conditions in their native lands reduced the pressure to migrate. Those coming had job skills enabling them to blend in more easily.

The success of group integration and economic equality had also brought about a significant change in bilingual education. Controversy no longer swirled about such programs, since all students now studied in two languages. The presence of such a large Spanish-speaking subculture had broadened the cultural perspective of other Americans. The United States was no longer the only monolingual developed nation. Its students no longer studied ''foreign'' languages, but ''contemporary'' or ''world'' languages, the title indicating that Americans had become less ethnocentric in their view of the world. Not only Spanish, but Arabic, Chinese, German, Japanese, Russian, and other languages were commonly studied as well.

Problems remained, of course. Tensions and occasional flareups reminded people that America, now called the ''Switzerland of the Western Hemisphere,'' because of its successful pluralism, still was filled with different kinds of people not always understanding and appreciating each other. Yet America of 2025 was as different a place for Blacks and Hispanics compared to 1985, as America of 1985 was for Germans, Irish, Italians, and Jews compared to the late nineteenth and early twentieth centuries.

SUMMARY

1. Americans' faith in education as the route to upward mobility overlooks biases in the system. For some minority children, the schools are an alien world with different value orientations and frequent insensitivity. Busing has worked in some areas, especially regionalized school districts. It has been a divisive program though, and some urban public school systems are now even more segregated.

2. Although minority workers have made some gains, they remain disproportionately unemployed and vulnerable to economic downturns. Median black family income is less than two-thirds that of white families, and the three times greater black poverty rate has been constant for several decades. Affirmative Action programs generate reverse discrimination charges and are of little aid among low-skilled workers where a labor surplus exists.

3. Housing segregation remains a serious problem, particularly among Blacks and Hispanics. Part of the situation is an outgrowth of past government discriminatory policies, combined with migration patterns and employment realities. The criminal justice system also reflects serious inequalities in the overrepresentation and treatment of minorities.

4. Native Americans live under incredible hardship on reservations, with a high incidence of pathologies resulting from the widespread poverty. Despite some recent court victories, they continue to suffer. Some black Americans have made progress but the presence of a large urban underclass, punctuated by extensive teenage and young adult joblessness, threatens to create permanent poverty among this population segment. Hispanics are a diverse and rapidly growing group, with many experiencing serious poverty problems. Migrant workers, comprised of several minority groups, remain a heavily exploited group without any prospects of improvement in their situation. The problem of illegal aliens is of major concern to everyone, prompting debate and proposals for correction of the problem.

5. The individual faults perspective looks to personality, frustration-aggression, scapegoating, and self-justification as reasons why people discriminate and blame the victim. Functionalists emphasize a system imbalance becoming entrenched, necessitating reform to eliminate the discrimination and build new relationships among people. Conflict theorists examine the economic exploitation of minorities and efforts of the privileged class to maintain their status. Interactionists discuss the problems arising because of misunderstandings and the lack of shared realities.

SUGGESTED READINGS

Bahr, Howard M., Bruce A. Chadwick, and Robert C. Day. *Native Americans Today: Sociological Perspectives.* New York: Harper & Row, 1972. An informative anthology of articles providing insights into both reservation and urban Native Americans, their problems and reactions.

Novak, Michael. *The Rise of the Unmeltable Ethnics.* New York: Macmillan, 1971. A provocative and influential book examining assimilation problems of "white ethnics" and their reactions to efforts for today's identified minorities.

Parrillo, Vincent N. *Strangers to These Shores: Race and Ethnic Relations in the United States,* 2d ed. New York: John Wiley, 1985. A readable and comprehensive look at all minorities in the United States, with strong material on prejudice, discrimination, intergroup relations, and current problems.

Sowell, Thomas. *Ethnic America: A History*. New York: Basic Books, 1981. A comparative analysis of major racial and ethnic groups in the United States, with discussion of reasons for their varying success in American society.

Willie, Charles V. *A New Look at Black Families,* 2d ed. New York: General Hall, 1981. Excellent study of black American families, debunking myths yet identifying their problems engendered by poverty and racism.

Wilson, William J. *The Declining Significance of Race: Blacks and Changing American Institutions*. Chicago: University of Chicago Press, 1978. A controversial argument that, with Blacks now divided into the affluent and poor, social class is more important than race in their gaining status and power.

GLOSSARY

Affirmative Action Antidiscriminatory policy to enhance the hiring of members of designated minority groups.

Assimilation The process by which members of racial or ethnic minorities are able to function within a society without indicating any marked cultural, social, or personal differences from the people of the majority group.

Authoritarian personality A set of distinct personality traits, including conformity, insecurity, and intolerance, said to be common among many prejudiced people.

Discrimination Differential and unequal treatment of other groups of people, usually along racial, religious, or ethnic lines.

Frustration-aggression A theory that aggression toward others is a response to frustration somewhere in the individual's environment.

Institutionalized discrimination Differential and unequal treatment of a group or groups deeply pervading social customs and institutions, often subtly and informally.

Pluralism A state in which minorities can maintain their distinctive subcultures and simultaneously interact with relative equality in the larger society.

Scapegoating Placing blame on others for something that is not their fault.

Self-justification A defense mechanism whereby people denigrate another person or group to justify maltreatment of them.

FACTS ABOUT POVERTY

About 35.3 million people—15 percent of the population—live in poverty, according to federal government statistics.

Of all those living in poverty, 62.6 percent are White, 26.6 percent are Black, and 10.8 percent are Hispanic.

One out of ten Whites lives in poverty, while one out of three Blacks is poor and one out of four Hispanics is poor.

One out of three female-headed families lives in poverty.

Children under 18 and adults over 65 comprise more than half of the nation's poor.

More than half the poor live in rural or suburban areas.

The infant mortality rate among the poor is twice that of other Americans.

9
POVERTY

Despite the accomplishments and affluence of many of its people, the United States does have a significant poverty problem. In his 1937 Inaugural Address, Franklin D. Roosevelt identified "one-third of our nation [as] ill-housed, ill-clad, ill-nourished." Matters had not changed much by 1964 when President Lyndon B. Johnson launched the War on Poverty. Four years later during his ill-fated campaign for the presidential nomination, Senator Robert F. Kennedy remarked that millions of Americans go to bed hungry every night. In 1984 the federal government identified 35.3 million Americans—15.2 percent of the population—as living in poverty. Another 30 million live on the edge of poverty, according to the National Advisory Council on Economic Opportunity.

Many economists, social scientists, and activists such as Jesse Jackson consider the government figures too low, arguing that the poor are undercounted because of such factors as their transitory or illegal alien status, their residence in illegally reconverted multifamily dwellings, or inaccessibility in remote rural areas. Other critics argue that the official number of poor is too high, that if noncash benefits such as food stamps, housing subsidies, and health benefits were included with cash income, the actual number of poor may be less than the number claimed.[1]

For most readers of this book, poverty is not something that has been experienced firsthand. In fact, the probability is extremely high that you, as a college graduate, will never personally confront this problem in your entire life. So why would you be concerned about the misfortunes of others if, as the Bible says, "the poor you will always have with you"?[2] Is poverty really a social problem, the responsibility of society, or an individual problem the poor themselves must overcome?

Although many different opinions exist, most social scientists agree that the poverty problem can be fully understood only within the larger context of the social system, not just by focusing on the subculture of the poor. Poverty may be an economic reality, but the failure of American society to eliminate it can be better explained through sociological analysis. As you will learn in this chapter, the value orientations of the American nonpoor and the focus of corrective efforts by government agencies more often serve to thwart a solution than end the degradation and suffering that poverty brings to millions of Americans.

THE NATURE OF POVERTY

At first thought, poverty may appear to be a simple enough concept to explain. Generally, most of us would agree that anyone is poor who lacks enough money to afford the basic necessities of life: food, shelter, clothing. But how much money is enough? What standard must be attained for even these necessities? For example, what minimum conditions should one's living quarters meet to be above the poverty standards? What about transportation and entertainment? Are people poor if they do not own a car, or if their only car is more than 7 years old? If a family does not own a television set or cannot afford to go to the movies, are they also poor?

A precise definition of poverty is actually very difficult to determine. Where does one draw the line between those who are poor and those who are not? Difficult as it may be, we must attempt to identify the poor if we are to help them. Many experts

FIGURE 9.1 Number of Americans Living in Poverty 1960, 1965–1983 (in millions)

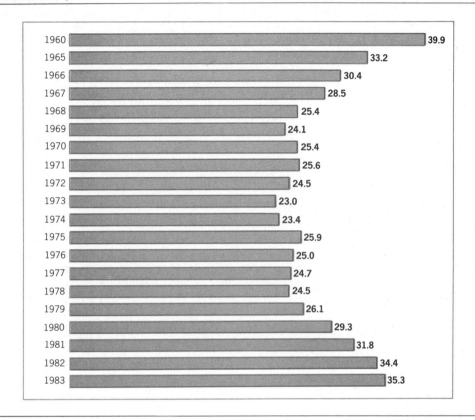

SOURCE: U.S. Bureau of the Census, *Current Population Reports,* Series P-60, Nos. 138 and 140 (Washington, D.C.: U.S. Government Printing Office, 1984).

have grappled with this problem; their proposals generally fall into two major approaches, based upon either absolute deprivation or relative deprivation.

Absolute Deprivation

To avoid the pitfalls of subjective measurement of poverty, the federal government and other official agencies use the **absolute deprivation** approach, in which income is the determinant. Here the assumption is that a family requires a minimum amount of money to secure the basic necessities of life, and it is poor if unable to earn that minimum amount.

Since government research has shown that poor families spend one-third of their income on food, and the Department of Agriculture provides cost estimates of average food prices for a minimum nutritional diet, the Social Security Administration (SSA) uses these data to set annually the official poverty income line. The SSA triples the annual food cost figure, factors in changes in the overall cost of living as shown in the Consumer Price Index (CPI), and then establishes cut-off numbers for the poverty level depending on size of family and farm or nonfarm family status. For example, in 1983 the poverty threshold for an urban family of four was $10,178.

Poverty Index Changes

In absolute terms, the number of impoverished Americans declined during the War on Poverty, going from 39.9 million in 1960 to 23 million in 1973. For the next 6 years the total remained around 25 million, but by 1983 it had risen to 35.3 million. Since 1979, about 5 million people have slid below the poverty line, the victims either of the recession or of structural unemployment caused by the deterioration of old-line industries.[3]

Arbitrary Indicator

Using family income levels to determine those living in poverty is a direct measurement approach, but also an arbitrary one. For example, if a family earns just one dollar more annually than the cut-off poverty figure, it is not included among the poor. Moreover, the cost of living varies from one urban region to another. Another important factor is that the federal experts setting the minimal food costs make assumptions about nutritional habits and consumer expertise among the poor which might not be correct. Unlike the middle class, the poor cannot afford to stock up on food sales items, buy newspapers and magazines to clip food coupons, buy more economical, larger-size food packages, or avoid shopping in the usually higher-priced food and merchandise stores in their neighborhood.[4]

One indication of the arbitrary nature of the division between the poor and the near-poor can be seen in the results of federal social program cuts since 1980. Seeking to reduce the huge federal deficit through domestic spending cuts while at the same time attempting to protect the "truly needy," the Reagan administration toughened the eligibility requirements for food stamps, Medicaid, housing subsidies, and Aid to Families with Dependent Children. While disagreement continues over whether or not a social safety net has protected the "truly needy," most authorities agree that the working poor—those families with incomes near or slightly above the poverty cut-off level—have been hardest hit. Loss of government assistance—the linchpin by which the working poor had previously made ends meet—plunged many into a quagmire of higher rents, food bills, and living costs on less income. Countless examples of the spreading misery have been documented throughout the country.[5]

Relative Deprivation

The absolute deprivation approach of considering the poor in terms of their needs may be the most commonly accepted, but other experts argue that the relationship of the poor to the nonpoor, or of the U.S. poor to the world poor, is far more significant. With the **relative deprivation** approach, the definition of poverty rests upon what the people believe are their minimal needs.

Some of the U.S. white poor stand in line in Oregon, awaiting their turn to receive a portion of the cheese and butter surplus distributed by the Reagan administration to the needy. Although welcome, such efforts hardly begin to ease their hardship and suffering.

Poverty Comparisons

Many of today's American poor—especially if they have indoor plumbing, electricity, and a television set—are better off than the poor of yesteryear, but then the present standard of living is higher than in the past. Today's poor view their situation not only in terms of their needs but also in relation to the affluence of the average American. Yet the poorest of our poor—the migrant workers—appear better off to the Mexican peasants entering this country legally or illegally to join their ranks. Mexico, in turn, is one of the richer of the world's poor countries, and hundreds of millions of Africans and Asians would luxuriate in a Mexican peasant's life in comparison to their own.[6]

Psychological Dimensions

Consideration of the psychological dimensions of poverty, in addition to the economic, focuses our attention upon those aspects of poverty usually disturbing the nonpoor: apathy, crime, deviance, poor educational performance, and social disorganization. A slum, for example, is not necessarily a neighborhood of old, dilapidated buildings if a strong community cohesiveness exists; a slum is more a state of mind of hopelessness, despair, and apathy possibly found in a modern high-rise housing project. If people feel so far removed from the average American standard that they cannot identify with the society, then the various lower-class pathologies will manifest themselves.[7]

WHO ARE THE POOR?

Because most Americans do not come into direct contact with the poor, they rely upon the media for their information. Unfortunately, the overemphasis on urban minorities distorts the reality of poverty in this country and fosters many popular misconceptions. In an influential book of the 1960s that helped launch the War on Poverty, Michael Harrington spoke about the ''invisibility'' of the poor to most Americans.[8] The average person lives and works in areas containing few impoverished people, this isolation further enhanced by zoning restrictions, highways bypassing poor neighborhoods, and heavily enforced local ordinances against ped-

One of New York City's homeless citizens dozes on the sidewalk outside the luxurious Plaza Hotel. In all U.S. cities can be found the street people, living in poverty, struggling daily to survive, without hope or direction in their lives.

dling, panhandling, and the presence of "undesirables." When we examine what we do know about the nation's poor, however, the picture is quite different from commonly held stereotypes.

Minority Status

Despite popular belief, most of the U.S. poor are white, not black. In 1982, the U.S. Department of Commerce reported that 62.6 percent of those living in poverty were white, 26.6 percent were black, and 10.8 percent were Hispanic. In actual numbers, these percentages convert to approximately 21.5 million, 9.2 million, and 3.7 million respectively.[9]

While this information gives us an accurate overview of the American poor, a different perspective emerges when we examine the data more closely. Two-thirds of the total poor may be white, but minority peoples are disproportionately represented in that total. Specifically, slightly more than 1 out of 10 Whites lives in poverty, but 1 out of 3 Blacks is poor and 1 out of 4 Hispanics is poor. Blacks comprise almost 12 percent of the nation's population, but they represent 26.6 percent of the total poor, while Hispanics are 6.3 percent of the country's population but account for 10.8 percent of the U.S. poor.

Minorities are overrepresented among the poor for several reasons. You will recall reading a few pages earlier that, since the Irish migration in the mid-nineteenth century and that of others thereafter, many poor from other lands have come to this country to improve their economic situation. While some achieved economic security rather quickly, most immigrants did not enter the economic mainstream until often into the second or third generation. Part of the explanation for large numbers of minority poor lies then in the continuing arrival of impoverished immigrants and the time required for them to move up the socioeconomic ladder (see Figure 9.2).

However, upward mobility can prove elusive to many minority people. Racial discrimination, for example, long denied equal educational and employment opportunities to Blacks. Poor nonwhite minorities today are usually concentrated in decaying urban areas where both the quality of education for the children and the job opportunities for the adults are often very limited. Whether they are Native Americans living on or near a reservation, Chicanos in the Southwest, or Blacks and other Hispanics throughout the country, their lack of educational attainment and occupational skills in comparison to the bulk of the population restricts their job marketability.

Family Structure

The 1980 Census revealed that one out of every eight children, and nearly half of all black youngsters now lives in a single-parent home. Because of the rising divorce rate and the increasing incidence of out-of-wedlock births, the number of single-parent families soared from 21.7 million in 1970 to 35 million in 1980. Since a household's composition has a direct relationship to the family's economic health, this statistic offers considerable cause for concern. For example, in 1982 the annual

FIGURE 9.2 Who the Poor Are (in millions)

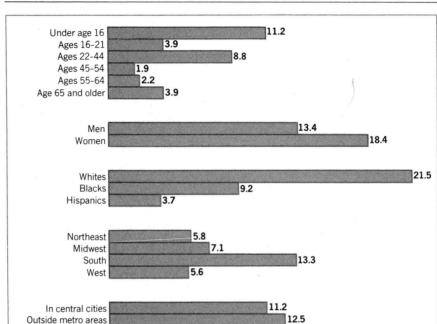

SOURCE: U.S. Department of Commerce.

median income for a traditional family, with both husband and wife present was $23,141, compared to $9,320 for a female-headed household.[10]

Nine out of ten single-parent families are maintained by the woman. With many women lacking skills and education, with poor job and earning opportunities for women, and with child-care centers often unavailable or too expensive, the female-headed households are more likely to live in poverty. In fact, a continual upward trend of such families living in poverty has been occurring, up from 1.8 million in 1969 to 3.0 million in 1980.[11] Thus, female-headed families are the fastest growing segment of the population living in poverty; one out of three female-headed families now lives below the government's official poverty line.

Critics maintain that government efforts to assist these families have actually contributed to this **feminization of poverty.**[12] In many states male-headed families receive less welfare aid than female-headed families, even if no difference in family incomes exists. No Medicaid assistance is available at all to male-headed families, regardless of income. The Aid to Families with Dependent Children program (AFDC) primarily benefits female-headed families.[13] If males are unable to find work to support their families, some people argue, they may well desert their families both to escape the painful daily reminders of their inability to provide and to make their families eligible for higher welfare benefits.

BOX 9.1

PORTRAIT OF POVERTY: I

Phyllis Sublett, 46, is not, by the definitions of Reagan's America, a "truly needy" person. She is nonetheless poor, a widow who has great difficulty eking out an existence for herself and three children on a $729-a-month social-security payment that began when her husband was killed in a train accident. Sometimes there is no money left for food at the end of the month. . . .

There was a time in America when $729 per month would have seemed generous income to the poor. But the ravages of inflation have made it at best a bare minimum to get by on. So that the house will keep running, Mrs. Sublett always pays her utility bills first. These consist of $126 for 100 gallons of fuel oil, which she must buy at least once a month in the cold weather. The other utilities—gas, electricity, water and sewer—come to $73 per month. Rent for her cramped home on Ninth Street in Sterling (Illinois) is $200 per month. Groceries are at least $80 a week, leaving $100 or less for all other expenses. "There are days at the end of the month when there's not a nickel in the house," she says, "and I'm scared, real scared."

Mrs. Sublett's difficulties are compounded by the rules under which the poor must play in Reagan's America. Because she receives social security, she is not entitled to the $50 a month in food stamps that once served as the linchpin of her budget. Because of social security, she is also not entitled to Medicaid. "All I know," she says, "is that if something happens to one of my children, someone is going to pay. Someone *has* to pay." . . . Phyllis Sublett's life consists of small strategies that all amount to the same thing—denial and trying to hold on to what little she has. Sometimes she must depend on the good graces of her landlady, who will bring food at the end of the month when the Subletts are down on cash. "Timmy wants to go to college," she says. She laughs—and in the laugh is acid irony. "What hope is there going to be of that?"

. . . But the outlook for Phyllis Sublett and her family is bleak. Burned in the furnace of inflation and locked to a fixed government income that is simply not enough, the Subletts and millions like them spend each day wondering how they will get though the next.

SOURCE: *Newsweek* (April 5, 1982), p. 22. Reprinted by permission.

Age

Together, children and youth under the age of 18 and adults over 65 comprise more than half of the nation's poor. Representing 38.4 percent of the total poor, the young are the largest single category living in poverty. The old are also disproportionately represented among the nation's poor, constituting about 14 percent of the total. Although 14 percent of the total population lives in poverty, about 16 percent of those over 65 and about 18 percent of those under 18 are poor.[14]

BOX 9.2

STARVING IN THE SHADOW OF PLENTY

I found her by accident, trying to crawl out of her doorway and down the broken concrete steps in an effort to get food. She was eighty-four and living alone in what looked like an abandoned house near the corner of Ninth and Bainbridge streets in South Philadelphia, less than a mile away from my comfortable town house. . . . Her name was Martha Roca. She had almost starved to death.

That afternoon in 1974 I went with my seven-year-old daughter Rebekah to our local supermarket and bought food for Mrs. Roca. In the months that followed it became our habit to take several bags of groceries to her each Saturday afternoon. Rebekah thought of it as the best part of our week. There was something in the experience of giving that moved and delighted her. When Martha Roca laughed with tears streaming down her face, saying, ''Thank you, thank you, darling dear, when I feel better I'll crochet,'' Rebekah felt her joy and believed we were solving the problem. But by then I had met Julia, who also lived nearby.

Down a narrow alley where renovated and dilapidated houses stood side by side, Julia, whose weight had dropped from 150 down to 90 pounds, was sitting in her doorway on a torn green plastic chair and hoping, as she always did, that someone would visit her. She was wearing the dark blue dress that she usually wore—the better of the only two she owned. Julie peered up at me from the darkness of her room. Then she smiled. She had no teeth, and her toes peeked through the holes in her straw slippers. She invited me in, and I sat down on the couch where she slept. I felt something on my leg. Automatically I went to brush it off, and then I saw them—hundreds of roaches running across the filthy green-and-white linoleum, over the fading flowered wallpaper, across the biblical scenic calendar and the postcard smile of John Cardinal Krol, archbishop of the Philadelphia diocese. Everywhere. Even if there had been any food in Julia's kitchen the roaches would have consumed it before she could.

Julia didn't see or hear too well, which was probably a blessing. Wanting to be hospitable to me, she raised her arm and pointed to a faded photograph of herself and her family. She, young and plump at twenty-one. Around her neck was a silver crucifix.

The overrepresentation of young people can be partly explained by their membership in single-parent families, as we discussed earlier. Although most poor families have an average of only two children, almost 15 percent have five children or more. Large families are overrepresented among the poor, as indicated by the fact that over 40 percent of the 11.3 million children living in poverty are in families with five or more children.[15] Another significant factor is the alarming increase of nonmarital births among teenagers, from 199,900 in 1970 to 271,801 in 1980.[16] Among white teenagers, 33 percent of all births were illegitimate, while black teenagers had 86

"I am High Episcopalian. I was christened in Camden (New Jersey) on June 28, 1899. There's no one left but me," she said sadly, "so I know God left me here for some purpose."

I couldn't help wondering exactly what purpose it was that God had in mind for her.

"Do you get much food? Do people go to the store and get you food?" I asked, seeing how thin she was.

Her voice cracked. "No," she said sadly, "there ain't been nobody around at all."

Once, on a Saturday, she had tried to go to a local supermarket, but she tripped and fell in the gutter. She lay there for a long time before a little boy stopped and helped her up. She tried once again, on a Tuesday. That time she got to the store and managed to buy a few things, but on the way home someone grabbed her bag of groceries and ran away. After that she was afraid to even try, so she sat there on her torn green chair among the roaches, waiting for the guests who never came and waiting also, rather patiently, for God to let her know the special purpose He had in mind for her.

I knew that Rebekah and I could add Julia to our list and take her food on Saturdays along with Mrs. Roca. We could help them, but I had done some research and had learned that there were tens of thousands of other people—men, women, and children—in Philadelphia alone who were desperate for food.

They were America's hidden poor, forgotten in the midst of our prosperity. They had been identified by the government; they were represented by statistics stored in government computers and filed in government cabinets. They were among those President Lyndon Johnson had intended to include when he declared his War on Poverty ten years earlier in 1964.

But the Johnson administration had failed to redeem its promises to the hungry and poor, and in 1969, Richard Burns, one of Nixon's top domestic advisers, had confidently announced that poverty was only "an intellectual concept defined by artificial statistics."

SOURCE: Reprinted by permission of The Putnam Publishing Group from *Starving in the Shadow of Plenty* by Loretta Schwartz. Copyright © 1981 by Loretta Schwartz.

percent of all births out of wedlock. Because most teenage mothers drop out of school and lack solid job prospects, a disproportionate number of teenage mothers are living in poverty and on welfare.[17]

Like so many of the young, the old also experience difficulty in finding a job to keep themselves from poverty. Compulsory retirement rules and age discrimination in hiring have excluded those 65 and older from the labor market. Consequently, many live on modest fixed incomes from social security, savings, and retirement benefits. An increasing number of the elderly and women are non-Whites, whose often low earnings when they were younger mean their retirement income will also be minimal. Despite older persons receiving increased attention in recent years, partly due to their organizing and lobbying efforts, the percentage of people over 65 living in poverty has remained fairly constant for the past 10 years. However, that figure of about 15.3 percent is far better than the 35.2 percent elderly poor reported in 1959 and in earlier years.[18]

Locale

Most of us are familiar with urban poverty because of extensive media coverage and the concentration of poor people in the central cities. However, more than half the nation's poor live in rural or suburban areas. Both the unemployment and poverty rates in rural areas are higher than the national average. The mechanization of agriculture and the lessened viability of small, independent farms have left many unskilled rural workers without means of support. Nonfarm rural people—like those living in Appalachia, the Ozarks, the Southwest, and the Upper Great Lakes—also find only irregular or seasonal employment, if any, and face little prospect of improved opportunities.

A fairly high proportion of the rural population lives throughout the southern half of the United States. It is not surprising, then, that almost 42 percent of the nation's

Less visible to most Americans are the rural poor, living in more isolated regions of most states. Their dwellings, such as this one in Appalachia, are substandard in structure, warmth, and plumbing, although they often have electricity and television.

poor live there,[19] especially when we realize this area also includes Native Americans on reservations, Mexican-Americans, and migrant workers—the country's three largest impoverished minority groups. Still, the majority of the rural poor are White.[20]

Repeating a centuries-old pattern, many of the rural poor migrate to urban areas to seek a better life. Instead, they find virtually no job openings, higher living costs, tenements to replace their shacks, unsafe streets, unhealthy and unsanitary living conditions, and the other urban problems encountered by the poor already living there. Lacking education, job skills, and employment prospects, and unable to fish, raise vegetables, or trap small game as they once could in their rural areas, many rural migrants wind up on city welfare rolls to secure the needed funds to survive.

THE IMPACT OF POVERTY

The costs and consequences of poverty are detrimental not only to the poor themselves, but to the rest of society as well. As long as poverty remains as extensive as it is, American society loses a sizable and productive labor force whose tax payments and increasing purchasing power would stimulate further the national economy. Also, until poverty is vanquished, taxpayers must shoulder immense burdens in underwriting the burgeoning social and welfare programs, slum clearance and urban renewal projects, and ongoing crime control activities. For the poor, their lack of income has both devastating and degrading effects on virtually every aspect of their lives.

Health

A 3-year study by the Public Health Service revealed that, in comparison to the nonpoor, the poor have four times as much obvious iron deficiency anemia and twice as many borderline cases. The poor also have twice the obvious deficiency in vitamins A, C, and Riboflavin. These diet deficiencies are an important cause of infant mortality and disease. The pregnant woman's lack of essential vitamins and minerals often means her child will be born prematurely, with fewer brain cells, a smaller brain, and damaged nerve tissue. Infants receiving inadequate nutrition in their early years are likely to suffer irreversible physical or mental impairment.[21] Related statistics prove quite shocking:

1. The infant mortality rate among the poor is twice that of other Americans and the national infant mortality rate is higher than that of Western Europe.
2. Premature births among poor women are triple the rate among the nonpoor.
3. Poor women die in childbirth at a rate four times greater than the nonpoor.
4. Prenatal malnourishment results in 5 percent of all babies in poor families being born mentally retarded, far above the national average.

5. Malnutrition after birth has caused brain damage to more than one million babies and young children.[22]

Inadequate nutrition, substandard housing (particularly heating), poor sanitary conditions, air pollution, and inadequate medical attention all make it quite likely the poor will be sick more often. They also suffer acute or chronic ailments more frequently and have an average life span that is 6 years less than the nonpoor.

Mental illness is another health area wherein notable differences occur among the social classes. Doctors diagnose problems of psychosis, particularly schizophrenia, more frequently among the poor, and they are far more likely to be institutionalized, receiving shock treatment or chemotherapy instead of the longer-range psychiatric treatment. Even those few accepted for psychotherapy received only limited assistance and from less qualified personnel because of social class value differences (see Chapter 14).[23]

Housing

Poor Americans usually live in substandard housing, surrounded by others like themselves living in drafty, dilapidated buildings likely to have rats, roaches, poor heating and plumbing. More than half of this housing lies in rural areas, where such living conditions remain relatively hidden from public view and the costs of living are lower than in the rest of the country. In the more visible urban areas, rents are proportionately higher than middle-class homes of similar living space, and without the equity and tax credit mortgage payments provide. Relatedly, the urban poor must shop at nearby stores where prices are often higher than at slightly more distant stores to which they cannot travel.

The outward migration of the urban middle class to suburbia, the suburban zoning regulations requiring large property lot size and restricting multiple-family structures, together with urban renewal and low-income housing projects, have combined to produce a highly segregated urban poverty class. Because the urban poor are more likely to be non-White, unlike the rural poor, these areas are racially segregated as well. Such economically depressed areas offer little attraction to investors, developers, or builders because the poor cannot afford to buy or rent new or rehabilitated housing units. Unless the area gets targeted for office buildings or middle-class housing (thereby driving off the poor to another neighborhood), it will continue to experience decay and decline.

Family Life

As social scientists have consistently found among lower classes of all backgrounds and time periods, family instability tends to be a more frequent occurrence among the poor. Marriages and pregnancies occur at an earlier age. Divorces and desertions are also more common, as are incidents of family disputes and violence. Since family life is an important factor in personality development, the greater possibility of stress and discord in the home rather than a stable emotional support system may serve as a causal factor of subsequent antisocial behavior.

Psychological Scars

To be poor is degrading, since all other segments of society both reject and despise the poor, considering them lazy, incompetent, and immoral. Others see them as failures, and often unable to find work and escape poverty no matter how hard they try, feelings of hopelessness and apathy set in among the poor. This fatalistic attitude, encouraged by the lack of power to effect any change, leads to several possible coping strategies for survival. These can range from hostility and aggression (vandalism, theft, assault) to withdrawal and total apathy. Others simply accommodate themselves to the situations, working as they can to survive. Another means of coping is escapism through religious fervor, drinking, or drugs.

Education

Lack of education is both a cause and effect of poverty. Almost three-fourths of the heads of low-income households did not graduate from high school, with about half completing less than 1 year of high school.[24] Their children are less likely than the nonpoor to graduate from high school or enter college. Part of the reason for this is they do not do as well in school as the children of high-school graduates. With no academic encouragement or assistance at home, and with the low expectations of their teachers intensifying their low achievement, these low-income students often drop out. As a result, they wind up in low-paying jobs, if any, and continue a new generation of poverty. The multigenerational dimension of poverty is intimately intertwined with education.

Besides a shorter length of education, the poor are also more likely to experience a lower quality of education. Formal schooling among the rural poor is often quite rudimentary or nonexistent. The urban poor usually attend overcrowded schools with limited resources due to budget constraints, less skilled teachers, and greater discipline problems. Labeled early as unlikely college material, these students are assigned to the "slow" or general track and destined therefore to be unqualified as adults for most better-paying jobs in our technological postindustrial society.

Work

Most poor people do work, but their jobs are low-paying and often unstable. Farm laborers eke out an existence with seasonal employment, subject to the erratic weather. Droughts, heavy rains, floods, hurricanes, early frosts, all can wreak havoc on crops and thus on the need for laborers for harvest. Nonfarm laborers are easily susceptible to downturns in the economy, finding themselves among the first to be laid off. Many find the kinds of work they are able to do becoming less available because of technology or the relocation of companies elsewhere. With dwindling employment opportunities and the remaining low-paying, dead-end jobs all they can hope to keep if they are fortunate, the working poor struggle from one day to the next to survive. Their health problems—ranging from frequent minor ills to stress-related problems of heart disease—more frequently cost them loss of income when they miss work, since their jobs often lack the sick benefits others take for granted.

WHO IS TO BLAME FOR POVERTY?

Perhaps no other social problem has stirred so much controversy among leaders, social scientists, and the public concerning its cause, as poverty. Since correct identification of the cause is critical for finding the solution, these differences of opinion can and have impacted upon how we as a society have addressed the problem and paradox of poverty in this "land of opportunity."

Individual Faults and Deviant Behavior

Blaming the poor for their circumstances has been a common American practice for at least 150 years, since large numbers of Irish immigrants settled in urban slums and struggled to overcome bigotry and achieve a better life. Because America has long served as the beacon light of economic opportunity to millions of impoverished immigrants, native-born American perception of poverty and minorities often became closely intertwined. Regardless of which minority group was at the bottom of the socioeconomic ladder in the past or present, their contemporary American hosts often have believed the group's cultural values or innate abilities were at fault for the poverty.

Value Orientations

Understanding how such thinking has prevailed for so long is not difficult. An integral part of the American belief system centers around individualism and the existence of widespread opportunity. In this country, advocates maintain, you can "make it" if you work hard and try to succeed in competition with others. With many rags-to-riches examples to demonstrate the validity of this belief, economic failure is attributed to a lack of effort, incompetence, and other character defects in the individual or in the members of a particular group.[25] Several national surveys of public opinion about the causes of poverty have illustrated that this attitude is widely held. One researcher found an average of four out of five people believed that a lack of thrift and proper money management among the poor, as well as their lack of ability and talent, loose morals, and drunkenness, were important reasons for their poverty.[26] Similar findings have been reported by Harris and Gallup polls in 1972, and in a 1978 *New York Times*–CBS News poll.

Contributing to this tendency to find fault in individuals for their poverty have been the controversial analyses of several social scientists. Richard Herrnstein, for example, has argued that the poor have a lower intellectual capability than the nonpoor, they marry other people of low intelligence, thus producing children of low intellectual capacity.[27] This argument is not a new one; similar claims have been made in the past against many immigrant poor, particularly southern and eastern Europeans.[28] However, substantial evidence exists to refute such arguments.[29] Changes in people's economic conditions result in changes in intelligence test results. Also, many poor people have raised children who rose to prominence in virtually every field of endeavor.

BOX 9.3

PORTRAIT OF POVERTY: II

In the leaky wooden house that the Champions built themselves, the only appliance is a small black-and-white TV set hooked up to an auto battery. For want of electricity, light is provided by kerosene lamp. For want of plumbing, water comes from a creek a mile away.

Yet this homestead is one of the better things that have happened to Lizzie Champion and her brood—a source of pride and comfort for a family that has coped with poverty for generations. Lizzie, 68, cannot read because she dropped out of school in the third grade to go to work. "I had to work all the time," she recalls. "I've been working on the farm all my life."

The cycle of limited income, education and opportunity has repeated itself in her children. Says son W.C. Champion, 29, the man of this household: "My father left when I was young, and we kids had to help our mother make a living. I went as far as the third grade."

Today Lizzie, W.C. and eight relatives and in-laws occupy the two-bedroom home and a nearby trailer on Wilhite Mountain, about 20 miles south of Decatur, Ala. The house sits on land purchased—using the installment plan at $48 a month— when W.C. worked for a nearby furniture manufacturer. He has since been laid off. The family's main income source now is Lizzie's Social Security and disability payments, W.C.'s unemployment checks, and food stamps.

Still, the Champions are proud of their modest home and dream of expanding it. "We're going to stay with it," says W.C. "We're just going to hang on to the mountain."

SOURCE: Reprinted from *U.S. News & World Report,* August 16, 1982. Copyright, 1982, U.S. News & World Report, Inc.

Culture of Poverty

Another explanation, more widely accepted, is that the poor develop a **culture of poverty,** as a means of adapting to their situation. According to anthropologist Oscar Lewis,[30] and others such as Edward Banfield,[31] the cycle of poverty is continually reinforced because children learn poverty-related values and attitudes from their parents. This set of beliefs and behavior includes attitudes of apathy, resignation, and fatalism; a deemphasis on schooling; immediate gratification instead of thrift; early sexual experience and unwanted pregnancies; unstable family life, often authoritarian and female-centered; and a distrust of authority, whether police, school, government, or social agencies. As the children mature into adults, their negative orientation to life and work makes them ill-equipped, Lewis argued, to enter the societal mainstream.

Raised in squalor and severe deprivation, what chance do these and other poor, nonwhite, urban children have to grow up and out of the slums? Many social scientists worry about the creation of a permanent underclass, trapped by poor education, job skills, and job opportunities.

War on Poverty

In the 1960s the federal government launched a short-lived War on Poverty, based on the premise of the perpetuation of poverty through parental socialization. According to the Council of Economic Advisors:

> Poverty breeds poverty. . . . Poor parents cannot give their children the opportunities for better health and education needed to improve their lot. Lack of motivation, hope, and incentive is a more subtle but not less powerful barrier than lack of financial means. Thus the cruel legacy of poverty is passed from parents to children.[32]

The government programs that followed attempted to counteract self-defeating aspects of the poverty subculture through early intervention programs of cultural enrichment for children (Operation Head Start, preschool centers, Sesame Street). The resocialization of adults, through various training programs (Job Corps, Comprehensive and Employment Training Act [CETA], Volunteers in Service to America [VISTA], and Community Action programs), was intended to build self-confidence and reorient adult work attitudes, as well as generate earning opportunities. Although a few programs were successful, such as those for consumer advocacy and legal services, or of limited success (Head Start, Job Corps, VISTA), the War on Poverty had little effect upon resolving the problem of poverty.

Opposing Views

Critics such as William Ryan and Charles A. Valentine, contend that poverty can only be eliminated by first recognizing that the problem is caused by society and that lower-income people are the victims, not the offenders.

To Ryan, **blaming the victim** results in misdirected social programs: by rationalizing away the socially acquired stigma of poverty as the result of a genetic character defect, we ignore the continuing effect of current victimizing social forces. As a result, we attempt to help the "disorganized" black family instead of overcoming racism, or we strive to develop "better" attitudes and skills in low-income children rather than revamping the poor quality schools they attend.[33]

Valentine argues that many of Lewis's "class distinctive traits" of the poor are either "externally imposed conditions" (unemployment, crowded and deteriorated housing, lack of education) or "unavoidable matters of situational expediency" (hostility toward social institutions, low expectations and self-image).[34] The poor, suggests Valentine, possess many positive values and behavior patterns similar to the middle class, but their life situation has obliged them to develop also some distinctive subcultural traits in order to cope and survive. Only changes in the resources made available to the poor and in the total social structure will bring about changes in any poverty subcultural traits.

This discussion about the fault for poverty resting in the individuals themselves should remind you of our consideration in Chapter 1 about the character-flaw fallacy and quasi-theories. Here we have the case of the poor analyzed to determine how they are different from the rest of us because they suffer deprivation. These differences are identified and incorrectly defined as the cause of the social problem of poverty, prompting publicly funded programs to eradicate or lessen these differences. Such programs are doomed before they begin because they fail to get at the root causes of poverty.

Institutional Faults and System Disorganization

Under the functionalist or system theory approach, we can understand poverty from two perspectives. One view is that the scope and very nature of poverty is the result of rapid social change throughout this century. Automation, high technology, the decline of low-skilled rural and urban labor opportunities, discrimination, and shifting residential patterns have altered needs and demands. Consequently, a large segment of the population has been caught in the middle, vulnerable and untrained for this postindustrial society. Much like the social upheaval caused by the Industrial Revolution, the people of this century have also experienced substantial economic changes which the social system has not completely absorbed.

Another view is this: instead of a breakdown in social institutions, our values make poverty a necessary part of the social system. The threat of poverty serves as an important function to motivate people to work, but if the work one does is not highly regarded (picking crops, washing dishes, custodial work), then the economic rewards are low. Conversely, we give more money and prestige to those whose work we do consider important, more difficult or complex, and which requires long and arduous training.[35] While all work contributes to the functioning of the entire society, a hierarchy of rewards creates a system of social stratification wherein some people at the bottom receive little.

Negative Functions

Although poverty exists as a negative incentive to work or as a weak reward for low-valued work contributions, according to this view, it can also become dysfunctional to the society as well. If poverty becomes too widespread, it then becomes a serious drain on the economy, necessitating large amounts of public expenditures or else making possible violent disruptions within the society. Also, if the pay incentives for the low-paying jobs are less than one could receive in welfare benefits, then a twofold problem exists: unfilled jobs and excessive unemployment. The functionalist solution is a more efficient economic system which effectively utilizes job training and educational programs and thereby meets the needs of agriculture, business, and industry.

Positive Functions

Yet poverty also persists because it is functionally beneficial to many others who resist efforts to change the situation. Herbert Gans has identified numerous positive functions the poor provide for the more powerful and affluent:

1. The poor offer a low-wage labor pool to do the "dirty work" no one else wants to do and which subsidizes the economic activities of these employers.

2. Their activities make life easier for the affluent, relieving them of daily chores, by working as servants, gardeners, etc.

3. Their poverty creates many jobs for the nonpoor: social workers, penologists, police, pawnshop owners, numbers racketeers, liquor store owners, drug sellers, loan sharks, and so forth.

4. Poor people subsidize merchants by purchasing second-hand, dilapidated products others don't want (cars, housing, appliances, stale bread, fruits, and other vegetables).

5. The poor provide a convenient target for condemnation and punishment to uphold the legitimacy of the traditional values of hard work, thrift, honesty, and morality.

6. The poor provide an opportunity for the nonpoor to feel good about themselves through altruistic or charitable activities, as well as serving as a reference point of favorable comparison.

7. The poor aid in the upward mobility of others, since they are removed from the competition for a good education and good jobs.

8. The poor are powerless and so can be made to absorb the cost of

change in a society (displaced from their homes by urban renewal, expressways, or civic projects; being among the first victims of unemployment because of technological advances or inflation-fighting government actions to tighten the money supply).[36]

Although functional alternatives to poverty exist, Gans concludes, they would be dysfunctional to the affluent by requiring higher costs and a redistribution of some wealth and power. Only when the existence of poverty becomes dysfunctional to the nonpoor or when the poor obtain enough power to change society will the situation change.

Inequality and Inevitable Conflict

Gans's analysis of the positive functions of poverty actually bridges over into conflict theory as well inasmuch as he examines how the powerful have a vested interest in the maintenance of a poverty class. Perhaps no other social problem has brought forth as much conflict theoretical analysis as poverty. Economic inequality prompted Karl Marx more than 100 years ago to argue that a capitalistic society promotes the interests of those owning the means of production while exploiting those who do not. Sociologist Ralf Dahrendorf, considering the new forms of ownership in modern society (stocks, mutual funds), has offered a neo-Marxian explanation that authority rather than ownership is the basis of class dominance and oppression of the poor.[37]

Blaming the System

Socialist Michael Harrington shares this view of capitalism as the root of all problems facing the poor.[38] He maintains inadequate programs and misdirected priorities have hampered the solution of this solvable problem. Only when a full national program, comparable to those of the democratic socialist countries of Western Europe, addresses the capitalist class inequities in income, housing, public transportation, education, medical and dental services, will poverty be overcome.[39]

Conflict theorists reject the notion that the victims of poverty are to blame because of inadequate socialization or "improper" values. If anything, the system is at fault in fostering a false consciousness among the poor that they cannot achieve more than they have and must therefore be dependent upon others. Alienated, robbed of human dignity, and filled with low self-esteem, the poor remain disorganized and apathetic. As long as they accept their plight, they remain in a set of chains negating their escape from poverty. Until poor people mobilize and take political action and gain some support from those in power, conflict theorists do not believe economic inequalities can be reduced much. Some evidence exists to support this contention. Michael Betz, for example, found the 23 riot-torn cities in 1965 and 1966 received a dramatic increase in welfare benefits thereafter compared to 20 similar cities not having riots.[40]

Frances Fox Piven and Richard A. Cloward also documented the expansion of welfare benefits in the late 1960s in response to the riots.[41] Noting that eligibility rules have been more permissive in times of high unemployment and more restrictive in times of low unemployment, they conclude welfare programs function as a safety measure to prevent disorder by absorbing and controlling the unemployed. Because capitalism requires a pool of low-skilled workers from which to draw during times of economic growth, it must also provide a place for laid-off workers when the economy contracts to avoid political turmoil. Additional proof of this view that only when the poor become a threat does the government initiate or expand welfare relief to diffuse social unrest, is the fact that these programs are reduced and even eliminated when conditions improve. Thus efforts to aid the poor are situational responses to potential instability of the society rather than a genuine drive against poverty itself.

Guaranteed Annual Income

In a subsequent work Piven and Cloward advanced a radical strategy for ending poverty.[42] They called for a coalition of all militant civil rights organizations, antipoverty organizations, and the poor to create a major political and economic crisis to force Congress to enact a **guaranteed annual income** for everyone. Their plan is to conduct a massive recruitment drive of all eligible welfare recipients not presently receiving any benefits which, they claim, would double the number. Such a massive increase of recipients would cause such political and fiscal turmoil that Congress would be forced to act to end the poverty that generates the problem. This strategy could lead to class conflict and violence, the authors admit, but so could continuing existing conditions.

Although Piven and Cloward's proposal is more radical than most, the concept of a nationally guaranteed annual income is not new. In Scandinavia, for example, poverty has been eradicated through such a program of providing a minimum decent income for all. The U.S. government also experimented between 1975 and 1979 with various forms of income maintenance programs for low-income families. A commitment was made so that thousands of people could receive different levels of support over a period of 3 to 5 years, with only a slow decrease during that period if they began to earn more money. Contrary to the negative expectations of some, most of the poor continued to work, spent the extra money on better housing, durable goods (refrigerators, TVs, cars), housewares and clothing, not on luxuries or entertainment.[43] However, a significant number of marriages also broke up, disturbing Congress which was unwilling to support a program encouraging women in unhappy relationships to leave their husbands.

Interaction and Social Interpretation

The interactionist perspective, as you recall, concentrates on the ways people perceive and define the events that influence their lives. That perception and definition among the poor, the outgrowth of daily interaction with others, could reinforce the existence of poverty. For example, despite the popularity of some minority superstars in sports and entertainment, the main reference group for the poor are those living in their neighborhood. If this area is an urban slum with high unemployment, serious crime, drugs and alcohol abuse, as well as a high school absenteeism and dropout rate, then few positive role models exist. The "successful" person to pattern oneself after may be the clerk in a nearby store with a steady job, or the pimp, hustler, or numbers runner in the streets. Or, one may fall victim to the pervasiveness of a dropout life-style with erratic, low-paying employment, early pregnancies, and overwhelming, defeating responsibilities.

Effects of Labeling

Another aspect of this view of poverty is the impact of societal **labeling** upon concepts of self among poor people. If we apply the blaming-the-victim approach we discussed earlier to how the poor may respond to such stereotyping, we can understand how society helps perpetuate poverty. If we define the poor as lazy, incompetent, immoral, apathetic, and without the necessary competitive determination to succeed, then those individuals may well accept these definitions as accurate. This is especially probable if socialization sources, including family, friends, school, and the media continuously apply such labels.[44]

Attitudes and expectations of others often occasion behavioral responses which conform to those views. In one study, for instance, black mothers and other adult female relatives tended to label the male youths as unreliable and irresponsible, and many internalized this view of themselves and behaved accordingly.[45] In the schools, low expectations can be devastating. If teachers have high achievement expectations for their students, their chances of realizing that level of accomplishment are high. However, low expectations tend to produce low student motivation and achievement.[46] Labeling a low-income child as a probable failure puts that child at a disadvantage and sets in motion a self-fulfilling prophecy: without encouragement and self-confidence the child is indeed more likely to perform poorly and possibly quit school when old enough to do so.

Continuous Reinforcement

Not all low-income people internalize inferior feelings about themselves or conform to low expectations. Many adults attempt to emphasize a good education for their children, and many young people set their sights on lofty goals and work hard to achieve them. Still, social class value orientations are widely shared by the members of each stratified tier of society. Labeling theorists suggest a long and continuous process of identifying the poor as inadequate often conditions them to believe that they are, and this self-concept is reinforced from within and without the poverty subculture.[47]

What this perspective is implying, therefore, is that the ongoing interactions and interpretations in people's daily lives function to keep people at the bottom of the socioeconomic ladder. Poverty is a psychological trap as well as an economic one. The poor tend to define their social environment as the result of their own shortcomings, because that is the prevailing view. This negative self-image causes a passive, fatalistic acceptance of the situation. Only through an interruption of that continual negative definition—encouraging a more positive redefining of oneself and one's possibilities—can the poor overcome the economic hardships imposed on them. Such enrichment efforts to improve self-concept must be accompanied, however, by employment income opportunities.

WORK AND WELFARE

In the nineteenth century, Europeans and Americans had workhouses to provide employment and industrial training for the poor. Today we no longer have workhouses, but the general public attitude still holds that poverty could be virtually eliminated if the poor were forced to work instead of allowed to freeload.

The Nonworking Poor

Studies have consistently shown that most of our poor people do not fit this categorization of freeloaders. Current Census Bureau analysis indicates the following composition of the poor:[48]

Children under 14	34.4%
Elderly, 65 and over	18.2
Ill and disabled	4.7
In school, 14 and over	6.6
Total	63.9%

Almost 64 percent of the poor are thus unable to work because of age, health, or educational pursuits. What about the remaining 36.1 percent?

Worked	23.8%
Did not work	12.3
Total	36.1%

Significantly, almost one-fourth of the poor *do* work, but their incomes are not sufficient to propel them above the poverty level. They either work full-time at low-paying jobs or else can find only seasonal employment.

If we look more closely at the 12.3 percent not working we discover that 10.9 percent were female and 1.4 percent were male.[49] Most of these unemployed able-bodied males lack job skills, live in areas of high unemployment, or were the victims of layoffs, bankruptcies, or automation and have not yet found other work. A significant number of these males are also between the ages of 60 and 64. Most of the unemployed women were unable to work because they had to care for small children at home, and day-care centers were unavailable or too expensive.

In certain regions where minorities are heavily concentrated, such as urban centers and Indian reservations, the male unemployment can sometimes be as high as 45 percent. Nationwide the black unemployment rate has remained about twice the white unemployment rate for almost 25 years. The unemployment rate for the Native Americans and Hispanic Americans has remained well above that of other Americans, as we have discussed in Chapter 8 on Race and Ethnic Relations.

BOX 9.4

PORTRAIT OF POVERTY: III

For Richard and Helen Telehowski (in Detroit), sudden poverty means scrambling to feed five kids, sacrificing comforts, accepting welfare—blows to the spirit and the body.

Yet nothing dramatizes the plunge of this family into the ranks of the newly poor like their decision to become squatters in an abandoned house this summer. "I've never done anything like this," says Richard, 27, "but my wife and kids needed a new place. Sometimes you've got to take a chance."

Telehowski, a machinist, was laid off from his $8-an-hour job with an automotive-parts firm in 1979. Until then, he says, "I felt secure about the future—we weren't rich but we didn't need welfare either."

What followed was two years without work in Detroit's depressed economy. Helen Telehowski went through the early stages of a nervous breakdown trying to provide for the children, then recovered with timely medical help. When the family car wore out, it was junked. There was no money for a replacement.

When jobless benefits ended, the family sought welfare aid. "We didn't want to because my husband is a proud man," says Helen. "But the children had to eat."

Finally Telehowski found factory work at $4 an hour, though 40-hour weeks are not always possible. Food stamps and dependent-children aid are still needed to supplement a meager income.

Now, they are repairing the decayed inner-city house they've occupied, hoping to find the owner and make what payments they can. Meantime, they'll take squatter's rights. "The American dream is to buy your own place," says Helen, "but our chance was taken away."

SOURCE: Reprinted from *U.S. News & World Report* issue of August 16, 1982. Copyright, 1982, U.S. News & World Report, Inc.

The Welfare Poor

Since the 1930s, **welfare**—public assistance programs for the poor—has resulted in the spending of hundreds of billions of dollars, generated intense controversy among all socioeconomic levels, and yet failed to bring the problem of poverty under control. How can we spend so much money for so many years, enact dozens upon dozens of major social programs, and still have one out of every seven Americans living in poverty? Part of the answer lies in misdirected efforts: treating the symptoms not the causes, or, as in the case of the War on Poverty, placing emphasis upon combatting the "pathological" culture of poverty as the cause of the problem.

Another dimension is that a large and cumbersome bureaucracy, composed of about 4,000 federal and 342,000 state and local officials, administers the various programs, but not in a systematic or consistent manner.[50] Eligibility requirements

These New York City demonstrators for employment rights call attention to a major aspect of poverty: lack of jobs. Often single parents and lacking appropriate job skills, they are frustrated in their desire to extricate themselves from the poverty trap.

and payment amounts vary considerably from one state to another. In some states people eligible for certain forms of welfare assistance are ineligible in others, or maximum income requirements may actually be below or slightly above the poverty line, or AFDC payments in some states may not necessarily require an absent father.

A third factor is the paternalistic attitudes of some welfare agency personnel who believe it is in their job security self-interests to discourage those poor dependent upon them to extricate themselves from poverty. Finally, the stigma attached to welfare recipients disheartens many eligible poor, particularly the aged, from seeking assistance.

The more than 50 federal programs of public assistance fall into four major categories: insurance programs, services programs, employment programs, and cash programs.

Insurance Programs

This form of public assistance is by far the most widely accepted. It includes Social Security payments to retired people or their survivors, and unemployment compensation for those having lost their jobs. Such programs benefit those who have worked at steady jobs and have had payroll deductions applied to these programs. Even though many recipients receive more than they may have paid in, the public attitude is that this is their due for past work. Social Security assists primarily senior citizens no longer working and unemployment compensation enables out-of-work individuals to meet daily living expenses while seeking other work.

Services Programs
Either low-income working or unemployed people can qualify for such services and nonmonetary aid as food stamps, housing, Medicaid, and Medicare—the "in kind" benefits that, if counted as income, would cut the official number of impoverished Americans in half. Two main reasons exist for working- and middle-class hostility against these programs. First, the recipients have not made any contributions to the funds from which they are paid, making them less deserving in the eyes of the nonpoor. Recipients of these benefits often surpass in total income (earnings plus benefits) many of the working class nonpoor, as hypothetically illustrated below:

	Poor Family	Nonpoor Family
Annual Income	$ 9,000	$10,500
Food Stamps	792	0
Housing	1,200	0
Medicaid	1,500	0
Total Income	$12,492	$10,500

Another services area has been Community Action programs, designed to mobilize the poor, enhance their self-confidence, and enable them to control the poverty programs in their neighborhood. When local politicians objected to placing power in the hands of others, they took action and the program was restructured to function through the local mayors. Even so, over 900 locally run community action groups ran many programs to benefit the poor, including Head Start, Upward Bound, legal services, and job counseling.

Employment Programs
Efforts under this category attempt to improve educational and job skill levels to enhance the labor marketability of the poor. The most ambitious of these federal programs was the 10-year Comprehensive Employment and Training Act (CETA), begun in 1973. Costing more than $12 billion, it provided training, paraprofessional jobs, and incentives for employment in the private sector for the unemployed poor. The Neighborhood Youth Corps offered part-time work during the school year and summer jobs for urban youths. The Job Corps gave job skill training, remedial education, and counseling assistance within each urban low-income community. Most of these programs, however, have now ended.

Cash Programs
A number of cash benefit programs exist, including aid to the elderly, the blind, the permanently and totally disabled, through the Supplemental Security Income (SSI), and aid to families with dependent children (AFDC). The latter program draws the most fire from Middle America because of concern over increasing nonmarital births and female-headed households. Because low-income males often cannot sup-

port a family and the AFDC regulations in most states allow payments only to females where no adult male is present, the result has been an alarming increase in female-headed households among the poor. Although originally intended to assist children whose fathers had died, the program—together with the bleak earning prospects of males—has often prompted involuntary desertions and a reluctance to marry. Forty-three percent of AFDC mothers have not been married, 28 percent are separated, and 18 percent are divorced.[51] Among Blacks, who are disproportionately represented among the poor, 31 percent of the households are female-headed compared to 12 percent among Whites.[52] It is also important to note that more than half of all welfare families have only one or two children; the average monthly payment of $35 for an additional child is not enough to meet expenses of raising that child. The poor do not have more children to make more welfare money.

Another serious drawback to the welfare cash payment programs is the reduction of dollars paid in equal proportion to dollars earned by working. In effect, this is a 100 percent tax rate which does not allow for any transitional period for people to become a little financially secure and self-sufficient before the loss of monetary assistance. Consequently, few are encouraged to seek employment in the arduous or monotonous low-paying jobs that immediately impact upon their total income and benefits from services programs for the poor.

Welfare Fraud

Despite the widespread belief of fraud among welfare recipients and the occasional media publicity of some "welfare queen" caught bilking the government of tens of thousands of dollars, the reality is that less than one-half of 1 percent of all welfare claims are fraudulent. All claims are investigated, and in most cases the occurring overpayments result from errors by agency personnel. Far more fraud occurs among middle-class income tax reporting and unemployment claims (including college students) costing the government millions of dollars.[53] In 1980 the Internal Revenue Service (IRS) estimated that concealed income in excess of $100 billion cost the government over $18 billion in taxes which could have totally eliminated poverty.

Lifetime Welfare

Many Americans believe the welfare poor remain perpetually living off government relief programs. While that is true for a small number, the government reports most welfare families have been receiving it for less than 21 months. Generally, what occurs yearly is an upward movement out of poverty by about 10 million people but a slippage into poverty by others.[54] In a major longitudinal study covering 9 years, from 1967 to 1975, researchers at the University of Michigan followed the fortunes of 5,000 families (altogether about 16,000 individuals) living in poverty throughout the United States.[55] Among the major findings was that relatively few "hard-core poor" remain in poverty year after year. Only one in five were poor in all of the 9 years. For most people poverty is a temporary situation, often arising out of divorce or leaving a parental home. The "persistently poor" most often have heads of households over age 65, or with little formal education, or who are Black, female, or disabled. So, while one out of seven Americans may be identified as poor in any single year, less than a fourth of them stay poor over a multiyear period. Instead, others fall into poverty yearly.

The Welfare Rich

The term *welfare* is not used for the public assistance programs for the nonpoor, but a great many exist. Largely ignored by the public, these programs also have the same objective: to raise the incomes of those the government chooses to help. This "dual welfare" or "**wealthfare**" system is what conflict theorists seize upon to illustrate the maintenance of structured inequality in American society.[56] The two major categories of these income supplements are in individual tax breaks and corporate incentives.

Individual Tax Breaks

Despite tax reform legislation in 1978, numerous loopholes remain favoring the rich. Among these are:

1. Tax-free interest on state and municipal bonds.
2. Capital gains tax of only one-half of profits from sale of investments.
3. Rapid depreciation formulas on buildings, vehicles, and machinery.
4. Charitable deductions (often to family foundations established out of family corporate profits).
5. Homeowner deductions for property tax and mortgage interest.
6. Home office deductions, where a proportion of all house expenses can be written off if one room is exclusively used for work by qualifying individuals.
7. Trust fund payments of up to $10,000 annually per child from each parent eliminating that money from taxation for the parents.
8. No inheritance tax on estates up to $600,000.
9. Tax shelters allow postponement of taxes (often indefinitely) on certain investment income.

Although many believe the income tax is progressive—the greater one's income is, the greater one's taxes are—these tax exemptions enable the affluent to pay considerably less. In fact a recent IRS report revealed that in 1976, 244 people with annual incomes over $200,000 legally paid no taxes at all, including five people who earned more than $1 million.[57] The houseowner deductions, also used by the middle class, cost the government more than $5 billion a year, over four times that spent on the poor.

The actual distribution of wealth in this country has barely changed since 1860.[58] The top 1 percent, then and now, own one-fourth of the nation's wealth. About 1.6 percent owns 80 percent of all stock, 88.5 percent of all corporate bonds, and virtually 100 percent of all state and municipal bonds. In terms of annual income, the top 20 percent of the population receives about 42 percent of all income compared to 5 percent for the bottom 20 percent (see Figure 9.3).

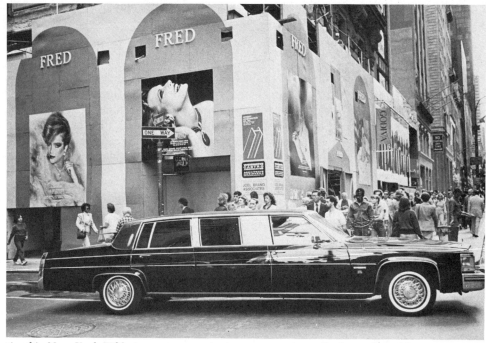

As this New York Fifth Avenue scene depicts, ostentatious displays of wealth contrast with other urban images of poverty. Matching this visual dichotomy is an attitudinal one, in which government programs for the affluent have no stigma like those for the poor.

FIGURE 9.3   Distribution of Income in the United States, 1980

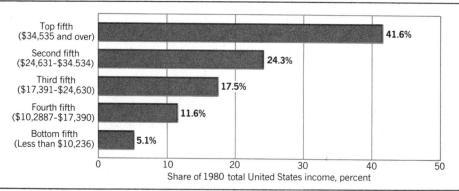

SOURCE: U.S. Bureau of Census, 1981d:15.

As is evident, there is an unequal distribution of income in the United States. In fact, the 5 percent of the population with the highest income (people who earned more than $54,060) received 15.3 percent of all income in 1950.

Corporate Incentives

All capitalist governments assist key industries in order to keep the national economy healthy. The effect, however, is to help the rich rather than the poor. For example, a recent law permits corporations with unused tax credits to sell them to other corporations, creating, suggests economist Alan Greenspan, a form of food stamps for undernourished corporations. General Electric took advantage of this law in 1981. Through the purchase of tax credits, it received a tax refund of $90 million rather than paying any taxes at all on its 1981 earnings of $1.65 billion.[60] Other incentives include investment tax credits, rapid oil depletion allowances, bailout loans to corporations like Lockheed and Chrysler, and subsidies to agriculture, railroads, shipping, and other special interests. Most farm assistance goes to agribusiness corporations (not small, independent farmers) in the form of payment for not growing crops or the purchase of surplus crops, food, and livestock to keep market prices high. In one case, the corporate family farm of U.S. Senator James Eastland, who was a staunch opponent of welfare for the poor, received $250,000 yearly in farm subsidies.[61]

One could make a strong case for each of these programs, just as one could make a strong case for each of the poverty programs. The key difference is that no stigma attaches to the programs for the affluent, no cries of government handouts are heard, no claims that the recipients are undeserving. Both programs give public money to people, but values and attitudes can and do place one group in a far more negative perspective.

ELIMINATING POVERTY

As you have read throughout this chapter, the problem of poverty has concerned many people, generated various causal explanations, and inspired many different attempts at solution. Yet poverty remains. What do we do now? As always, no shortage of suggestions exists. We shall look at three major approaches: "trickle down," Robin Hood, and interventionist.

The "Trickle-Down" Approach

The Reagan administration has approached poverty and the nation's economic ills with a supply-side policy. Utilizing the expression "A rising tide lifts all boats," their efforts have been to cut taxes and government spending, to eliminate cumbersome federal regulations and red tape that restrict the growth of business and industry, and to provide incentives in the private sector for expansion and greater employment. While these policies have been controversial, federal policymakers argue their efforts will keep inflation in check and create a period of prosperity that will trickle down to the lowest strata so all will benefit. Critics contend these policies will instead widen the gulf between the rich and poor and that some poor—the aged, disabled, or unskilled—do not gain from others' improved economic situations.

The "Robin-Hood" Approach

Advocates of this position seek a redistribution of wealth in this country. Some recommend the radical action of nationalizing large corporations and seizing large fortunes, proposals unlikely to gain much support in a society built upon the principle of free enterprise. However, more moderate suggestions center around tax reform eliminating the loopholes which enable the wealthy to avoid paying millions of dollars in taxes each year. The extent of this legal tax evasion was reported in 1979 by the IRS: in 1975 almost 21 million people paid no income tax at all on $49.4 billion income because they declared exemptions totaling $35.3 billion and tax credits sufficient to cover the remaining taxable income.[62] One significant individual example was that of the late J. Paul Getty, oil billionaire; in the 1960s he was earning about $300,000 a day, for which his annual income tax would have been $70 million. However, effective use of tax loopholes resulted in his paying only a few thousand dollars.

The Interventionist Approach

Others say bold and direct federal action, similar to that of the Roosevelt administration during the Great Depression, is the only solution. A variety of proposals have been advanced, all involving the government more fully in assisting the poor.

Employment

Providing job training for unskilled workers was a major part of the War on Poverty that had mixed results. Creating jobs for the unemployed was a successful approach by the FDR administration. However, this action is extremely expensive for taxpayers and fuels inflation—not a problem in the 1930s. Current federal policy is to stimulate the economy and provide tax incentives for the private sector to expand in depressed areas and hire the unemployed.

Education

Since education often provides the means for upward mobility and lack of its tends to produce poverty, some have argued for greater educational effort. Michael Harrington, for example, has pressed for a GI-type bill in education wherein the federal government would pay for the poor to go to school, pay all education expenses, and give them a living allowance if they have a family.[63] After World War II such legislation was extremely effective in raising the educational levels and life opportunities of millions of war veterans. Similarly, a compensatory payment program for law enforcement personnel in the 1970s, also covering their education expenses, succeeded in raising dramatically their educational achievement levels. Once again, however, education alone is not the answer; jobs have to exist once the poor complete their education.

Welfare Reform

The present system is an inconsistent patchwork of federal, state, and local regulations and agencies. It is ineffective, inefficient, and disliked by both taxpayer and welfare recipient alike. Additionally, it treats symptoms not causes, encourages absentee fathers, and discourages the poor from earning money because benefits are immediately reduced or eliminated. We need a drastic overhaul in both the way the program is administered and its approach. Perhaps the answer lies in Canada's approach, which eliminates eligibility red tape, and offers medical care, family allowances for children, and small retirement pensions for all. Since all benefit, fraud and the costs of detecting chiselers are significantly reduced, and people are not discouraged from working.

Increasing Income

Another means of simplifying the present bureacratic welfare system would be to raise the income of the poor. Instead of spending tax dollars on current programs with their complex procedures and detection systems, the government would give each family below the poverty line the amount necessary to push them above it. This "negative income tax" or guaranteed annual income has been proposed by several presidents and successfully trial tested in New Jersey.[64]

THE FUTURE

If we examine the course of poverty throughout the twentieth century, considering programs which have worked here and in other countries, we can project several futuristic scenarios. As in previous chapters, the scenarios are in direct contrast to each other but are a logical projection of present-day tendencies.

Pessimistic Scenario

Technology has brought significant changes in work and life-style to middle-class America by 2025. For the majority of Americans, their affluence enables them to enjoy a life of comfort and leisure-oriented enjoyment in their electronic cottages, with work and entertainment self-contained at home, away from those wretches living so dreadfully in other areas. Computers hooked into main terminals, video conference phones, and information/store-order connections, together with holographic home entertainment systems brings in plays, concerts, and all other entertainment forms, and it is unnecessary to travel through those urban blighted areas. Those rural poor have remained as invisible as in previous generations. Avoidance has further lessened the sensitivity of most Americans to the continuing plight of the poor.

Concerning the poor themselves, their suffering and degradation has not changed much since the late twentieth century, except that the gulf between the nonpoor and themselves has widened considerably. While the past two generations of nonpoor became computer literate and moved with increasing knowledge and competency into the twenty-first century, the continuing low education levels of the poor kept them at a standstill. By remaining constant in low skills and education while everything around them was accelerating, the poor fell even further behind. Seldom does anyone speak of eliminating this inequality; the imbalance is viewed as far too severe ever to be corrected.

Schooling remains of limited interest. Achievement difficulty and low motivation foretell probable dropping out. Besides, literacy isn't too important. Print media has virtually vanished; video novels and learning tapes are commonplace and computerized machines handle routine purchase transactions. In actions reminiscent of Roman bread and circus provisions, the government regularly distributes surplus food and gives free entertainment programs. Why should a poor youth waste time seeking lofty but unattainable goals? It's smarter just to discover how to make your way as best you can. To be poor is to live without hope and only to cope. Public assistance programs still provide the means to survive, as do low-skill clerical and blue-collar jobs yet remaining. This is barely enough to get by, however, as reflected in their deplorable living conditions, undernourishment, and high rates of infant mortality, sickness, and chronic ailments. Crime and violence remain serious problems among them, and they live, if you can call it that, surrounded by continuous reminders—in the forms of dilapidated buildings, debris-strewn neighborhoods, and discarded people—of what they are and will become.

Optimistic Scenario

Of all the many achievements and improvements in the standard of living in 2025, perhaps the finest accomplishment has been the elimination of poverty in America. Social classes remain, but the stratified layers of society are much closer together, now that the great disparities between the affluent and less affluent have been reduced. No dramatic change in form of government effected this change, only a reawakened social conscience and public determination to deal more directly with the problem.

After years of false starts and intense counterlobbying by special interest groups, the government finally succeeded in instituting expansive tax reform and in completing a thorough overhaul of the welfare system. Soaring budget deficits, middle-class rebellion against still further tax increases, and lower-class social unrest had prompted government officials to take bold steps. Legislation rolled through the Congress and Senate, speedily signed by the president.

Corporations and wealthy individuals now paid a proportionately fair share in taxes, generating billions of dollars in additional revenues. Sufficient deductions remained so as not to undermine business reinvestment, state, and municipal bonding, or cultural and charitable activities. Scrapping the welfare system and its replacement by a guaranteed annual income for all Americans restored dignity and self-esteem among the former poor. Crash programs in job training and job placement, as well as education incentives for the poor, created in one generation the upward mobility they had desired. Government pension plans for the elderly and disabled allowed them to live in reasonable comfort.

One of the job-training programs was in child care, to provide personnel for the publicly funded day-care centers that opened so female heads of low-income households could go to work while their children benefited from learning enrichment activities. Others found work in such gentrification tasks as masonry, carpentry and remodeling, and painting, as the rising incomes in previously poor regions sparked neighborhood improvement efforts.

Strangely, this turnabout in people's lives did not occur at greater public expense. Rather, it was made possible by streamlining the bureaucratic system and redirecting monies from the Treasury from the now obsolete old programs. Additionally, it was augmented by additional revenues from an expanding national economy due to the increased purchasing power of the no-longer-poor and the no-longer-nontaxpaying wealthy.

SUMMARY

1. One way of measuring poverty is the absolute deprivation approach, wherein failure to earn a minimum amount set by the government to secure basic necessities constitutes being poor. A second approach is relative deprivation wherein poverty is considered in comparison to the living standards of others.

2. Although two-thirds of American poor are white, minorities are disproportionately represented among the poor. Female-headed families are the fastest growing segment of the poor population, creating a "feminization of poverty." Those under 18 or over 65 constitute more than half the poor, as do those living in rural or suburban areas.

3. Poverty has both devastating and degrading effects upon the poor. Inadequate nutrition causes high incidence of premature births, infant deaths, and mental retardation. Living in a less stable family environment in substandard housing, the poor may develop feelings of apathy, fatalism, or hostility and aggression. Most poor people do work, but their low-paying jobs are often unstable and vulnerable to downturns in the economy. Both the education and judicial systems work to the disadvantage of the poor concerning equal opportunity and treatment.

4. Blaming the poor for their poverty because of their values or abilities is a popular view and was the basis for many War on Poverty programs. Other views include system dysfunctions or positive functions of poverty in a society, the exploitation of the poor by those in authority, and the reinforcement of stigmatic labeling, fostering conformity to those views.

5. Almost all poor on welfare cannot work, since they are children, elderly, disabled, or mothers of young children. Only 1.4 percent are able-bodied males who cannot find jobs. Most welfare programs (services and cash) treat the effects of poverty, not the causes. Insurance programs, such as social security, help the elderly poor and are widely accepted. Employment programs get to the cause, but most have now been phased out. Welfare fraud is actually quite small, less than a half of 1 percent, and most people (about 80 percent) remain in poverty less than 21 months.

6. Although the term *welfare* is not used, similar government programs exist to raise the incomes of the nonpoor through individual tax breaks and corporate tax credits and other incentives.

7. Conservatives suggest eliminating poverty through a healthy economy and encouraging the private sector to hire the unemployed. Radicals urge nationalizing large corporations and seizing large personal fortunes, while other moderates call for tax reform to create a more equal distribution of wealth. The interventionists recommend direct federal action in job training, creating jobs, education pay incentives, welfare reform, and income provisions.

SUGGESTED READINGS

Feagin, Joe R. *Subordinating the Poor: The Welfare Class System.* Englewood Cliffs, N.J.: Prentice-Hall, 1975. A very informative analysis of prevailing beliefs about America's poor and how the welfare system operates to keep the poor in a dependent state.

Harrington, Michael. *The Other America.* New York: Macmillan, 1962. Still quite relevant today, this very readable modern classic was highly influential in launching the War on Poverty. It movingly portrays the many types of poverty in the United States.

Lewis, Oscar. *La Vida* New York: Random House, 1966. In his preface, Lewis discusses fully his "culture of poverty" hypothesis and then illustrates it through a detailed portrait of Puerto Rican families in New York City and San Juan.

Piven, Frances Fox, and Richard A. Cloward. *Regulating the Poor: The Functions of Public Relief.* New York: Pantheon, 1971. Representing the radical perspective, the authors give a provocative argument that our welfare system functions more to isolate and control the poor rather than to help them.

Reiman, Jeffrey H. *The Rich Get Richer and the Poor Get Prison.* New York: John Wiley, 1979. A provocative account of the disparities in the American social system between the affluent and the poor.

Ryan, William. *Blaming the Victim,* rev. ed. New York: Vintage, 1976. A very effective analysis of how society incorrectly blames the poor for their poverty, with a systematic piercing of the myths supporting this type of thinking.

Schwartz-Nobel, Loretta. *Starving in the Shadow of Plenty.* New York: McGraw-Hill, 1982. A moving, first-hand account of the suffering of America's hungry people. This hard-hitting and eloquent exposé is the result of 7 years spent traveling across the country and speaking with the poor.

GLOSSARY

Absolute deprivation   A standard of living below the minimum necessary to secure the basic necessities of life.

Blaming the victim   Identifying the poor or some other individual or group as responsible for their poverty or other problems instead of considering externally imposed conditions such as unemployment or lack of education.

Culture of poverty   A controversial viewpoint arguing that the disorganization and pathology of lower-class culture is self-perpetuating through cultural transmission.

Feminization of poverty   A term describing the rapid rise of female-headed households living in poverty.

Guaranteed annual income   Providing a minimum income for all through government-funded income maintenance programs for low-income families.

Labeling   A theory explaining negative effects of societal labeling on concepts of self among poor people.

Relative deprivation   A standard of living below that of most others in society, but not necessarily threatening to life or health.

Wealthfare   A term conflict theorists use to designate government support to affluent individuals and corporations through tax breaks and incentives.

Welfare   Government economic assistance to societal members with incomes below an established minimum for securing basic necessities of life.

FACTS ABOUT SEXISM

Females are half the world's population, work two-thirds of the work hours, receive a tenth of the world's income, and own a hundredth of the world's property.

In many countries females eat only after men have eaten. Girls suffer chronic malnutrition and starve to death much more frequently than boys.

In 1980 in the United States, for every 1,000 men earning between $20,000 and $25,000 there were only 187 women. For every 1,000 men earning over $50,000 there were only 30 women.

Male high-school dropouts often earn $1,000 more per year than female college graduates.

If girls continue to be socialized to feel uncomfortable with mathematics and computers they could be shut out of the future.

Many women have recently joined the labor force but most entered the "female ghetto," jobs that are at least 90 percent female.

In the federal government alone, during 1978–1980, absenteeism and job turnover caused by sexual harassment cost $189 million.

10
SEXISM

BIOLOGICAL JUSTIFICATIONS FOR SEXISM

False notions about male-female differences are not confined to any branch of science. In fact, Gould in *The Mismeasure of Man,* attributes the most biased statement to an early social-psychologist/sociologist:

> In 1879 Gustave LeBon . . . published what must be the most vicious attack upon women in modern scientific literature. . . . LeBon was no marginal hate-monger. He was a founder of Social Psychology and wrote a study of crowd behavior still cited and respected today . . . .
> "In the most intelligent races, as among the Parisians, there are a large number of women whose brains are closer in size to those of gorillas than to the most developed male brains. This inferiority is so obvious that no one can contest it for a moment; only its degree is worth discussion. All psychologists who have studied the intelligence of women, as well as poets and novelists, recognize today that they represent the most inferior forms of human evolution and that they are closer to children and savages than to an adult, civilized man. They excel in fickleness, inconstancy, absence of thought and logic, and incapacity to reason. Without doubt there exist some distinguished women, very superior to the average man, but they are as exceptional as the birth of any monstrosity, as, for example, of a gorilla with two heads; consequently, we may neglect them entirely."[1]

Weakness of the Biological Argument

Fixed biological sex differences cannot account for any of the differences between male or female behavior in different societies or time periods. Why is one tribe much more warlike than another? Why does one society aggressively try to conquer the world while others choose peace? Similarly, why are women often physical laborers in the Soviet Union, as well as being about one-third of the engineers and 75 percent of the doctors?[2] The answers lie in the society's historical definitions of gender roles. Modern evidence suggests that the weakness of the strict "biological differences" position is ironic. It actually is most at fault because it does not not go far enough.[3] There are differences between people and among all people. The differences between the sexes are much smaller than individual differences within the male sex or within the female sex.

Biological differences among people should cause many different types and levels of individuals. This seems to be evident in male society. Many different occupations and a number of roles exist. But females, until recently, were confined to one role, no matter what their emotional or intellectual equipment.

The traditional idea of females as the weaker sex is directly challenged by women's increasing participation in physically demanding sports. These bodybuilders confront us with the evidence that females have very effective muscles that social standards have kept them from developing until recently.

SOCIALIZATION AND SEXISM

Sociologists call gender identity an ascribed status: one given at birth that determines the way we are defined and treated by others for our entire lives. Society shapes people's identities in three ways: (1) by presenting certain selected values and goals as desirable and correct; (2) by training the individual to internalize, that is, take on as an integral part of themselves, the societally acceptable role; and (3) by providing and justifying a self-evaluation that fits their position in society. People in lower positions are kept feeling satisfied.

Values and Goals

Religious Writings and Sexism

The ideology that supports the biased gender identification has been invisible and largely accepted until recently. Supernatural justifications for male supremacy are easily found in the sacred books of the three major religions.[4] Islam's Koran states, "Men are superior to women on account of qualities in which God has given them pre-eminence." In the New Testament, Saint Paul orders, "Let the woman learn in silence with all subjection. But I suffer not a woman to teach, nor to usurp authority over the man, but to be in silence . . . she shall be saved in childbearing, if they continue in faith and charity and holiness with sobriety." Finally, the morning prayer of the Orthodox Jew includes the line: "Blessed art Thou, oh Lord our God, King of the Universe, that I was not born a woman."

Feminization and American Religion

Ann Douglas makes us aware of the close relationship between the Protestant religions and the acceptance of the passive, powerless place of women.[5] As the success of business and the popularity of competitive economic values secularized American life in the early 1800s, the Protestant clergy and the women who were their main supporters were pushed out of everyday life. They were confined to the moral-cultural realm of good manners, politeness, and sensitivity to the arts. Both were excluded from the "'male' world of politics, fighting, cigars, and business."[6] Ministers encouraged the process because it gave them many female supporters. They and other men of that period admonished their females to "be above all unselfish" and to cling to religion because "it is far more necessary to you than to self-sufficient men."[7] In other words, men should be left to do all the "dirty work" of business and decision making. For a woman to do *anything* in the "real" world might destroy her unassertive purity and her presentation of a moral example.

It should also be noted that males, except Protestant ministers, were segregated out of cultural pursuits. It became unmanly to be interested in books or music, or anything not associated with aggressive competition.

Internalization of Roles

The roles are already there, waiting for the infant at birth. Studies have shown that parent's expectations shape behavior from the earliest moments. When adults are asked to describe the behavior of babies, they respond first to sexual cues. They attribute to the children characteristics they don't yet have. If a group of babies wear blue, pink, or yellow diapers, those in blue are described as active and loud, while those in pink are described as quiet and sweet. The babies in yellow confuse the observers, who even attempt to peek inside the diapers to find out the sex in order to know how to treat them.

Bem and Bem report that 6-month-old girls are usually touched and talked to more by their mothers while infant boys are influenced to explore and play independently. The girls, therefore, tend to cry more frequently when separated from their mothers.[8]

Children also identify with their parents and learn by modeling their sex roles. This involves more than dressing up in Mommy's clothes. Children also assume the attitudes and evaluations of their gender. They can learn that Mommy is proud to be a "moron" about mechanical things while Dad feels at home with them.[9]

The sexes even learn to play differently. Girls are more often found in exclusive dyadic friendships in which they learn to exchange intimacies and self-disclosures. Boys are found in larger groups in which organized games teach skills related to

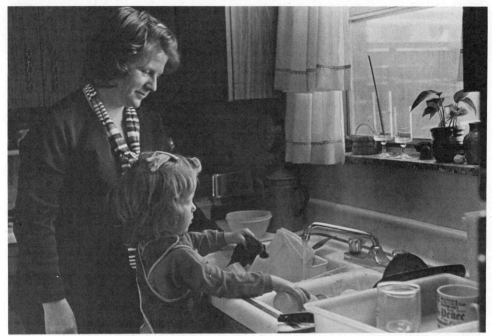

When a child models her gender behavior solely on a parent's behavior it introduces a strong conservative element into society. The generations stay similar and it reduces adaptation to modernizing conditions.

group process and leadership.[10] But in a school with open classrooms, it was found that the opportunity to meet and talk in the nongame structured situation broke down these patterns.

Children learn differential territoriality for the two sexes. Men are given more territory in the home: a special room or a special chair is set aside for their exclusive use. Women's "places" are often smaller and always more open to invasion, or they are, like kitchens, totally public.[11]

Finally, the segregation into women's and men's types of work starts early. "The major changes in women's adult roles within the last two decades have yet to reach childhood."[12] While there is no difference in boys and girls in the *amount* of chores they do, there is a clear sex-typing of *what* they do inside the home. The differences become even more exaggerated when they take their first jobs outside the home. This means that if equality in work life is to become the role-standard of their later lives, they will have to somehow overcome a large amount of biased learning in their early socialization.

All of these factors contribute to **role entrapment,** the culturally defined need to be "feminine," often preventing women from doing things they might otherwise do to achieve success and self-realization.

EFFECTS OF SEXISM

Women as a Minority Group

Women are singled out from other groups in society for differential treatment, they receive an unfairly small amount of society's rewards, and their opinions and social contributions are less valued. This has caused some sociologists to study women in the same way as they do the groups who are objects of racial or ethnic prejudice. In his landmark study of sex prejudice, Goldberg demonstrated a basic dimension of women's minority status. Women are not respected and even their professional work is considered less adequate:

> Goldberg gave 149 college women six articles in both "masculine" fields (e.g., law and city planning) and "feminine" fields (e.g., art history and dietetics). There were two identical sets of each article signed by "J. T. McKay." Some named the author John T. McKay, others Joan T. McKay. The students rated the articles for value, persuasiveness, profundity, writing style, professional competence, professional status, and ability to sway the reader. In both male and female fields, the students thought John McKay more impressive; out of 54 comparisons, 44 favored John. The experiment illustrates not only the belief that females are inferior and the distorting effect of that belief on judgment, but also the women's sensitivity to something as apparently irrelevant as the author's sex.[13]

The pervasiveness of sex prejudice is most powerfully demonstrated by the fact that it was *women* who made these biased judgments in Goldberg's experiment. The societal values had malstructured their perceptions and evaluations. When Gloria Steinem was asked if she thought that the Women's Movement had made progress, she replied that it had: many of the damages and costs of being a woman were invisible and undiscussed and not legally recognized only 10 to 15 years ago; now at least they have names; at least women are conscious of them. Here are some of the "newly discovered" social problems: (1) biological limitation and deformation; (2) inordinate insecurity about appearance; (3) powerlessness in social interaction; and (4) sexual harassment.

Biological Limitations and Deformations

Many of us are familiar with the practice of tightly wrapping the feet of Asian infant girls, thereby stunting normal growth. These women were not able to walk normally. We can see a less drastic but parallel effect in the high heels that inhibit and "beautify" Western women.

A much more direct and drastically deforming process is still practiced in the Middle East and parts of Muslim Africa. The female relatives, or sometimes the father, of a young girl cut off her clitoris (the central sexual organ). In some societies, the labia is removed as well. The World Health Organization estimates that

Some Chinese women's feet are bound tightly when they are very young. They become deformed to fit their culture's standard of female beauty. Our high heels are not as final a solution, but they severely limit females' participation in social life.

BOX 10.1
ABOUT THE MULTILATED HALF

Ten years ago in Cairo I met an Egyptian woman of whom I recall the following: She was 35 years old, handsomely dressed, spoke three foreign languages fluently, worked as a bilingual researcher, had lived five years in Toronto with her engineer husband; also, she had been married off by her father at 15, had four children by the age of 22 and was kept housebound by her husband, who was otherwise kind and worthy of her affection and of whom she remarked sadly, "I know that my husband will not take four wives, but the fact that under the law he is permitted to do so colors his emotions, and mine." One last thing about this woman. She had been circumcised at the age of 6; that is, her clitoris had been surgically removed from her body.

In Egypt today under the law a man may take four wives; a girl may be married off by her father without her consent; no woman may petition for divorce; a man may obtain a divorce by the simple act of repudiation; a woman has no right of custody of her children; a husband need not pay alimony or child support if his wife has withheld herself sexually; a husband has the right to forbid a wife to work or to travel or even to move freely in her own environment; a husband has the right to have his wife forcibly returned to his home if she has left it without his consent. While a fraction of urban university-educated women escape their "destiny," the mass of women in Egypt live out their lives in the manner ordained by such social conditions.

about 75 million women have had this excision. The apparent goal is to remove sexual temptation and assure women's faithfulness in marriage (see Box 10.1).

While this practice may seem horrifying to Westerners, it is not that far removed from similar *social* deformations used in the recent past in our society. Women's sexuality had been officially kept from them, and considered to be an aberration, until the 1970s. When a woman was unsatisfied in marriage, it was likely that a doctor would tell her it was proper and normal for women to be frigid. In a famous study of gynecological textbooks, "A Funny Thing Happened on the Way to the Orifice," Scully and Bart demonstrated the dangers and biases inherent in the medical system, in which 93 percent of gynecologists were men. Masters and Johnson fully demonstrated what Kinsey had discovered in the late 1940s; that American females were not only capable of sexual satisfaction, but had a capacity far beyond that of most males. The texts used to train our doctors, however, still maintained, in the early 1970s, that women should be passive and entirely oriented to what were regarded as the dominant and much more powerful needs of males.[14]

Popular sex manuals also kept the myth of female unsexuality alive until 1973–1974.[15] Until then women's sexuality was described as part of the institution of marriage, in which male needs were all-important, not as a loving activity between

"The Hidden Face of Eve" is divided into discussions of life for women in contemporary Egypt, women in world history, women in Arab history and literature. The longest and by far the most powerful section is called "The Multilated Half." Its subject is the equation still prevalent in the Arab world between a man's honor and a woman's virginity. Consistent with this all-absorbing concern that a "girl" not be a "woman" on her wedding night is the barbaric practice of female circumcision, designed to insure that a woman will not be tempted to give away what is clearly not hers to give. Dr. Saadawi's discussion of modern-day circumcision in Egypt is eloquent. She begins with herself. The daughter of a provincial Controller of Education, she was seized in her bed in the middle of the night and dragged into the bathroom, where her legs were pried apart and her clitoris slashed off. Eyes shut tight, she cried out in pain and terror for her mother; when she opened her eyes she saw her mother standing above her, smiling among the murderers.

Nawal grew up, became a doctor and spent years listening to patients repeat this experience, almost word for word, as they sought to explain their fear and hatred of sex. Female circumcision became an obsession that led her to realize that "amputation of the clitoris . . . goes hand in hand with brainwashing of girls, with a calculated merciless campaign to paralyze their capacity to think and to judge and to understand."

SOURCE: Vivian Gornick, *The New York Times Book Review* (March 14, 1982) p. 33, a review about Nawal L. Saadavi's book *The Hidden Face of Eve: Women in the Arab World* (Boston: Beacon Press, 1982). Copyright © by the New York Times Company. Reprinted by permission.

two people. In 1973–1974 the manuals began to reflect the social change toward sexual autonomy and women were instructed to seek their own satisfactions through independence and the development of sexual competence.

Powerlessness in Interaction

There is nothing natural about boys being "strong and silent" and girls "chattering." They have the same vocabularies at the age of 3 and the same capacities for further growth. One of the paradoxes of our male-female stereotypes is that while females are thought to be more verbal, men are expected to dominate conversations. This is not a recent nor an entirely American tradition. In the sixteenth century, speech in England was so segregated that males and females spoke almost different dialects. In Japan, when men mean to emphasize a sentence and demand its acceptance, they add "yo" to it. This is the equivalent of saying "you'd better believe it." If a woman adds "yo" to a phrase, however, it is interpreted as "I pray that you will believe me when I tell you."[16]

A number of studies have shown that women speak more hesitantly than men, displaying an **interaction powerlessness.** They often, for example, end their phrases with a rising intonation signifying the apparent questionableness of what they have just said.[17] Women in many cultures sit in rigid closed postures during cross-sex interactions, contrasting with the relaxed, more spread, postures of men.

Functionalist sociologists ascribed these sex-interaction differences to the fact that all social groups have basic needs that must be fulfilled. Groups will only succeed if both *instrumental* and *emotional* needs are met. Males were seen as concentrating on getting things done, on decision making and leadership. Females perform a socioemotional function. They worry about keeping everything running smoothly. More recently, this functionalist view has been questioned and sociologists tend to

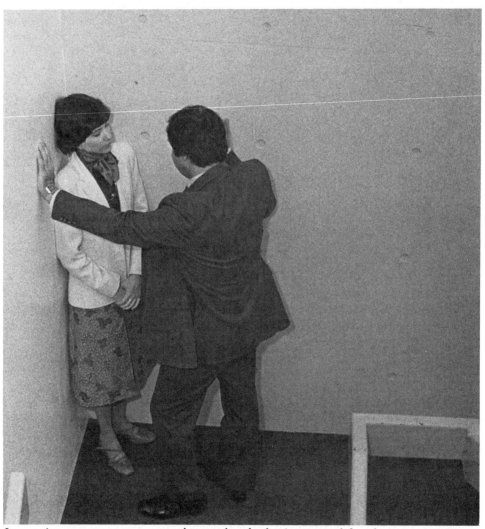

Interaction patterns are structured around male dominance and female passivity. Women tend to ask questions and be unsure, and their body language expresses these feelings. Men exhibit a commanding posture and assume they will be listened to.

see the gender-based interaction differences as originating in male social power.[18] Males are dominant in the general society and also in the microinteractions that make it up. The proof of this reasoning is found in observations of other higher-lower status interactions. Bosses treat workers, old treat young, and parents treat children with styles that are similar to the ways that men interact with women. For example, women get touched more often and very seldom initiate touching. They get called by diminutive, cute names such as ''honey'' and ''baby.'' Men frequently interrupt women, but are rarely interrupted. If there is an awkward silence, women will usually fill it because they have been taught that to do so is their responsibility. Finally, women ask the questions. Fishman said that when analyzing her interaction tapes for the study, ''Interaction: The Work Women Do'': ''At times, I felt that all women did was ask questions.'' They have been given responsibility for the process, but must play the role of subservient ''asker'' to the men's role of ''provider'' of answers.[19]

Sexual Harassment

Sexual harassment is one of those severe social problems that was, for the first time, given a name during the mid-1970s. Before that, women suffered alone or told a close friend, but were unable to refer to any societal sanction or legal remedy.

It took *Redbook* magazine's 1976 survey to define the extent of the problem. Of the 9,000 women who volunteered answers, 90 percent said that at some time in their work lives they had been harassed. An even larger and more scientific study was done by the U.S. Merit System Protection Board. Its results demonstrated the shocking economic costs of sexual harassment. In the 2 years from 1978–1980, $189 million was lost because of hiring, training, absenteeism, and job-turnover expenses caused by harassment. This estimate was for the federal government alone: the enormous additional costs in the private sector can only be guessed at, but they must be in the billions.[20] The personal costs were also severe. Using the same federal government survey, researchers conservatively estimated that 1 percent, or about 9,000 women, had been victims of attempted rape by supervisors or co-workers.

Definitions of Harassment

Here are three examples that we can probably all agree on as harassment:

> . . . a military policeperson was assigned to the midnight shift. On her first night of training, her supervisor said he wanted to test her ability to maneuver a police sedan at high speeds. ''He advised me to go real fast and weave in and out of the airstrip's flashing lights . . . When I was going about 60 mph, he started grabbing me all over my body.''[21]

> . . . a woman was pinched on her breast by a co-worker and told later that there had been a bet about it with the manager who had watched the activity through binoculars.[22]

> . . . a woman was fired because her daughter would not sleep with or marry her supervisor.[23]

Sexual harassment has been accepted until quite recently. It is very unlikely that this woman is the man's girl friend or wife. What he is doing is a public act of disrespect and dominance.

Motivations and the Context of Harassment

The typical harasser is older, in a supervisory position, married, considered unattractive by the victims, and usually harasses a number of women.[24] The sexual content of the harassment is often used as a screen for pure dominance or discrimination. Often sex is merely used to disguise and confuse a heavy power content in which women are being punished for presuming to work with men.

Typical excuses or cover-ups are: that it was "only fun" or flattering to the woman; that such attention is only forced on women who "ask for it"; or that any woman who "really wants to" should know how to handle such situations on her own. On the contrary, it has been proven over and over that women need help to defend themselves from some men's assumption that being their superior on the job also involves sexual privileges:

> Sexual harassment by a boss or supervisor harkens back, in a way, to the medieval practice of "droit du seigneur," which gave the feudal lord the right to sleep the first night with the bride of any of his vassals. Although feudalism ended many centuries ago, some people still feel that to be a boss is to be at least semi-divinely ordained—to have certain inalienable rights. . . . The idea of using a paycheck as a license for sex seems ludicrous, if not sick, but it happens all the time. Men who would never think, or at least never follow through on, the idea of pinching a woman's breast in a bus or on the street, feel free to

subject their secretary to this humiliation as if it were a job-given right.[25]

The prospects for reduction of this type of harassment seem promising. Though it is deeply entrenched in the attitudes of some men, it has survived mainly because it was kept secret. Women now know that it is not their fault and will less frequently hesitate to expose such incidents. The EEOC guidelines also change the legalities of the situation and make the business firm or other employer responsible for preventing the development of harassment.

ARENAS OF CHANGE

During the 1970s women substantially increased their participation in education and work. These changes were vitally interconnected with revisions in our social definitions of women's family and reproductive roles. It is remarkable, however, how far there still is to go; how much it is still a man's world.

Education

The decade of the 1970s saw a sizable reduction, from 16 percent to only 7 percent, in the number of colleges that were not coeducational.[26] A similar dramatic shift has taken place in overall college enrollments. As late as 1972–1973, 59 percent of college students were male. By 1980, equality had not yet been achieved, but males were only a majority of 52 percent.

Women's percentage of all college degrees awarded rose from 44 percent to 50 percent between 1971–1972 and 1980–1981. There was substantial change in some areas formerly thought to be male. For example, engineering degrees awarded to women increased by 830 percent and business degrees by 247 percent.[27] The traditional female areas of home economics, education, and foreign languages, however, have remained stably segregated.

Professional Degrees Awarded to Women

The percentage of medical degrees awarded to women rose from 9 percent to 24 percent, and there were similar changes in law degrees (7 to 32 percent) and veterinary medicine (9 to 33 percent) from 1972 to 1981.

The current area of disappointment and potential change is at the level of professional degrees. In education, for example, where 73 percent of the B.A.s are awarded to women, only 53 percent of the Ph.D.s are received by women. This is by far the most female-segregated of the professions. For example, only 4 percent of engineering and 10 percent of computer science advanced degrees went to women in 1980–1981.

Being Allowed to Use Education

At present more than a third of the candidates for M.B.A.s are women, but only 5 percent of the business executive positions are held by women.[28] Both numbers indicate possible future changes. Only recently, there were very few female executives, but there is an obvious imbalance: unless occupational discrimination and segregation are quickly reduced, much educational effort will be wasted.

Working for Less

Working outside the home seems to be both an established societal fact and beneficial for women. The first major entrance into the labor force by women was during World War II. "Rosie the Riveter" was the projected role model of the women who took "fighting men's" places in the factories. But when the men came home, the women returned to motherhood in the biggest "baby boom" in modern history. It was not until 1980 that women achieved a hallmark of stable employment. In that year the female unemployment rate was lower for the first time in 30 years than the male unemployment rate. Previously females had been the least adaptable, most expendable workers, but the unemployment statistics' reversal demonstrates a new stability of employment.

Two studies by Kessler and McRae examine a number of surveys of the changes in psychological distress over time.[29] They show that modern woman's role as a housewife contributed to distressful symptoms. Employed women report *less* stress in an apparent benefit from changing female role expectations. The transition to work does not seem to produce stress as some have expected, but reduces the stress of the nonworking wife.[30]

These are signs of positive change, but three major problems are still prominent: (1) women who work often enter the female occupational ghetto; (2) they work for less money than men; and (3) they are often shut out of formal and informal network systems, therefore receiving fewer promotions.

The Female Occupational Ghetto

Historical study of the sex segregation of work shows that women move into occupations that are already sex typed as female or into new occupations that become classified as female.[31] This has similarities to the racial typing of jobs in military life. Until recently the "real" military roles were reserved for Whites, and Blacks were relegated to nonfighting support jobs. Kanter has studied sex typing of occupations within large organizations. She found managers and clerical workers to be in two distinct classes, or even rigidly separated castes. They have "separate hierarchies, rules, and reward structures, and practically no mobility between them."[32] Women are not usually found in the managerial class. More than 95 percent of secretaries and receptionists are female, as are more than 90 percent of all bank tellers, phone operators, bookkeepers, nurses, and dieticians. The **occupational ghetto** also includes cashiers, sales clerks, librarians, health technicians, and noncollege teachers. All of these positions are at least 70 percent female.

One explanation sees this segregation as a combination of paternalistic overprotection and discrimination.[33] Blue-collar and lower-middle-class men are channeled by society into the dirty and hard jobs that pay more but have lower prestige. Women are paternalistically protected from such work by being pushed into the office where they are paid much less (see Table 10.1).

Work is still segregated, but it is changing. The "girl" who serves coffee at the man's desk is probably disappearing. But females are still forced into the "female ghetto" of support services, and it is hard for them to break through into management.

TABLE 10.1 No End to the "Women's Ghettos"

Despite their entrance into many jobs formerly held exclusively by men, women complain that they still are concentrated in positions that consistently pay less than those held by men with comparable skills. Among such jobs, and the percentage held by women—

	1973	1983
Sectetaries	99%	99%
Child-care workers	96%	97%
Registered nurses	98%	96%
Billing clerks	83%	88%
Waiters, waitresses	92%	88%
Librarians	83%	87%
Health technicians	72%	84%
Elementary-school teachers	81%	83%
Bank tellers	90%	81%
Retail salesclerks	69%	70%

SOURCE: U.S. Department of Labor, February 1984.

TABLE 10.2 Male-Female Income Ranges

	Men	Women	Women per 1,000 Men
Over $75,000	442,000	12,000	27
$50,000–$75,000	1,103,000	37,000	34
$35,000–$50,000	2,644,000	128,000	48
$25,000–$35,000	7,133,000	600,000	84
$20,000–$25,000	7,550,000	1,414,000	187
$15,000–$20,000	8,571,000	3,691,000	431
$10,000–$15,000	8,366,000	8,089,000	967
$5,000–$10,000	4,574,000	7,612,000	1,664
Under $5,000	1,495,000	1,276,000	854
Total	41,881,000	22,857,000	546

SOURCE: Andrew Hacker, *U/S: A Statistical Portrait of the American People* (New York: Penguin Books, 1983), p. 148. Reprinted by permission.

Sex ratios in some traditionally male areas, however, are changing. Female assembly line workers are now in the majority, and more than a third of college teachers, accountants, and buyers or purchasing agents are now female—all major changes from 1960. Female physicians have doubled in number to constitute 13 percent of all doctors. And women are becoming managers (about 40 percent) in their "own" areas of food service and sales.[34]

Income Inequality

But even in these areas of change enormous inequalities in pay remain (see Tables 10.2 and 10.3). The new female retail sales managers can expect to be paid only 56 percent as much as their male counterparts; the assembly line workers only 68 percent, and the female bank officers, only 57 percent.[35]

Unequal pay is clearly demonstrated in Table 10.4 in which full-time year-round employees' incomes are shown by both occupational prestige category and educational preparation. Only among laborers does female income rise to be even three-

TABLE 10.3 Individuals' Incomes at Various Age Levels

Age	Men's Median	Women's Median	Women's Incomes as Percentage of Men's
15–19	$1,801	$1,673	92.9%
20–24	$7,923	$5,286	66.7%
25–34	$15,580	$6,973	44.8%
35–44	$20,037	$6,465	32.3%
45–54	$19,974	$6,403	32.1%
55–64	$15,914	$4,926	31.0%
65 and up	$7,342	$4,226	57.6%

SOURCE: Andrew Hacker, *U/S: A Statistical Portrait of the American People* (New York: Penguin Books, 1983), p. 146. Reprinted by permission.

TABLE 10.4 Male-Female Median Incomes by Occupational Categories and Education

	Men	Women	Women's Incomes as Percentage of Men's
Professional	$23,026	$15,285	66.4%
Managerial	$23,558	$12,936	54.9%
Sales	$19,910	$9,748	49.0%
Clerical	$18,247	$10,997	60.3%
Craft	$18,671	$11,701	62.7%
Operatives	$15,702	$9,440	60.1%
Laborers	$12,757	$9,747	76.4%
Service workers	$13,064	$7,853	60.1%
5+ years college	$27,690	$18,100	65.4%
4 years college	$24,311	$15,143	62.3%
1–3 years college	$20,909	$12,954	61.9%
4 years high school	$19,469	$11,537	59.3%
1–3 years high school	$16,101	$9,676	60.1%
Less than high school	$13,117	$8,216	62.6%

SOURCE: Andrew Hacker, *U/S: A Statistical Portrait of the American People* (New York: Penguin Books, 1983), p. 148. Reprinted by permission.

quarters of their male equivalents. Professional women receive only 66 percent of men's income, and college education makes little difference. Women average about 61 percent of men's salaries in whatever status is examined. In 1980 the average man earned $19,173, while the average woman earned $11,591, or 60.5 percent.[36]

Isolation of Women

A significant part of the inequality that women experience begins only after they have secured a career job, especially if it is a management job or a formerly male-typed job. The experiences of women police officers provide vivid examples.[37] Among police, the gossip network is very important for acceptance as a trustworthy officer-colleague and for finding promotion opportunities. But women are excluded from the male networks. They are mistrusted because "the men fear that women will gain exemptions and favorable assignments by taking advantage of their sex (i.e., using something that men cannot use to gain favor, thus changing the rules of competition)"[38] Male officers often seek to be friendly with superiors who can help them, but women are isolated and often exclude themselves from such helpful contact so as not to be labeled as using their sex.

Political and Legal System Sexism

One of the most startling discrepancies between our democratic expectations and the actual result is in the segregation of women from political power. More than 52 percent of voting age Americans are female. The proportion will continue to increase because women live longer than men and our population is aging. But almost all our elected politicians are male. One of the better feminist statements makes this point profoundly and very simply by presenting "The View from the Sexual Ghetto," a series of photographs of the United Nations, the Russian leadership, the Chinese leaders, the U.S. Senate, the Cabinet, the Supreme Court (recently changed), the floor of the Stock Exchange, leaders of the black movement, the 1960s protest leaders, the College of Cardinals, the Joint Chiefs of Staff, the NASA control room, and so on. Everyone is male.[39]

Sexism in the Courts

This imbalance has caused some discriminatory definitions and practices in our courts. The law defines women as passive and in need of protection from active males. But the courts tend to reserve protection for women who can clearly prove they deserve it; they must be blameless.[40] In rape or abuse cases, even when very young females are involved, the tendency has been to interrogate them and suspect them until they can prove they did not provoke the crime. This prejudice is now beginning to be recognized, but there are many others not yet documented.

In 1983 New Jersey completed the first review anywhere of sexism in the state court system. It showed that (1) women received lower personal injury settlements, especially if they were housewives, because juries failed to recognize the value of their work; (2) judges were failing to enforce the new law against wife beating and domestic violence; and (3) child-support payments in divorce cases were set much too low and there were no strong enforceable sanctions against nonpayment by fathers. The female attorneys also said that 86 percent of their colleagues and 66 percent of the judges had made demeaning jokes or hostile remarks about their sex.[41] The state is calling for an end to all such practices. Pressure for change will probably increase because of the rapid rise in the percentage of law degrees granted to women: from 7 percent in 1971–1972 to 30 percent in 1979–1980.

The outlook for change in the political system is not as bright. The very limited cultural definition of women's political place seems to be the basic cause of our male-oriented politics.

Women's Political Place

A study of the wives of presidents and other elected officials reveals that they are consistently portrayed as loyal, stable, and in particular, as symbols of a strong traditional family orientation.[42] The public wife is presented as "Mrs. Morality" and this demands that she be, above all, circumspect. This usually means that she must avoid doing anything that has any political import. She is presented at ceremonial occasions, but if there is any real work to be done, the cast of characters again becomes all-male. This public image reinforces the "cultural lag" of the desirability of exclusive family orientation for wives in order to protect the appearance of the maximum respectability for the politician.

Women fare no better at the grass-roots end of the political process. When they join local political parties they are relegated to the role of "invisible hands" or political drudges, while males make public presentations and political contacts.[43] In a New England town's Democratic and Republican organizations, women were found to work twice as many hours and to have up to three times as many political interactions as male workers. They were, however, unnoticed and unrewarded because the men usually held the visible leadership posts.[44]

Margolis concluded that the role of "behind the scenes drudge" was a direct transference of traditional family structure to politics. Men have specific and narrow political and family functions; they are "heads" and "breadwinners." But the women, just as in the family, are the ones who do everything else. They not only fill in the gaps, they have learned to *find* the gaps and take care of them without "bothering" the men.[45] They have become used to working in seclusion while men seek center stage.

Margolis's analysis may not apply to all women's political experiences, and we have seen that the traditional family is changing. But it does clearly remind us of the powerful interconnection of sexist definitions and practices in the institutions of society. Family values reinforce political discrimination and this, in turn, supports other prejudices and discriminations.

Let us turn to the areas that sociologists highlight as causal and basic for future change.

SOCIOLOGICAL PERSPECTIVES

Individual Faults: Women Seen as Deviants from the "Male Norm"

The search for stable sex differences has not yet revealed any that could be exclusively ascribed to biological or inborn characteristics. The findings that have been most regularly reported find females to have greater verbal abilities, and males to be more skilled at spatial-mathematical thinking and to be more aggressive. Most sociologists feel that these findings must be judged very carefully. They seem to be too closely associated with socially created interests, attitudes, and roles to be basic sex differences.

Developmental Stage Theories
These have a central place in psychological thought. They lend substance to the underlying idea of the Individual Faults perspective: that it would be necessary to change people (in this case women) before they could take advantage of the institutional opportunities available to them.[46] Kohlberg's six stages of human moral development place the highest value on selfless principles that transcend social or national affiliations. Women, according to Kohlberg, are not capable of achieving this high level of development. Their development gets "stuck" at stage 3, at which morality is based on pleasing and helping others. This controversial assumption of one universal set of stages that applies to all humans would be accepted by few anthropologists or sociologists. Women's concern for others, rather than for abstract principles of morality, even if this is in fact a stable characteristic, should not necessarily be judged as only half way up the moral ladder.[47]

In summary, the weakness of this Individual Faults orientation to sex differences is that it only "dimly recognizes" the possible effects of the status differences assigned to sex-role activities. Particularly among girls who accept and internalize the system, "male" behaviors will be avoided as "unnatural."[48] In one experiment attempting to develop boys and girls further with already outstanding mathematical potentials, a number of girls dropped out because they did not see the point of continuing. They felt math wouldn't take them anywhere.[49] They also found the meetings dull and the boys involved to be "little creeps."

Institutional Faults: Gender Problems as System Disorganization

Division of Labor

Functionalist sociologists see sex roles originating in the essential division of labor. Males and females have always in the past been ascribed different family and economic duties. With the reduction in agricultural and household labor due to technology, women now frequently find that their family responsibilities must be fulfilled as wage earners. Functionalists concentrate on the disruption caused by such changes and compare current confusions to the supposedly stable past. They do not usually emphasize females' freedom or opportunities, but instead worry about how the

---

TABLE 10.5 Comparable Worth

As Some Experts See the "Wage Gap"—Studies by "job evaluators" in Washington State, Minnesota, and Illinois found these disparities in monthly salaries in male-dominated and female-dominated state-government jobs ranked of roughly "comparable worth":

Predominantly Male Job		Comparable Predominantly Female Job	
Washington			
Carpenter	$1,654	Social-service worker	$ 961
Security officer	$1,114	Telephone operator	$ 808
Mechanic	$1,462	Medical-record analyst	$ 892
Highway engineer	$1,654	Registered nurse	$1,392
Illinois			
Accountant	$2,470	Nurse	$1,794
Electrician	$2,826	Secretary	$1,486
Highway worker	$1,816	Clerk-typist	$1,075
Minnesota			
Delivery driver	$1,382	Pharmacy assistant	$1,202
Auto-parts handler	$1,505	Dining-hall director	$1,202
Game warden	$1,808	Behavior analyst	$1,590

Source: *U.S. News & World Report* (February 20, 1984), p. 73, from basic data reported by Washington State, Illinois Commission on the Status of Women, and Minnesota Commission on the Status of Women. Copyright, 1984, U.S. News & World Report, Inc.

functions fulfilled by traditional roles might be overlooked in a more open sex-role structure.

It is interesting that one of the more powerful legal tools of the current movement for equal pay for women is based on what would seem to be functionalist concepts. Job evaluations, that is, the standardized judgment of how much each occupational slot contributes to the system, have been upheld in a number of lawsuits. No longer must a man and a woman be doing exactly the same work to deserve equal pay. Equal pay should now be given to workers in equally functional or equally difficult jobs. For example, registered nurse and vocational education teacher have been judged to be of equivalent worth, as have secretary and maintenance carpenter. In the current reward system, the traditionally male jobs of carpenter and vocational teacher receive roughly 40 percent more pay, and this may now become the cause of lawsuits under the equal pay laws (see Table 10.5).

> One of the earliest studies of the equity-pay issue was commissioned in 1974 by Washington Governor Dan Evans, now a U.S. senator. A private firm, Norman D. Willis & Associates, rated as comparable many kinds of work in which men consistently received fatter paychecks than women. . . .
>
> After studying the Willis report and state wage scales, U.S. District Judge Jack Tanner ruled [in December 1983] that Washington State had "historically engaged in employment discrimination on the basis of sex." Tanner ordered wage increases and four years' back pay for more than 15,000 workers, 90 percent of them women. The ruling will cost the state between 500 and 800 million dollars. . . .
>
> Union leaders predict that this scenario will be repeated in state after state as discriminatory patterns are uncovered and challenged.[50]

Establishing "comparable worth" wage scales is an increasingly popular concept among states and cities. In July 1984, the House of Representatives approved such a measure for all federal employees by a 413-to-6 vote.

Inequality and Inevitable Conflict: Women as an Oppressed Class

Attached Women

Acker points out how biased even social scientists' assumptions can become.[51] Most theories, whether Marxist or functionalist, assume that the family is the basic unit of social structure. Even in this time when traditional families are a shrinking minority, we tend to judge the social status of the family by the status of the main wage earner, the "head of the household." "Women determine their own social status only when they are not attached to a man."[52] At other times, they are as ignored in our research studies as they are in people's everyday evaluations of social status. Acker points out that it is damaging to treat women as invisible; it is important that sociologists recognize sex as an "enduring ascribed characteristic" which affects the social evaluation of persons and positions and "is the basis of the persisting sexual division of labor and of sex-based inequalities."[53]

Women as Property

The conflict-oriented *Realpolitik* view demonstrates how women's lower status benefits men and supports the capitalist consumer economy.[54] The traditional sex roles are nothing but ideological justifications of men's power. Women have been seen as private property, and are still encouraged to sell themselves on the marriage market and to concentrate on preparing for this sale by competing with other women to become attractive commodities.[55] Their long history of being in a subordinate status has made women more sensitive to the behavior of others. They do not naturally desire to please others, they have had to learn indirect manipulation because they were denied equal or direct power.[56] Unless actively counteracted, this system will continue as long as men continue to profit from it.

Sexist Consumerism

Advertising helps to maintain women's position. It is directly related to the changing needs of the economy's form of production. In the early 1800s industrialization created the first excess wealth and the need to find new markets to reabsorb the new products. Women were encouraged to dedicate themselves to becoming consumers and maintainers of spotless, well-furnished households.[57] Advertising capitalized on a woman's anxiety that this was entirely her responsibility. Gloria Steinem's comment on a famous commercial highlights the ridiculous extent of this creation and manipulation of guilt. She asks that, just once, when the "ring around the collar" commercial comes to the moment when the guilty dirt has been discovered, the wife would turn to her husband and say, "wash your neck," instead of cringing.

Lasch has provided the most devastating analysis of the advertising industry's motivation for the promotion of women's liberation. He says that the need for even more consumption has stimulated the economic powers to appear to free women in order that they will earn more and buy more. "The logic of demand creation requires that women smoke and drink in public, move about freely, and assert their right to happiness instead of living for others . . . disguising freedom to consume as genuine autonomy."[58]

Interaction and Social Interpretation

Interactionists see gender as a master status that is central to the way we view and evaluate each other and ourselves. For example, in many social situations the racial status of a black surgeon might unfortunately supersede all her other statuses. Biased definitions are often difficult to change because everyday interaction is organized around the master statuses.[59] It is easier for many people to use consciously or unconsciously biased categories than it is for them to be uncertain of what to expect of others. Interactionists, however, emphasize that social expectations are not fixed or rigid categories. Symbolic interaction is the most hopeful of the orientations: sexist definitions are seen as products of self-other interactions. That is, **gender roles** are cultural-verbal constructs that we use to understand each other. If, however, we decide not to confirm them, or to use others that better fit the current environment, they can and will change.

Let us select three interactionist emphases for discussion: (1) the **situationality of sex differences;** (2) the importance of early interaction; and (3) the real effects of social definitions.

Situationality and Multiple Realities

Society members share common master-status definitions, but we usually see most situations through the specific subcultural and other special definitions we have learned in the social statuses we have occupied. When an interactionist studies the sexes, the first points of focus are the differences between the social realities in which they live. Just as we now accept that many I.Q. tests are ethnically biased because they only test knowledge of middle-class white reality, we must also accept that "male reality" is not the standard reality.

In an example related to our previous discussion of differences in spatial judgment abilities, Stoneall examined gender differences in cognitive mapping of communities. "Men tend to follow the political township boundary . . . whereas women seem to have certain people in mind whom they want to include in the community and draw their maps according to what roads they live on."[60] There is clearly a difference, and in terms of reproducing the official map, men were more accurate. But is one more able, or correct, than the other? The women were, in fact, closer to what sociologists mean by the real, day-to-day "community." The difference in definition of their common physical environment came out of how their *social* environment guided their experiences.

Early Categorizations and Evaluations of Self

The self is formed through internalization of the expectations and evaluations of others. Gender evaluations are waiting for the infant even before birth. Parents' immediate concern is the sex of the child. Studies show that new parents will rate the characteristics of their newborn boys and girls differently even before they have any physical contact with them.[61] The evaluations of "good" and "bad" quickly get associated with the child's choosing appropriately or incorrectly between "boy stuff" and "girl stuff." Girls internalize as desirable images of themselves that would seem to be irrationally limiting or subservient. This is not just a process of adopting what is comfortable. Society dictates appropriate behaviors, ambitions, and even emotions. These social definitions can erroneously appear to be "natural" differences because they start so early, and because they are accepted by those they define.

The Consequences of Social Definitions

It should not be assumed that because interactionists see gender differences as based on social definitions that they see them as trivial. W. I. Thomas's famous phrase was stated using a sexist pronoun, and that makes it even more socially true: "If men define situations as real, they are real in their consequences." Our definitions of the situation guide our behavior and they can lead us down false paths to dangerous conclusions.

BOX 10.3
AGNES

THE ANOMALY

"Agnes" is the pseudonym for an intersexed person who applied for a sex-change operation at the Medical Center of the University of California, Los Angeles. She was born with a normal penis and scrotum, and, accordingly, was named, registered, and raised as a male child. However, by the age of nineteen when she came to the medical center, she had developed large well-developed breasts, rounded, feminine hips, and displayed no facial hair. In addition, she had elected to live as a female and was wearing feminine clothes and affecting feminine mannerisms. In short, Agnes had the appearance of a normal female when clothed and behaved appropriately for a female in our culture. However, Agnes had a fully developed penis and scrotum.

Garfinkel's case study of Agnes is a paradigmatic illustration of ethnomethodological interests. First, human sexuality is usually considered to divide the population into unambiguous males and unambiguous females. Further, the supposed "best test" of gender involves the nature of the primary and secondary physiological sexual characteristics. This test, though, founders on Agnes' anomalous physiology. She is not, by this usually unapplied test, either a normal male or a normal female: she has male primary sexual characteristics and female secondary sexual characteristics. Second, the confounding of this test of gender has little, if any, sociological relevance. Agnes was not treated in her daily life as a "freak" or physiological anomaly. She was treated as a *female* by her employer, by her female roommate, by her friends, and by her fiancé until she told him about her condition. In terms of serving as the basis for social relationships, there are very few occasions in which the physiological test of gender is relevant, appropriate, or applied. Rather, other procedures are employed to determine gender and the physiological characteristics that nominally define gender are assumed to be in line with the results of these other procedures.

We will use an example of the very real cost for *males* of sexist gender images. Recent studies of male and female death rates attribute as much as three-quarters of the 8 year difference in life spans to differential socialization. Infant males are more delicate than females. They are more prone to some birth defects and illnesses, but we treat them as tougher than girls and sometimes withhold necessary protections. During later socialization the inculcation of the "macho" achievement/aggression orientation makes men prone to stress-related diseases. One of the most obvious dangers is smoking, long a male behavior signifying toughness, but in reality related to anxiety. The male sex role is dangerous to your health.[62]

Because gender is one of the sociological variables usually regarded as subject to objective measurement, the existence of ambiguous cases is interesting in itself. But Agnes' ability to pass as a normal female is more important as a source of insight into the ways in which gender is established as a social characteristic under more typical conditions. It is hard to believe that there are a surfeit of anomalous cases, such as Agnes, among our social contacts. Nonetheless, we must recognize that there are relatively few people of whose physiological normalcy we can be sure, and few situations in which this matters. Agnes' ability to be defined and treated as a female by other people serves as a reminder that most practical social purposes do not require physiological proof for gender to be determined. Her case indicates that, in addition, one need not even be able to pass such a physiological test in order to be defined and treated as a female in many situations. Finally, her case indicates strongly that some other procedure for assigning gender is actually employed. At least as far as the word "female" is concerned, Agnes' case indicates that meaning is not based on objective or ideal ways of categorizing people but on some other practical procedures.

SUMMARY OF IMPLICATIONS OF AGNES' CASE

We are now in a position to consider what one needs and what one does not need to be accepted as a woman in social situations. One does not need to be a physically normal female. Choice of clothes and other devices can conceal even extreme irregularities. One does not need extensive preparatory practice and experience in the female role. Apparently, one can learn and perform the role at the same time. One must be able to anticipate the sorts of background information and practical investigative procedures that will be employed in various settings, or at least fulfill the expectations they lead to in social settings. In short, to be a female one needs only to be competent in the use of interpretive skills, including reasonable assessments of relevant background knowledge and the nature of the reasoning others will use.

SOURCE: Robert H. Lauer and Warren H. Handel, *Social Psychology: The Theory and Practice of Symbolic Interaction* (Boston: Houghton Mifflin, 1977), pp. 286–289, quoting from H. Garfinkel, *Studies in Ethnomethodology* (Englewood Cliffs, N.J.: Prentice-Hall, 1967), pp. 262–284.

THE FUTURE

We have had a spasm of recognition of the inadequacy, waste, and unfairness inherent in the traditional female role.[63] It is unlikely that women will ever go back to blaming themselves for, or accepting, their low status. Bernard describes a "click" analogous to that which happens during religious conversion.[64] Traditional sex roles are no longer the "natural order," they are in the spotlight of social focus. Evidence from surveys of sex-role attitudes shows that men as well as women have substantially increased their acceptance of women in nontraditional sex roles. In fact, by 1978 men's attitudes resembled those of women.[65] Finally, sex-role changes were made necessary and inevitable by technological changes. The main function of the feminist movement has been to recognize these changes and to make society aware of the futility of resisting them.

The remaining questions are how long and how difficult will the period of transition be? The political confrontation has not yet occurred, either in the legislatures or the boardrooms. Women are the majority of voters but the politicians are still men, and it is unclear how long this disproportionate situation will persist. Women are forming networks to help secure jobs and powerful positions for "their own kind." They are called **new woman networks** after the model of the "old boy" networks that have been so effective for generations in England and the United States in placing the alumni of male private schools in powerful positions. What happens when these networks collide?

One more element clouds the future. How entrenched are the male-macho individual-achievement oriented competitive values that define America's version of success? Will women bring or create a more rational, cooperative, less driven approach that modifies the pressure and aids the integration of work into life? Or will there be a long period in which everyone uses the old success values and competition is accelerated by equality?

Pessimistic Scenario

By the year 2025 America resembled today's South Africa. Women's power became too threatening and the men realized that if a small minority of Whites can control a majority of Blacks, then a larger male minority should have no trouble staying in complete control. Women's castes are officially legislated with the cooperation of the male-dominated unions. It began in the military service during the 1980s when women were officially segregated out of any of the important fighting roles. The female jobs are now officially listed in civil service and in official "equal pay guidelines." Women found that they could not break into the informal "old boy" networks that more and more controlled hiring. They had to work exclusively through the courts.

The legal resolution to the equal pay for equal work dispute was the familiar "separate but equal" segregation. When a new job is created through technological change, a board of psychologists and biologists decides if sex differences are relevant and which sex should monopolize it. Women are at a disadvantage because of their well-known computer shyness. All technological occupations became male.

When frustration and economic repression led to violent protests and the beginnings of a female guerrilla movement, the government reacted with an elaborate control system and a limitation of political rights.

Personal life has suffered because of the official segregation. Men and women interact with great hesitancy because they do not know what to expect of each other. Many men sympathize with the cause of women's equality, but are afraid to make their feelings overt because it could bring them economic sanctions from the power structure. Men and women tend to live more and more separately; marriage and families are becoming infrequent, and men and women only meet in what is called the "competition for pleasure."

Optimistic Scenario

Women realized that they could influence the political process through direct participation and by making use of their numerical majority. The overemphasis on aggressive-competitive values in government policies was modified. Legislators became less willing to sacrifice social needs to maintain a huge male-dominated defense establishment. For a few decades, when this trend began to strengthen, it was in doubt whether the armed services and male political structure would accept change, but they seem to have chosen democracy, even when they are not the majority.

The major changes have taken place in the relationship of work and home. Marriage is more egalitarian. The tradition of a dominant male choosing among available females 2 years younger faded away, because the end of population growth made fewer and fewer younger females available.[66] Couples tended to meet in school because educational sex segregation into different career programs had ended. Corporations often hire "company couples" to fulfill a joint responsibility and full day-care facilities and parental sharing make childraising easier than before. Flex-time schedules and the large market for part-time workers has also led to experimentation in many forms of work-home divisions of labor. The power struggles between male and female networks were neutralized by this couple-work pattern, and by many men realizing that their own wives might be treated badly if they supported a closed system.

SUMMARY

1. We find sexism even in early social science theory. Women were thought of as biologically inferior. This bias continued through the Freudian era, which saw "anatomy as destiny." But the weakness of the argument that biological differences shape social differences is that it does not recognize the wide range of differences within both males and females, nor can it explain why men play many types of roles and women have been traditionally expected to fit themselves to a limited social position.

2. The socialization of sexist gender roles starts so early and is supported by such a consistent and integrated structure of values, norms, and ideologies that it fools us into thinking that gender roles are natural, instead of social.

3. Religious history and sacred books also contain limited definitions of women's inherent abilities and moral capacities. The Protestant clergy in America joined in the "feminization" of religion, and thereby the further segregation of social life into the "women's world" of art, culture, and religion, and the "men's world" of power, money, and decision making.

4. The effects of sexism are so powerful that many sociologists think women's position is best understood as that of a minority group or social caste. They suffer

prejudice and discrimination, and even a trained devaluation of their own self-images.

5. The specific effects of sexism include: (a) the alteration of women's biological natures by the physical or social limitation of sexual capacity; (b) a highly increased self-consciousness and fear of displeasing others due to the requirement to compete in the marriage market; (c) powerlessness in day-to-day verbal interaction with men so that a hesitant subservient attitude and an increased feeling of anxiety concerning the success or smoothness of the interaction are accepted as normal; and (d) sexual harassment on the job, both as exploitation of their inferior positions and as retaliation for daring to try to do "men's work."

6. The current arenas of change in sexism are: (a) education, in which there is clear evidence of the desegregation of both colleges and their career programs. Women are increasingly completing professional degrees in formerly male-dominated areas; (b) Equal pay for equal work is far from a reality, in fact, recently the income gap widened and the average woman only makes about 60 percent of what the average man makes; (c) women are still socially guided into working in the female occupational ghetto. They are thereby segregated in most organizations from the career ladder leading into management; and (d) there has been the least amount of progress in the political area. The female majority of voters is almost exclusively represented and judged by males.

7. Sociological orientations to the study of sexism emphasize very different causes of the problem. Those concentrating on individual faults ascribe women's position to their failure to cope due to innate biological limitations of logical thought or moral development. Functionalists see a continuing division of labor as necessary, but are concerned that technological innovation has caused such a disruptive transition to the next workable organization of family and economic functions. Conflict theorists see sexism as clear-cut domination of one sex by the other, and the traditional family model as merely a justifying ideology for the continuation of male superordination. Interactionists see gender role definitions as flexible. Now that they are in the spotlight of social concern their unfairness and irrationality will probably cause society members to no longer confirm them in everyday life. They warn, however, that even the effects of changeable definitions can be socially destructive until they are forgotten.

SUGGESTED READINGS

Davison, Jane. *The Fall of a Doll's House: Three Generations of American Women and the Houses They Lived In*. New York: Avon, 1980. Personal and historical description of America's "moral obligation to keep house."

Douglas, Ann. *The Feminization of American Culture*. New York: Avon, 1977. How American women were segregated from the "dirty" parts of life (money and power) and into domesticity, sentimentality, and "culture."

Gilligan, Carol. *Psychological Theory and Women's Development*. Cambridge, Mass.: Harvard University Press, 1983. An analysis of the weaknesses of prevailing theories which present women as unable to reach the higher levels of moral development.

Horn, Patricia, and Jack C. Horn. *Sex in the Office: Power and Passion in the Work Place*. Reading, Mass.: Addison-Wesley, 1982. The current arena of change with all its complexities and problems of harassment and confusions of purposes.

Huber, Joan. *Changing Women in a Changing Society*. Chicago: University of Chicago Press, 1973. A collection of articles summarizing sociological knowledge and perspectives. Many are still the best statements to date.

Key, Wilson Bryan. *Subliminal Seduction*. New York: Signet, 1973; and *Media Sexploitation*. New York: Signet, 1976. How the advertising industry exploits women and their sexuality, vividly illustrated and described.

Komarovsky, Mirra. *Dilemmas of Masculinity: A Study of College Youth*. New York: W. W. Norton, 1976. Description of male college seniors' feelings of ambiguity and role strain, and experience of contradictory expectations.

Pleck, Joseph H., and Robert Brannon (eds.). "Male Roles and the Male Experience." *Journal of Social Issues*. Vol. 34, No. 1, 1978. The changing social dimensions of masculinity and their psychological costs, described in a series of articles.

Sex Roles: A Journal of Research. New York: Plenum Press, 1975. Current research on sex role concepts and issues.

Shapiro, Evelyn, and Barry M. Shapiro (eds.). *The Women Say, The Men Say: Issues in Politics, Work, Family, Sexuality, and Power*. New York: Dell, 1979. A compilation of provocative fiction, social science observations, and statements on sexism.

Tripp, Marge (ed.). *Woman in the Year 2000*. New York: Dell/Laurel, 1974. Twenty-one interesting speculations and provocative extensions of changing female roles.

U.S. Bureau of the Census. *A Statistical Portrait of Women in the United States: 1978*. Washington, D.C.: Government Printing Office. Facts and figures to assess the changing status of women.

Yorburg, Betty. *Sexual Identity: Sex Roles and Social Change*. New York: Wiley Interscience, 1974. An historical and cross-cultural analysis of biological and gender differences, their origins, and potential changes.

GLOSSARY

Gender roles   The set of cultural expectations and rules making up society's view of proper masculinity or feminity.

Interaction powerlessness   As demonstrated in experimental findings, the usual confinement of women to the more submissive "follower role" in social interaction.

"New-woman" networks   Recent organizations of working women pledging to help each other's professional progress just as the "old-boy" networks have helped men.

Occupational ghetto   Confining women to the less important support jobs and away from decision making or high-paying positions.

Role entrapment   The culturally defined need to be "feminine" that prevents many women from doing things that would help them achieve success and self-realization.

Sexual harassment   Sexual advances or requests, and sexual remarks or behaviors that are intimidating, hostile, or offensive in the working environment, especially if rejection of the advance is used as the basis of a future employment decision.

Situationality of sex differences   Environmental demands, not biological differences, determining the responsibilities of males and females.

All societies, past and present, attempt to meet their basic social needs through organized patterns of beliefs and behavior that sociologists call social institutions. Examples of major social institutions are family, religion, education, and the economic, legal, medical, and political systems. Each of these contains a stable cluster of values, norms, statuses, roles, and participating groups to handle the demands and problems of everyday living. The exact nature of these social institutions will vary, depending upon a society's culture and stage of development.

Because they shape our expectations and values, social institutions are of critical importance to a society. Their effectiveness in fulfilling their culturally prescribed purpose determines the extent of that society's sense of well-being. Moreover, social institutions are "hooked into" one another; political and legal systems, for instance, affect the economic and educational systems, while family size, structure, and stability have relevance to the medical and educational systems. Changes in one social institution therefore impact upon the others. If any social institution favors only certain segments of society or loses its effectiveness, then the society's stability is threatened and not all experience a satisfying life.

In Chapter 11 we study the family, which provides for the care of children. Is the family still offering the nurturance and emotional support it should? A high divorce rate, increase in single parents, family violence and lessened cohesiveness have provoked much concern.

Education, discussed in Chapter 12, has been heavily criticized in recent years. One area of attack has been poor quality in terms of teacher competency, academic standards, and individual stimulation. Another has been the disparity between urban and suburban schools.

The focus of Chapter 13 is on the concentration of political and economic power within a small segment of society. Many believe the advent of megacorporations, political action committees, and the disproportionate sharing of the nation's wealth pose dangers to most American citizens.

The skyrocketing expenses exaggerating the social inequities of health care, the moral dilemma of life or death decisions, and problems of mental health care comprise the subject matter of Chapter 14. Also covered is the irony of lower effectiveness of our health care compared to many other countries.

Throughout this section you should note the continuing themes of socioeconomic variation within each social institution and of the need to improve their quality provisions for all people.

FOUR
CHALLENGES TO SOCIAL INSTITUTIONS

FACTS ABOUT THE FAMILY

The U.S. divorce rate more than doubled between 1965 and 1979.

One-third of all children experience family disruption by age 15.

Female-headed households constitute over 15 percent of all white families and over 48 percent of all black families.

Every year 16 percent of American couples produce at least one incident of physical abuse among themselves.

Every year 14 percent of American children are victims of severe parental violence.

One study found sexual victimization of children occurs among 19 percent of females and 8.6 percent of males.

11
THE FAMILY

The most compelling question about the family today is how to define it. Swept by the currents of change, the family exists in a variety of forms, and appears to be chiefly characterized as "in transition." Most families have someone in their midst who is divorced. Many know individuals who are living together rather than legally marrying. Others have had household routines upset by mothers or wives returning to work; and some have observed the disappointment of would-be grandparents as career-oriented couples decide not to have children. In the circle of the family we hear these and other changes discussed. The assessments range from a viewpoint that family life is better now, since individuals are no longer locked into traditional marital and parental roles, but instead can make a choice, to a pronouncement that families are falling apart and that the disorganization will soon bring the society to the brink of ruin.

Table 11.1 displays some of the prominent changes which occurred between 1970 and 1980: the increase in female-headed households, the increase in the number of individuals living alone, the decrease in the average size of households, the increase in the number of families with women working, especially women with children under 6, the increase in divorce. We will attempt to understand these changes by examining the empirical studies and to analyze their impact upon society. Some of the changes are distressing only to a small proportion of individual families. Others, however, have widespread consequences, serious enough to be considered social problems.

CONTEMPORARY FAMILIES IN TRANSITION

As the feminist movement began to gain followers, the status of women began to change and to have a significant impact upon family life. First, the divorce rate doubled between 1965 and 1979, when many women, beginning to take jobs, found they could support themselves. Second, childlessness among married couples increased as career pursuits became more satisfying. A survey conducted by the *New York Times* in December 1983 found that women valued jobs as much as family life. Only 26 percent of 927 women cited motherhood as one of the best parts of being a woman, half the percentage of 1970.[1] Third, the number of singles increased, since marriage was only one of several female choices. Finally, roles and power balances shifted within the family. Studies show the act of juggling careers and children has been fairly stressful, although the satisfactions generally outweigh the costs. So many women have embarked upon careers that Betty Friedan, whose book *The Feminine Mystique* was a catalyst for the feminist movement in the 1960s, now sees women at a "second stage":[2] employment opportunities are available but the pressing concern is whether jobs can be combined with marriage and particularly with parenting. Is there a family option?

Clearly, momentous changes are occurring in families. It would be fallacious to attribute the transformation to women alone, however. The changes are fueled by an economy that is now consumer-oriented, encouraging high material standards, escalating the costs of children, and requiring two-paycheck families. Concurrently,

TABLE 11.1   American Families, 1970–1982

	1970	1982
Family households	51,456,000	61,019,000
Married couple family	44,728,000	49,630,000
Without own children under 18	19,196,000	25,165,000
With own children under 18	25,532,000	24,465,000
Other family, male householder	1,228,000	1,986,000
Without own children under 18	887,000	1,306,000
With own children under 18	341,000	679,000
Other family, female householder	5,500,000	9,403,000
Without own children under 18	2,642,000	3,535,000
With own children under 18	2,858,000	568,000
Nonfamily households	11,945,000	22,508,000
Male householder	4,063,000	9,457,000
Living alone	3,532,000	7,482,000
Female householder	7,882,000	13,051,000
Living alone	7,319,000	11,872,000
Average size of household	3.14	2.72
Average number of children ever born to all women		
18–44 years of age	1.9	1.4
Proportion childless among married women 25–29 years		
of age	15.8	27.5
Percent 25–29 years of age never married		
Female	10.5	23.4
Male	19.1	36.1
Number of divorced persons per 1,000 of married		
persons living with spouse		
Female	60	137
Male	35	92
Number of children living with only one parent	8,250,000	13,700,000
Number of children living with mothers never married	527,000	2,800,000

SOURCE: U.S. Bureau of Census, *Current Population Reports,* Series P–23, No. 130, "Population Profile of U.S.: 1982" (Washington, D.C.: U.S. Government Printing Office, 1983).

more individualistic values prevail, responsive to and supportive of today's social and economic structure. Are any of these phenomena simply long-term adaptations of the family to an evolving society, or are they social problems for individuals, society, or both?

Social Change or Social Problem?

Let us take the example of **cohabitation.** Cohabiting couples, individuals living together without legal marriage, now number nearly 2 million. You may be cohabiting or know someone who is; your parents, parents of friends, or other relatives may disapprove on moral grounds. Research indicates that the majority of cohabitors find the arrangement both convenient and/or pleasurable. There is no firm evidence as

Traditional parental roles of mother as nurturing agent and father as provider have been merging in American society. Many males now share the responsibilities and emotional fulfillment of child care as greater numbers of wives also work full-time.

yet on its impact on any future marriage. Traditional sex roles do tend to be maintained within the cohabiting context.[3] Additionally, "palimony" suits have emerged with disputes over shared property. To guard against this latter problem, it is likely that cohabitation will become more institutionalized, more regulated by contractual agreements. Cohabitation, then, is a change affecting the family, which although morally disapproved of by some, is not yet a social problem.

How might cohabitation become a social problem? If cohabitation were to become so common that few bothered to marry legally, and if this depressed the birthrate, society might eventually suffer a loss of new recruits to the labor force. A high incidence of childlessness among married people might similarly become a social problem if we were not able to sustain our economic production levels because of too few workers. A social and economic restructuring of society might be required or technological revolution. We have an inkling of a related problem today in the precariousness of our social security system (see Chapter 7).

DIVORCE

The divorce rate in the United States had been relatively stable for decades. A downward fluctuation occurred during the Depression when people could not afford divorce or maintenance of two households. An upward surge followed after World War II due to unstable marriages hastily contracted before or during the war, or from changes wrought by the effects of separation. Between 1965 and 1979, however, the divorce rate rose from 2.5 divorces per 1,000 population to 5.4, more than double.[4] Since 1975 the number of divorces has increased, but the rate of increase has been much more gradual. In response to those alarmed by the high divorce rate, seeing it as the death knell of the family, analysts quickly point out that, although declining slightly in recent years, the remarriage rate continues to be between 75–80 percent of all divorced individuals, seemingly a vote of confidence for the institution.

Factors Contributing to the High Rate of Divorce

Changing Roles of Women

When we examine the social factors associated with the rise in the divorce rate, certainly the change in women's roles must be acknowledged. Women in the past who were dependent on males for support might have hesitated to terminate their marriages, but now many have the ability to become self-supporting. Likewise, the option may be open to more males who will not be saddled with alimony. Research shows that women of higher status and better paid occupations are more likely to separate and least likely to remarry.[5]

Attitudes, Laws, and Demographic Factors

Attitudes toward divorce have changed, with more tolerance and acceptance of the divorced and less discrimination. Beliefs about divorce have also changed: in particular, that it is better to stay together for the sake of children. Liberalized divorce laws, beginning in California in 1970, when no-fault divorce was instituted, have made divorces easier to obtain. (No-fault means neither party is blamed for the divorce; the decision is seen as mutual.) Now all but two states have no-fault provisions. Further, in the early part of the 1970s the rise in the divorce rate was affected somewhat by the end of the Vietnam War, and finally, by sheer demographic fact: divorce for women most often occurs between the ages of 20–24 and for men between 25–29.[6] In the 1970s there were large numbers of individuals in these age categories due to the growing up of the baby boom generation. In the future there will be fewer people in these age categories reflecting the lower birthrate in the 1960s and 1970s, so that we may even find a decline in the number of divorces.

Changing Expectations for Marriage

Even more fundamental to explaining the high divorce rate, however, is the change in expectations for marriage: the underpinnings of marriage today are largely psychological. Individuals seek self-fulfillment through a union with another person, and if their emotional needs are unmet, then the basis of the contract no longer exists. Ann Swidler discusses the emerging love ethic today which emphasizes the rebellious, free, individualistic side of love, endorsing flexibility and avoiding permanence.[7] In the past, the "success" of the marriage might have been judged on how well individuals fulfilled their social roles (the man as a good provider and the woman as a skilled housewife and good mother). Because it is easier to become an experienced baker or to make more money for the family than to become a day-to-day expert in interpersonal relations, marriage has become much more risky.

The Impact of Divorce on Adults

With such a high rate of divorce—nearly one in two marriages—the long-term effects on individuals are of concern to the society. Ann Goetting, reviewing the various studies on the impact of divorce, draws the following conclusions: (1) problems of household maintenance and of economic and occupational difficulties may accompany divorce; (2) social participation may decrease when marriage becomes unsatisfactory and then increase somewhat after divorce; (3) while at least temporarily divorce may lead to an enhanced sex life, especially for men, casual sex among the divorced leaves something to be desired; (4) both physical and mental health are best among the happily married, worst among the unhappily married, and somewhere between these two extremes among the divorced.[8]

The medical profession has recently begun to examine the long-term effects on health, particularly the biological links between emotional stress and the development of physical illness. The divorced have higher suicide rates, more alcoholism, higher rates of admission to psychiatric hospitals and outpatient clinics, and make more visits to nonpsychiatric doctors than married, single, or widowed individuals.[9] For men, who have been found to remarry sooner than women, remaining unmarried for more than 6 years increases their rates of car accidents, alcoholism, drug abuse, depression, and anxiety. For divorced women, the most serious long-term health

The stresses and strains upon many marriages today have led to a high number of divorces. Marriage counselling and couples therapy are two increasingly growing means of reducing tensions and conflicts by examining roles and expectations.

effects come from the stresses of poverty, continued conflicts with former husbands, and problems in childrearing.[10]

Divorce as a Process

Paul Bohannan describes divorce as a multistage process of separation: the emotional divorce, the legal separation, the economic divorce, the custodial divorce regarding care of children, the community divorce when family and friends must be informed, and the psychic divorce, a time when individuals must crystallize a new identity for themselves, since the former identity is shaken by the loss of the spouse.[11]

Robert Weiss has categorized the various stages of marital separation wherein individuals experience separation distress, anxiety, panic, and depression as the object of attachment becomes detached. This stage is sometimes followed by or alternates with a sense of euphoria that one no longer needs the former partner and then periods of intense loneliness.[12] The bonds of attachment are found to last much longer than each expected, even between people who wanted the divorce. Recovery comes most assuredly from remarriage or the formation of new intimate relationships.[13]

The Impact of Divorce on Children

The Rising Proportion of Children
Experiencing Divorce

With the increase in the divorce rate has come the rise in the number of children involved. Sixty percent of divorces involve children. Two researchers, Larry Bumpass and Ronald Rindfuss, basing their findings on a 1973 survey, estimated that one-third of white children and nearly three-fifths of black children would experience marital disruption by age 16.[14] A national study conducted in 1981 by Furstenberg, Nord, Peterson, and Zill corroborated the estimates by finding that nearly one-third of all children have experienced family disruption by the time they reach age 15. When children of never-married parents and those living with neither parent are included, the proportion rises to 39 percent. Further, they estimate that since some will experience disruption in their midteens, close to one-half of all children living in the United States will reach age 18 without having lived continuously with both biological parents. Blacks were 1½ times as likely as Whites to have experienced divorce by early adolescence. Finally, in the national sample, only 3 percent of respondents had a joint custody arrangement.[15]

The Consequences of Divorce

From the Goetting survey cited earlier,[16] the following generalizations can be made regarding the impact of divorce upon children: (1) a higher rate of school absence occurs among children from divorced homes when compared to children from intact homes; (2) children from happy marriages may display more positive personality traits such as self-esteem than either children from unhappy intact marriages or divorced marriages; (3) adolescents from happy homes appear to have closer relationships with their parents than adolescents from both unhappy intact homes and homes where the parents have divorced.

Adolescents from divorced homes may have more distant relationships with their fathers than do adolescents from unhappy intact homes. Adolescent women who are the children of divorced parents may have closer relationships with their mothers than do adolescent women from unhappy homes; (4) women whose parents have divorced may marry younger and are more likely to be pregnant at the time of marriage than women from intact homes; (5) men and women whose parents have divorced are themselves more likely to divorce; (6) diabetes may be more common among children of divorce; and (7) if there is a positive relationship between parental divorce and delinquency, divorce alone may be of no greater importance to the incidence of delinquency than is family discord.

The Effects of Divorce over Time

The most comprehensive study of the impact of divorce on children has now spanned over 10 years. Wallerstein and Kelly,[17] beginning in 1971, followed 60 divorcing families and their 131 children who ranged from age 3 to 18 at the time of the marital separation. Contact was established at 18 months, 5 years, and 10 years after the divorce to determine the impact and coping mechanisms. The perspectives of children often differed from that of their parents: unlike their parents, children did not perceive divorce as a solution to unhappiness until many years after the divorce. Frequently children would have preferred the unhappy marriage to the divorce.

Divorce impacts differentially on children depending upon their developmental age. Wallerstein and Kelly divided the respondents into four age groups: (1) 3–5½; (2) 6–8; (3) 9–12; (4) adolescents. In the youngest group the predominant emotion was fear, along with irritability and for some, guilt that they might have caused the divorce. The 6–8-year-olds' most striking response was grief and sadness, with a yearning for the departed parent, conflicts in loyalty, and anger at the custodial mother. The 9–12 year olds displayed anger, alignment with one parent, a shaken sense of identity, and somatic symptoms. Finally, in the oldest age groups, teenagers worried about their own sexual identities and marriage, had loyalty conflicts, and at times competed with their parents.

At 18 months, when 20 percent of the men and 17 percent of the women had remarried, 60 percent of the women and 40 percent of the men reported a decline in their standard of living. One-fifth of the children were still anxious over the divorce; one-fourth were depressed. The remainder were more realistic and had a less fear-dominated view of the divorce.[18] The gap between the sexes had appeared. While women were worse off than their former husbands, with one-half of them still depressed and two-thirds lonely, the average father was close to reestablishing his psychological equilibrium. For children and adolescents the reverse held true: more boys were evidencing stress, were preoccupied, longing for the departed father, and fantasizing about reconciliation. Girls coped more successfully, apparently because of their stronger support network of friends.[19]

At 5 years after the separation, two-thirds of the men and one-half of the women viewed divorce as beneficial. For the children, one-fifth still evidenced anger, regret, and longing; the others had made a successful adjustment.[20] Divorce obviously impacts differently on each family member.

Finally, preliminary results of the impact on children 10 years later find that they have generally outgrown their anger and have come to understand the reasons for divorce but wish that their parents had made their decision before having children.[21] Their childhood and adolescence have been irreparably influenced by the divorce.

The recent studies like that of Wallerstein and Kelly have led us to be more cautious in assuming that divorce benefiting parents will necessarily benefit the children. We recognize that the happiness and adjustment of divorced children is better than that of children in intact conflict-ridden homes, but lower than that of children in happy homes with both parents. The impact cannot be lightly dismissed.

The research on the impact of divorce points out the need for a stronger societal response in the form of counseling and other services to ease people through difficult transitions. Although the percentage of adults remarrying is high, the incidence of suicide, alcoholism, depression, and so on bespeaks a serious problem

SINGLE-PARENT FAMILIES

The increase in the divorce rate has meant a rise in the number of **single-parent families** in the United States (Figure 11.1). There has been an increase in the number of men awarded custody of their children, but the actual proportion as well as the

FIGURE 11.1   Households Headed by Women

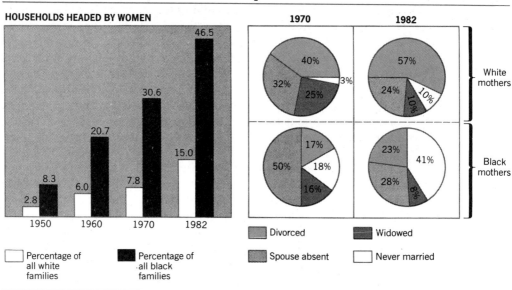

HOUSEHOLDS HEADED BY WOMEN

Percentage of all white families / Percentage of all black families

| 1950 | 1960 | 1970 | 1982 |

2.8 / 8.3 / 6.0 / 20.7 / 7.8 / 30.6 / 15.0 / 46.5

1970 · **1982**

White mothers — Black mothers

Divorced · Widowed · Spouse absent · Never married

SOURCE: U.S. Bureau of the Census.

percentage of couples electing joint custody remains small. More attention is being directed toward the single-father families, however, where men are found to suffer some of the same problems as single mothers: notably, the need for financial help to acquire day and home care, problems of loneliness, childrearing, and general overload.[22] The role of the single father, especially in caring for daughters, is not yet institutionalized in the society, nor are men as likely to seek help or advice.[23]

Families Headed by Women

Overwhelmingly, however, the national concern over single-parent families is centered on the problem of families headed by women. Currently, 15 percent of white families, with children under 18 and 48 percent of black families are headed by women.[24] In view of the latter startlingly high percentage, many black leaders and scholars have begun to address the issue of family structure as one of the most serious problems facing the black community.[25] The heart of the problem is the fact that families headed by women are twice as likely to be poor as two-parent families, and half of all families headed by black women have incomes below the poverty line. Where other types of black families have begun to advance socially and economically, the gains are offset by black female-headed households falling increasingly behind. Black women do have a higher divorce rate than white women and also tend less often to remarry. The fear is that even larger numbers of black children will be disadvantaged in the next generation because of their present-day circumstances.

Nonmarital Births

The major contributor to the higher proportion of female-headed households among Blacks is the incidence of **nonmarital births.** As Figure 11.1 indicates, 41 percent of households headed by black women are women who have never been married, while for Whites the figure is 10 percent. Further, the rate of nonmarital births is greatest among black teenagers. More than one in four Blacks was born to a teenage mother in 1979.[26] The birthrate among black teenagers did drop in the 1970s, but birth rates declined even faster among older black women so that the proportion of teenage births increased. The rate of teenage pregnancy among Whites increased in the same decade.

Factors Linked to the Incidence of Teenage Pregnancy

The factors contributing to a high rate of teenage pregnancy are varied: some of the main reasons are greater sexual activity among teens today (70 percent of 19-year-old females have had sexual intercourse),[27] psychological motivations such as the need for affection or desire to leave the parental home, and inconsistent or nonuse of contraception. The latter is more common among Blacks and at the lower status levels. In addition, black teenagers are less likely to seek abortions, since there appears to be less stigma in being a single parent in the black community.

The Consequences of Teenage Pregnancy

The negative consequences of teenage pregnancy are that young women are more likely to drop out of school, have low-paying jobs, or be unemployed. Additionally, infants of adolescent mothers are at higher risk healthwise.[28] The black infant mortality rate is considerably higher than that for Whites.

In examining the problem of single-parent families, then, it is clear that a societal response is demanded. Individual teenagers need more sex education and counseling, apparently at a younger age. The larger response required, however, is structural change aimed at reducing levels of poverty in the society. Many analysts think that the absence of males in such a large proportion of black families is directly linked to high levels of unemployment, the attendant inability to play any sort of provider role in the family, and to hopelessness about the future which impedes advancement. Needed structural changes are linked to broader problems in the society, notably racial discrimination and among many of the poor, lack of skills required in fields where jobs are expanding.

VIOLENCE AND ABUSE

When Dr. Richard Gelles, a nationally recognized expert on family violence, made the statement in 1972 that "more violence occurs within the nuclear family than within any other social group,"[29] we might have thought he was exaggerating in order to draw our attention to something. We have become painfully aware, how-

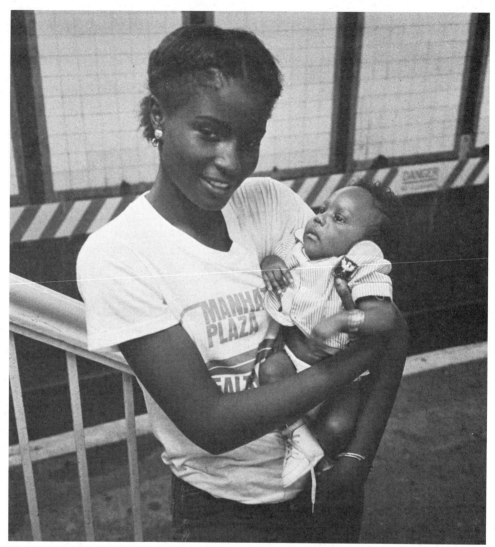

This teenage mother and her baby personify the serious problem of nonmarital births among teenagers. One of four black babies born now has a teenage mother, leading to school dropouts, unemployment, or low-paying jobs.

ever, of just how common is intrafamily violence. Far from being an idyllic retreat from the pressures of everyday life, for many the family is a battlefield and a training school for future violence. Although abuse has always existed, the problem of battered children was not publicly identified until 1962;[30] spouse abuse, specifically wife beating, was not raised as a serious concern until the mid-1970s, and abuse of elderly parents has surfaced even more recently. The term *abuse* can be used in a broad sense to include both physical and psychological harm, or, oftentimes, more narrowly to refer to the former alone since empirical evidence such as police records may exist.

Incidence of Family Violence

Table 11.2 presents the findings from a nationally drawn sample on the incidence of violence in the United States.[31]

Violence Between Spouses

Looking first at spouse abuse, the figures tell us that each year about 16 out of every 100 American couples experience at least one incident of one partner using force upon the other. Projecting that rate to about 47 million couples at the time of the survey, would mean violence between spouses takes place in 3 million homes each year. The incidence of wife abusing husband is comparable to that of husband abusing wife, but the wife's action is frequently a retaliation; additionally, in terms of

TABLE 11.2 Percentage Engaging in Violence or Severe Violence by Family Role Relationship, 1976

Family Role Relationship	Violence Indexes[a] Sex of Respondent			Severe Violence Indexes[b] Sex of Respondent		
	Male	Female	Both	Male	Female	Both
Husband-to-wife	12.8	11.3	12.0	3.5	4.1	3.8
Wife-to-husband	11.2	11.7	11.5	5.1	4.3	4.6
Couple	15.8	15.3	15.6	6.2	6.0	6.1
Father-to-child	57.9	*	*	10.1	*	*
Mother-to-child	*	67.8	*	*	17.7	*
Parent-to-child	*	*	63.5	*	*	14.2
Excluding hit with object						
Father-to-child	—	—	—	2.7	*	*
Mother-to-child	—	—	—	*	4.4	*
Parent-to-child	—	—	—	*	*	3.6
Child-to-father	13.7	*	*	7.5	*	*
Child-to-mother	*	20.2	*	*	11.1	*
Child-to-parent	*	*	17.7	*	*	9.4
Sibling-to-sibling	69.5	78.5	75.5	43.8	52.2	48.4

SOURCE: Murray Straus, Richard J. Gelles, and Suzanne Steinmetz, *Behind Closed Doors: Violence in the American Family* (Garden City, N.Y.: Doubleday, 1980), p. 266.

* = Data not available because parent-child questions were asked only about the respondents.

— = Not applicable because these rows are concerned only with severe violence.

[a] Based on percentage engaging in any of the following violent acts: (a) threw something at the other one; (b) pushed, grabbed, or shoved the other one; (c) slapped the other one; (d) kicked, bit, or hit with a fist; (e) hit or tried to hit with something; (f) beat up the other one; (g) threatened with a knife or gun; (h) used a knife or gun.

[b] Based on percentage engaging in any of the following violent acts: (a) kicked, bit, or hit with a fist; (b) hit or tried to hit with something; (c) beat up the other one; (d) threatened with a knife or gun; (e) used a knife or gun.

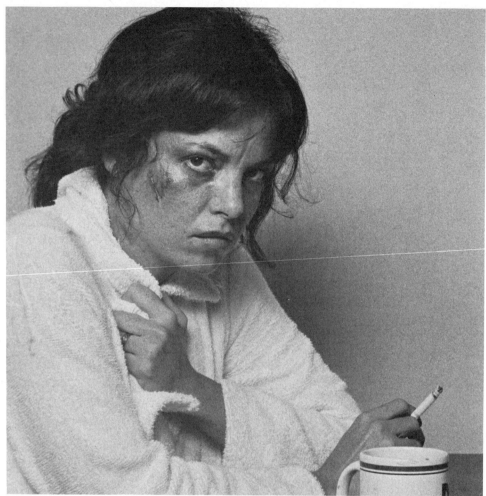

Only in the mid-1970s did wife beating emerge as a publicly recognized social problem. Violence between spouses occurs in 16 of 100 families each year, with women more often injured due to inequities in strength and weight. Homes for battered women now exist in many communities providing refuge and assistance to those seeking escape.

actual physical harm, women, due to inequities of strength and weight, are more often injured.

Child Abuse

Examining Table 11.2 for the incidence of child abuse, we find that 14 out of every 100 children yearly are the victims of severe parental violence. The projections are that between 1 and 2 million children are beaten while growing up.[32] The general expectations in the society are such that physical force is considered an acceptable way to control children, with widespread approval for spanking.

Most common are the attacks of siblings to the point that they are not recognized as anything but "kids being kids." Such "playfulness," however, does result in substantial bodily harm and contributes to a general acceptance of violent behavior.

Abuse of the Elderly

The category in Table 11.2 "child-to-parent" includes children up to 17 years. Currently, interest has been kindled over the issue of elderly abuse or what Jean Renvoize called "granny bashing."[33] Very similar to the acknowledgment back in 1962 that bruises on babies might not be accidental, doctors are discovering injuries among the aged inflicted by family members caring for them. More research and attention will certainly be forthcoming as the proportion of elderly increases in the society.

As individuals live longer, some, especially widows, may be welcomed by adult children only to have the relationship go sour under daily rounds of demands, complaints, and conflicts. Other elderly are taken in reluctantly to begin with, and the abuse may be an eventual expression of resentment. Still, for others, abuse of the elderly parent may be an additional display of the violent responses already exhibited in the family. Some data reported by Renvoize in England[34] found attackers were frequently unmarried daughters living with widowed mothers.

Unlike the care of children where constant demands are mitigated by the pleasures of watching the child develop, the older person faces continuing disabilities and may raise the level of stress within the family. Now that abuse of the elderly has been identified, much work remains to alleviate the problem: the need for hot lines, for support groups, for a large number of day-care centers for the aged, and for temporary residential shelters where the elderly relative could be left while the remainder of the family enjoyed a weekend or vacation.

Social Factors Linked to Violence

Richard J. Gelles, in summarizing the research done in the 1970s on family violence, identified the social factors related to abuse.[35]

The Cycle of Violence

Violence tends to run in families where individuals are socialized into it as a mode of response. Those individuals who were abused are more likely to grow up to become child and spouse abusers than individuals who have experienced little or no violence.

Socioeconomic Status

More cases of abuse are known to occur among the lower classes. More cases of abuse among the lower class are reported through use of hospital emergency rooms, clinics, and differential treatment by the police. It must be underscored that family violence does occur at all socioeconomic levels of society, but upper- and middle-class families effectively conceal it. Still, to deny a greater incidence in the lower class would be to ignore the social basis of family violence. In other words, if all classes had the same levels of violence then abuse could be explained as individual psychopathology, a sickness needing psychiatric treatment without societal response. The very real differences in class behavior, however, force us to acknowledge that society itself contributes to the behavior. Murray Straus has stated:

Rather than psychological factors being anywhere nearly equal in importance to the social causes of family violence, I am now convinced that they account for only a miniscule proportion of the violence which occurs in families—at the outside 10 percent. In short, at least 90 percent of the violence which takes place in American families grows out of the very nature of the family and of the larger society, rather than out of individual aberrations.[36]

Stress
Domestic violence is linked to stress, specifically, unemployment or part-time employment of males, pregnancy, being a single-parent family, and financial problems.

Social Isolation
Those families more socially isolated, less tied into a network of kin, neighbors, or friends who might lend support or intervene, have a greater risk of abuse.

Family Structure
Nuclear families—husband, wife, and children—are expected to meet members' emotional needs. Individuals in a setting of intense intimacy are vulnerable to the remarks of others; violence is more easily sparked. In previous generations, the **extended family**—grandparents and perhaps uncles and aunts also living with the nuclear family—diffused the emotional conflict, helping restore family stability. Further, a family structure where the power of males over females and parents over children is emphatic will be subject to demonstrations of that power. Instances where power is threatened become dangerous.

Cultural Norms
American cultural norms condone violence, stemming, according to some, from our frontier/cowboy tradition. A quick glance at television programs from the prevalence of police shows to children's cartoons reflects the propensity toward physical force.

Additional Factors
Other studies examined by Gelles noted additional factors related to violence toward children: larger than average family size, low birth weight or premature children, presumably requiring more attention, lack of attachment between mother and child, sometimes associated with low birth weight.[37] Victims are more likely to be infants and young children or older adolescents. Both groups are incapable of or not inclined to "listen to reason." Females are more likely to abuse their children since they are most continuously with the child and motherhood is a more essential element in their identity; also, handicapped, retarded, or any child perceived as "different" is at greater risk.

The studies on wife abuse found it more common when husband and wife report low job satisfaction of the male, when husband has no religious affiliation, and when there are alcohol problems.[38]

Runaways

Child abuse is linked to the growing number of runaways in the society. The U.S. General Accounting Office (GAO) estimates that at least 1 million young people are absent from their homes.[39] Although about 80 percent of runaways return home within two days, those who do not have a high probability of getting involved in criminal activity either as a perpetrator or as a victim. Many become drifters, turning to shoplifting, prostitution, pornography, or drugs in order to support themselves. Few have any prior work experience or job skills. The link with abusive families is strong: estimates are that between 25 and 50 percent of runaways are fugitives from homes where beatings, sexual abuse, and alcoholism are common. Up to one-half are described as "throwaways," pushed out by families who no longer want them or cannot afford to keep them.[40]

There is a growing network of shelters to house the runaways. In some cases youth workers can contact the parental homes and solutions can be worked out, such as instances where child-rearing practices are overly rigid, or there is a specific dispute, or the youth does not want to live with the court-assigned parent in divorced families.

Throwaways pose a different problem. There is no home within which to reintegrate the youth; the danger is in the creation of a large class of urban nomads drawn heavily from low-income households. Unfortunately, the ages of runaways have been dropping with an increase in the number of 11–13 year olds.[41]

SEXUAL VIOLENCE AND VICTIMIZATION IN THE FAMILY

Out of the dark closets of families, **sexual victimization** has been unearthed. The term is utilized here to refer to cases of marital rape or instances of **incest.**

Marital Rape

There are no official statistics so that the incidence of marital rape is unknown. Finkelor found 10 percent of a sample of 330 women in Boston reporting it, most often when a marriage is breaking up or during separation. From interviews with 50 women admitting to rape, in 40 percent of the cases the husbands did not intend to harm their wives physically.[42] This nonbattering type of rape seemed to be an exercise of power. Other types of marital rape that might be subsumed under physical abuse included battering rape where pain is deliberately inflicted to punish the wife or to retaliate, 48 percent in Finkelor's study. A small percentage (6) were classified as perverted rape with husbands aroused by violence and forcing wives into bizarre acts. In all types the lingering effects of the rape experience led many women to have problems of sexual adjustment and problems in trusting future intimate relationships.[43]

The same pattern is often true in cases of marital rape as in cases of physical assault: women do not recognize or define their forced sexual compliance as deviant. They assume that they are the sexual property of their husbands and if they deny them satisfaction, then they themselves are frigid or deserving of punishment—the blaming-the-victim perspective. In the next 10 years more cases of women claiming marital rape are expected, pressuring the courts to acknowledge women's rights within the appropriate circumstances.

Incest

On January 9, 1984 the American Broadcasting Company aired a movie, *Something about Amelia,* which dealt with father-daughter incest. Although talk shows and news reports had been probing the topic for 2 or 3 years previously, this was the first time that the subject was treated nationally on prime time television. Finkelor's study of 796 college students found that 19 percent of the women and 8.6 percent of the men had been sexually victimized as children, and over one-half of the time, coercion forced compliance.[44] **Sexual victimization** is the term used to emphasize that a child is victimized because of age, naiveté, and relationship to the older person rather than because of aggressive intent. The narrower category of incestuous sex includes incidents between siblings, other relatives, as well as parent-child. Twenty-eight percent of the victimized women in Finkelor's study had had incestuous relations while for men the figure was 23 percent.[45] In parent-child cases the pattern is overwhelmingly father-daughter incest; mother-son incest seems to be rare in the society, although "seductive mothers" are widely written about. The older the partner is, the more unpleasant the experience is for the child.

A Traumatic Experience

Judith Herman's study of 40 victims of father-daughter incest found that sexual contact with an adult, especially a trusted relative, is a significant trauma. Long-lasting deleterious effects include a variety of problems later in life and the introduction in many cases to a life of repeated victimization by men.[46] Herman found that 13 of the 40 victims ran away from home and 18 became pregnant, hoping to escape. Interestingly enough, many of them idealized men and hated women, the latter animosity stemming from their own self-contempt and guilt, and their anger toward their mothers who failed to intervene.[47]

Social Factors Related to Incest

The structural factors characterizing the family that lend support to incest seem to be a **patriarchal unit** where fathers assume they have the right to use female members of the family as they see fit, first wives, then daughters. Mothers in incestuous families have been found to be weak, incompetent, subservient, alcoholic, or largely absent and unable to protect their daughters. Many are unresponding when informed of the situation.[48] They themselves are victims of the patriarchy; if they are economically dependent upon their husbands with few alternatives, they may fear jeopardizing the marriage with a confrontation. One of the main thrusts of treatment of a victim is to build the mother's confidence and to improve the mother-daughter relationship. Herman suggests that when there is less male supremacy and a less rigid division of labor, especially when males become involved in the nurturant behavior required of childrearing, cultural supports will begin to crumble.[49] Institutional clarification of the role of stepfather would be useful too: Finkelor noted that having a stepfather or a stepbrother is associated with a higher risk of sexual victimization, either because the steprelatives take advantage of the female victim or increase the likelihood that a nonfamily member may do so.[50] Finally, rather than depicting the power of the relative over the vulnerable child, young girls have often been portrayed as little "Lolitas," seducing their adult victims. Advertising today widely uses young girls in forms of soft pornography to sell products by exploiting their emergent sexuality.

VIOLENCE AND VICTIMIZATION: THE NEED FOR SOCIETAL INTERVENTION

Since the sheer numbers of people who are abused within the family has reached alarming proportions, many believe a need exists for immediate intervention to protect victims.

Services for Battered Wives

In England, Erin Pizzey's book *Scream Quietly or the Neighbors Will Hear* led to the founding of Women's Aid of Chiswick, a house which became a model for battered women's shelters around the world. Such shelters not only provide food and lodging but can offer both individual and group counseling to begin to build self-esteem. Job referrals may also be made or advice on training for work, since a major problem is that so many battered wives are financially dependent. Richard Gelles pointed out that many battered wives remain with their abuser husbands since they see no alternatives.[51] Unfortunately, many more places of refuge are needed in the society.

Intervention in Child Abuse

For children, intervention generally means placement in a foster home while charges of abuse are investigated. With doctors and counselors required to report abuse cases, expansion of social service efforts is desperately needed. Currently we have a poor allocation of resources to deal with the large number of child abuse cases. Too often there is a delayed response to the crisis situation, temporary placement of the child in another home, then reinstatement in the unchanged, abusing home. Meanwhile, the foster-care arrangements may have created further psychological confusion for the child. Most children do not want to be separated from parents and usually interpret their removal as "their fault." We need more extensive follow-ups on families instead of short-term monitoring. Again, resources are the bottom line here: society, through leaders and public pressure has to decide that social goals ought to be given a priority.

The Police

In the past the response of police and the courts to family violence, especially battered wives, was oftentimes part of the problem. Police, unwilling to intervene, tended to dismiss cases of domestic violence as something for the parties to work out

A Gallup, New Mexico, police officer watches over a distraught wife as she packs to leave her husband. Police have become more trained in domestic intervention, as cases of family violence have become of increasing concern.

privately. Today, however, more police are trained in domestic intervention. In the past, wives were required to press charges against abusive husbands. Many did not, seemingly downgrading the seriousness of the offense. Some states such as New Jersey now allow an officer to make an arrest if his or her own assessment of the situation warrants it, despite refusal on the part of the wife.[52]

Prevention of Family Violence

Beyond the need for greater resource allocation for intervention is the larger need for prevention of family violence. Here research points the direction for social and economic change in the society. First, changes reducing stress in families need attention: reduction in unemployment, poverty, and more family planning to cut down on unwanted children. More day-care centers where parents might drop off children so they might have more free time, as well as more hot-line services, should be established. Second, training in the role of parenting would benefit many, since abusive parents often have unrealistic expectations of children. Third, measures promoting sexual equality may, in the long run, alleviate the problem of violence, because the male dominance emphasis over wives and children in past years encouraged the potential for abuse. Ultimately, an egalitarian family structure will discourage abuse.[53]

WHY ARE FAMILIES IN TROUBLE?

When we try to explain the social problems within the family, we can again turn to our four different orientations.

Individual Faults and Deviant Behavior

Carl Zimmerman described 4,000 years of family life[54] as a pendulum swinging between one extreme, the trustee family, to the midpoint, the domestic family, and finally to the opposite extreme today, the atomistic family. In the trustee family no concept of individual rights existed. The authority of the family as embodied in the patriarch was absolute, untempered by any outside agents. In this absolute control, however, lay the seeds of the trustee family's destruction: wives and children as property of males were subject to abuse. Eventually, as Church and State evolved during the Medieval–Renaissance periods, they came to intercede on behalf of the victims and power was shared in the domestic family type. The concept of individual rights emerged. Zimmerman praises this form of the family as the ideal because of its balance between the interests of the unit and the needs of individuals.

The Growing Emphasis on Individual Rights

The spirit of individualism grew, however, leading to the atomistic family of today. Now more emphasis is placed on the protection of the rights of individual family members, each of whom expect their own self-fulfillment. These rights, protected by the State, take precedence over the maintenance of the family unit. One example of this would be the courts deciding in favor of surgery on a deformed baby against the parents' wishes to deny treatment. Zimmerman sees examples of "rampant individualism" stemming from the atomistic family: juvenile delinquency, women's liberation, and high divorce rates.

Zimmerman's theory illustrates two points. First, an emphasis on individualism will portray family members as ego-centered, immersed in their own aggrandizement, willing to sacrifice the stability of the family unit to their own concerns. In this regard today, women are generally "blamed" for their unwillingness to serve their families any longer, and in their thrust for equality, for upsetting the family structure. Thus, women pursuing jobs and careers leave behind unsupervised children who, according to some research, have higher rates of delinquency. This perspective, however, fails to focus on the social, economic, and political structures which promote individualistic values and ignores the costs of women's subordinate status.

The second point demonstrated by Zimmerman's theory is that selection of one family type as ideal will result in judging all others in some way as deficient or deviant.

Deviant Families and Sick Individuals

In the past divorced families were treated as deviant. With divorce so much more prevalent today, however, this is increasingly less often the case, although we still hear the phrase, "broken families." Black families with a high incidence of single parenthood and out-of-wedlock births are still frequently stigmatized.

In the area of abuse the explanation of individual faults has been commonplace. Abusers have been seen as "sick," as psychopaths with serious personality disorders. Child abusers were those unable to delay gratification, individuals whose emotional needs went unmet in their own childhood. Now they seek satisfaction from their children, even from infants, who are not capable of filling such emotional voids. In addition, parents or other relatives sexually victimizing young family members are treated as "perverts."

As we have seen, the pathological or sick individual approach ignores the concentration of abuse within certain groups and fails to explain the social patterns that are observed.

Institutional Faults and System Disorganization

The social systems perspective views the family as one institution within a societal system for which it performs essential functions.

The Loss of Family Functions

According to Ogburn,[55] the family in Colonial times was charged with at least seven functions: (1) the economic function wherein the family was a production unit supplying its own food, clothing, and shelter; (2) education, in that the family passed on to the children the knowledge and skills necessary for participation and survival in the society; (3) protection, especially in the figure of the father who protected members from outside physical harm without reliance on a police force; additionally, the family protected its members by caring for them in old age or during illness; (4) recreation occurred within the home in the form of family activities such as singing and dancing; (5) religion, as beliefs were taught by family elders and worship took place within the home; (6) status placement wherein the family determined the status and prestige of its members; and (7) reproduction and affection among members.

When we analyze the family today, we find that these functions are largely being performed by outside agents, by schools, by police, nursing homes, insurance agencies, and so on. Industrialization removed the production function from the family and as other social and economic changes occurred, most of the remaining functions were stripped away. The family, left with few tasks to perform, becomes a fragile unit. The disturbing question posed by Robert Nisbet[56] is whether a unit stripped of functions can remain a source of psychological identification for its members. Divorce and its attendant negative consequences for the society would stem from this weakened family, which is no longer perceived as essential for individual survival.

New Functions: Emotional Gratification

On the other hand, some theorists, notably Talcott Parsons,[57] see the contemporary family free to specialize in a small number of tasks. The family, linked to the impersonal world of bureaucracies, specializes in providing affection and supplying emotional gratification for its members, thereby performing an essential function for both society and the individual. Parsons' ideas, however, have come under attack by feminists because women were the ones expected to create the emotional refuge for family members while many of their own needs went unmet.

New Functions: Consuming

Following the functionalist line of thought, the economy today is described as consumer-oriented, based increasingly on the growth of the service sector. The family's adaptation to such change is reflected in the declining birth rates and the increase in the number of women working in the society. More two-income households allow the family to consume more. At the same time, consumer standards have risen and parents expect to provide each child with more goods and more lessons, and so on. Except perhaps for the wealthy who can afford more children or the very poor who have no control, two children or less has become the norm.

The consumer family is still expected to meet its members' emotional needs, however. Since the number of members is fewer and since more women are now working, there is oftentimes little time or energy left over to meet the psychological demands of others within the home. A high rate of divorce is not surprising when so much is expected from one, two, or three other people.

Disorganization

We can conclude, then, that the social systems' perspective would view the family as disorganized in response to changes in the larger society. Until a new stabilized system or a new equilibrium is attained, family-related social problems can be expected. Some abuse by husbands can be explained as men resisting the democratic family structure which will increasingly promote both the family's and society's survival. Instead, they seek to maintain the roles and values of an older, patriarchal industrialized social system.

Inequality and Inevitable Conflict

The perspective of conflict and inequality has only been recently applied to family studies, given the strong ideological press to portray the family as a harmonious unit.

The Inequality of Women

An early depiction of the family from the framework of inequality, however, was Engels's classic work, *The Origin of the Family, Private Property and the State,* wherein Engels claimed that the family was the source of female oppression. In fact, the only difference between a wife and a prostitute was that the former had sold herself for life! Engels attributed the subjection of women to the capitalistic system with its fundamental tenet of private property. Industrialization was taking men out of the home and enslaving some children as well, leaving women economically dependent on males.

Today conflict theorists direct our attention to the power relationships in the family. We are able to understand that women who return to work gain a measure of power. Following the Marxian line of thought, women whose consciousness of their oppression has been unearthed, are engaging in pitched battles with their male oppressors. The struggle is waged in the home as well as in the marketplace, and for many women, divorce represents a certain victory, a release from inequity. Some of the violence in the home also derived directly from the changing balance of power where males, no longer social and economic dominants, resort to force to keep women in their place.

Conflict with External Organizations

On the macrolevel, the family unit, rather than interdependent with and adapting to the other institutions of society as functionalists maintain, can be seen as pressured by external organizations. Economic organizations pursue profit-making activities and expect families to conform to bureaucratic schedules. With more women working, now two members of the family are under external pressures, while children must meet the demands of educational and recreational organizations. The family tries to maintain the ideology that it is a retreat, but individuals find it difficult to compartmentalize their public and private lives. Unfortunately, many people blame themselves for personal failures in marriage when, in fact, the major contributing factor may be the unrelenting stress created by extrafamilial organizations. Feldberg and Kohen[58] express this by noting that the family exists in an "antifamily setting." The outside organizations of society are not sympathetic to and are in conflict with the values held important to family life.

The Class Structure

Finally, the perspective of inequality directs our attention to the higher incidence of many family-related problems such as divorce and violence in the lower classes. The inequalities of the social structure resulting in scarce resources mean that poorer families must struggle to keep the unit intact. Ill-health, unemployment, and larger family size are only some of the stresses linked to poverty, contributing to the instability of family life.

Interaction and Social Interpretation Emphasis

Throughout our discussion we have seen that a basic process occurring today is the reinterpretation of family roles.

Change in the Meaning of Marriage

As noted previously, the meaning given to marriage itself has changed; gratification of emotional needs has assumed primary importance. This has made the marriage contract more precarious, a major explanatory factor in the high divorce rate. Furthermore, society has reinterpreted the nature of the contract itself, from a sacred to a civil to a personal bond between two people. This change in the definition of marriage has been accompanied by a reinterpretation of divorce. A growing number do not blame their divorce on personal failure, but rather, assess it as a stage in their on-going personal development, a relationship that "did not work out." Divorce is no longer as stigmatized. One family sociologist even describes individuals today as being "permanently available" in the mate selection process.[59]

Shifting Marital Roles

The interactionist orientation directs our attention to the changing expectations for family roles. The clash over shifting interpretations of what is properly the husband, wife, parent, or child role results in power struggles as each tries to impose his or her own definition. Men who beat their wives or children or who sexually victimize their daughters are a prominent example of a dominant group trying to retain the traditional definition of the male role. Increasingly, marital roles are defined by the two persons involved, custom made to their particular situation and life-styles: the allocation of tasks in the home, for example, may be decided by who has the time or preference rather than according to some stereotyped division of labor. Since marital roles are less often defined by society, lengthy processes of negotiation are often required before two people can come to an equitable agreement on the expectations each has for the other. Currently, most women are still burdened by traditional definitions of the female role. Women do most of the housework and in the job market earn only about 65 percent of male incomes.

Change in the Meaning of Childhood

In the case of child abuse, the symbolic interactionist can look at the changing meanings given to childhood: from historical periods when children were regarded as miniature adults to be seen and not heard,[60] to modern times when children, now economic liabilities, are begotten for emotional gratification. The standards for child care have risen, and the results are judged by experts—nutritionists, psychologists, educators. The pressures on parents to meet new performance levels has intensified, along with the meteoric rise in costs. Currently, discussion has shifted to "the disappearance of childhood,"[61] as children learn from television at an early age many of the "secrets" kept from them in previous generations, as programs reveal the problems, concerns, and weaknesses of the adult world. Violence, politics, and sexual matters are vividly present in the media and much of adult mystery has been literally laid bare. At the same time, a new generation in many cases surpasses the technical knowledge of their elders as in the case of computer whiz kids. The definitions and redefinitions and attendant confused role expectations may be cited in the general pool of stress-related elements suffered by families today.

Defining Family Matters as Social Problems

Finally, many of the concerns we have discussed have only recently been defined by the society as problems. Child abuse and wife beating have been thrown into the public arena only within the last 20 years, although the occurrence goes back to ancient times. Previously they were defined as "family matters" and police and courts only reluctantly intervened. As we have come to recognize their social basis, however, society has had to acknowledge its responsibility and to redefine its role.

WHAT CAN BE DONE TO HELP FAMILIES?

In order to help families, should the federal government intervene? Some favor a national policy to strengthen families while others oppose any form of government involvement.

Some social observers suggest children now grow up too quickly because television prematurely reveals all the secrets of the adult world. Besides sex and violence, children also see on family shows parental indecision in child rearing, a view previously not experienced.

A National Family Policy?

A **national family policy** would require agreement on the essential nature of the family, a notion of what is a "healthy" family, with government measures introduced to achieve this end. At this point in time, unlike several European countries, the United States does not have a national family policy nor are we likely to have one in the near future. Widespread disagreement exists over who should be included under "family" legislation. Should "family" be restricted to two parents and their children, or should the term *family* also extend to single persons and homosexuals among others? Just as there is little agreement over what properly constitutes a family, so is there little accord on which type among the variant forms should most benefit from public funds. Should more attention be directed to single-parent families who have more difficulties or to traditional families, helping to maintain them and thereby reducing the incidence of divorce and single parenting—or both? Resources are always limited, however, so choices would have to be made.

Liberals Versus Conservatives

Liberals favor the rights of the individual, equality of sex and race, and do not want to stigmatize anyone because one family type is preferred. They support more opportunities for women, which probably would increase the divorce rate in the short run. They favor more government intervention to help families. Conservatives want to restore the traditional family which essentially is patriarchal in nature. They laud the services of the homemaker and lament women having to work, but as we have discussed, such inequality and rigid division of labor does contribute to situations of abuse. Conservatives favor less government involvement and restoration of autonomy and control to the family to handle its own affairs.

THE FUTURE

It is time now to look ahead and examine the state of the family in the society. We have two pairs of glasses for our viewing and we will look through each.

Pessimistic Scenario

Let us put on a pair of dark glasses and take a look at a bleak future. It is the year 2025. The society is composed of a large number of elderly people, the aged baby boom generation. They have held political power for a number of years, acting in their own interests to provide monies for housing and health care. These costs have fallen on a small pool of workers, the result of years of low birthrates, and as a result, the society is experiencing antagonistic clashes between age groups. Younger family members, however, are often required to take in their elderly since the expanded programs have still not been able to provide for them all. Since insufficient funds have been allotted to day-care and temporary shelters, incidents of elderly abuse abound in the society.

The divorce rate has leveled off and even declined from that of the late twentieth century, largely because fewer people are getting married. Men, finding no advantages in marriage, and women who are enjoying careers, think that marriage is not worth the effort. Men have continued to resist involvement in child care and domestic duties, and more women have accepted the male model of achieving status and recognition through occupational mobility. Men and many more women are loyal to organizations, meeting the demands of bureaucracies, with little time for personal involvements. Rather than accommodate the needs of employees' families, bureaucracies have created pseudofamily environments. Organizations are the center of social life and individuals think of them as their families; meanwhile, their emotional needs go unmet and they are pawns of profit-oriented companies.

Birthrates are generally low since the costs of childbearing are prohibitive, given the high material standards. Rapid advances in biology and genetic engineering have resulted in a professional class of breeders. Concerns over the "quality" of those reproducing have resulted in vicious attacks and charges of elitism and racism between groups in the society. The ability to determine the sex of a child has resulted in an imbalance of males who, in a carryover from the twentieth century, are preferred. A masculine orientation, therefore, continues to dominate the society, fostering aggressiveness and competition.

The majority of children whose parents are both working, are cared for from birth in day-care centers and later remain in schools until 6 o'clock. The government has attempted to ensure standardization of practices and values by these caretakers.

Childhood has further disappeared, since children's activities are structured round the clock by adults.

Society has failed to enact legislation that would have aided and strengthened poor families, and each generation has fallen further behind. Advances in computer technology have widened the gap between rich and poor and shrunk the proportion of individuals who are middle class. The inequitable structure of the society is reflected in a sharp division of families into stable and unstable types. For the poor, the strain of their circumstances has maintained spouse and child abuse at the levels of the 1980s. Teenagers, for whom jobs are not yet a priority, continue to have a large number of out-of-wedlock births.

Finally, liberals and conservatives have continued to disagree on appropriate forms of the family, so that instead of strengthening families, many functions have been further taken over by government and outside agencies. The family for many has become an empty shell, a unit with which there is little psychological identification. The weak attachment of people to primary groups, however, has resulted in a high incidence of mental illness and suicide.

Optimistic Scenario

Let us remove our dark glasses and put on a pair of rose-colored ones. This time in the year 2025 sex roles have changed significantly, especially for males who are now more involved in child care and housework. Women are pursuing careers or jobs, but are less burdened because domestic concerns are shared. Organizations have responded to family needs by establishing day-care centers on the work site, by expanded and more generous maternity and paternity leaves, and by more flexible work hours. Individuals are recognized by society for their contributions to family life. The family structure has become more democratic and there is less abuse stemming from attempts to control members.

The electronic revolution has allowed some families to become a work unit, processing information at home with computer terminals. Teenagers are equal contributors in the family endeavor. Restoring functions to the family has helped to strengthen the ties. Electronics has also allowed families to be linked to blood relatives or more often to a network of friends. Large video screens bring this network into the home for frequent "visits." Family problems are discussed with the network members, thereby reducing the stress and intense emotions of the nuclear family.

The government has recognized the value of communal groupings and has given grants and tax breaks to enable their formation. Food, baby-sitting, and exchange-of-service cooperatives link people to a broader network, strengthening primary group attachments in the society. These new extended families have reduced the isolation of families, helping to alleviate violence.

The birthrate has remained low so that fewer children are affected by divorce, which has also declined. Children are more highly valued, since with fewer young people and a large proportion of elderly requiring support, society has come to recognize their contribution. For those individuals who do experience divorce, a full range of counseling services is available to them; the single-parent family has been aided also by the new communal networks and expanded day care. Marriage and parenting courses are required in school so that individuals have more realistic expectations.

The government has given priority to the needs of poor families with income maintenance programs, job training, and more day-care centers. The incidence of teenage pregnancy has thus begun to drop in the society, and a generation of youth is beginning for the first time to experience some upward mobility.

Lobbyists have succeeded in pressuring the media to reduce the shows involving violence and the ads exploiting men, women, and children. Humane concerns are more often celebrated. Because of the problem of scarcity of resources globally, cooperation has been seen as a value necessary for survival. Control over environment and people is seen as a destructive thrust. Children are being socialized into the appropriateness of less violent responses.

Liberals and conservatives have managed to smooth out some of their differences, and the society has a healthy balance between public support for nuclear families embedded in a broader communal network and tolerance for variant forms.

Finally, the impact of computer technology and the age of information has been felt on all levels of society and the rate of social change has slowed. The period in which families are struggling to adapt to a rapidly changing world has largely ended and family forms suited to this transformed society are prevalent and stabilized.

SUMMARY

1. In the 1960s, the women's movement began to initiate a change in the status of women. As more women began to pursue jobs and careers, there was an increase in divorce, childlessness, singlehood, and shifting roles within the family. The transformation of contemporary families is not due to women alone, however, but also to changes in the economy which, encouraging consumption, demand two paycheck families, and to more individualistic values. Some of the changes are simply manifestations of the family's adapting to an evolving society; others constitute social problems.

2. The divorce rate doubled between 1965 and 1979, but since then the rate of increase has been more gradual. The high rate of divorce is attributed to the changing roles of women, to softening attitudes toward the acceptability of divorce, and to more liberalized divorce laws. During the 1970s, large numbers of individuals were in the age brackets when the risk of divorce is greatest. A change in the expectations for marriage occurred making the nature of the contract more precarious.

3. Divorce, shown to occur in stages, has a number of negative consequences for adults such as higher rates of suicides, alcoholism, and physical and mental health problems. Sixty percent of divorces involve children, so that close to one-half of all children can expect to experience marital disruption by age 18. The impact of divorce on children varies according to the developmental age of the child, but in general, even children who come to understand and accept the divorce, wish their parents had made their decision before having children.

4. A sharp rise has occurred in the number of single-parent families in the United States, especially among Blacks, the majority of them headed by women. These families are twice as likely to be poor. A major contributor is out-of-wedlock births, an increasing proportion of all births, especially among teenagers. Teenage pregnancy results from greater sexual activity today, psychological motivations, lower status, and inconsistent or nonuse of contraceptives. The consequences are a greater likelihood of poverty and a higher health risk to infants.

5. Violence between spouses and abuse of children are widespread. Abuse of elderly parents has been more recently uncovered. Social factors linked to a greater incidence of abuse are the experience of abuse in one's own background, lower-class status, stress, social isolation, the nuclear family structure, and cultural norms condoning violence.

6. Sexual victimization within the family includes both marital rape and incest. Both have lingering deleterious effects on women, linked to male supremacy and a rigid division of labor.

7. Given the widespread incidence of family violence, a need exists for more shelters and counseling services for battered wives, more extensive intervention in child abuse cases, and police training for domestic situations. Preventive efforts would include alleviating family stress, training in the parent role, promoting sexual equality, and reducing the overall level of violence in the society at large.

8. Family-related social problems are inadequately explained by attributing them to selfish individuals (divorce) or to sick personalities (abuse). Some see the family as disorganized, having lost its traditional functions in the society, and under stress trying to specialize in the emotional gratification of its members. Conflict theorists view family problems as a function of a shifting balance of power between men and women, as engendered by conflicts with external organizations, and linked to the inequities of the class structure. Finally, new definitions of marriage, marital roles, and childhood lead to confusion and greater stress in families today.

9. The United States has no national family policy and is unlikely to adopt one because of the widespread disagreement between liberals and conservatives over the nature of the family, acceptance of variant forms, and the desirability of government intervention. Family legislation in the future is likely to proceed piecemeal.

SUGGESTED READINGS

Dempsey, John J. *The Family and Public Policy: The Issue of the 1980s.* Baltimore, Md.: Paul H. Brookes, 1981. A thorough discussion of public policy and the family including a historical overview, coverage of the 1980 White House Conference on Families, and the current controversies.

Gelles, Richard J. *The Violent Home: A Study of Physical Aggression Between Husbands and Wives.* Beverly Hills, Calif.: Sage, 1972. An important sociological study which was instrumental in calling attention to family violence as a major social problem.

Finkelor, David. *Sexually Victimized Children*. New York: Free Press, 1979. A study of 796 college students revealing a surprising incidence of sexual victimization as youths.

Finkelor, David, and Kersti Yllo. *License to Rape: Sexual Violence Against Wives*. New York: Holt, Rinehart and Winston, 1983. A study of 50 wives admitting to marital rape, clarifying the types of violence, and describing the lingering effects.

Skolnick, Arlene S., and Jerome H. Skolnick. *Family in Transition*. 4th ed. Boston: Little, Brown, 1983. A collection of 40 articles, both theoretical discussions and empirical research, focusing attention on the major issues confronting the family today.

Straus, Murray A., Richard J. Gelles, and Suzanne K. Steinmetz, *Behind Closed Doors: Violence in the American Family*. Garden City, N.Y.: Doubleday, 1980. An important study of family violence documenting the widespread incidence and analyzing the social factors contributing to this serious problem.

Wallerstein, Judith S., and Joan B. Kelly. *Surviving the Breakup: How Children and Parents Cope with Divorce*. New York: Basic Books, 1980. A study of 60 divorcing families and their 131 children over a 5-year period, showing how divorce impacts differently on each family member.

GLOSSARY

Cohabitation   An arrangement where a man and a woman share a common dwelling without being legally married.

Extended family   A nuclear family extended to include the parental generations and also sometimes to include relatives such as aunts and uncles.

Incest   Sexual relations between close relatives in violation of societal norms.

National family policy   A nationally agreed upon course of action directed at the family to influence both its structure and the functions it performs.

Nonmarital birth   The birth of a child to an unmarried mother.

Nuclear family   A unit consisting of husband and wife and their children.

Patriarch unit   A form of the family in which the male has dominance over the females.

Sexual victimization   Sexual abuse because of age, naiveté, and relationship to the abuser, such as in father-daughter incest.

Single-parent family   A family unit consisting of one parent and his or her children, the consequence of divorce, illegitimacy, or death of a spouse.

FACTS ABOUT EDUCATION

In the past 10 years, average SAT scores have dropped 40 points on the verbal section and 25 points in math.

Minority students outnumber Whites in 33 of the 50 biggest central city school districts.

Private school enrollments increased 31 percent in the South and 19 percent in the West while public school enrollments declined 6 and 11 percent, respectively.

Education majors scored 80 points below the 1982 national average in combined SAT scores.

Thirty-eight percent of California teacher education graduates failed a minimum competency test in 1983.

The average teacher's salary of $20,531 in 1983 was well below that of other white-collar professionals, plumbers, and electricians.

Only 12 to 15 percent of teachers are still in the classroom 10 years after entering the profession.

12
PROBLEMS IN EDUCATION

Ever since Thomas Jefferson first advocated mass education to produce an enlightened citizenry to sustain democracy, Americans have looked upon the educational system as the springboard for individual achievement and national well-being. Not until the mid-nineteenth century, however, did free public education for all become the norm. In the early twentieth century, native-born Americans also relied heavily on the schools to Americanize the large numbers of diverse groups coming from southern and eastern Europe.

Value orientations have since changed very little among the American public, who still place great faith in education as the social institution capable of solving both personal and societal problems, including alcohol and drug abuse, teenage pregnancies and reckless driving, crime, poverty, and prejudice. People tend to view schools as the great equalizers, the pathway to success, the transmitters and preservers of all that is good about America: the work ethic, the belief in democracy and free enterprise, and a sense of responsibility to one's family and community. Such lofty goals identify education as a means to an end, rather than as an end in itself. Basic skills are taught, of course, but the greater emphasis is neither on them nor on the value of intellectual growth or learning for its own sake. Rather, through education one gets to be something, to get somewhere else, to be successful.

Ironically, the greater demands on American education have a negative correlation with the status of educators, who are held in lower esteem here than in African, Asian, or European countries. By expecting so much from the educational system, people make it an easy target for criticism from all directions. Liberals, conservatives, and radicals all find fault, as do feminists, minorities, parents, teachers, and students. In spring 1983, President Ronald Reagan struck a responsive chord among many Americans when he attacked the poor quality and teaching ineffectiveness in the nation's schools. Others have lambasted education for helping maintain inequality instead of eliminating it. Problems of school discipline, integration, and financing have also drawn fire from many sides.

CHARACTERISTICS AND CONTRADICTIONS

A land of many diverse peoples and continuing new arrivals, the United States faces numerous challenges in its educational goals. As already mentioned, we place great faith in the educational process both to improve society and to cure its ills. Our values and beliefs make the American educational system quite unique in the world, but simultaneously cause frequent disillusionment or dysfunctional practices.

Compulsory and Universal Education

In other countries education either remains available mostly to the property-owning elite or else a meritocractic reward for the test-proven competent. In the Soviet Union and its satellite countries, for example, the sorting process begins after the 10th grade when the lower third of achievers are sent to vocational schools. The others, based upon written examinations, will go on to 2- or 4-year specialty schools and universities. Comparable programs exist in Western Europe. The

United States, in contrast, has the prevailing attitude that every individual is entitled to as much education as each desires. Universal higher education is a generally accepted national phenomenon.[1]

Insisting upon extended educational opportunities for everyone, however, does have its price. One frequent complaint is that mass education results in a lowering of academic standards, thereby reducing the quality of education received. The philosophy in other industrialized nations has been to emphasize high standards for university study, even though this denies entrance for the less academically able. Forty percent of American high-school graduates now attend college compared to about 10 percent in Europe. The American paradox of greater quantity but lesser quality can be illustrated by the following: (1) over 80 percent of American students now graduate from high school; (2) verbal test scores fell from a 466 average in 1967 to 426 in 1982 while mathematics scores dropped from 492 to 467;[2] (3) since a high-school diploma does not now necessarily guarantee even basic literacy any more, many states are beginning to follow the lead of Arizona, Colorado, and New Jersey in requiring a passing score on a basic skills test in order to receive a high-school diploma.

Community Control

"Home rule" has long been a cherished aspect of American life. People zealously fight to preserve local control over all aspects of community life, including education. In most states the greatest proportion of funding for the public schools comes from the local communities themselves, augmented by some state and federal assistance. While certain state and federal guidelines must be observed, local decisions guide most aspects of the educational process. Sometimes community control means a segment of a municipality; in 1968, for example, black parents in the Ocean Hill–Brownsville section of New York City successfully fought for a direct voice in personnel and curriculum decisions, rather than the monolithic bureaucracy that ran the schools for a city of 8 million.

Local control allows a community voice in meeting the needs of one's children, but it also presents problems as well. Since tax bases vary widely on a continuum from affluent to poor communities, the quality of education will vary according to the available funding for teachers, facilities, equipment, and supplies. Curriculum content will also vary from one district or state to another. Thus, variance may be from the grade level material first introduced (for example, multiplication and division in primary grades, or American and English literature in high school) to how subjects are taught (such as creationist or evolutionist teaching in science or biology).

Education is susceptible to local pressures, whether to ban certain books or fire a coach because the team is not winning. Typically, local school boards are elected and are comprised of business and professional people, with little representation, if any, from working-class or minority people. Those elected make policy decisions tending to echo the views of one segment of the community, not those of other local residents from different backgrounds. Only in defeating school budgets and bond proposals do community taxpayers get to express their frustration or dissatisfaction with expenses and policies.

THE SCHOOL AS A BUREAUCRACY

Supposedly, schools stimulate intellectual curiosity, encourage creativity and individualism, develop critical thinking, and provide opportunity for students to reach their potential. In practice, the schools either fail to do these or they are biased, favoring certain categories of students. Part of the reason for this lies in social class differences, which we shall discuss in the next section. Another part of the explanation lies in understanding that each school system is a complex organization, and the difficulties in education are similar to those in other forms of bureaucracy: an emphasis on efficiency; elaborate rules and regulations; regimentation and conformity; a weakness for handling nonroutine situations.

Schools are frequently compared to factories and prisons. Alvin Toffler suggests that assembling large masses of students (raw material) processed by teachers (workers) in a centrally located school (factory) under discipline and regimentation was an acceptable system to the assembly-line age.[3] The prison analogy offers a warden (principal), guards (teachers), prisoners (students) forced to be there, a repressive atmosphere (hall passes and monitors, quick punishment for rule infractions), and demands for total silence, straight lines, and movement only upon permission.[4]

Conformity and Obedience

Traditionally, the schools have been geared toward teaching large groups of learners, requiring them to fit into the bureaucratic framework rather than structuring the school to meet individual needs. What has emerged is an authoritarian system demanding submissiveness to an elaborate set of rules and regulations in order to maintain order and efficiency. In a highly influential book which redirected educational aims in the 1970s, Charles Silberman in *Crisis in the Classroom* warned that the high schools are even more repressive that the elementary schools and the values being transmitted are "docility, passivity, conformity, and lack of trust."[5]

In some school districts, progressive educators have succeeded in creating a more open, diversified classroom environment where creativity, curiosity, and an individualized pace of learning is encouraged. Lessening the rigidly controlled, collective uniformity of learning approach is a positive shift in educators' focus, but unfortunately most schools remain preoccupied with regimentation and discipline. Obedience to time modules, lesson plans, dress and hairstyle codes, approved reading lists, emphasis on silence and straight lines, and conformity to teacher performance expectations instead of individual inquiry and pursuit of study are all still the norm in most schools. The result is a student body with a slave mentality, which sacrifices its real feelings and intuition, losing the growth potential for self-reliance and self-motivation, and becoming instead apathetic, conforming, and obedient drones.[6]

Hierarchy of Authority

Because the schools are bureaucracies, they function through a multitiered strata of personnel wherein the limits of authority are clearly set and specific procedures are delineated for various situations. Teachers especially find themselves enmeshed in a quagmire of paperwork (grading papers, writing lesson plans, reports, recommendations, evaluation studies, etc.). Specific content material must be covered, specific textbooks used, and classrooms must be quiet and well ordered. Administrators pressure teachers to report tardy students, to patrol restrooms for smoking or drug use, and when not teaching to serve as cafeteria, hallway, or study hall watchdogs or general detention monitors. Teachers do not set policy, but are required to implement it. Their job performance evaluations depend heavily upon the teachers' ability to command respect and maintain order.

In a rather cynical observation, Christopher Jencks suggested the hierarchy of school authority rests upon the premise of distrust: ". . . The school board has no faith in the central administration, the central administration has no faith in the principals, the principals have no faith in the teachers, and the teachers have no faith in the students."[7] Although there is much truth in this statement, quite obviously situations vary from one school district to another. Still, bureaucratic structures everywhere emphasizing conformity will produce more rigid personalities among those in the hierarchy, thus tending to stifle creativity and innovation.

EDUCATION AND SOCIAL CLASS

Our insistence upon universal public education opens the schools to young people from all social classes. Citizens have long believed that formal education could decrease social inequalities and provide the means for lower-class youth to achieve a higher socioeconomic status than their parents. For the past 20 years, though, many research findings have offered contrary evidence. Although some low-income individuals do offer proof of success through education, it would appear for most youngsters that their degree of educational achievement is strongly related to their race and family background.

Dominance of Middle-Class Values

As we said earlier, the schools reflect the prevailing values and attitudes of the society, and in the postindustrial United States, this means the middle class. To provide a standard education for all, schools stress certain value orientations and behavior patterns. In early grades teachers place emphasis upon cleanliness, neatness, quiet, orderliness, straight lines in going to and from recess or fire drills, punctuality, and conformity. In later grades teachers replace the earlier thrill of discovery learning and success in learning how to do things (self-realization) by emphasis upon simply learning subject matter, with grade competition and deferred gratification (good grades for college for good jobs) as the primary motivating factors.

As part of their teacher preparation, educators are taught to recognize individual differences among their students in the classroom. Unfortunately, the orientation is usually upon "intellectual" differences, with little or no education about class or cultural differences which may impact upon perceived intellectual differences. Consequently, many teachers evaluate classroom performance as it conforms to middle-

In a typical classroom, such as this junior high school class, each student is part of the competitive process. Class discussions, question-answer sessions, and tests can enhance or impair one's self-identity, depending upon how one fares against one's classmates.

class expectations. Let us now look at some of these intervening class and cultural variables.

Language

In all countries, the "correct" grammar and pronunciation is that of the upper class. Consider the basic premise in George Bernard Shaw's *Pygmalion* or its musical version *My Fair Lady:* acceptance comes when one overcomes a lower-class dialect. Students who speak Black English or a lower-class white dialect which both differ from the standard American English—or students of immigrant families who have a limited ability to speak any English—are at a disadvantage in school. They will have difficulty in understanding what they read and hear, and get lower grades for their grammatical errors when they write. Many such students entering school will never overcome this initial language barrier because they fall behind their classmates, become discouraged, and set lower educational goals for themselves.

Family and Peer Influence

Since family and peers are the two most influential agents of socialization during one's formative years, their attitudes about high school and college will play a major role in an individual's motivations about education. In the past, for example, the value orientations in most Italian and Polish immigrant families was to enter the work force after high school in contrast to Armenian, Greek, Japanese, and Jewish immigrant families for whom a college education was stressed.[8] Today is no different for other groups. Family expectations among the middle and upper classes assume academic success and a college education, which is less the case among lower- and working-class families.

Learning potential is also increased in middle- and upper-income families because they possess more books and educational toys, can take trips to zoos, theaters, museums, planetariums, and other cultural centers, and emphasize long-term goals (deferred gratification). The plans and actions of one's school or neighborhood friends will also affect a student's aspirations, regardless of teacher efforts at motivation.

Teacher Expectations

A **teacher's expectations** often serve as a positive or negative motivating factor in student conformity. If a teacher believes a student can achieve highly, various forms of encouragement in attitude, comments, allowing more time to respond, or having a second chance will serve to promote better performance. If instead the teacher doesn't expect much from an individual, the teacher's attitude and behavior convey to the student a distinct message that may well discourage further effort.

In a provocative experiment which has stirred some controversy, Robert Rosenthal and Lenore Jacobson administered intelligence tests in a San Francisco elementary school and then randomly identified 20 percent of the students tested as "spurters," ones whom teachers were asked to watch.[9] Eight months later, all were retested and the "spurters" scored significantly higher and their teachers evaluated them as happier, better adjusted, and more appealing, interesting, and curious than their class. Actually, the only real difference had been in teacher expectations in the arbitrarily chosen "spurters," suggesting, said the researchers, that the change in the teacher's attitudes had affected the students' progress. Subsequent similar experiments have had mixed results, however, indicating more research is needed to identify precisely how the self-fulfilling prophecy works in the classroom.[10]

Ability Grouping

The basic premise of **ability grouping** in the public schools appears sound. Instead of a class with students of greatly varying ability where high achievers are not sufficiently challenged and low achievers may feel intimated or overwhelmed, why not group students of similar ability in the same class to provide a proper standard of instruction for everyone? Such a system does indeed have some merit, but simultaneously creates behavioral patterns that work to the detriment of many students. Two aspects of this ability grouping system we shall consider are the means by which the grouping decisions are made and the effects of this system.

Testing

IQ tests are widely used as a basis for ability grouping because most people associate educational achievement with intelligence. A number of difficulties, however, surround the use of IQ tests to measure intelligence. Considerable disagreements exist among psychologists concerning what these tests actually measure and how valid the scores are in predicting achievement. The major argument surrounds the cultural bias in the tests, since they use language, concepts, and basic information much more familiar to white middle-class America.[11] Critics argue IQ tests are measuring not innate abilities necessarily but environmental opportunities as well. Moreover, only certain intellectual aptitudes are tested: language, mathematical reasoning, and spatial and symbolic relationships. Not measured are such intellectual capacities as artistic aptitude, creativity, imagination, and intuition or the social skills of persuasiveness, perseverance, cleverness, and charm—all of which can help a person do well in life.

The question of heredity and intelligence has been argued for generations, but the genesis of modern debate on the subject is psychologist Arthur Jensen's article in the *Harvard Educational Review* in 1969.[12] Jensen argued that environment played only a minor role in test scores, that lower-class youths score equally to middle-class youths in tasks requiring memorization or rote learning but consistently lower in problem solving, seeing relationships, and abstract reasoning. This difference in conceptual performance, he argued, is due to genetic factors, not testing bias.[13] Others such as William Shockley and Richard Hernnstein, also maintained that genetic differences, not environmental opportunities are the basic determinants of success or failure.[14]

Of all the criticisms leveled at this position, two of the most compelling have been those of Lee J. Cronbach and Thomas Sowell. Cronbach's position is that the differences in conceptual scores are not because of lesser ability but lack of training in

Perhaps no testing experience places greater stress on high school students than taking the SATs or ACTs for college admission. Pressure is often overpowering, as students realize their scores may open or close certain doors to them.

conceptual skills.[15] Indeed, we have empirical evidence demonstrating that lower-class children, initially scoring lower than middle-class children in conceptual ability tests are able to raise their scores even above the middle-class children after receiving brief training in conceptual skills.[16] Economist Thomas Sowell observed that all lower-class newcomers—such as the immigrants from southern and eastern Europe in the early twentieth century—scored lower in the abstract portions of intelligence tests.[17] After experiencing upward mobility, however, the IQ scores also rise, suggesting that whatever IQ tests do measure, it varies according to environmental influences.

Despite all the controversy, using standardized tests such as the Stanford-Binet Intelligence Test (IQ) and the California Achievement Tests (CAT) as placement tools is widespread. Although they may accurately measure certain forms of intellectual ability at a particular point, the problem is that they result in differential grouping for instructional purposes, where teacher expectations and student self-image may stifle further growth in intellectual capacity, as we shall next discuss.

Effects of Tracking

Ability grouping often begins as early as the first grade, with reading groups of comparable ability. From that moment on throughout elementary school, students receive different challenges and assignments, with curriculum material oriented to their perceived ability to comprehend. The benefits of these differential educational ''fits'' between capabilities/needs and instruction are real, but they often remain fixed instead of pursuing a long-term goal of greater challenge to intellectual growth potential. Too frequently this labeling process of who is above average, average, or below average sets in motion a cumulative set of teacher expectations and student conformity to those expectations.

High-school students are well aware of how they are grouped and it affects their self-image and motivation. Those in the upper track often develop a smug attitude of superiority while those in the lower track may have a negative self-image or sense of inferiority. Assignment to the lowest track carries with it a stigma. These students, seeing how educators and other students identify and relate to them, lose much of their self-esteem and see themselves as stupid and less deserving (see Box 12.1).

Significantly, a highly disproportionate number of students in the lowest track are from low-income families; students from upper middle-income families are disproportionately represented in the upper, college-bound track. The tracking system thus both reflects and reinforces the American social class structure. A sifting and sorting process occurs in the schools to fit each individual to a place in society. The combination of social class bias and tracking affects teacher and student attitudes, motivation, self-image, curriculum choice, career goals, dropout and further education decisions, and subsequent earning power. Conflict theorists argue further that the schools thereby deny equality of educational opportunity. The courts have also recently partly adopted this position, ruling that standardized test scores used to assign children to different tracks violates the principle of equal educational opportunity.[18]

BOX 12.1

THE EFFECTS OF TRACKING AND LABELING

. . . Nobody . . . can fix things now. The only thing that matters in my life is school, and there they think I'm dumb and always will be. I'm starting to think they're right. . . . Even if I look around and know that I'm the smartest in my group, all that means is that I'm the smartest of the dumbest, so I haven't gotten anywhere at all, have I? I'm right where I always was. Every word those teachers tell me, even the ones I like most, I can hear in their voice that what they're really saying is, all right you dumb kids, I'll make it as easy as I can, and if you don't get it then, then you'll never get it. Ever. . . .

. . . I used to think, man, that even if I wasn't so smart, that I could talk in any class in that school, if I did my studying, I mean, and have everybody in that class, all the kids and the teacher too, think I was all right. Maybe better than all right too. . . .

. . . I used to think that all the time, man. Had myself convinced that whenever I had to stand up and give a little speech, you know, about something, that I'd just be able to go to it and do it. . . .

I could have once, but not anymore.

. . . Because last year just before they tested us and talked to us, you know, to see what we were like, I was in this one class and doing real good. As good as anybody else. Did everything they told me to do. Read what they said, wrote what they said, listened when they talked.

. . . Then they told me, like on a Friday, that today would be my last day in that class. That I should go to it today, you know, but that on Monday I had to switch to this other one. They just gave me a different room number, but I knew what they

INTEGRATION AND THE QUALITY OF EDUCATION

For generations Americans have possessed a deeply ingrained belief that education is the gateway to success for economically disadvantaged minorities. Social and technological changes in our lifetime have made higher levels of education a necessity. With this increased emphasis has come a national reassessment of the quality of education minority children receive. Particularly, the focus has been upon achieving a racial balance in the schools and a more equitable funding among school districts. As efforts in the past two decades have attempted to correct these inequities, they have generated intense controversy and impassioned reactions at the local level. Today the problems remain and some of the response patterns have only served to increase the difficulties.

Although the 1954 U.S. Supreme Court ruling declaring segregated schools uncon-

were doing. Like they were giving me one more day with the brains, and then I had to go to be with the dummies. So I went with the brains one more day. . . . But the teacher didn't know I was moving, so she acted like I belonged there. Wasn't *her* fault. All the time I was just sitting there thinking this is the last day for me. This is the last time I'm ever going to learn anything, you know what I mean? Real learning.

. . . From now on . . . I knew I had to go back where they made me believe I belonged. I didn't even argue. I was just sitting there thinking I was like some prisoner, you know, who thought he was free. Like they let him out of jail and he was walking around, like you and me here, having a great old time. Then the warden meets him on the street and tells him they made a mistake and he has to go back to prison. . . .

So then the teacher called on me, and this is how I know just how smart I am. She called on me, like she always did, like she'd call on anybody, and she asked me a question. I knew the answer, 'cause I'd read it the night before in my book which I bought, and then my mother read the book to me too, after I'd already read it. So I began to speak, and suddenly I couldn't say nothing. Nothing, man. Not a word. Like my mind died in there. And everybody was looking at me. You know, like I was crazy or something. My heart was beating real fast. I knew the answer, man. And she was waiting, and I couldn't say nothing. That's how I know how smart I am. That's when I really learned at that school, how smart I was. I mean, how smart I *thought* I was. I had no business being there. Nobody's smart sitting in no class crying. That's the day I found out for real. That's the day that made me know for sure.

SOURCE: Thomas Cottle, *Barred from School* (Washington, D.C.: The New Republic Book Company, 1976), pp. 138–140.

stitutional redirected American educational efforts, the 1964 Civil Rights Act served as the catalyst for widespread implementation. Part of this legislation mandated the U.S. Office of Education to prepare a report on the "lack of equal education opportunities" in the public educational institutions at all levels because of race, color, religion, or national origin. Two years later the government released this report—one of the most extensive social science studies ever conducted, involving achievement tests given to almost 600,000 students and survey forms to 60,000 teachers at 4,000 schools.[19] Popularly known as the Coleman Report, the findings included the following:

1. Most black and white students attended different schools.

2. White and Asian-American students had higher achievement test scores than Blacks, Hispanics, and Native Americans.

3. Family background was of major significance in the students' level of achievement.

4. Differences in school facilities, teacher experience, teacher-student ratios, and curriculum had little impact upon test scores.

5. Poor minority children performed better in schools predominantly middle class than those in homogeneous lower-class schools.

The implications of these findings were clear: social class, not race, is the key factor and lower-class youngsters achieve better if placed in a learning environment with classmates who have strong educational backgrounds. The Coleman Report became a major influence in school integration efforts, both voluntary and under court order.

By the mid-1960s a significant shift in residential patterns had intensified the problem of racial and ethnic imbalance in the schools. Hundreds of thousands of Whites moved out of the northern cities into the suburbs while equally large numbers of black migrants left the South to settle in the decaying urban centers. As a consequence, the neighborhood schools—a long-cherished American tradition—became increasingly segregated by race and social class. City schools now ranged from 40 to almost 100 percent Black.[20] Problems of order and discipline, low motivation and achievement, high absenteeism, and dropout rates marked many of the urban public schools. Local school boards and governments, as well as the courts, attempted to desegregate the schools and improve the learning environment.

Shifting residential patterns have resulted in highly segregated schools in many cities in the Northeast and West. Differing in quality, schools in 23 major cities and hundreds of smaller cities now have minority students exceeding two-thirds the total enrollment.

Busing

The most common solution tried was busing. This usually occurred within city boundaries only, but in a few states where school districts cut across local boundaries (e.g., California) or involved county jurisdiction (e.g., Maryland), busing became more regional. Most school systems became desegregated by busing without a problem, but in other cases anger and violence greeted such efforts. Most notable were Louisville and Boston in 1975, when police escorts in riot gear were necessary to protect the school buses carrying black children to white schools from rock throwing and to control angry crowds at the entrance to the schools.

In 1977 the U.S. Commission on Civil Rights issued a report stating that desegregation was working and that 82 percent of all desegregation efforts occurred without serious disruption. For every Boston and Louisville, it maintained, in dozens of other communities desegregation was proceeding smoothly without major incident, newspaper headlines, or television coverage.[21] The experience of cities which have used busing for school integration, even where initial opposition was intense, has been one of eventual general acceptance by the community. Still, Americans remain opposed to busing while simultaneously supporting school integration. Nationwide opinion polls in 1975 (Gallup) and 1979 (Harris) found most Whites and almost half of the Blacks surveyed opposed to busing. In 1981 the Reagan administration shifted federal policy from seeking court-ordered busing to voluntary busing programs, such as that organized in the St. Louis metropolitan region the same year. The problem so far with voluntary busing is that, although it worked well without conflict where utilized, other white segregated school districts resist busing efforts.

School Funding

Perhaps the most significant educational problem today is finances, for it affects all other aspects of the quality and effectiveness of the learning environment. Tax dollars pay for public education, but since the federal government provides only 8 percent of needed school revenues, the state and local levels generate most funds. Because states and communities within those states vary greatly in their ability to generate revenues, the wealthier ones are able to spend more per student than the poorer ones. For example, Wyoming ranks second nationally in its $1,014 per student spending compared to neighboring Idaho whose $587 per student expenditure places it 37th (see Table 12.1).

Local communities with a strong tax base can spend more per student while costing individual taxpayers less. One illustration is in New Jersey: Newark residents pay 1.5 times the tax rate of residents in Waldwick, an older suburban town of smaller lot sizes and virtually no industry. Yet Waldwick residents pay twice the amount of those in Mahwah, a sprawling 26-square-mile township with large lot sizes and industrial parks. Yet Mahwah's junior and senior high schools are situated on a modern, multibuilding campus in comparison to Newark's dilapidated schools. So the amount individuals pay for the school budget does not necessarily correspond to the quality of the schools.

TABLE 12.1 State Spending on Public Education, 1982 Kindergarten through College

	Total Spent	Per Capita		Total Spent	Per Capita
Alaska	$0.8 bil.	$1,896	Hawaii	$0.6 bil.	$625
Wyoming	$0.5 bil.	$1,014	Louisiana	$2.6 bil.	$624
Washington	$3.4 bil.	$824	Texas	$8.7 bil.	$614
New Mexico	$1.0 bil.	$795	North Carolina	$3.6 bil.	$612
Oregon	$2.1 bil.	$788	Illinois	$7.0 bil.	$609
Utah	$1.1 bil.	$756	South Carolina	$1.9 bil.	$604
Delaware	$0.4 bil.	$753	Indiana	$3.3 bil.	$603
Michigan	$6.9 bil.	$748	South Dakota	$0.4 bil.	$599
Colorado	$2.2 bil.	$747	Connecticut	$1.8 bil.	$593
Wisconsin	$3.5 bil.	$743	Massachusetts	$3.4 bil.	$593
North Dakota	$0.5 bil.	$733	Ohio	$6.4 bil.	$592
Arizona	$2.0 bil.	$731	Idaho	$0.6 bil.	$587
New York	$12.7 bil.	$724	Nevada	$0.5 bil.	$585
California	$16.9 bil.	$716	West Virginia	$1.1 bil.	$583
Iowa	$2.1 bil.	$716	Dist. of Columbia	$0.4 bil.	$564
Montana	$0.6 bil.	$715	Pennsylvania	$6.6 bil.	$557
Minnesota	$2.9 bil.	$713	Mississippi	$1.4 bil.	$553
Maryland	$2.9 bil.	$688	Alabama	$2.2 bil.	$553
Vermont	$0.4 bil.	$686	New Hampshire	$0.5 bil.	$547
Nebraska	$1.1 bil.	$679	Georgia	$2.9 bil.	$531
New Jersey	$5.0 bil.	$674	Florida	$5.1 bil.	$527
Kansas	$1.6 bil.	$669	Kentucky	$1.9 bil.	$525
Rhode Island	$0.6 bil.	$645	Missouri	$2.6 bil.	$524
U.S.	**$145.8 bil.**	**$644**	Arkansas	$1.2 bil.	$522
Oklahoma	$1.9 bil.	$637	Maine	$0.6 bil.	$522
Virginia	$3.4 bil.	$628	Tennessee	$2.2 bil.	$479

SOURCE: U.S. National Center for Education Statistics, *Digest of Education Statistics*, 1983.

Court Actions

Some effort to correct this inequity has occurred. In a landmark 1971 decision, *Serrano* v. *Priest,* the California Supreme Court struck down that state's system of using local property taxes to finance public education as discriminatory, because it made the quality of children's education dependent on the wealth of their parents and neighbors. Several years later the New Jersey Supreme Court made a similar ruling. Those two states and others have since attempted to provide a more equitable means of funding public education through channeling state monies to local communities. In New Jersey, for example, the state sets a budget cap or maximum for each municipality and proportionately allocates financial support based on need; cities thus receive more funds than affluent suburbs.

California and New Jersey, however, are two of the nation's wealthier states. Nationwide the inequities continue and other court and government decisions have not been encouraging. In 1973 the U.S. Supreme Court let stand the local property tax funding of education in Texas, ruling the Constitution does *not* guarantee education as a right. In 1982 the Colorado Supreme Court rules that the state's constitution did not require equality among school districts in per-student spending. Under President Reagan federal aid has been reduced by 25 percent and the administration's philosophy is that funding should be more the responsibility of state and local governments.

Financial Strain

The states, however, have been hard hit by several years of recession and inflation, federal cutbacks, and, in some states like California and Massachusetts, voter referendums limiting property taxes. Some school districts have reduced or eliminated teacher or librarian positions, field trips, equipment, or maintenance expenditures. Other local school boards now require students to pay fees to participate in such extracurricular activities as athletics, music, and theater. Needless to say, this practice eliminates or sharply reduces participation by the poor and denies them an equal right to benefit from these activities along with students whose parents can afford to pay the fees.

At present we have a decidedly mixed situation. While some states have attempted to provide equal access for all to a quality education, other states have not. Discrepancies remain among the states and among school districts within many states. Until such time as a more equitable distribution of educational funding occurs, equal opportunity will remain an American myth.

THE DECLINING QUALITY OF EDUCATION

In recent years many indicators have been pointing to problems in the caliber of teaching and learning in our schools. Throughout the 1970s and early 1980s, scores on the Scholastic Aptitude Test (SAT) consistently declined. In 1974 the Association of American Publishers had to rewrite its reading textbook guide for college freshmen down to a ninth-grade reading level. Nonetheless, a majority of 13-year-olds and 45 percent of 18-year-olds in a 1978 Gallup poll did not think their schoolwork was difficult enough. Yet a 1979–1980 study of reading, writing, and analysis of skills, conducted by the National Center for Education Statistics, found few students able to write coherent essays about their reading assignments.

What's Wrong with Our Schools?

In May 1983 The National Commission on Excellence in Education issued a scathing report of its findings after an 18-month study.[22] It asserted "a rising tide of mediocrity" had devastated public education in all aspects: teacher competency, curriculum, and achievement. So inadequate was the quality of education, maintained the commission, that we were moving backward in intergenerational educational progress:

> Each generation of Americans has outstripped its parents in education,
> in literacy and in economic attainment. For the first time in the history

of our country, the educational skills of one generation will not surpass, will not equal, will not even approach, those of their parents.[23]

What were the reasons for such a blunt condemnation of American education? Let's look at some of the problem areas.

Teacher Competency

Although 9 out of 10 teachers are adequate in their performance, increasing cases of incompetence are being brought to public attention. Frequent complaints include teachers employing bad usage and misspelling words, poor communication skills, insufficient knowledge of the subject, and low mental ability.[24] Many who are concerned about the decline in the quality of education are discouraged by some of the current signs.

Future Teachers

Teaching is not attracting many individuals of strong academic ability. Students entering college as education majors had combined verbal and math SAT scores 80 points below the 1982 national average. Of 29 academic fields surveyed, future teachers ranked twenty-sixth in SAT scores (see Table 12.2).[25]

Why doesn't education attract more competent people? Low pay is a major reason. In 1983 the average starting salary for a public school teacher was $12,800 compared to an average beginning salary of $16,000 for accountants and $20,000 for many business trainees. In the words of a 1981 study for the National Institute of Education, the United States "gets approximately what it pays for: the bottom one

TABLE 12.2 1982 Combined SAT Scores by Intended College Major

	Test Score		Test Score
1. Physical sciences	1,054	15. Health and medical	896
2. Mathematics	1,024	**National average**	**893**
3. English, literature	995	16. Communications	892
4. Engineering	986	17. Music	890
5. Biological sciences	976	18. Psychology	882
6. History and cultures	960	19. Theater arts	878
7. Foreign languages	955	20. Forestry conservation	876
8. Philosophy and religion	945	21. Geography	868
9. Social sciences	936	22. Business and commerce	847
10. Library science	932	23. Agriculture	838
11. Undecided	925	24. All other fields	832
12. Military science	908	25. Art	822
13. Computer science, systems analysis	906	26. Education	813
		27. Home economics	792
14. Architecture, environmental design	898	28. Ethnic studies	744
		29. Trade and vocational	739

SOURCE: College Entrance Examination Board, Annual Report, 1983.

third of the college-going population is seeking positions paying salaries in the bottom one third of the economy.''

In an effort to weed out the inept and poorly prepared, 20 states now require teacher competency tests before certifying new teachers. California administered its first **minimum competency test (MCT)** in 1983, and 38 percent of nearly 7,000 prospective teachers failed.[26] In Florida, 16 percent of all those taking the MCT failed, but 63 percent of the black students in education failed, raising concerns about the ability of recent top-quality black students as teachers.[27] In 1984, Texas began to test-screen prospective teacher education majors as well as testing them again before certification.

Current Teachers

Low pay and morale are two most common reasons for the exodus of many competent teachers from the classroom. Many teachers find immense personal satisfaction in their profession, but others become discouraged because of classroom disruptions, inadequate supplies, and low economic incentives. Many teachers are forced to take part-time jobs to supplement their income and 24 percent of the nation's 2.2 million public school teachers polled by the National Education Association (NEA) said they ''probably would not'' choose teaching as a career again, compared to 8 percent in 1961. Only 26 percent of high-achieving teacher education graduates still planned to be teaching by age 30, compared to 60 percent of the lowest-achieving college graduates, according to a study for the National Institute of Education.[28]

Of equal concern to educators is how to improve the quality of teachers now in the field. Texas is considering eliminating lifetime certification and requiring periodic reexamination. An effort in Houston requiring that the system's 3,000 teachers take a competency test in early 1983 resulted in anger, resentment, and defiant open cheating in protest. Still, the public is increasingly demanding greater accountability from its teachers and we may well expect more action on the subject of teacher competency.

Subject Matter

The National Commission on Excellence in Education blasted the curriculum offerings in secondary schools. By permitting a drift away from academic subjects, the schools had undermined the traditional purpose of education and placed the United States at a disadvantage to other industrialized nations.[29]

"Cafeteria-Style" Curriculum

A smorgasbord of electives has subverted academic standards and emphasis on the challenging courses necessary to prepare students for advanced study in scientific and technological fields. Since 1969, academic subjects had suffered a drop from 70 to 62 percent of allotted classroom time while nontraditional subjects like driver education grew from 8 to 13 percent of allotted time.[30] In 70 percent of the states, only 1 year of math and science are required, and no state mandates taking a foreign language. The result, said the commission, is a ''cafeteria-style curriculum in which the appetizers and desserts can easily be mistaken for the main course.''

Compulsory Instruction

To reverse the poor preparation of young people for a new era of computerized technology and global competition, the commission has recommended mandatory courses for everyone. It suggests "the new basics" include 4 years of English, 3 years each of math, science, and social studies, and a half-year of computer science. Additionally, college-bound students would have to take 2 years of foreign language study.

Academic Standards

Another aspect of education attacked by the commission was declining academic standards. In the drive to provide everyone with the credentials of a high-school diploma or college degree, educators all too often graduated functionally illiterate students (reading below the sixth-grade level). Long before the commission's report, however, much attention had focused on the problem of graduating students unable to meet minimum achievement standards. One example which drew national attention in 1976 was of a young man who graduated at the top of his class from a Washington, D.C. high school and was the class valedictorian. Despite his perfect attendance record and determined study habits, he apparently had not been taught reading or mathematical skills for college study. His SAT verbal score of the 13th percentile nationally and math score in the lowest 2 percent illuminated the problems of social promotions, grade inflation, and student competency.[31]

Social Promotions

Until the 1960s, children would be "left back" and required to repeat a grade if they were unable to meet the minimum requirements at that level. Then the prevailing attitude changed, as educators kept moving children through grades with their age peers regardless of actual learning achievement. The new operative philosophy was that those not promoted were stigmatized, suffered a loss of self-esteem, and became less motivated. **Social promotions** became the common standard practice to avoid any impediments to learning because of self-image and social interaction networks. Whatever merit this practice has had, it produced graduates who were deluded into thinking they had gotten an education when, in reality, many lacked even the basic skills.

Another consequence of social promotions was a watering down of course content because of the gradual but steady lowering of general class ability. At the college level, remedial courses in basic skills became both necessary and commonplace. Many professors abandoned assigning term papers or giving essay exams because so many students had poor writing ability. For many students, reading and writing skills were not essential to getting a high-school diploma or even, in some cases, a college degree. All one had to do was listen in class to what the instructor emphasized, then find or guess at the multiple-choice answers on the exams.

Grade Inflation

During the unpopular Vietnam War, college students dismissed for low scholarship lost their draft deferment. Whether from protest against the war or guilt at being partially responsible for sending someone to a maiming in combat or possible death, professors became more liberal in their grading practices. Although a C grade had once been both average and respectable, now higher grades became commonplace, with an A or B grade often accounting for at least half the total grades given out. This **grade inflation** distorted the picture of what had really been learned.

Grade inflation also extended down into the elementary and secondary schools. Teachers frequently interpreted giving high grades as a sign of their effectiveness and as a means of opening the high-school academic track or college opportunities to youngsters who might otherwise have a less promising figure. Grades were defined, like education itself, as a means to an end rather than a measure of level of attainment. Like the Washington, D.C. high-school student mentioned earlier, many barely literate students received high grades.

Student Competency

If students have the freedom to avoid traditional academic skill subjects, and if watered-down courses, social promotions, and grade inflation are usual, a decline in achievement test scores is not unreasonable. As we have already mentioned, SAT scores have been dropping for the past 20 years. Some educators have suggested that this decline is due to the larger percentage of minority students taking the SAT, but actually that percentage has remained fairly constant (about 13 percent) while the decline continued.[32]

As more Americans complained about poor student competency, a "back-to-basics" movement gained support across the country. Many school systems began to stress more the learning of fundamental reading, writing, and math skills. As we said earlier, about 20 states now have MCTs as a condition of earning a high-school diploma. Support is quite high for these tests; 82 percent of Americans surveyed in 1979 favored use of a standardized test to determine eligibility for a high-school diploma.[33]

The MCT measures the level of proficiency achieved in basic skills, but critics argue it is not an accurate indicator of a student's ability and will encourage teachers to prepare students to pass the test without truly learning anything. Others maintain its positiveness in restoring credibility to the high-school diploma. Many colleges also now require an MCT for first- or third-year entry. In a credential-oriented society, the MCT is emerging as another necessary credential.

SOCIOLOGICAL PERSPECTIVES

As we have examined educational concerns throughout this chapter, various sociological considerations have been interwoven with that discussion. Now we shall focus more sharply on the sociological perspectives as they relate to the goals, practices, and problems of our educational system.

Individual Faults and Deviant Behavior

Educators continually encounter students with poor attendance records, low motivation, incorrigible behavior, poor achievement, and early termination of their schooling. Because they are committed to a lifetime career of helping young people learn, develop their minds, and prepare for the future, instructors do not get any satisfaction out of failing students or seeing them turn their backs on their education. As educators search for a rationale for the inability of students to learn and achieve, under this perspective they may either resign themselves to accept certain students as simply "lost" due to a "bad" attitude or misdirected priorities or else seek a means to change student value orientations so they may take full advantage of the educational opportunities society offers them.

Character Flaws

To fault others for the disintegration of any form of interaction pattern is a fairly common defense mechanism called self-justification. If teachers, despite what they consider their best efforts, have students not conforming to the rules or achievement standards, they quite normally explain that failure as inherent in the problem individual. With experience, teachers find such failures emerging as a common pattern among certain groups, perhaps those living "on the wrong side of the tracks" in town or belonging to a particular minority group. Many educators assume that, since they are giving everyone an equal chance to learn, "what else can you expect" from "those kinds of kids?" If this interpretation is the prevailing one, educators often adopt a fatalistic attitude with suspensions, expulsions, dropouts, failures, or social promotions rather frequent.

Resocialization

A more positive approach under this emphasis is to identify why the "underachievers" do not follow the educational pathway of preparation for success and to change them so they will. Beginning with the assumption that the educational system is the only correct approach to fitting into societal roles, a concerted effort occurs to reshape the values and attitudes of those identified as deviating from the norms and goals of the rest of society. Rather than believing these differences are inherent defects, this orientation focuses upon redirecting adaptive responses to years of discrimination and discouragement. Psychologist B. F. Skinner, famous for his advocacy of operant conditioning—the gradual shaping of individual behavior through a system of rewards and punishments—recently spoke about the failure of education to use behavioral science effectively to achieve its goals (see Box 12.2).

Ranging from slogans such as "Play it cool, stay in school," to television vignettes such as Bert and Ernie telling Cookie Monster if he eats all his cookies now that he won't have any to enjoy later (deferred gratification), a multipronged effort attempts to inculcate appreciative attitudes about the value of a good education. Schools bring in career speakers, cite role models, and concentrate on developing conforming value orientations as well as skills and intellectual abilities.

Institutional Faults and System Disorganization

All developed countries look upon formal education as critically important to the welfare of their societies. Schools have the dual responsibilities of transmitting the culture from one generation to the next and teaching young people the knowledge and skills necessary to function in a technologically advanced society. In the United

BOX 12.2

A CURE FOR AMERICAN EDUCATION

PT: You once said we already have all the behavioral science we need to solve our social problems. Do you think that holds true for solving our educational problems as well?

SKINNER: Yes. It's not so much our failure to support behavioral science as our failure to make use of it. If we could simply change the way educators think about human behavior, we could solve all our problems. But people who are designing courses at the present time are simply not facing reality.

PT: How do you get them to face reality?

SKINNER: All I'm doing is creating a noise. I don't know whether that will work or not. I believe that those who are suffering from our present educational system should be the ones to act. Those who pay for education ought to demand their money's worth. Teachers ought to demand a situation in which they can teach well. Teacher burnout is a very real thing. It is due primarily to teachers' realization that they're not accomplishing much. If you show teachers how to teach well, and give them the material they need, including devices of some kind, it will increase the morale of the profession enormously, and it will keep good teachers teaching.

PT: But let's look at what usually happens when taxpayers demand their money's worth. The school board institutes an achievement test and then blames the kids because they haven't learned or the teachers because they haven't taught them.

SKINNER: If you blame the students, you flunk them. But how can students learn if they're not properly taught? If you blame the teachers, you can fire them. But it's not the teachers' fault; they haven't been taught to teach properly. It must be the fault of the schools of education. But they haven't been given good behavioral science. Then it must be the fault of behavioral science. No, our culture doesn't allow good behavioral science to be used effectively. So you wind up blaming the culture, but you can't punish the culture. I firmly believe that America will be punished if it does not support the kind of behavioral science that makes good education possible. The culture will fail, and another culture will come along to take its place.

SOURCE: Elizabeth Hall, "A Cure for American Education," *Psychology Today* (September 1983), pp. 26–27. Copyright © 1983, American Psychological Association.

States, the schools are also expected to be the means of solving such social problems as alcohol and drug abuse, reckless driving, sexual promiscuity, prejudice, and poverty. Above all, curriculum is to be "relevant" and teaching methods adaptable to the varying abilities of the students. Functionalists maintain educational problems are a consequence of system strain due to the schools trying to be too many things to too many people simultaneously.

Extensive Demands

If all the schools had to do was teach the traditional subjects and basic skills, it might not even do these jobs very well because the educational bureaucratic system is often disorganized or subject to contradictory pressures both from within the school itself or from the outside community. The probability of system dysfunctions is greatly increased, however, with the addition of other roles. Part of the social movement of the 1960s was directed toward making education "relevant"; thus a wide array of elective courses was introduced into the public schools. Often these courses represented educators' personal preferences or courses in college they had liked; previously exclusive college-level courses such as psychology, sociology, race and ethnic relations, or specialized humanities courses became quite common in many high schools.

Other competing courses in art and music—with a wide selection of interests—together with those in theater, computers, first aid, driver education, personal health, shop, home economics, typing, stenography, accounting, and many others made the traditional subjects less appealing to students. Excused class absences for athletic events, pep rallies and assemblies, play rehearsals, band competitions, field trips, and guidance sessions further intensified the clash of educational goals. An unintended consequence of these multipronged educational efforts was all too often misdirected priorities, a deemphasis of mastery of basic skills, and goals lacking a unified and coherent approach.

Social Engineering

Through the schools Americans have sought to correct the inequities in society and fit individuals into various adult slots available. Sometimes this effort has interfered with the learning process; for example, in the case of the antagonisms generated by integration solutions. When the curriculum changes to lessen potential discouragement to weaker students, the more able students are not sufficiently challenged. When students are placed in academic tracks by ability grouping, the dysfunctions of self-image and expectation fulfillments occur, as we have discussed earlier. When the schools attempt to educate uniformly without school prayer but in areas of sex and health education, evolutionary theory, or certain literary books, they frequently are in conflict with the other social institutions of family and religion. The resulting value conflicts present difficult learning environments for parents, teachers, and students.

Inequality and Inevitable Conflict

Conflict theorists reject the concept that the schools have ever functioned as the great equalizer in American society by providing opportunity for the poor to achieve upward mobility. To them the schools reflect the inequities in society, favor the ruling class, and thus help perpetuate both social and economic disparities. Class biases in the schools and socioeconomic differences among the school districts are their primary concerns, as we shall now examine.

The Schools as Selectors

Theoretically, the schools sift and select students for higher educational attainment on the basis of each child's ability. In practice an individual's educational success is closely linked to social class background. We have already discussed, you will recall, the presence of class bias in the schools. Many studies have confirmed strong correlations between socioeconomic background and educational performance as well as level of attainment. The Carnegie Council on Children reported that low-income children will have at least 4 years less schooling than higher-income children.[34] A similar finding emerged from the research of Bowles and Gintis, who found a 4.9-year educational achievement differential between those of the same IQ scores, but of the highest or lowest 10 percent in socioeconomic background.[35]

Many factors contribute to these differences in educational level, which have nothing to do with ability. Many poor children have no choice but to drop out of school to help support their families. Others are cooled out through the tracking system (see Box 12.1) and low expectations, motivation, or reinforcement. Because occupational opportunity and economic earnings are heavily dependent upon educational success, the schools tend to reinforce the social class ranking of the next generation to be the same as that of their parents.

School District Inequities

Local school funding difficulties result in significant differences in the quality of school facilities, staff, and instruction. The poor are primarily concentrated in poorly funded and poorly staffed schools, which continue to deteriorate in discipline and quality. From the conflict perspective the current system of economically segregated schools, in which minorities are disproportionately represented within the urban schools, operates to keep the "oppressed" peoples in the lowest strata of society. The affluent and powerful make certain they benefit from the educational system and resist efforts at change which would impact negatively upon the advantage they hold. Possessing the resources to be geographically mobile or to enroll their children in private schools, the nonpoor can avoid any public school system they dislike. They also hold sufficient political clout to influence busing and redistricting decisions. Most conflict theorists therefore believe inequities in the educational system can be eliminated only by changes in society itself.

Interaction and Social Interpretation

Education serves as an important part of the socialization process through which individuals develop their personalities and learn their culture. Through the formal structure of the schools and the informal structure of peer relationships, each student experiences many years of continuous interactions which help shape a concept of self. The impact of education upon an individual extends far beyond the subject matter taught in the classrooms. For example, if you now constructed two lists of the first 10 memories you recall from elementary and from high school, you would most likely have your two lists heavily filled with emotion-charged events in your life which affected your self-esteem (being hurt, embarrassed, ridiculed, rejected, loved, honored, etc.). Try it and you'll see what we mean. What is important for you to realize is that the shared interpretations of these day-by-day interactions determine whether school will be a positive or negative experience.

Positive Encounters

For many students, exposure to an ongoing system of rational discipline and work tasks develops within them goal orientations, a sense of responsibility, initiative, perseverance, and a work ethic. Immersed in a microcosmic world of rules and regulations with competing students, they are prepared to function more effectively in the outside world. Students learn how to develop social relationships, work together, and face challenges. Some social psychologists therefore believe most traditional schools are quite beneficial in helping children learn, develop, and function. While no school can ever be the perfect ideal, they view the schools as capable of providing opportunities for personal growth and fulfillment.

Negative Encounters

Other behavioral scientists are less optimistic. Too many schools are authoritarian and demand unquestioning conformity to rules, procedures, and teacher expectations. Such a repressive atmosphere, they state, stifles creativity and encourages a passive compliance to authority in later life, dangerous for any democracy. Also, with their competitive nature and use of the fear of failure as a motivation, the schools create feelings of anxiety, insecurity, and inadequacy among many students. Poor performance or even expected poor performance, together with the tracking system, sets in motion a series of interpretations and reinterpretations that works against individuals and instills in them a negative self-image. Once labeled by themselves, their peers, and/or their teachers as less than average, that definition becomes reinforced through subsequent interactions. From this perspective, the daily interactions and interpretations in school can actually impede the ability of children to learn, to develop positive personality characteristics, and eventually to function effectively as adults in society.

HOW CAN WE IMPROVE EDUCATION?

Some problems in education are political and economic, requiring changes within the structure of society itself to correct. Other problems are more manageable, but necessitate bureaucratic changes and a greater accountability from the educational system as to its effectiveness and efficiency. Indeed, some of the suggestions have already been implemented in private schools and a few public school systems. Efforts at educational reform may be examined at four levels: school districts, schools, teachers, and students.

Equitable School Districts

As we have seen, the nation's public schools do not provide equal educational opportunity. School populations are frequently imbalanced racially and socioeconomically due to residential patterns. Urban, rural, and even small-town school districts lack the revenue base of affluent suburbs in financial support of school needs. Busing to achieve minority integration has been successful in some areas, but it has hastened white flight from many urban areas, and now government officials and many black leaders no longer see this approach as viable.[36] Some states have also tried to equalize school expenditures per student, but nationwide great disparities remain. Alternative proposals, some already tried in certain areas, offer some promise.

Redistricting

Redrawing the boundary lines within a community concerning which school students attend preserves the neighborhood school concept, eliminates or reduces the need for busing, yet creates a better balance in student enrollment. White Plains, New York, was among the first to adopt an integration program, declaring that no school would have less than 10 percent nor more than 30 percent black enrollment. Through redrawn boundary lines and integrated housing, children at six of the nine schools walk to a neighborhood school, while those at the other three utilize busing.[37]

Another **redistricting** approach creates school districts independent of municipal boundaries to establish equitable revenue bases and integrated schools. This may work in Los Angeles, for example, where the county instead of the city provides

Once the preserve only of the wealthy, private schools have spectacularly grown, whereas public school enrollments have declined. Whether escaping integrated schools or seeking better discipline and quality schools, many parents have lost faith in the public schools.

other services, such as fire fighters and ambulance paramedics. In the Northeast, however, local resistance to this type of solution is quite strong because of the longer presence of traditional local boundaries and the "home rule" philosophy of local control.

Magnet Schools

Large cities or smaller metropolitan areas can keep white students in urban public schools by offering special learning experiences. As the term implies, **magnet schools** attract talented youngsters to an exceptional program in computer science, music and art, science, or special teachers' techniques unavailable at the other schools. These special high schools offer excellent facilities and intense programs that make the busing worthwhile to parents and motivate students to attend and gain a valuable educational experience.

Educational Parks

Much like an industrial park or shopping center, educational facilities are concentrated in one campus setting. Since all students in an area come to one central location, the integration and funding parity are more easily achieved. With most school buildings already existing in scattered neighborhood settings, however, this approach can only be attempted in places of growth or development.

Grade Grouping

Another method of desegregating schools is grade grouping; the concentration of only certain grade levels in each school. One neighborhood school might contain all the kindergartners, first, and second graders in the school district. Another could house the third, fourth, and fifth graders while still another school would have the sixth through eighth graders. This plan ensures all schools will be equal in their quality. Equally important, the burden of busing is fairly shared among all families, and all children spend a few years in their neighborhood school.

Voucher Plans

Different proposals exist for using school vouchers, but generally all call for the schools to compete with each other to attract students. For each of their school-age children, families receive a **voucher** which they give to the state-certified school—public or private—they select. Public schools would operate on the money they qualify for from the vouchers, not from levied tax revenues. Stipulations in some voucher plans mandate acceptance of a broad spectrum of students including the poor, handicapped, and slow learners. Voucher plans thus attempt to promote better quality schools equally sharing responsibility for educating all students.

James S. Coleman suggests a voucher plan would enable low-income families to send their children to private schools and thus desegregate them.[38] Critics attack the subsidizing of parochial schools, as violating the doctrine of separation of church and state. Most teacher and school administration organizations oppose voucher plans because they would spawn hucksterism and dubious recruiting methods. Others contend that small population areas would still have little choice of other schools to attend, while many other parents would still continue sending their children to neighborhood schools.[39]

Learning Environment

Several approaches attempt to reduce middle-class biases in the schools. Many school systems run mandatory in-service workshops for their teachers to develop greater sensitivity to cultural and social class differences. Bilingual classes and minority studies programs are now standard in most urban regions. An innovative curriculum approach begun 25 years ago at the Dale Avenue School in Paterson, New Jersey, attracted nationwide attention and served as a model for similar programs in other cities and at Indian reservation schools in the American Southwest. This system effectively motivates students and gets them to grade reading level or beyond by using curriculum materials and teaching illustrations completely reflective of their cultural background instead of such "alien" readers as, for example, the white middle-class Dick and Jane books.

Numerous school systems use the open classroom to stimulate individual ability and creativity in a less restrictive but supportive setting. Begun in the 1960s and continuing today on a widely adopted basis, the open classroom eliminates or rearranges the traditional classroom apparatus: student chairs in neat rows with the teacher's desk set as a barrier in front and confined work spaces. Instead, the classroom becomes student-centered instead of teacher-oriented in this still carefully designed environment, as teachers guide, encourage, and stimulate individual achievement through multiple learning approaches, including varied curriculum materials and cooperative student learning tasks. Although the open classroom replaced the repressive authoritarianism of the classroom with a more positive learning environment, it did not necessarily improve academic achievement. Some teachers lacked the necessary training for this new role and could not handle the children. Generally, this approach has worked best in middle-class suburban schools, where it was more consistent with family child-rearing practices.

Knowledge and Technology

We live on the leading edge of a massive social change in our society brought about by high technology—what Alvin Toffler calls the "third wave" of revolutionary change after those of agriculture and industrialism.[40] We are experiencing a knowledge explosion, having doubled the total span of human knowledge in the past 30 years. Four out of every five scientists who have ever lived are alive today, and that fact is evident in the scientific breakthroughs and new technologies that keep impacting upon our way of life.[41] Schools cannot maintain this rapid expansion of new and specialized information. Further, students can learn much more outside the school, particularly through home microcomputer systems.

To face the challenge of providing effective education in the midst of a knowledge and technological revolution, the schools must utilize more technology in the classroom and redefine the pedagogical emphases in education.[42] As continuing changes in occupational work patterns, social relationships, and life-style test one's ability to make choices and adapt, schools must focus more on developing independent think-

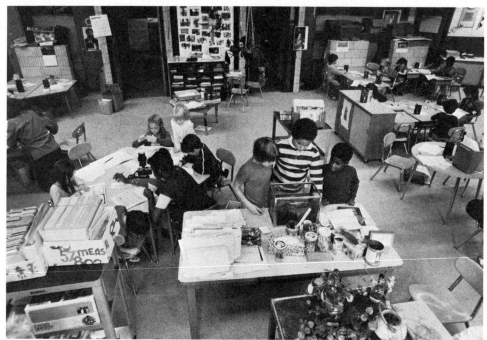

In an open classroom setting, multiple learning experiences occur simultaneously in different areas of the student-centered classroom environment. This approach appears to work best in stimulating creativity and achievement in middle-class suburban schools.

ing and self-reliance. The emphasis needs to be more on enhancing conceptual understanding than on memorizing names, dates, and formulas. Classroom computers used to develop an individual's thought processes, not just to drill and review material, is another possibility for creative learning.

Better Teachers

The demand for a quality education effectively given all students obviously requires highly competent and committed educators in the classroom. Although many such people comprise the profession, we pointed out earlier the decline in the quality of those entering teacher education programs. Moreover, many teachers in the elementary and secondary schools are as obsolete as much of the material they teach. To improve education we need to attract more competent people into teaching, and we need to maintain a high level of competence among the teachers throughout their careers.

Salaries

In 1983, the average starting salary for teachers was $12,800, compared to $16,200 for accountants and $20,364 for computer scientists.[43] The average salary for all public schoolteachers was $20,531, well below the $24,000 for plumbers and $26,000 for electricians.[44] Quite obviously, education cannot attract or keep very many good people with such poor economic incentives. Merit pay proposals and implementations, in which superior performance earns teachers additional pay, usually adds only an additional $1,000 that particular year, still far below average incomes in other occupations.[45] Master-teacher plans are a variation of merit pay, allowing good teachers both to receive extra pay and to serve as peer counselors to less experienced colleagues and as curriculum development consultants.

Another important variable is that a generation ago teaching was about the highest profession most women could attain, and many competent and capable females became educators because other higher-paying careers, for the most part, were not open to them. Today that is no longer true; women now have a wide choice of better-paying occupational roles. Finally, more pay for teachers means higher school budgets, and in a time of fiscal difficulty at all levels of government, no one has yet found a way to provide more revenues for education.

Competency and "Burnout"

Financial compensation is a critical factor in restoring teaching as an attractive profession, but its prestige and quality are also heavily dependent on the caliber of its members. Most teacher colleges have raised admission standards and curricula, according to a follow-up report from the National Council on Excellence in Education.[46] Increased use of MCTs for prospective teachers also helps ensure quality personnel. Other, more controversial proposals include eliminating lifetime tenure for teachers and replacing it with, say, a 5-year renewable contract based upon an evaluation of classroom performance.

A serious problem in American education is our inability to keep effective teachers. Many become **"burned out"** by their role conflicts (instructor, disciplinarian, and employee); excessive demands (paperwork, meetings, committee tasks); and low work rewards (pay, prestige, parental criticism, undisciplined students.) Only 12 to 15 percent of teachers are still in the classroom 10 years after entering the profession. More than one-fifth of beginning teachers leave the profession after just 1 year.[47] Until we address both the economic and intrinsic rewards of job satisfaction, teacher quality and attrition will remain a grave cause for concern.

Compensatory Education

The back-to-basics movement and the correlation between social class and achievement have focused attention on the need for special programs and assistance for disadvantaged youngsters. Project Head Start, begun in the 1960s, has been the biggest and best-known effort to offer preschoolers early education in basic skills, as well as medical and nutritional care. Early gains made by those in the program, however, are eroded by the second or third grade, suggesting the possible need for longer-range efforts. Transitional bilingual programs (the gradual phasing in of English usage only), sequential grade level competency testing, and systematic programs aimed at improving skills are some types of **compensatory education** aimed at helping each student achieve grade level performance.

Learning Environment

Effective education appears to occur best where a balance is achieved between discipline and self-expression in a warm, friendly atmosphere. Schools consistent in democratic but orderly classroom management, having positive life-goal orientations for students, and treating and trusting students to act with maturity and responsibility, have better student achievement despite their inner-city location.[48] Social organization—expecting students to study hard, succeed in their tasks, and accept responsibility, together with a cohesive teacher cooperative effort—was more important in producing significantly better outcomes than age or size of school facilities, or student socioeconomic background.

THE FUTURE

In the next several decades education will become even more important to success in life, and the way we educate may even change dramatically. Perhaps, as Alvin Toffler suggests, more formal learning will occur outside the classroom than inside, with it more interspersed and interwoven with work.[49] Computers and video teaching machines may replace competitive classroom interaction. While we await the determination of how high technology changes education, let us now examine some possible outcomes from current behavioral trends in education.

Pessimistic Scenario

By 2025 education in the United States had dramatically changed. Federal and state governments had abandoned integration efforts after their regionalization of school districts had driven not only the middle class, but a large proportion of the more affluent working class, out of the public school system. Their children were now all in private schools, often in buildings bought or leased from cities and towns. Public schools were solely the repository of America's underclass, and regardless of where you lived, attending or teaching at a public school earned a social stigma.

Efforts to attract better teachers to the public schools had failed despite greater economic or "combat pay" incentives. Working in an area where vandalism, car theft, muggings, rape, and drug abuse were commonplace was too unattractive. Public schools were filled with unruly students and severe discipline problems, even though school police forces attempted to maintain order in the halls, stairwells, restrooms, and on the school grounds. Working with young people who see little value in education, where the efforts of reaching even a few motivated students were impeded by frequent disruptions, discouraged many potential teacher candidates. As a result, public schools could employ only less qualified and competent teachers, often with a "holding pen" mentality rather than a life-preparation orientation.

"Real" education now only occurred in the private schools. However, they retained the authoritarian and competitive atmosphere of earlier generations. Students now not only had to conform unquestioningly to teacher expectations but also to the programmed learning simulations on their classroom computers. Stimulating creativity, curiosity, and self-actualization were not teaching objectives. Since the school socialization process emphasized adherence to rules, procedures, and controlled learning situations, development of critical thinking and decision-making skills were virtually ignored.

The schools not only reflected the social stratification in American society, but intensified its rigidity as well. Upward mobility was no longer part of the educational philosophy. Your socioeconomic background predetermined the type of school you would attend, and consequently the type of education you would receive. Like all other students, you would be programmed to fit into a slot considered ''appropriate'' to your background. As an adult, you would enter an occupation similar in pay and status to that of your parents.

Optimistic Scenario

The computer age had revolutionized the educational system by 2025. Once the technology had been put into use at all grade levels, it occasioned unintended but positive consequences in student creative enrichment and self-realization. Minority leaders, who had in the late twentieth century urged improvement in the quality of neighborhood minority schools as a viable alternative to busing, found the extensive utilization of computers in the classroom an effective means of achieving this goal. What made computers change schooling so well was not simply their presence, but the way they were utilized and the attitudinal and behavioral modifications they caused.

A new generation is growing up and learning in school how to use computers. If properly utilized, computers have the potential of providing better individual instruction, assistance, reinforcement, and creative stimulation than a classroom teacher could.

With students each at their own computer station, they received far more individual instruction, assistance, and reinforcement than they could from a classroom teacher. Freed by computers from basic chores, teachers had more time also to work with students. Students also mastered basic skills through computer programming in drill, execution, review, and self-testing. Another key factor was the use of discovery-type programming which encouraged students to explore and learn. This form of presentation of materials rewarded creativity and self-reliance.

One result of classroom computer usage was the demise of ability grouping or tracking systems. Since computer systems allow each student to proceed at his or her own pace, grouping students by ability levels for a class to learn at the same rate was unnecessary. Teachers could give a lesson in any subject to a class of mixed abilities, and then the supplemental computer program could individually assist each student in subject mastery. Returning to mixed ability grouping and the personal tutoring/creative stimulation of computers ended class stigma, development of negative student self-image, and low teacher expectations while promoting intellectual growth and development in each individual. Because they were motivated, most students remained in school.

Not insignificantly, computer mastery gained in learning about one's culture prepared each student, regardless of background, with skills essential to employment in a high technological society. Wise application of computer technology had also provided students with creative interests and the ability to make their own decisions in a world of complex choices. Through the combination of computers and nonfrustrated, unbiased teachers, education had at last become the great equalizer in fully preparing all students for a promising future.

SUMMARY

1. Americans have long believed in education as the means to economic success and the curing of society's problems. The advocacy of universal educational opportunity and insistence on local community control are deeply ingrained in the American way of life.

2. As a bureaucracy, the school system allows little flexibility through its hierarchy of authority. Curiosity, creativity, and individualism decline at the insistence on uniformity, obedience, and conformity to a structured approach.

3. Middle-class values dominate the schools, often at the expense of low-income students. Ability grouping and teacher expectations affect self-esteem, motivation, and achievement. With a disproportionate number of low-income students in the lowest track, schools tend to reinforce the social class structure rather than serving as the great equalizer.

4. Busing to achieve minority integration has had mixed results. Because of white migration to the suburbs and the growth of private schools, particularly in the South and the West, most large cities today have a disproportionate minority student

population. While Americans favor integration, most Whites and many Blacks oppose busing as the solution.

5. Local property taxes, supplemented by state funds, are the primary means of financing education. States and communities vary greatly in their ability to generate revenues. Consequently, the quality of education has been directly dependent on the wealth of one's parents and neighbors, but recent court decisions have led some states to seek more equitable funding alternatives.

6. Several national reports and surveys have called public attention to serious shortcomings in education. These problems include declining achievement scores, teacher competency, a "cafeteria-style" curriculum, grade inflation, and graduating functional illiterates.

7. Solutions depend upon how the problem gets defined. Do students require resocialization? Is the educational system attempting to do too much? Do the schools simply reinforce inequities that can only be corrected by major changes in society itself? Do the years of daily interaction in school enhance or distort personal growth and development?

8. Educational reform efforts include creating more equitable school districts through redistricting, magnet schools, educational parks, grade grouping, and voucher plans. Improvements in the learning environment through innovative and less authoritarian teaching, including use of classroom computers, can create better schools. However, better teachers are necessary and this requires improved salaries, higher standards, and prevention of "burnout."

9. If education is to achieve its goal of maximizing individual development, it must allow all students equal educational opportunities. The most effective schools are those that achieve a balance between discipline and self-expression, treating students as mature, responsible persons in a cooperative, orderly, and democratic atmosphere.

SUGGESTED READINGS

Bowles, Samuel, and Herbert Gintis. *Schooling in Capitalist America*. New York: Basic Books, 1976. A conflict perspective analysis of how the American educational system maintains social class and economic inequities in society.

Hurn, Christopher J. *The Limits and Possibilities of Schooling*. Boston: Allyn and Bacon, 1978. A helpful sociological analysis of the current problem issues in education. It offers a practical evaluation of societal change through the schools.

Jencks, Christopher, et al. *Who Gets Ahead? The Determinants of Economic Success in America*. New York: Basic Books, 1979. A thorough analysis of the interrelationships among educational attainment, family backgrounds, and economic success.

Lortie, Dan C. *Schoolteacher: A Sociological Study*. Chicago: University of Chicago Press, 1975. An insightful examination of the problems and conflicts that teachers encounter which restrict their effectiveness.

Silberman, Charles E. *Crisis in the Classroom*. New York: Random House, 1970. The result of a 4-year study of 100 schools, this clear and thorough criticism of American educational practices is still very pertinent today.

Yarmolinsky, Adam, Lance Liebman, and Corinne S. Schelling (eds.). *Race and Schooling in the City*. Cambridge, Mass.: Harvard University Press, 1981. A series of insightful articles on the immense difficulties facing urban schools in giving a quality education.

GLOSSARY

Ability grouping   Also known as tracking; placing students of comparable ability in the same class to maximize effective instruction.

Burnout   The loss of motivation and satisfaction among teachers due to role conflicts, excessive demands, low salaries, and little sense of accomplishment.

Compensatory education   Special programs teaching basic skills and knowledge to disadvantaged youngsters.

Grade grouping   Concentrating certain grade levels in each school of a community, to achieve integration and make busing evenly shared.

Grade inflation   A liberal grading practice resulting in disproportionate numbers of high grades and distorting the picture of what really was learned.

Magnet school   An urban school offering special, exceptional programs making busing worthwhile and maintaining a racial balance.

Minimum competency tests (MCTs)   Standardized tests measuring knowledge of basic skills in reading, writing, and math, often a precondition to earning a high-school diploma.

Redistricting   Redrawing boundary lines within a community to achieve a racial balance yet retain neighborhood schools.

Social engineering   Use of the schools to correct the inequities in society and to fit individuals into adult occupational slots.

Social promotion   Moving children through grades with their age peers regardless of actual learning achievement.

Teacher expectations   The positive or negative influence of an instructor upon student achievement.

Voucher plans   Providing families with tuition vouchers, payable by the state to any public or private certified school.

FACTS ABOUT ECONOMIC AND POLITICAL POWER

One-tenth of 1 percent of all U.S. corporations control 60.8 percent of all manufacturing assets.

One percent of the U.S. population owns 25 percent of the nation's net worth, a figure unchanged since 1860.

The 2.7 million federal employees in 1982 were 23 percent greater than the 2.2 million in 1960.

Political Action Committees spent $88 million in 1982 to elect sympathetic congressmen.

Because only about half the voting public cast ballots, recent presidents have received only about a 27 percent "mandate."

Multinational corporations comprise the world's third largest economy, after that of the United States and Soviet Union.

Most regulatory agencies have top echelon executives from industry who often resume their careers after leaving government.

13
THE CONCENTRATION OF ECONOMIC AND POLITICAL POWER

American society today reflects the changes wrought by the industrialization process. The division of labor within a much larger, heterogeneous, and interdependent population necessitated a new form of social organization. America's economic and political institutions also changed. Bureaucratization, centralization, consolidation, and concentration of power became characteristics of contemporary American society. An individual's influence diminished as corporate and national goals, priorities, and policies dominated.

Traditional American values—democracy, freedom, equality, individualism, achievement, humanitarianism—fostered contradictory beliefs in people. For example, we believe in local autonomy and control but we want the federal government to intervene to correct our social problems. Government should help people, yet it should not interfere in people's lives. We believe in the free enterprise system, but we want government to regulate big business. We distrust both big business and big government, and yet we regard them as necessities.

How do we reconcile these conflicts? How do we encourage greater business productivity and government protection without impinging on individual rights? With the continuing growth of conglomerates and lobbies, does the government represent the public interest or special interests? Who really runs America?

Power is cumulative. That is, when one group has more power, others must have less. If economic and political power is concentrated in the hands of a few, individual choice and the democratic process are endangered. Moreover, the roles of government and big business affect the solutions of all social problems discussed in this book. To handle them we must more properly utilize our economic and political institutions. But how? In this chapter we shall confront these issues as we examine the nation's power structure and its accountability to the public.

CORPORATE AMERICA

Through diversification and concentration of resources, a few huge corporations now dominate the American economy. Instead of a free enterprise system based upon competition, in many fields we actually have a few corporations with little competition, who control demand rather than respond to it. These corporate giants are so large and deeply immersed in an interdependent economic system that they also have a concern about maintaining national stability. It is in their best interests to preserve the socioeconomic order, so they use their accumulated power to influence legislation through intensive lobbying and campaign support of sympathetic politicians.

The term used when a few producers dominate an industry is **oligopoly,** which means the division of wealth and power among very few competitors. When only a few producers control an entire market, they frequently engage in price leadership, which is a polite term for coordinated pricing or parallel pricing to avoid price competition. When one major auto, oil, or steel company raises its prices, the others quickly do the same. They gain far more this way through added revenues than by keeping a lower price. Sometimes the increases are justified, but many instances of artificially inflated prices also occur. One of many examples is the oil industry's tripling of gasoline prices in the late 1970s, far beyond the increases by OPEC.

The extent of big business dominance of the economy becomes apparent when one realizes that one-tenth of 1 percent of the almost 2 million corporations in this country controlled 60.8 percent of the total assets in 1982; in 1950 these 200 corporations controlled 47.7 percent.[1] The largest 200 companies produce 44 percent of the total value of manufactured products, up from 30 percent in 1947.[2]

Who Owns the Corporations?

If a small number of corporations play a major role in the nation's welfare, who owns the corporations themselves? The question is hidden in complex layers of corporations owning stock in other corporations which in turn own other stock, and so on; corporate investors acting on behalf of private investors; and concealed trust funds. Numerous people have investigated this matter, of course, and all indications point to a small wealthy elite as the ultimate owners of much of the corporate stock. Millions of private investors may be involved in the stock market, but the bulk of the stock is owned by a few.

The Wealthy Elite

One study found that the top 1 percent of income earners owned 51 percent of all corporate stock, but that did not include the 20 to 25 percent of stock held by institutions, often on behalf of private investors.[3] Michael Parenti reported an even more provocative finding: only 0.2 percent of the population owns almost 60 percent of the nation's corporate wealth.[4] Less than 2 percent of the population owns 100 percent of all state and municipal bonds, 88.5 percent of all corporate bonds, and 80 percent of all stock.[5] This immense concentration of wealth—the top 1 percent owning about 25 percent of the nation's net worth—has remained unchanged since 1860.[6]

Using two famous families—the Du Ponts and Rockefellers—Parenti illustrates how a wealthy elite dominates corporate ownership:

> The Du Ponts control ten corporations, each with over $1 billion in assets, including Penn Central, General Motors, Coca-Cola, Boeing and United Brands, along with many smaller firms. Over a million people work for Du Pont controlled firms. . . .
>
> Another powerful family enterprise is that of the Rockefellers. They hold over $300 billion in corporate wealth, extending into just about every industry, in every state of the Union and every nation in the nonsocialist world. The Rockefellers control five of the twelve largest oil companies and four of the largest banks in the world. They have holdings in chemicals, steel, insurance, sugar, coal, copper, tin, computers, utilities, television, radio, publishing, electronics, agribusiness, automobiles, airlines—indeed, in just about every known natural resource or manufactured commodity and service.[7]

Interlocking Directorates

Besides corporate investment, another effective means of control is **interlocking directorates.** This occurs when executives or directors from one corporation sit on the board of directors of another corporation. Such linkage can either be direct (one person on the board of directors of two companies) or indirect (two companies each having someone on the board of directors of a third company). Either way provides a concentration of economic or fiscal control in the hands of a few who can effectively chart the production and investment in one of several industries without outside interference.[8] A tight interlocking network of business executives creates unified power, shared information, policy coordination, and reduced competition.

Interlocking directorates, both direct and indirect, are extremely common throughout American business. A 1981 study offered the example of the 13 largest corporations, which together possess one-eighth of the country's corporate assets, averaging 4.5 direct links and 122.5 indirect links with the other 12.[9] Numerous other studies have given evidence of the control of major banks and corporations through the widespread use of interlocking directorates.[10]

When competition becomes virtually nonexistent, when a few corporate giants have great concentrations of wealth and power, when these corporations—controlled by a small wealthy elite—have little accountability or regulation, then the free enterprise system is not functioning. Interlocking directorates are not illegal as long as direct competitors do not sit on each other's boards or those of suppliers and customers. Nevertheless, this practice guarantees a privileged position of power to the huge corporations and no protection to consumers.

Engulf and Devour

A recent phenomenon has been the growth of monolithic **conglomerates** through mergers and acquisitions. This trend toward conglomerates—large firms that own businesses in greatly diversified fields—increases the probability of corporate oligopolies and their greater influence on government policy. The trend has reached large proportions. The peak period was 1965–1969, when 8,213 acquisitions took place. Another 7,466 occurred in 1970–1979.[11] As the number of acquisitions declined, the value of these conglomerate mergers skyrocketed because of the greater holdings of the acquired companies. In 1978 the value of these mergers had been about $5 billion, but by 1981 the 50 biggest transactions alone totaled $49.9 billion, almost matched by 1982's $48.2 billion.[12]

Hostile Takeovers

As recently as the mid-1970s, no respectable corporation or its investment banking advisors would consider a hostile raid on another company.[13] Since then tumultuous takeovers have dominated the business scene, prompting television commentator Bill Moyers to label the spectacle one of "cannibals gorging on one another."[14]

The largest 1982 deal was the almost $6 billion paid by U.S. Steel to acquire Marathon Oil. The largest deal of all was in 1981 when Du Pont purchased Conoco (the ninth largest oil company) for $7.4 billion.[15] The $10 billion takeover bid in 1984 of third-ranked Texaco for seventh-ranked Getty Oil surpassed that deal, itself topped by the $13.2 billion takeover action of Standard Oil of California for Gulf Oil Company. Experts expect continuing combinations of financial service companies, insurance companies, oil companies, and banks.[16]

Corporate Technostructure

Impersonal corporate entities set the tone for today's economic environment, not identifiable power brokers like a Ford or Rockefeller of a bygone era. Occasionally certain corporate leaders become media celebrities, such as Lee Iaccoca of Chrysler or Frank Borman of Eastern Airlines. Even then their charismatic leadership depends upon an anonymous group of specialists who serve as the guiding intelligence in organizational decision making. Power may be concentrated in boards of directors, but modern corporations depend heavily upon a faceless management team of talented and experienced experts for input and direction.

Economist John Kenneth Galbraith calls this remote leadership group within the organization the "technostructure."[17] If oriented toward maximizing corporate profits, these **technocrats** wield enormous power in decisions that affect national policy and the quality of life.[18] The public may not know who they are, but this key group acts to produce profits for stockholders, with public welfare a secondary consideration. For example, toxic waste disposal and air and water pollution become corporate concerns only after governmental regulation and enforcement.

Giant Slaying

What if we act to break up the corporate giants to make them less powerful and more accountable to the public? The case of AT&T offers a mixed picture. Gradual chipping away at this communications monopoly brought competitors into the field selling telephone equipment and long-distance service. Consumers benefited from greater choice and lower costs. Then came the breakup of AT&T, with its regional telephone subsidiaries becoming independent companies as of January 1, 1984. Most AT&T stockholders retained shares in the parent company and gained shares in each of the seven spin-off companies. Consumers, however, had to pay higher telephone bills. AT&T had kept local call charges low through inflated prices for telephone equipment and long-distance calls. Now the local companies had to charge more realistically for normal usage since they did not have this financial underpinning. As a result, consumers paid much larger telephone bills than ever before, in many cases twice as much.

The question then is, do we really benefit by slaying the giants, or should we put a leash on them? Would a federal consumer protection agency or an end to lax enforcement of antitrust legislation in existence since 1914 be better alternatives? Is bigness necessary? Is it more cost-efficient? If so, how can we make the megacorporations more responsive to public benefits and welfare? (See Box 13.1).

The Irrelevance of Evil

Individuals acting alone will first evaluate the situation in terms of available information, their intent, and anticipated results by the action to be taken. Organizations, however, have a momentum of their own and transform the meaning of each individ-

BOX 13.1

"BIG" IS NOT "BAD"

American business—especially *big* business—appears to be widely unpopular. . . . Why do people distrust big companies even more than some other institutions? I believe there are two fundamental reasons:

First, there is a widespread lack of understanding of the *relative* importance and influence of big business in the total economy. People simply do not know enough about how big companies fit into the total economic system, nor do they understand the manner in which big firms are managed.

Second, there is a similar lack of understanding of the essential role and contributions of large business enterprises in achieving national goals.

The attitude of many toward big companies can be understood more readily if it is viewed as a traditional reaction to "bigness" in general. Americans equate size with power, whether economic or political, and have always viewed the growth of large institutions with apprehension. When people think of business, they like to think of the corner grocer, the town druggist, or the service station at the neighborhood shopping center. *Small* business, which is perceived as being accessible, personalized, and understandable, has been the national ideal. . . .

The perception that "big" is "bad" is reinforced in our schools, which tend to emphasize the past excesses of the business system—such as attempts to create monopolies and efforts by some businessmen to control political affairs. As the nation has grown to maturity, it has learned to control the potential excesses of the

ual's actions as well as the focus of responsibility for one's deeds. Because the nature of organizations is to fragment tasks and limit authority in individuals, it also obscures a person's relationship to the organization's actual goal achievement. Large corporations so diffuse knowledge and responsibility that persons throughout the hierarchy may feel blameless. The "noninvolvement" in organizational actions permits the individual to feel devoid of responsibility for any secondary negative consequences as the organization gains its objectives.[19]

In a famous experiment, Stanley Milgram effectively demonstrated the high obedience tendency of individuals to a recognized authority.[20] Using the prestige of Yale University, Milgram convinced his subjects to administer "painful" shocks to another person as part of a teaching experiment. As the "victim" pretended great pain through screams and protests, the experimenter ordered increasingly higher shock levels. Despite their own personal anguish, over 60 percent of the subjects did so. Applying the results of this experiment to an organization, we see how individuals become role performers obeying an authority to help achieve a larger goal. Since they do not decide the shock levels, when to terminate the shocks, or even what the actual goals are, the individuals are relieved of responsibility for their actions and find themselves able to do something they ordinarily would not have done acting alone.

In an analysis of this organizational impact on individual actions, Maury Silver and

business system—and the human beings in it—through powerful deterrents such as the antitrust laws. As a result, business and businessmen today are as a rule quite unlike some of their historical counterparts. . . .

Today's large corporation is responsive to broad social goals because it is managed for the long run. Because businessmen ordinarily speak in economic terms, it is somehow perceived that they look *only* at short-term profits. The public believes—and rightfully—that in a democratic society such a narrow objective for any institution is unacceptable. But the realities of the business system are quite different. The lingering presumption of great and unbridled power exercised by corporate management rests on out-of-date concepts. . . .

Successful capitalism means that business must profit from others' well-being, rather than taking advantage of people. Business must conduct its affairs in a way that adds to the general good, making a mutually rewarding contribution to the achievement of worthwhile human goals. The measurement of business' success in doing this is profitability over time. *Profit-making* and not *profiteering* is the only basis for the continued existence of business. Thus, large business enterprises are managed so as to respond to broad social goals, thereby helping assure the growth and long-term viability of the business. That is the standard by which the performance of corporate management is judged.

SOURCE: Excerpted from an address by Randall Meyer, President of Exxon Company, U.S.A., "The Role of Big Business in Achieving National Goals," Florida State University, November 26, 1974. These remarks are at variance with many points discussed in this chapter.

Daniel Geller point out that even higher level functionaries can disentangle themselves from responsibility.[21] They see their actions as role requirements separate from their own desires. The morality of the bureaucrat lies in fulfilling assigned duties, not in disregarding rules and organizational needs. Individuals can thus rationalize their morality and sense of responsibility because the organizational structure encourages their doing so.

Price-Fixing

Theoretically, our free competitive system benefits consumers with better products at lower prices. In reality, corporations realized long ago that avoiding price competition was far more profitable to them. Although price-fixing is illegal, it is very widespread. One survey of top manufacturing executives revealed that 47 percent of those at the 500 largest U.S. companies agreed that price-fixing is standard practice, while 70 percent of the executives polled in the next 500 largest firms also agreed.[22]

The illegal collusion of major companies setting uniformly high prices costs unknowing customers millions of dollars each year. These coordinated pricing actions become possible when a few producers dominate an industry. Probably the most notorious example—only because the federal government succeeded in convicting the violators—was the admission of top executives at General Electric, Westinghouse, and McGraw-Edison that for years they had fixed prices in the electrical equipment industry which unnecessarily cost the public over $1 billion.[23] The prevailing attitude of many business executives was perhaps summed up in the words of one convicted GE executive who said, "Sure, collusion was illegal, but it wasn't unethical."[24]

Consumer Manipulation

In an advanced industrial society where most people's primary needs of food, shelter, and clothing are satisfied, corporations create artificial needs for new products through advertising. A generation ago, Vance Packard warned in *The Hidden Persuaders* how advertisers deliberately exploit our psychological needs and desires to make us buy their products.[25] More recently, Wilson Bryan Key called our attention to advertisers' successful use of subliminal seduction—the subtle use of images to appeal to our subconscious—to increase sales.[26] Today it remains equally true that advertisers effectively manipulate us to consume unnecessary products, as the 1983 consumer stampede to buy Cabbage Patch dolls so well illustrates.

Advertisers play to our anxieties and insecurities. They sell us acceptance, affection, beauty and youth, sexual attractiveness, and the good life. You may think the commercials and print media advertisements do not influence you, but sales figures demonstrate how consumers succumb to their promise. Mass advertising encourages a philosophy of behavior which exerts an indirect influence on cultural value patterns in our personal desires and daily activities.

With little real difference between products, corporations create imagined or artificial differences. Bayer may be "the most trusted name in aspirin," but since all aspirin is alike, advertising made it so well received. Similarly, Anacin may "contain the ingredient most doctors recommend," but that ingredient happens to be aspirin. And whether we fly the "wings of man" or the "friendly skies" of another airline, we are really getting into the same type of plane and getting the same service. You can "taste the difference" in coffees, sodas, or beers, but that product satisfaction is mostly psychological, not actual.

Deception and misrepresentation are fairly common in advertisements. The Federal Communications Commission (FCC) polices against deceptive product claims, but often an advertising campaign has extensive play before the violator agrees to withdraw the offending ad. Jules Henry once observed that, to advertisers, "truth is what sells" and "truth is what is not legally false."[27] Although many people may not literally believe all advertisements, they are nonetheless often convinced through them to buy products to achieve status, happiness, and the good life. After all, "You only go through life once, so live it with gusto."

GOVERNMENT-CORPORATE ALLIANCES

Big business had enjoyed a close relationship with several administrations in the past, such as those of McKinley and Taft, but its real partnership with government was forged in World War II. The immense demands of that global conflict prompted creation of a War Production Board which coordinated all industrial efforts to meet wartime needs. When the war ended, the federal government continued and expanded its activities in the economic area to promote full employment, low inflation, and sustained economic growth. Successful business executives provided a pool of skilled administrators to head cabinet departments and agencies. Long-range planning and business incentives (research subsidies, tax allowances) linked the government and corporate giants more closely, as business executives realized their best interests were served by maintaining a favorable climate with public officials.

Financial Benefits

In many ways individuals benefit from governmental involvement in the economy. Student loans and Educational Opportunity Funds (EOF) enable hundreds of thousands of people each year to obtain an otherwise unattainable college education, which will allow them to get better-paying jobs, make a greater contribution to society in their lifetimes, and also generate more tax revenues for the government. Similarly, government-guaranteed mortgages enable more people to have better housing, which in turn stimulates the housing industry (construction, building supplies, plumbing, electricity, painting, and so on).

Government assistance to business also benefits the public frequently. Whether the financial rescue of a major employer like Chrysler Corporation or the tax incentives for research, development, or capital expansion, such actions encourage economic growth, thereby providing more jobs, products, and higher living standards. However, what appeals to business may not necessarily benefit the public. Corporations have large resources to draw upon to press an unfair advantage in influencing policy decisions. Herein lies the danger of a concentration of economic and political power combining to work against the public interest.

Political Funding

In a media-dominated society where candidates are packaged and marketed much like commercial products, political campaign expenses run into millions of dollars at the national level and hundreds of thousands in statewide elections. Since most of this money comes from contributions, candidates can easily become indebted to and influenced by big-money contributors. Since 1972, when Richard Nixon's campaign received $14 million from just 100 people (including $2 million from insurance executive W. Clement Stone), presidential campaigns have contribution restrictions and receive matching financing from public funds. Congressional candidates, however, do not receive public funding and continue to depend upon contributions from individuals and special interest groups.

Political Action Committees

Most alarming has been the growth of **political action committees (PACs).** A PAC can contribute a maximum of $10,000 to one candidate—$5,000 each in the primary and general election campaigns. Intended to reduce the influence of big money on the political process, they are having the opposite effect. PACs have grown from 600 in 1974 to 3,500 in 1982, with their contributions increasing from $12.5 million in 1974 to $88 million in 1982.[28] In the 1982 congressional election, 1,450 corporate PACs contributed $25 million to elect sympathetic legislators.[29] Mostly they supported incumbents who served on committees dealing with matters affecting their fields.

Companies which do business with the government are especially likely to set up PACs; 19 of the top 20 federal contractors have PACs.[30] Corporations account for

A delegation of Right to Lifers lobby their New York congressman, Hamilton Fish, Jr., for a constitutional amendment prohibiting abortion. Another approach is campaign contributions to sympathetic legislators or challengers through political action committees.

the largest number of PACs, but labor unions, trade associations, doctors, teachers, realtors, and other groups also form PACs. The most rapid growth is among independent PACs, which grew from 165 in 1978 to 644 by 1982.[31] Most are organized around a single issue: abortion, nuclear freeze, conservatism.

No one can prove conclusively these special interest campaign contributions buy votes, but enough evidence exists to suggest this is a reasonable conclusion. For example, 83 percent of those who voted to defeat a proposed regulation to require used car dealers to reveal known defects in a vehicle to prospective buyers had received campaign contributions from the dealers' PAC.[32] In 1979, 43 of the 51 first-term congressional representatives who voted to weaken government enforcement power in real estate fraud cases had received contributions from the realtors' PAC.[33]

The Military-Industrial Complex

One of the most closely studied and debated areas of government-corporate alliances is that of military spending. By 1961, the relationship between defense industries and the military branch of the government had become so intertwined that Dwight D. Eisenhower warned the nation about its dangers in his farewell presidential address to the nation:

> Until the latest world conflicts, the United States had no armaments industry. American makers of ploughshares could, with time and as

required, make swords as well. But now we can no longer risk emergency improvisation on national defense: we have been compelled to create a permanent armaments industry of vast proportions. . . . This conjunction of an immense Military Establishment and a large arms industry is new to the American experience. The total influence—economic, political, even spiritual—is felt in every statehouse, every office of the Federal Government. We recognize the imperative need for this development. Yet we must not fail to comprehend its grave implications. Our toil, resources, and livelihood are all involved: so is the very structure of our society. In the councils of government we must guard against the unwarranted influence, whether sought or unsought, by the military-industrial complex. The potential for a disastrous rise of misplaced power exists and will persist.[34]

This oft-quoted but largely ignored admonition came from a man who had been a career army officer, Supreme Commander of Allied Forces in Europe during World War II, and a political conservative who himself had corporate executives in his Cabinet. Such a background made his words even more ominous, but in the quarter of a century since then, the interlocking cooperative relationship and informal influencing about weapons systems has grown even more pronounced. As a result, the **military-industrial complex** is even more firmly entrenched in the American economy.

The Department of Defense (DOD), located in the Pentagon—the world's largest office building—employs almost one million civilians, about 35 percent of all federal civilian employees.[35] The Pentagon owns more property than any other corporation or organization in the world, with $372.1 billion in property assets.[36] With annual defense purchases exceeding $179 billion and over 6.8 million employees in defense-oriented industries, the Pentagon exercises enormous influence on the economy.[37] Its expenditures are not confined to just a few geographic areas; more than three-fourths of the nation's congressional districts receive some DOD money.[38]

How much defense spending is really necessary is a fiercely debated topic. Pentagon lobbyists, on behalf of corporate defense contractors or the Defense Department, continually provide information to the members of Congress about the necessity of proposed budget expenditures. Global reports of aggression, subversion, insurrection, and repression help shape public opinion about the necessity of greater military spending for our national survival. Yet critics charge the pressures of contract-seeking corporations stir the arms race more than real strategic need. Again, the question of the social definition of a situation becomes the determinant of policy decisions.

Wasteful Spending

Senator William Proxmire, a key watchdog of wasteful governmental spending, has repeatedly warned about the community of interest between the military and defense industries which perpetuates the ''old boy network'' of influencing budget decisions.[39] Two examples can serve to support the Wisconsin senator's statement. In 1960 a secret Air Force guideline from 1946 was declassified which instructed that

Employees at McDonnell Douglas Corporation in St. Louis, Missouri, work on new fighter planes for the U.S. Air Force. Although necessary, the military-industrial complex also tends to generate wasteful spending of tax dollars, according to critics.

contracts be "Parceled out among the old established manufacturers on an equitable basis so that they may be assured enough business to perpetuate their existence."[40] Such an arrangement both undermines the free competitive system and violates antitrust legislation. The second illustration was the then unprecedented $250 million government loan in 1971 to Lockheed Aircraft. Lockheed's difficulties stemmed from civilian aircraft contracts, but the bailout was based upon the company's potential demise delaying delivery of some military hardware.

Waste of taxpayer dollars occurs for several reasons. First, about 80 percent of all defense contracts are awarded without competitive bidding, and are usually of a higher profit rate than the general industry average. The nation's top 100 corporations who monopolize these contracts often subcontract to smaller companies who produce the product more quickly and inexpensively, allowing the contract-holding corporation to then sell it to the government at a substantial profit; if the government dealt directly with the actual manufacturer, it could save much money.

The Pentagon also allows massive **cost overruns** beyond the contracted price. Supposedly these cost overruns are permitted because of unforeseen rising production costs over the multiyear project. However, these checkbook guarantees do not encourage greater economy and production efficiency to hold down costs. Final costs to the taxpayers are never known at the time when the decision is made to adopt a new weapons system or aircraft model. In the case of Lockheed's C-5A cargo plane, the expenditures were $2 billion higher and only 81 planes were delivered instead of the 120 originally contracted.[41]

Another important factor in wasteful spending lies in the cozy relationship between the military and industry. The Pentagon sometimes approves proposals without sufficient critical evaluation, does not demand repayment if the product fails to meet performance standards, and even pays compensation to companies when it cancels a contract due to the incompetence of the corporate supplier. Among the dozens of examples of scrapped project payments are: $1.5 billion for the B-70 aircraft which was so poor that only two unused models were ever built; $679.8 million for the Navaho missile; $511.6 million for the nuclear ANP aircraft; $330.4 million for the Seamaster aircraft; and $215 million for the F-111 aircraft.

Another major problem area is ordering spare parts simply by federal stock numbers, resulting in frequent abuses, such as paying $1,118 each for plastic caps costing 31 cents each or $2,043 each for nuts costing 13 cents each.[42] The Pentagon tolerates this ineptitude because it remains dependent on its suppliers and its classified, highly technical projects protect it from public accountability.

The Revolving Door

The **revolving door** interchange of personnel between corporations and the government/military further illustrates the warnings of Eisenhower and Proxmire. Presidents frequently recruit corporate executives. Eisenhower's Secretary of Defense was Charles F. Wilson, former President of General Motors (which also produces military hardware), who exclaimed at his appointment hearing, "What is good for General Motors is good for the country." A few of many other examples are Robert McNamara, former President of Ford Motor company as Kennedy's and Johnson's Secretary of Defense; David Packard, founder and principal stockholder of the major defense contractor Hewlett-Packard Company, as Nixon's Undersecretary of Defense; and Reagan's Secretary of State George Schultz, former corporate executive at Bechtel, a multinational engineering construction firm.

Dependent upon government contracts for much of their income, or concerned about regulatory legislation and enforcement, corporations frequently hire former military and government officials as influence peddlers. With their established contacts, these individuals have informal access and influence over those in decision-making positions. In turn, the decision makers, whether in regulatory agencies or the military, see a bright future for themselves in a similar position when they leave office.

> It used to be called the "revolving door"—the way prominent Washingtonians alternated between serving the government and getting rich by influencing it. Indeed, it was sometimes argued that allowing them to cash in afterward was the only way to get good people into government service. Today the service part is increasingly regarded as superfluous. . . . Washingtonians have been selling connections or the appearance thereof, ever since the town was a swamp.[43]

An average of nine ex-congressmen registered as lobbyists after each election between 1946 and 1966. In 1980, of the 85 congressmen who left office, one regis-

Pictured at a 1983 meeting in the Oval Room of the White House are Caspar Weinberger, Secretary of Defense; Brent Scowcroft, president of the Bipartisan Commission of Strategic Forces; President Ronald Reagan; George Schultz, Secretary of State; and members of the commission. Cabinet and commission members, past and present, have usually been corporate executives, as conflict theorists quickly note.

tered as a foreign agent, 20 as lobbyists, and another 15 went to work for consulting firms, interest groups, or law firms in the Washington area where their contacts would be of benefit to their employers.[44] Between 1970 and 1979, approximately 2,000 people moved back and forth between the government or military and the eight largest defense contractors.[45] Over 5,000 former Pentagon officials now work in defense-related industries.[46] This disproportionate high number of people in influential corporate positions raises important questions about the impact of this intimate relationship and the public interest, national priorities, and the economy.

MULTINATIONAL CORPORATIONS

Since midcentury some corporate giants have evolved into such large concentrations of power and wealth that they are prominent forces in the world economy. These **multinational** corporations operate across national boundaries, with plants and investments in many countries. Not under the authority of any one nation or international organization, these gigantic business enterprises conduct business freely in the pursuit of profits. Yet their decisions, possibly made in a boardroom thousands of miles away, affect nations' domestic and foreign policies, as well as their economies.

The multinationals, most of which are American companies, comprise the world's third largest economy, after that of the United States and the Soviet Union.[47] Al-

The westernizing influence of multinationals takes many forms, including changing culinary tastes within a culture, such as the popular Dairy Queen franchise in Japan. One can easily find a MacDonald's or Kentucky Fried Chicken franchise throughout many parts of the world.

ready accounting for more than one-fourth of the global economic production, their share will rise to over one-half within 20 years.[48] Some of these global companies—General Motors, International Telephone and Telegraph (which has diversified into hundreds of industries), and the major petroleum companies—have annual sales greater than the GNP of all Third World countries and several industrialized countries, such as South Africa and Switzerland.[49] Exxon, which does business in almost 100 countries, has a tanker fleet equal in size to the entire British navy.

International Impact

Driven by the goal of profit maximization, the multinational corporations locate their manufacturing and production in underdeveloped countries with low labor costs. This causes loss of jobs and increased import of foreign goods in industrialized nations but does not, analysts observe, improve poverty conditions in the poor countries.[50] Several sociologists have found that after an initial gain in the host nation's wealth, economic inequality actually increases, since only the upper and middle classes really benefit from economic expansion.[51] This is because foreign investment is limited to certain areas, which impedes economic growth in other areas.

Many countries encourage foreign investment in the hope of becoming more developed societies. These countries often lack the financial resources of the wealthier multinationals and become dependent on tax revenues from the corporations for a sizable portion of government expenditures. For example, in the 1970s Anaconda and Kennecott generated 20 percent of Chile's domestic GNP and up to 40 percent of its national budget.[52] In Chile and other countries in a similar position, it then becomes almost impossible to pursue policies that conflict with these corporate interests. Their withdrawal from the country would have devastating economic consequences.

Supporters of multinationals maintain they promote global interdependence, thereby reducing the risk of war. Instead of hurting the economy, they suggest, foreign sales increase, creating more jobs for American workers and more markets for American goods.

Abuse of Power

Since the multinational corporations wield such power, what happens when their goals are in conflict with the economic, political, or social goals of the countries in which they do business? With such a broad and immense field of operations, these global titans pursue interests and foreign policies that transcend national concerns. Sometimes these corporations use their influence in subtle, indirect, and legitimate ways to prevent adoption of national policies not in their interests. However, the potential for illegitimate actions not only exists, but unfortunately has occurred.

Multinationals regularly use bribery and kickbacks to protect their investments and secure foreign orders; over 500 American-based corporations have admitted doing so. Between 1969 and 1975, Lockheed paid $202 million in payoffs to government officials in several countries, with the subsequent scandals implicating the prime minister of Japan, the prince of the Netherlands, cabinet members in Italy, and military leaders in Colombia. Exxon paid almost $60 million in bribes to government officials in 15 countries, half the amount in Italy alone, to secure tax breaks. United Brands gave $1.25 million to one Honduras official to get a reduction on the export tax on bananas. In a 5-year period, Tenneco spent $12 million in bribes to leaders in 24 countries. These and other corporate bribes to individuals and political parties illustrate the common practice of multinationals to influence foreign politics to protect their own economic interests.[53]

Most notorious of all corporate intervention in a nation's internal affairs was that of the International Telephone and Telegraph Company (ITT) in Chile. In 1970 ITT feared the election of Marxist presidential candidate Salvador Allende because he had pledged to seize ITT's $150 million Chilean property. John McCone, a director of ITT and former head of the CIA, offered the CIA $1 million to help block Allende's election. The CIA spent $13 million to do so, including bribing the electoral delegates. When Allende won anyway, in what observers say was a fair and democratic election, ITT planned his overthrow, by creating economic chaos. Assisted by CIA economic sabotage efforts, U.S. banks cutting off financial credit, and U.S. corporations boycotting shipment of machine parts, the plan worked. In 1973, President Allende and many of his supporters were killed in a bloody military coup. Replaced by a military dictatorship frequently denounced for its violation of human rights, the regime did adopt a policy of unconditional support of U.S. policies and business interests.[54]

Whether Allende would have been overthrown without ITT's meddling is uncertain, but its action shows the extent to which a multinational corporation can go to protect its profits and involve the United States. The complicity of the U.S. government and ITT in the matter greatly damaged this nation's image throughout Latin America.

WHO REALLY RUNS AMERICA?

We pride ourselves as a nation of participant democracy, where the majority rules but all have freedom of choice. But is our democracy working? Are we under the domination of an elite, as radicals insist, or is our society diverse enough to have sufficient countervailing power bases?

The Power Elite Model

Conflict theorist C. Wright Mills was one of the first to claim the existence of a coalition of high-ranking leaders from similar backgrounds who are in the strategic command posts of the social structure.

> There is no longer, on the one hand, an economy, and, on the other, a political order, containing a military establishment unimportant to politics and to money-making. There is a political economy numerously linked with military order and decision. This triangle of power is now a structural fact, and it is the key to any understanding of the higher circles in America today. For as each of these domains has coincided with the others, as decisions in each have become broader, the leading men of each—the high military, the corporation executives, the political directorate—have tended to come together to form the power elite of America.[55]

Mills did not see the **power elite** as either a conspiracy or an attempt to gain political power and influence. They did, however, head the dominant institutions of our society and comprised a unified, self-conscious social class. Though they did not conspire, their shared interests did bring them together both professionally and socially.

The power elite, said Mills, is at the top of a three-tiered power structure, functioning invisibly but informally deciding major policy decisions. The middle levels of power are the more visible special interest groups and U.S. Congress where competing influence pressures still occur. At the bottom level is mass society, the unorganized, almost powerless individual citizens who usually are unaware of the power machinations taking place.

Similar Backgrounds

According to Mills, members of the power elite are mostly white, native-born Protestant males from the East, whose families have been wealthy for at least two generations. They attend the same Ivy League colleges, generally share the same values and attitudes, and remain closely interconnected through a social network of clubs, charities, and leisure activities.

They enter the corporate, military, or political bureaucracies, moving rapidly into powerful positions, due in part to their contacts in the "old boy network." Sitting together on government commissions and corporate boards, they comprise informal interlocking directorates where they coordinate their policies and actions to protect their mutual community of interests.

Interchangeability

Earlier we discussed the revolving door syndrome—the interchange of government, military, and corporate executives. In recent years sociologists have extended Mills's analysis to demonstrate the similar backgrounds of these shifting leaders. Of the approximately 5,500 top positions in business, government, and the military, Thomas R. Dye found that 30 percent were filled by those from the upper class (1 percent of the total population) and 60 percent from the upper-middle class (21 percent of the total).[56] Other studies have shown that, between 1897 and 1973, 90 percent of all cabinet officials were from the upper social strata, and that over 40 percent were corporate executives both before and after serving in the Cabinet[57]

The Pluralist Model

Pluralists accept the reality of an unequal distribution of power in society, but deny a single elite group coordinates and controls the major policy decisions. Instead, as suggested by David Riesman, they point to a two-tiered power structure.[58] At the top are different elites in various decision-making spheres who have different, and some-times conflicting, interests. The lower level consists of the unorganized public, who are not so much dominated as sought after as allies by the competing elite groups.

Veto Groups

Reisman felt that at the upper level, powerful interest groups act to protect them-selves from encroachment by others. To block such efforts, these **veto groups** form alignments with other groups and exert pressure on the decision makers. Since no one group maintains the same interest on all issues, the coalitions continually shift and so the balance of power also shifts, preventing any one group from influencing policy decisions on all matters. For Riesman, this was the critical factor in keeping a dispersed power balance.

Other pluralists, most notably Arnold M. Rose, expanded Riesman's concept to suggest that interest groups initiate action on their own behalf rather than mainly reacting against unfavorable proposals.[59] As interest groups compete with each other and bargain with government agencies, the government policies which emerge reflect compromises in which all groups, to some degree, are represented. Thus government resolves conflict by moderating between the varying power alignments.

The Voter Elite

A democratic, pluralist society works well if all its citizens participate in the govern-ment through their voices and their votes. An informed and involved citizenry can collectively act to protect their interests against the power brokers. At times this

Labor unions are often an important interest group within the pluralist model acting to protect themselves. Here textile workers protest against imports in Boston, seeking to call public and government attention to the matter and to do something about it.

voter activism manifests itself, as in the recent tax revolts—the 1983 recall of several Michigan state legislators who voted a tax increase in a state with high unemployment; the passage of Proposition 2 in Massachusetts in 1980; the passage of Proposition 13 in California in 1978.

Voter apathy is more common, however. Voter turnout has declined in each presidential election since 1960. In 1984 only 51 percent voted. In off-year elections, state and local elections, even fewer people vote. Studies of voting patterns show nonvoters are mostly young, poor, black, and uneducated. High-income individuals are twice as likely to vote as low-income individuals.[60] By defaulting on their voting privileges, the lower- and working-class nonvoters have created a **voter elite** which elects our government leaders. (see Box 13.2)

Comparison of the Two Models

Is one model a more accurate description of power in the United States? The mere presence of people from a similar background does not necessarily indicate a cohesive elite group. While they may share certain general values—preservation of the status quo and certain economic and political advantages—their specific interests do not always coincide and may, in fact, clash. At the same time, taking a pluralist view

BOX 13.2

WHY VOTERS HAVE A BAD
CASE OF THE BLAHS

Antipathy toward candidates and disillusionment with elections are not new to American politics. In fact, since the beginning of the Republic there has never been a president elected by a majority of the voting-age population. . . .

"We tend to believe that we're a country that governs itself, but the people are not acting that way," notes Jonathan Moore, director of the Institute of Politics at Harvard University. "They're not active, not getting good candidates and not participating. And the more they turn off and gripe, the more the system will not work."

Some blame flagging voter enthusiasm on boredom with the long road to presidential nomination that begins in the snows of New England and ends in the summer swelter of party conventions. By the time formal campaigning begins, voters are limp from months of unceasing political rhetoric.

The candidates themselves do not escape unscathed. Their carefully polished images are ground down by remorseless public scrutiny focused by what many regard as a predatory news media. No scar goes unexamined, no contradiction unexplored. Result: By the time the fall campaign peaks, there is little left to revere.

"We're overexposed to the candidates," suggests one political observer. "As a result, you'll never again have a chosen candidate who's truly popular. Put anybody under a microscope, and you'll find things you don't like."

The recent decline of political parties also contributes to voter apathy. Younger voters, in particular, are cast adrift without the basic political philosophy that strong parties can provide. Lacking the private contributions and federal funding that now go to candidates, party machinery rusts between elections and there is insufficient time to get it back into shape once campaigning begins. . . .

Citizens of [European] countries . . . have a strong sense that government policy directly reflects their vote.

"Voting is considered a duty," notes a German official. "Only people outside of society fail to vote. It's not something to be proud of."

Experts say this element—the sense of actually controlling the national destiny by ballot—is fading steadily in the American electorate.

SOURCE: Reprinted From *U.S. News & World Report,* issue of October 13, 1980. Copyright, 1980, U.S. News & World Report, Inc.

can shut one's eyes to the reality that a small number of interest groups possess enormous resources and power to influence the decision-making process.

The actual situation probably lies somewhere between these two extreme views. In fact, the two sides have many areas of agreement, as G. William Domhoff has indicated:

> These disagreements often reflect differences in style, temperament and degree of satisfaction with the status quo as well as more intellectual differences concerning the structure and distribution of political power. . . . There are areas of agreement between us, and on certain questions our disagreement is primarily one of degree.[61]

Powerful interest groups do compete with each other and elites do have substantial power. The questions remain whether the elite comprise a cohesive unit and whether the competing occurs at the top or middle range of power.

SOCIOLOGICAL PERSPECTIVES

Because we focused on the economic and political institutions of society in this chapter, our application of the four sociological perspectives will be somewhat different from that in other chapters. Through the macrosocial views of functionalist and conflict theorists, we shall be attentive to the structure of our social system. The deviant approach will provide us with a public perception of the situation, while the interactionist approach will offer an analysis of the impact of our economic and political systems upon the active participants and the general public.

Individual Faults and Deviant Behavior

To many Americans, the words *politics* and *corruption* are almost synonymous. Certain leaders may possess charisma, integrity, or the respect to inspire people, but throughout the nation's history, the generalized belief that politicians were "liars and thieves" has been a rather constant one. Revelations about voting fraud, machine politics, scandals, Watergate, Abscam "sting" operations have all reinforced the public image of politicians as an "unworthy lot."

Despite outsider Jimmy Carter's election as president in 1976 on the basis of "personal trust," public confidence in elected officials plummeted still further. Public opinion polls in 1979 revealed 68 percent of Americans believed "their leaders regularly lie to them," and 66 percent responded the "government is run for the benefit of a few."[62] Reagan's defeat of Carter in 1980 (by less than a third of the potential electorate) continued a pattern of no president since Eisenhower in the 1950s serving two full terms. Reagan's reelection in 1984 restored the reality of a two-term president, however.

The perception that business ethics are often sacrificed for profits is held not only by much of the general public. In 1976 Leonard Silk and David Vogel reported a finding that the top leaders of large U.S. corporations believed unethical behavior was both widespread and a daily reality.[63] Of course, many companies do have high ethical standards, but those which tolerate or rationalize their unethical and illegal behavior smear the others as well.

What we have in our society, then, is a tendency of people to blame politicians and business executives for the problems that exist. The system does not produce bad government, or environmental pollution, or poor products, or unresponsiveness to public concerns. Rather, the greed, insensitivity, and self-centeredness of the people in leadership positions do.

Institutional Faults and System Disorganization

Our current problems, functionalists maintain, are the result of rapid economic and social changes which have thrown the system out of balance. The emergence of huge corporations and powerful labor unions, together with greater government involvement in the economy, radically altered the free enterprise system. Moreover, continuing rapid technological and economic changes create even more problems before the old ones can be resolved. As government and corporations grow ever larger and more powerful, the means of their social control become more and more elusive.

Economic Dysfunctions

In the past 100 years, the growth of large corporations was functional for society in providing investment capital and extensive expertise to sustain the massive economic development that occurred. At the same time, this corporate growth has been dysfunctional in that a small number of companies now dominate the national and world economies, with little accountability to the public. The economic system fails to function smoothly because of a lack of coordination between the economic institutions and other social institutions. In addition, social control mechanisms have become inadequate to monitor and deter improper and illegal corporate actions.

The old American value of individualism is virtually lost with the mammoth organizations which shape and control most people's lives. So too is the cherished value of equality undermined when powerful groups with large resources at their disposal can pursue goals, while most individuals lack adequate resources to pursue theirs. When a society's basic values are incompatible with its social institutions, then its normative integration—the social cement which binds it together—is seriously threatened and requires correction.

Political Dysfunctions

Government should provide enforcement of norms through laws and the criminal justice system as well as social planning and direction. However, government fails most often to perform effectively, particularly in deterring corporate crime and in protecting the public interest. Rapid technological changes and creaking, antiquated organizational methods render government inadequate in coping with its responsibility to preserve order and stability.

Government has also grown so big that it is no longer responsive to input from individual citizens. Elected officials, the representatives of the people, lack the time, staff, and expertise to scrutinize government agency activities. This breakdown of system checks and balances permits government abuses of power or dereliction of duties to occur. Until each cog in the government machinery adjusts or is corrected to function efficiently and effectively, this perspective holds, the social problems will remain.

Inequality and Inevitable Conflict

The study of economic political power and competing interest groups provides fertile ground for conflict theorists since such competition for limited resources is the heart of this perspective. It sees in society numerous groups continually struggling to gain advantages over the others. Social problems arise when those who succeed in accumulating power then act to advance their own interests at the expense of the rest of society.

Economic Inequality

Large corporations and conglomerates in business and industry have achieved so much power that they dominate most aspects of the economy. When they work for their own selfish interests, particularly if they form a coalition of mutual interest groups, curtailing them is extremely difficult. As a result, the danger of an abuse of power is a real one. The corporate giants can also create a false consciousness among the populace through extensive media campaigns to shape public opinion. One example is ITT's counteracting the criticism over its intervention in Chilean politics by spending $6.4 million in a media blitz; within a year a specifically commissioned poll showed their public image had climbed favorably from 20 to 43 percent.[64]

Exploitation of workers by employers, who either are or represent the elite, is a fundamental cause of economic problems, according to this perspective. Labor unions have provided the organized unity to protect workers in some areas, but relocation of plants to the nonunionized sunbelt or to foreign countries with cheap labor—as well as union-busting tactics of bankruptcies/reorganized companies under new names—continue the exploitation.

Political Inequality

The economic elite of a society, said Karl Marx, are the political elite as well. They are able to use their vast financial resources to gain political power and influence. Government officials are simply agents of the ruling class, maintaining that class' privileged position by protecting its interests. The state, under the control of the rich and powerful, repress conflict rather than resolve it and thus maintain the inequality. The special interest groups exploit the masses by using the law and government to preserve the status quo, if not to enhance further their wealth.

Average citizens and less influential groups simply do not have the same access to political leaders. They could therefore be victimized by collaborative acts of government-corporate alliances. Only when organized social movements like Civil Rights seek a redress of grievances, does the collective power of ordinary citizens bring about change. Whether peaceful or violent, these actions of the oppressed come about when they develop a class consciousness about their exploitation and organize to do something about it.

Interaction and Social Interpretation

Rather than a structural analysis of corporate and governmental problems, interactionists examine the impact of the economic and political systems upon people's attitudes and behavior patterns. This approach can take two directions: the perceptions and actions of individuals within society or within the organization for which they work.

Public Perceptions

Before the rise of the big corporations and big government, Americans felt more independent and powerful, in greater control of their destinies than many people do today. Whether they actually were so autonomous is less important than their belief that they were. By acting in accordance with their beliefs, they often succeeded in their self-directed goals, in effect creating a self-fulfilling prophecy. Today's mammoth bureaucracies intimidate many people, causing feelings of impotency and dependency. If indifferent or fatalistic attitudes lead to inaction or passive compliance, people obviously do lose control over most things which affect their lives.

Since Americans measure success through achievement, individual competitiveness in an organizational society can breed considerable anxiety, dissatisfaction, insecurity, and hostility. Attitudes of cynicism and mistrust of others are likely under such circumstances, except among those economically secure. Combatting such negative factors are family and religious influences, the shaping of public opinion by corporations and government alike through the media, and various ego gratification activities outside the work place (clubs, hobbies, and so on).

Employee Perceptions

The very nature of organizations, with their hierarchy of authority and limited area of responsibility for each person, requires individuals to work for corporate goals if they wish to succeed with that company. The "culture" of a corporation pressures those at all levels to develop attitudes and behaviors necessary to advance the interests of their company. The individual's promotion or continuance with the firm is dependent upon his or her contribution to the company's financial well-being. This overriding preoccupation with meeting organizational goals may oblige some to take actions that contradict their personal values and ethics.

Rationalization is a common means for individuals to resolve their conflict between personal morality and corporate demands. If one believes "everybody's doing it," the pervasiveness of unethical or illegal behavior becomes the excuse to do so also. After all, "business is business." Another example is the argument that too much government interference exists, thereby justifying one's ignoring certain laws or regulations. Perhaps one might also think certain actions are necessary to keep an industry stable or profitable. Whatever the rationale, what is important here is that employees become socialized into seeing things from the company's perspective, which enables them to act in harmony with that interpretation.

POWER TO THE PEOPLE

Concentration of power and bureaucratization in business and government have not been entirely unchecked. A rallying slogan of social activists in the 1960s and 1970s was "Power to the People" and, indeed, organized citizen groups, as we shall shortly discuss, did succeed in making government and the corporate world more responsible. In the 1970s, the abuses of power revealed in the Watergate scandal and in the end of the 48-year reign of FBI Director J. Edgar Hoover brought about a Congress more assertive in its dealings with the executive branch of government. In redefining their role, representatives now scrutinize more thoroughly the actions of all parts of the executive branch.

At present two areas almost defy watchdog inspection. Because national security mandates secret activity in research, development, and manufacture, Congress is limited in its overseeing activities of the military-industrial complex. Since multinational corporations operate different parts of their economic activities simultaneously in various countries, only the coordinated actions of those nations can control these companies. At present no such coordination exists.

Regulatory Agencies

The creation of regulatory agencies usually comes about as a result of aroused public concern. For example, extensive lobbying by environmental groups like the Sierra Club and the National Wildlife Federation produced establishment of the Environmental Protection Agency (EPA). The EPA is intended to be a countervailing force to big business, setting standards for industrial pollutants and automobile engine emissions, cleaning up hazardous toxic waste sites, and enforcing other environmental policies. Even though the EPA is a government agency, other public-interest groups oversee its activities. Consequently, in 1983 its top two executives were forced to resign with public exposure of their contrary actions to the original purpose of the EPA.

A frequent problem with the regulatory agencies is their "capture" by industry. The "revolving door" is the culprit; former business executives, not consumer advocates, staff the upper echelons of these agencies. Their former positions were in the very industries they are supposed to regulate, whether they are now on the SEC, the FCC, the ICC, the FDA, or other regulatory agencies. While it makes sense, on the one hand, to appoint people familiar with the industry, these appointees retain their loyalties and personal business associations, which may prevent their objectivity. They have to deal with old friends and perhaps act on a project they once helped create, such as recall of an auto model. Further, many return to industry after their term as government officials, and their careers could be seriously jeopardized by an anti-industry reputation.

Perhaps the most effective federal agency is the General Accounting Office (GAO). It scrutinizes the expenses of other government departments and saves the taxpayers over $300 million each year by eliminating the unnecessary expenditures it uncovers. Although it has retained more independence than other federal regulatory bodies, its scope of supervision is limited, preventing it from challenging many other instances of abuses and waste.

Citizen Groups

Where "People Power" has been most evident in recent years is in the actions of organized citizen groups. Most effective have been those organized by consumer advocate Ralph Nader and John W. Gardner, former Secretary of Health, Education, and Welfare (HEW).

Consumer Advocacy

Nader quickly emerged as a powerful national spokesperson in the late 1960s with his book, *Unsafe at Any Speed,* in which he accused General Motors of manufacturing a dangerous car—the Chevrolet Corvair—ignoring public safety in pursuit of profits.[65] Nader subsequently won $280,000 in damages against General Motors when it hired private investigators in an attempt to discredit him. With that money and other funds, Nader formed various citizen watchdog groups—Nader's Raiders, the Center for Auto Safety, the Center for the Study of Responsive Law, and the Public Interest Research Group. His investigations uncovered many abuses, prompted corrective legislation, and forced corporations to be more responsive to the public interest.

Nader's Raiders exposed extensive inefficiency and ineffectiveness at the FTC, which brought about a thorough reorganization of that agency. Other investigations resulted in the following legislation: the National Traffic and Vehicle Safety Act of 1966 (which established the Highway Traffic Safety Administration), the Wholesome Meat Act of 1967, the Gas Pipeline Safety Act of 1968, the Radiation Control for Health and Safety Act of 1968, the Coal Mine Health and Safety Act of 1969, and the Comprehensive Occupational Safety and Health Act of 1970. Nader remains an activist for the public today, providing a spectacular example of how even one dedicated person can make a difference.

Political Advocacy

John Gardner formed Common Cause, an important citizen group comprised of over 300,000 dues-paying members. This middle-class activist group focuses on government corruption and waste. It too has been credited with legislative changes, particularly election financing. One major mission of this movement is to keep pressure on elected officials to serve the public interest through continual exposure of the lobbying activities of special interest groups upon them.

Other smaller citizen groups have had some notable successes also. Most often their technique has been a class-action suit. This legal approach enables a citizen group to sue on behalf of all affected parties, who individually could not afford the high legal costs and would be unlikely to take on the government or big business. If the court decides in favor of the plaintiff, the people all benefit. Sometimes companies voluntarily recall unsafe or defective products to avoid court costs and unfavorable publicity. State government actions contrary to federal law or local assistance

Whether in Philadelphia—as pictured here—or elsewhere, more and more organized citizen groups are challenging public utilities and major corporations, demanding accountability to the public. These groups have often been successful in their efforts.

cutbacks without legislative approval have also been successfully challenged by this method.

The continued effectiveness of class-action suits has been severely curtailed, since the U.S. Supreme Court ruled each injured party represented must be individually named when the suit is filed. Since these suits involve tens and hundreds of thousands of people, usually identified through company warranty records or government records, the likelihood of securing this information from them so they can be defendants in a class-action suit is rather remote.

THE FUTURE

Of all the possible social changes within the next 40 years, perhaps our freedom of choice in political leadership and economic activity is of most concern. With the current trend of increasing concentrations of economic and political power, the danger of the dominance of the few over the many is quite clear. Democracy and freedom are fragile realities, and every generation has to redefine them and make tough choices to keep them. Nothing is inevitable; our children can live in a better or worse society depending upon the choices we make. Let's take a look at the two extreme possibilities.

Pessimistic Scenario

By 2025 voter apathy, evident even in the late twentieth century, had become so widespread that hardly anyone bothered to vote anymore. Candidates were selected by a few, elected by a few, and primarily represented the interests of those few. A wealthy elite and powerful corporate interests so thoroughly dominated the political decision-making process that most individuals saw no purpose in their own involvement. Instead, most of the general public allowed themselves to be led by others and passively accepted the political actions and interpretations given them by the corporate media.

Big corporations had become even bigger to compete against their foreign counterparts all over the globe. Continued mergers and takeovers, combined with manufacturing streamlining, meant fewer competing companies producing the same product. These oligopolies were thus able to set prices, control demand, and reap huge profits. Extensive corporate influence over government officials, virtually unchallenged because of public indifference and unawareness, had resulted in reduced government regulations and restrictions, as well as less corporate accountability for the safety and quality of its products.

The government-corporate alliance had taken one ominous direction: the marriage of government computers and industry data banks. Through massive data banks and instant retrieval systems, both government and corporations kept tabs on nearly every aspect of people's lives: their education, religion, family, job, credit, medical history, organizational activities, and voting record. With surveillance technology in place, people feared doing anything which might jeopardize their situation, and so they refrained from any challenges to or criticisms of the status quo.

Actually, any challenges to the corporate state were rather unlikely. The rich and powerful were too firmly in control, and the generally good living standards were not fertile grounds for creating social unrest. Corporate socialization of employee attitudes and behavior were augmented by continual opinion shaping through the media. People defined their world as quite good, not realizing their liberty was far less than that of their grandparents in the late twentieth century.

Optimistic Scenario

Primitive two-way television communication experiments in the 1970s in Washington state and in Columbus, Ohio, had led to active participant democracy by 2025.[66] *Teledemocracy*—the term for electronically aided, rapid, two-way political communication—involved people directly in government. Through use of a television set and attached small box with buttons to press as directed, people became educated on issues, facilitated discussion of important decisions, registered instantaneous polls, and voted directly on public policy. A purer democracy now existed, since real power was diffused and decentralized, resting in the will of the public itself. People were eager to get involved in politics, knowing their opinions were valued and seeing how the decisions directly affected their lives.

With a computer in every household, campaign costs had tumbled, making candidates far less dependent upon financing from special interest groups. Through computers people had access to campaign headquarters to get printouts about the candidates and positions on issues. Use of television campaigning was more widespread, particularly "narrowcasting"—the use of cable television to reach special audiences, such as a message in Spanish over a cable station serving an Hispanic audience. People now cast ballots by means of their home computer for local, state, and national elections. Initiatives and public referendums were more common, including national issues such as gun control and nuclear freeze.

Corporations were bigger than in the previous century; a large federal bureaucracy still existed also. Both, however, were far more accountable to the public than in earlier decades. It all had to do with the return of power to the people through teledemocracy and televoting. People had redefined their roles in the society. Having gained control of their political system through direct power, people looked to the economic system as their concern as well, and insisted their elected representatives be active in protecting the public interest. Even multinational corporations fell under closer scrutiny, as tighter global interdependence, higher expectations in the more recently developed nations, and advances in communications technology prompted international coordination. Once the populace became linked together through computer technology, public opinion became the law of the land.

Companies and politicians still worked hard to promote favorable images through the media and influence public opinion about products and performance. Some people were swayed by these efforts, of course, but most were too enlightened and active in the decision process to be naive or gullible. They insisted upon full disclosure, responsible leadership, and proven excellence. A value orientation toward cooperation, public trust, mutual gain, and a recognition of the power vested in the people had pervaded both business and government. The electronic information age had packaged the spirit of ancient Athens and old New England town meetings into a bright national reality.

SUMMARY

1. One result of the emergence of corporate giants is oligopolies, the control of entire markets by a few producers. With little competition, these companies can set artificially inflated prices.

2. The largest 200 companies control 60 percent of this nation's assets and produce 44 percent of all manufactured products. Less than 1 percent of the population controls most of the nation's corporations and one-fourth of the nation's wealth.

3. Another threat to the free enterprise system is the shared decision network through interlocking directorates. Friendly and hostile takeovers have created immensely powerful conglomerates, whose anonymous technocrats provide input and direction which affect national policy.

4. Fragmentation of tasks and responsibility in the pursuit of corporate profits enables individuals to rationalize their morality into role requirements. Thus price-fixing, consumer manipulation, and selling unsafe products all become personally blameless activities.

5. Government has grown to huge proportions also, and in many ways has forged a partnership with big business. Three significant illustrations of this alliance are the campaign contributions of corporate PACs, the cozy relationship of the military-industrial complex, and the revolving door of executive position interchange between government/military and industry.

6. Multinational corporations presently have little regulation but significant impact on national economies. Many have annual sales exceeding most nations' gross national product, and abuses of power (bribery, kickbacks, interference in internal politics) have occurred. Though some countries encourage foreign investment, studies show the economic inequality in those countries usually worsens afterward.

7. Some believe America's power structure consists of a power elite, who share similar backgrounds and dominate corporate and government executive positions. Pluralists maintain interest groups both initiate and block various measures, through continually changing alignments which prevent any permanent power base from dominating.

8. People often blame politicians and business executives, not the system, for many of our social problems. Functionalists suggest rapid societal changes and growth have thrown the system out of balance, politically and economically. Conflict theorists point to worker exploitation, corporate domination, and political power under the control of the economic elite as causes of our social problems. Interactionists emphasize the system's impact upon people's attitudes, noting evidence of cynicism, fatalism, and rationalized compliance.

9. Though regulatory agencies should protect the public interest, too often industry "captures" them and they lose their independence and effectiveness. Citizen groups, most notably those of Ralph Nader and John Gardner (Common Cause), have been successful advocates for the public welfare.

SUGESTED READINGS

Clinard, Marshall B., and Peter C. Yeager. *Corporate Crime*. New York: Free Press, 1980. A thorough analysis of corporate wrongdoing of all kinds, including defective products, tax evasion, unsafe working conditions, and white-collar crime.

Domhoff, G. William. *The Higher Circles*. New York: Vintage Books, 1971. An extension of earlier writings, this book examines the nature of the upper class, their involvement in the government process, and critiques pluralist and ultraconservative views.

Friedman, Milton, and Rose Friedman. *Free to Choose*. New York: Avon, 1981. A long-time best seller now in paperback, these economists offer a well-written endorsement of the free enterprise system.

Nader, Ralph, Mark Green, and Joel Seligman. *Taming the Giant Corporation*. New York: Norton, 1976. A critical, consumer-advocate analysis of the functioning of modern corporations, their abuse of power, and suggestions for their social control.

Orum, Anthony M. *Introduction to Political Sociology*. Englewood Cliffs, N.J.: Prentice-Hall, 1978. An excellent, concise sociological overview of politics and political institutions, highlighting the work of Karl Marx, Talcott Parsons, and Max Weber.

Sampson, Anthony. *The Sovereign State of ITT*. Greenwich, Conn.: Fawcett Books, 1978. An intriguing, carefully documented exposé of International Telephone and Telegraph's abuse of power, with fine analysis of the beneficial and harmful potentials of multinational corporations.

Silk, Leonard, and Mark Silk. *The American Establishment*. New York: Basic Books, 1980. A lively, sociohistorical analysis, supported by powerful anecdotes, of the people, ideas, and institutions that shape America's destiny.

Vernon, Raymond. *Storm over the Multinationals: The Real Issues*. Cambridge, Mass.: MIT Press, 1973. A clear and useful examination of the development of multinational corporations and their impact, both good and bad upon other nations.

GLOSSARY

Conglomerate A large corporation owning businesses in greatly diversified fields.

Cost overruns Expenditures allowed because of unforeseen production costs incurred in a multiyear project.

Interlocking directorate Occurs when executives or directors from one corporation sit on the board of directors of another corporation.

Military-industrial complex Term coined by President Eisenhower to describe military establishment and private firms doing business with it.

Multinationals Large corporations operating across national boundaries, with plants and investments in many countries.

Oligopoly When a few producers dominate an entire industry and thus control pricing in that market.

Political action committee (PAC) A political action committee formed by any organization to raise funds for political candidates.

Power elite Assertion by conflict theorists of the existence of a coalition of high-ranking leaders with similar backgrounds and interests.

Revolving door The continual interchange of administrative personnel between corporations and the government/military.

Technocrats Those with technical expertise providing the input and direction for corporate decisions affecting national policy and the quality of life.

Veto groups Concept of special interest groups continually shifting alignments and thus the balance of power.

Voter elite Tendency of voters to be mostly middle- and high-income individuals.

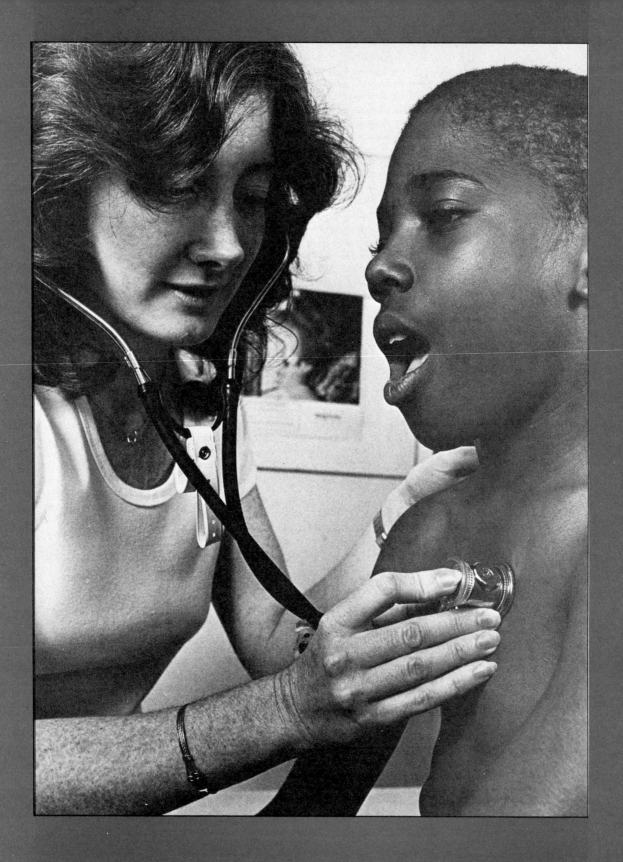

FACTS ABOUT HEALTH CARE

The U.S. infant mortality rate ranks eighteenth worldwide today compared to fifth in 1950.

Active U.S. physicians increased from 279,000 in 1970 to 420,000 in 1980.

The number of operations increased by 23 percent in the 1970s, although the nation's population grew by only 5 percent.

Hospital costs have been doubling every 5 years, far greater than the nation's inflation rate.

Physician-caused deaths number about 150,000 annually.

Almost 7 million people receive mental health patient care each year.

14
HEALTH CARE

Good health is one of our more prized personal possessions, something very closely associated with our satisfaction with life.[1] Such health is easy to take for granted, especially when you are young and feel the world lies before you. Only when our health is threatened or lost do we recognize how important it is. Worry, fear, depression, torment, disability, loss of self-sufficiency, and heavy financial burden can then dominate and change the focus of our daily lives.

Health and sickness are, however, much more than personal, physiological, or psychological factors. Sociocultural factors can be the cause of many health problems. For example, the United States has few people dying from such contagious diseases as diphtheria, typhoid, cholera, tuberculosis, influenza, and pneumonia compared to preindustrial societies in other parts of the world today. However, our lifestyle—alcoholic drinking, smoking, polluted air and water, food additives, fatty foods, little exercise, recreational sex—cause other health problems such as heart disease, cancer, and herpes, not as common in preindustrial societies. Bad health is also a matter of societal concern because it means lost worker productivity, the social waste of children denied the right to become contributing adults to society, the cost of institutional care for the elderly and mentally ill, and the social commitment to provide everyone, regardless of income, with adequate medical care to prevent as much pain and suffering as possible.

Health care in the United States is one of many paradoxes. This nation spends more money on health care than any other country in the world. Our expenditure of $362.3 billion in 1983 constituted 10.5 percent of the Gross National Product (GNP), almost $150 billion more than for defense.[2] Yet we are the only industrialized society today without a national health insurance program or a health-system designed to make health care available to all. Despite our vast expenditures, health care services are unequally distributed, with poor quality care or none at all available to rural and small town America and to the urban poor. Despite our vast expenditures, we now rank eighteenth in our infant mortality rate compared to 1950 when we ranked 5th.[3] Male life expectancy in the United States is sixteenth worldwide, and female life expectancy in the United States ranks eighth.

How did we reach this situation? Why are health costs soaring faster than any other part of the economy? Why do Americans fare more poorly than many other peoples in adequate health care and life expectancy? Why do we pay more but get less? Why are we unable to provide everyone with equal health care?

PHYSICAL HEALTH

Certainly as a society we have come a long way in our health achievements. Americans born in 1776 had a life expectancy of 35 years compared to the 73 years of today's newborn child. We have conquered most contagious diseases that had previously claimed many lives—smallpox, diphtheria, whooping cough, typhoid, cholera, scarlet fever, and polio. Yet medical care had far less to do with these dramatic health gains than did scientific discoveries and the improvement of living conditions (better nutrition, sanitation, education, and economic well-being).[4] Still, our technological and scientific advances have enabled us to save a great many lives, reduce pain and suffering, and allow people to live normal lives longer. Our advances, though, have also created problems as they reshaped our values and attitudes, the structure of the health-care system, and the quality of personal care.

The Medicalization of Life

As medical science advanced in the twentieth century, personalized medical care declined. The nostalgic and sentimental image of the old-fashioned family doctor who made house calls and maintained a personal interest in the well-being of patients dates from a period when specialization in medicine was rather limited.[5] Beginning in the early twentieth century, but accelerating dramatically after World War II due to the massive growth of medical knowledge and technological capabilities, medical specialization became the norm. Keeping abreast of all developments in all areas of human illness was simply unrealistic. The general practitioner lost prestige and popularity; new medical school graduates opted more and more for a specialization. To illustrate, in 1923 only 11 percent of all U.S. physicians were specialists compared to 72 percent today. Not included as specialists are primary-care physicians, such as general practitioners, pediatricians, and internists. Actually, only 14 percent of all doctors are general practitioners, compared to 30 percent in 1960.[6]

Changes in the Health Care System

At first the advent of specialized medicine spurred a greater tendency toward hospital care and treatment rather than home care and doctor's visits. Since specialized medicine also necessitates advanced training and scientific expertise, medical schools and research-oriented medical centers or major teaching hospitals grew into medical empires. Bolstered by extensive federal funding but with little public accountability, they achieved many medical breakthroughs, trained a new medical elite, and replaced the small, independent hospitals as the primary medical care unit.

Medical Businesses
This growth of large institutional medical care and training spawned hundreds of corporations profiting from the medical business. Mostly they sell diagnostic and therapeutic equipment to the hospitals, whose staff is fascinated by the latest gadgetry. The result is higher overhead costs, sometimes from the acquisition of equipment whose limited use does not justify its purchase, as well as increased personnel costs for technicians and support staff.

Patient Care
One significant change has been that the sick rarely have a doctor come to them. Instead they travel to laboratories for tests, to doctors' offices for examination, and to clinics or hospitals for treatment. Because health care is so fragmented due to specialization, people frequently must see several physicians for the same health problem, thus increasing their medical bills. Such an arrangement has served to depersonalize the practice of medicine, with physicians viewing patients as objects instead of human beings and with patients seldom feeling a close rapport with their doctors.

Dominance of Modern Medicine

People believe in the power of medicine and demand more from it than earlier generations. While one's grandparents and those before them looked upon death as something natural and inevitable, today many tend to think death can be controlled. We expect the impossible, and if a doctor loses a patient, for many the first thought is to charge medical malpractice. Often physicians employ heroic methods to prolong life, at considerable expense, even though no hope of recovery exists.

Overmedicalization

What has happened in America, critics maintain, is the **overmedicalization** of life—the medical establishment exercising too much control over people's lives and society becoming much too dependent on medical care. Ivan Illich, one of the harsher critics, claims we are "overmedicalized" in that we have been stripped of our rights regarding sickness and death.[7] The medical profession has achieved a "mystification" of knowledge and expertise beyond the average person's grasp; now physicians exclusively determine what constitutes sickness, what medicines to use, when to admit someone to the hospital and when to discharge them. An outgrowth of this is that expensive institutional care has replaced personalized home care. Having babies at home, convalescing there from a serious illness, or dying at home in the warmth and comfort of one's home is no longer considered proper by most people.

Medicine can do relatively little about the major causes of death today. Our

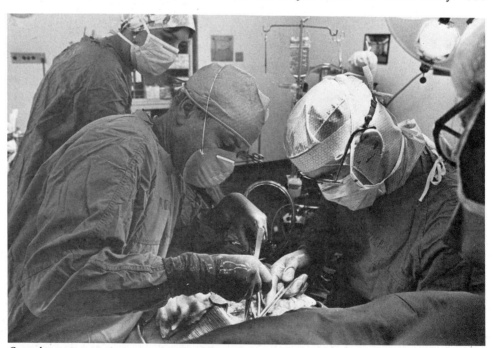

Open heart surgery is a recent medical breakthrough allowing prolonged life for thousands of Americans. Yet the excess number of U.S. surgeons has meant other unnecessary operations also take place, resulting in perhaps 10,000 deaths annually.

chronological age, life-style, genetic weaknesses, or environmental pollutants bring about accidents, arteriosclerosis, cancer, cirrhosis of the liver, diabetes, or heart attacks and strokes. Little benefit comes to these patients from the elaborate and expensive treatments given in the hospital. Clinical medicine has been very effective in, say, polio, pneumonia, and venereal disease. Advances in microsurgery allowing severed limbs to be restored, or in heart surgery, enabling infants to live normal lives or adults to live longer, active lives are but two examples of medical progress. Yet some people believe that we have paid a heavy price for the miraculous achievements.

> Medicine undermines health not only through direct aggression against individuals but also through the impact of its organization on the total milieu. . . . It obtains when medical bureaucracy creates ill-health by increasing stress, by multiplying disabling dependence, by generating new painful needs, by lowering the levels of tolerance for discomfort or pain, by reducing the leeway that people are wont to concede to an individual when he suffers, and by abolishing even the right to self-care. [It] is at work when health care is turned into a standardized item, a staple; when all suffering is "hospitalized" and homes become inhospitable to birth, sickness, and death; when the language in which people could experience their bodies is turned into bureaucratic gobbledegook; or when suffering, mourning, and healing outside the patient role are labeled a form of deviance.[8]

The Social Organization of Health Care

Among the positive indicators of American health care is the reduction of our doctor-to-patient ratio, with the number of professionally active physicians now exceeding 420,000 from approximately 279,000 in 1970;[9] the countertrend against fragmentation of care by the continuing growth of integrated medical group practices instead of solo practice; and the impressive equipment and facilities at most of the nation's 6,100 general hospitals, among the most modern in the world. Although we rank fairly high globally in our health standards, problems remain in the high cost and access to medical care, and inequalities in the quality of that care. To understand more fully why these problems exist, we need to examine the structure of the American-care system.

The AMA and the Business of Medicine

In the late nineteenth century, the American Medical Association (AMA) began a successful campaign to upgrade the profession by having state legislatures require licensing procedures and by forcing poor quality medical schools out of business. It then worked to curtail admissions and improve the standards of medical training. A substantial increase in the physician-to-patient ratio then followed until it stabilized in the late 1940s. Arguing that an increase in the quantity of doctors would reduce the quality, the AMA resisted efforts to increase the number of doctors despite increased demands.

Not until the 1960s did the AMA admit to a doctors shortage and take a more flexible position.[10] Even then the supply continued to lag so behind demand that by the 1970s, graduates of foreign medical schools—both immigrants and Americans unable to get accepted to American medical schools—constituted one-fourth of all newly licensed physicians each year.[11] By 1980, however, the number of medical schools had grown from 101 in 1970 to 126, and the number of graduates had nearly doubled, from 8,387 in 1970 to 15,135 in 1980.[12] Consequently the number of active physicians has grown and promises to reduce the doctor-patient ratio still further (see Figure 14.1).

Uneven Health-Care Delivery Systems

While the supply of physicians may have improved, their availability to all people fluctuates by region and type of locale. An oversupply of doctors exists in suburbs and affluent urban neighborhoods, particularly those near teaching and research-oriented hospitals (see Table 14.1). Few doctors locate in low-income neighborhoods or rural communities. Estimates place the number of doctors per person in metropolitan counties at triple that in rural counties.[13] The ranking of the United States below other countries in infant mortality rate and life expectancy is partly due to this inequity of medical care access.

Several socioeconomic factors influence this uneven distribution of physicians. As educated, upper-middle-class professionals, physicians are no different from others in comparable occupations in preferring life-style, cultural, and recreational opportunities available in metropolitan areas. Small town and rural America cannot provide the expensive, sophisticated equipment and technical support personnel that today's physicians have come to depend upon; and not enough patients exist there to justify these high capital costs. Finally, as we shall discuss more fully in the next section, physicians can earn much greater incomes in affluent, more densely populated areas than in poor and/or more sparsely inhabited regions.

FIGURE 14.1   Doctors in Active Practice
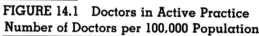
Number of Doctors per 100,000 Population

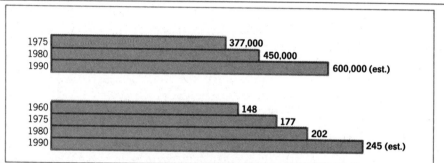

SOURCE: Congress of the United States, Office of Technology Assessment, *Forecast of Physician Supply and Requirements* (Washington, D.C.: U.S. Government Printing Office, 1980), p. 22.

**TABLE 14.1   U.S. Active Health Personnel by Geographic Region[a]
Number per 100,000 in 1980**

	Number	U.S.	Northeast	North Central	South	West
Physicians	422,310	191.4	233.6	175.0	163.7	212.3
M.D.s	405,800	183.9	224.9	162.5	159.4	208.0
D.O.s	16,510	7.5	8.7	12.5	4.3	4.3
Dentists	121,240	54.9	65.2	53.1	44.4	63.7
Optometrists	22,330	10.1	10.2	11.2	8.0	12.3
Pharmacists	142,780	64.7	60.8	67.7	65.0	64.6
Podiatrists	8,880	4.0	6.3	3.9	2.5	4.1
Registered nurses	1,164,000	520.1	620.3	547.4	423.8	529.7
Veterinarians	36,000	16.3	10.8	19.9	16.0	18.5

[a] Excludes federal service and those in U.S. possessions. Ratios for physicians and dentists based on civilian population; other ratios based on resident population.
SOURCE: Division of Health Professions Analysis, Bureau of Health Professions, *Supply and Characteristics of Selected Health Personnel,* DHHS Pub. No. (HRA) 81–20 (Hyattsville, Md.: Health Resources Administration, June 1981).

Since few doctors locate their offices in low-income neighborhoods, patients such as these must go to a hospital clinic to see a physician. There they often find longer waiting times and less personalized care than others do who see doctors in private practice.

Health Care for Profit

Despite its professed ideals about serving humanity, the health-care system is a business designed to make profits. As recently as 1968, the president of the AMA publicly argued that health care should be available only to those able to pay.

The AMA still forbids doctors to advertise, and a highly effective informal network utilizes peer pressure to keep fees comparable among physicians. This price-fixing monopoly prevents any economic competition. In addition, doctors are relatively unconcerned about their prices affecting patients because of third-party payments from insurance companies or the government. Even then, the public still pays more through higher taxes and insurance premiums.

Private medical practice is the most lucrative small business in the country, with the average physician earning five times as much as the average American wage earner. In 1982, a family physician's median net income was $84,185, with surgeons having a median income of $141,600.[14] The argument usually given for high doctors' fees is that they invest more time and money in their training than other professionals, work longer hours, and have heavy expenses, including malpractice insurance. Two economists, Roger Feldman and Richard Scheffler, determined that physicians earned a 22 percent return on their investment in 1970, compared to 10 or 11 percent in other professions; since then, the figure has fallen only slightly.[15]

Surgeons earn their incomes by performing surgery; the more they operate, the more they make. With twice as many surgeons per capita as in Britain, the United States also has twice as many operations per capita. How many are necessary? The U.S. population grew by 5 percent in the 1970s, but the number of operations increased 23 percent in the same period.[16] Although obstetricians delivered twice as many babies in 1965 than in 1979, they delivered three times more by cesarian in 1979 than in 1965.[17] One-sixth of all U.S. births are now by cesarian section, for which the obstetrician receives a higher fee than for a natural childbirth.

According to a 1975 study of the American College of Surgeons, we have an excess of 20,000 surgeons. By 1979, the number of hysterectomies performed had reached 639,000, cesarian deliveries 599,000, tonsillectomies 501,000, and cardiac bypass operations 114,000.[18] Several studies have found the number of these operations, including appendectomies, that were unnecessary range from 15 to 30 percent.[19] And, these operations are not without risk: as many as 10,000 Americans die each year from unnecessary surgery (see Figure 14.2). As two medical researchers cynically observed, "The 1970s and 1980s will be remembered as the decades when the medical profession trained so many surgeons that they ran out of patients who needed surgery and began to do it on those who didn't."[20]

The Hospital Industry

Hospitals are also often private, profit-making concerns. Within them, doctors have enormous power—determining a patient's length of stay, deciding what tests to administer and what drugs to prescribe. As much as 40 percent of all hospital stays have been found to be unnecessary.[21] However, the extended stay increases a hospital's income, as well as providing a significant portion of doctors' incomes.

FIGURE 14.2 Nurses' Opinions About Surgery

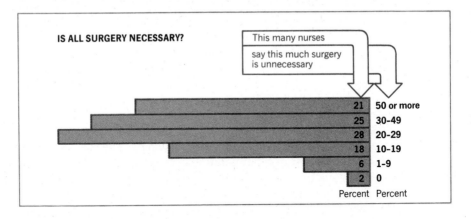

SOURCE: *RN Magazine.*

Hospitals were once almost all locally controlled, nonprofit places of refuge for the sick and dying, yet that has been changing in the past 15 years and shows indications of accelerating. Today one out of five hospitals is owned by a profit-making chain. One out of three hospital beds belongs to a chain, with one out of eight to a for-profit chain.[22] Almost 40 percent of all hospitals are linked by multihospital systems; this pattern is expected to reach 60 percent by 1990.[23] The growth of multihospital systems run by powerful corporate management suggests loss of control by local authorities and thus even more impersonal medical care.

In 1982, investor-owned hospitals reaped $11.2 billion in revenues and $520 million in profits. The five largest are the Hospital Corporation of America, Humana, American Medical International, National Medical Enterprises, and Lifemark. Hospital Corporation of America, called the "McDonald's of the Hospital Business," owns 367 facilities utilizing 40,000 physicians who treat 7.5 million patients daily. It was founded in 1968 by two physicians and Jack Massy, one of the founders of Kentucky Fried Chicken. These investor-owned institutions frequently use extensive marketing techniques—birthday parties for babies born in the hospital, and flying airplane-pulled banners over football stadiums.

A Blank Check

No evidence indicates the profit-making chains are any more efficient than nonprofit hospitals, but they are very efficient in securing maximum funds from insurance and government-supported medical protection plans.[24] Nonprofit hospitals also utilize reimbursement programs heavily to meet their operating expenses. Since hospitals and doctors are paid for whatever they do, regardless of whether the care actually benefits the patient, the temptation is strong to use every test, technique, or treatment available. As much as 30 percent of all such medical treatment is probably unnecessary.[25]

Unlike most business ventures based on supply and demand, health service providers have almost total control. People have medical care because of need, not choice. Hospitals and doctors set the price, and people have no alternative but to pay—either directly or through public and private insurance programs. Given in essence a blank check or guaranteed payment whatever the cost, hospitals have had little incentive until now to hold down costs. A significant new development, to be discussed shortly under Medicare, promises to change such cost matters significantly.

Increased Hospital Expenses

Hospital costs have risen about 14 percent every year since 1970, a far greater pace than the inflationary rise in the cost of living.[26] The reasons for this rise being more rapid than the cost of other goods and services are not just the acquisition of needed expensive equipment and hospital workers' higher wages. Part of the answer also lies in wasteful expenditures, which place a heavy financial burden on hospitals. Roughly a third of increased hospital costs are attributed to medical technology.[27]

Hospitals compete with each other over which has the most prestigious or fashionable, high-cost equipment. Acquiring some of this expensive, though perhaps seldom used equipment adds to a hospital's fixed operating expenses which is passed along in part to all patients. For example, nuclear-magnetic resonance (NMR) is the latest "prestige" technique, capable of detecting tumors in the brain, lungs, respiratory

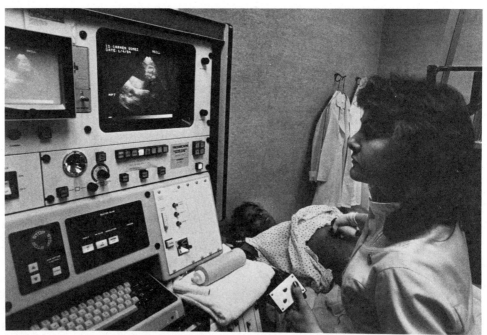

Using an ultrasound machine, a medical technician examines the size and position of the baby growing within the mother's womb. Expensive equipment, sometimes seldom used, increases a hospital's fixed operating expenses, which are then passed on to all patients.

tract, and liver nonfindable even by such sophisticated means as computerized axial tomography (CAT scans).[28] While NMR devices can be an immense help in certain cases, their $2 million apiece price tag suggests a multihospital shared purchase and utilization might be a cost-saving approach rather than individual hospitals raising their status by buying their own.

To understand fully how these capital expenditures accelerate hospital costs, realize that hospitals are seldom filled to capacity. When hospitals operate below capacity, the cost per patient increases since fewer persons are helping pay fixed operating expenses. One consequence is for people to be hospitalized unnecessarily because hospitals need income-producing patients. Moreover, since hospitalization plans reimburse hospitals on a flat daily fee for patient care, a strong incentive develops to keep patients in the hospital for processing, diagnostic tests, surgery, and postoperative care. But after that, patients require less care and therefore create less expense to the hospital. By keeping the patient a little longer, hospitals realize greater net income.

Doctors and Nurses

Increased impersonal treatment by specialists instead of family doctors, together with soaring health costs and occasional reports of medical incompetence, unnecessary surgery, or fraud, have combined to lessen the public esteem for doctors. One public opinion poll, for example, noted a decline from 73 percent in 1966 to 43 percent in 1977 of those expressing a "great deal" of confidence in the medical profession.[29] Part of the attitude shift may be a reaction to the increase of foreign-trained doctors, from 1970 to 1979 accounting for one-fifth of the annual active physician supply.[30]

Nurses remain in critically short supply, particularly in the sunbelt. The American Hospital Association estimates there are 100,000 unfilled nursing positions in American hospitals. The Bureau of Labor Statistics projects a need for 85,000 new nurses each year through 1990, but the number of nursing graduates has been steadily declining for years. Besides more attractive career opportunities in other fields, nurses blame lack of autonomy, physicians' disrespect, low salaries, and limited opportunities for advancement. The shortage also creates heavier work loads, leaving nurses unable to be as caring or as careful as they want and were trained to be.[31]

The Ideal and the Real

Many Americans have a romanticized vision of the concerned family physician. This image, often stemming from past personal recollections, is fostered by the media through books, films, and television. The idealized doctor—pictured on such old shows (now in reruns) as *Gunsmoke, Little House on the Prairie, Marcus Welby,* and *Dr. Kildare*—is someone today's physician cannot match. Family medicine is now an accepted specialty in medical schools, but most physicians are sophisticated medical specialists who, while highly skilled technicians, are nonetheless impersonal professionals.

A great many of this nation's physicians, both male and female, are dedicated professionals with rigorously high standards. Some are less idealistic, however, and

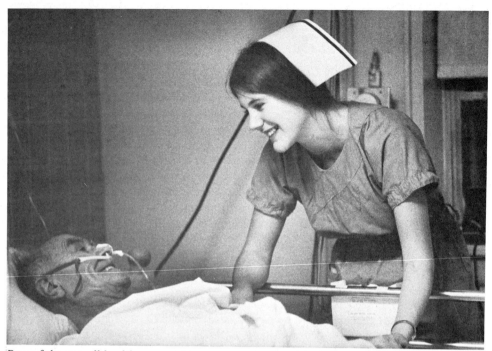

Part of the overall health-care problem rests upon the critical shortage of nurses, a situation worsening each year. With so many other career opportunities now open to women, many far more rewarding in income and responsibility, fewer women now choose nursing.

the lure of big money is more attractive. Sociologist Howard Becker headed a team of investigators who examined the impact of the socialization process in medical school upon the students.[32] They found that the initial idealism of beginning med school students often modifies into pragmatic career and achievement goals, while some become rather cynical, seeing medicine simply as a vehicle to high social status and affluence. The public's loss of confidence in physicians rests heavily upon their role in the greater cost–lesser quality care so many experience.

Malpractice

Perhaps nowhere is the alienation between doctor and patient as evident as in the rising number of **malpractice** suits. They have spiraled to such an extent, that one researcher found an intensifying cycle of mutual distrust. Doctors tend to look upon all patients as potential litigants; patients see the doctors as potential threats to their well-being.[33] Including out-of-court settlements, plaintiffs have won almost 80 percent of the time, though the amount is $5,000 or less about half the time. If the case goes to court, the doctors win about three-fourths of the time.

High legal costs, as well as the costs of settlements, have increased premiums for malpractice insurance, which doctors pass on to their patients, thereby escalating health costs. Also, doctors now practice "defensive medicine."

> . . . Fear of malpractice litigation has forced individual physicians to rely more on standard testing procedures than on individual judgment. . . . Since nonmedical considerations enter the decision process, that is, considerations of lawsuits and what other physicians are doing, certain actions may be legally and economically rational, but medically irrational . . . [on the hazard of extra tests] It is estimated that 30 percent of X-rays are unnecessary, and the excessive radiation may account for 1,000 cancer deaths annually.[34]

What about incompetence as a cause of malpractice? The American Association of Trial Lawyers, with an obvious vested interest, maintains only actual malpractice causes malpractice suits, while the AMA argues many suits, based upon unrealistic expectations of a full cure for every treatment, are unreasonable.[35] Doctors are human; and they do make mistakes occasionally. Some are the result of failure to maintain knowledge of current medical techniques or of doctors who have received inferior training at dubious foreign medical schools, or simply human error. At most, perhaps 5 percent of all doctors are incompetent.[36] Still, that is a large number, and the self-policing actions of the AMA have not been very effective. For example, at Yale–New Haven Hospital, a highly respected teaching hospital, a study found that 20 percent of the patients were injured by their medical treatment.[37] The national yearly number of physician-caused deaths has been estimated at 150,000.[38] So, while most doctors are highly skilled and competent, a suspicious public increasingly suspects the worst and files malpractice suits with greater frequency.

Medical Insurance

Almost all medical bills were paid directly to doctors and hospitals until the Great Depression made people unable to pay. Thereafter medical insurance programs emerged, particularly when labor unions successfully negotiated their inclusion as a fringe benefit during the 1940s and 1950s. However, 45 million Americans today—the poor, many rural residents, nonunion or seasonal workers, for example—have little or no health coverage.[39] Additionally, millions of workers have only medical insurance as long as they are working; if they are fired or laid off—a harsh reality for many during the recession of 1981–1982—they and their families lose their medical coverage. Even for the 80 percent of the population covered by health insurance, they still had to pay one-third of their medical costs out-of-pocket because of deductibles on their coverage or services not covered (e.g., office visits, routine examinations, inoculations).

The "Blues"

When the Great Depression of the 1930s created widespread destitution, people obviously could not pay their hospital bills. To protect themselves against this loss of income in future years, the hospitals created Blue Cross, a nonprofit organization, to collect individual insurance premiums to pay for eventual hospitalization expenses, at least a substantial portion of them. Later came Blue Shield to pay medical and surgical doctors' fees incurred in hospitals. Both "Blues" programs have state or regional executive boards dominated by hospital doctors and other medical professionals. Today the national network of Blue Cross and Blue Shield plans, intimately linked with the hospitals, provides about 35 percent of the private patient coverage.[40]

Since the AMA-sponsored Blue Cross and Blue Shield plans have always been hospital oriented, they tend to encourage waste and inefficiency. They offer little or no reimbursement for less costly nonhospital expenses but a much higher percentage for hospital expenses, even for the same procedures. For example, kidney dialysis costs $28,000 annually per patient in a hospital, but half that amount at home. Because hospital plans will reimburse up to 80 percent for hospital treatment, however, the percentage of patients treated in their homes has dropped from 40 percent in 1972 to 10 percent today.[41]

Medicare and Medicaid

Despite strenuous lobbying by the AMA, Congress created, as part of its War on Poverty, the **Medicare** and **Medicaid** health assistance programs. Medicare is funded from federal and social security taxes, and pays for some medical services for people over 65. Medicaid is funded from federal and state taxes, and assists the poor, blind, and disabled. Because Medicaid is administered by the states, its eligibility requirements and number of benefits vary considerably from state to state. Medicare, on the other hand, is fairly uniform throughout the country. However, both require patients to pay part of the initial treatment costs and have a coinsurance provision, requiring patient payment of 20 percent of all additional costs.

These well-intended programs of medical payment assistance to the elderly and the poor created a whole new social problem themselves. When the AMA realized it could not prevent passage of Medicare and Medicaid, it changed tactics to ensure the fees for services rendered through the programs would be set by the doctors and hospitals. Within 2 years, these programs had raised physicians' income an average of $7,000, even though virtually no increase of health care had occurred.[42] Not surprisingly, the attitude of physicians changed from only 38 percent in favor of the legislation at the time of its passage to 92 percent in favor by 1970.[43]

With little accountability or control, just unchallenged reimbursement, doctors and hospitals had no incentive to keep costs down; and so the costs skyrocketed. "Medicaid Mills" came into existence—storefront clinics in low-income neighborhoods indiscriminately giving unnecessary tests and treatment to as many people as possible to gain six-figure incomes for the owners. Besides such fraudulent abuse, however, legitimate medical establishments used Medicare and Medicaid to gather whatever income they could; the impact on inflation was extensive, as health costs rose from $41.7 billion in 1965 (the year before Medicare and Medicaid began) to over 362 billion in 1983 (see Figure 14.3).

Beginning in October 1983 and phased in over a 3-year period, Medicare pays for the elderly at predetermined rates for 467 types of medical problems based on severity of illness, type of hospital, and geographic region. The government—not the doctors or hospitals—decides in advance how much it will pay. Hospitals exceeding their dollar limit must cover the extra expenses themselves, but hospitals with lower charges can pocket the difference—an incentive to reduce costs. Unable to bill patients for nonreimbursed charges and no longer paid for itemized daily charges,

FIGURE 14.3 U.S. Health Costs in Billions of Dollars

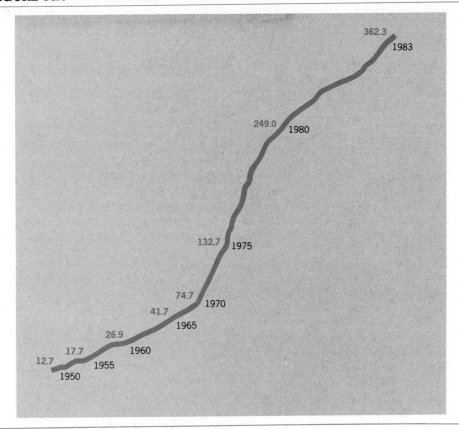

SOURCE: Health Care Financing Administration.

hospital administrators place greater pressure on doctors to prescribe only necessary care and decrease extra tests.

State governments are also requiring fixed-fee hospital–reimbursement plans which will cut hospital revenues and reduce support personnel. Some express fear the standard of health care will be lowered, larger hospitals which attract the more seriously ill will suffer, and perhaps as many as 1,000 hospitals will be forced to close by 1990.[44] Others see this cost-control system as encouraging efficiency and stability, while reducing waste and the taxpayers' heavy burden.

Rise of the Private Sector

One of the most significant developments in the health-care industry is the rapid rise of corporate and private sponsorship of prepaid group plans. Since U.S. companies pay $77 billion annually in health insurance premiums for their workers, more than they pay in dividends, they are becoming more and more interested in such plans. Chrysler Corporation, for example, pays $373 million in health-insurance benefits, which adds more than $600 to the price tag of each car it manufactures.[45] Insurance companies also find group health care attractive in both cost and quality. "We're saving about six dollars for every dollar we spend," said a Prudential vice president for group insurance, "and we think the quality of care is better, because most patients do better at home."[46]

Health-Maintenance Programs

Known popularly as **HMOs,** the health-maintenance programs have quadrupled in enrollment since 1973, from 3 to 12 million members by 1983, or about 4 percent of the population.[47] Despite attacks from the medical profession as a form of socialized medicine, they are expanding rapidly and their lower cost makes them very attractive to large corporations.

Essentially, HMOs are prepaid group health programs. Subscribers pay an annual fee of a few hundred dollars instead of paying fees for services they use. Because the group physicians only have a fixed annual fee for their income, they are motivated to keep costs down and patients out of the hospital. Indeed, studies have shown patients in HMOs in comparison to people with conventional insurance plans, pay up

This health-care facility in Cherry Hill, New Jersey, is typical of the private, prepaid group health programs rapidly rising throughout the country. These lower-cost HMOs quadrupled in number between 1973 and 1983, growing from 3 to 12 million enrolled members, or about 4% of the population.

to 40 percent less, spend only half as much time in hospitals, and undergo far less surgery.[48]

Preferred Provider Organizations

Referred to as PPOs, these are one of the fastest-growing innovations in the private sector. Under this plan a group of doctors agrees to provide comprehensive health services to contracting companies at a discount. For example, Philip Morris and Reynolds Aluminum Company in Richmond, Virginia, have a PPO contract through the Blue Cross plan. This option is so cost-efficient to American companies that more than 80 PPOs have been established in 30 states.[49]

BIOETHICS: LIFE AND DEATH DECISIONS

Our medical advances enable us to save prematurely born babies under two pounds and other "distressed" newborns with genetic defects, including serious heart problems, who just a few years ago would have died. Just as we can save a new life we would have previously lost, so too can we prevent a new life through abortion if the mother does not want to have that baby. Doctors now have the drugs and machinery to prolong the lives of the terminally ill and the hopelessly injured. We have it in our power, at over $800 a day, to maintain, with life support systems, lives that can't be saved.

The common question in all these instances is this: what should we do? Abortion pits medicine against religion. Is abortion an act of murder? Is prolonging life among the dying a duty, a humanitarian act, or an unnecessary extension of suffering? The toughest ethical dilemma in ending treatment is if the patient cannot express his or her wishes, or is a very small child. Nurses sometimes let their charges die. For example, they may respond slowly if a terminally ill patient takes a turn for the worse, or give a little extra morphine to a child with terminal cancer which not only dulls pain, but also suppresses respiration and hastens death.[50]

Abortion

Since the 1973 U.S. Supreme Court ruling that abortions were legal, they have so increased that abortion is now one of the most common surgical procedures in the United States. A total of 1,554,000 legal abortions occurred in 1980, one-fourth of all pregnancies, a total which is more than twice the 600,000 legal abortions in 1972.[51] Although black women have a disproportionately high number of abortions, white women have two-thirds of all abortions. Three-fourths of all women having abortions are unmarried, more than half are childless, and two-thirds are between 15 and 24. Although some abortions occur to prevent the birth of babies with serious genetic defects such as severe mental retardation, cystic fibrosis, or Down's syndrome—cystic fibrosis, for example, leading either to paralysis or death from spinal meningitis before age 20—most are simply unwanted pregnancies because of age, social stigma, or economic considerations (see Figure 14.4).

FIGURE 14.4 Changes in Abortion Attitudes in the U.S. in 1965, 1972 to 1980 By Percent Approving

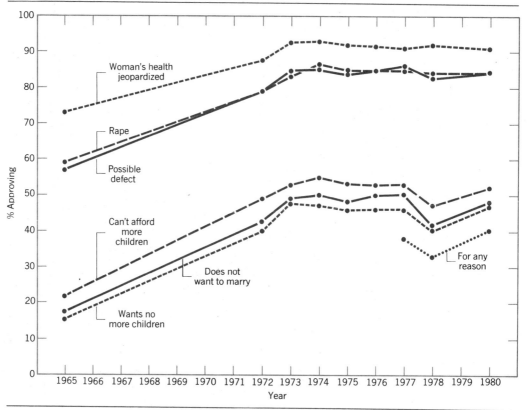

SOURCE: National Opinion Research Center.

Many doctors will not perform abortions, but physicians' groups, like the AMA and American College of Obstetricians and Gynecologists, oppose government restrictions. Can we justify compulsory pregnancy? Is it moral to force a woman to have a child she does not want? Doesn't that unborn child have a right to live? When is a fetus a human being?

The dilemma exists because we cannot scientifically determine when human life begins. Prolife advocates maintain life begins at conception, that a fetus is human and its termination is murder. One medical researcher has argued that life, like death should be defined by the existence of brain activity—usually eight weeks after conception.[52] Other medical researchers say such a precise answer is impossible. Social scientists have long argued a fetus is not human, that humanity is an achievement occurring after birth when socialization occurs and social motivation begins in the first weeks after birth.

Emotion-charged debate continues. Prochoice advocates argue that making abortions illegal discriminates against the poor unable to pay a private physician or travel to secure a legal abortion. A return to dangerous self-induced or backstreet abortions is likely if abortions are banned. These methods often cause death, serious injury, and sterility. However, prolife advocates argue that a fetus is a living and growing life form, entitled to the same protection and rights of other living persons.

Keeping the Dying Alive

A slowly dying 86-year-old woman in a hospital bed goes into cardiac arrest. Quickly the medical staff takes emergency measures (CPR), cardiopulmonary resuscitation—cardiac injections, and possibly defibrilation—and the woman returns to life. In the next two weeks this situation repeats itself three times before the woman dies. This actual event, with slightly varying particulars, is a common occurrence in hospitals nationwide. Should that woman, and others like her, have been allowed to die without such "heroic efforts"? In other hospital beds there are many other patients, their bodies wasted by cancer and their pain relieved by frequent doses of morphine. Some would have died sooner, but for short-term life-prolonging drugs and surgery. Yet they lie in their beds, with no possibility of recovery, and suffer. Still others are comatose, hooked up to expensive machines that perform their life-support functions, without which patients would probably die.

Euthanasia, also called **mercy killing,** is the deliberate allowing or causing of the death of someone with a serious illness. Most religions and governments forbid it. But is the deliberate withholding of life-sustaining efforts in which the dying succumb to their own natural causes an act of euthanasia? Since state laws hold the physician responsible for maintaining life, most hospital doctors do not terminate life-preserving measures unless the patient has made a living-will declaration against "heroic measures" or the family gives "no code" instructions, that is, take no "heroic measures" to prolong life.

Without a living will or "no code" instructions, though, the life-prolonging efforts continue for the majority of dying patients. Interestingly, in 1957 Pope Pius XII, a very conservative leader of the Roman Catholics, decreed that the primary duty of the physician is to relieve pain in hopeless cases, even if that means taking action inconsistent with prolonging life. Today many hospitals use a staff committee of experts to make decisions in such cases, rather than placing this heavy burden on one doctor (see Box 14.1).

MENTAL HEALTH

To most Americans the problems of physical health are more real than mental health problems. All of us have been physically sick, some of us more seriously than others, and we have had friends and relatives who were seriously ill, had surgery, or died. Some of us might also have sought psychological counseling to sustain us through a stressful period in our lives or we might know someone who suffered a nervous breakdown or committed suicide while in a depressive mental state.

When many people hear the terms *insanity* or *mental illness,* their minds conjure up images of frenzied-looking mad people acting in a random, violent fashion, or of

BOX 14.1

WHAT WOULD YOU DO?

Every day, doctors, nurses, patients, and patients' families face life-and-death decisions. There is rarely an obvious "right" choice; each of them is, in some way, bad. Here are some real cases that present painful alternatives. The choices made by those responsible—and the results of their actions—appear below.

1. Doctors at a university hospital examined a 10-year-old boy whose bone cancer of the upper arm had recurred in spite of radiation treatments. The physicians advised amputation of the limb and warned that without the operation, the child would almost certainly die. But the boy, an enthusiastic Little Leaguer, begged his parents and the doctors to let him keep his arm so that he could continue to play baseball.

2. A 7-year-old girl was suffering from a progressive neurological disease that had made her totally dependent on a respirator. She could talk and think normally, but the rest of her body functions were deteriorating rapidly and she was obviously in pain. Attempts to "wean" her from the respirator were unsuccessful, and doctors eventually realized it was unlikely she would ever recover. The parents, who were deeply religious, agonized over a decision about whether to turn off the machine.

3. A young woman, who was dying of multiple sclerosis, finally lapsed into an irreversible coma. She remained totally unresponsive for about a week, and her doctors agreed there was nothing more they could do to help her. One evening the patient, still comatose, began to gasp for breath. Her parents, who were sitting by the bedside, summoned the nurse and asked her to call a doctor.

1. The family decided against surgery. Now, nearly a year later, the boy is receiving radiation and chemotherapy—and playing baseball. Physicians say it is too soon to estimate his chances of recovery.

2. The physician asked the parents if they wanted to discover whether God wished the child to breathe on her own. The distraught couple agreed and, as they set vigil, the respirator was removed; the child died about four hours later.

3. The nurse requested that the parents leave the room. Instead of summoning the doctor immediately, she waited until the patient had stopped breathing. Then she went, with a physician, to tell the parents that their daughter had died. "It was the hardest thing I ever did in my life," the nurse admits.

someone vacantly staring into space, lost in a private reality and unable to communicate with anyone in the real world. Such people do exist, but most mental disorders are less obvious—occasioned by stress, anxiety, and depression. Unlike recognizable physical ailments, especially serious ones, mental disorders often go unrecognized by the affected individual, particularly the more serious they are.

4. A 6-year-old boy had severe renal failure from both kidneys; his best chance of survival would be a transplant from a sibling. Each of his two older sisters, 8 and 12, was willing to donate a kidney in an effort to save the boy. The risk to either girl—from the operation or from living with one kidney—was quite small. But common medical practice dictated that young donors should not be used, except in the case of a twin.

5. At the student-health service of a major university, a young man told his psychotherapist that he wanted to kill a young woman who lived nearby but who was then on a trip abroad. The therapist conferred with two colleagues and, in a limited breach of confidentiality, informed the campus police; they picked up the student and detained him for questioning. Concluding that the youth was harmless, the police decided to release him after extracting a promise that he would not bother the woman he had spoken of murdering. The health service thought it unnecessary to take any further action.

4. The doctors refused the sisters as donors, on the ground that they were too young to make a major medical decision that could affect their whole lives. The brother has survived for four years on dialysis.

5. Two months later, shortly after the woman's return, the student went to her home and killed her. Her parents sued the university—and won. The state supreme court ruled the campus police and the university had a "duty" to warn the girl of the threat on her life.

SOURCE: *Newsweek* (August 31, 1981), p. 52. Copyright, 1981, by Newsweek, Inc. All Rights Reserved. Reprinted by Permission.

Mental health problems in the nation are more widespread than many realize. Almost 7 million people receive patient care annually at some form of mental health facility, either public or private, inpatient or outpatient.[53] In addition, the President's Commission on Mental Health suggested that between 20 and 30 million Americans, or 10 percent of the population, require mental health care of some form at some point.[54] The latter estimate does not include those suffering mild emotional distress brought on by stress, anxiety, or depression, which would add many millions more to the statistics. Clearly then, mental health is a social problem which affects a large segment of the population. As we shall see, it becomes more complex a problem because of the lack of consensus about the nature and causes of mental disorders, the interplay of social class, the social stigma attached to mental illness, and the inadequacy of quality treatment.

The Nature of Mental Disorders

When it comes to defining mental illness, everything is relative, with neither agreement among mental health experts on how to classify or diagnose mental disorders, nor a consistency of public perception. Joan of Arc heard supernatural "voices," Mormon leader Joseph Smith conversed with an archangel, and Mohammed heeded the voice of Allah. They all became religious leaders, not patients in an asylum. In modern times a person who attempts to communicate directly to God through prayer, either silently or aloud, is considered normal, but a person who talks to the spirits of nature or the deceased is considered, at the very least, to be "strange." One can "get away" with unique behavior more easily in a city than a small town, or if one is affluent, not poor. Even court psychiatrists examining the same defendant often disagree about the sanity of that person.

Mental disorders can take many forms. They may range from personality disorders or **neuroses** (including deep anxiety or depressive states, hypochondria, phobias, compulsive actions, and psychosomatic illness) to more severe disorders or **psychoses** (including paranoia, schizophrenia, manic depression, and melancholia brought on by physiological life changes like menopause or physical decline). From a sociological viewpoint, our interest centers on the variations in social definition of the problem and the resulting social reaction and treatment. First, however, we shall examine the prevailing medical model among professionals and the socioeconomic factors involved.

The Medical Model

The most widely accepted approach to mental disorders is to view the problem as an illness that requires professional treatment so it does not worsen. A humane approach which arose in reaction to earlier views that the mentally disturbed should be chained, beaten, or killed, the medical approach assumes mental illness can be treated through therapeutic treatment of the individual. In some cases the cause may be physiological, resulting from such biochemical abnormalities as an inadequately functioning thyroid gland or atrophied cerebral cortex or lack of certain chemical substances in specific regions of the brain. Other mental disorders, according to this model, are rooted in psychological causes, a disturbance of certain perceptual or personality processes. This perspective sees the abnormality as the result of a lack of personality integration or emotional imbalance, requiring insight into those hidden causes and patient awareness of them to restructure that person's personality development and restore him or her to a "normal" state.

Deep depression is one of the more common forms of mental illness, unlike the images of violent madmen in the public mind. This unclothed young woman, depressed and withdrawn, sits impassively beside her doll in a deteriorating urban apartment.

Criminal Defense

Psychologists, psychiatrists, as well as nurses and social workers, have all been advocates of this mental health viewpoint. Most notable and controversial has been its utilization in criminal defense. Each year, 20,000 persons charged with crimes or convicted of crimes are placed in mental institutions. Those who successfully plead insanity spend time in a mental hospital, but remain there for an average 35 percent shorter duration than those sent to prison.[55] To combat this earlier release, nine states have laws allowing juries to find defendants "guilty but mentally ill," to insure the person will serve as much time as another convicted person and still receive psychiatric help. Public pressure is on in dozens of other states to effect a similar verdict option.[56]

Supporting Evidence

Some evidence exists to support the medical model. Psychoactive drugs have been used successfully on mental patients to curb their aggressive behavior. Therapy has brought some people back into normal, functioning lives. Studies have found some schizophrenics to have biochemical abnormalities, and children of a schizophrenic parent are more likely to become schizophrenics themselves than people without schizophrenic parents. Critics argue, however, that in the latter instance, children may have learned to become schizophrenic rather than inheriting that tendency, and therein lies the major criticism of the entire medical model. By restricting the focus to the individual, one ignores the impact of the social environment and the way it affects individual behavior. After we first examine the socioeconomic factors related to mental disorders, we shall take a look at alternative sociological explanations for mental disorders.

Socioeconomic Factors

Numerous investigators have examined the relationship between the prevalence of mental disorders and varying socioeconomic factors. Their findings, while capable of some generalized conclusions, require some caution in their interpretation. First, we have the problem of the reliability of the psychiatric diagnosis since, as we have indicated a few paragraphs earlier, mental illness is not as easy as physical illness to identify; even psychiatrists disagree often with each other on a diagnosis. In addition, not everyone requiring treatment is in fact undergoing treatment, and the more affluent and educated may distort their group's incidence rate by seeking mental health care for even the most minor problems. It is also far more difficult to obtain statistical information about those being treated in private practice than for those being treated in mental hospitals, clinics, or outpatient facilities. Fourth, changes in social conditions—war, depression, rapid social change—can intensify rates of mental disorders.

Despite these not unimportant considerations, sociologists have been able to make several conclusions which have remained fairly consistent over 50 years of investigation. Of the hundreds of studies conducted, three major studies have dominated, reinforced by the findings of many others. In 1939 investigators of patients at Chicago public and private mental hospitals revealed that mental disorders followed a pattern, not a random distribution among the population.[57] In 1958 researchers in New Haven, Connecticut, included patients under private care, clinic, or hospital treatment, and also found significant differences when they controlled for social class.[58] Another team of investigators did a midtown Manhattan study in 1954, with a follow-up study in 1974, in which they interviewed a cross section of 1,660 adults to determine if they ever had mental problems, obtained treatment, or displayed neurotic symptoms.[59] Again, the findings revealed patterns found in earlier studies, which are all summarized below.

Social Class

An inverse correlation exists between social class and mental disorders. Members of the lowest classes have the higher rates of mental disorder and those of higher socioeconomic status have lower rates. The poor and deprived are much more likely to suffer cases of psychosis, particularly schizophrenia. On the other hand, neuroses were far more common among those of high socioeconomic status and income than among the lower classes.

Treatment also varied considerably according to social class. Lower-class people are less likely to receive treatment, but their rate of hospitalization is much higher and their stay in those mental hospitals much longer. Probable explanations for this pattern are that the poor cannot be protected or supported by their family, must turn to public facilities which tend to institutionalize them, and have more contact with social workers, welfare agencies, and the courts who make referrals about recommended hospitalization. In contrast, middle- and upper-class Americans are more likely to use outpatient or expensive private facilities, and if institutionalized, it is only for a brief period. Psychotherapy is the likely treatment for the more affluent, but drug treatment or electroshock therapy are the more common treatments for lower-class patients.

Race

Since a disproportionate number of black people are poor, it is not surprising that their hospitalization for mental disorders is about 33 percent higher than that of Whites. Their higher incidence of psychosis is comparable to that of low-income Whites, meaning this high rate of incidence appears to be a social class variable not a racial one. As we just mentioned, people of lower social status are more likely to be hospitalized than receive private therapy and to have greater contact with social agencies, including mental health officials. Moreover, health-care professionals are usually of a different cultural background; psychiatrists and psychologists at the doctoral level are mostly middle-class Whites, with only 0.9 percent of them Black and 0.4 percent Hispanic.[60]

Sex

Although men and women are equally likely to be treated for mental disorder, some significant differences exist in the patterns of diagnosis and treatment. Not yet clear, however, is whether these differences truly reflect gender differences or prevailing sexist orientations in society influencing the diagnoses of the mostly male psychiatric profession. One study, for example, found that women were more likely to be identified as schizophrenics for behavior considered acceptable for males.[61]

Males experience a much higher hospitalization rate for mental disorders in all marital status groups (see Figure 14.5). The number of males aged 14 years and older, controlled for an admission rate per 100,000 population, has been about twice that of females. Women are more likely to be diagnosed as neurotics, receiving outpatient care, while men more often are diagnosed as psychotics and hospitalized. Women are more likely to be treated for depression and alcoholism, especially when their traditional motherly role lessens when their children are grown and leave home.[62]

Marital Status

One's marital status appears to be an important factor in mental disorder cases (see Figure 14.5). Married people have much lower rates of treatment and hospitalization. Both males and females who never married have considerably higher rates, though for males this is much more so. The most difficult situation for males is that of separation or divorce, where their problem requires admission to state or psychiatric hospitals and surpasses all other categories. Especially vulnerable are those in the 18–24 year age group with a hospitalization admission rate of 2,224 and those in the

FIGURE 14.5 Age-adjusted Admission Rates (14 years and over) to State and County Psychiatric Hospitals By Sex and Marital Status, United States 1975

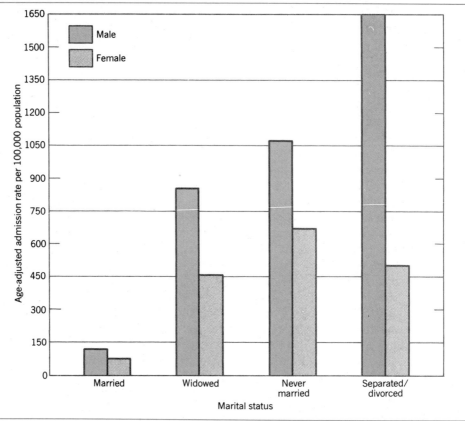

SOURCE: National Institute of Mental Health.

45- to 54-year age group (2,360). The highest rate for females (916) in an age group is found among the never married, age 35–44, while overall the highest female rate is among the widowed (666.2). It would seem that in a couples-oriented society, the emotional support of a mate is an important intervening variable concerning mental health.

SOCIOLOGICAL PERSPECTIVES

The concepts of physical and mental health are deeply rooted in sociocultural as well as organic explanations. Sociologists have offered various analyses to enhance our understanding of the social problems surrounding public expectations, incidence of illness, actual health care, and recovery.

Individual Faults and Deviant Behavior

Some diseases, even fatal ones, receive cynical and unsympathetic response from many people because they see the diseases as the result of an immoral or unwise life-style. Since AIDS primarily strikes the male homosexual community, a common reaction has been, "It's their own fault for living that way." Response to this epidemic has ranged from calling it "moral retribution" to public indifference, including a reluctant government research funding effort, until the disease spread to other population segments. Similarly, those contracting herpes are branded as sexually promiscuous, tubercular patients are undesirable aliens living in overcrowded housing, alcoholics are weak-willed people, lung and throat cancer victims are paying the price for their smoking habits, overweight or physically inactive people invite their own heart attacks. In an advanced society like ours, too often we blame the victim for getting sick, thinking it could have been avoided.

Personality as Villain

In addition to blame for their condition because of poor health habits, taking unnecessary risks, or disapproved life-style, people also are faulted for their personality. One study identified "Type A" personalities—those more aggressive and achievement-oriented, impatient, restless—as more likely to suffer heart disease than "Type B" personalities having a more easy-going nature.[63] Evidence supporting this also extends to those likely to suffer ulcers. While such factors may be true, they tend also to place blame on the victim. This blame can in turn produce a cavalier attitude about one's own risk of heart disease by comparison.

Mental Disorder as Deviance

In a highly influential work, Thomas Scheff offered insight into the social stigma attached to mental disorders.[64] Within a society there exist **residual norms,** so totally taken for granted that they are assumed to be a part of human nature. For example, people talking to each other do not stare only at the ceiling or face in the opposite direction, but face each other instead. One does not laugh at a funeral or suddenly get angry when paid a compliment. Violating any residual norm frightens other people because it is not "natural." They therefore label the violator as unbalanced, crazy, or mentally ill. With such a label, expectations about behavior change; that person is expected to be irresponsible, erratic, and strange and is treated differently from others. Possibly confused and frightened by their own behavior and under stress, they may be highly impressionable and accept the label. Once the individual takes on the label, casting it off is difficult (see Box 14.2).

Institutional Faults and System Disorganization

From the functionalist perspective, the problems of health care are the result of rapid social change and altered public attitudes. Advances in medical technology have shifted the focus of medical practice from the family doctor to specialists and large hospitals. Despite its high financial cost to patients, the hospital-based system is very functional in providing income for physicians, hospitals, pharmaceutical companies, and medical suppliers. The American concept of free enterprise and the fee-based

BOX 14.2

The Mental Illness Hoax

California psychiatrist D. L. Rosenhan attracted national attention in 1973 when he published the results of an experiment about the problems of diagnosis and treatment of mental disorders. He selected 12 different mental hospitals in five states on either the West Coast or East Coast, including some of the most prestigious, where he sent eight colleagues—none with any history of mental disorder—to seek help. Each pretended in the admissions interview to have heard a voice say a word, such as "thud," "hollow," or "empty." Otherwise they gave correct life histories except for their names and occupations.

In each case they were diagnosed as schizophrenic and admitted. Thereafter the pseudopatients acted normally and no longer said they heard voices. Nevertheless all the staff reacted to them on the basis of their diagnosis and not their behavior. One humorous instance of this was when one of the pseudopatients was seen taking notes of what was happening, which was recorded as "engages in note-taking behavior" by a staff note-taker who thought the pseudopatient's note-taking was a pathological symptom.

Interestingly, the real mental patients almost immediately detected the normality of the pseudopatients, and insisted they were either academics or journalists who were "checking up on the place." No one on staff ever found out though. The pseudopatients remained hospitalized anywhere from 7 to 52 days, averaging 19 days each. Even then, they were released because schizophrenia was "in remission."

When officials at another mental hospital, after this study was published, were disbelieving and claimed they could detect phony patients, Rosenhan announced he would send them pseudopatients also. They alerted their staff to be on guard and, over the next three months, they identified 41 imposters sent by Rosenhan. Actually, Rosenhan had sent no one and all 41 cases had been genuine. Once again, he had demonstrated the subjective nature and difficulty of diagnosis of mental disorders.

medical system have encouraged an unregulated, unplanned rapid growth of a medical industry, which fails to function efficiently or properly within the entire social system.

Dysfunctions

One consequence of the patchwork growth of group or corporate medicine has been its depersonalization. Instead of being the well-known patient of a family doctor, one is now "the eighth patient" sitting in the waiting room, "the pregnancy" in hospital room 254, or "the broken leg" in the emergency room. Another dysfunction has been the growth of third-party payments which have raised medical costs because the money has often been wasted because of fraud, or on nonessential expenditures, instead of on improving the quantity or quality of health care. Still another dysfunction has been the imbalanced doctor-patient ratio in different parts of the country. Finally, a cultural lag exists in the public belief in private, personalized professional care and the reality of a diversified large-scale medical industry. Functionalists would say that the system is correcting itself through the evolution of lower-cost outpatient clinics, alternative health-care plans, and cost controls on third-party payments.

The Sick Role

Over 30 years ago, Talcott Parsons identified an interdependent functioning as a process wherein the sick person assumes a mostly passive behavioral stance.[65] In the sick role, the ill person is not held responsible for the sickness and is exempted from normal role obligations. However, the cooperation of the sick person in seeking expert help and in wanting to get well is necessary. Otherwise the individual is considered lazy or goldbricking and others will no longer excuse that person's absence from normal role obligations. Through the social control mechanism, society regulates both the illness and the behavior that accompanies it. This analysis, while helpful, does not explain ethnic behavioral variations, avoidance of doctors for minor ailments, or diseases for which the victims are blamed.

Inequality and Inevitable Conflict

Conflict theorists look upon the problems surrounding the health-care delivery system as the result of the domination of the rich and powerful. Because physicians want to maximize their incomes, one comprehends why their offices and the superior medical facilities are disproportionately located in urban and suburban areas where the affluent and influential live, and not in rural or ghetto areas. Additionally, one realizes that rates of infant mortality and diseases, are higher amongst low-income people, while life expectancy is lower, and they have less access to medical services than the more affluent. Health care is not only a profit-making industry, but a monopoly which totally controls prices, maintains high demand through limiting the number of new physicians, and effectively opposes any efforts at outside regulation.

The AMA Lobby

Of the many health industry groups lobbying intensively in their own self-interest, the AMA offers conflict theorists a prime example of the wielding of political and economic power not in the public interest. The AMA has successfully fought off many attempts over the past 50 years to create a national health-insurance system. Although such a system exists in every other industrialized nation and would help people in this country cope with runaway medical costs, the medical profession feared it would impair their right to set their own fees and undermine their independence from outside regulation. Consequently, the AMA has branded such proposals as "socialized medicine" or "Marxist medicine." Besides successful lobbying to defeat such proposals, the AMA has donated millions of dollars to opponents of congressional advocates of national health insurance plans, helping to defeat many of them. Congressional fear of the AMA lobby and its continuing campaign contributions to sympathetic legislators demonstrate how a powerful special interest group can thwart the public good.

System Inequities

Besides exploiting illness for financial gain, the health-care industry also comes under attack from conflict theorists for its treatment of the mentally disturbed. Those who can afford private care receive it while those who cannot are ignored until they create a problem. Then they are put in mental hospitals where they receive inadequate attention because of the shortage of funding and expert professional staff (see Box 14.3).

Conflict theorists also emphasize stress and anxiety produced by our economic system. The constant competitive struggle to achieve breeds tension and intense pressure, setting the stage for some form of mental breakdown. Those economically exploited, who feel alienated and powerless to change the conditions in which they live, develop a frustration which can lead to serious mental problems. The high incidence of psychoses among low-income peoples, this perspective holds, is the result of economic, political, and social exploitation.

Interaction and Social Interpretation

Already mentioned in this chapter have been some aspects of the interactionist perspective: socializing med school students into less idealistic, more pragmatic doctors; the impersonal doctor-patient relationships engendered by specialization and hospital-based health care; the effects of labeling on a physically or mentally sick person. What interactionist theorists concentrate upon, as they focus on the problems of health care, are the means by which people communicate, define, and alter the social reality of illness. Whether a person is considered healthy or ill depends upon how others define that person and the resulting self-concept. Two further examples will demonstrate how social interaction patterns help explain mental illness.

Problems in Living

According to psychiatrist Thomas Szasz, mental disorders are not illnesses, but an unconscious excuse to avoid an unpleasant reality. Some social factor—an unbearable personal and emotional situation, an unresolved problem in living—causes the person unable to deal with the problem to adopt a defective strategy to escape one role and assume another. Since the psychiatrist makes a value judgment based on his or her behavioral norms, the identification of much mental illness is a "myth" and penalizes people with involuntary treatment, thereby depriving them of their freedom and facing responsibility (See Box 14.2).

Total Institutions

About a quarter of a century ago, the noted sociologist Erving Goffman worked for a year as a hospital aide at a mental hospital, where he had complete access to the patients and took notes on his impressions. What resulted was a very important work that led to a change in the discharge rates. Goffman found a lengthy stay was counterproductive in a **total institution,** a place where a large number of like-situated

BOX 14.3

NO SNAKE PIT, NO ROSE GARDEN   WAYMART, Pa

Farview State Hospital here is typical of similar institutions around the nation: It is no longer a snake pit of brutality and deprivation, but neither is it a shining model of medical treatment.

The 70-year-old hospital's 225 inmates don't live in luxury, although the place is more relaxed than a prison. As a maximum-security institution for mentally ill persons charged with or convicted of crimes, it keeps its outer doors securely locked. Yet inmates can move around wards that each house about 40.

When not watching television or playing pool, they can participate in therapy. They sleep in a spacious dormitory. Says one inmate: "I was scared before I got here, but I don't have a bad thing to say about it now."

Farview once was packed with 1,400 inmates as men with seemingly untreatable mental defects stayed for years and sometimes decades. Little care was offered; instead, guards ran the place with iron fists. A grand jury reported in 1978 that many inmates had died after being "severely and unmercifully kicked, beaten and punched by groups of guards."

By then, the hospital already had begun changing. Psychologists and social workers were hired. New administrators curbed abuses. Drugs were introduced to keep most inmates under control. Lawsuits forced release of hundreds to other hospitals or community treatment. Today, Farview inmates stay only a few months on average—counting the many who come for a short spell for mental-competence tests.

"REVOLVING DOOR"

Despite improvements, a catalog of problems persist. One is the "revolving door": 3 of every 5 new inmates have served a previous stint. Explains social worker Tom Glacken: "Patients go back to prison and stop taking their medication. They deteriorate, and all of a sudden they're back."

Many inmates are idle. Fewer than half take part in therapy, which fills only a few hours a week in any case. "It's hard to motivate patients, and we can't force them to participate," says chief nurse Irene Vauter. Most are on constant medication. Observes an armed robber: "It slows your metabolism down; you don't feel like doing nothing." Care is expensive. Nearly $100,000 is spent annually per patient, much of it to pay 248 guards—now called psychiatric security aides.

Farview has several staff psychologists and four part-time psychiatrists. But another statistic shows how far it must go: Experts say seven full-time psychiatrists are needed, but the hospital's rural site and low pay have made it impossible to recruit even one.

SOURCE: Reprinted from *U.S. News & World Report* issue of June 27, 1983. Copyright, 1983, U.S. News & World Report, Inc.

individuals are cut off from the rest of society and together lead an enclosed, formally administered life.[66] Individuals must forsake their former, self-determining role and assume that of an inmate, totally dependent on the institution for all physical needs. The staff tended to treat the patients in terms of the institution's expectations, ignoring normal behavior but recording any aspect of abnormal behavior. Anyone who challenged the system was considered a problem, others went into withdrawal, while others passively conformed to the rules.

Goffman found the atmosphere of a mental institution worsens people's mental problems, and as they adapt to their sick role more and more, their chances of being released decrease the longer they are confined. Today the long-term effects of such institutionalized interaction are widely recognized, and mental health professionals now strive to release new patients within a few months before they become unable to assume personal responsibility.

THE FUTURE

Medical advances and genetic research promise a revolution in health care by 2025. By then we should have a complete map of all the human genes, and thus be able to cure many diseases by altering genes. Spare parts medicine—replacing damaged body parts with artificial and natural substitutes—will prolong life. Identifying the several hundred neurotransmitters in the brain, the chemical messengers, will enable doctors to use specific drugs to combat mental disorders such as depression, schizophrenia, and senility. Many present-day operations will become obsolete through advances in radiation and drug therapy, as well as new techniques with lasers.[67]

Our future scenarios, though, do not focus on technological advances. At the beginning of this chapter, you will recall, we discussed how the quality of health care had not improved despite the medical achievements of the past few decades. As long as social inequalities remain within the society, no health-care system will be able to solve the problems created by poverty, prejudice, and discrimination. Therefore, what our bipolar scenarios emphasize below are the possible direction of the present variables affecting access, care, cost, and recovery.

Pessimistic Scenario

Technological marvels and miraculous medical achievements had been accompanied by soaring health costs. The increasing complexity of high-technology medicine had driven national spending on health care to 15 percent of the Gross National Product, with a rise to 20 percent forecast within 20 years. Despite the clamor for reform, the health system had changed in only two respects. Profit-making medical companies now dominated the hospital industry and a two-class health system had evolved: one for privately insured patients and another for the poor and disabled. The latter fared poorly in decisions about using the costly new technologies and resources, including artificial hearts.

Although medical achievements by 2025 were impressive, they had little effect upon the social and environmental causes of a large proportion of the health problems. Poverty still fostered higher rates of illness than that of the affluent, and environmental pollution had increased body illnesses from the contamination. Continuing bad health habits and overindulgence caused a large segment to suffer health problems in their late middle age and senior years. A larger elderly population suffering from incurable degenerative diseases strained both the health facilities and the financial resources of their families. Life seemed more stressful than ever, and the pressures upon people often created both physical and mental health problems.[68]

Few people were housed long in mental hospitals, given the advances in drug therapy. Yet continuing outpatient care—so important for the rehabilitation of former mental hospital patients—was not very satisfactory. Public fears about the mentally disturbed were still strong and resistance to establishing community mental health centers in one's own neighborhood was so widespread that only an insufficient number existed. Institutions remained understaffed, with insufficiently trained paraprofessionals being the ones that the patients mostly saw. Only the affluent could afford private outpatient treatment.

We had come a long way in medicine, but in many ways, we had gotten nowhere. The medical monopoly prospered and many people suffered. Some regions still had a shortage of doctors and quality health care. The infant mortality rate, incidence of illness, and life expectancy still were worse among the poor. The average family worked eight weeks a year just to pay its medical bills, while other families went into debt to pay the heavy expenses occasioned by the lingering serious illlness of one family member. Those with mental disorders still experienced a social stigma and their care was heavily dependent on their social class.

Optimistic Scenario

Of all the changes in medicine by 2025, perhaps the most far-reaching was a transformation of the health-care system into three major components of preventive, corrective, and environmental medicine. Many physicians and surgeons still provided emergency care and treatment for illness as most had in the twentieth century. However the surplus of doctors (about 144,000 at the turn of the century) and the cost controls on hospitalization and surgery had obliged other physicians to redirect their career goals.

Preventive medicine offered a promising future, especially with prepaid group medical insurance providing steady income and a clientele. With offices set up in all communities in shopping centers, urban neighborhoods, and medical parks, these practitioners were easily accessible. Through inoculations and health education about diet, nutrition, exercise, the effects of alcohol, tobacco, and other drugs, emphasis was on preventing diseases before they occurred. Regular checkups, blood pressure readings, and brief tests for chronic diseases all helped reduce health risks among the entire population. Those involved in environmental medicine, either research or application, were finding satisfaction in improving the quality of the environment and promoting better health thereby. Hospital admissions and surgery had dropped almost 25 percent because of the preset individual medical fees.

A national health insurance program, with stringent cost controls, was a reality. Physicians had been forced to surrender some of their exclusive control over fees and certain health-care decisions, but despite ferocious AMA objections, they remained able to earn comfortable incomes without bankrupting the funding program.

More importantly, social class no longer meant inequitable health care, and the United States had attained parity with other industrialized nations in the quality of life for all its inhabitants. Infant mortality rates were lower and life expectancy rates higher. Poverty was still a concern, but its debilitating effects upon health were now under control.

An enlightened public now knew more about mental disorders, thanks to the discoveries in neurobiology. Mental health professionals now received more intensive training, with coursework in the behavioral sciences mandatory. As a result, they could offer more help and be more effective. The use of drugs to act upon the chemical messengers in the brain had been a boom to the mentally ill. They not only corrected the problem but enabled the staff to diagnose accurately the problem initially. Almost all mental patients were discharged within a month, reporting to outpatient clinics in their neighborhoods for periodic checkups.

What was ironic about the improved health care was that it did not occur from any scientific or altruistic breakthrough. Physicians realized it was in their economic self-interests to redirect their energies, given their surplus and the payment reform brought about by consumers, corporations, and politicians. Mental health personnel had improved and increased in sufficient number because of the job opportunities available there when other occupational areas for hospital staff declined.

SUMMARY

1. The United States has made many advances in medicine, spending more money on health care than any other nation. Paradoxically, the quality and equity of our health-care delivery system is rather uneven, with our health statistics not as strong as those of many other countries.

2. Advances in medical science have engendered the medicalization of life, wherein people submit to the dominance of the health practitioner. Increased specialization and the growth of institutions have brought about impersonalized medical care and hospital-based treatment. Although modern medicine cannot do much about the major causes of death, critics charge it has stripped patients of their rights and can even be a threat to one's health as a result of errors in diagnosis, drug therapy, or surgery.

3. Because the medical profession is based upon a fee-for-service, the distribution of physicians and medical facilities is uneven, with affluent suburbs and urban areas oversupplied and small towns and low-income neighborhoods underrepresented. Private medical practice is extremely lucrative, but an excess number of surgeons exists. As a result, many unnecessary operations occur.

4. Both profit and nonprofit hospitals benefit from extended patient stays. Until recently, hospitals had complete control over determining costs from diagnosis, treatment, and patient care, unquestioningly reimbursed through third-party payments. Costs skyrocketed, caused by hospitals securing expensive new equipment and running extensive tests. Fear of malpractice suits has driven up insurance costs and forced physicians to rely more heavily on tests than on personal judgment.

5. Medical insurance brings some coverage to some people. Whether employer-employee supported (the "Blues") or government-supported (Medicaid and Medicare), the former blank check payment is being replaced by preset fee payments. The rise of Health Maintenance programs (HMOs) and Preferred Provider Organizations (PPOs) is a private sector response to high health costs.

6. Mental health problems affect about 10 percent of the population. It is widely accepted that they are illnesses requiring professional help. Social scientists have found significant correlations between the incidence and treatment of mental disorders by social class, race, sex, marital status, and age.

7. The deviance approach is most readily seen in public response to sexually transmitted diseases and the stigma attached to those with mental disorders. The functionalist view examines the functional advantages of the health-care system to health practitioners and suppliers, as well as the dysfunctional problems of depersonalization, high costs, cultural lag, and uneven quality care. Conflict theorists emphasize the exploitation by the medical elite and related special interest groups of the rest of society and how the system generates many of the health problems. Interactionists focus on the many ways social interpretations of illness and behavior affect diagnosis and treatment.

SUGGESTED READINGS

Conrad, Peter, and Joseph W. Schneider. *Deviance in Medicalization: From Badness to Sickness*. St. Louis, Mo.: Mosby, 1980. An excellent sociological analysis of the historical process by which society redefined its social problems in medical terms and the resultant implications of these changed values and attitudes upon American life.

Corea, Gena. *The Hidden Malpractice: How American Medicine Mistreats Women*. New York: Harcourt Brace Jovanovich Jove Books, 1977. An angry indictment of the health system's mistreatment of women, both as patients and healers. Included is an analysis of the ways in which nineteenth-century males excluded women from many health practitioner roles.

Goffman, Erving. *Asylums: Essays on the Social Situation of Mental Patients and Other Inmates*. Garden City, N.Y.: Doubleday, 1961. This classic participant–observer study still offers the reader a fine insight into how daily interaction patterns in a mental hospital can be counterproductive to a patient's well-being.

Illich, Ivan. *Medical Nemesis: The Expropriation of Health*. New York: Pantheon, 1976. A carefully documented attack on the inability of modern medicine to cure disease despite highly expensive procedures. Not only is faith in medicine unjustified, the author argues, but health care is often harmful instead of helpful.

Starr, Paul. *The Social Transformation of American Medicine*. New York: Basic Books, 1982. A comprehensive study of the social and economic development of medicine in America through the nation's history, with an analysis as to why we are now confronted with problems of quality health care, corporate medicine, and physician dominance.

GLOSSARY

Bioethics   Refers to the moral considerations in prolonging or aborting lives.

Euthanasia (mercy killing)   The deliberate allowance or causation of death of someone with a serious illness or injury.

HMOs   Health maintenance organizations offering lower-cost preventive and corrective health care through prepaid group health plans.

Malpractice   Improper professional action or treatment by a physician out of negligence, ignorance, or error.

Medicaid   State-administered health payment program, partly federally funded, to assist the poor, blind, and disabled.

Medicare   Federally funded health payment program to assist those over 65.

Neuroses   Personality disorders including deep anxiety or depression, hypochondria, phobias, compulsive actions, and psychosomatic illness.

Overmedicalization   The view that the medical establishment has too much control over society and people's lives.

Psychoses   Severe personality disorders including paranoia, schizophrenia, manic depression, and melancholia.

Residual norms   Rules of behavior so totally taken for granted that they are assumed to be part of human nature.

Total institution   A place of work or residence, such as a mental institution, where individuals are physically and socially insulated from the outside world.

Social forces—much as migration patterns, scientific engineering advances, value shifts, and government policies—often initiate changes throughout a society, and have an impact on the life experiences of everyone. Some of these changes may be an indirect outgrowth of a society's technological evolution, like the problems caused by the invention of the automobile. Others may reflect our ever-increasing interdependence on the world's ecosystem. Whatever the impetus or consequences, sociologists use the term *macrosocial* to describe the magnitude of this aspect of the human experience.

All social change, even that apparently beneficial, has some negative consequences since it either disrupts people's lives or creates new problems while resolving old ones. For example, medical advances in conquering fatal contagious diseases sharply lowered the infant mortality rate, but in underdeveloped countries—where cultural values still prize large families—a high birthrate remains, causing a world population problem. Technology may produce many labor-saving machines but it may also cause loss of jobs, alienating or depersonalized work situations, as well as difficulties with self-identity and satisfying use of leisure time. In this section we shall examine some of these macrosocial factors influencing our quality of life: where we live, how we work and play, population pressures, and the interdependence of our ecosystem.

Chapter 15 addresses the problems confronting both America's older cities and the rapidly expanding sunbelt cities. Transportation policy and practice also receive our attention because, as you will see, they heavily affect our urban centers. What if you don't live or work in a city? Because of the interdependence of city and suburb, and continuing urban sprawl, you will learn that your quality of life still depends upon what happens in our cities.

Chapter 16 explains our interconnectedness with other cultures—what happens in other countries affects our own quality of life. As the world's population grows at an alarming rate, the drain on our natural resources rapidly increases. How much should we help the developing countries? Should we attempt to shape their population policies? Can our food and water supply, as well as the earth's raw materials, continue to meet this burgeoning demand? Large population masses and industrialization also strain the planet's ability to cleanse itself, as pollution, poisons, and toxic waste overload the ecosystem.

As Chapter 17 shows, technological advances, together with increased female and minority labor force participation, have dramatically altered the work environment. Problems of job displacement, unemployment, job dissatisfaction, occupational hazards, and satisfying use of leisure time all remain, however. How do we deal with them? Until we do, the quality of life for many Americans will suffer the stress and anguish of economic insecurity and the emptiness of meaningless work.

Throughout this section you should note that the vastness of the problems minimally require national policies and safeguards. Pay attention also to the social definitions and accompanying value orientations influencing efforts to resolve these problems.

FIVE
CHALLENGES TO THE QUALITY OF LIFE

FACTS ABOUT CITIES

Six of the 10 largest American cities lost population between 1970–1980.

Seventy-four percent of the population lives in an urbanized area.

Rural population growth rate in the 1970s almost equaled the urban, for the first time since 1810–1820.

By the year 2000, 60 percent of the population will be concentrated on 8 percent of the land.

An increase in middle- and upper-middle-class population has occurred in 75 percent of large American cities.

Older cities continue to suffer a loss of manufacturing jobs, but an increase of white-collar jobs.

The 1980 census showed the South and West containing more people for the first time than the North and Midwest.

15
URBAN DECLINE AND GROWTH

Cities have always represented the best and worst of a society. Because of the concentration of a large heterogeneous population, cities have frequently magnified the social problems existing within the entire society. At the same time, cities have been centers of economic, cultural, governmental, and religious influence; they have been the centers of civilization. As beacons of opportunity, cities have always attracted people seeking an end to their problems elsewhere.

The key to successful cities, past and present, lies in their mutual interdependence with the surrounding regions. As long as each benefited from the other—enjoying a reciprocity of relationships—both cities and outlying regions prospered. Serious social problems resulted when this symbiotic exchange ended: for example, farmland no longer able to sustain an urban population or a city becoming parasitic on surrounding areas due to loss of industry, population, or tax revenues.

Cities themselves are not problems. In fact, they contribute much to improvement of a society. However, a large concentration of people living in a small area intensifies societal problems, making them more visible. Then, too, the breakdown of mutual interdependence accentuates the problems even more.

CHANGING URBAN AMERICA

For the first 60 years of this century, central cities contained the large majority of the U.S. population, expanding their influence to surrounding towns and villages. Since 1960, older American cities, like many European cities, have lost population and industry to other regions. Most of the population redistribution, however, has been to nearby places, creating extended metropolitan areas.[1] Major cities have become part of a larger urban complex; we are an urban people now, even though most of us do not live in cities per se.

Urban Sprawl

The spread of an unrelenting **megalopolis** concerns many people. As Americans move farther away from the cities into the outlying regions, so also do all the trappings of urban life: stores, offices, factories, hospitals, crime, congestion, and pollution. Developers gobble up more and more land as the population increases and disperses. One town looks like another, stores on the highways erect signs to shout out their wares to the fast-moving traffic going by, and every activity requires a separate trip by car.

We pay a high social cost for urban sprawl. By spreading residences, medical and commercial offices, and industries throughout the region on large tracts of land, we create a major dependency on automobile transportation. Everything and everyone is too spread out to make public transportation economically feasible. With insufficient coordination of work sites and highways, traffic congestion results. Nor can everyone get around by car; a life-style requiring a car discriminates against poor families, the elderly, the disabled, and the young. Suburban teenagers, for instance, usually lack sufficient activities in their town but are unable to travel to locations where they do exist. Suburban parents thus spend a large portion of their time chauffeuring their children to stores, juvenile activities, and other events.

When a business relocates to a suburban location, the city loses jobs, tax revenues, and the loss of income for stores, restaurants, and business services previously dependent on that business. Other problems occur in the new setting. Several studies show that the average employee trip to work increases by several miles after relocation, thereby increasing traveling costs.[2] Low-income workers without a car must depend on a car pool or look for another job, both risky ventures. The company faces higher costs: maintenance of grounds and parking facilities, a subsidized cafeteria, messenger service to specialized support firms in corporate law, marketing, bond transactions, or similar services. Not unimportantly, the cost of providing utilities to an isolated site is a cost passed on to the general public.

According to the nonprofit Regional Plan Association, if the office space needed for each 5 million increase in population were built on suburban campuses, it would cut a swath one-half mile wide and 54 miles long.[3] In a large city with skyscrapers, 200 acres would fulfill this same need. Each 1 million square feet of suburban office space averages 80 acres (25 acres for parking lots) as compared to 1 acre in a large city, half of that for an office plaza. In smaller cities, this same 1 million square feet would require about 6 acres (25-story buildings with landscaping and parking lots).

HOUSING PROBLEMS

Beginning in the 1930s, the federal government began to subsidize the movement of Whites to the suburbs. Through the Federal Home Bank System (1932), the Home Owners Loan Corporation (1933), and the National Housing Act (1934) setting up the Federal Housing Authority (FHA), banking practices became more liberal; people without much capital could afford to buy homes. The Housing Act of 1949, together with Federal Housing Administration (FHA) loans and GI benefits to World War II veterans, funded the building of homes on vacant land, launching the suburban boom of the 1950s and 1960s. Significantly, during this booming postwar construction period, the FHA had an official policy against underwriting construction in racially integrated areas.

Redlining and Abandonment

Long after the FHA discontinued its discriminatory practice of refusing financial support in "undesirable" areas, the banks and savings and loan associations continued it. **Redlining,** the literal drawing of a red line on a map around "bad risk" neighborhoods, marks areas where lending institutions refuse to give mortgages or home improvement loans. Consequently, the older housing in these areas deteriorates further, attracting few buyers and reinforcing the bankers' supposed wisdom. Though illegal, redlining continues. Bankers defend their actions as a response to deteriorating housing, not its cause.[4]

Beset by rising fuel and maintenance costs, city demands for compliance with housing codes, higher taxes, rent control laws, and spreading urban blight, urban landlords find themselves in a no-win situation. Unable to get higher rents, improve, or sell their property, many owners squeeze the last ounce of profits from rental properties, ignoring necessary repairs and tax payments. After that, they abandon the buildings to junkies, looters, and arsonists.

Once the decline starts, it's hard to stop. Anyone who can move out, does so. The poor and helpless are left behind to cope with degenerating city services and increasing crime. As many as 150,000 houses and apartment buildings are abandoned each year.[5] Arson, a rapidly increasing crime by profiteering landlords or local vandals, becomes a frequent occurrence, with over 150,000 cases each year.[6] Parts of the South Bronx in New York are tragic examples of this downward process.

Urban Renewal

Launched by the Housing Act of 1949 with the lofty goal of improving city neighborhoods with planned redevelopment, urban renewal was not only a failure, but a destructive force as well. First, slum clearance displaced the poor without provision for their relocation. This action destroyed local neighborhoods, shattering sentimental attachments to old residences, neighborhood cohesiveness, friendships, and a whole way of life. Second, the city sold the cleared land to private developers who chose the most profitable forms of housing, almost never low-income housing.

One study found replacement construction was 36 percent housing, mostly for the upper middle class, 27 percent for commercial and industrial, and 37 percent for institutional and public use.[7] Another study showed that from 1949 to 1965, only 166,288 new housing units replaced the 311,197 units demolished through urban renewal.[8] At an expenditure of $3 billion, urban renewal substantially reduced low-cost housing in American cities.[9]

Undoubtedly the most notorious instance of community destruction through urban renewal is the West End of Boston. Because it was an area of old buildings, city planners slated this tight-knit Italian neighborhood—popularized by Herbert Gans in *The Urban Villagers*—for urban renewal.[10] Noted urban sociologist Jane Jacobs, fighting the decision, said of this neighborhood filled with pride, cohesiveness, and stability, "If this is a slum, we should have more of them." Nevertheless, the ethnic neighborhood was bulldozed into oblivion and the people scattered, replaced by high-rise luxury apartments and office buildings.

Public Housing

Another ill-conceived plan, created by the Housing Act of 1937, was public housing for the poor. The problem here was that policymakers ignored fundamental social concepts about human needs and interaction. Old, dilapidated buildings do not alone constitute a slum; a slum is a condition in which personal disorganization, apathy, alienation, lack of community, frustration, despair, and lack of opportunity exist. By attempting only a physical solution to the social problem of poverty, government simply created new slums.

The architectural design of the "supertenements" or "federal ghettos" as they came to be called, intensified further the isolation, alienation, and crime prevalent in disorganized low-income areas (see Box 15.1). Living in such a segregated place for impoverished minorities stigmatized the residents, and the poor considered such projects as residences of last resort. Moreover, income limits meant the eviction of the upwardly mobile and the concentration of only the very poor, thereby providing few legitimate successful role models for children.

Housing Subsidies

When government leaders realized that public housing projects were not the answer, they turned to direct subsidies to the poor to purchase homes or rent apartments of their choice. Greedy speculators, able to exploit the government and the poor through criminal collusion, undermined this program (the Housing and Urban Redevelopment Act of 1968). Typically, a real estate broker or speculator either bought rundown ghetto housing at low prices or frightened white owners in transitional neighborhoods into selling at low prices. By bribing government appraisers, this speculator then sold the property at much higher prices to low-income buyers qualifying for the federal subsidies. Their marginal existence forced some low-income buyers to default on their mortgage. More often, they abandoned the property because cosmetic repairs made before the sale had not corrected very serious defects in heating, plumbing, or structure. In either case, having guaranteed the bank its money, the FHA or VA found itself owning another house no one wanted. Although several hundred people were convicted of fraud in Detroit, St. Louis, and other older cities, the urban blight and abandonment remained.

Rent subsidies have had mixed results. The Experimental Housing Allowance Program (EHAP), beginning in the early 1970s, gave direct housing assistance (an average of $70) directly to tenants. The RAND Institute in 1980 reported that one cause of apartment abandonment was that these welfare recipients often did not pay the rent, even though they received the money to do so. Now under the current Section 8 Housing Assistance Payment Program, the U.S. Department of Housing and Urban Development (HUD) pays the landlords directly at least two-thirds of the "fair rental value."

Housing subsidies have become the nation's fastest-growing welfare program, doubling in cost every 5 years. Subsidies amounted to $2 billion in 1974, $5 billion in 1979, and the Office of Management and Budget projected them at $10 billion in 1984. The programs have had limited impact on housing low-income families, however. Recipients did not move any more often than nonrecipients, nor did rents become inflated because of demand for acceptable housing.

Defensible Space: A Successful Concept

Responding to the failures of public housing projects such as Pruitt-Igoe in St. Louis, Rosen Apartments in Philadelphia, Columbus Homes in Newark, and Columbus Point in Boston, architects and planners finally began to take human factors into consideration in determining the physical layout. By building low-rise structures (no more than six stories) in a design which allows families to share stairwells, interact, and develop proprietary attitudes, their security and liveableness improved greatly.

Oscar Newman demonstrated the value of such planning in his comparison of New York's adjacent Brownsville and Van Dyke Projects.[11] Although their population composition is similar, the two projects are strikingly different in physical design. Van Dyke is the typical housing project: 13 14-story monolithic buildings, each with

BOX 15.1

THE FAILURE OF PRUITT-IGOE

The central feature of the design was a "skip-stop" elevator system that would only stop at every third floor, which would have an open gallery containing laundry facilities and storage bins. The galleries were to be "vertical neighborhoods," providing, in addition to the laundry and other facilities, a "close, safe playground." In order to increase neighborliness, no more than twenty families would use a gallery. The floors in between the galleries would consist only of apartments. The entire complex was to be located on a large site (57 acres) with a "river of green running through it, and no through streets."

Pruitt-Igoe was completed in 1955, with thirty-three buildings of eleven stories each. A few changes had been made. The plan to mix some townhouses in with the high-density units was rejected on the basis of a cost-benefit analysis done by the Public Housing Authority. There were also other economies, such as eliminating the landscaping, not painting the cinder-block galleries and other public areas, eliminating public washrooms on the ground floor, leaving steam pipes uninsulated, and not providing screens for the gallery windows. Although the project won an award in 1958 for architectural design, very serious problems were beginning to emerge. The economies listed above had some unexpected consequences: children urinated in hallways, burned themselves on exposed pipes, and fell out of gallery windows.

The project had been designed for a racially mixed population—one-third white and two-thirds black—but a heavy influx of hard-core families with numerous social problems soon drove out all who could escape. Demographically, the project soon became inhabited mainly by black households headed by women, with a large number of children—five to twelve per household—and on welfare. Of the 10,736 people living in Pruitt-Igoe in 1965, there were only 900 men—many of them elderly—but over 7,000 children, of whom 70 percent were under twelve years of age.

During the 1970s, Pruitt-Igoe became a symbol of all that is wrong with public housing projects, with elevators battered and out of order, stairwells with lighting fixtures ripped out, galleries unused and unsafe, and laundry rooms that invited robbery and rape. Laundry rooms, stairwells, and halls in Pruitt-Igoe were used by adolescents for sex. Making many "conquests" was one of the few ways for a boy there to achieve status with his peer group, and the girls viewed sex as a way of achieving popularity and maturity. The mean age for becoming sexually active was thirteen, and half the girls in the projects became pregnant at least once before age eighteen. Mothers found it practically impossible to supervise children. They feared to go out of their apartments; and this was a reasonable fear: a survey of residents disclosed that 41 percent of the adults had been robbed, 20 percent physically assaulted, and 39 percent insulted by teenagers. The absence of men and the physically unsafe design features, such as the skip-stop elevators and the open galleries, resulted in a constant threat of mugging or rape for female inhabitants.

By 1972, only the most desperate of the poor remained in the dangerous foul-smelling buildings. Occupancy was down to a total population of only 2,788 persons. One by one, the buildings were simply abandoned by their tenants. Even the most down-and-out welfare recipients were unwilling to tolerate the degradation and the constant threat of personal danger. Rehabilitating the buildings to make them fit for human habitation, it was estimated, would cost more than $40 million, and then there was no guarantee that addicts and vandals would not destroy and terrorize the buildings again.

In the fall of 1972, the Housing Authority took the drastic action of blowing up the two worst buildings and began dynamiting the top seven stories off others in order to convert them into more manageable four-story buildings. It was hoped that the resulting low-rises would be easier for the tenants to control against outsiders and would provide some sense of defensible space and physical security. This effort was not successful, and in 1973 the Housing Authority began to demolish the remainder of the buildings. Today Pruitt-Igoe is a wasteland.

Fifteen years after its construction, the Pruitt-Igoe Housing Project in St. Louis was dynamited into oblivion by the federal government. Winning an "excellence in architecture" award in 1958 this high-rise complex rapidly became so unsafe that no one wanted to live there.

SOURCE: J. John Palen, *The Urban World*, 2d ed., (New York: McGraw-Hill, 1981), pp. 279–80.

a common entrance for the 112 to 136 families, and two elevators in the middle of the corridor stopping at every floor. In contrast, the older Brownsville Houses are three- and six-story structures with six families sharing a floor. Several apartments are a few steps above the lobby, encouraging surveillance over activity in this entryway. The elevator stops only at odd-numbered floors, requiring residents to go up or down one floor through use of an open stairwell around which the apartments are clustered. This arrangement assures frequent use and supervision through vertical communication and tenant exercise of territorial prerogatives in building corridors, hallways, and stairs. As a result, Brownsville has had significantly fewer problems than Van Dyke with crime, vandalism, child supervison, and maintenance.

Today, high-rise housing projects are no longer built in the United States. Multiple family construction for low-income families is now low-rise dwellings with courtyards and other features to enhance social interaction, cohesiveness, and safety.

Gentrification

Some of the older cities in the snowbelt—Baltimore, Boston, Chicago, New York, and Washington, D.C.—have been experiencing a renaissance of sorts, with middle-class families moving into dilapidated neighborhoods and restoring them. In most major European cities, **gentrification** has long been a significant movement, but only

The gentrification process occurring in the nation's older cities in recent years has revitalized many neighborhoods, bringing back the middle class while simultaneously displacing the poor. Pictured above is one of many streets of row houses in Baltimore undergoing restoration.

in recent years have affluent, young professionals in America rediscovered the cities. An Urban Land Institute study in 1979 found that, in about 75 percent of large American cities, a significant resettlement of middle- and upper-middle-income families had occurred. Numerous factors have contributed to this trend: the increased proportion of young adults in the population, the high level of professional jobs in the city, the high cost of suburban living, the low cost of much inner city real estate, the lessening of commuter time and costs, the accessibilty to urban activities.

Many signs give evidence of the beginnings of gentrification. Brownstone houses in previously depressed city areas get renovated, with colorful shops and restaurants opening in the neighborhood. In a few prime areas the brownstones now sell for as high as $500,000 in New York, but others elsewhere are still available for as little as $40,000. When you compare their four stories with 5,000 square feet, fireplaces and oak or mahogany woodwork, to the typical suburban house with 1,200 square feet selling for over $80,000, the bargain often becomes irresistible.

While gentification revitalizes city neighborhoods and returns the middle class to the cities, it has its negative aspects as well. The influx of affluent families, mostly white, results in higher rents and property taxes, forcing poor and minority residents from their neighborhoods into less desirable ones or new ghettos outside the city. Encouraging economic redevelopment thus creates the dilemma of how to protect the poor and prevent the spread of urban blight elsewhere.

Not all cities have benefited from city neighborhood revivals. Newark, Cleveland, and St. Louis, for example, continue to experience residential and business decline. While a definite trend is occurring in most cities, it is too soon to tell whether the gentrification process will spread throughout the cities or remain confined to a few select neighborhoods.

Urban Homesteading

Begun in Wilmington, Delaware in 1973 and a moderate success in other cities also, urban homesteading offers one example of how gentrification works. Cities sell abandoned or foreclosed dwellings for a token price to people who agree to rehabilitate the home, usually within 18 months, and live there for at least 3 years. Through city efforts and federal support, they receive low-interest bank loans for the needed renovations. For a cost of perhaps $60,000 or less, considerably less than the purchase price of suburban homes, they can restore these city residences to meet housing code standards. Such costs put this type of housing program beyond the reach of the urban poor, although ''sweat equity'' projects of low-income people, such as the People's Development Corporation (PDC) in the South Bronx have been successful in reclaiming abandoned tenements.

Urban homesteading is a relatively small program. Slightly over 40,000 homes have been rehabilitated since 1973, while over 1 million inner-city homes have been abandoned. Many abandoned properties are beyond the rehabilitation stage, and often those salvageable are surrounded by others which are not, or by cleared land. Unless an entire neighborhood can be improved, urban homesteading alone is not the answer. Still, the program has been successful in Baltimore, Chicago, Cleveland, Pittsburgh, Oakland, and Wilmington where it all began.

The grafitti on these buildings in New York's lower east side protest against their planned gentrification, demand speculators keep out, and that the buildings be repaired for low-income people instead. One continuing problem in most older cities is adequate housing for both middle- and low-income residents.

Low-interest City Mortgages

Another attractive program luring the middle class has been using below-market interest rates on mortgages. In the late 1970s cities began selling tax-exempt municipal bonds to raise money for mortgages which in turn pay off the bonds to the banks. Such a practice costs the cities very little while generating new tax revenues and improving the quality of the housing stock.

Condo Fever

The conversion of urban rental apartments to condominium units has been extensive in recent years. Caught in a squeeze between increasing operating costs and narrowing profit margins, owners have found it advantageous to convert their buildings. Middle-class tenants gain both property ownership and the accompanying tax advantages. As the condo trend continues, the ones most adversely affected are the working poor who cannot afford the financing, yet do not qualify for subsidized housing. They could easily be forced out of their rented apartment building if it converts to condominium units.

TRANSPORTATION PROBLEMS

Transportation technology defines a city, determining its size, shape, and character; makes different types of cities possible; and causes the great changes that cities presently are experiencing. Being chosen as a station on the American railroads certainly helped to locate early cities, but the auto has been the main force in urban change. The American city "exploded" into the dispersed **metropolis** much earlier than most of us realize. Auto registrations jumped from 2.5 million to 26.5 million during 1915–1930. Today urban auto congestion is extensive, leading to the remarkable statistic that the average speed in New York City's borough of Manhattan has decreased over the past 50 years from 11 miles an hour to 7 miles an hour.[12]

At first glance the extension and improvement of rapid transit systems appear to be an ideal solution for all the problems the cities have accumulated from the overabundance of autos. A rapid transit track moves 40,000 persons past a given point in an hour while, at 1.8 persons per car, it would take a 16-lane highway to do the same job.[13]

In most large American cities, transit is in an impossible mixed-definition position. The government owns and operates the lines and sees them as a "public service" while insisting they should pay for themselves. Comfort, even necessary maintenance, are seldom paid for because politicians set low fare structures they think will please the voters. If we knew whether transit was private or public, a government-run business, or a utility, then better planning would be possible. In most European cities rapid transit has gone the whole definitional route and is considered a public utility. Transit is better there.[14]

Mass transit has been failing financially for many years. The precipitous decline in ridership is not merely due to people leaving for the suburbs, or to deteriorating

Wherever large concentrations of people live and work, traffic congestion and noise and air pollution also exist. Yet Americans prefer driving to using mass transit, unlike urbanites in other countries. Note the number of cars with just one person in them.

conditions. The deterioration is part of a vicious cycle of loss of income–deterioration–loss of ridership–loss of income. Political neglect has aggravated the cycle. In 1980 the Boston transit system was briefly closed because no government body would take responsibility for its debts. A similar battle has been raging for years in New York City over how much of the massive deficit should be assumed by the city, state, or federal budgets. One of the Reagan administration's first pronouncements was that mass transit subsidies were inefficient and should be phased out. The inescapable fact is that in 1930, 15.2 billion riders used the country's transit systems, but only 7.3 billion by 1970.[15]

Over 90 percent of all trips in large metropolitan areas occur by private, not public, transportation. Only about 1 percent of city trips are by rail, mostly in large cities; remaining public transport is by bus.[16] Only in a few of the largest cities (Boston, Chicago, Jersey City, New Orleans, Newark, Philadelphia) does public transportation play a significant role by carrying 25 to 44 percent of the people, and about 50 percent in New York. Only Atlanta, Boston, Chicago, Cleveland, New York, Oakland, Philadelphia, San Francisco, and Washington, D.C. have subway systems. In smaller metropolitan areas, public transit accounts for less than 2 percent of trips, a pattern unlikely to change.

Mass transit need not be oppressive, ugly, and grafitti marred. The scene above at Marta Station in Peachtree Center in Atlanta, Georgia, shows a fast, quiet, efficient, and aesthetically pleasing system. Similar systems exist in San Francisco, Toronto, and Washington, D.C. Older mass transit systems in other cities lack this pleasant environment.

CAN SNOWBELT CITIES COMPETE WITH SUNBELT CITIES?

The 1980 census confirmed the long-publicized growth of sunbelt cities and decline in population of snowbelt cities. The South and West now contain over half the U.S. population and 5 of the 10 largest cities (#3 Los Angeles, #5 Houston, #7 Dallas, #8 San Diego, #10 San Antonio [see Figure 15.1]). As of 1980, the five fastest growing cities were all in the Southwest: San Jose, Phoenix, El Paso, Houston, and San Diego. Those with the most rapid population loss were St. Louis, Cleveland, Detroit, Pittsburgh, and Washington, D.C. The 1980s also saw a large exodus of business and industry from the older central cities away from high taxes, energy costs, wages, congestion, and outmoded plants. The combination of loss of people and manufacturing jobs led some observers to sound the death knell for the older cities.

Are the older cities dying? Some "experts" have predicted economic disaster for them because of these loss of jobs to suburban or sunbelt locations. A closer look, however, reveals a more balanced picture. For example, as the sunbelt cities rapidly expand, the familiar urban problems develop: overcrowding, lack of housing, con-

FIGURE 15.1   U.S. Resident Population by Region, 1850–1982

Northeast
1850	37.2%
1900	27.6%
1950	26.0%
1970	24.1%
1982	21.4%

Midwest
1850	23.3%
1900	34.6%
1950	29.4%
1970	27.8%
1982	25.5%

South
1850	38.7%
1900	32.2%
1950	31.2%
1970	30.1%
1982	33.7%

West
1850	0.8%
1900	5.7%
1950	13.3%
1970	17.1%
1982	19.4%

SOURCE: Bureau of the Census, *Statistical Abstract of the United States: 1984,* pp. 6–10.

gestion, pollution, an increasing crime rate (see Table 15.1). In recent years, such supposedly declining snowbelt cities as St. Louis and Baltimore have had lower unemployment rates than the sunbelt cities of Atlanta and Los Angeles. Unemployment in the Northeast's 26 million-member work force was lower in 1983 than was the national average.[17]

Northeast Resurgence

Many indicators point to both the strength and rebound in the Boston–Washington, D.C. corridor. The region's 49 million inhabitants (22 percent of the population) produce more than their share (25 percent) of America's wealth, compared to the 48.2 percent produced by the South and West, which contain 50.2 percent of the population. Nearly 50 percent of the $5.9 billion in investment capital available nationwide in 1981 was concentrated in the Northeast, where bank assets of $1.7 trillion accounted for 37 percent of the nation's bank assets.[18]

Even more significantly, the northeastern states have been cutting various business taxes and aggressively seeking industrial development. In 1981 Massachusetts broke its annual record for plant expansion, and then set another record in 1982 despite the recession. Pennsylvania was fourth from 1979 to 1982 in attracting new investments, trailing only Texas, Louisiana, and Florida. Over 400 foreign companies are located in Pennsylvania, employing over 250,000 people and shipping over $15 billion worth of Pennsylvania-made goods to foreign markets.[19]

Why does this region still attract job-creating investments? From interviews with employers and state secretaries of commerce, Rushworth Kidder identified the following factors.[20]

1. *Market concentration.* The region is the most concentrated market in the nation (one-fifth the population on one-twentieth the land mass). A centrally located manufacturer in the BosWash corridor can reach over half the U.S. and Canadian manufacturing firms and retail sales outlets within 24 hours by truck. Also, the corridor states are, by air and sea, close to the 271 million people in the European Community countries.

2. *Education.* The 11-state region has the highest concentration of higher education, sending 2.8 million students annually to 875 colleges and universities. Proximity to top colleges influences location choice of high technology firms. Massachusetts's famous Route 128 (now called ''America's Technology Highway'') is near MIT and Harvard. New Jersey, with only 3.3 percent of the nation's population, has laboratories, many near Princeton University, doing 9 percent of America's research and development work.

3. *Infrastructure.* Although in need of repairs, the region's **infrastructure**—roads, bridges, and water systems—are already in place. Many fast-growth cities have not yet developed adequate systems and the cost of doing so, including obtaining the necessary lands, is rising rapidly.

4. *Quality of life.* Many people recognize the region as the artistic and cultural center of the country. Access to the seacoast, lakes, and mountains brings a rich mix of city and country, work and leisure opportunities.

A New Economic Function for the City

Only recently have American central cities become centers of positive change. Even though the days of heavy manufacturing in the cities are gone, these cities are now emerging as centers of sophisticated services in finance, advertising, entertainment, and corporate management. As British urbanologist Peter Hall observes, the central business district is now an ideas-industry area: producing, processing, and trading specialized intelligence.[21]

New York, for example, is the headquarters for 80 organizations with assets exceeding 1 billion dollars. Of the 14 American companies with assets of $25 billion or more, 10 are based in New York. Another exciting aspect of the city's economic development is the influx of foreign capital; 280 foreign financial institutions are now located in New York. A recent study by the London *Economist* noted that ''New York is becoming the capital of the world even as it is becoming noticeably less the all-dominating city of the United States.'' In another recent survey of foreign busi-

TABLE 15.1 Changes in Quality of City Life, 1970–1982

	Population Density				Crime		
	Persons per Square Mile				Serious Crimes per 1,000 Persons		
	1970	1980	Change		1970	1982	Change
New York	26,345	23,455	Down 11%	New York	66	97	Up 47%
Chicago	15,136	13,174	Down 13%	Chicago	38	61	Up 61%
Los Angeles	6,060	6,384	Up 5%	Los Angeles	62	108	Up 74%
Philadelphia	15,175	12,413	Down 18%	Philadelphia	23	56	Up 143%
Houston	2,841	2,867	Up 1%	Houston	49	104	Up 112%
Detroit	10,968	8,874	Down 19%	Detroit	84	128	Up 52%
Dallas	3,179	2,715	Down 15%	Dallas	60	128	Up 113%
San Diego	2,200	2,736	Up 24%	San Diego	33	75	Up 127%
Phoenix	2,346	2,437	Up 4%	Phoenix	50	96	Up 92%
Baltimore	11,568	9,793	Down 15%	Baltimore	69	93	Up 35%

NOTE: Serious crimes are murder, forcible rape, robbery, aggravated assault, burglary, larceny-theft and auto theft.

	Families			Taxes		
	Percentage of Population over Age 14 Married (with spouse present)			Local Taxes per Person		
	1970	1980		1970	1981	Change
New York	56.0%	45.7%	New York	$383	$1,053	Up 175%
Chicago	54.5%	43.3%	Chicago	$113	$ 263	Up 133%
Los Angeles	55.1%	46.1%	Los Angeles	$110	$ 255	Up 132%
Philadelphia	53.5%	43.4%	Philadelphia	$183	$ 500	Up 173%
Houston	63.1%	52.2%	Houston	$ 82	$ 253	Up 209%
Detroit	54.9%	40.7%	Detroit	$148	$ 300	Up 103%
Dallas	62.5%	50.7%	Dallas	$106	$ 260	Up 145%
San Diego	57.9%	48.7%	San Diego	$ 63	$ 155	Up 146%
Phoenix	65.1%	56.9%	Phoenix	$ 72	$ 161	Up 124%
Baltimore	51.9%	39.4%	Baltimore	$222	$ 442	Up 99%

ness, New York was the overwhelming choice over London, Paris, and other major cities as the place to live and work.[22]

In other major cities, business rebirth is also occurring. Detroit's Renaissance Center, a striking tourist attraction of office towers, and hotel-shopping-business complex costing over $420 million, has brought thousands of jobs and millions of property-tax dollars to that city. Chicago's central business district (CBD) is experiencing its greatest corporate expansion in history, with about two dozen new skyscrapers built or under construction, costing over $1 billion.

Urban sociologist J. John Palen offers two additional facts to counter the prophets of urban doom.[23] White-collar jobs increased 7.2 percent in the older cities from 1960 to 1970, the pattern accelerating during the 1970s. The downtowns of most large cities are experiencing new business construction. Within a 10-year period Chicago

TABLE 15.1 (cont'd)

	Health Care				Education		
	Physicians per 100,000 Persons (suburbs included)				Share of Persons Age 25 and over with College Degrees		
	1970	1980	Change			1970	1980
New York	278	349	Up 26%	New York		10.6%	17.3%
Chicago	170	235	Up 38%	Chicago		8.1%	13.8%
Los Angeles-Long Beach	202	267	Up 32%	Los Angeles		13.9%	19.8%
Philadelphia	202	257	Up 27%	Philadelphia		6.8%	11.1%
Houston	152	209	Up 38%	Houston		14.9%	23.1%
Detroit	139	183	Up 32%	Detroit		6.2%	8.3%
Dallas-Fort Worth	136	175	Up 29%	Dallas		14.0%	22.0%
San Diego	186	258	Up 39%	San Diego		15.8%	24.0%
Phoenix	166	221	Up 33%	Phoenix		11.7%	16.5%
Baltimore	232	304	Up 31%	Baltimore		7.2%	11.3%

	Public Transit			Parks	
	Share of Workers Commuting by Public Transit			Acres of Park per 100,000 Persons	
	1970	1980			
New York	61.8%	55.8%	New York		352
Chicago	36.2%	32.4%	Chicago		344
Los Angeles	9.3%	7.0%	Los Angeles		494
Philadelphia	37.1%	30.2%	Philadelphia		515
Houston	7.8%	4.8%	Houston		1,255
Detroit	18.4%	11.8%	Detroit		384
Dallas	10.6%	8.3%	Dallas		2,151
San Diego	5.5%	3.3%	San Diego		2,056
Phoenix	1.7%	2.7%	Phoenix		3,515
Baltimore	27.0%	25.4%	Baltimore		763

SOURCE: Bureau of the Census, *Statistical Abstract of the United States: 1984.*

and New York increased office space by 50 percent. The trend may take a further upswing if the indications of new concentrations of "managerial industries" in the older cities continues.

Remote-Control Transactions

In some ways the new development of the urban core is reminiscent of the cities' earliest function as crossroads centers of trade. They are acting again as the bases for transactional activities. Instead of processing raw materials as they did during their manufacturing phase, they act as remote-control centers of the now widespread production and distribution systems. As early as 1961, Jean Gottman suggested that the old classification of economic activities into three sectors (primary: producing raw materials; secondary: processing them into finished goods; tertiary: providing

Now the seventh largest city in the nation, Dallas typifies the rapid growth of sunbelt cities while snowbelt cities decline in population. Such dramatic changes produce problems for both types of cities, especially in the infrastructure and support services.

services) was no longer adequate. **Transactions** are a new fourth sector, becoming a major part of America's business in cities.[24]

Urban Centrality

Only urban centers can provide the support services and the elements of centrality necessary to the service and transactional industries:[25]

1. *Accessible location:* through ports, railroads, and airports.

2. *Information flow:* knowledge is power; the old London coffeehouses and the modern media center serve similar functions.

3. *Labor market:* abundant specially trained support personnel.

4. *Amenities and entertainment:* necessary personnel, experts, and customers attracted by cultural activities.

5. *Expert consultants:* often necessary and available in less time than it would take to fly them in.

6. *Banking:* instant discussion of large-scale credit availability, often crucial for transactions.

7. *Education:* knowledge and technical training are a lifetime commitment of the modern business staff.

The Automated Office

Will the new "automated office" and "electronic cottage" make possible the total dispersal of transactional business, just as the truck dispersed manufacturing? Urbanologists and futurists are already trying to estimate the impact of home computers and word processors that will be "on-line" to central computers through phone lines from around the country, and of two-way or even multichannel videophones that would seem to make the conference-phone call the equivalent of a real conference. Some futurists feel that major dispersal of white-collar activities is inevitable, and being able to work at home will substantially reduce the need for central management locations.

Others, particularly interactionist sociologists, disagree. They argue that phone calls or computer outlets, however convenient, cannot fulfill the same needs as social proximity and direct interpersonal contact. Frequent face-to-face relations are needed to gain opinions, new ideas, judgments of their latest efforts, and something that could be called the emotional support of being with others who "understand." Some call this having to "be where the action is." These social functions of the specialized city districts, advocates maintain, make it unlikely they will be destroyed by increased automation of communication.

POLITICAL FRAGMENTATION

The inability of our political structure to adapt to the needs of metropolitan regions explains much about the causes and continuance of many urban problems. Traditional local boundaries are irrelevant to services needed by adjacent communities. Crime control, education, housing, pollution, solid waste disposal, transportation, and water supply require planning and control over an entire region, not within single localities. Museums, major city libraries, sports arenas, convention halls, cultural centers, and parks all attract many suburbanites, but the city bears the cost of staff, police, sanitation, and transportation services.

We function in metropolitan regions but do not govern that way. The existence of multiple small governing bodies within the metropolis means duplication of services (departments and agencies of government, fire and public safety, roads and sanitation, and so forth). Each municipality pursues its own course, without coordination and often in competition with others for ratables, creating unnecessary conflict and waste (inefficiency and high cost).

Cities actually have little control over their own affairs. Subject to many state and federal regulations, dependent upon other levels of government for funding and policy decision, urban government is impotent to deal with many of its problems with mass transit, poverty, pollution, and others. Until the 1970s, cities lacked political power in the rural-dominated state and federal legislatures, despite their greater population concentration. When the Supreme Court ruling on one-man, one-vote mandated reapportionment to balance legislative district representation, the majority of the population had shifted to the suburbs. Added to the rural/suburban bias against cities is the frequent political split of Democratic-controlled city governments and Republican-controlled state legislatures further impairing urban problem solutions.

Another aspect of **political fragmentation** is the presence of so many decision-making points in a large city, making overall coordination difficult. One consequence of the 1960s reform movement eliminating political machines has been the creation of new machines—semiautonomous city agencies and bureaucracies staffed by career professionals. These agencies shape important policies, but their leadership is relatively self-perpetuating, not easily subject to a higher authority. A city mayor, never certain-if the bureau chiefs and career commissioners look beyond their vested interests at the larger picture, is more a mediator between conflicting interest groups than someone in control.[26]

HOPE FROM PAST POLICY FAILURES

The early optimism and the belief that nonscientific analysis (that we all know what the answers are to poverty, crime, etc.) are giving way to realization that it is not enough to want to help, that social problems are just as in need of professional attention as medical problems. This attitude is not yet dominant among the public, but is becoming widespread among social scientists and members of the political system itself. Let us list some suggested modifications of the policy system.

Self-Help Rehabilitation

Replace the notion of slum clearance in housing policy with local rehabilitation. Geoffry Payne suspects that self-help rehabilitation, the poor remaking their own homes, never got a chance because it didn't fit into the existing bureaucratic structure.[27] Condemning whole city blocks and replacing them with new buildings was a simple, if monumentally expensive, process. Government did not have to deal with people, with human complications.

Collaborative Planning

As part of program planning, use a need-assessment survey to learn people's opinions and needs. Ask local residents: What should the facility contain? Will they use a new facility if it is offered? Too often an already prepared plan has been presented at a community meeting, or to selected "key people." Sometimes "hard-sell" techniques were used such as: "We experts thought we would let you amateurs get a brief look at what we've designed for you so that you can give us your blessing." This was not the best atmosphere for **collaborative planning.**

When planning research is coupled with continuous monitoring of the expected changes, again by scientifically surveying the people supposedly affected, you are able to tell quickly if an effort is really causing the desired change. Citizen-based planning provides two-way communication between government and people, deflects pressures from lobbies and special-interest groups, deescalates unreasonable expectations, and reduces public hostility and crisis atmospheres.[28]

Systematic need assessment will also end paternalistic planning. Beginning in the 1960s, when politicians frequently mentioned the feelings of "the people," they assumed those spokespeople who were most noticeable in the community were the "duly elected" representatives of the people involved. The policy shortcut of going to the presumed representative, rather than directly to the people, frequently produced biased reports. The situation became so bad in New York City that the mayor and others used the ugly term "poverty pimp" to describe the self-serving representatives who distorted "facts" to try building one sector of the service-provider establishment.

Unplanning Streets and Sidewalks

Why are the streets only defined as transportation conduits of the neighborhood? This one redefinition could have a radical impact on city life. Suppose the streets were sanctuaries in which the children could grow up? This is not total possibility, but the effort could be made outside main commuter routes. In some areas the streets would have to be won back from autos, in some from muggers. Donald Appleyard says the only difficult part is to reorient our thinking, to turn it from the surrender we have made.[29]

Jane Jacobs has been perhaps the most eloquent proponent of reclaiming the sidewalks for the community. She sees the destruction of social community and the substantial increase in urban violence and fear as results of antipeople, anticity planning concepts:

> . . . that the sight of people attracts still other people is something that city planners and city architectural designers seem to find incomprehensible. They operate on the premise that city people seek the sight of emptiness, obvious and quite. Nothing could be less true.[30]

A safe street is a continuously busy street that has a lot of "eyes upon it." Modern planners aim for the widely spaced, scientifically ordered city in which "the presence of many other people is, at best, a necessary evil." This creates noncommunities and areas that are, literally, out of social control, and, therefore, open for street crime.

The Belmont neighborhood in the South Bronx, a seven-block Italian community of 25,000 people, illustrates this concept. Life exists on the streets after dark, with no bars or steel gates on shop windows; old people walk the streets alone and young people play in the park in the evenings. The crime rate is low and break-ins and looting did not occur during the 1978 blackout. The key difference is community cohesiveness, the people acting together as the eyes and ears of the street. Nothing goes unnoticed; the people help and watch out for each other. Police of the neighborhood's 48th Precinct say it is not unusual to receive a call that some resident has caught a thief and to send an officer to get him. Captain Robert McGowan said, "The word is around that if you want to make trouble, don't go to Belmont or you'll wind up losing."[31]

Social Utilities Not Social "Services"

The final redefinition has to do with helping those in obvious need. Alfred Kahn has deplored our lagging definition of social "services" or "charities."[32] He pointed out that we totally accept any number of physical functions as "necessary" to individual survival in the city: water, street lights, postal and telephone communication, and fire fighting. No one expects victims of power blackouts to be carrying their own flashlights, and no one blames them for not being equipped to "adjust to" that form of city failure. This is because we define these things as utilities, even setting up highly subsidized monopolies to provide them. Our culture has a great deal of difficulty extending this form of acceptance to social or individual problems. But, until such things as "social service," unemployment, ill-health, transportation, and decent housing are seen as beyond individual control, then the causes of social problems burdening our central cities will not receive the attention needed for solution.

SOCIOLOGICAL PERSPECTIVES

In this chapter we have examined perceptions and problems of cities, effects of past policies and the potential of policy redefinitions. While doing so, the contributions of various urban sociologists guided our understanding of specific areas of concern. Within this section we shall consider the differing analytical viewpoints regarding the entire array of problems besetting the cities.

Individual Faults and Deviant Behavior

This perspective is popular both with the general public and some social scientists. Public opinion polls sampling reasons for people avoiding or leaving the city often find complaints about crime, overcrowding, or other negative aspects of life people believe are inherent in the city. Since population density correlates highly with deviant behavior—crime, drug addiction, mental illness, disapproved sexual orientations, suicide, vandalism—some theorists seek a causal explanation.

Sociologist Louis Wirth and other determinists see the scale, density, and heterogeneity of cities weakening social bonds and social control mechanisms, thus generating alienation and disorder. Some biological scientists and psychologists suggest overcrowding leads to antisocial activity, citing animal studies to support their position. Critics state humans do not actually live or work within massive scale, density, or heterogeneity, but within the enveloped protection of their small group memberships. Animal studies provide only suggestive conclusions, not proof; humans possess rationalizing capabilities about the reality they see, giving them adaptive flexibility lacking in animals.

Because cities offer anonymity and a more tolerant environment through their size and diversity, they probably attract more deviants from other areas. This factor of critical mass, a sufficient number of people generating supportive social institutions, appeals to like-minded individuals seeking to escape notice and disapproval in smaller communities.

The diversity of cities could possibly create anomie, confusing the individual about acceptable social norms. With no clear guidelines to follow and a wide range of lifestyle options to emulate, some will choose an unconventional behavior form. The deviance approach thus holds the city responsible for enabling such aberrant behavior to continue.

Institutional Faults and System Disorganization

Functionalists blame rapid urbanization for disrupting the social organization of society. First, large masses of rural residents and immigrants came to American cities, creating intolerable living conditions. Unprepared to assimilate the new-comers who themselves were ill-equipped for urban living, the cities experienced increasing pathologies in sickness, disease, death, crime, and social disorganization. Before the urban system could regain equilibrium, it suffered another jolt as the exodus to the suburbs happened. Factories, stores, offices followed the former ur-banites, leaving the city core unable to assist the nonwhite minorities replacing them.

Much of this social change was functional. Modern manufacturing technology required horizontal plant expansion which cities could not provide but suburbs could. Suburban expansion created many job opportunities for the building trades, automotive, and transport industries. It also took the population pressure off cities, reducing their density. Business and industry benefited from lower taxes and greater ease of shipping products. Workers gained the satisfaction of home ownership and travel flexibility by automobile. Yet many dysfunctions flowed from these social changes as well. Cities lost tax revenues, became disproportionately inhabited by the poor, and lacked employment opportunities and sufficient resources to provide adequately for them. Housing and schools deteriorated, demands for services increased, and the inner city declined into a near-comatose state.

To restore stability and equity in the system, functionalists maintain that adjustments must occur. Since our communities have merged with each other all ways but politically, perhaps reorganization along more realistic lines would return the governing and financial balance needed. Regional planning and coordination would insure more rational land use and a greater sense of mutual interdependence. Problems knowing no geographic boundary—water supply, pollution, traffic—could be addressed more effectively. The problems of employment and housing might be more easily resolved if a redefined community through a metropolitan form of government worked to provide a coordination system of business locations, housing, and transportation.

Another possibility of restoring balance in the social system may be further social change. Perhaps the cities need to evolve further out of their previous manufacturing role into their new transactional one. The processes already occurring—gentrification, new office buildings, revitalized downtowns—need to be encouraged further. Reduced density and vacant lots provide the opportunity to rebuild the city, improving its aesthetic beauty while providing new opportunities for its poor. Urban enterprise zones offering tax incentives to industry, together with job training programs, could bring the jobs to the people who need them. Cities do not exist in isolation; their welfare hinges upon taking steps to place them on an economic parity with other regions.

Inequality and Inevitable Conflict

Conflict theorists view the problems in cities as the uneven outcome of various interest groups competing against each other for limited resources. This struggle takes many forms, often pitting more powerful groups with little concern for particu-

BOX 15.2

STREET PEOPLE: ADRIFT
AND ALONE
Alcoholic and penniless, Albert Pierpont expects to die on the streets of the nation's capital. In Manhattan, an elderly "bag lady" known only as Dianne scrapes by on handouts. In the boom town of Houston, a young job seeker from New Jersey has ended up on skid row, broke and without hope.

They are among an estimated 200,000 homeless adults roaming the country—a problem of mounting concern across the nation. Destitute street people, once a big-city phenomenon, today are found almost everywhere. Efforts to provide food and shelter are costing charities and taxpayers millions of dollars, and still the drifters keep dying in distressing numbers.

Some of contemporary America's hobos are no different from the thousands who crisscrossed the land during the Great Depression, thrown out of work by a sagging economy. But experts say that the largest percentage are mentally ill or hopeless alcoholics, unable to cope with society. Some seem wild-eyed and menacing, but most threaten only themselves and one another.

Scores perish each year—victims of exposure, starvation, disease or predatory thugs who want what little they have. No one knows for sure how many freeze to death each winter, but church groups believe it could be several hundred. Many are killed when the abandoned buildings in which they have built fires for warmth go up in flames.

EXODUS OF MENTAL PATIENTS

The number of vagrant Americans began climbing in the 1960s, when state and federal governments started to encourage the release of mental patients judged no threat to society or to themselves. The number confined fell from nearly 560,000 in the mid-1950s to about 138,000 today. The plan was for the mental inmates to be

lar urban problems against the directly affected, less powerful groups. The arena of conflict is often among groups within the city as well as with others outside the city.

Urban heterogeneity makes potential conflict among different groups quite likely. Should a city's limited funds improve the downtown shopping district, build low-cost housing for the poor or elderly, build recreation centers, improve the schools or public transportation? All cannot be accomplished at once, yet all needs are immediate. Merchants and citizens of different constituencies thus vie with one another, pressing for their own interests. Added to this oft-seething caldron of conflict are the vested interests of the civic bureaucracies, seeking higher salaries and improved working conditions or preservation of their domain. As unresolved issues continue, the likelihood of organized protest—demonstrations, protest meetings, noisy confrontations, rent strikes, union job actions, or violence—increases.

Within the city lies another focal point for conflict analysis: the exploitation of

treated as outpatients in places closer to home. But often it has not worked out that way. "Many former patients, because of their condition, did not know how to get to community centers," explains Lee Carty, administrator of the Washington-based Mental Health Law Project. "So after they were released from hospitals, that's the last anyone saw of them until they showed up in doorways."

Lacking any sort of identification, a fixed address or job history, [most qualify] for no government relief benefits. . . . Many others do qualify for welfare benefits, but few are able to negotiate the bureaucratic maze. "They are so sociologically disintegrated that they can't stand in line long enough to fill out the form or cash the check," explains Dr. Stuart Schwartz, a psychiatrist at San Francisco General Hospital.

The vagabonds travel different paths to life on the street, but for all of them existence is precarious. Days are spent wandering and begging strangers for change. Medical care usually comes only when they show up at a hospital's emergency room. Most get just one meager meal a day, usually at a soup kitchen.

BEDROOMS IN THE OUTDOORS

Those with money spend nights in vermin-infested $5-a-night flophouses like the ones in New York's Bowery and San Francisco's Tenderloin. Others take refuge in shelters run by charitable groups. Derelicts without cash and for whom space cannot be found in shelters must shift for themselves. These are the "untouchables" found on the sidewalk steam grates of Washington, in packing crates in San Francisco and New York, in the alleyways of Portland and Houston. . . .

Most of the homeless can testify that street life is marked by violence as well as privation. The puny among them are robbed and assaulted by the strong. Women are easy prey for rapists. The young and aggressive displace the old and weak from precious places of warmth.

SOURCE: Reprinted from *U.S. News & World Report* issue of March 8, 1982. Copyright, 1982, U.S. News & World Report, Inc.

others. When cities were manufacturing centers, powerful industrialists often maximized their profits by exploiting the available cheap labor; their one-sided gain meant widespread poverty and neighborhood deterioration for large sections of the city. Similarly, slumlords seeking maximum profits through "rent gouging" and/or minimal maintenance accelerated the decline. Forced eviction of low-rent tenants to upgrade a building into a middle-income rental facility, or engineering condemnation of an area to build more lucrative structures, are but two instances of the ability of potent real estate entrepreneurs to garner profits at others' expense. Political machines and crooked politicians often bilked cities of millions of dollars to the detriment of the public welfare.

The perception by many social analysts of a rural/suburban anticity bias and of political fragmentation intrigues conflict analysts. With political power in state and national legislatures vested in rural and suburban regions, their representatives use their dominance primarily for their own benefit. Besides feathering their own nests with government monies, these regions resist any efforts to redistribute resources in any other fashion. Programs giving cities more financial support or restructuring tax levies upon affluent suburbs for city treasuries encounter fierce resistance. Until urbanites become more aware of their common interests and become more organized, they are unlikely to develop sufficient power to gain an equitable allocation of resources.

Interaction and Social Interpretation

Focusing upon how people subjectively define reality, interactionists examine how values, shared expectations, and perceptions apply to social problems in cities. Traditional American values have always stressed the small town ideal with its personal cohesiveness and sense of community. Warnings against the corruptive influences of cities, while common throughout world history, have been especially pronounced in the American experience. Predominant rural America mistrusted the cities. Later the influx of millions of culturally distinct immigrants and then of American Blacks and Hispanics engendered prejudices and avoidance responses. Acclimation to suburban living provoked disdain for urban life-styles. One's perception of the city as a place inhabited by "lesser types" removed any sense of social responsibility to improve the situation. Anticity value orientations prompt the response that cities bring on their own problems rather than reflect an intensity of societal problems.

Because cities house large concentrations of poor people, nonurbanites stereotype cities as almost exclusively urban jungles and slum neighborhoods. While sections of cities do fulfill that perception, other areas are safe, cohesive, and beautiful. Even in the poor sections, problems of overcrowding, substandard housing, crime, and health are not as severe as 50 years ago. They remain matters of concern in a relative sense because they still contrast with conditions elsewhere. The rise in living standards and expectations (car, TV, hot water, and other necessities once thought luxuries) cause the poor to feel deprived compared to the nonpoor possessing such items.

Another common interaction difficulty has been between the poverty-stricken urban minorities and the police and city government agencies. Beginning with the Irish in the mid-nineteenth century and continuing to the present day, those responsible for maintaining the formal social control mechanisms of the city often viewed the minority groups as the enemy. Their physical and cultural differences, the pathologies flowing out of their poverty, and the ethnocentric attitudes of the middle class all served to reinforce this perception. Mutual antagonisms developed and a vicious circle of attitudes, actions, and reactions ensued. By the time the minority achieved economic and political power, another group replaced it at the bottom of the ladder and the cycle began anew. Presently Blacks and Hispanics are gaining a stronger representation in elected and appointive positions, suggesting improved social policy reinterpretations and actions for their constituents.

THE FUTURE

Our cities today offer both encouraging and disheartening signs. We appear to be going in two directions at the same time. On the one hand, we see an influx of the middle class, refurbished neighborhoods, new office buildings, much cultural and economic activity. Yet, we can also see decay and decline, congestion and pollution, crime and poverty, suburbanites shunning the city. Which trend will prevail?

Pessimistic Scenario

By 2025 cities had become an anachronism. Most Americans neither lived in, worked in, nor even visited them. What had been a fairly substantial population loss in the 1970s had become a massive exodus by the turn of the century. Sunbelt cities had not escaped the antiurban population shift; their rapid growth in the 1980s had generated serious urban problems of congestion, pollution, crime, and inadequate housing. These problems, compounded by a lack of an infrastructure of roads, bridges, and water systems and local resistance to their high costs, had caused the sunbelt cities to lose their allure, declining almost as rapidly as their earlier growth.

Federal and state government cutbacks had sent mass transit into such a tailspin that service deteriorated while fares increased and ridership declined. The antipathy toward traveling to or within the city became so extreme that businesses could no longer remain in the city and retain their best people, who were being lured away by suburban firms. Cutbacks in housing subsidies, public housing, and mortgage loans accelerated the urban housing problem. The valiant efforts of a few to preserve or restore neighborhoods were overwhelmed by the neglect, deterioration, abandonment, arson, and razed buildings that turned much of the urban landscape into a wasteland. The decaying or vacant properties created a kind of "urban black hole," drawing entire neighborhoods into its blight. As the loss of ratables mounted, the cities sank deeper into a financial abyss, and what property, business, and services remained suffered even more.

The suburbs meanwhile had prospered, although their nature had changed somewhat. Seizing upon the transactional activity trend that had once promised an urban renaissance, the suburbs began building commercial parks—office buildings, financial institutions, advertising and marketing firms, computer specialists and support systems, restaurants, conference centers, health spas, large parking areas, and minibus service within the vast park complex. Nearby shopping malls had completely replaced the old urban downtowns, offering a multitude of stores within walking distance, as well as theaters, concerts, ballet, and symphony orchestra performances, fairs, festivals, and excitement. Individual creativity, formerly found in urban artist subcultures, had been replaced by computer art and music created by random selection programming.

Suburbs sprawled into each other, all lacking a sense of identity or community. The automobile was a critical need, but roads were crowded and transportation costs a major part of the family budget. The combination of computer dominance and suburban sameness had homogenized much of America. Conformity in values, fashions, and actions had brought civilization to a plateau existence—a high plateau to be sure—but a plateau nonetheless.

What remained of the cities though, were not plateaus, but sinks of decay and despair. The filth, poverty, crime, and violence made these places seem worse than in the times of Dickens and Engels. Cities no longer had any redeeming features. They were considered un-American, a national commission recommending their dismantling to make room for additional suburbs.

Optimistic Scenario

Several major factors had sparked the rebirth and dominance of American cities by 2025. Most significantly, the suburban population had become alarmed over the urbanization of their towns and surrounding countryside. Acting to protect their own interests, the suburban civic leaders joined forces with urban leaders to keep large offices and stores in the metropolitan areas, linked by a more reliable, comfortable public transportation system. Such action had helped revitalize the cities while at the same time helping the suburbs preserve their residential character, leaving undeveloped parcels of land for recreational use and ending urban sprawl. The increasing scarcity of fossil fuels had caused Americans to rely more on mass transit, locating nearer to the social, cultural, and economic activities of the city.

The continued influx of middle-class professionals into the city had broadened the gentrification process. As more neighborhoods blossomed into refurbished areas of pleasant homes, stores, and eateries, a ripple effect had occurred. City neighborhoods became good places to raise children again, and the schools, playgrounds, and parks reflected that change. Each improvement prompted another, and the rebuilding spirit had spread to other neighborhoods. Changed values and attitudes, successful role models, had ignited an urban renaissance.

In an age when technology had revolutionized the nature of work and the length of the work week, cities had provided the most advantageous location for the interplay of business transactions and leisure pursuits. Choosing to live closer to their work, the middle class now lived mostly in cities, while the working class lived farther away to be near the plants in which they worked. Yet the appeal of the cities' activities brought the working class frequently to the urban areas, while middle-class city dwellers often traveled into the suburban hinterland to enjoy the countryside.

Regional government planning, together with county educational and emergency services (police, fire, ambulance), had drawn the urban-suburban communities closer. Recognizing their social problems and needs were interrelated with each other's, both the urbanites and suburbanites worked together to improve the quality of life for all. With a strong, healthy urban center and a surrounding region remaining truly suburban in form and character, Americans could enjoy a fine life-style in either location of their choice.

Conclusion

Either eventuality is a possibility. The exact future of our cities rests upon many variables. The key one, however, lies in the prevailing attitude toward cities by policymakers and the general public. If the problems of the city are understood as also the problems of the suburbs, that the whole region is interrelated and mutually affected by the problems of housing, poverty, crime, congestion, and pollution, then they can be tackled directly and more effectively. If the urban problems are not perceived as regional, with cities remaining politically impotent to deal with them, they can only worsen and American cities suffer even more drastically.

SUMMARY

1. About 75 percent of the American population lives in urbanized areas. Many of these metropolitan areas have overlapped and interpenetrated each other, forming megalopolises. This urban sprawl uses up large tracts of land, increasing dependency on automobiles, and raising living costs.

2. Redlining has been an institutional contributor to housing deterioration. A cycle of abandonment by landlords, caught in an increasing costs–declining income syndrome, spreads urban blight. Urban renewal was a disastrous public program, destroying neighborhoods and reducing available low-cost housing. High-rise public housing projects ignored human needs, causing stigmatization, alienation, vandalism, and crime. Housing subsidies have had mixed results and are skyrocketing in cost.

3. Some positive housing steps have been incorporation of human factors in planning buildings with defensible space, gentrification, urban homesteading, low-interest city mortgages, and condominium conversions. Those benefiting the least from these measures, often displaced by them, have been the poor.

4. Massive federal funding from the Highway Trust Fund launched an extensive road-building program, some of them unnecessary. Negative side effects included inefficient land use, family displacement, loss of manufacturing jobs to outlying regions, auto congestion, and reduction in mass transit. Some approaches to improve city transportation problems might be commuter minibuses for low-income workers, electric cars to reduce pollution, and vehicle-free zones to return streets to people.

5. Older cities in the Northeast are enjoying a resurgence, thanks to their market concentration, high education concentration, established infrastructure, and cultural attractions. Central business districts of many older cities are building new office buildings, utilizing their centrality of support services to emerge as transactional centers over the dispersed production and distribution systems.

6. Although a functional interdependence exists between cities and suburbs, each municipality governs itself independently, usually resulting in unnecessary conflict and waste. Fragmentation of political authority prevents cities from controlling their own affairs, and makes them dependent upon state and federal bodies often biased against them. Competing civic bureaucracies within the city also negate coordinated effort, since they seek their own narrow objectives.

7. Past policy failures do offer hopeful alternatives. Providing the poor with self-help

rehabilitation instead of massive slum clearance keeps neighborhoods intact and instills pride. Collaborative planning makes the affected people the guiding experts, ending paternalistic efforts. Returning streets and sidewalks to the people can create safe and positive living environments. Redefining social needs as utilities, not services, will enable us to address social problems more effectively.

8. The deviance approach emphasizes the impact of the city on individuals, creating anomie, improper role models, and antisocial behavior. Both urbanization and suburbanization were functional for society, maintain functionalists, but the dysfunctions require some adjustment: new political boundaries, new financing structures, or further evolution of cities as transactional centers. Conflict theorists point to competing urban constituencies, profiteering exploiters, and outside political powers as causes of urban problems. Interactionists stress value-biased perceptions, relative definitions of deprivation, and cultural differentiation as important to our understanding of interaction patterns.

SUGGESTED READINGS

Downs, Anthony. *Opening up the Suburbs: An Urban Strategy for America*. New Haven, Conn.: Yale University Press, 1973. A specific proposal for political and financial integration of cities and suburbs to resolve their similar problems.

Fischer, Claude S. *The Urban Experience* 2nd ed. New York: Harcourt Brace Jovanovich, 1984. A highly readable, excellent overview of the social and psychological consequences of urban life, with clearly presented theory and findings.

Freedman, Jonathan L. *Crowding and Behavior*. New York: Viking Press, 1975. A comprehensive report on the research findings of crowding studies, concluding they fail to prove a causative link to pathological human behavior.

Gans, Herbert J. *The Urban Villagers*, expanded ed. New York: Free Press, 1983. A classic case study of life in a tight-knit, working-class, white ethnic community destroyed by urban renewal.

Jacobs, Jane. *The Death and Life of Great American Cities*. New York: Random House, 1961. Still pertinent and provocative, an indictment of urban planning and urban renewal, with specific, actual alternatives given.

Palen, J. John. *The Urban World,* 2d ed. New York: McGraw-Hill, 1981. A fine basic book on urban growth, life, and problems, with a cross-cultural emphasis and discussion of contemporary debates.

Suttles, Gerald. *The Social Order of the Slum,* rev. ed. Chicago: University of Chicago Press, 1968. An important participant-observer study of status, communication, and territorial prerogatives among Blacks, Chicanos, Italians, and Puerto Ricans living together in a slum neighborhood.

GLOSSARY

Collaborative planning Unlike paternalistic planning, this effort involves the people affected in the decision-making process.

Defensible space Incorporation of the human factor in physical planning to reduce alienation, crime, and vandalism.

Gentrification The buying and rehabilitation of buildings in decaying urban neighborhoods by middle- and high-income families.

Infrastructure A region's system of roads, bridges, water supply, and waste disposal to support its population.

Megalopolis The interpenetration of previously separate metropolitan regions in commerce and communications.

Metropolis The linking of a city and its surrounding communities through communications, economic, and social networks.

Political fragmentation The governance structure of numerous local municipalities in a metropolitan region, resulting in inability to adapt to regional needs.

Redlining The designation of certain neighborhoods as "bad risk" areas for mortgages or home improvement loans.

Transactions The new fourth sector of economic activities, rapidly emerging as a major part of America's business in cities.

FACTS ABOUT POPULATION AND ECOLOGY

Mexico City may have 32 million inhabitants by 2000, an almost fourfold increase in less than three decades, to become the world's most highly populated city.[1]

Over 500,000 species of plants and animals now alive may be extinct by 2000.[2]

In the United States, every man, woman, and child creates at least six pounds of solid waste per day, over a ton per year.[3]

The acidity of rain—destructive enough to kill entire lakes and rot stone buildings—has increased fortyfold in the last 25 years.[4]

In the cities of India, millions live in the streets without sanitation and with rampant disease.[5]

In the time it takes an American family to have dinner, 418 people starve to death.

Hunger has killed more people in the last 5 years than have been killed in all the wars, revolutions, and murders in the last 150 years.

Every day the sun sets on 200,000 additional new human beings in the world.

16
POPULATION AND ECOLOGY

THE SCOPE OF THE PROBLEM: IMAGES OF THE WORLD SYSTEM

Rapid population growth drives many of the other forces that could destroy the world's ecological balance. Population growth spurts can also cause dislocations and imbalances in social structures and traditional values, disrupting societies and disorienting their members.

Malthusian Pessimism

Thomas R. Malthus authored one of the most pessimistic statements ever made about the world's future. He was responsible for economics getting the nickname "the dismal science." In 1798, the year of publication of *An Essay on the Principle of Population,* the atmosphere was filled with hope for the future. Science and political reform were in their first productive stages and anything seemed possible. Malthus dimmed this hope by stating that progress might never outrun population growth: that, unless restrained, population will always grow faster than the food supply. Each procreating couple usually produced more than enough children to replace itself. And, people will continue to do this until the checks of disease, starvation, or war raise the death rate and cut the population back to the sustainable level.

It was the apparent inevitability of Malthus's doctrine that was so upsetting. It was called, "That black and terrible demon that is always ready to stifle the hopes of humanity."[6] The first implication seemed to be that nothing could be done to help the situation. If the food supply is increased by some technological invention, population will increase enough to, literally, eat up the progress. And then, people will have more children, in expectation of more progress, until some devastation kills off enough to rebalance the ratio of people to resources.

Malthus's only solution was "moral restraint," "the postponement of marriage until a man is able to support a wife and at least six children in conjunction with total pre-marital sexual abstinence."[7] Malthus did not believe in birth control because he thought that people were unreformedly indolent, and unless given the burden of having to support a family, they would do nothing.

Criticisms of Malthus

We now believe that population does not inevitably outrun resources. Technology might have the potential to keep ahead of reasonable population growth.

We should not blame Malthus for not anticipating the Industrial Revolution and the popularity of birth control devices. But we must modify Malthus's assumption that the sex drive is so strong that without enormous moral restraint births will be uncontrolled. Birth control, in some form or other, is practiced everywhere in the world. Birthrates are not usually controlled by all-powerful biological or environmental forces. We now know that changes in social values surrounding how and when it is proper to have children powerfully affect couples' desired family sizes. Not long ago in the United States, many wives said they would like to have "as many children as God would allow," and desired family sizes of five to seven were common. But there has been a major shift in family attitudes and Americans now typically have the two children that Malthus would have found acceptable. We will examine what changes in social conditions caused this drastic shift in fertility attitudes and behavior.

Earth as a System: The Limits to Growth Study

Meadows's study is a famous example of the **neo-Malthusian** image of our future. It extends to its ultimate conclusions the idea that populations and their needs grow exponentially and overburden limited resources. Meadows's research constructed statistical world models interrelating the production and consumption rates of all known resources with expected rates of population growth. The early conclusions seemed disastrous. They foresaw no possibility that technology could alter the coming scarcity of resources or food, and they predicted a substantial "dieback" of the world's population, or a massive armed conflict in competition for the limited supplies.

The second report of the Club of Rome, *Mankind at the Turning Point,* and more recent statements[8] have concentrated on international cooperation, long-term planning in a global context, and the need for individual attitude changes. The neo-Malthusian pessimism is tempered by the hope that "a new ethic in the use of material resources" can be developed that will be compatible with the coming scarcity, an attitude based on harmony with nature, not its conquest. They warn, however, that the strongest threats to future survival of the world system are the short-term reductions in fertility, the apparent successes that make a nation, like the United States, satisfied with its own condition and less concerned with the global dangers.[9]

Criticisms of Meadows

The *Limits to Growth* study has faults similar to those of Malthus. It made significant omissions, dealt in limited, fixed physical systems, and used some false assumptions. Meadows proved that no matter how elaborate your statistical models, it is possible to leave out factors that might change all the conclusions, such as the possibilities of synthetic food, or sea-farming. Meadow's model is similar to Malthus's in assuming control by overwhelming physical forces, instead of the flexibility that is possible because people can change decisions and invent new social and scientific solutions when a threat is recognized. The question remains, however, can they do this in time?

The Earth as a Lifeboat

One of the Meadows team's conclusions was superpessimistic: "There is no possibility of bringing the vast majority of those living in the developing countries up to the material standard of living enjoyed by the developed nations."[10]

International population ethics, questions about what social responsibilities the nations-of-abundance owe to the nations whose populations are starving, was brought to world attention by the debate over the **lifeboat ethic.** Hardin advocated a harsh solution:[11] the *triage* system used in battlefield medical stations. Those in need of aid are divided into three classes: (1) those in need of only minor aid, who could wait; (2) those who could be saved with immediate attention; and (3) the mortally wounded with so little hope that no time or resources should be wasted on them. The metaphor of the lifeboat demands that we imagine the world as containing about 50 countries that have "made it out of the sea" and are in no imminent danger of drowning. They are surrounded by about 100 nations still floundering in danger. Hardin maintained that it would do no good to try to "pick up" the other nations; "the boat" would only sink from their weight. Hardin returns us to the old nationalistic notions of each country as a specific geographic unit with its own "carrying capacity" that is, its own set of resources and economic possibilities, with the potential to support only so much population.

Hardin further maintains that if we try to help other countries by providing a World Food Bank or some other mechanism, we will only disrupt the natural order of these smaller nations' systems, and keep them from finding their own level of balance. Hardin's main point is political: we are not in one system because we don't have a sovereign captain who can make decisions about what parts are too damaged to be saved, or what drastic measures are absolutely necessary in order to save the whole. Without this central leadership, the world will remain as competing nation-units, and we might as well adopt an "ethic" that fits harsh reality.

Criticisms of the Lifeboat Ethic

Objections were quickly raised against this extremely pessimistic proposal. For example, what would it do to the ethical values of the people of a developed country to have to decide consciously exactly which people were to be left to starve? In addition, Hardin's assumptions contained many factual inaccuracies: (1) He assumed that massive efforts had already been made to help undeveloped countries with their problems and that they have failed. The truth is that most efforts have been "token" or "pilot" projects, or specific disaster relief efforts. (2) He assumed that the world cannot produce enough food, but it is actually more a problem of maldistribution of already available food.[12] (3) Hardin assumed that poorer nations would stand idly by without resistance and watch while developed nations sentenced them to inevitable misery. It is more likely this would cause political disruptions.

Demographic Transition Theory

The final model of population change is more hopeful. It postulates that people will spontaneously change to a desire for smaller families when their countries become economically and scientifically developed. If this is true, then there is hope for the future and our political course is clear. We should do all that is possible to help nations to develop. Just as with the other three models, however, the evidence is not clear. The **demographic transition** remains a theory.

Hope for decreased population growth in undeveloped countries is based on the history of the Western world and Japan; they *have* gone through a three-phase transition. Up until about 1700, birth- and death rates were both very high and they canceled each other out, causing little growth. Then sanitation and medical improvements caused many more infants to survive and an increase in the life span. This second phase is happening in much of the non-Western world today. Rapid population growth is being caused by a sharp lowering of the death rate. The third phase began around 1850 in Europe and spread to North America. The birthrate started to recede to approach the already lowered death rate. Except for the "baby boom" in Post-World War II America, the birthrate downtrend has been steady and continues today and could cause population growth to stabilize early in the next century.

The theory of the demographic transition assumes that this three-phase change was due to modernization, industrialization, and increased standards of living.[13] The theory expects that when people leave farming for industrial jobs, they will realize that children are not needed to tend the fields, nor to inherit and work the farm when the parents are too old and must be supported. People will, therefore, voluntarily reduce their number of children. This attitude transition should take place in all countries, according to the theory, and the population problem could be solved automatically just through industrialization.

Criticisms of Demogaphic Transition

Criticisms of the demographic transition theory are centered on two of its fallacies. First, it is limited by Western ethnocentrism. It assumes that there is only one road possible to development: the one that Europe took in the last century. But development in the new nations is taking many forms and often happens much more rapidly than in the past. This quick transition from agriculture to industrialization may be the reason for the second fallacy. Studies have shown that economic development does not necessarily bring smaller families. In fact, in many countries the higher standard of living increases the desire for children because they can be more easily supported. For example, Miller and Inkeles interviewed men in Pakistan, India, Nigeria, and Israel, who had had extended contact with industrial occupations and Western-style schooling.[14] This contact had little effect on the men's ideas about family limitation. Unless the men had adopted the full set of Western attitudes, including a strong belief in the value of science, technology, and modern medicine, they retained traditional desires for large families. Miller and Inkeles concluded that cultural values exist separately from structural changes, like industrialization. This suggests that family-size desires are not going to change inevitably due to development, and the demographic transition may not take place.

POPULATION PRESSURE ON THE WORLD

Five trends are causing substantial changes in our world environment. Each is the direct result of the human population explosion. First, even the most optimistic forecasts see population growth continuing for almost 100 years. Second, people are depleting the ecological assets they need to support themselves. Third, undernourishment is chronic in many developing countries. Fourth, many species of animals and plants that share our ecosystem are becoming extinct as humans spread out across the entire planet. Finally, our industrial economy is transforming natural processes, like the weather, into lethal forces.

Crowded urban conditions demand a life-style that is different from the agricultural world of the past. Large families are not economically useful and overcrowding is a central problem of work and home life, as well as in commuting, shopping, and recreation.

Continuing Growth

Population change cannot level off to zero-growth before the year 2090 (see Figure 16.1). Even using the unrealistically optimistic assumption that all the world's families will average two children by the year 2000, the world's population will still reach almost 8.5 billion. The earth will have to support twice as many people as it does now. If current trends continue, world population could reach over 36 billion, or about *nine times what it is now,* in less than 100 years.

Figure 16.2 shows that growth will be most rapid in the underdeveloped countries least able to support the increased burden. Europe is expected to grow 18 percent and North America 31 percent by the year 2000. Latin America, however, will more than double, increasing in population by 119 percent. The developing countries have populations with many more young couples in the childbearing ages contributing to the growth spurt.

We are, therefore, faced with two types of population problems: (1) the underdeveloped countries are growing so fast that it is inhibiting and possibly negating their

FIGURE 16.1 **World Population Growth Scenarios**

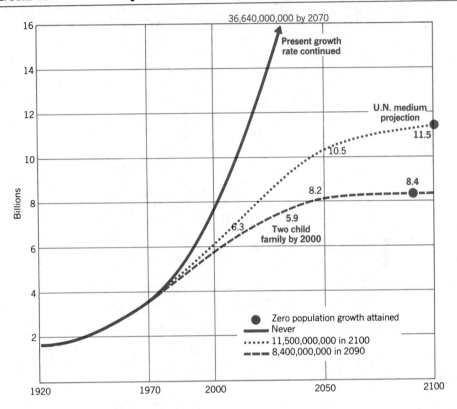

Three alternative scenarios for world population growth: The solid line shows the enormous potential for growth if present birthrates continue; the dotted line gives the U.N. medium projection; and the dashed line shows the reduction possible if a two-child per family average is attained worldwide by the year 2000. Even taking the last, extremely optimistic outlook, world population will not stabilize for over a century, and when it does the earth will be occupied by nearly twice as many people as are living today.
SOURCE: Rafael M. Salas, "World Population Growth: Hopeful Signs of a Slowdown," *The Futurist* (October 1978), p. 279. Unpublished data from the Population Reference Bureau, Washington, D.C., and the U.N. Population Division.

development. Social and economic change is retarded because government investment that could stimulate modernization must be used to avert starvation, prevent disease, and provide social services. It has been estimated that each 1 percent increase in the population "costs" a 3–4 percent investment of the country's Gross National Product.[15] (2) Population growth is not rampant in the developed countries, but because of past growth spurts, there are enough people in the childbearing ages to potentially cause expansion for the foreseeable future. This is a serious problem

FIGURE 16.2   The Population Explosion: Where the People Are Likely to Be in the Year 2000

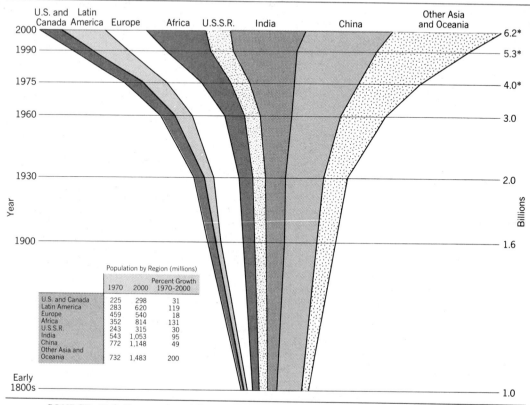

Population by Region (millions)

	1970	2000	Percent Growth 1970-2000
U.S. and Canada	225	298	31
Latin America	283	620	119
Europe	459	540	18
Africa	352	814	131
U.S.S.R.	243	315	30
India	543	1,053	95
China	772	1,148	49
Other Asia and Oceania	732	1,483	200

SOURCE: U.S. Department of State, "Population Growth and Foreign Policy," *Current Policy #263* Washington, D.C.: Bureau of Public Affairs (January 27, 1981).
   * U.N. medium projection variant.

because each member of these societies is "technology-assisted." That is, each has the potential to be a powerful polluter and a prodigious waster of natural resources.

Resource Depletion: The Scarcity of Cropland

We are beginning to use up many essentials; energy is the resource most spoken of, but our water and our cropland are also becoming scarce. There have always been localized droughts and famines, and we tend to think of them as "natural" disasters. But now, even the more fortunate countries may soon have shortages of cropland.

Other economic uses compete with farming for the use of the land: housing and urban sprawl; dam building, with its massive flooding, which is necessary to supply water to new cities; and stripmining, are but a few. Cropland in the United States has been shrinking for at least three decades.[16] At first, this was due to increased productivity: better machines made less land necessary. But the new efficiency caused by technology and chemicals has already made its contribution, and the total productivity of U.S. cropland began to decline starting in 1971. It may have passed its peak. Most farmers near city-access roads must turn down attractive offers from "developers" in order to keep the family farm in business. Because these other uses for land are becoming increasingly profitable, "it is difficult to see how the world can achieve much more than a 10 percent increase in cropland area during the final quarter of this century without a dramatic rise in the price of food."[17] Japan has had severe shortages for generations. It has strict government zoning that requires that certain regions must remain agricultural, no matter what alternative profitable use is available. This is a severe restriction on the farmers' freedom to buy and sell their personal property. But, as we will see throughout this chapter, shortages caused by overpopulation have powerful implications for personal and political freedom.

Hunger in Developing Nations

Starvation and famine have killed more people in the last 5 years than all the wars. revolutions, and murders of the last 150 years.[18] Even though India has made progress, 46 percent of its population is still below the $110 per year income poverty line.[19] But chronic malnutrition is an even more serious problem. Estimates of the number of people who are malnourished have ranged from 500 million to 932 million.

Cropland is disappearing as the cities, their sprawling suburbs, and managerial headquarters move farther out. If development is not checked we could find ourselves paying much more for food produced on scarce land.

Even using very conservative procedures, it is estimated that 100 million are chronically malnourished.

The malnourished are found mostly in 45 countries that are least developed, and most subject to economic and food crises. "The groups that suffer most frequently are the urban poor and . . . the landless laborers, subsistence farmers and nomads. Within these groups small children and lactating mothers are most affected; in the most seriously affected countries one-quarter to one-half of young children suffer from malnutrition."[20]

The problem is not simple. Many social, political, and economic forces limit food production and distribution. As one example of these complexities, look at the interconnection of female infanticide and food production (Box 16.1). When food is in short supply, young females are allowed to, or even helped to, die. But since females still perform so much of the agricultural labor, their smaller population affects future production.[21]

Extinction of Species

It is estimated that 500,000 species will become extinct by the end of the century.[22] As humans spread out to cover the entire earth, they destroy the habitats of all other species. Those they do not domesticate are gone forever. While animal species usually get the most attention (we can identify with koala bears, orangutans, and

Hunger is a basic problem in developing nations. Even if starvation is controlled, weakness due to malnutrition increases disease and keeps individuals from reaching their full mental and physical potentials. Unlike dying Ethiopians, these people typify the world's hungry.

BOX 16.1

THE CONTINUING VICIOUS CYCLE OF FEMALE MALNUTRITION AND FOOD SHORTAGES

. . . In a traditional [Third World] setting, a woman is so dependent on her sons for immediate status and future security that she is apt to nurse them longer and feed them better than her daughters. In Bangladesh the result is a mortality rate for girls under age five that is 30 to 50 percent higher than the rate for boys in the same age group. Similarly, researchers attributed higher death rates among girls admitted to a large university hospital in Africa to the girls' inferior nutritional state. More girls than boys died from routine infectious diseases like measles, which seldom kill unless a child is weakened by malnutrition.

. . . India's obsession with male offspring is age old. It is one of the few countries where males outnumber females. The sex ratio decreased yearly from 972 women per 1,000 males in 1921 to 930 women per 1,000 males in 1971. Female infanticide was a common method of disposing of unwanted girls. Another was sheer neglect. Female mortality rates are 60 percent higher than for males up to the age of five.

. . . In many parts of the world women and children . . . must wait to eat until the men have finished. Where there is little protein available, the men get most of it, leaving mainly carbohydrates for the women and children. Female children fare worst of all in this regard.

. . . In Third World countries, women are the foundation of the agricultural system. [In many developing countries women are responsible for 50 to 80 percent of agricultural production.] Any substantial improvement in the food picture will depend largely on improving the health, productivity and overall role of women. In fact, the role of women is at the center of the hunger problem in spite of the fact that nearly all western experts of development have managed to ignore their role for years. . . .

SOURCE: The Hunger Project, *World Development Forum* 1, no. 6 (January 31, 1983), pp. 3–4.

whales), it is really the loss of plants that is potentially the most costly. Any one of the many as yet unstudied plants might have the potential of quinine, curari, or rubber. About 10 percent of the world's plants are "endangered" or "threatened." The loss of one plant has intricate ramifications for the surrounding ecosystem. It is estimated that a plant's extinction "can take with it 10 to 30 dependent species such as insects, higher animals and even other plants."[23]

Transformation of Natural Processes: Acid Rain

Population pressure also disturbs the balanced operation of the world's ecological system. One striking example is the transformation of rain into a destructive force by the addition of pollution acids. The sulfur and nitrogen dioxides that go up industrial chimneys can fall thousands of miles away as acid rains that blight plant life, make forest growth slow down, and cause fish to suffer chronic chemical stress that alters their biochemistry, leaving behind dead rivers and lakes. The acidity of the rains has increased fortyfold in the last 25 years.[24] It even erodes buildings and automobiles. This is a global problem. Acid-producing communities and nations need to be forced, or given some incentive, to save the waters of others who are downwind.

ECOSYSTEM PROBLEMS

Ecosystem Thinking

The word **ecosystem** was coined by Tansley, a British plant ecologist, in 1935. He realized that in order to understand any plant, one also needed to know about the soil, the climate, and animals: the plant's total environment. When we apply this concept to social problems, we think of human ecosystems and their psychological and social-cultural elements.[25] Problems should be treated holistically, with the environment seen as a nondivisible whole which must be considered all-at-once when studying ecological problems. Holistic thinking sounds relatively simple, but it is difficult for most Americans because they have been brought up in the scientific tradition of analytic thinking: we are taught to break down each problem into its parts and to deal with only one part at a time. For example, farmers are oriented toward one species. Their goal is to increase crop yields in the shortest amount of time. Any plant that competes with the "crop" is defined as a "weed" and defoliated. Any animal or insect in the area is a "varmint" or pest and poisoned or trapped. We do have the high crop yields, but some of the side effects have been devastating.

We don't mean to single out farmers. Most of us share this type of singlemindedness. In fact, we are taught that goal-oriented concentration on production is the key to success. But we are beginning to realize that we live in a context which has limits. Three aspects of this context are the critical elements of ecosystem thinking: interconnectivity, instability, and overload.

Interconnectivity

Every part of the system is potentially connected to every other part. Effects can be caused in parts of the system that are very far removed from the original action. **Food chains** are a basic example of interconnectedness. Their importance became clear when the poisonous effects of DDT were discovered. The most publicized result was the near extinction of our national symbol, the Bald Eagle. Think of the complexity of the "chain" of species involved: a human is worried that an insect will eat a crop plant, so DDT is sprayed over farmland and runs off into waterways, contaminating shellfish and minnows that larger fish eat; eagles eat the fish, and the highly concentrated DDT severely affects the reproductive system by making their eggs too fragile to survive.

Simplicity Equals Instability

Modern technological thinking sets out to simplify all systems, not only in order to understand them analytically, but also to make them "work better," to do their "job" better by producing more for human consumption. Nature's goals are defined in terms of humans' desires, not in terms of nature's own real design.

By understanding what is happening to other species, we can see that when the complexity of the system is destroyed, our own existence is endangered. Koala bears and orangutans are becoming extinct now because they are both one-plant animals. Koalas, for example, only eat eucalyptus leaves, and, now that their forests are being cut down, they may survive only in zoos. The more complex the system is, the more likely that if one element is taken away, the balance will be maintained. For example, even if one predator, say, the fox, is hunted to extinction, it is still unlikely that the forest will be overrun with mice, because owls will increase and maintain the balance. Now think of a human-made farmfield instead of the forest. There is only one type of plant allowed. All animals have been "simplified-out." If some new imbalance in weather, or blight, or insect invasion occurs, the farmer has only technology to save the system. Our dependence on technology is best understood in the context of the natural law that *simplicity leads to instability* and jeopardy. We tend to eliminate the many elements that make up the natural balance and replace them with only one new element, mechanical manipulation of the environment.

Overload: Thresholds and Triggers

The ecosystem can handle a good deal of pollution. Rivers can transform raw sewage to harmless chemicals, just as soil microorganisms can transform manure into fertilizer. At some point, however, a threshold is reached, and the system can handle no more and begins to die. This began to happen to the Atlantic Ocean outside of New York City. Large areas were found to contain no life at all, just green slime and the city's sewage sludge. The frightening fact is that *we don't know where the thresholds are* for most of our natural systems.[26] Trigger effects are even more dramatic: the natural balance can be totally upset by relatively small human-made inputs. This has frequently happened when a new species is imported into an ecosystem. When it has no controlling predators, it multiplies too rapidly, destroys the balance and takes over. Australians, for example, suffered greatly from a plague of rabbits and now have to maintain a "rabbit-proof" fence across a good portion of their continent in order to contain them. Ehrlich and Holdren provide another "trigger" effect of gigantic proportions: when a dam is built, the weight of the accumulated water might be powerful enough to make a geological fault line slip and cause an earthquake.[27] This happened in 1967 in India and the earthquake killed 200 people. After Lake Mead was filled in 1935–1939, there were hundreds of seismic events of significant magnitude.

Let us now see how some ecological threats illustrate the three principles just described.

Current Ecosystem Problems

Pesticides

DDT was an outstanding case because it was the first time we discovered we were guinea pigs for a worldwide chemical laboratory. DDT went from a heralded miracle chemical to a banned dangerous substance in just 20 years. In 1948, P. H. Muller won the Nobel prize for his discovery of DDT. It had controlled many insect-borne diseases, like malaria, in the tropical areas of the world.[28] DDT saved millions of lives: the population of Madagascar had been stable for many years, but it doubled in the 12 years following a DDT antimalaria campaign.[29] But, scientists began to find DDT "in the fatty tissues of animals over a global range of life from penguins in Antarctica, to the children in Thailand's villages, to your tissues and mine."[30]

Concentration of Poisons by Food Chains

There is another ecosystem fact about food chains that we should be concerned about. Not only do food chains transmit poisons, they also tend to concentrate them as you go higher and higher in the chain. The cattle we eat, just like the fish that the eagles ate, are collecting, filtering, and passing along very dense dosages. Remember, humans are not only at the end of food chains; we also are the omnivores who eat both the herbivores and carnivores, so we get all their accumulations.[31] In 1970 it was estimated that each of us carried about 12 parts per million of DDT in our fatty tissues.[32]

Weather Modification and Atmosphere Alteration

A number of our activities could alter the world's climate: burning fossil fuels, creating agricultural dust bowls, deforestation of large areas, construction of large dams and bodies of water, developing the Arctic and Antarctic, and, of course, intentionally modifying the weather.[33] We have already altered some local weather patterns significantly with industrial pollution. St. Louis has had a 20–30 percent increase in thunderstorms and a 100 percent increase in hailstorms due to polluting industries.[34]

Two effects of adding pollutants to the atmosphere are particularly worrisome. The *greenhouse effect* occurs when carbon dioxide is produced by the combustion of fossil fuels. The accumulation of this gas could form a layer that might reflect back the earth's heat instead of letting it radiate off into the atmosphere. A slight increase in temperature could alter the planet significantly. Even a slight melting of the polar ice caps could raise the ocean levels enough to drown some coastal cities.

The *ice-age effect* cools the earth due to particulate matter forming clouds and dust layers that screen out the sun, as does the airborne debris from volcanic eruptions. Even minor cooling could reduce food production significantly.[35]

We will soon have the technology to modify local weather significantly, but we will probably be afraid to use it because of possible unintended consequences. We can chemically seed clouds to create rain, suppress hail to protect crops at harvest time, and control local temperatures by forming clouds to block the sun. Since most weather moves continuously from West to East across our continent, however, each

BOX 16.2
WHO OWNS THE CLOUDS?
People no longer are just talking about the weather; in a growing number of areas they are doing something about it—and not everyone is happy about it.

A cloud-seeding program passed recently by the Washington state legislature in an effort to save the state's wheat and fruit crops from a devastating drought immediately triggered charges of "cloud rustling" from officials in neighboring Idaho.

Idaho Attorney General Wayne Kidwell, claiming that the cloud seeding would deprive Idaho of needed rain, threatened to file lawsuits in an attempt to stop the program. One suit would accuse Washington of causing "inverse pollution" by removing rain from the atmosphere.

Because of the western drought, more than a dozen western states have adopted weather modification plans this year. A total of 29 states in the United States currently have weather modification laws.

The question of ownership of the water in clouds is still up in the air, and weather experts say that it is still not known if cloud seeding actually will decrease rainfall downwind.

"Sooner or later there's going to be a need for some kind of federal operational licensing for weather modification," says Ray J. Davis, a University of Arizona weather-modification law specialist. Mounting charges of cloud rustling may hasten the coming of federal intervention.

SOURCE: André Van Dam, "Water: The Wells Need Never Run Dry," *The Futurist* (June 1977), pp. 163–67. Published by the World Future Society, 4916 St. Elmo Avenue, Washington, D.C.

---

local modification might affect many other local patterns. This raises a very interesting political question: *Who owns the clouds?* Who will be allowed to seed and tap their moisture as they travel east? (See Box 16.2.)

Dangerous Practices and Regulation Difficulties

Difficulties of Air Pollution Regulation

In 1273, King Edward I attempted to prohibit the burning of coal, but it did not solve London's stifling air pollution problem.[36] It was not until the middle of this century, when the millions of home-heating coal fires were totally outlawed, that Londoners got to see the sky on most days.

Our government's program suffers from a severe lack of enforcement capability. This is typical of the middle stages of the social problem development cycle. The air pollution problem has reached a stage advanced enough for there to be organized governmental recognition, and the beginnings of program definition. But it has not yet developed enough support to force the allocation of the significant funds necessary for monitoring and enforcement.

> Present federal law gives primary responsibility for enforcement to the states. Yet inspection personnel at the state level are totally inadequate, both in numbers and in training. New York State, for example, must check 90,000 major heating plants and 25,000 incinerators for compliance, plus over 100,000 industrial-emission sources, some of which must be analyzed by actual stack testing. With present stack testing personnel—two teams of three men each—only about fifty stacks per year can be tested. "The work requires the nerves of a steeplejack and the mentality of an engineer," said a state official. "Not only can't we afford them, we can't even find them."[37]

Water Pollution and Chemical Dumping

The first water regulation laws were enacted in Hammurabi's Code over 3,500 years ago.[38] There have been notable successes. "Philadelphia, in the early 1900s, introduced sedimentation in their well-water supply, letting it filter through a sand bed. The daily mortality in Philadelphia went down about 20 percent. . . . A year later they introduced chlorination of the filtered water and the death rate went down about 50 percent—absolutely striking."[39]

We are currently plagued by a series of threats: (1) eutrophication of our fresh water; (2) disruption of the ocean's essential contribution to photosynthesis; and (3) poisoning of our well-water supplies by chemical dumps.

Eutrophication is one result of overfertilization of fresh water bodies. Farmers' heavy applications of phosphate and nitrogen fertilizers run off into local streams and speed up the growth of algae in surrounding lakes. The algae population explosion uses up all the oxygen, choking off other life. The dead plants and fish and the inevitable death of the overabundant algae foul the lake. This is another case of an apparent benefit (powerful fertilizer) having side effects. In Third World countries where food is scarce, the increased harvest is very welcome until it is noticed that the fish catch has been reduced by the deoxygenization of the water. Animal wastes are also fertilizers, and the great feedlots where animals are fattened for market can cause almost as much eutrophication in rural areas as do the outdated sewerage systems of our cities.

Photosynthesis is the process of plant growth using sunlight, water, and carbon dioxide. It creates oxygen that refreshes the planet's biosphere. Each large area deforested or jungle reduced affects the world's balance of carbon dioxide to oxygen to some small degree. We do not yet know the threshold of danger from deforestation, but we do know that another part of the process is under potentially severe stress. Over a decade ago, the Food and Drug Administration (FDA) had already estimated that over a half-million substances were being ocean dumped.[40] The major portion of our oxygen supply is from ocean photosynthesis, and if the pollution reaches the threshold where the ocean plants (plankton or diatom) populations are reduced, the entire biosphere is jeopardized.

Illegal dumping is an almost irreversible disaster. Toxic or carcinogenic chemicals lie in the earth like grounds in a coffee pot. Rain percolates through a landfill or illegal dump, creating a polluted leachate. The Environmental Protection Agency (EPA) estimates that the average dumpsite of only 17 acres can generate 4.6 million gallons of leachate each year.[41] It can last for up to 100 years, and the plume of poison can extend for long distances, fouling or secretly poisoning any subterranean water it contacts. About 80 percent of municipal water systems are dependent on **aquifers:** water collected in underground porous rocks, caverns, or sand beds. They are particularly important in the drier West and southwestern United States (where they may be the only sources of water). In these areas their use has been growing exponentially in the last decade. Once they are tainted, little can be done; the people must move on.

Victimization without Realization

Many of these landfill sites are covered up by the dumpers. Michael Brown's *Laying Waste* is a terrifying catalogue of government timidity, mismanagement, and criminal coverups abetting short-sighted corporate greed. Perhaps the most frightening and damaging effect of chemical dumping is that it makes people less able to fight off normal diseases. For example, ducklings experimentally fed pesticidal material and then exposed to hepatitis died four times more often than those not fed with the

The pollution of waterways and underground reservoirs went on for so long that we now find it difficult to correct it. So many jobs are tied to industries that dump dangerous wastes that officials hesitate before causing economic dislocations in order to ensure clean water.

pesticides.[42] It is very hard to detect and expose such environmentally induced weaknesses.

What Can Be Done about Pollution?: New Jersey's Program

New Jersey is the state with the worst problems with landfill pollution and illegal dumping. It is a leader in the production of petrochemicals and, although no clear link has been proven, many believe this makes a contribution to New Jersey residents having the highest chances of contracting cancer in America.[43]

Every 12 months 14,000 people were dying from what was ambiguously termed "environmental cancer." The state has reacted by pioneering control efforts:

1. Fast reaction and a disregard for costs are important in dangerous situations. The normal procedure had been to use court orders to get the polluters to clean up their own messes. Anyone could form a company, rent space in a warehouse, fill it with drums of toxic materials, and when it got full or discovered, go bankrupt leaving the waste behind. Now they do not wait to catch the dumpers; they clean up immediately and prosecute later.

2. New Jersey has also gone into the surveillance business. Illegal dumping was so rampant that tank trunks were driving the highways in rainstorms with their jets open, spreading pollution to wherever the run-off water was carried. "Midnight dumpers" are now being combatted by special law enforcement spys who use elaborate "night sight" technology and "stake out" likely dump sites.

3. Early-warning recording systems have also been set up to report new cases of environmental cancer or unusual outbreaks of diseases so that potentially dangerous areas can be examined as soon as possible.

4. Social and environmental impact statements are now requirements for projects seeking government funding. In New Jersey, they have learned that foresight is the only protection. The federal government, on the contrary, still has too little interest in anticipating the social impacts of its actions. Freudenberg and Keating exposed two shocking omissions.[44] When the government drew up plans for both the MX missile system, the largest construction job ever contemplated, and for the dumping of radioactive wastes, there were *no* reports ordered about estimating their possible effects on social life.

THE PERSISTENCE OF ECOLOGICAL AND POPULATION PROBLEMS

Not everyone agrees that population pressure is a problem. Even those who accept the need to reduce growth disagree on the need for special measures to change peoples' fertility attitudes and behaviors. In addition, a number of elements of American culture promote population growth by affecting our ideas and values.

Positions That Deny the Need for Action

Teitelbaum[45] has isolated a dozen current and powerful arguments used by political, medical, religious, and ideological groups against population limitation programs. The conflict of so many opposing positions confuses even the most dedicated policymaker seeking the proper level for his or her nation's future growth. We hope to promote discussion of possible costs and benefits of alternative policies by summarizing Teitelbaum's list of arguments into the five most prevalent arguments.

1. *Pronatalism.* Especially in small developing nations, population growth may be seen as a way to provide more workers, consumers, and soldiers in order to increase the power of the economy or the ability to protect the country from attack. Even when these nation-building ideas are no longer present, **pronatalist** policies often still persist. The income tax credit that each new child allows an American family is a small but direct probirth encouragement.

2. *Revolutionist* and *genocide* positions. Population control programs are often seen as attempts to distract people from the real problems. For example, some Marxists feel that the environment is to be utilized as fully as possible because only full economic development can end exploitation. Ecological problems, therefore, have low priority. Among nations with histories of exploitation by colonialists, there is often the suspicion that aggressive population limitation programs suggested by their former rulers might be attempts to keep them small and dependent, or to keep them from using up their own resources, which the Western nations desire. This suspicion is also prevalent among minority groups in developed countries. When American Blacks, for instance, are asked to use birth control aggressively, they begin to wonder if the majority groups are not trying to limit, or even diminish, their numbers. Their fear is that the majority has begun a program of covert racial genocide against them.

3. *Redistribution position.* All over the world we find *under*populated areas. Even within most countries' borders, there are places that could easily accommodate overflow from crowded areas. The American Southwest could accept "excess" people from the industrial cities. The answer is not population control, but applying technology to make the land productive, or applying political and economic expertise to creating jobs that would support people who moved to the empty areas.

4. *Religious doctrinal position.* There are two levels of this position: (a) the fundamentalist belief that "God will provide" and that humans should not interfere with the mystery of procreation; (b) religious objections focused on the *means* of population control. The Catholic Church, for example, tacitly accepts the need to limit births and an individual's right to determine family size, but states that the usual instruments of birth prevention are unnatural.

5. *Medical risk position.* Although overpopulation is seen as a problem, the risks to women from IUD implantation and "the pill" are also strong, and population control is not considered worth the price of jeopardizing

human life. All efforts should be put into the development of safe contraceptive devices.

Cultural Supports for Population Growth and Resource Depletion

Culture can be defined as the ideas, values, and social norms that are internalized by every human being as they are socialized into society. Our Western tradition contains many elements that strongly promote unlimited population growth and ecosystem exploitation. Three of the most powerful are: (1) the *Dominant Western World View,* encouraging us to conquer nature; (2) *the business ethic,* biasing our values toward accelerating growth; and (3) the **motherhood mandate** that creates a biased social position for women, forcing them to become mothers in order to be socially acceptable.

The Dominant Western World View has ruled our thinking for hundreds of years and is only recently being challenged by events. It promotes an anthropocentric and overly optimistic view of our relationship to nature. **Anthropocentrism** is the belief that people are fundamentally different from all other creatures and that we are earth's natural rulers. It is our right and even duty to have our way with the rest of the planet because we are "the highest form of life" around which the whole world revolves. Optimism is even more deeply entrenched in our thinking. It is represented by three beliefs:

1. People are masters of their destiny; they can choose their goals and learn to do whatever is necessary to achieve them.

2. The world is vast and thus provides unlimited opportunities.

3. The history of humanity is one of progress; for every problem, there is a solution and thus progress need never cease."[46]

This view is presently exemplified by the group that other futurists call the "Technological Optimists."[47] They believe that as soon as a problem "gets bad enough," our governmental attention and investment capital will be directed toward its solution, and technology will solve it. Many disagree and say that it is industrialization aided by technology that has *created,* not solved, our problems.

The Business Ethic values rapid growth above all else. Paul Ehrlich says that "our entire economy is geared to growing population and monumental waste."[48] We are also so in love with newness and change that we purchase deliberately perishable products so that we can buy new ones sooner than we really need to. Just as a business's profits must increase every year for the business to be thought successful, so individuals measure personal success by continuous movement. "Getting ahead" only stops with forced retirement. We get programmed by our own momentum.[49]

Those who feel that the economy is fueled by more customers never mean more *poor* customers.[50] But the system is already strained. Harmon estimates that "real unemployment," those who want to work but are squeezed out as too young, or too old, or too discouraged to look, and those in holding institutions, may total as much as 35 percent of the work force.[51] Cetron and O'Toole estimate that, by the year

2000, there will be 300 million unemployed in the world economy. Many jobs have been lost to computers and robots and if population keeps increasing, the imbalance will be severe.[52] Consider J. J. Spengler's admonition: "It is high time that business cease looking upon the stork as a bird of good omen."[53]

The Motherhood Mandate

One powerful force maintaining population growth is the cultural norm mandating that "a woman have at least two children (historically as many as possible and preferably sons) and that one raise them 'well.'"[54] Women are now almost expected to work outside the home, and "the pill" and other devices give them some control over their reproductive decisions. But the mandate remains strong. Even a "working wife" is expected to place "someday having children" uppermost in her concerns. This status requirement is so deeply embedded in our culture that it is taken for granted: deviation has been unthinkable. It can be called a dominant **unconscious ideology.** As one consequence, at present there is a mini-baby boom among women in their early thirties who feel they are "catching up" with the "family responsibilities." Therefore, even if a perfectly safe and morally acceptable method of birth control were to be invented tomorrow, this role prescription of raising-two-well-adjusted children in order to be a "true" woman, would keep population growing in the United States well into the middle of the next century.

The Motherhood Mandate, the societal insistence that a woman's first responsibility is to bear children, seems to be weakening, somewhat, but only in developed countries.

SOCIOLOGICAL ORIENTATIONS AND SOLUTIONS

Many of the confusions keeping experts from agreeing on an effective population policy can be understood by collecting the many directions that proposed changes could take into the four underlying sociological emphases. Solutions to population problems are oriented toward either: (1) individuals' control of their fertility behavior; (2) the structure or values of society's institutions; (3) the underlying conflicts caused by social inequality and the profit motive; or (4) the social interpretations that individuals create during social interaction about fertility.

The Individual Faults Emphasis: Excess/Unwanted Fertility

The **unwanted fertility hypothesis** holds that the population problem is the consequence of a lack of control of fertility by individuals who have insufficient access to fertility control techniques, or who were not educated about the need for such control. The broad social impact, and even the international issues involved, are seen as stemming from individuals being poorly equipped or socialized to handle their fertility responsibilities. Bumpass and Westoff found that if people were able to have only the births that they had planned, population growth in the United States would almost immediately reach stability.[55]

System Disorganization Emphasis: Changing Institutions

Sociologists who emphasize the structure of society see population growth and the resultant ecological problems as a leftover, nonmodern behavior pattern that will fade away as societies reach full development. Large families are seen as survivors of the agricultural age, when they served an economic function. Similarly, women are now undergoing a drastic change in role prescriptions mainly because their older, hard-labor functions have been automated. This encourages outside employment and the seeking of status in institutions other than the child-centered family.

Optimistically, smaller families are expected to become the norm in all modernized societies. Structural-functional sociologists expect that growth will reach a sort of stable balance, supplying fewer people *because fewer are needed* in a modern society.

New Value Consensus

Another group of sociologists and futurists also believe that industrialization was central in forming our life-style, but that it is now outdated; a new value consensus is necessary for human survival. Elgin and Mitchell (see Box 16.3) contrast the old industrial ideas and values with those of a new counterculture, *voluntary simplicity,* that attempts to reverse the present values.[56] Instead of economic complexity, it would substitute **appropriate technology** in which each local area uses only the tools and methods it needs in order to become self-sufficient.[57] All production would be scaled down. Elimination of desires for conspicuous consumption, material wealth, and technological gadgetry would reduce the pressure on resources. Schumacher eloquently expresses the need for new values. He wants us to give up being "people of the forward stampede,"[58] and instead to become "homecomers." He observes that the people in "advanced" countries, where technology is supposed to save so much labor and time, work much harder and have much less time for their homes and families than in undeveloped countries.[59]

But many sociologists would argue that no matter how pressing the ecological need, you cannot forcibly change just the consumatory values of a society without changing many other institutions. For example, the current corporate structure and advertising methods would have to be altered before any major economic value shifts could be realized. This is the emphasis of the next group of sociologists and environmental activists.

Inequality and Inevitable Conflict Emphasis

The conflict orientation attributes population problems to social inequality and our lack of ecological concern to the underlying idea of the capitalist system, the profit motive.

Population pressure is not a high priority problem. Unwanted fertility is a symptom of unequal opportunity and would soon diminish if ethnic injustice and class bigotry were erased. If a redistribution of wealth could be implemented, then individuals could choose their own life-styles, and family size decisions would be more effective.

Both conflict theorists and the ecological hawks feel that those who promote voluntary simplicity and rely on individual value changes to solve ecological problems are naive. Commoner presents evidence that pollution is profitable and will be very difficult to eliminate as long as the profit motive is the basis of the economic system.[60] Dumping of radwaste, the radioactive leavings of nuclear energy or uranium mining, is encouraged because it is more profitable than proper storage or treatment. There are more than 50 known large dumpsites. For example:

> Within fifteen miles of Salt Lake City, a weed-choked railroad track
> was flanked by a 4.3 billion pound collection of uranium residues, what
> Governor Scott Matheson described as "the largest microwave oven in
> the West."[61]

Commoner discusses another less obvious danger of the profit motive, the drive to create new technologies. "For about four to five years after a new, innovative chemical product reaches the market, profits are well above the average" (innovative firms enjoy about twice the rate of profit of noninnovative firms due to the temporary monopoly enjoyed by the firm that developed the materials).[62] Unless these innovations are monitored, they proliferate, as they did after World War II, when they caused so many of today's dumpsite problems.

It is actually profitable for owners of whaling fleets to kill off all the whales. It seems irresponsible and ridiculous to wipe out your own industry's source of income. But the capitalist entrepreneur can use the temporary high rate of profit to

BOX 16.3

CONTRASTS BETWEEN THE INDUSTRIAL WORLD VIEW AND THE WORLD VIEW OF VOLUNTARY SIMPLICITY

EMPHASIS IN INDUSTRIAL WORLD VIEW	EMPHASIS IN VOLUNTARY SIMPLICITY WORLD VIEW
Value Premises	*Value Premises*
Material growth	Material sufficiency coupled with psycho-spiritual growth
Man over nature	Man within nature
Competitive self-interest	Enlightened self-interest
Rugged individualism	Cooperative individualism
Rationalism	Rational and intuitive
Social Characteristics	*Social Characteristics*
Large, complex living and working environments	Smaller, less complex living and working environments
Growth of material complexity	Reduction of material complexity
Space-age technology	Appropriate technology
Identity defined by patterns of consumption	Identity found through inner and interpersonal discovery
Centralization of regulation and control at nation/state level	Greater local self-determination coupled with emerging global institutions
Specialized work roles—through division of labor	More integrated work roles (e.g., team assembly, multiple roles)

reinvest in some other business. It's "profitable" to kill the goose that lays the golden eggs, so long as the goose lives long enough to provide sufficient eggs to pay for the purchase of a new goose.[63] Commoner's point is that we can't rely on the present system to control pollution or ecological assaults so long as it is based on short-run profits.

Social Interaction: Interpretation Emphasis

Symbolic interactionists remind us that each decision to have another child or to buy a "gas-guzzler" is made using culturally provided definitions of the situation. Sudden shifts can take place in peoples' values and tastes. Americans seemed totally in love with the biggest cars they could buy. Then, for a time, these cars crowded

EMPHASIS IN INDUSTRIAL WORLD VIEW

Social Characteristics
Secular
Mass produced, quickly obsolete, standardized products
Lifeboat ethic in foreign relations
Cultural homogeneity, partial acceptance of diversity
High pressure, rat race existence

EMPHASIS IN VOLUNTARY SIMPLICITY WORLD VIEW

Social Characteristics
Balance of secular and spiritual
Hand crafted, durable, unique products
Spaceship earth ethic
Cultural heterogeneity, eager acceptance of diversity
Laid back, relaxed existence

The authors comment:

"Voluntary simplicity seems to constitute a broadly-based attempt to moderate, in the short run, and transcend, in the long run, the industrial world view. VS implies going beyond material growth to include evolution among more subtle dimensions of life.

"A second pattern revealed by this table is that the values cluster embraced by voluntary simplicity represents at least as coherent a world view as the industrial world view (which has powered our social vision and industrial development for nearly two centuries).

"Lastly, voluntary simplicity does not appear to be a movement whose domain of social impact can be narrowly defined; rather, it reaches out and touches a great many aspects of life."

SOURCE: Duane S. Elgin and Arnold Mitchell, "Voluntary Simplicity: Life Style of the Future?" *The Futurist* (August 1977), p. 20. Published by the World Future Society, 4916 St. Elmo Avenue, Washington, D.C.

dealers' lots. Now they are beginning to sell again. The baby boom suddenly ended, just as the present value of "two-children-is-enough" could evaporate tomorrow. Or, similarly, why does one ecological problem get singled out for action when so many others are ignored?

To understand these seemingly irrational and apparently random decision shifts, we must study the specific contexts in which individuals construct their behaviors. For example, Margaret Mead summarized the conclusions of an international conference on population policies by stating that nationwide birth control programs would inevitably fail. We cannot set goals and standards for a whole country or design one service for all people: "individuals do not make choices in the rarified atmosphere of nation states":[64] they react to their regional, or even village conditions and traditions.

The policy recommendation of the symbolic interaction emphasis is that neither economic development nor technological advances such as "the pill" will be the panaceas that solve our population problem. Before they can have impact, they must be fitted into the social-cultural values guiding individuals' decisions. In spite of all the obvious dangers of auto pollution and the wastefulness of driving to work in your own car instead of using public transportation, only 1 in 16 Americans now use buses or trains to get to work, a marked decrease from the 1 in 12 who did so 10 years ago.[65] Interactionists remind us that policies that ignore social definitions of the situation are doomed to be forgotten.

POPULATION POLICY AND THE CONTROL DILEMMA

Very soon we will be able to pre-design our offspring. Do you want your first child to be male or female? Almost every American says, "a boy." If this freedom is allowed there will be too many males in the next generation. Now, go one step further into the technological future; do you want the boy to grow up to look like Robert Redford? This engineering will also be possible: what should we do, if anything, to control it?

> If it is argued . . . that the state has no right to determine how many children its citizens may have, it could similarly be argued that it has no right to determine how many wives or husbands they may have. To this invasion of freedom, of course, we have all accommodated ourselves.[66]

In the future we may not be able to rely on the unaided "good sense" that individuals derive from their cultural heritages any more than we can count on the "morality" of industrial leaders. The question is: How much do we interfere? Harman calls this the control dilemma.[67]

Beyond Family Planning

It is not just population hawks who propose sweeping, coercive measures. Some sort of a subsidy for people who do not have the third child, and some sort of penalty for those who do, are often discussed. For many years, there have been science fiction stories and movies about what it would be like to live in a future society where childbearing was outlawed or totally decided by lottery. Aldous Huxley's *Brave New World* was predicated on the idea that parenthood would be abolished and all new society members would be test-tube created and trained to government specifications. These draconian measures do not exist just in science fiction. Recently, the government of India became so worried about the failure of its population limitation program that it forced men to sterilization clinics at the point of machine guns. The

Chinese government has instituted very strict and intrusive measures (see Box 16.4). The entire country is organized by local community committees and someone is assigned the task of keeping track of each woman's menstrual cycle. If she misses a period and does not have government permission to conceive, she is ordered to get an abortion.[68]

Policy Proposals for Population Reduction

Many proposed population limitation programs would radically intervene into people's lives. Others would reward couples for having small families. The most far-reaching are those that would change the institution of the family. The following list is adapted from Berelson's "Beyond Family Planning."[69] A good way to judge your own feelings about the population problem is to see how many of the following programs you think might become necessary. If you are willing to institute most of them, you are a population hawk.

1. Assistance for *voluntary family planning:* provision of medical advice and birth control to all who want them, in any country. The next step being *liberalization of abortion* and its free availability (a policy already used in Japan).

2. Intensified, extensive *education campaigns:* inclusion of birth control lectures in all primary and secondary school curricula. Establishment of a special cable TV station with constant birth control information and propaganda.

3. *Incentive programs:* gifts and payments for accepting sterilization, for the successful spacing of children far apart, or "responsibility prizes" for each year of nonpregnancy.

4. Taxation and other penalties: withdrawal of maternity leave or insurance after one pregnancy; withdrawal of the family allowances that exist in many countries; a *direct tax* levied for every "excess" birth; a limitation on the number of years of free schooling provided by the state, to be allocated among all children in the family; tax incentives to stay unmarried.

5. Political changes: modification of *foreign aid* policies allowing no food or support unless substantial population control is demonstrated; and within the United States, establishment of a Cabinet level *Ministry of Population Control* charged with promoting and enforcing **Zero Population Growth (ZPG).**

6. *Involuntary Controls:* introducing a mass fertility control agent into the water systems of the country, or a temporary sterilizing agent to supplies of staple food; the marketing of licenses to have children, or allowing women to have one child only after the accumulation of "credits"; *compulsory sterilization* of all men with three living children; implantation in

BOX 16.4

CHINA'S POLICY ON BIRTHS

PEKING—China's rigid plan to control population growth conflicts sharply with the liberal economic policies it is pursuing in the countryside, where family planning has met renewed resistance from 800 million peasants now armed with greater economic rights.

The growth of China's huge population—last year officially estimated at 982.55 million—must be limited if the country's modernization strategy is to succeed. Hoping to quadruple the gross national product, per capita, to $1,000 by the end of the century, Peking in 1979 announced a new plan to prevent the population from growing larger than 1.2 billion. The ultimate goal is to reduce the population to 650 million to 700 million in the year 2080.

The previous limit of two children per family has been replaced by a drastic "one couple, one child" policy, designed to restrict the families of the 160 million young people who will reach marriageable age between 1980 and 1985.

China's centralized political and economic system has helped execute the new plan. Rewards and punitive economic measures—affecting grain allocation, housing, medical care, schooling and, employment—have been established to deter couples from producing "excess children."

About 10 million couples are complying with the program. However, most live in cities where the Government maintains strong economic and administrative control. An article in The People's Daily laments: "At present, it is quite easy to implement the 'one couple, one child' policy in the cities. But it is very difficult to do so in the countryside due to the economic interests and 'backward ideology' of the peasantry. But it is in the countryside where the policy will win or fail."

Agricultural reforms have given China's 135 million peasant households greater economic power with which to defy harsh birth-control programs. The highly collectivized and egalitarian commune system—which in the past helped to enforce Peking's population policy—is giving way to a new system of "production responsibility" that encourages private farming and greatly reduces commune leaders' authority.

The expansion of private plots of land and the new policy of assigning output quotas to individual peasants or households have tremendously boosted peasants' enthusiasm and productivity. But the new official policy also allows some peasant households to get rich ahead of others—and households with more laborers will have a significant advantage.

"We now work on our own. We don't ask for grain, money, or cloth from the Government. If we produce some more children, that's our own problem and nobody can interfere," said a peasant in Sichuan Province, where the birth rate has risen considerably in the last two years. The national family-planning office denounces local leaders' reluctance to tackle "planned parenthood" work for fear of "antagonizing the masses and losing votes."

In Kiangsi Province, couples who produce a child not provided for in the Government's plan are fined 1,000 yuan ($571). "Between playing with my baby and playing with 1,000 yuan, I'd prefer my baby," said a young mother of two. Besides, the additional labor power will surely mean more than 1,000 yuan in the long run.

China's Ministry of Justice recently denounced as "illegal and criminal" operations to remove internally worn loops—the most common birth-control device in rural areas. Such operations are reportedly rising as more peasant women wish to conceive again.

Peking is aware of rural people's opposition to its population policy and has undertaken measures to weaken peasants' resistance. In some areas, for example, the Government is alloting smaller private plots and grain fields to recalcitrant households.

Peking's Guangming Daily has also aired an open call for family-planning legislation—a move that would make birth control compulsory for all, including the country's national minorities, hitherto exempt from family planning.

In the meantime, a system of rewards and punishments is being brought to bear on the rural bureaucracy. Not too long ago, a prefecture in Kwangtung Province counted about 100,000 pregnant women who would be having their second or third babies. Then, during May and June, hundreds of local leaders began hunting around the countryside for pregnant women—and the figure suddenly dropped to 47,000. Even women nine months' pregnant were forced to undergo abortions. The local bureaucrats apparently are determined to get rewards, not reprimands or punishment, from the Peking family-planning office.

There's no mistaking Peking's determination to limit population growth. But as its economic reforms continue to encourage peasant families to produce more children, the issue of population control will remain a source of painful conflict between the Chinese peasantry and the Communist state.

SOURCE: John Erik, "China's Policy on Births," *New York Times* (January 3, 1982), p. E-19. Copyright © 1982 by The New York Times Company. Reprinted by permission.

all females of a "time capsule" sterilizing device reversible only by a government medical service.

THE FUTURE

The recently published *Yearbook of World Problems and Human Potential* lists no fewer than 2,653 separate widespread problems that have the potential for aggravating social tensions.[70] What is even more startling is that over 3,300 international agencies already exist to deal with them. Sometimes there are too many answers! The best available general forecasts about the *world's alternative futures* were provided earlier in the theories of the neo-Malthusians, the technological optimists, and the proponents of the demographic transition. Here we confine our predictions to the future of American population.

Pessimistic Scenario

Life in 2025 is ruled by lotteries. If you are between the ages of 25 and 30, you look at the daily news release to see if your number has been selected as a potential parent. If it was, you have one year in which to find a mate and conceive a child, or your chance at "family-time" is gone. If you are over 55, you look at the numbers with fear; if you find yours on the Black List you have one year to get your life in order before "voluntary resignation," also called "depressuring" society. Most people do not try to escape "resignation" because the shortages caused by severe population pressure, and the breakdown of the world's economic system have made life quite nasty. The yearly quotas of how many new births will be allowed, and how many deaths will be forced, are keyed to the Gross National Product. The population growth equation has been simplified because there is no more immigration. The world is divided into hostile nations, each jealously guarding its own natural resources and technology. Much of the world is barren now; the nations without mechanized farming were wiped out during the drought of 1995–2000. Their surviving peoples have banded together and become the Third Horde, a Confederation of Nomadic societies organized by the idea of seeking vengeance against the Developed Countries for their criminal inaction during the drought. All nations' borders must be defended, and all internal political changes are suspended by harsh regimes on the basis of this threat.

Because of isolation from the international oil fields, atomic power is the main source of energy. Contamination from radwaste dumping, and from nuclear power plant leaks is a constant threat. People are forced to live near the atomic generators or go without power. Autos are battery operated, and the only recharge stations are in the cities. Long trips are very expensive, and so the cities as well as the nations are becoming isolated. The cities are separated by wide expanses of open land. All the underground aquifers were found to be contaminated. All towns served only by well water had to be abandoned. Only cities large enough to run reservoirs or desalinization plants are populated.

Communication is through computervision, but that too is limited by the danger of overloading the energy plants. People do not have the resources to do very much, so they spend most of their time watching government-controlled computervision, or tinkering with their consciousnesses with drugs. The government promotes cheap synthetic drugs as the alternative to the older forms of leisure activities and family life.

Besides, it is much safer to stay inactive and indoors. Your apartment-warren's air filter system is more efficient in reducing the pollution than your gas-mask-upper-body pack would be. And, there is always the danger that it might rain. If you are caught without your acidproof umbrella and boots, you are forced to stay indoors until the street neutralizer trucks come around.

Optimistic Scenario

In 2025 the world has come through the end of the Industrial Age and into the Age of the Quality Life-style. It took luck and significant technological breakthroughs, but the four trends that the Optimists predicted were realized. The age of 2025 is characterized by: (1) sexually equal families that center on providing quality nurturance for their children; (2) stability of life and a beneficial and productive age distribution; (3) a recognition of the need for simplicity of life-style; (4) a world context that has improved because of successful development and demographic transition by all nations.

The motherhood mandate has faded and women no longer feel that they must produce children to be valid members of society. Instead of thinking of children as inevitable, couples are planning to give the best environment they can to their wanted children. The breakthroughs in bioengineering and early childhood training have been fully developed. Parents are now able to choose the characteristics, as well as the time of birth of their babies. Though some couples still waste this opportunity by just choosing the best *looking* children, most are selecting among the new psychological and intelligence traits that have been discovered. As soon as possible, parents place their infants in a Stimulation School that maximizes the child's chances of developing the potential they genetically planned. Child rearing is finally being managed by experts, instead of being left to amateurs.

Population growth had been predicted to level off in 2025, but it stopped even earlier as people became involved in the stable life-style that developed. As the population aged, there were more and more productive workers to support fewer dependent young people. Without this burden, and with the additional productivity of working women, society produced an abundance. There was less crime because there were many fewer younger people. The cities shrank to become efficient, as the great sunbelt migrations settled down into a new pattern.

The trend toward simplicity of life-style and concern for environmental quality has been encouraged by scientific breakthroughs. Science began concentrating on cleaning up, rather than creating, new elements. Most dangerous chemicals and experiments are handled on space stations, and the solar winds carry away the contaminants into the void. Efficient and compact electrical batteries power our

Recycling is now economically feasible for paper and many metals. Our new attitude toward preserving and cleaning up the environment will encourage the discovery of more new technologies.

transportation, reducing pollution and noise. The electricity is produced in underground caverns that are pollution controlled. All air and solids are "scrubbed" before their release. The greenhouse effect was stopped in time. Individual families are increasingly concerned with activities rather than new things. The medical confirmation that exercise and relaxation lengthen life spans even beyond the 90 years now expected has stimulated interest in travel and outdoor sports. Preservation of wilderness is now seen as essential.

The Demographic Transition did take place in the Third World. Their government budgets were redirected away from the old priority on weapons and defense toward economic strength. Back in the 1980s, in the Developing Countries, there was only one doctor for every 3,700 people, but there was one soldier for every 250 people.[71] This colonialist-militarist influence has now faded, as the regions have politically stabilized. Economic cooperation has allowed the countries to choose their own appropriate technologies in order to use their particular resources for maximum employment. Some have chosen self-sufficiency, and they hardly participate in the world community. The mechanization of agriculture and the fading of the farm-family life-style influenced a drop in the desired family size from eight children to an average of three to four, and it is expected that soon all couples in the world will choose the replacement level goal of two or fewer children.

SUMMARY

1. Malthus's pessimism was the original warning about population pressure. He said that the population's geometric increase would always outrun the resources available for its support. This view was revitalized by the Meadows team's *Limits to Growth* study's prediction of the collapse of the world system due to resource depletion. There are also two optimistic views: (a) the theory of the Demographic Transition predicts that the developing countries will follow the West's three-phase pattern and that their fertility will come to be in balance with mortality; (b) Technological Optimists see scientific progress as geometrically increasing and more than able to handle any problem that arises.

2. Even taking the most optimistic projection, (all families having only two children by the year 2000), world population will not stabilize for over a century. If present growth rates continue, the world could have more than six times its present population, or 35 billion people, by the year 2070.

3. Population pressure creates two major problems. The developing nations suffer chronic malnutrition and poverty and are inhibited in their attempts to industrialize. The technologically assisted production and consumption of the developed nations allows them to be powerful polluters and prodigious wasters of resources. We are facing shortages of water, cropland, and the rapid extinction of plant and animal species.

4. Ecosystem thinking means understanding the relationships between all elements in the environment. We cannot separate out the goals of humans; they must be seen in their holistic interconnectivity. Ecosystems are fragile and can be destroyed by: (a) simplifying them too much so that they become unstable, or (b) triggering an overload of their normal waste-handling capacities. We are already in danger of overloading our food chain with pesticides, modifying our weather and atmospheric balance, poisoning our aquifers, killing our lakes and streams, and polluting rain with acids.

5. Ecological and population problems persist partly because of many beliefs that deny the need for action. Pronatalism, revolutionary, religious, and economic redistribution viewpoints all deny that population is the primary problem. There are also cultural supports for continuing growth and "the conquering of nature." The Dominant Western World View, the Business Ethic, and the Motherhood Mandate each uphold the traditional value on growth.

6. The individual faults position sees excess fertility and resource waste as the inability to control individual wants or desires. It proposes that both eduction and birth control devices be distributed to remedy population problems. Functionalists' System Disorganization view adheres to demographic transition theory. Excess fer-

tility is seen as a cultural lag in attitudes that will automatically disappear as family life catches up to economic life. Conflict theory emphasizes inequality and places population problems in a low priority. Excess fertility is merely another instance of people not being allowed to control their own destinies. It would disappear with economic equality. Interactionists emphasize the interpretation of family life and the place of children as they are seen by the potential parents within their own surroundings. Policies or international efforts that ignore these cultural elements, no matter how technologically efficient, are doomed to failure.

SUGGESTED READINGS

Brown, Michael. *Laying Waste: The Poisoning of America by Toxic Chemicals.* New York: Washington Square Press, 1981. A vivid, frightening account of chemical pollution by the reporter who exposed Love Canal and the twisted government/industry cooperation that caused it.

Cole, H. S. D., et al. (eds.). *Models of Doom: A Critique of the Limits to Growth.* New York: Universe Books, 1971. A collection of papers examining the strengths and weaknesses of the Meadows' team's world model of resource-population interaction.

Ehrlich, Paul R. *The Population Bomb.* New York: Sierra Club/Ballantine, 1968. Still a classic popular exposition of the extent and degree of the ramifications of population pressure's dangers.

Johnson, Warren. *Muddling Toward Frugality: A Blueprint for Survival in the 1980's.* Boulder: Shambhala, 1979. A suggestion for voluntary scaling down of our goals and projects to human proportions in order to avoid calamity. Underdevelopment for the future rather than affluence.

Kahn, Herman, W. Brown, and L. Martel. *The Next 200 Years: A Scenario for America and the World.* New York: William Morrow, 1976. The very elaborate, fact- and theory-filled, presentation by the optimistic futurists. The answer to the Limits to Growth Study from those who believe that technology will save us.

McPhee, John. *Encounters with the Archdruid: Narratives About a Conservationist and Three of His Natural Enemies.* New York: Farrar, Straus, and Giroux, 1971. The "archdruid" is the head of the Sierra Club; those who disagree with radical conservationism say "he worships trees and sacrifices people." A lively discussion of basic issues.

Peccei, Aurelio, *One Hundred Pages for the Future: Reflections of the President of the Club of Rome.* New York: Pergamon Press, 1981. The update of the Limits to Growth model, with suggestions for how disaster might be avoided.

Schumacher, E. F. *Small Is Beautiful: Economics as if People Mattered.* New York: Harper and Row/Perennial Library, 1973. The proponent of Buddhist economics and appropriate technology presents his simple and sensible plan for developing the Third World and remaking our own.

GLOSSARY

Anthropocentrism   The belief that humans are the center and rightful rulers of the planet; the rejection of the idea we are only part of the ecosystem.

Appropriate technology   The main idea of Schumacher's *Small Is Beautiful,* that economic production need not be industrialized, but should fit the social and ecological environment.

Aquifer   Natural underground water storage, easily polluted by seepage from chemical dumps.

Business ethic   The belief that growth is always good and resulting pollution and shortage problems can be handled by new technologies.

Demographic transition   The theory that non-Western countries will follow the three-stage transition, from high fertility and mortality to low fertility and mortality, that occurred in Western countries.

Ecosystem   The total interconnected, nondivisible environment, in which in order to understand one element we must study the whole.

Eutrophication   Fertilizer pollution of lakes and streams, stimulating heavy growth of algae that can kill the waterway by depleting its oxygen.

Food chain   Humans eat animals which eat plants which, if chemically treated, those chemicals get passed along into humans.

Lifeboat ethic   The hard-line view that nothing can be done for undeveloped countries ("drowning" in overpopulation) and that developed countries (inside the lifeboat) should take care of themselves.

Motherhood mandate   The societal requirement that to be a complete woman a female must give birth.

Neo-Malthusian   Renewed concerns about population pressure and the depletion of resources because of the belief population will grow much faster than the food supply.

Pronatalist   Policies or values favoring high birthrates.

Unwanted fertility hypothesis   The theory, based on extensive survey evidence, that the different fertility levels of social classes and ethnic groups in America are based not on different desired family sizes, but on unavailability of acceptable or effective birth-control techniques.

Zero Population Growth (ZPG)   A stabilized population in which the number of annual births equals the number of annual deaths.

FACTS ABOUT WORK

Manufacturing jobs have declined from 34 percent of total jobs in 1950 to 24 percent today.

Computer technology has eliminated several layers of middle-management positions in many corporations.

Long-term unemployment often produces mental stress, family violence, and pathological behavior.

Good pay is less important a factor in job satisfaction than having some challenge, responsibility, and sense of personal achievement.

At least 50,000 chemicals used in the workplace are toxic, many obscurely labeled or unregulated.

It would take 100 years to regulate known chemicals, yet new ones are produced every 20 minutes.

17
WORK AND OCCUPATIONAL TRENDS

As independent adults, work is an important focus of our lives, consuming an enormous part of our time and energies. Our social status rests primarily on our occupation, which also heavily influences our sense of self—who and what we are. In a society like ours where we emphasize the work ethic, work gives us a feeling of usefulness, fulfillment, and self-respect. Through work we meet other people and form friendships. For many, identity or self-image is immersed in their work, and to be unemployed or retired creates not only a loss of income but a loss of a sense of self and one's place in society as well.

German sociologist Max Weber (1864–1920), in his provocative work called *The Protestant Ethic and the Spirit of Capitalism* (1904), explained how such Protestant leaders as Martin Luther and John Calvin successfully transformed the meaning of work in their preachings. Work was more than an imposed duty, they said, for it was also a calling, a service to God. Calvinists also believed in predestination, and success in work could thus be interpreted as a sign of God's blessings that one was to be saved. Because they worked hard, Weber continued, they reaped profits which their Puritan beliefs forbade for any self-gratification, and so they were reinvested to make even more profits. This argument for the genesis of capitalism remains controversial, but the evolution of a secular work ethic—hard work, self-denial, and thrift—did become an important feature of American culture and remains so today.

Because work dominates so many aspects of an individual's life and is a critical ingredient to the welfare of all of society, the social problems related to work are of concern to all. In this chapter we shall discuss the three major areas that receive the most attention: the changing work force, job satisfaction and occupational health. The first category includes the impact of automation, high technology, and the participation of men and women in career positions.

OCCUPATIONAL TRENDS

For the past 35 years, the American economy has been undergoing a major restructuring. Just as industrialization brought enormous changes a few generations ago, so too are the present trends revolutionizing how we make our living, who is working, and who is unemployed. Demographic patterns are having a pronounced effect on the composition of the work force, and value shifts about the role of women have also brought an unprecedented number of women into the workplace in many different jobs.

Rise of the Service Sector

In 1956 the United States became the first nation to have more than half of its labor force engaged in a service or **tertiary occupation** rather than in a primary industry (farming, fishing, forestry, mining) or secondary industry (manufacturing). Tertiary jobs are mostly white-collar jobs such as clerical, administrative, research, or professional, but they also include maintenance and repair trades. With more than two-thirds of the American labor force in tertiary industry, we are living in what Daniel Bell has called a "postindustrial society."[1] The process of occupational restruc-

Telephone repair work is just one of many previously all-male occupational fields in which women now work. Despite the entry of women into many fields of work, four out of five females still remain in "pink collar" occupational roles.

turing still continues, and for many caught in the transition, its effects can be devastating.

The Rust Bowl

For more than a century, manufacturing has been the major activity of the Midwest. From a handful of states (Indiana, Illinois, Ohio, Michigan, Wisconsin) have come more than two-thirds of all our steel and more than half of all new cars.[2] Until recently, workers on assembly lines or running machinery were higher paid than equally skilled workers in other industries. All that changed with the 1981–1982 recession and foreign competition. Factory closings, layoffs, and business failures across America's industrial heartland sent unemployment rates to around 15 percent, about one-half greater than the national average.

From western New York and Pennsylvania through midwestern "Smokestack America," the fear has been that the region is likely to become a "rust bowl" similar to the agricultural dust bowl of the 1930s. While unemployed workers nationwide were victims of the recession and were eventually recalled, social observers identified most of the jobs that had disappeared as being bunched in the rust bowl region. Estimates of the number of permanently displaced workers range from a low of 60,000 to a high of 1.6 million. The trend away from manufacturing jobs toward service jobs is seen in the decline of manufacturing jobs from a 34 percent share of total jobs in 1950 to 24 percent by 1978.[3] Geography presents the greatest problem to the displaced workers in the rust bowl, since the greatest job growth is in the sunbelt. Wages are lower there, however, and the displaced workers often lack the necessary upgraded skills, and many simply do not move. Enticing new jobs to the depressed region to absorb the unemployed will be a slow, painful process.

White-Collar Bloat

Until recently, nonproduction employment had been a constant growth process. When bad times came, the white-collar employee remained but the production worker was laid off. The 1981–1982 recession forced American business to trim costs in managerial and white-collar ranks. Most vigorous were the badly hurt Big Three automakers, who slashed 55,000 salaried jobs, 27 percent of the total number.[4] Most other companies also streamlined their middle-management personnel, including such strong corporations as Xerox (13,500 jobs eliminated) and Texas Instruments (10,000 jobs eliminated).[5]

Significantly, this redefinition of unnecessary layers of management has brought about a lean management orientation which extends beyond bad economic times. Nissan Motor Company opened a highly automated light-truck plant near Nashville and boasted that it had only 5 layers of management instead of the 11 to 15 layers common among U.S. auto manufacturers. Other companies in and out of the auto industry quickly realized that eliminating layers of management not only reduced costs, but that extending more responsibility to remaining managers, aided by computer technology, created a more efficient operation.

The theory is that, with responsibility for more workers, managers are forced to spend less time in close supervision and more time planning and instructing. That means more authority and responsibility are delegated to the workers, who then achieve a larger degree of autonomy. As many experts see it, the result is a more efficient, more productive work force.[6]

What this trend also means in the long run is that companies will have less middle-management positions to offer. This changing perception of how companies are run portends less middle-management opportunities for the average white-collar worker within any given company.

The Impact of Automation

We live in the midst of rapid technological change, a time when electronic achievements are making many traditional methods of work obsolete. In 1964 a presidential commission warned that technological innovation would displace many workers from their jobs.[7] Since then automation has indeed eliminated many jobs. For example, direct dialing made many long-distance operators unnecessary, and automated plants required fewer workers to monitor machines that perform tasks previously done by a three times larger work force.

Computer technology has directly affected all our lives, whether at the bank, supermarket, department store, at home, or at work. These computer-caused changes in the way we live, play, and work have been compared to the major changes brought on by the Industrial Revolution.[8] The changes in the past 20 years which have already revolutionized our lives in many ways are only a small sample of what is to come. Yet already they have incredibly reduced the time to do things and we struggle to keep abreast of it all.

> We now have computer-operated microprinters capable of turning out 10,000 to 20,000 lines per minute—more than 200 times faster than anyone can read them, and this is still the slowest part of computer systems. In twenty years computer scientists have gone from speaking in terms of milliseconds (thousandths of a second) to nanoseconds (billionths of a second)—a compression of time almost beyond our powers to imagine. It is as though a person's entire working life of, say 80,000 paid hours—2,000 hours per year for forty years—could be crunched into a mere 4.8 minutes.[9]

As electronic machines shorten the time to perform various tasks, they obviously achieve by themselves more than humans could working with now obsolete machines (Box 17.1). Consequently, decreases in the number of jobs in occupations already affected by automation will continue (e.g., postal workers, printing compositors, certain textile operatives, certain railroad jobs). Other occupations will change because of the implementation of electronic automation (e.g., managers, production workers, statistical clerks, bank tellers). Other occupations will grow in number because of automation (e.g., accountants, computer service technicians, sociologists, systems analysts) (see Table 17.1).[10] Even though some jobs lessen in number and some workers are displaced, the number of jobs available continues to grow. The Bureau of Labor Statistics predicts that by 1995 the labor force will number about 131.5 million, compared to 111.5 million in 1983.[11] Some jobs may be disappearing, but new ones are taking their place.

For the blue-collar worker, the modern technology eliminates some monotony and demands more skills and greater responsibilities. One is no longer a laborer, but a technician who monitors the proper functioning of the machinery. While cynics may call such work machine-sitting, the work has become cleaner, lighter, and in many cases has given workers more freedom and autonomy on the job.

Many social consequences of electronic automation at work are evident among white-collar workers. One of the first was "flex-time," an arrangement which allows workers, within predetermined limits, to set their own working hours. Since information can be stored and retrieved anytime, it becomes less necessary for everyone to begin and end work at the same time. About 17 percent of all American companies have flexible working hours and the trend is continuing.[12] This personalized work schedule gives the individual greater freedom but does not disrupt the work of others. As a result, employers report higher productivity and reduced absenteeism.[13]

The computer age does not necessarily mean job satisfaction, however, as we shall discuss shortly. Many of the jobs may require different skills, but not necessarily any change in the level of skill. Back in 1966, the editors of *Fortune,* a major business publication, noted that computers simply require "a different kind of rote, but it is still rote."[14] Many clerical computer jobs often are low paying and create another form of monotony for workers.

A computer controls the cutting of a Boeing airplane wing as a worker-technician watches the monitor. Computer technology allows cleaner, automated factories requiring fewer workers. Other new jobs are created but some workers find their job skills have become obsolete.

UNEMPLOYMENT PROBLEMS

Joblessness is undoubtedly the most serious problem that confronts any society's work structure. Economists study unemployment rates and analyze their impact on the economy in terms of lost income, decreased productivity and consumerism, and cost to the government in benefits paid out. Sociologists examine the interrelationships of unemployment and group membership by age, race, sex, and occupation, as well as the effects of prolonged unemployment upon people's behavior and sense of self-worth. Unemployment therefore is more than a reflection of economic downturns and jobs becoming obsolete. It can also reflect inequities in the social system when it disproportionately hits one population segment, and it can be the cause of many devastating social consequences.

Who Is Unemployed?

The 1981–1982 recession, the eighth since World War II, caused the highest unemployment rates since the Great Depression, with more than 12 million people pounding the pavements. One-tenth of a percentage point shift in the unemployment rate indicated either economic and social well-being or deprivation for over 100,000 families. As you have read, blue-collar workers—particularly in the Midwest, once the bedrock of wealth that made the United States the envy of the world—face chronic unemployment even with economic recovery. In addition, other groups experience widespread unemployment for different reasons.

The Demographic Victims

As the post–World War II "baby boom" moved into the adult labor force, they left behind declining enrollments in public schools and colleges. Many towns across the country closed schools and cut back on the number of teachers, while in colleges the jobs for academics became harder to find. Education no longer was a growth occupation.

For many displaced workers, whether blue collar or white collar, growth was occurring in the sunbelt, not where they lived. Migration patterns and economic development have obliged many to move to that section of the country to make a living. They leave behind not only idle factories and shrinking town populations, but a depressed economy among other businesses—such as stores, bars, diners, restaurants, and recreational/entertainment facilities—which depended on their patronage.

The Economic Victims

Certain jobs are very vulnerable to even slight changes in the economy. When the demand for products falls, production line workers quickly become expendable in management cost-cutting measures. So too do all suppliers, distributors, and retailers of their products suffer loss of income. With a tight or retracting economy and high interest rates, individuals and businesses will be less inclined to build new

BOX 17.1

EXAMPLES OF AUTOMATION IN VARIOUS INDUSTRIES AND/OR OCCUPATIONS

INDUSTRY (OCCUPATION)	HOW AUTOMATION IS BEING USED
Printing and publishing (*Printing compositors-typesetters*)	The most advanced electronic photo-typesetting equipment allows an operator, using a keyboard, to select the size and style of type as well as the column width, and to provide spacing instructions. This data, as well as the characters, are keyed and stored in a computer which displays columns of type on a cathode ray tube ("TV screen"). That way, the text can be verified and any necessary corrections made. Photography is then used for printing. Automated photographic equipment can prepare entire pages of type while previously used hand and semiautomated methods required more manual effort and prepared only single lines of type at a time.
(*Telephone operators*)	Traffic service position systems automatically feed data about each telephone connection into a computer. The data includes the length and cost of a call and allows billing statements to be prepared automatically. Previously, this information was tabulated by an operator who transferred it to the bill. Electronic switching systems are also being used more. They eliminate the need to manually switch telephone calls.
Insurance (*Agents and brokers*)	Agents and brokers are using computers to perform necessary clerical tasks such as preparing reports, maintaining records, drawing up lists of prospective customers, and planning programs tailored to the

homes, offices, or plants, and so construction workers and their suppliers also find less work and income. Similarly, those whose livelihood is based upon leisure activities—for example, travel agents, theaters, beach or ski resorts, audio/video stores and arcades—find fewer people with extra money to afford what they offer. Bad economic times impact directly upon production workers, but the ripple effect also causes service occupations to suffer as well.

	prospects' needs. In the past, much of this work was done manually.
Various (Bookkeeping workers)	Functions such as maintaining records of accounts and business transactions in journals and ledgers as well as preparing financial statements are now done more by computer than by the previous method of manually processing such data.
(Railroad Yard workers)	Freight cars are sorted in a yard with a photoelectric reading unit which is connected to a computer. When codes on the cars are read, the computer automatically switches the tracks for car sorting. This automation has eliminated the necessity for yard employees to read the freight car destination in order to assemble and disassemble trains.
Steel (Various)	Greater use is expected of computers to control plant equipment, such as in hot finishing mills and other steelmaking operations. In the automatic hot mills process, an attendant feeds instructions to the automatic equipment through a card reader. The manual operation of equipment used previously is eliminated.
Various (Credit managers)	Computers and telecommunications will enable credit-related information to be more efficiently processed, stored and, most importantly, immediately retrieved. This will slow the growth in the number of credit managers needed.
Apparel (Various)	Computers are being used to draw patterns, mark cloth for cutting, and, combined with laser technology, cut cloth. Without computers, more pattern gradercutters, markers, and machine cutters would be needed. Other automation includes sewing machines that position needles and trim threads, and devices that automatically position fabric pieces under the needle as well as remove and stack completed pieces.

SOURCE: U.S. Bureau of Labor Statistics, 1984.

The Discrimination Victims

Many of the unemployed are young and/or minority-group members (see Figure 17.1). Some are caught up in societal changes—rapidly disappearing low-skill jobs, the malaise of central cities, and economic fluctuations. Most, however, are caught up in the larger problems of past discrimination and unequal opportunity, and lack the necessary qualifications and skills for today's jobs. A major factor is their usually

TABLE 17.1 Occupations Expected to Grow Because of Automation and Other Factors

In a detailed analysis of the impact of automation upon occupational opportunities, the Bureau of Labor Statistics identified 26 occupations as most likely to benefit from expansion:

Accountants	Industrial engineers
Bank clerks	Instrument makers (mechanical)
Bank officers and managers	Librarians
Business machine repairers	Maintenance electricians
Ceramic engineers	Mathematicians
City managers	Medical record administrators
Computer operators	Metallurgical engineers
Chemical engineers	Physicists
Computer programmers	Political scientists
Computer service technicians	Sociologists
Economists	State police
Electrical engineers	Systems analysts
Engineering & service technicians	Technical writers

SOURCE: Bureau of Labor Statistics, "Advances in Automation Prompt Concern over Increased U.S. Unemployment" (Washington, D.C.: U.S. Government Printing Office, May 25, 1982), p. 15.

FIGURE 17.1 Selected Characteristics of the Civilian Labor Force and the Unemployed, 1982

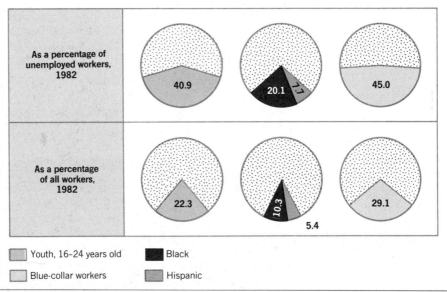

SOURCE: U.S. Department of Labor, *Workers Without Jobs: A Chartbook on Unemployment* (Washington, D.C.: U.S. Government Printing Office, July 1983), p. 7.

low educational level, which makes them unqualified for many existing job opportunities (see Figure 17.2).

Effects of Long-term Unemployment

Unemployment means far more than financial hardship for workers. Social and psychological consequences reverberate throughout the entire family from the ensuing intense emotional turmoil (see Box 17.2). Separated from the companionship of their fellow workers and an important part of their daily lives, the newly unemployed must cope with disruption and financial strain. Even when the plant shutdown or layoff is beyond their control, people tend to blame themselves for their job loss. Feelings of helplessness, inadequacy, disorientation, and depression set in.

As the nonworking days stretch into weeks and then months, problems intensify. From feelings of apathy, boredom, embarrassment, despair, and bad temper, the frustrated worker may lapse into heavy drinking, child or spouse abuse, and even attempted suicide. Wives sometimes become hysterical. Children may retreat in some form from the harsh reality, as illustrated by one unemployed steelworker's family which sought counseling because its child had stopped speaking.[15]

Mental Stress

Human flotsam adrift in a sea of despair, the unemployed find themselves unable to find the shore of employment. Their society places a high value on work and so do they themselves, but they cannot find any. The contradiction takes its toll as they find it difficult to face daily reminders of their situation. One steelworker stayed in bed for nine days after being laid off.[16] "When you're asleep, nothing hurts," remarked another laid-off worker who slept most of the time.[17]

One researcher found mental hospital admissions increased during economic downturns and decreased when the economy improved. Similarly, suicide studies show this inverse correlation with economic changes.[18] Other studies have found

FIGURE 17.2   Unemployment Rates of Persons 25 Years of Age and Over By Years of School Completed, March 1982

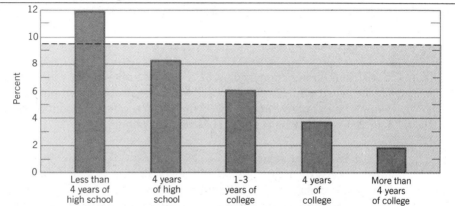

SOURCE: U.S. Department of Labor, *Workers Without Jobs: A Chartbook on Unemployment* (Washington, D.C.: U.S. Government Printing Office, July 1983), p. 11.

BOX 17.2

A GROWING DESPAIR

Now what will happen to me? The wording suggests an uncharacteristic passivity, even despair. But the lesson of the past several years is that taking charge doesn't always yield results. Fred O'Connor, a 40-year-old lathe operator from Rockford, trekked across the Midwest in search of new employment after his layoff six months ago. From Logansport, Ind., to Marysville, Ohio, the response has been the same: no vacancy. "I've been practically spit on when I've tried to apply for a job," he says. "They don't want to hire you; they don't even want to see you coming."

. . . Hunger is a new and humiliating experience. "At first I felt really depressed about having to come here," says former Chevrolet worker Dave Anderson, 25, over a bowl of barley gruel at the Northside soup kitchen in Flint." But I'd run out of food stamps if I didn't." Even the Gospel missions, traditionally the refuge of drifters and drunks, are filling up with out-of-work factory hands and their families. "When the money runs out, we have to rely on the mission," says Michael Hartwell after a dinner of mashed potatoes and ham at the Flint Rescue Mission with his wife Lynn and four-year-old son Shawn. "The boy needs to eat and we need to eat. When it's time, it's time."

Pride prevents many of the new unemployed from taking advantage of either public or private assistance.

Others take the help but hate it. George Papson swallows hard every time he picks up his unemployment check, recalling the times he looked down on recipients: "I used to say, 'Jesus Christ, look at those guys standing in line for handouts.' I started from scratch. Nobody gave me anything. Now look at me."

Daytime drinking is on the rise throughout the industrial states, and one of the predictable results is an increase in family abuse. "They sit in the tavern all day and then head home to kick the wife and kids around a while," says Don Brooks's wife, Diane. "I don't know whether there is more violence, but I do know the severity has increased," adds Jo Sullivan of Range Women's Advocates in Chisholm, Minn.

disorientation common, including avoidance of wearing watches since they had no reason to structure their time.[19] Psychiatric problem symptoms are highly evident among involuntarily unemployed males by the fourth month, while their wives by that time exhibit depression, anxiety, and phobia.[20]

Social Transformation

Most studies of the emotional and social effects of long-term unemployment have been fairly consistent in their findings. Headaches, high blood pressure, overeating, and heavy drinking are common. Feelings of inadequacy, incompetence, worthless-

"It's no longer the pushes and shoves and slaps. Now it's the stitches, the wired jaws, and broken ribs."

Unemployment may mean more togetherness than is good for a family. Says Paul Kapsch, the director of the psychiatric-services unit at the Central Mesabi Medical Center in Hibbing, "Now dad's home, making comments about mom's cooking and child-rearing methods and other things he never noticed before. He's feeling inadequate, and if he's like most males, he's having difficulty expressing that." Instead, the housebound husband erupts in anger. . . ."

Even more disturbing in the long run is the resentment and cynicism growing within the next generation. When older children are forced to look for work to help their families scrape by, there is "a great deal of tension," according to Carl Robertson of the Pittsburgh area Christian Family Services. "The kids feel, 'You had your chance, and you took it. Then you blew it. Now I'm being forced to pay for your mistakes.'" Alternatively, many children may respond by lapsing into a permanent helplessness. "I'm worried that the children will get the idea that life isn't worth living, that they'll be on welfare for the rest of their lives," says Maj. Alvin R. Nelson, Coordinator of the Rockford Salvation Army services.

On welfare for the rest of their lives: it is an idea no industrial worker could even have conceived of 20 years ago, when American factories were pouring forth an endless stream of finished goods, and you could walk out of a job one day and have your pick of two others the next. There were recessions now and then, of course, but they seemed no more than momentary stumbles in the economy's ever-upward march. Of all the damage this last recession has inflicted on the industrial heartland, none is more worrisome than its undermining of the old optimism, for optimism is a precondition of economic health. Without it, people stop planning, stop saving, stop cooperating with each other. Without it, they tacitly concede defeat in the growing global economic competition.

ness, and depression prevail. One study of unemployed white-collar and professional men, most of them college graduates and out of work for the first time in their lives, found a permanent change of attitude remaining after they found new jobs.[21] These men lost much of their self-esteem while unemployed and felt alienated from society, feeling themselves to be insignificant, a statistic, easily replaceable even in their own families. When they returned to work, they did not fully recover their self-esteem and maintained a deep cynicism toward other people and toward the political system and other social institutions. Their trauma of unemployment triggered a social transformation lasting well beyond the problem situation.

JOB SATISFACTION

Three major contributors to early sociological theory—Emile Durkheim, Max Weber, and Karl Marx—all expressed concern about growing alienation among workers. Durkheim believed increased division of labor and specialization brought to workers a state of anomie, or loss of direction, because their limited work responsibilities no longer offered personal fulfillment. Weber provided insight into the inherent characteristic of impersonality found in bureaucratic organizations. Marx detailed the **alienation** of workers—their sense of powerlessness, isolation, and meaninglessness—brought on by the restrictive demands of production. In varying ways, each of these pioneers of sociological thought saw work becoming an enforced activity, not a creative or satisfying one.

There was certainly much evidence throughout the nineteenth and early twentieth centuries to support these views. Until the bitterly contested efforts of labor unions succeeded in improving their wages, benefits, and working conditions, workers labored in prisonlike factories and mines for long hours at low pay under hazardous conditions with no sickness or injury benefits.

Since the 1930s employers have taken great interest in reducing worker alienation and providing a pleasant work environment in order to achieve increased productivity. Industrial sociologists offer valuable assistance in this area to many companies. Nevertheless, worker dissatisfaction has remained a serious problem in American business and industry, though its presence varies considerably from one field to another.

Measuring Workers' Satisfaction

An extensive number of surveys and studies have been conducted to measure worker satisfaction, but the findings have been contradictory. In virtually all public opinion polls asking workers if they were satisfied with their jobs, between 80 and 90 percent generally say yes. For example, a 1981 national survey of manual workers resulted in 80 percent expressing satisfaction with their jobs.[22] Yet in a highly discussed 1973 report, *Work in America,* issued by the U.S. Department of Health, Education, and Welfare, millions of American workers reported dissatisfaction with the quality of their working lives. When asked if they would pick the same job over again, only 43 percent of the white-collar workers and 24 percent of the blue-collar workers said they would.[23] As shown in Table 17.2, people in occupations where they had some measure of control over what they do (e.g., professors, scientists, lawyers) tended to express far greater satisfaction in their work than those in less autonomous jobs.

The national study drew attention because its findings were contrary to conventional wisdom that alienation was primarily a blue-collar worker experience and that high income is the most important variable in job satisfaction. Actually other studies had also long been reaching conclusions that contradicted popular belief. Perhaps most notable have been the extensive studies of worker attitudes by the University of Michigan Institute for Social Research. While income was important, these studies found dissatisfaction varied from job to job, regardless of income. Of all age groups, workers under 30 were the most dissatisfied of any category of workers. The

TABLE 17.2 Percentages of People in Different Occupational Groups Who Would Choose Similar Work Again

Professional and Lower White-Collar Occupations	(%)	Working-Class Occupations	(%)
Urban university professors	93	Skilled printers	52
Mathematicians	91	Paper workers	42
Physicists	89	Skilled autoworkers	41
Biologists	89	Skilled steelworkers	41
Chemists	86	Textile workers	31
Firm lawyers	83		
Journalists (Washington correspondents)	82	Blue-collar workers (cross section)	24
Church university professors	77		
Solo lawyers	75	Unskilled steelworkers	21
White-collar workers (cross-section)	43	Unskilled autoworkers	16

SOURCE: Special Task Force of Secretary of Health, Education, and Welfare, *Work in America* (Cambridge, Mass.: MIT Press, 1973), p. 16.

sequential studies of the University of Michigan Institute showed a general decline in job satisfaction between 1973 and 1977, particularly among college graduates.[24]

When the Michigan researchers asked workers to rank the most important factors in their work, good pay ranked fifth. In priority order ahead of it were: (1) doing interesting work; (2) sufficient help and equipment; (3) sufficient information about what should be done; (4) sufficient authority to get the job done. After pay, other priorities in order were growth opportunities, job security, and seeing the results of one's work.[25] These findings reinforce the views of Durkheim and Marx about workers' need to gain intrinsic satisfaction from the challenge, variety, control of, and results from, their work.

Blue-Collar Blues

The Work in America report reaffirmed earlier studies about worker alienation, particularly among auto assembly workers. In his 1955 study of "Autotown," Eli Chinoy had found 80 percent of the men he interviewed were frustrated in their repetitive, dead-end jobs, and had at one time considered leaving.[26] Many subsequent studies also found high worker dissatisfaction. Harold L. Sheppard and Neil Q. Herrick, whose 1972 book *Where Have All the Robots Gone?* is a definitive work on the subject, concluded that one-third of male union workers—particularly young ones—were alienated from their jobs and could not be assuaged with the typical rewards of more money, shorter hours or longer vacations.[27] Another researcher found job dissatisfaction a common reaction to boring and repetitive work, fragmented tasks, and extensive supervision.[28] In a newly automated Chevrolet plant in Lordstown, Ohio, almost 100 percent of the workers voted to strike. Researchers had a field day investigating, since money was not the issue but worker dissatisfaction with the assembly-line process and lack of a voice in the decision-making pro-

Seabrook construction workers head home after a day's work. Various studies have shown work satisfaction among blue-collar workers depends more upon their sense of challenge and control over the results of their labors than the pay they receive.

cess.[29] In *Working,* Studs Terkel also reported the negative consequences of powerless work experiences.[30]

In contrast, Japanese autoworkers have high job satisfaction, but this results from the collective orientation of Japanese culture (see Box 17.3). Japanese workers identify closely with their company, whose management takes a lifetime paternalistic interest in them and their families.[31] Comparative research of British and French workers performing almost identical tasks at their respective nation's highly automated oil refineries found a sharp contrast in job satisfaction. British workers, who participated in many day-to-day decisions such as who would work each shift, were very content compared to the strong dissatisfaction among French workers, over whom management exercised total control.[32]

Some American studies have had similar findings to these cross-cultural studies. For example, Robert Blauner reported back in 1964 that printers, working in small shops and occasionally supervising apprentices, had strong job satisfaction.[33] More recently, Edward Greenberg's 2-year study revealed that participation in the governance of industrial enterprises significantly enhanced the sense of satisfaction at work.[34] In a case study of aircraft factory workers about to undergo changes in job characteristics including a shortened work week, researchers found among the employees significantly higher general satisfaction, growth satisfaction, internal work

BOX 17.3
THE JAPANESE YEN FOR
WORK

Japanese workers aren't motivated primarily by money or the prospect of climbing to the top. Basically, they work for the team. Their attitude is a throwback to feudal days when daimyo (feudal lords) protected and provided for their followers and demanded loyalty and obedience in return. Today, the daimyo are gone, replaced by corporations—but the tradition of obedience remains. Company presidents often take a paternalistic interest in their employees. For example, Takeshi Hirano, president of one of Japan's leading fishing and canning firms, attends ten or more employee weddings a month, and members of his board go to ''many, many more.''

As a result, the Japanese worker usually feels a deep loyalty to his firm, which almost always employs him until he retires or dies. Working for the advancement of the company is elevated into a life goal for the worker. Japanese society encourages this by identifying a man not by his profession, but by the company he works for. ''If you ask a man what he does,'' says one Japanese businessman, ''he will say he is with Mitsubishi regardless of whether he is a driver or vice president.'' Often a Japanese employee's life revolves more around his company than his family. A government poll revealed that almost one-third of Japanese employees felt that work was the most meaningful part of their lives.

Company officials work hard at maintaining a team spirit among employees. In many firms, the work day starts with group exercise, the chanting of a company song or a slogan-packed speech by the president. Sometimes whole plants are shut so workers and employers can go off together for company-paid overnight trips. Along with teamwork comes harmony. Most firms have management-labor councils that hold year-round discussions with employees—not just on wages and vacation issues, but also on production rates, new machinery, and how to improve working conditions. As a result of this team effort, strikes are infrequent, and when they occur, they are usually symbolic and end after a day; workers just care too much that other companies will get ahead of their own.

There is also a philosophic basis for the Japanese work ethic of which Westerners are often not aware. It is based on Confucianism, which promulgates the doctrine that work is a virtue.

SOURCE: Bernard Krisher, *Newsweek* (March 26, 1973), p. 82. Copyright, 1973, by Newsweek, Inc. All rights reserved. Reprinted by permission.

motivation, and a sense of increased meaningfulness and responsibility for work that had occurred several months later.[35]

The 1981–1982 recession appears to have had a sobering effect on the way blue-collar workers feel about their jobs, returning to them after long layoffs. Both management and union officials agree the changes are dramatic: virtually no absenteeism, grievances, or turnover, but improved productivity and a more positive attitude than before. Whether such changes are short term or longer lasting remains to be seen.

White-Collar Woes

A 1972 national survey identified only 43 percent of the white-collar workers willing to choose the same occupation over again. Like blue-collar workers, many white-collar workers also confront repetitive, fragmented, mechanical tasks providing little meaning or self-fulfillment. Most especially so situated are the low-level clerks, office workers, keypunch or computer terminal operators, accountants, and book-keepers. As members of an impersonal organization, they frequently feel they are unappreciated cogs in the bureaucratic machinery, with little opportunity for advancement and better pay. When a clarity of goals and feedback about performance exist, as a study of pharmaceutical sales personnel showed, job satisfaction increases.[36]

Recent studies suggest white-collar job discontent reflects the changed work orientations of a new generation of better educated workers. Called the "New Breed" by Daniel Yankelovich, they value individuality, independence, and leisure activity as much, if not more than the traditional benefits of work.[37] Consequently they have less personal identity with their work, less loyalty to their employer, but a willingness to remain in jobs they dislike if flexible or favorable work schedules permit more personal freedom.[38] With greater education and higher expectations among professional workers, they place more value on fulfillment in work and are thus more sensitive to alienating conditions.[39]

Fittingly, the Opinion Research Corporation reported a 1980–1982 study of white-collar workers in a variety of occupations were much less satisfied with their bosses than they were from 1975 to 1979.[40] The slide was at all levels: from 62 to 47 percent among clerical workers; from 73 to 57 percent among middle- and lower-management employees; from 66 to 50 percent among professionals (accountants, teachers, doctors in organizational settings); and from 53 to 35 percent among hourly employees. The decline, interviews revealed, reflected lack of communication, insensitivity, and unnecessary tight control.

Attributes of Job Satisfaction

If job dissatisfaction has increased in so many occupational fields, what can be done to ameliorate the situation? This question has long intrigued social scientists and perplexed employers. Of the many analyses and attempted solutions, two seem most helpful: an understanding of the complexity of human needs and greater worker participation in the decision-making process.

What Do We Really Want?

Psychologist Abraham Maslow observed that human needs exist in certain priority levels. When the most immediate need has been met, then the next level of need becomes more keenly felt until it too is fulfilled and the next unfulfilled need demands greater attention. Maslow identified this **hierarchy of needs** as first, the basic needs of food, clothing, and shelter; second, the need of safety and security; third, the need for companionship and affection; fourth, the need for self-esteem and the esteem of others; fifth, the need for self-actualization.[41] Our affluent society enables most Americans to satisfy the first three needs, but its large-scale organizational structure often thwarts the fulfillment of the higher needs. This inability of work to meet the higher expectations of workers, except for those in prestigious occupational positions, in turn generates job dissatisfaction and a search elsewhere for those need gratifications (family, church, clubs, leisure).

Utilizing a different focus, Frederick Herzberg reached a conclusion similar to that of Maslow. Instead of a sequential needs hierarchy, Herzberg suggested both **intrinsic** and **extrinsic** factors influence job satisfaction. Income, supervision, and working conditions exemplify extrinsic factors while a sense of personal achievement, responsibility, and challenge characterize intrinsic factors.[42] If the inherent nature of our work denies us fulfillment of our potential, then the extrinsic factors alone, however good, cannot eradicate dissatisfaction. Therefore, the contradictory research findings on job satisfaction or dissatisfaction may result from the workers' interpretation of the question to refer to either the intrinsic or extrinsic factors, and so answer differently from one survey to the next.

Workplace Democracy

You will recall our mention of greater job satisfaction among British oil refinery workers because they played an active role in many of the day-to-day decisions. Beginning in 1970 at the Gravy Train dog food plant in Topeka, Kansas, and then spreading to over 100 other factories, short-lived experiments in worker self-management brought high productivity and employee morale, low turnover and rate of accidents.[43] Workers did the hiring, disciplined their colleagues principally through informal sanctions (stares, glares, comments), determined quality control standards, and worked in almost autonomous units. Despite the success of the Topeka and similar experiments, by 1980 almost every experimental plant had returned to more traditional hierarchical standards.[44]

Still, the idea had worked, and so it took on new form through a growing movement called **quality of work life (QWL).** Well over 1,000 companies in virtually every industry now have programs aimed at tapping the experience, resources, and advice of their rank-and-file employees. "QWL enleashes the talents and knowledge of people who know where the 'bodies are buried,' who know where the waste is, but have never been asked," says Jerome Rosow, president of the Work in America Institute.[45] This trend encompasses many different programs, tailored to specific plant or office needs. Perhaps most popular are the Japanese-inspired "quality circles"—regular small-group meetings of employees on company time to solve production problems.[46]

Other popular QWL techniques include semiautonomous work teams, profit-sharing incentive plans, flexible working hours, earned free time based on certain performance standards, custom-designed benefits for medical, life-insurance, disability, vacation-time, and retirement. Dual-income families covered by the spouse's job benefits can pare back medical benefits, for example, to increase vacation time. One-fourth of the U.S. labor force is now engaged in some type of QWL program. Significant productivity gains, cost savings, and improved job satisfaction are dramatic proof of this labor-management cooperative approach.

SOCIOLOGICAL PERSPECTIVES

So far we have been discussing concerns about the impact of demographic and technological changes upon the nature of work and workers' attitudes. Before examining the social problems regarding occupational health and safety, let us first consider the different sociological perspectives shaping our understanding of all aspects of work and leisure.

Individual Faults and Deviant Behavior

Economic hardship impacts directly on individuals, their families, and society itself, but it is the social definitions of its causes and cure potential which can exacerbate the situation. When one takes a blaming-the-victim attitude about those not working, indifference or prejudice toward that group or depressed area will likely prevent harnessing societal resources to correct the problem. Instead the problems continue, their symptoms treated through unemployment and welfare benefits, with an undercurrent of resentment smoldering on both sides of the have and have-not economic chasm.

The Work Ethic

Americans may no longer subscribe to the **work ethic** emphasis on the value of work for its own sake, but other aspects of this Calvinist legacy remain. We still believe everyone should work and that those who do not are not useful members of society. Work bestows dignity on a person as a measure of personal worth and reflection of desirable personal characteristics. By working hard anyone can overcome life's obstacles, for one's own efforts are the direct link to success.[47]

Prolonged unemployment, as we have seen, adversely affects one's sense of self-worth. This negative self-image, in large measure, results from the shared value orientation about work and identity. A person often feels ineffective and worthless by not working, and indeed, society reinforces that feeling. The character flaw among the unemployed is alleged to be either their inability to develop a job skill, acquire new skills to keep up with the changing times, or to apply themselves with the necessary vigor.

The American Success Syndrome

Our society stresses success goals. Built into the American socialization process is the belief that individuals must each "make it" in the world or be a "failure."[48] We hold in high esteem those whose occupation and life-style denotes success and we tend to look down upon those not working or in low-paying jobs. With a pervasive value orientation about individual achievement, economic opportunity, and upward mobility as basics in American society, those who miss the mark receive little sympathy.

To explain all work-related problems—job dissatisfaction, absenteeism, low productivity, unemployment, and low occupational status—the **American success syndrome** perspective looks to individual character flaws. A person has a "bad attitude" or "wants something for nothing." Laziness, ineptitude, and irresponsibility emerge as interpretations of limited or nonexistent work effort. Sometimes entire groups of people, usually minorities, are castigated for their perceived deficiencies in "proper" values about work.

The major shortcomings of this entire perspective is that it assumes all individuals are masters of their own destiny. In reality, many social forces beyond an individual's control affect work opportunities, including economic fluctuations, technological change, blocked life opportunities, and discrimination. While some individuals' work difficulties are indeed of their own making, attempting such a generalist explanation for all problem situations ignores the intervening factors and enables one to avoid social responsibility to address the causative social conditions.

Institutional Faults and System Disorganization

From the functionalist perspective, work is a key element in the social organization of a society. Under ideal conditions an equilibrium of society exists when the supply of all the differently skilled workers evenly complements the available jobs, with a steady, continuous economic growth to absorb the increasing population. In reality, an industrial society is particularly vulnerable to economic fluctuations, technological changes, and outside influences such as the Organization of Petroleum Exporting Countries' (OPEC) sharp rise of oil prices which in turn fueled worldwide inflation, recession, and unemployment. Sudden or unexpected changes usually cause dysfunctions in a nation's economy, which result in a ripple effect throughout the social system (unemployment, bankruptcies, alienation, social unrest, even violence). The inability of the social system to adapt quickly to social changes causes such problems, according to this view.

Another dimension to the functionalist perspective centers on maintaining the motivation to work for the mutual exchange of goods and services among all societal members. If an office or factory prevents employees from achieving a sense of personal fulfillment in their work, as well as adequate informal interaction, the workplace becomes dysfunctional in its organization; alienation and job dissatisfaction become commonplace. Additionally, changes in cultural values and attitudes about work as the central focus of one's life—together with a greater emphasis on leisure activity—can make workers less tolerant of problems in the work environment.

Demographic Dysfunctions
Studies in **demography** show that changes in the age structure of American society have created work problems. For example, an expansive child-oriented industry (clothing, toys, furniture, games, schools) was fine for the post–World War II baby

Older workers, such as this lathe operator in Nashville, Tennessee, are not as common as in earlier years. This trend is expected to continue as the percentage of workers over 55 is expected to drop from 13.9 to 10.9 percent by 1995.

boom, but as it ebbed and the sharp decline in the birthrate continued, widespread unemployment occurred. Many towns closed schools or consolidated school districts, and so teaching vacancies virtually dried up. As the median age of the population edged upward, the growing number of retired workers in proportion to active workers caused funding difficulties for social security (Chapter 7) and health-care benefits (Chapter 14).

Technological Dysfunctions

In the long run, technological innovations like computers and robots create new job opportunities such as manufacture, maintenance and repair, programming, and support services. In the short run, however, they displace workers whose skills are no longer needed, causing them much stress, anxiety, hardship, and deprivation. These unemployed workers must acquire new skills if they wish to make a decent living, and many must move to another region of the country for those other jobs. Retail businesses dependent on these customers and all government levels dependent on their tax revenues also experience problems.

In time the self-regulating mechanisms of society restore a balance. One example is Nashua, New Hampshire, a town of 68,000 people whose textile mills moved south in the 1950s, causing widespread depression in the area for a quarter of a century. Today it is a booming success story; its unemployment rate was only 3 percent in 1983, thanks to its concentration of high-tech firms and defense-electronics contractors. Yet this recovery took 30 years to produce and many workers suffered much hardship during that time.

Inequality and Inevitable Conflict

For the conflict theorist, the social and economic inequalities within the society provide the basis for understanding social problems pertaining to work. In a capitalist system, powerful corporate interests have a profound influence on national policy and the economy. Since their major objective is profit, employers and management exercise their power and influence to that end, usually at the expense of the weaker groups.

Who Benefits?

Because of our global interdependence, all countries go through cycles of booms and slumps. However, when a recession or depression occurs in a capitalist society, those who own or control the means of production are likely to dismiss workers as part of their cost-saving actions to maintain profits. The groups which suffer the highest rates of unemployment in such times are the less powerful societal members: minorities, women, and blue-collar workers.

Conflict theorists argue it is no mere coincidence that the less powerful are the ones most affected in difficult economic times. The pursuit of personal profit in a capitalist system dooms the less powerful in the competition for scarce resources such as jobs and income. Some even suggest that the affluent favor some degree of unemployment, for it keeps down wage demands, grievances, and absenteeism while improving productivity among the employed.[49]

Alienation

A conflict of interest between employers and workers serves as this perspective's explanation of the problems of alienation and worker dissatisfaction discussed earlier. Industrialization separated people from the products of their labor. The meaningfulness of labor and the intrinsic satisfaction from one's craftsmanship have been replaced. Nowadays the division of labor fragments work assignments. In a manufacturing plant the product belongs to the owner, not the various employees who work on it; in an office the product is less tangible since employees are in support service positions. As a result, the goals of employer and employee take different directions.

Denied intrinsic satisfaction from many of today's jobs, workers find themselves performing boring, repetitive, unsatisfying, and demeaning tasks. Workers experience difficulty finding fulfillment in their work. Their full human potential is unrealized. Work becomes a social problem because some groups of workers do not feel they receive sufficient rewards from work. It is an enforced activity in which the profits from one's labors go to someone else. Little creativity or satisfaction emanate from the work, for the worker has little to say in the decision-making process.

Conflict Resolution

Although inevitable conflict occurs between employers and employees in virtually every aspect of work, conflict theorists maintain it often results in positive social changes. The abuses of the Industrial Revolution ended when workers united through the labor union movement; although a bitter struggle ensued, they ultimately improved their pay, working hours, working conditions, and benefits. More recently, employees have gained improvements in work participation and satisfaction through adoption of various QWL techniques, as discussed earlier. Few would argue that the combination of foreign competition and poor productivity due to worker dissatisfaction were principal reasons for the rapid acceptance of QWL.

Interaction and Social Interpretation

Our subjective interpretations about our work, its meaning in our lives, and the work situations of others constitute the focal point of this perspective. Changing times bring about different interpretations as, for example, the arrival of high technology and increased leisure time caused a shift in value orientations about work as the central focus of our lives. The rise in the standard of living increased our life expectations and reshaped our view of what it took to satisfy us (remember Maslow's hierarchy of needs). People in different situations will have different perceptions of work, and interactionists attempt to analyze the conditions under which certain groups view work as a social problem.

Occupational Identity

Part of the problem with job dissatisfaction is that technological changes have forged numerous new jobs whose content does not provide people with a firm profile. Peter Berger has suggested, for example, that saying "I am a railroad man" can be a source of pride, but saying "I am an electroencephalograph technician" means nothing to most people.[50] His point is that many individuals are unable to enjoy a full sense of identity from their work because others will not understand what it entails and because the worker is unable to obtain any sort of self-identification from such occupations. In a society which assigns prestige and esteem based upon occupation, the vagueness of one's work limits its value as a source of dignity and satisfaction.

For many workers, white collar and blue collar alike, work has therefore been redefined. Instead of being the central focus of one's life from which self-respect and societal acceptance flow, work is often a neutral area one simply tolerates in order to enjoy the more important things of life.[51] This significant shift means more than a lessening of the work ethic; it impacts upon the presentation of self in the workplace. People are more likely to play roles as workers, restricting their real or actual selves for family and close friends.

Husband-wife Interaction

One of two discernible patterns affecting the tension or dissatisfaction within many working-class families is the unrealized expectations of the wives. Their perception of reality has been altered by images of the affluent life portrayed on television, the women's movement, equal rights, and abortion issues. The women's expectations rise, but housebound and without the heralded liberation in their own lives, they are frustrated and lonely. Working-class males, providing what they think are all the attributes of a good life—home, car, necessities, and luxuries—are puzzled by their wives' unhappiness. In her field research and analysis of this problem, Lillian Rubin found working-class husbands and wives experiencing great difficulty in communicating with each other because their value orientations had become sex-segregated.[52]

The second pattern concerns dual-career families, which now comprise more than half of all married couples. Increased participation of women in the labor force has created some marital strain, according to a survey of 32,500 respondents, of whom 80 percent were female.[53] This survey was particularly helpful because it was based upon a large sample whose income, education level, and home-ownership rates were all considerably higher than the national average. The 1981 median household income was $31,250, with 84 percent homeowners, 87 percent married, 79 percent with children; 71 percent of the males and 75 percent of the females had attended or graduated from college.

Of these respondents, 70 percent reported that work pressures frequently or occasionally create a serious strain on their marriage. Follow-up questions revealed that trouble on the home front was not due to a spouse too involved with work, guilt over giving insufficient time to children, or employer's attitude. Instead the stress factors were home-centered: family expectations, child-care concerns, parental responsibili-

This professional couple getting ready for work typify a growing pattern of dual-career families in the United States. This trend indicates important changes in the family structure and interaction patterns with children and spouse.

ties, household responsibilities, financial pressures, and too little time to do all that must be done. Employed women remain primarily responsible for child care and household chores, getting little help from husbands. The popular image of the super-woman who "does it all"—singlehandedly juggling home, child care, work, and personal time did not set well with those surveyed. Carrying an unfair burden of domestic chores, more true of those forced to work because of financial pressures than those who freely choose to work, was high on female respondents' gripe list.

OCCUPATIONAL HEALTH AND SAFETY

Concern about health problems related to work is at least as old as the times of the ancient Greeks and Romans, whose miners, metalworkers, and weavers of asbestos cloth suffered high incidence of lung disease. Throughout the Renaissance and Enlightenment periods, physicians grappled with special illnesses found only among certain crafts. The Industrial Revolution brought new occupational hazards—poor ventilation, exposed machinery gears that mangled hands and feet, toxic fumes and particles—that labor unions would fight to overcome.[54] In some areas progress occurred but in others, the picture is grim.

One of the bright spots is in on-the-job injuries and deaths, which have been steadily declining in recent years. In 1982, the 11,100 occupational fatalities were 1,000 less than in 1981, continuing a downward trend since 1945. Work-related, disabling injuries in 1982 totaled 1.9 million, down from 2.1 million in 1981. Agriculture, including forestry, and mining remain the most dangerous occupations for lost workdays due to injury, remaining at twice the national average.[55] Elsewhere the reduction reflects enforced safety regulations, heightened worker awareness, a smaller blue-collar work force, and greater use of robots to perform dangerous tasks.

Most serious are the growing problems of work-related illnesses and the long-term degenerative and fatal effects of exposure to suspected toxins and carcinogens (cancer-causing substances). While some substances have a negative impact within a fairly short time, others may take years to demonstrate their deadly effect. Then arguments arise as to whether those chemicals were responsible or if other factors of heredity, life-style, or life experience were contributing variables. Consider the difficulty of Vietnam war veterans exposed to Agent Orange or veterans exposed to atomic bomb radiation and the difficulty they have encountered over many years in convincing the federal government of that link to their high cancer rates.

Government Intervention

Growing concern over occupational illness in the 1970s resulted in the passage of two significant legislative acts. The Occupational Safety and Health Act of 1970 created the **National Institute for Occupational Safety and Health (NIOSH),** and the **Occupational Safety and Health Administration (OSHA).** In 1976 the Toxic Substances Control Act set the guidelines and systems for screening and controlling dangerous substances.

NIOSH

Situated in the Department of Health and Human Services, this agency researches work hazards. Its task is a formidable one, since chemicals are used in the manufacture of virtually every product we eat, wear, or use. The institute has identified at least 50,000 chemicals which are toxic that could be used in the workplace.[56] As its scientists analyze the products for regulation, the agency makes only slow headway. The General Accounting Office (GAO) in 1977 estimated that it would take 100 years to regulate known chemicals on a substance-by-substance basis, while new ones are produced at the rate of one every 20 minutes.[57]

Seriously complicating the matter is obscure labeling of chemical ingredients. Many manufacturers are unaware of any toxic dangers from chemicals used in their plants and may therefore not take the necessary precautions. This unawareness is due to the use of either thousands of unscreened and unregulated substances or brand names which disguise the identity of regulated toxic materials or carcinogens. The institute discovered in the 1970s that in 70 percent of cases of exposure in the workplace, obscure labeling masked the chemical identification.[58] Since then OSHA has been attempting to get passed a ''right to know'' law, requiring the use of generic and brand names, with a complete list of ingredients on all packages so that workers would know of chemical exposure and be able to take safety precautions.

The institute recently reported scary findings that almost all work gloves used for protection against hazardous chemicals were ineffective. Of the 11 different types used, all but one became permeated by a variety of cancer-causing chemicals, including benzene, PCBs, cleansing fluids, industrial solvents, and chlorinated ethane fumigants.[59]

OSHA

This agency is part of the Department of Labor and sets industrial health standards. However, its budget appropriations have suffered the double whammy of Reagan administration cutbacks and industrial lobbyists influencing sympathetic and powerful legislators to pressure OSHA to cease plant inspections or cut back their funding so there will be fewer inspectors. Even when OSHA succeeds in fining a violator of health standards, industry prefers to pay the relatively small fine than pay the larger costs on new equipment or plant remodeling.

As OSHA continued to be a thorn in industry's side, arguments ensued over so-called petty regulations and cost-benefit ratio. Critics argued that cost analysis should determine compliance requirements to health standards. In June 1981, the U.S. Supreme Court ruled in favor of OSHA, stating only that workers' health was the issue, even if the needed cleanup is costly. The Occupational Health and Safety Administration still must demonstrate that health and safety standards are technically feasible, and the budget cutbacks do hamper their effectiveness, but the decision gives them muscle to accomplish more.

Health Hazard Occupations

All occupations contain some measure of stress, risk, and work-related illnesses, even white-collar and professional ones. Blue-collar workers, however, face excessive health risks because of the prevalence of hazards in the mines, on the farms, and in the factories and mills. Many workplaces are cleaner today but they also contain more new hazardous substances. Recently NIOSH estimated that over 10 million full- or part-time workers are exposed to identified human carcinogens.

Mining

Statistically, miners have the nation's most dangerous occupation. They risk death from cave-ins, explosions, and sudden flooding as well as a variety of respiratory diseases. From 8 to 10 percent of the nation's coal miners suffer from black lung, known since 1813 to be caused by years of breathing coal dust.[60] This incurable lung ailment scars the lung tissue, rendering it useless; gradually the miner is unable to work, later gasps for breath, and ultimately dies from the disease. Ventilation technology for the control of coal dust has existed for years, according to the National Academy of Sciences. However, limited enforcement of the permissible dust levels set by the 1969 Coal Mine and Safety Act has prevented any significant improvement.

Another common respiratory disease is silicosis, caused by dust in mines, quarries, and foundries. So prevalent worldwide, silicosis is the major cause of death and disability among all occupational illnesses, according to the World Health Organization (WHO).[61] Dust-control technology exists but has limited application and is not utilized in all situations where it could be effective.

Farming

The second greatest occupational hazard group are farm laborers. They comprise only 4 percent of the labor force but account for 16 percent of the nation's occupational deaths. The primarily culprit is the widespread spraying of herbicides and pesticides. Migrant workers in the fields, 25 percent of whom are children, live in shacks or work in fields adjacent to those sprayed from the air. The inevitable drift and residue when they move to work in the sprayed fields cause itching, nosebleeds, nausea, and diarrhea. No one is certain about the long-range effects, but the life expectancy of migrant workers is only 49 years.

Textile Workers

Cotton dust in the air of textile mills and cottonseed oil plants causes an irreversible and fatal respiratory disease called byssinosis, more commonly known as brown lung. Although the disease was diagnosed in the eighteenth century and Britain began a compensatory disability program in 1941, American industry refused to recognize its existence until 1968.[62] Prior to that, company doctors in the mill towns labeled the workers' ailment as emphysema. It took 8 more years of labor union lobbying to get minimum standards set (200 micrograms of dust per cubic meter of air), but industry was given until 1983 to comply. Meanwhile, brown lung disease continued to spread. Of 800,000 textile workers in this country, almost one-fourth have brown lung.

Asbestos Workers

The chemically induced health problems from asbestos did not become known for several decades. As a fireproof mineral, its fibers were used for many purposes: fire fighters' gloves, theater curtains, ceilings, and manufacturing work stations. Over a million Americans working in the shipyards during World War II had extensive exposure to asbestos. Minute particles falling from school ceilings or clinging to workers' clothes, handled by wives and washed with other family clothes, spread the contact. The inhalation of these minute particles, we now know, causes a rare form of lung cancer. Asbestos ceilings have been ripped out of thousands of buildings and industrial workers in dozens of industries using asbestos wear protective clothing against its carcinogenic effects.

Chemical Workers

A great many synthetic products dominate American life in virtually every category of consumption. The chemicals used to create such diverse products also create two serious social problems: the toxic chemical dump sites discussed in Chapter 16 and the health hazards to the workers in the plants. Government studies found unusually high rates of cancer malignancies among those who produced and processed such carcinogenic chemicals as benzene, acrylonitrile, beryllium, ethylene oxide, and vinyl chloride. The current surge in synthetic organic chemicals, as yet unscreened by NIOSH and their long-term effects unknown, presents a potentially dangerous work environment to the health of millions of workers.

Workers unearth a toxic waste dump on a pig farm in Coventry, Rhode Island. Exposure to various poisonous and cancer-causing substances is a serious health hazard for many types of workers, and the dump sites themselves endanger those living nearby.

THE FUTURE

Professional and amateur futurists alike in substantial numbers have depicted scenarios about the future of work.[63] The miniaturization of computer technology, dramatic cost reductions, and the seemingly endless number of microprocessor applications create enormous potential impact. Sophisticated word processors and computerized information storage and retrieval systems are increasingly affecting office jobs. Industrial robots, which bear little resemblance to the creations of science fiction authors and screenplay writers, are rapidly revolutionizing the manufacturing world. Despite all the predictions about how and where the "techtronic age" will take us, little consensus exists on the subject. From a sociological perspective, let us project where our current social problems relating to work may lead through future technology.

Pessimistic Scenario

By the year 2025, technology had abolished far more jobs than it had created. Robots had replaced all manufacturing operatives in the automotive, electrical equipment, machinery, and fabricated-metals industries. More than two-thirds of the factory work force had been eliminated. Office jobs had dropped by more than 30 million, as managers acted to invest in cost-efficient computerized equipment, thereby eliminating the cost of high salaries and fringe benefits. As plants and offices now operated with the smallest number of employees possible, higher unemployment than in the late twentieth century was a constant reality.

Gods and Clods

With the fewer jobs in the complex technology performed by an elite of highly trained professionals, the majority were useless to the nation's formal economy. Although they were in the way because they were unable to operate and control the words and mathematical symbols of the information society, this large group nevertheless fulfilled useful functions as "shadow workers."[64] The highly technological environment had increased many artificial personal needs of the elite: drivers, pilots, accountants, child care, car and machine maintenance, personal consumer purchasing agents. Those doing shadow work worked hard, but theirs was primarily a service function to the technocrats.

Meaninglessness

Most fundamental of social problems was the disappearance of the work ethic, the core of industrial society upon which the entire social structure had been based. High unemployment, unchallenging work which often amounted to little more than "machine-sitting," and abundant leisure time fostered little work motivation, intrinsic job satisfaction, or self-identity through work. Working less hours, days, and weeks than any of their predecessors, Americans were uninspired and bored by their work, restless with too much free time, and without a sense of purpose to their existence.

Bread and Circuses

To combat the social unrest, street crime by the roving unemployed, and potential rebelliousness of the populace, the elite—the high priests of technology—had opted to distract the public through the ancient Roman technique of amusements and giveaways. A highly permissive environment encouraged narcissistic self-expression, sexual freedom, and hedonistic pleasure, but the diversions could not completely still the gnawing feeling of many that something was missing in their lives.

Optimistic Scenario

Work had scarcely become obsolete by 2025, but advanced computer technology had liberated workers from much of the drudgery of factory and office work. Over the years new products and new services had generated new needs, which in turn demanded new efforts to fulfill them. Consequently, more jobs existed than ever before to meet rising public expectations and support a higher standard of living. Thanks to the widespread utilization of automated machines, computers, and robots, the quality of life at work, home, and play had greatly improved.

The Half-Half Week

Contributing to full employment in the nation was the nearly universal 3½-day work week at factories and offices. Huge capital investments in complex electronic technology necessitated continuous operation to maximize cost-efficiency. Around-the-clock work shifts of three eight-hour days and one four-hour day meant six different work groups functioned in any given company. The typical worker spent half of the week at work and the other half in free-time activities. This system was beneficial to workers as well as management, for it provided a wide choice in work schedule, large blocks of leisure time, and availability of all services at any time.

The Electronic Cottage

Working at home was another common labor experience. Whether routine, creative, or specialized work tasks, people worked at home computer terminals to create and update data banks, write programs, and respond to inquiries. Electronic networking allowed access to financial, legal, or medical information with appointments, traveling, or waiting in an office. Banking, shopping, library research, even some psychological counseling was doable through home computers. With home as the central workplace for many, social scientists had observed a revival of the nuclear family, fewer transient human relationships, greater participation in community life, and more closely knit relationships.[65]

Satisfying Leisure Activities

Freed from the stress and alienation of earlier time-consuming work environments, people were now more highly motivated to engage in productive leisure pursuits. Depending upon an individual's interests, these ranged from the intrinsic pleasures (gardening, music, painting, repairs, or building projects) to self-improvement activities (further schooling, training, personal development), and shared activities such as more time with one's children or friends, traveling, and community projects.

SUMMARY

1. Work is a major focus of our lives upon which our social status, self-identity, and self-worth depend. As a dominating factor in a person's life and a critical ingredient to societal welfare, work-related problems are of concern to everyone.

2. Technology has been changing the structure of the labor force. Blue-collar jobs are disappearing, causing serious economic problems in the manufacturing Midwest. Although white-collar jobs in tertiary occupations dominate, computer technology has revolutionized the office as well. Fewer administrative levels are needed, which has eliminated many middle-management positions and advancement opportunities. Automation is generating the reduction of some jobs (operatives, postal workers, printing compositors) while increasing others (accountants, sociologists, technicians).

3. Unemployment hits hardest those most vulnerable to economic downturns—production workers, suppliers and distributors, leisure activity occupations, and minority workers. Long-term unemployment can have more devastating social effects: depression, heavy drinking, violence, mental stress, and prolonged cynicism.

4. Lack of job satisfaction exists among both blue-collar and white-collar employees. Recent findings have shown alienation often results from a lack of self-actualization; work fails to offer challenge, some measure of control, and a sense of personal achievement. In recent years many companies have successfully adopted quality of work life (QWL) techniques to improve worker moral and productivity.

5. The legacy of the work ethic influences some people to look upon jobless or poorly motivated employees as deficient in attitude and character. Functionalists, in contrast, view such problems as dysfunctions caused by inability to adjust to demographic changes, technological advances, or organizational problems. Conflict theorists see exploitation and a conflict of interest between employers and workers as the culprits, although they can foster worker movements to improve conditions. Interactionists focus on changed interpretations of occupational identity, the meaning of work, and husband–wife interaction as the basis for either work satisfaction or dissatisfaction, as well as on societal perception of the unemployed.

6. Occupational hazards are a dangerous problem to the health and safety of many workers, especially those in mining, farming, textiles, and chemicals. Two government agencies—NIOSH and OSHA—attempt to regulate and protect people but they are overwhelmed by the rapidly increasing number of chemical compounds to investigate.

SUGGESTED READINGS

Berger, Peter L. (ed.). *The Human Shape of Work*. New York: Macmillan, 1964. Sparked by a fine essay by Berger on the meaning of work, this book offers a timeless anthology of helpful readings on the human factors in work.

Eckholm, Eric. *The Picture of Health*. New York: Norton, 1977. Well written by an expert, this book provides a detailed look at often unnecessary health hazards faced by coal miners and other workers.

Kanter, Rosabeth. *Men and Women of the Corporation*. New York: Basic Books, 1977. An analysis of corporate management conservatism, it also profiles those who climb the corporate ladder while Blacks and other minorities find missing rungs.

Ritzer, George. *Working: Conflict and Change,* 2d ed. Englewood Cliffs, N.J.: Prentice-Hall, 1977. A valuable sociological examination of the problems and changes found in many forms and levels of the American workplace.

Rubin, Lillian. *Worlds of Pain: Life in the Working-Class Family*. New York: Basic Books, 1976. A revealing portrait of the communications gap and differing gender value orientations about self-fulfillment, work, family, and life satisfaction.

Terkel, Studs. *Working*. New York: Random House, 1974. Fascinating series of interviews with workers of all occupations, revealing both fulfillment and alienation, with intriguing human interest comments.

Toffler, Alvin. *The Third Wave*. New York: Morrow, 1980. This popular futurist projects current trends into the future world of work and leisure, evaluating their social impact on family life and social interactions.

Zwerdling, Daniel. *Workplace Democracy*. New York: Harper & Row, 1980. A captivating report on workers in the United States, Great Britain, Spain, and Yugoslavia who were given production control and self-management responsibilities.

GLOSSARY

Alienation Disconnection from meaningful or authentic social participation resulting from loss of control of one's life or being forced to do senseless work.

American success syndrome Robert Merton's term for American societal emphasis on achieving success.

Demography The scientific study of the population, such as birth- and death rates, migration, median age, and so on.

Extrinsic satisfaction Factors enhancing job satisfaction, such as income, supervision, and working conditions.

Hierarchy of needs Abraham Maslow's concept that human needs exist in certain priority levels.

Intrinsic satisfaction Factors enhancing job satisfaction, such as sense of personal achievement, responsibility, and challenge.

National Institute for Occupational Safety and Health (NIOSH) Researches and reports on work hazards.

Occupational identity Development of self-identification, self-respect, and prestige from one's work.

Occupational Safety and Health Administration (OSHA) A federal agency setting and enforcing industrial health standards.

Quality of work life (QWL) A growing movement modeled after the Japanese, tapping the resources, experience, and advice of the rank-and-file.

Tertiary occupations Jobs providing services, such as banking, commerce, education, health care, and legal services.

Work ethic Emphasis on the value of work for its own sake, offering one a sense of fulfillment.

Chapter 1

1. Jeffrey Katzer, Kenneth H. Cook, and Wayne W. Crouch, *Evaluating Information: A Guide to Users of Social Science Research* (Reading, Mass.: Addison-Wesley, 1982), pp. 22–32.

2. Peter Collier and David Horowitz, *The Rockefellers: An American Dynasty,* (New York: Signet, 1976), pp. 62–63.

3. Fay Lomax Cook, *Who Should Be Helped* (Beverly Hills, Calif.: Sage Library of Social Research #83, 1979), p. 173.

4. Richard A. Cloward and Frances Fox Piven, "The Acquiescence of Social Work," in John E. Tropman, Milan J. Dluhy, and Roger M. Lind (eds.), *New Strategic Perspectives on Social Policy* (New York: Pergamon Press), pp. 276–94.

5. John P. Hewitt and Peter M. Hall, "Social Problems, Problematic Situations, and Quasi-Theories," *American Sociological Review* 38 (1973): 367–74.

6. John Stimson and Ardyth Stimson, "Quasi-Theories and Research Origination, Part I: Quasi-Theories as Substitute Cures," *Sociological Practice* 2 (1977): 38–48.

7. Dluhy, Milan, J., "The Changing Face of Social Policy," in Tropman, Dluhy, and Lind (eds.), *New Strategic Perspective on Social Policy,* pp. xi–xxvii.

8. Martin Rein, *Social Science and Public Policy* (Baltimore, Md.: Penguin, 1976), p. 82.

9. Earl Rubington and Martin S. Weinberg (eds.), *The Study of Social Problems: 5 Perspectives* (New York: Oxford University Press, 1971), p. 19.

10. Rein, *Social Science and Public Policy,* p. 82.

11. David Matza, *Becoming Deviant* (Englewood Cliffs, N.J.: Prentice-Hall, 1969), p. 15.

12. Ibid.

13. Robert K. Merton, *Social Theory and Social Structure* (Glencoe, Ill.: Free Press, 1957), pp. 132f.

14. Joe Bailey, *Social Theory for Planning* (Boston: Routledge and Kegan Paul, 1975), p. 77.

15. Travis Hirschi, "Procedural Rules and the Study of Deviant Behavior," *Social Problems* 21 (1973): 159–73.

16. Edward Cornish, *A Better Future World* (Washington, D.C.: World Future Society, 1981), pp. 9–12.

17. Edward T. Cahill, "Sociologists as Planners," in A. B. Shostak (ed.), *Putting Sociologists to Work* (New York: David McKay, 1974).

18. Bailey, *Social Theory for Planning,* p. 142.

19. Willard Waller, "Social Problems and the Mores," *American Sociological Review* 1 (1936): 926f.

NOTES

Chapter 2

1. Angus Campbell, *The Sense of Well-Being in America* (New York: McGraw-Hill, 1981), p. 4.
2. Ibid., p. 7.
3. Emile Durkheim, *Suicide,* 1897, translated by John A. Spaulding and George Simpson (New York: Free Press, 1951).
4. Philip G. Zimbardo, *Shyness* (New York: Jove/HBJ, 1977).
5. Stanley Cohen and Laurie Taylor, *Escape Attempts: The Theory and Practice of Resistance to Everyday Life* (New York: Penguin, 1976), p. 18ff.
6. David A. Karp and William C. Yoels, *Symbols, Selves, and Society* (New York: J. B. Lippincott/Harper & Row, 1979), p. 45.
7. C. Wright Mills, "Situated Actions and Vocabularies of Motive," *American Sociological Review* 5 (1940): 904–13.
8. Robert Nisbet, *Sociology as an Art Form* (New York: Oxford University Press, 1976), p. 120.
9. Robert MacIver, "The Great Emptiness," in Eric and Mary Josephson (eds.), *Man Alone: Alienation in Modern Society* (New York: Dell Laurel, 1962), p. 49.
10. Louise Bernikow, "Alone: Yearning for Companionship in America," *The New York Times Magazine* (August 15, 1982), p. 25.
11. Arthur C. Norton, "Life Becoming a Chronicle of Changes," interview by Sally Squires in *The Sunday Star Ledger* (N.J.) (October 2, 1983), Section 1, p. 71.
12. Nisbet, *Sociology as an Art Form,* p. 123.
13. Emile Durkheim, "Anomic Suicide," in K. Thompson and J. Tunstall (eds.), *Sociological Perspectives* (Baltimore, Md.: Penguin, 1971), p. 111.
14. Nisbet, *Sociology as an Art Form,* p. 123.
15. Anton C. Sijderveld, "Industrial Society Tends to Reduce Man to a De-humanized Functionary," p. 70, in George McKenna and Mirella Baroni-Harris (eds.), *Taking Sides: Clashing Views on Controversial Social Issues* (Guilford, Ct.: The Dushkin Group, 1980).
16. William H. Swatos, Jr., "Revolution and Charisma in a Rationalized World: Weber Revisited and Extended," paper presented at the Max Weber Colloquia/Symposia, University of Wisconsin, Milwaukee, October 30, 1979, p. 6.
17. Peter L. Berger, "Secularization and the Problem of Plausibility," in K. Thompson and J. Tunstall (eds.), *Sociological Perspectives,* p. 455.
18. Ibid., p. 447.
19. A. James Rudin and Marcia R. Rudin, *Prison or Paradise: The New Religious Cults* (Philadelphia: Fortress Press, 1980), p. 14.
20. Irving Louis Horowitz, "The New Fundamentalism," *Society* (November/December 1982), pp. 40–47.
21. Ibid.
22. Ibid.
23. Rudin and Rudin, *Prison or Paradise: The New Religious Cults,* p. 299.
24. Elliot Krause, *Why Study Sociology?* (New York: Random House, 1980), p. 169.
25. Ibid.
26. E. Schur, *The Awareness Trap* (New York: McGraw-Hill, 1976).
27. Karp and Yoels, *Symbols, Selves, and Society,* p. 199.
28. Andrezej Walicki, "Marx and Freedom," *The New York Review of Books* (November 24, 1983), p. 52.
29. Paul Goodman, *Growing Up Absurd* (New York: Vintage, 1960).
30. Richard Sennett and J. Cobb, *The Hidden Injuries of Class* (New York: Vintage, 1972).
31. Ibid.
32. Arnold W. Green, *Social Problems: Arena of Conflict* (New York: McGraw-Hill, 1975).
33. Sennett and Cobb, *The Hidden Injuries of Class,* p. 179.

34. Christopher Lasch, *The Culture of Narcissism* (New York: Warner Books, 1979), p. 137.

35. C. Wright Mills, "The Competitive Personality," in Lewis A. Coser (ed.), *The Pleasures of Sociology* (New York: Mentor, 1980), p. 270.

36. Ralph Keyes, "We the Lonely People," in Kurt Finsterbush and George McKenna (eds.), *Taking Sides* (Guilford, Conn.: Dushkin, 1982), p. 79.

37. Peter L. Berger, *Invitation to Sociology* (Garden City, N.Y.: Doubleday/Anchor, 1963), p. 129.

38. Joseph Bensman and Robert Lilienfield, *Between Public and Private: Lost Boundaries of the Self* (New York: Free Press, 1979), pp. 12–13.

39. Elaine Walster, "Playing Hard to Get: Understanding an Elusive Phenomenon," in T. Blass (ed.), *Contemporary Social Psychology* (Itasca, Ill.: F. E. Peacock, 1976), p. 94ff.

40. Walter R. Gove, M. Hughes, and M. R. Geerkin, "Playing Dumb: A Form of Impression Management with Undesirable Side Effects," *Social Psychology Quarterly* 43 (1980): 89–102.

41. Karp and Yoels, *Symbols, Selves, and Society,* p. 74.

42. Andrew Hacker, quoted in Paul Blumberg, "The Decline and Fall of the Status Symbol," *Social Problems* 21 (1974): 489.

43. Alvin Toffler, *Future Shock* (New York: Bantam, 1970), p. 358ff.

Chapter 3

1. H. Meyer, *Old English Coffee Houses* (Emmaus, Pa.: Rodale, 1954).

2. National Commission on Marijuana and Drug Abuse, *Report to the President* (Washington, D.C.: U.S. Government Printing Office, 1973), p. 9.

3. Much of this material is derived from Jules Saltman, *Children and Drugs* (New York: Public Affairs Committee, 1980), pamphlet no. 584.

4. Bureau of the Census, *Statistical Abstract of the United States, 1984,* Table 195, p. 126.

5. Department of Health, Education, and Welfare, *Alcohol and Health* (Rockville, Md.: Public Health Service, 1975).

6. Department of Health, Education, and Welfare, *Third Special Report to the U.S. Congress on Alcohol and Health* (Washington, D.C.: U.S. Government Printing Office, 1978), p. 8.

7. Erich Goode, *Drugs in American Society* 2d ed. (New York: Knopf, 1984), p. 134.

8. John Timson, "Is Coffee Safe to Drink?" *Human Nature* 1 (1978): 57–59.

9. Oakley Ray, *Drugs, Society, and Human Behavior,* 2nd ed. (St. Louis: Mosby, 1978).

10. Oswaldo Tippo and William L. Stern, *Humanistic Botany* (New York: Norton, 1977).

11. Richard Ashley, *Cocaine: Its History, Uses and Effects* (New York: St. Martin's Press, 1975).

12. *Statistical Abstract of the United States, 1984,* Table 195, p. 126.

13. Jean Seligman, et al., "Getting Straight," *Newsweek* (June 4, 1984), p. 62; "Cocaine: Middle-Class High," *Time* (July 16, 1981), p. 57.

14. *Federal Strategy for Drug Abuse and Drug Traffic Prevention* (Washington, D.C.:. U.S. Government Printing Office, 1979).

15. Michael J. Hindelang, Michael R. Gottfredson, and Timothy J. Flanagan (eds.), *Sourcebook of Criminal Justice Statistics—1980* U.S. Department of Justice (Washington, D.C.: U.S. Government Printing Office, 1981); Gallup Poll, "Teens Oppose Easing of Anti-Pot Laws," 1982.

16. Susanna McBee, et al., "How Drugs Sap the Nation's Strength," *U.S. News & World Report* (May 16, 1983), p. 55.

17. *Marihuana: A Signal of Misunder-*

standing, First Report of the Commission of Marihuana and Drug Abuse (Washington, D.C.: U.S. Government Printing Office, 1972), p. 109.

18. McBele, et al. "How Drugs Sap the Nation's Strength."

19. Patricia M. Fishburne, Herbert I. Abelson, and Ira Cisin, *National Survey on Drug Abuse: 1979* (Rockville, Md.: National Institute on Drug Abuse, 1980), pp. 45–47.

20. "Marijuana: The Grass Is Getting Greener," ABC Television Special Report (April 11, 1977).

21. Fishburne, Abelson, and Cisin, *National Survey on Drug Abuse: 1979.*

22. Sidney Cohen, "A Program Report on Marijuana as Medicine," *Psychology Today,* 11 (April 1978), pp. 60–73; Joann S. Lublin, "Government Helping Develop Ingredient in Marijuana as Aid to Cancer Patients," *Wall Street Journal* (February 4, 1980), p. 1.

23. Fishburne, Abelson, and Cisin, *National Survey on Drug Abuse: 1979.*

24. Ibid.

25. Joel Fort and Christopher T. Cory, *American Drugstore* (Boston: Educational Associates, 1975), p. 41; *Statistical Abstract of the United States, 1984,* Table 198, p. 127.

26. William A. Hunt and Joseph D. Matarazzo, "Habit Mechanisms in Smoking," in William A. Hunt (ed.), *Learning Mechanisms of Smoking* (Chicago: Aldine, 1970), p. 76.

27. Fort and Cory, *American Drugstore,* p. 42.

28. Ibid.

29. Statistics are from Department of Health, Education, and Welfare, *Surgeon General's Report on Smoking and Health* (Washington, D.C.: U.S. Government Printing Office, 1979).

30. *Statistical Abstract of the United States, 1984,* Table 198, p. 127.

31. Vincent Dole and Marie Nyswander, "Heroin Addiction—A Metabolic Disease," *Archives of Internal Medicine* 120 (1967): 19–24.

32. See, for example, Nancy S. Cotton, "The Familial Incidences of Alcoholism: A Review," *Journal of Studies on Alcohol* 40 (1979): 89–116.

33. See A. Roe, "Children of Alcoholic Parents Raised in Foster Homes," in *Alcohol, Science, and Society* (New Haven: Quarterly Journal on Studies of Alcohol, 1945), pp. 115–28.

34. Alfred Lindesmith, *Opiate Addiction* (Bloomington, Ind.: Principia Press, 1947), pp. 67–89.

35. Jonathan D. Cowan, et al., "Drug Abusers: Defeated and Joyless," in Louis S. Harris (ed.), *Problems of Drug Dependence* (Rockville, Md.: National Institute on Drug Abuse, 1979), pp. 170–76.

36. Ray, *Drugs, Society and Human Behavior.*

37. Peter H. Odegard, *Pressure Politics* (New York: Octagon Books, 1966).

38. Patricia A. Morgan, "The Legislation of Drug Law: Economic Crisis and Social Control," *Journal of Drug Issues* 8 (1978): 59.

39. Ashley, *Cocaine: Its History, Uses and Effects.*

40. James M. Graham, "Amphetamine Politics on Capitol Hill," *Transaction* 9 (1972): 14–15.

41. Larry Sloman, *Reefer Madness: The History of Marijuana in America* (Indianapolis, Ind.: Bobbs-Merrill, 1978); Donald Dickson, "Bureaucracy and Morality: An Organization Perspective on a Moral Crusade," *Social Problems* 16 (1968): 146–56.

42. Barry Glassner and Bruce Berg, "How Jews Avoid Alcohol Problems," *American Sociological Review* 45 (1980): 647–64.

43. Georgio Lolli, et al., *Alcohol in Italian Culture* (Glencoe, Ill.: Free Press, 1958).

44. Richard Stivers, *A Hair of the Dog: Irish Drinking and the American Stereotype* (University Park, Pa.: University of Pennsylvania Press, 1976).

45. See, for example, Bruce D. Johnson,

Marihuana Users and Drug Subcultures (New York: Wiley, 1973).

46. This concept of criminal activity as reinforced by differential association was formulated by Edwin H. Sutherland in *Principles of Criminology* (Philadelphia: J. B. Lippincott Company, 1934).

47. Department of Health, Education, and Welfare, *Third Special Report to the U.S. Congress on Alcohol and Health,* p. 64.

48. Ibid, pp. 158–63.

49. Alex Thio, *Deviant Behavior* (Boston: Houghton Mifflin, 1978), p. 302.

50. Charles Winick, "Physician Narcotics Addicts," *Social Problems* 9 (1961): 174–86.

51. John A. Volpe, chairman of Presidential Commission on Drunk Driving, quoted in *U.S. News & World Report* (January 17, 1983), p. 71.

52. Robert C. Petersen, *Marijuana and Health: Seventh Annual Report* (Rockville, Md.: National Institute on Drug Abuse, 1977).

53. Department of Health, Education, and Welfare, *Third Special Report to the U.S. Congress on Alcohol and Health.*

54. Department of Health, Education, and Welfare, *Drug Dependence in Pregnancy: Clinical Management of Mother and Child* (Rockville, Md.: Public Health Service, 1979).

55. Quoted in McBee, et al., "How Drugs Sap the Nation's Strength," p. 56.

56. John Brecher, et al., "Taking Drugs on the Job," *Newsweek* (August 22, 1983), pp. 53–58.

57. McBee, et al., "How Drugs Sap the Nation's Strength," p. 55.

58. Brecher, et al., "Taking Drugs on the Job," pp. 53–58.

59. Ibid.

60. Alvin P. Sanoff, "How Drugs Threaten to Ruin Pro Sports," *U.S. News & World Report* (September 12, 1983), pp. 64–65.

61. National Commission on Marijuana and Drug Abuses, 1973, p. 152.

62. *Marijuana: A Signal of Misunderstanding,* p. 109.

63. Richard H. Blum, Eva Blum, and E. Garfield, *Drug Education: Results and Recommendations* (Lexington, Mass.: Heath, 1976).

64. Barry Leach, "Does Alcoholics Anonymous Really Work?" in Peter G. Bourne and Ruth Fox (eds.), *Alcoholism: Progress in Research and Treatment* (New York: Academic Press, 1973), pp. 245–84.

65. Edward Preble and Thomas Miller, "Methadone, Wine, and Welfare," in Robert S. Weppner (ed.), *Street Ethnography: Selected Studies of Crime and Drug Use in Natural Settings* (Beverly Hills, Calif.: Sage Publications, 1977).

66. George DeLeon and Mitchell S. Rosenthal, "Therapeutic Communities," in Robert L. DuPont, Avram Goldstein, and John O'Connell (eds.), *Handbook on Drug Abuse* (Rockville, Md.: National Institute on Drug Abuse, 1979), pp. 40–41.

67. Horace F. Judson, *Heroin Addiction in Britain: What Americans Can Learn from the English Experience* (New York: Harcourt Brace Jovanovich, 1973).

Chapter 4

1. Marston Bates, *Gluttons and Libertines* (New York: Vintage Books, 1967), p. 75.

2. Ibid., p. 80.

3. James Henslin and Edward Sagarin (eds.), *The Sociology of Sex* (New York: Schocken, 1978), p. 14.

4. Bates, *Gluttons and Libertines,* p. 86.

5. Ibid., p. 80.

6. Paul H. Gebhard, "Human Sexual Behavior," in Donald S. Marshall and Robert C. Suggs (eds.), *Human Sexual Behavior: Variations in the Ethnographic Spectrum* (Englewood Cliffs, N.J.: Prentice-Hall, 1971), p. 21.

7. Ibid., p. 210.

8. Ibid., p. 212.

9. Arno Karlen, *Sexuality and Homosexuality* (New York: Norton, 1971), p. 445.

10. Ibid., p. 3.

11. Ibid., p. 25.

12. Ibid., p. 34.

13. Ibid., p. 121.

14. Gebhard, "Human Sexual Behavior," p. 215.

15. Karlen, *Sexuality and Homosexuality,* p. 476.

16. Ibid., p. 502.

17. Elizabeth Ogg, "Changing Views of Homosexuality," *Public Affairs Pamphlet No. 563* (New York: Public Affairs Committee, 1978), p. 9.

18. Ibid.

19. *Newsweek* (April 5, 1982), p. 75.

20. Karen Stabine, "Tapping the Homosexual Market," *New York Times Magazine* (May 2, 1982), p. 80.

21. Karlen, *Sexuality and Homosexuality,* p. 18.

22. Ogg, "Changing Views and Homosexuality," p. 9.

23. John Gagnon and Simon William, "Sexual Deviance in Contemporary America," *American Annals of the American Academy of Political and Social Sciences* 376 (1968): 106–22.

24. Karlen, *Sexuality and Homosexuality,* p. 543.

25. Ibid., p. 540.

26. Ibid., p. 544.

27. Ibid., p. 545.

28. Nikki Meredith, "The Gay Dilemma," *Psychology Today* (January 1984), p. 56.

29. Arno Karlen, "Homosexuality: The Scene and Its Students," in Henslin and Sagarin (eds.), *The Sociology of Sex,* p. 245.

30. Martin S. Weinberg and Colin J. Williams, "Gay Baths and the Social Organization of Impersonal Sex," *Social Problems* 23, no. 2 (December 1975), p. 125.

31. Meredith, "The Gay Dilemma," p. 56.

32. Ibid., p. 61.

33. Joann S. Delora and Carol B. Warren, *Understanding Sexual Interaction* (Boston: Houghton Mifflin, 1977), p. 291.

34. Karlen, *Sexuality and Homosexuality,* p. 372.

35. Delora and Warren, *Understanding Sexual Interaction,* p. 307.

36. Robert J. Stoller, "The Term 'Transvestism,' " *Archives of General Psychiatry* 22 (1971): 232.

37. Delora and Warren, *Understanding Sexual Interaction,* p. 308.

38. Karlen, *Sexuality and Homosexuality,* p. 359.

39. Delora and Warren, *Understanding Sexual Interaction,* p. 309.

40. Duncan Chappell, et al., "Forcible Rape: A Comparative Study of Offenses Known to the Police in Boston and Los Angeles," in Henslin and Sagarin (eds.), *The Sociology of Sex,* p. 112.

41. Vicki McNickle Rose, "Rape as a Social Problem: A Byproduct of the Feminist Movement," *Social Problems* 25, no. 1 (October 1977), p. 86.

42. Ibid., p. 48.

43. Lynda Lytle Holmstrom and A. W. Burgess, "Rape and Everyday Life," *Society* 20, no. 5 (July/August 1983), p. 33.

44. Ibid., p. 34.

45. Rose, "Rape as a Social Problem," p. 80.

46. Ibid., p. 79.

47. Ibid., p. 80.

48. Delora and Warren, *Understanding Sexual Interaction,* p. 370.

49. Ibid., p. 332.

50. Susan H. Gray, "Exposure to Pornography and Aggression Toward Women: The Case of the Angry Male," *Social Problems* 29, no. 4 (April 1982), p. 388.

51. Susan Brownmiller, *Against Our Will* (New York: Bantam Books, 1976), pp. 442–43.

52. Nanette J. Davis, "Prostitution: Identity, Career, and Legal Economic Enterprise," pp. 195–222, in Henslin and Sagarin, *The Sociology of Sex.*

53. Ibid., pp. 216–17.
54. Karlen, *Sexuality and Homosexuality,* p. 140.
55. Delora and Warren, *Understanding Sexual Interaction* , p. 10.
56. Brownmiller, *Against Our Will,* pp. 442, 446.
57. Karlen, "Homosexuality: The Scene and Its Students," p. 240.
58. For a fuller discussion, see Edwin Lemert, *Social Pathology: A Systematic Approach to the Theory of Sociopathic Behavior* (New York: McGraw-Hill, 1951).
59. Rose Weitz, "From Accommodation to Rebellion: Tertiary Deviance and the Radical Re-definition of Lesbianism," paper presented to the Society for the Study of Social Problems, San Francisco, September 1982, p. 1.
60. Ibid., p. 9.
61. Ibid., p. 31.
62. Robert R. Francoeur and Anna K. Francoeur, "The Pleasure Band: Reversing the Anti-Sex Ethic," *The Futurist* X (August 1976), p. 176.
63. Ibid.
64. Ibid., p. 201.

Chapter 5

1. David Matza, *Becoming Deviant* (Englewood Cliffs, N.J.: Prentice-Hall, 1969), pp. 41–66.
2. Robert MacIver, *Social Causation* (Boston: Ginn, 1942), pp. 88–95.
3. Richard Quinney, *The Problem of Crime* (New York: Dodd, Mead, 1974), p. 14.
4. William Graham Sumner, "The Mores Can Make Anything Right," S. Rappaport and H. Wright (eds.), *Anthropology* (New York: Washington Square Press, 1972), pp. 212–20.
5. Quinney, *The Problem of Crime,* pp. 162–63.
6. Marvin Harris, *Cows, Pigs and Witches* (New York: Vintage Books, 1975), p. 207.
7. Ibid., pp. 208–209.
8. Gloria Vannote, "Old Laws," *Tele-News,* New Jersey Bell Telephone Company (1982).
9. Quinney, *The Problem of Crime,* p. 9.
10. William Ryan, *Blaming the Victim* (New York: Vintage Books, 1976), p. 209.
11. Ibid., p. 24.
12. For a complete breakdown, see: *Statistical Abstract of the United States, 1984* (Washington, D.C.: U.S. Department of Commerce , Bureau of the Census, 1984).
13. Alan Booth, David R. Johnson, and Harvey M. Choldin, "Correlates of City Crime Rates: Victimization Survey Versus Official Statistics," *Social Problems* 25 (1977): 187–97.
14. "The Prevalence of Crime," *Bureau of Justice Statistics Bulletin* (Washington, D.C.: U.S. Government Printing Office, March 1981), p. 1.
15. Gresham Sykes, *The Future of Crime* (Washington, D.C.: Alcohol, Drug Abuse, and Mental Health Administration, National Institute of Mental Health, 1980), p. 70.
16. Edwin H. Sutherland, "Crime and Business," *The Annuals of the American Academy of Political and Social Science* 217 (September 1941).
17. Gilbert Geis, "Toward a Delineation of White-Collar Offenses," in B. J. Cohen (ed.), *Crime in America* (Itasca, Ill.: F. E. Peacock, 1977), p. 397.
18. Ellwyn R. Stoddard, "Bluecoat Crime," in L. Radzinowicz and M. E. Wolfgang (eds.), *The Criminal in the Arms of the Law* (New York: Basic Books, 1971), pp. 189–205.
19. Ibid., pp. 194–95.
20. *U.S. News & World Report* (April 19, 1982), p. 80.
21. Erwin O. Smigel and H. Laurence Ross, *Crimes Against Bureaucracy* (New York: Van Nostrand Reinhold, 1970).
22. Robert G. Caldwell, "A Re-Examination of the Concept of White Collar Crime," in B. J. Cohen (ed.), *Crime in America,* pp. 388–96.

23. National Criminal Justice Information and Statistics Service, 1980.

24. Tom Shea, "The FBI Goes After Hackers," *Info World* 6, no. 13 (March 1984), p. 38.

25. Ibid., p. 39.

26. Grant Johnson, Tom Bird, and J. W. Little, *Delinquency Prevention: Theories and Strategies* (Washington, D.C.: U.S. Department of Justice, LEAA, 1979), p. 19.

27. Ted H. Rubin, *Juvenile Justice* (Santa Monica, Calif.: Goodyear, 1979), pp. 34–35.

28. Johnson, Bird, and Little, *Delinquency Prevention*, p. 20.

29. Rubin, *Juvenile Justice*, pp. 39–40.

30. Ibid., p. 20.

31. John Hagan, A. R. Gills, and Janet Chan, "Explaining Official Delinquency: A Spatial Study of Class, Conflict and Control," *Sociological Quarterly* 19 (1981): 75.

32. Travis, Hirschi, *Causes of Delinquency* (Berkeley, Calif.: University of California Press, 1969), p. 75.

33. Johnson, Bird, and Little, *Delinquency Prevention*, p. 49.

34. Sykes, *The Future of Crime*, p. 8.

35. Don C. Gibbons, *Crime and Criminal Careers* (Englewood Cliffs, N.J.: Prentice-Hall, 1973), p. 137.

36. Sheldon Glueck and Eleanor Glueck, *Physique and Delinquency* (New York: Harper & Row, 1956).

37. Sykes, *The Future of Crime*, p. 8.

38. Johnson, Bird, and Little, *Delinquency Prevention*, pp. 34–35.

39. Sykes, *The Future of Crime*, p. 9.

40. Charles L. Tittle, "Deterrents of Labeling?" *Social Forces* 53 (1975): 399–410.

41. Robert K. Merton, *Social Theory and Social Structure* (New York: Free Press, 1957).

42. Gibbons, *Crime and Criminal Careers*, pp. 186–87.

43. Richard A. Cloward and Lloyd Ohlin, *Delinquency and Opportunity* (New York: Free Press, 1960).

44. M. D. Wiatrowski, D. B. Grishold, and M. K. Probers, "Social Control Theory and Delinquency," *American Sociological Review* 46 (1981): 525.

45. Quinney, *The Problem of Crime*, p. 126.

46. Johnson, Bird, and Little, *Delinquency Prevention*, p. 73.

47. Sykes, *The Future of Crime*, p. 28.

48. Ibid., p. 29.

49. Jerome H. Skolnick, "The Policeman's Personality," in L. Radzinowicz and M. E. Wolfgang (eds.), *The Criminal in the Arms of the Law*, p. 149.

50. Lieber, "The American Prison," *New York Times Magazine* (March 8, 1981), p. 28.

51. *U.S. News and World Report* (October 12, 1981), p. 42.

52. Ibid., p. 38.

53. Lieber, "The American Prison," p. 60.

54. Bureau of Justice Statistics Bulletin, p. 1.

55. *U.S. News and World Report*, p. 42.

56. Lieber, "The American Prison," p. 26.

57. *New York Times* (November 22, 1982), p. 58.

58. J. McCord, "Early Criminals: Hands-Off vs. Intervention," *Human Behavior* 7 (1968): 16–17.

59. Dennis A. Romig, *Justice for Our Children* (Baltimore, Md.: Penguin Books, 1978).

60. Johnson, Bird, and Little, *Delinquency Prevention*, p. 79.

61. Ibid., p. 70.

62. Romig, *Justice for Our Children*, p. 56.

63. *New York Times* (January 15, 1981), C1.

64. *U.S. News and World Report* (July 13, 1981), p. 54.

65. Ibid. (June 21, 1982).

66. Ibid. (January 4, 1982), p. 8.

67. R. Rinaldi, *Prison Labor in Australia* (Canberra: Australian National University Press, 1973).

68. L. G. Moseley, "Finnish Labor Colonies," *Howard Journal of Penology*

and Crime Prevention 13 (1973): 317–30.

69. Lieber, "The American Prison," p. 34.

Chapter 6

1. Richard M. Brown, "The History of Extra-Legal Violence in Support of Community Values," in Thomas Rose (ed.), *Violence in America* (New York: Vintage Press, 1969), p. 87.
2. Ibid., p. 88.
3. Sandra J. Ball-Rokeach, "The Legitimation of Violence," in James F. Short, Jr. and M. E. Wolfgang (eds.), *Collective Violence* (Chicago: Aldine Atherton, 1972), p. 107.
4. Ibid.
5. David Burnham, "Most Call Crime Worst City Ill," *New York Times* (January 16, 1974), p. 1.
6. James D. Wright and Peter H. Rossi, *Weapons, Crime, and Violence in America* (Washington, D.C.: U.S. Department of Justice, 1981), p. 14.
7. Ibid.
8. Ibid.
9. "Juveniles Commit 25% of Crimes Against Persons," *Justice Assistance News,* Vol. 2, No. 7 (Washington, D.C.: U.S. Department of Justice, 1981).
10. Donald Lunde, "Our Murder Boom," *Psychology Today* (July 1975), pp. 35–42.
11. Ibid., p. 75.
12. Ibid., p. 36.
13. Ibid., pp. 36–38.
14. Natalie Jaffe, "Assaults on Women: Rape and Wife Beating," *Public Affairs Pamphlet,* No. 579 (New York: Public Affairs Committee, 1982), p. 2.
15. Ovid Demaris, *Brothers in Blood: The International Terrorist Network* (New York: Charles Scribner's Sons, 1977), p. 377.
16. Ibid., p. 378.
17. Ibid.
18. Ibid., p. 267.
19. Ibid., p. 380.

20. Michael P. Hamilton, "Terrorism: Its Ethical Implication for the Future," in John Stimson and Ardyth Stimson (eds.), *Sociology: Contemporary Readings* (Itasca, Ill.: F. E. Peacock Publishers, 1983), p. 353.
21. Ted R. Gurr, *Why Men Rebel* (Princeton, N.J.: Princeton University Press, 1970), p. 757.
22. William L. Chaze, "In the Mideast Terrorism Is a Tradition," *U.S. News & World Report* (November 7, 1983), p. 30.
23. Gurr, *Why Men Rebel,* p. 212.
24. "Warfare on the Cheap," *New York Times* (December 29, 1983), p. 13.
25. Ibid.
26. Ibid., p. 1.
27. Marvin Stone," Terrorism: Spreading Disease," *U.S. News & World Report* (May 16, 1983), p. 76.
28. Ibid.
29. William L. Chaze, "In War on Terrorists, Some Victories, but—" *U.S. News & World Report* (June 28, 1982), p. 27.
30. J. D. Elliot, et al. (eds.), *Contemporary Terrorism* (Gaithersburg, Md.: International Association of Chiefs of Police, 1978), p. 141.
31. Gwynn Nettler, *Social Concerns* (New York: McGraw-Hill, 1976), p. 293.
32. Kurt Finsterbusch and H. C. Greisman, "The Unprofitability of Warfare in the 20th Century," *Social Problems* 22 (1975): 450.
33. Ibid., p. 451.
34. Hugh D. Graham and T. R. Gurr, *Violence in America: Historical and Comparative Perspectives,* Vol. II (Washington, D.C.: National Commission on the Causes and Prevention of Violence, 1969), p. 407.
35. Graham and Gurr, *Violence in America,* p. 410.
36. U.S. Office of Technology Assessment, "The Effects of Nuclear War," in J. H. Skolnick and E. Curris (eds.), *Crisis in American Institutions,* 5th ed. (Boston: Little, Brown, 1982), p. 516.

37. May Klinghoffer, "Suicide or Medical Preparedness," *Society* 20 (1983): 20.

38. Elliot Abrams, "Deterrence as Moral Response," *Society* 20 (1983): 27.

39. John Monahan, "The Clinical Prediction of Violent Behavior (Rockville, Md.: Public Health Service, NIMH, 1980), p. 9.

40. Ibid., p. 107.

41. Michael D. Smith, "Hockey Violence: A Test of the Violent Subculture Hypothesis," *Social Problems* 27 (1979): 244.

42. Tamotsu Shibutani, "On Personification of Adversaries," in T. Shibutani (ed.), *Human Nature and Collective Behavior* (New Brunswick, N.J.: Transaction Books, 1973), p. 226.

43. Ibid., p. 232.

44. "Crime and Its Victims: An Official Look," *U.S. News & World Report* (December 12, 1983), p. 72.

Chapter 7

1. Sula Benet, "Why They Live to be 100, or Even Older, in Abkhasia," *The New York Times Magazine* (December 24, 1971); Grace Halsell, *Los Viejos: Secrets of Long Life from the Sacred Valley* (Emmaus, Penn.: Rodale Press, 1976).

2. Austin J. Shelton, "The Aged and Leadership Among the Ibo," in D. O. Cowgill and L. D. Holmes (eds.), *Aging and Modernization* (New York: Appleton-Century-Crofts, 1972), pp. 31–50.

3. C. T. Philblad, Eva Beverfelt, and Haktor Helland, "Status and Role of the Aged in Norwegian Society," in *Aging and Modernization,* pp. 227–42.

4. Population Reference Bureau, "America's Elderly: Policy Implications," *Policy Supplement to Population Bulletin,* Vol. 35, No. 4 (January 1984), p. 3.

5. Ibid.

6. National Council on Aging, *Perspectives on Aging* (July/August 1980), p. 3.

7. Population Reference Bureau, "America's Elderly: Policy Implications," pp. 5–6.

8. Robert Butler, *Why Survive? Being Old in America* (New York: Harper & Row, 1975).

9. Carole Offir, "At 65, Work Becomes a Four-Letter Word," *Psychology Today* 3 (1974): 40.

10. Alex Comfort, "Age Prejudice in America," *Social Policy* 17 (November/December 1976): 3–8.

11. Gail Sheehy, *Passages* (New York: E. P. Dutton & Company, 1976), p. 285.

12. Martin Shephard, *Someone You Love Is Dying: A Guide for Helping and Coping* (New York: Crown Books, 1975).

13. Donald Oken, "What to Tell Cancer Patients: A Study of Medical Attitudes," *Journal of the American Medical Association* 175 (1961): 1120–28.

14. Georgia M. Barrow and Patricia A. Smith, *Aging, Ageism, and Society* (San Francisco: West Publishing Company, 1979), p. 78.

15. James E. Birren, "Psychological Aspects of Aging and Intellectual Functioning," *Gerontologist* 8, no. 1, Part II (1968): 6–19; P. Baltes and W. Schaie, "Aging and I.Q.: The Myth of the Twilight Years," *Psychology Today* (March 1974), pp. 35–40.

16. William Masters and Virginia Johnson, *Human Sexual Inadequacy* (Boston: Little, Brown, 1970).

17. Norman Lobsenz, "Sex and the Senior Citizen," *New York Times Magazine* (January 20, 1974).

18. Ibid.

19. Susan Sontag, "The Double Standard of Aging," in H. Cox (ed.), *Focus: Aging* (Guilford, Conn.: Dushkin, 1972).

20. Ardyth Stimson, Jane F. Wase, and John Stimson, "Sexuality and Self-Esteem Among the Aged," *Research on Aging* 3 (June 1981), pp. 228–39.

21. T. Hickey, L. Hickey, and R. A. Kalish, "Children's Perceptions of the Elderly," *Journal of Genetic Psychology* 112 (1968): 227–35.

22. Robert Kastenbaum and N. Durkee, "Young People View Old Age," in R.

Kastenbaum (ed.), *New Thoughts on Old Age* (New York: Springer, 1964); T. Hickey and R. A. Kalish, "Young People's Perceptions of Adults," *Journal of Gerontology* 23 (1968): 215–19.

23. Connie Ivester and Karl King, "Attitudes of Adolescents Toward the Aged," *Gerontologist* 17 (February 1977), pp. 85–89.

24. Barrow and Smith, *Aging, Ageism, and Society;* C. G. McTavish, "Perceptions of Old People: A Review of Research Methodologies," *Gerontologist* 11 (April 1971), pp. 89–101.

25. Population Reference Bureau, "America's Elderly: Policy Implications," p. 7.

26. Scott Campbell Brown, "Educational Attainment of Workers: Some Trends from 1973 to 1978," *Special Labor Force Report* 225 (Washington, D.C.: Bureau of Labor Statistics, 1979).

27. Philip L. Rones, "The Retirement Decision: A Question of Opportunity?" *Monthly Labor Review* (Washington, D.C.: Bureau of Labor Statistics, November 1980), p. 15.

28. Ibid.

29. Ibid.

30. Ibid., p. 16.

31. Harold Sheppard and Sarah Rix, *The Graying of Working America* (New York: Free Press, 1977).

32. Thomas H. Holmes and Minoru Masuda, "Psychosomatic Syndrome," *Psychology Today* (April 1972), pp. 71–72, 106.

33. Vivian Wood, "Age Appropriate Behavior for Older People," *Gerontologist,* Part II (Winter 1971), pp. 74–75.

34. Robert C. Atchley, "Adjustment to Loss of Job at Retirement," in Mildred M. Seltzer, Sherry L. Corbett, and Robert C. Atchley (eds.), *Social Problems of the Aging* (Belmont, Calif.: Wadsworth, 1978), pp. 52–59.

35. Population Reference Bureau, "America's Elderly: Policy Implications," p. 7.

36. Bureau of the Census, "Characteristics of the Population Below the Poverty Level: 1981," *Current Population Reports,* Series P-60, No. 138 (March 1983), p. 18.

37. Population Reference Bureau, "America's Elderly: Policy Implications," p. 6.

38. U.S. Department of Commerce, *Statistical Abstract of the United States: 1984* (Washington, D.C.: U.S. Government Printing Office), p. 379.

39. Population Reference Bureau, "America's Elderly: Policy Implications," p. 6.

40. Ibid., pp. 5–6.

41. Ibid., p. 5.

42. Ibid., pp. 6–7.

43. Gari Lesnoff-Caravaglia, "The Five Percent Fallacy," *International Journal of Aging and Human Development* 9 (1978–79): 192.

44. Holmes and Matsuda, "Psychosomatic Syndrome," pp. 71–72, 106.

45. Martha Baum and Rainer C. Baum, *Growing Old* (Englewood Cliffs, N.J.: Prentice-Hall, 1980), p. 46.

46. Joseph T. Freeman, "A Survey of Geriatric Education: Catalogues of United States Medical Schools," *Journal of the American Geriatrics Society* 19 (1971): 746–62; Butler, *Why Survive? Being Old in America.*

47. Barrow and Smith, *Aging, Ageism, and Society,* p. 256.

48. James S. Henslin, "Growing Old in the Land of the Young," in J. M. Henslin and Larry T. Reynolds (eds.), *Social Problems in American Society,* 2nd ed. (Boston: Holbrook Press, 1976).

49. Rodney Coe, "Self-Conception and Institutionalization," in Arnold Rose and Warren A. Peterson (eds.), *Social Worlds* (New York: Macmillan, 1965); Jules Henry, "Human Obsolescence," in *Culture against Man* (New York: Vintage, 1963); Erving Goffman, *Asylums: Essays on the Social Situation of Mental Patients and Other Inmates* (Chicago: Aldine, 1961).

50. Robert N. Butler and M. I. Lewis, *Ag-*

ing and Mental Health (St. Louis: C. V. Mosby, 1977).

51. Mary Mendelson, *Tender Loving Greed* (New York: Knopf, 1974).

52. Lesnoff-Caravaglia, "The Five Percent Fallacy."

53. Elisabeth Kübler-Ross, *Death: The Final Stage of Growth* (Englewood Cliffs, N.J.: Prentice-Hall, 1975).

54. Robert S. Morrison, "Dying," in *Life and Death and Medicine: A Scientific American Book* (San Francisco: W. H. Freeman, 1973).

55. Barney G. Glaser and Anselm L. Strauss, *Awareness of Dying* (Chicago: Aldine, 1965).

56. Suzanne K. Steinmetz, "Battered Parents," *Society* 15 (July/August 1978), pp. 54–55.

57. U.S. Department of Justice, *Crime in the United States: Uniform Crime Reports* (Washington, D.C.: U.S. Government Printing Office, 1981).

58. Herman J. Loether, *Problems of Aging* (Belmont, Calif.: Dickenson Publishing Co., 1975).

59. Ernest M. Burgess, *Aging in Western Societies* (Chicago: University of Chicago Press, 1960).

60. Robert J. Havighurst, "Successful Aging," *Gerontologist* 1 (1981): 8–13.

61. Arnold M. Rose and Warren A. Peterson, *Older People and Their Social World: The Subculture of the Aging* (Philadelphia: F. A. Davis, 1965).

62. Elaine Cumming and William E. Henry, *Growing Old: The Process of Disengagement* (New York: Basic Books, 1961).

63. Butler, *Why Survive? Being Old in America;* H. P. Brehm, "Sociology and Aging: Orientation and Research," *Gerontologist* 8 (1968): 20–23.

64. Bernard Kutner, "The Social Nature of Aging," *Gerontologist* 2 (1962): 5–9; Samuel Granick and R. D. Patterson, *Human Aging II: Age 11–Up. Followup Biomedical and Behavioral Study* (Rockville, Md.: Public Health Service, 1971).

65. Robert C. Atchley, *The Social Forces in Later Life,* 3d ed. (Belmont, Calif.: Wadsworth, 1980).

66. Matilda Riley, et al., *Aging and Society, Vol. 3: A Sociology of Age Stratification* (New York: Russell Sage Foundation, 1972).

67. J. A. Kuypers and Vern L. Bengston, "Social Breakdown and Competence: A Model of Normal Aging," *Human Development* 16 (1973): 181–201.

Chapter 8

1. "Busing: Why the Tide Is Turning," *U.S. News & World Report* (August 11, 1975), p. 25.

2. *Current Population Reports,* Series P–60 No. 134 (July 1982), p. 29.

3. William B. Gould, "Discrimination and the Unions," in Jeremy Larner and Irving Howe (eds.), *Poverty: Views from the Left* (New York: Morrow, 1968), pp. 168–83; Julius Jacobson, "Union Conservatism: A Barrier to Racial Equality," in Julius Jacobson (ed.), *The Negro and the American Labor Movement* (Garden City, N.Y.: Doubleday, 1968).

4. Juan Cameron, "Black America: Still Waiting for Full Membership," *Fortune* (April 1975).

5. Thomas Sowell, "Debate: Equal Opportunity or the Numbers Game?" *American Educator* (Fall 1978).

6. U.S. Department of Labor, "Employment in Perspective: Minority Workers," Report 694 (First Quarter 1983).

7. Merrill Sheils, "A Portrait of America: The Work Revolution," *Newsweek* (January 17, 1983), p. 31.

8. Eunice Grier and George Grier, "Equality and Beyond: Housing Segregation in the Great Society," *Daedalus* 95 (1966): 82.

9. Rita M. James, "Status and Competence of Jurors," *American Journal of Sociology* 64 (1959): 565–66; Charles E. Ares, et al., "The Manhattan Bail Project," *New York University Law Review* 28 (1963), 67–92; Paul B. Wice,

Bail and Its Reform: A National Survey (Washington, D.C.: U.S. Government Printing Office, 1973).

10. Henry P. Fairchild, *Greek Immigration* (New Haven, Conn.: Yale University Press, 1911).

11. Steve Huntley, et al., "America's Indians: 'Beggars in Our Own Land'," *U.S. News & World Report* (May 23, 1983), p. 70.

12. Ford Foundation Report cited in *Chronicle of Higher Education* (February 3, 1982), p. 11.

13. Aric Press, et al., "The Indian Water Wars," *Newsweek* (June 13, 1983), pp. 80–82.

14. William J. Wilson, *The Declining Significance of Race: Blacks and Changing American Institutions* (Chicago: University of Chicago Press, 1978).

15. Diane N. Westcost, "Blacks in the 1970s: Did They Scale the Job Ladder?" *Monthly Labor Review* (June 1982), pp. 29–30.

16. John Herbers, "Women and Blacks Gained in Jobs, U.S. Says," *New York Times* (April 24, 1983), pp. 1, 38.

17. William J. Wilson, "The Black Community in the 1980s: Questions of Race, Class, and Public Policy," *Annals of American Academy of Political and Social Science* 454 (1981).

18. Ibid.

19. Lee Rainwater, "Crucible of Identity: The Negro Lower Class Family," *Daedalus* 95 (1966); Charles V. Willie, *A New Look at Black Families,* 2d ed. (New York: General Hall, 1981).

20. Wilson, "The Black Community in the 1980s."

21. A. Ramirez, "Miami Cubans Prosper by Sticking Together, Aiding Later Refugees," *Wall Street Journal* (May 20, 1980), pp. 1, 21.

22. Michael Satchell, "Bent, But Not Broken," *Parade Magazine* (October 10, 1982), pp. 6–9.

23. Ibid.

24. John D. Huss and Melanie J. Wirken," Illegal Immigration: The Hidden Population Bomb," *The Futurist* (April 1977), p. 114.

25. Saskia Sassen-Koob, "Immigrant and Minority Workers in the Organization of the Labor Process," *Journal of Ethnic Studies* 8 (1980): 1–34.

26. Elsa Chaney and Constance Sutton, "Caribbean Migration to New York," *International Migration Review* 13 (1979); Michael P. Piore, "Notes for a Theory of Labor Market Stratification," in *Labor Market Segmentation* (New York: Heath, 1976).

27. Sassen-Koob, "Immigrant and Minority Workers in the Organization of the Labor Process," p. 18.

28. Marvin Stone, "Help for Illegals— How Much?" *U.S. News & World Report* (August 16, 1982), p. 74.

29. T. W. Adorno, et al., *The Authoritarian Personality* (New York: Harper & Row, 1950).

30. George E. Simpson and J. Milton Yinger, *Racial and Ethnic Minorities: An Analysis of Prejudice and Discrimination,* 4th ed. (New York: Harper and Row, 1972).

31. Gordon Allport, *The Nature of Prejudice* (Reading, Mass.: Addison-Wesley, 1954).

32. Carl I. Hovland and Robert R. Sears, "Minor Studies of Aggression: Correlation with Economic Indices," *Journal of Psychology* 9 (1940), pp. 301–10; Donald Weatherly, "Anti-Semitism and the Expression of Fantasy Aggression," *Journal of Abnormal and Social Psychology* 62 (1961): 454–57.

33. Neal Miller and Richard Bugelski, "Minor Studies in Aggression: The Influence of Frustration Imposed by the In-group on Attitudes Expressed Toward Outgroups," *Journal of Psychology* 25 (1948): 437–42.

34. Edna Bonacich, "A Theory of Ethnic Antagonism: The Split Labor Market," *American Sociological Review* 37 (1972): 547–59.

35. W. Lloyd Warner and Leo Srole, *The Social System of American Ethnic*

Groups. Yankee City Series, Vol. 3 (New Haven, Conn.: Yale University Press, 1945), pp. 285–86.

36. Alfred Schutz, ''The Stranger,'' *American Sociological Reivew* 69 (1944): 449–507.

Chapter 9

1. Martin Andersen, *Welfare* (Stanford, Calif.: The Hoover Institute, 1978).
2. Matthew 26:4.
3. ''Life Below the Poverty Line,'' *Newsweek* (April 5, 1982), pp. 20–28.
4. David Caplovitz, *The Poor Pay More* (New York: Free Press, 1963).
5. ''Poverty Trap: No Way Out?'' *U.S. News & World Report* (August 16, 1982), pp. 31–35.
6. Kenneth E. Boulding, ''Reflections on Poverty,'' in *The Social Welfare Forum: 1961* (New York: Columbia University Press, 1961), pp. 45–58.
7. Lee Rainwater, ''The Problem of Lower-Class Culture and Poverty-War Strategy,'' in Daniel P. Moynihan (ed.), *On Understanding Poverty* (New York: Basic Books, 1969).
8. Michael Harrington, *The Other America* (Baltimore, Md.: Penguin Books, 1962).
9. U.S. Bureau of the Census, *Current Population Reports,* Series P-60, No. 138, ''Characteristics of the Population Below the Poverty Level: 1981'' (Washington, D.C.: U.S. Government Printing Office, March 1983).
10. Ibid., Table 5, p. 18.
11. Ibid.
12. Diana M. Pearce, ''The Feminization of Poverty: Women, Work, and Welfare,'' (Chicago: University of Illinois Press, 1978).
13. Irwin Garfinkel, ''What's Wrong with Welfare?'' *Social Work* (May 1978), pp. 185–86.
14. U.S. Bureau of the Census, *Current Population Reports* (March 1983), Table 1, p. 7.
15. Ibid., Table 5, p. 18.

16. U.S. Bureau of the Census, *Current Population Reports,* Series P-20, No. 369, ''Fertility of American Women: June 1981'' (Washington, D.C.: U.S. Government Printing Office, March 1982), Table 2, p. 4.
17. Wendy Baldwin and Virginia S. Cain, ''The Children of Teenage Parents,'' *Family Planning Perspectives,* 11 (January/February 1980), pp. 34–43.
18. U.S. Bureau of the Census (March 1983), Table 1. p. 7.
19. Ibid., Table 4, p. 16.
20. Ibid., Table 8, p. 30.
21. U.S. Public Health Service, Washington, D.C., 1981.
22. Michael Parenti, *Democracy for the Few,* 3d ed. (New York: St. Martin's Press, 1980), pp. 41–42.
23. Jerome K. Myers and Leslie Schaffer, ''Social Stratification and Psychiatric Practice: A Study of an Outpatient Clinic,'' *American Sociological Review* 19 (June 1954), pp. 307–10.
24. U.S. Bureau of the Census (March 1983), Table 5, p. 18.
25. Joe R. Feagin, *Subordinating the Poor: Welfare and American Beliefs* (Englewood Cliffs, N.J.: Prentice-Hall, 1975).
26. Ibid.
27. Richard Herrnstein, *I.Q. in the Meritocracy* (New York: Allan Lane, 1973).
28. See, for example, Vincent N. Parrillo, *Strangers to These Shores,* 2nd ed. (New York: Wiley, 1985), pp. 313–16.
29. Robert Holman, *Poverty: Explanations of Social Deprivation* (New York: St. Martin's Press, 1978); Thomas Sowell, ''New Light on Black I.Q.,'' *New York Times Magazine* (March 27, 1977), p. 57.
30. Oscar Lewis, ''The Culture of Poverty,'' *Scientific American* 215 (October 1966), pp. 19–25.
31. Edward Banfield, *The Unheavenly City Revisited* (Boston: Little, Brown, 1974).
32. *1964 Economic Report to the President* (Washington, D.C.: U.S. Government Printing Office, 1964), pp. 69–70.

33. William Ryan, *Blaming the Victim,* rev. ed. (New York: Vintage, 1976).

34. Charles A. Valentine, *Culture and Poverty: Critique and Counterproposals* (Chicago: University of Chicago Press, 1968).

35. Kingsley Davis and Wilbert E. Moore, "Some Principles of Stratification," *American Sociological Review* 10 (April 1945), pp. 242–49; Charles Hurst, *The Anatomy of Social Inequality* (St. Louis: Mosby, 1979).

36. Herbert J. Gans, "The Uses of Poverty: The Poor Pay All," *Social Policy* 2 (July/August 1971), pp. 20–24; also Gans, "The Positive Functions of Poverty," *American Journal of Sociology* 78 (September 1972), pp. 275–88.

37. Ralf Dahrendorf, *Class and Class Conflict in Industrial Society* (Stanford, Calif.: Stanford University Press, 1959); "Toward a Theory of Social Conflict," in Amitai Etzioni and Eva Etzioni (eds.), *Social Change: Sources, Patterns, and Consequences* (New York: Basic Books, 1973).

38. Michael Harrington, "Why We Need Socialism in America," *Dissent* 76 (May/June 1970), pp. 240–303.

39. Michael Harrington, *Decade of Decision* (New York: Simon and Schuster, 1980).

40. Michael Betz, "Riots and Welfare: Are They Related?" *Social Problems* 21 (1974), pp. 345–55.

41. Frances Fox Piven and Richard A. Cloward, *Regulating the Poor* (New York: Vintage, 1971).

42. Frances Fox Piven and Richard A. Cloward, *The Politics of Turmoil* (New York: Pantheon, 1974); see also Piven and Cloward, "Social Movements and Social Conditions: A Response to Roach and Roach," *Social Problems* 26 (1978), pp. 172–78.

43. Randall J. Pozdena and Terry R. Johnson, *Income Maintenance and Asset Demand* (Menlo Park, Calif.: SRI International, March 1979); Terry R. Johnson, Randall J. Pozdena, and Gary Steiger, *The Impact of Alternative Negative Income Tax Programs on Nondurable Consumption* (Menlo Park, Calif.: SRI International, October 1979).

44. Howard S. Becker, *Outsiders: Studies in the Sociology of Deviance* (New York: Free Press: 1963).

45. David A. Schulz, *Coming Up Black* (Englewood Cliffs, N.J.: Prentice-Hall, 1969).

46. Ronald R. Edmonds, "Some Schools Work and More Can," *Social Policy* (March/April 1979), pp. 28–32; Jonathan Kozol, *Death at an Early Age* (Boston: Houghton Mifflin, 1967); Robert Rosenthal and Lenore Jacobson, *Pygmalion in the Classroom* (New York: Holt, Rinehart & Winston, 1968).

47. L. Richard Della Fave, "The Meek Shall Not Inherit the Earth," *American Sociological Review* 45 (December 1980): pp. 955–71.

48. U.S. Bureau of the Census (March 1983).

49. Ibid.

50. *U.S. News & World Report* (August 8, 1977), p. 23.

51. U.S. Bureau of the Census (March 1982).

52. Ibid.

53. U.S. Department of Health, Education and Welfare, *Welfare: Myths and Facts* (Washington, D.C., U.S. Government Printing Office, 1972).

54. Ibid.

55. Robert Reinhold, "Poverty Is Less Persistent but Wider Spread Than Thought," *New York Times Magazine* (1978), p. 14.

56. A. Dale Tussing, "The Dual Welfare System," *Society* 11 (January/February 1974), pp. 50–57; Jonathan H. Turner and Charles E. Starnes, *Inequality: Privilege and Poverty in America* (Pacific Palisades, Calif.: Goodyear, 1976).

57. "Latest Figures Show 244 People with Incomes of $200,000 or More Paid No '74 U.S. Income Taxes," *New York Times* (May 6, 1976), p. 19.

58. Maurice Zeitlin, "Who Owns America? The Same Old Gang," *The Progressive,* 42 (June 1978), pp. 14–19.

59. Parenti, *Democracy for the Few,* p. 9.

60. James Peltz, "General Electric Stirs Controversy with Selling, Buying Tax Credits," *New York Times* (March 19, 1982).

61. Tussing, "The Dual Welfare System," p. 53.

62. Internal Revenue Service, Individual Income Tax Returns 1975 (Washington, D.C.: U.S. Government Printing Office, 1979).

63. Michael Harrington, "Introduction," in Louis A. Fernan, Joyce L. Kornbluh, and Alan Haber (eds.), *Poverty in America: A Book of Readings* (Ann Arbor: University of Michigan Press, 1965), pp. vii–xiv.

64. See Daniel P. Moynihan, *The Policies of a Guaranteed Income: The Nixon Administration and the Family Assistance Plan* (New York: Random House, 1973).

Chapter 10

1. Stephen Jay Gould, *The Mismeasure of Man* (New York: Norton, 1981), pp. 104–105.

2. Sandra L. Bem and Daryl J. Bem, "Training the Woman to Know Her Place: The Power of a Nonconscious Ideology," in H. Robboy and C. Clark (eds.), *Social Interaction,* 2d ed. (New York: St. Martin's Press, 1971), p. 91.

3. Ibid., p. 92.

4. Ibid., p. 87.

5. Ann Douglas, *The Feminization of American Culture* (New York: Avon, 1977).

6. Elliot Krause, *Why Study Sociology?* (New York: Random House, 1980), p. 40.

7. Douglas, *The Feminization of American Culture,* p. 50.

8. Bem and Bem, "Training the Woman to Know Her Place," p. 89.

9. Ibid.

10. Donna Eder and M.T. Hallinan, "Sex Differences in Children's Friendships," *American Sociological Review* 43 (1978): 247.

11. Irene Handler Frieze and Sheila J. Ramsey, "Nonverbal Maintenance of Traditional Sex Roles," *Journal of Social Issues* 32 (1976): 135.

12. Lynn K. White and D. B. Brinkerhoff, "The Sexual Divison of Labor: Evidence from Childhood," *Social Forces* 60 (1981): 181.

13. Goldberg's 1968 study is described by A. R. Hochschild, "A Review of Sex Role Research," in Joan Huber (ed.), *Changing Women in a Changing Society* (Chicago: University of Chicago Press, 1973), pp. 256–57.

14. William H. Masters and Virginia E. Johnson, *Human Sexual Inadequacy* (Boston: Little, Brown, 1970).

15. M. S. Weinberg, R. G. Swensson, and S. K. Hammersmith, "Sexuality in U.S. Sex Manuals from 1950 to 1980," *Social Problems* 30 (1983): pp. 312–24.

16. P. Farb, *Word Play: What Happens When People Talk* (New York: Bantam Books, 1974), p. 55.

17. Frieze and Ramsey, "Nonverbal Maintenance of Traditional Sex Roles," p. 137.

18. B. F. Meeker and P. A. Weitzel-O'Neill, "Sex Roles and Interpersonal Behavior in Task Oriented Groups," *American Sociological Review* 42 (1977): 91–105.

19. P. M. Fishman, "Interaction: The Work Women Do," *Social Problems* 25 (1978): 397–406.

20. P. D. Horn and J. C. Horn, *Sex in the Office: Power and Passion in the Workplace* (Reading, Mass.: Addison-Wesley, 1982), pp. 62–63.

21. "Stopping Sexual Harassment," U.S. Government Labor Education and Research Project, 1981.

22. F. S. Coles, "Definitions of Sexual Harassment," paper presented at the Annual Meetings of the Society for the Study of Social Problems, 1982, p. 6.

23. Ibid., p. 7.
24. Horn and Horn, *Sex in the Office,* p. 68.
25. Ibid., p. 70.
26. A. Hacker, *U/S: A Statistical Portrait of the American People* (New York: Viking Press/Penguin Books, 1983), pp. 240–41.
27. Ibid., p. 243.
28. "How Long Till Equality?" *Time Magazine* (July 12, 1982), p. 20.
29. R. C. Kessler and J. A. McRae, Jr., "Trends in Sex and Psychological Distress," *American Sociological Review* 46 (1981): 443–52.
30. Kessler and McRae, "The Effects of Employment," *American Sociological Review* 47 (1982): 216–26.
31. Krause, 1980, pp. 91–92.
32. Rosabeth M. Kanter, "Women and the Structure of Organizations," in Robboy and Clark (eds.), *Social Interaction,* p. 215.
33. L. Lyon, T. Abell, E. Jones, and H. Rector-Owen, "The National Longitudinal Data for Labor Market Entry: Evaluating the Small Effects of Racial Discrimination and the Large Effects of Sexual Discrimination," *Social Problems* 29 (1982): 524–39.
34. "When Women Take Over As Bosses," *U. S. News & World Report* (March 22, 1982), pp. 77–80.
35. Hacker, *U/S: A Statistical Portrait of the American People,* p. 148.
36. Ibid., p. 149.
37. S. E. Martin, "Sexual Politics in the Workplace: The Interactionist World of Policewomen," *Symbolic Interaction* 2 (1978): 44–60.
38. Ibid., p. 53.
39. Nancy Reeves, *Womankind: Beyond the Stereotypes.* (Chicago: Aldine/Atherton, 1977), pp. 135–52.
40. V. L. Swigert, "Sexuality and the Law: Review Article," *Contemporary Sociology* II (1982): 581.
41. "Scales Tilted Against Women," *New York Times* (November 27, 1983), p. E7.
42. J. B. Gillespie, "The Phenomenon of

the Public Wife," *Symbolic Interaction* 3 (1980), pp. 109–26.
43. D. R. Margolis, "The Invisible Hands: Sex Roles and the Division of Labor in Two Local Political Parties," *Social Problems* 26 (1979), pp. 314–24.
44. Ibid., p. 314.
45. Ibid., p. 323.
46. M. Rein, *Social Science and Public Policy* (Baltimore Md.: Penguin, 1976), p. 82.
47. Carol Gilligan, *In a Different Voice: Psychological Theory and Women's Development* (Cambridge, Mass.: Harvard University Press, 1982).
48. Hochschild, "A Review of Sex Role Research," p. 254.
49. Sheila Tobias, "Sexist Equations," *Psychology Today* (January, 1982), pp. 14–17.
50. "Comparable Worth," *U.S. News & World Report* (February 20, 1984), p. 73.
51. J. Acker, "Women and Social Stratification: A Case of Intellectual Sexism," in Huber (ed.), *Changing Women in a Changing Society,* pp. 174–83.
52. Ibid., p. 175.
53. Ibid., p. 178.
54. Hochschild, "A Review of Sex Role Research," p. 258
55. E. Goldfield, S. Munaker, and Naomi Weisstein, "A Woman Is a Sometime Thing," in F. Lindenfeld (ed.), *Radical Perspectives of Social Problems,* 2d ed. (New York: Macmillan, 1973).
56. Hochschild, "A Review of Sex Role Research," p. 258.
57. Krause, 1980, pp. 40–41.
58. C. Lasch, *The Culture of Narcissism* (New York: Norton, 1979), pp. 139–40.
59. D. A. Karp and William C. Yoels, *Symbols, Selves and Society* (New York: J. B. Lippincott/Harper & Row, 1979), p. 56.
60. L. Stoneall, "Cognitive Mapping: Gender Differences in the Perception of Community," *Sociological Inquiry* 51 (1971): 121–28.

61. S. E. Cahill, "Directions for an Interactionist Study of Gender Development," *Symbolic Interaction* 3 (1980): 127.

62. J. Harrison, "Warning: The Male Sex Role May Be Dangerous to Your Health," *Journal of Social Sciences* 54 (1978): 65–86.

63. Reeves, *Womankind: Beyond the Stereotypes,* p. 109.

64. Jessie Bernard, "Change and Stability in Sex-Role Norms and Behavior," *Journal of Social Issues* 32 (1976): 207–23.

65. P. B. Walters, "Trend in U.S. Men's and Women's Sex-Role Attitudes: 1972–1978," *American Sociological Review* 46 (1981): 453–60.

66. Amitai Etzioni, "The Sexual-Chase Ratio," *New York Magazine* (January 10, 1977), p. 41.

Chapter 11

1. Maureen Dowd, "Many Women in Poll Value Jobs as Much as Family Life," *New York Times* (December 4, 1983), p. 1.

2. Betty Friedan, *The Second Stage* (New York, Summit Books), 1982.

3. James Henslin, "Cohabitation: Its Context and Meaning," in James Henslin (ed.), *Marriage and Family in a Changing Society* (New York: Free Press, 1980), pp. 101–15.

4. U.S. Bureau of the Census, *Statistical Abstract of the United States: 1984* (Washington, D.C.: U.S. Government Printing Office, 1984).

5. Heather Ross and Isabel V. Sawhill, *Time of Transition: The Growth of Families Headed by Women* (Washington, D.C.: Urban Institute, 1975).

6. J. Ross Eshleman, *The Family: An Introduction* (Boston: Allyn and Bacon, 1981), p. 560.

7. Ann Swidler, "Love and Adulthood in American Culture," in Arlene Skolnick and Jerome Skolnick (eds.), *Family in Transition,* 4th ed. (Boston: Little, Brown & Co., 1983), pp. 286–306.

8. Ann Goetting, "Divorce Outcome Research: Issues and Perspectives," *Journal of Family Issues* (September 1981), pp. 243–57.

9. Jane Brody, "Divorce's Stress Exacts Long-Term Health Toll," *New York Times* (December 13, 1983), p. III-1.

10. Ibid.

11. Paul Bohannan, *Divorce and After.* (Garden City, N.Y.: Doubleday/Anchor Books, 1971).

12. Robert Weiss, *Marital Separation* (New York: Basic Books, 1975), pp. 48–56.

13. Brody, "Divorce's Stress Exacts Long Term Health Toll," p. III-1.

14. Larry Bumpass and Ronald R. Rindfuss, "Children's Experience of Marital Disruption," *American Journal of Sociology* (July 1979), pp. 49–65.

15. Frank F. Furstenberg Jr., et al. "The Life Course of Children of Divorce," *American Sociological Review* 48 (October 1983), pp. 656–68.

16. Goetting, "Divorce Outcome Research: Issues and Perspectives," pp. 243–57.

17. Judith S. Wallerstein and Joan Kelly, *Surviving the Breakup: How Children and Parents Cope with Divorce* (New York: Basic Books, 1980), pp. 4–11.

18. Ibid., pp. 150–65.

19. Ibid.

20. Ibid., p. 177.

21. "Reactions of Children of Divorce," *New York Times* (November 2, 1983), p. C-9.

22. Arnold Katz, "Lone Fathers: Perspectives and Implications for Family Policy," *The Family Coordinator* (October 1979), pp. 521–28.

23. Mendes, H. S., "Single Fathers," *The Family Coordinator* 25 (1976): 439–44.

24. Cummings, Judith, "Breakup of Black Family Imperils Gains of Decades," *New York Times* (November 20, 1983), p. 1, 56.

25. Ibid.

26. Ibid.

27. Pearila Brickner, Namerow, "Teenage

Pregnancy," in John Stimson and Ardyth Stimson (eds.), *Sociology: Contemporary Readings* (Itasca, Ill.: F. E. Peacock, 1983), pp. 338–44.

28. Ibid.

29. Richard Gelles, *The Violent Home: A Study of Physical Aggression Between Husbands and Wives* (Beverly Hills, Calif.: Sage Publications, 1972).

30. C. H. Kempe, "The Battered Child Syndrome," *Journal of the American Medical Association,* 181 (July 1962), pp. 17–24.

31. Murray A. Straus, Richard J. Gelles, and Suzanne K. Steinmetz, *Behind Closed Doors: Violence in the American Family* (Garden City, N.Y.: Doubleday/Anchor, 1980), Chapter 2.

32. Ibid., Chapter 3.

33. Jean Renvoize, *Web of Violence: A Study of Family Violence* (London: Routledge and Kegan Paul, 1978), pp. 113–27.

34. Ibid.

35. Richard J. Gelles, "Violence in the Family: A Review of Research in the Seventies," *Journal of Marriage and the Family* (November 1980), pp. 873–85.

36. Murray A. Straus, "A Sociological Perspective on the Causes of Family Violence," in Maurice Green (ed.), *Violence and the Family* (Boulder, Col.: Westview Press, 1980), p. 8.

37. Richard J. Gelles, "Violence in the Family: A Review of Research in the Seventies," *Journal of Marriage and the Family* (November 1980), p. 879.

38. Ibid.

39. Myron Brenton, *The Runaways: Children, Husbands, Wives and Parents* (Baltimore, Md.: Penguin, 1978), p. 35.

40. Arnold Madison, *Runaway Teens: An American Tragedy,* New York: Elsevier/Nelson Books, 1979), pp. 23–32.

41. Myron Brenton, *The Runaways: Children, Husbands, Wives and Parents,* p. 37.

42. David Findelhor and Kersti Yllo, *License to Rape: Sexual Violence Against Wives,* (New York: Holt, Rinehart, Winston, 1983).

43. Ibid.

44. David Finkelhor, *Sexually Victimized Children* (New York: Free Press, 1979), pp. 71–72.

45. Ibid., p. 96.

46. Judith Lewis Herman with Lisa Hirschman, *Father-Daughter Incest* (Cambridge, Mass.: Harvard University Press, 1981), p. 33.

47. Ibid., pp. 86–94.

48. Ibid., pp. 47–49.

49. Ibid., p. 62.

50. David Finkelhor, *Sexually Victimized Children,* p. 130.

51. Richard J. Gelles, "Abused Wives: Why Do They Stay?" *Journal of Marriage and the Family,* 38 (November 1976), pp. 659–68.

52. "Jersey Reports 18,000 Cases of Family Violence This Year," *New York Times* (December 11, 1983), p. 56.

53. Murray A. Straus, Richard J. Gelles, and Suzanne K. Steinmetz, *Behind Closed Doors,* pp. 237–39.

54. Carle C. Zimmerman, *Family and Civilization* (New York: Harper, 1947).

55. William F. Ogburn, "The Changing Family," *The Family* (1938): 139–43, reported in Robert F. Lynch and Louis Wolf Goodman, *Selected Studies in Marriage and the Family,* 3d ed. (New York: Holt, Rinehart, Winston, 1968), pp. 58–63.

56. Robert Nisbet, *The Quest for Community* (London: Oxford University Press, 1973), Chapter 3.

57. Hyman Rodman, "Talcott Parsons' View of the Changing American Family," *Merrill–Palmer Quarterly of Behavior and Development* (July 1965), pp. 209–27.

58. Roslyn Feldberg and Janet Kohen, "Family Life in an Anti-Family Setting," *The Family Coordinator* (April 1976), pp. 151–58.

59. Bernard Farber, *Family: Organization and Interaction.* (San Francisco: Chandler, 1964), pp. 106–109.

60. Philippe Ariès, *Centuries of Childhood: A Social History of Family Life* (New York: Random, 1965).

61. Marie Winn, *Children Without Childhood* (New York: Pantheon Press, 1983).

Chapter 12

1. Logan Wilson and Olive Mills (eds.), *Universal Higher Education* (Washington, D.C.: American Council on Education, 1972).

2. College Entrance Examination Board, *National Report on College-Bound Seniors* (New York, 1983).

3. Alvin Toffler, *Future Shock* (New York: Bantam, 1970), p. 400.

4. See Jonathan Kozol, *Death at an Early Age* (Boston: Little, Brown, 1968).

5. Charles E. Silberman, *Crisis in the Classroom* (New York: Random House, 1970), p. 324.

6. Ibid; see also Jerry Farber, *The Student as Nigger* (New York: Pocket Books, 1970) and John Holt, *Why Children Fail* (New York: Pitman, 1967).

7. Christopher Jencks, quoted in Silberman, *Crisis in the Classroom,* p. 133.

8. Vincent N. Parrillo, *Strangers to These Shores,* 2nd ed. (New York: Wiley, 1985), Chapter 6.

9. Robert Rosenthal and Lenore Jacobson, *Pygmalion in the Classroom* (New York: Holt, Rinehart, Winston, 1968).

10. John W. Ritchie, "The Magic Feather: Education and the Power of Positive Thinking," *Teachers College Record* 78 (1977), pp. 477–86; Janet D. Elashoff and Richard E. Snow, *"Pygmalion" Reconsidered* (Worthington, Ohio: Jones, 1971); William J. Gephart, "Will the Real Pygmalion Please Stand Up?" *American Educational Research Journal* 7 (1970): 473–74; Ray C. Rist, "Student Social Class and Teacher Expectations: The Self-Fulfilling Prophecy in Ghetto Education," *Harvard Educational Review* 40 (1970): 411–51.

11. See, for example, Joanna Ryan, "IQ— The Illusion of Objectivity," in Ken Richardson and David Spears (eds.), *Race and Intelligence* (Baltimore, Md.: Penguin Books, 1972).

12. Arthur R. Jensen, "How Much Can We Boost I.Q. and Scholastic Achievement?" *Harvard Educational Review* 39 (1969): 11–123.

13. In a later work, Jensen reaffirmed his position by arguing that the mean differences remain despite attempts to raise scores. See Arthur R. Jensen, *Bias in Mental Testing* (New York: Free Press, 1980).

14. Richard Hernnstein, "IQ," *Atlantic Monthly* 228 (September 1971), pp. 43–64.

15. Lee J. Cronbach, "Heredity, Environment and Educational Policy," *Harvard Educational Review* 39 (1969): 338–47.

16. Philip Scrofani, Anatas Suziedelis, and Milton Shore, "Conceptual Ability in Black and White Children of Different Classes: An Experimental Test of Jensen's Hypotheses," *American Journal of Orthopsychiatry* 43 (1973): 541–43.

17. Thomas Sowell, "New Light on the Black I.Q. Controversy," *New York Times Magazine* (March 27, 1977), p. 57.

18. Constance Holden, "California Court Is Forum for Latest Round in IQ Debate," *Science* 201 (1978): 1106–09.

19. James S. Coleman, et al., *Equality of Educational Opportunity* (Washington, D.C.: U.S. Office of Education, 1966).

20. Joint Center for Political Studies, Washington, D.C., 1983.

21. U.S. Commission of Civil Rights, *Reviewing a Decade of School Desegregation, 1966–1975* (Washington, D.C.: U.S. Government Printing Office, 1977). See also U.S. Commission on Civil Rights, *Fulfilling the Letter and Spirit of the Law: Desegregation in the Nation's Public Schools* (Washington, D.C.: U.S. Government Printing Office, 1976).

22. The National Commission on Excellence in Education, *A Nation at Risk:*

The Imperative for Educational Reform (Washington, D.C.: U.S. Government Printing Office, 1983).

23. Ibid.

24. Lucia Solorzano, "What's Wrong with Our Teachers?" *U.S. News & World Report* (March 14, 1983), p. 38.

25. Dennis A. Williams, et al., "Can the Schools Be Saved?" *Newsweek* (May 9, 1983), p. 56.

26. Solorzano, "What's Wrong with Our Teachers?" p. 40.

27. Ibid., p. 38.

28. Ibid.

29. The National Commission on Excellence in Education, 1983.

30. Clifford Adelman, unpublished report to The National Commission on Excellence in Education.

31. "The Valedictorian," *Newsweek* (September 6, 1976), p. 52.

32. College Entrance Examination Board and National Center for Education Statistics, *The Condition of Education,* 1982.

33. "Opinion Roundup," *Public Opinion* 40 (1981): 21–40.

34. Carnegie Council on Children.

35. Samuel Bowles and Herbert Gintis, *Schooling in Capitalist America: Educational Reform and the Contradictions of Economic Life* (New York: Basic Books, 1976).

36. See, for example, Thomas Sowell, "A Black 'Conservative' Dissents," *New York Times Magazine* (August 1, 1976), p. 14; Gary Orfield, *Must We Bus?* (Washington, D.C.: The Brookings Institution, 1978).

37. William A. Caldwell (ed.), *How to Save Urban America* (New York: Regional Plan Association, 1973).

38. James S. Coleman, "It's How Private Schools Are Better That Counts," *New York Times* (April 19, 1981), p. E14.

39. John Jarolimek, *The Schools in Contemporary Society* (New York: Macmillan, 1981); Christopher Jencks, "Educational Vouchers," *The New Republic* 163 (July 4, 1970), pp. 19–21.

40. Alvin Toffler, *The Third Wave* (New York: Morrow, 1980).

41. Daniel Bell, *The Coming of Post-Industrial Society* (New York: Basic Books, 1973).

42. See Christopher J. Hurn, *The Limits and Possibilities of Schooling* (Boston: Allyn and Bacon, 1978).

43. Bureau of the Census, *Statistical Abstract of the United States: 1984* (Washington, D.C.: U.S. Government Printing Office, 1984).

44. Carnegie Foundation for the Advancement of Teaching, reported in *Newsweek* (September 5, 1983), p. 10.

45. Dennis A. Williams, et al., "The Merits of Merit Pay," *Newsweek* (June 27, 1983), pp. 61–62.

46. "Survey of Teacher Education: Perceptions of Methods for Improvement," National Center for Education Statistics (Washington, D.C.: U.S. Government Printing Office, 1983).

47. Jonathan H. Mark and Barry D. Anderson, "Teacher Survival Rights—A Current Look," *American Educational Research Journal,* 15 (1978, pp. 379–83.

48. Edward L. McDill and Leo C. Rigsby, *Structure and Process in Secondary Schools: The Academic Impact of Educational Climates* (Baltimore, Md.: The Johns Hopkins University Press, 1973). Similar findings of a 3-year British study are found in Michael Rutter, et al., *Fifteen Thousand Hours* (Cambridge, Mass.: Harvard University Press, 1979).

49. Toffler, *The Third Wave,* p. 364.

Chapter 13

1. Bureau of the Census, *Statistical Abstract of the United States: 1984* (Washington, D.C.: U.S. Government Printing Office, 1984), Table No. 905, p. 538.

2. Ibid., Table No. 906, p. 538.

3. See Marshall E. Blume, Jean Crockett, and Irwin Friend, "Stock-ownership in the United States: Characteristics and

Trends," *Survey of Current Business,* 54 (November 1974), pp. 16–40.

4. Michael Parenti, *Democracy for a Few,* 3d ed. (New York: St. Martin's Press, 1980), p. 8.

5. Ibid.

6. Maurice Zeitlin, "Who Owns America? The Same Old Gang," *The Progressive,* 42 (June 1978), p. 15.

7. Parenti, p. 11.

8. U.S. Senate Committee on Government Affairs, *Interlocking Directorates Among the Major United States Corporations* (Washington, D.C.: U.S. Government Printing Office, 1978), p. 6.

9. Maureen Jung, Dean Purdy, and D. Stanley Eitzen, "The Corporate Inner Group," *Sociological Spectrum* 1 (1981), pp. 317–33.

10. See, for example, Johannes M. Pennings, *Interlocking Directorates* (San Francisco: Jossey-Bass, 1980); Samuel Norich, "Interlocking Directorates, the Control of Large Corporations, and Patterns of Accumulation in the Capitalist Class," in Maurice Zeitlin (ed.), *Classes, Class Conflict, and the State,* (Cambridge, Mass.: Winthrop, 1980), pp. 83–106; Peter Mariolis, "Interlocking Directorates and Control of Corporations: The Theory of Bank Control," *Social Science Quarterly* 56 (1975), pp. 425–39.

11. *Statistical Abstract of the United States, 1982–83,* p. 531.

12. Robert Steyer, "Deals of the Year," *Fortune* (January 24, 1983), p. 48.

13. Leslie Wayne, "The Corporation Raiders," *New York Times Magazine* (July 18, 1982), p. 18.

14. Quoted in John S. DeMott, "White Knights and Black Eyes," *Time* (February 14, 1983), p. 56.

15. Ibid.

16. Steyer, "Deals of the Year," p. 48.

17. John Kenneth Galbraith, *The New Industrial State,* 2d ed. (Boston: Houghton Mifflin, 1971), p. 71.

18. Leonard Silk and David Vogel, *Ethics and Profits* (New York: Simon and Schuster, 1979), p. 207.

19. Maury Silver and Daniel Geller, "On the Irrelevance of Evil: The Organization and Individual Action, *Journal of Social Issues* 34 (1978): 126.

20. Stanley Milgram, "Some Conditions of Obedience and Disobedience to Authority," *Human Relations* 18 (1965), 57–76.

21. Silver and Geller, "On the Irrelevance of Evil," pp. 125–36.

22. Mark J. Green, *The Closed Enterprise System: Ralph Nader's Study-Group Report on Anti-Trust Enforcement* (New York: Grossman, 1972), pp. 147–50.

23. Richard A. Smith, "The Incredible Electrical Conspiracy," *Fortune* 63 (1961), pp. 132 ff.

24. Ralph Nader and Mark J. Green, "Crime in the Suites: Coddling the Corporations," *New Republic* (April 29, 1972), pp. 17–18.

25. Vance Packard, *The Hidden Persuaders* (New York: Pocket Books, 1958).

26. Wilson Bryan Key, *Subliminal Seduction* (New York: Signet, 1974).

27. Jules Henry, *Culture Against Man* (New York: Vintage, 1965).

28. "Are PACs Good for Democracy?" *Economist* (February 19, 1983), p. 22; John M. Eddinger and Craig S. Brightrip, "The Power of the Political Action Committee," *Nation's Business* (May 1982), pp. 32–35.

29. "Are PACs Good for Democracy?" p. 22.

30. Alvin P. Sanoff, "PAC Spells More Than a Game in Politics," *U.S. News & World Report* (October 25, 1982), p. 37.

31. Herbert Cheshire, "Washington Outlook," *Business Week* (July 19, 1982), p. 193.

32. Sanoff, "PAC Spells More Than a Game in Politics."

33. Ibid.

34. President Dwight E. Eisenhower, *Fare-*

well *Radio and Television Address to the American People* (January 17, 1961), quoted in Seymour Melman, *Pentagon Capitalism: The Political Economy of War* (New York: McGraw-Hill, 1970), p. 235.

35. *Statistical Abstract of the United States: 1984,* Table 542, p. 336.

36. Ibid., Table 576, p. 352.

37. Ibid., Table 559, p. 346; Table 556, p. 345.

38. Stephen Cobb, "Defense Spending and Defense Voting in the House: An Empirical Study of an Aspect of the Military–Industrial Complex Thesis," *American Journal of Sociology* 82 (1976): 163–82.

39. See Stanley Lieberson, "An Empirical Study of Military-Industrial Linkages," *American Journal of Sociology* 76 (1971): 564.

40. Richard J. Barber, "The New Partnership: Big Government and Big Business," *New Republic* (August 13, 1966), p. 19.

41. Ralph Nader, et al., *Whistle Blowing: The Report of the Conference on Professional Responsibility* (New York: Grossman, 1972), pp. 39–40, 56; Seymour Melman, *Pentagon Capitalism: The Political Economy of War* (New York: McGraw-Hill, 1970), pp. 177–79.

42. Robert A. Kittle, "Pentagon Bogs Down in Its War on Waste," *U.S. News & World Report* (June 4, 1984), p. 74.

43. Robert M. Kans, "There's No Shame Anymore," *Harper's* (August 1982), pp. 9–10.

44. Ibid., p. 14.

45. Merrill Sheils, "Politics of Arms Spending," *Newsweek* (June 22, 1981), p. 68.

46. Michael D. Edwards, "Golden Threads to the Pentagon," *Nation* (March 15, 1975), pp. 306–8.

47. Neil H. Jacoby, "The Multinational Corporation," *Center Magazine* (May 1970), pp. 37–55; Abdul A. Said and Luiz R. Simmons, *The New Sovereigns: Multinational Corporations as World Powers* (Englewood Cliffs, N.J.: Prentice-Hall, 1975).

48. Ibid. See also Ralph Nader, Mark Green, and Joel Seligman, *Taming the Giant Corporation* (New York: Norton, 1976), p. 28.

49. Louis Turner, *Invisible Empires* (New York: Harcourt Brace Jovanovich, 1971), pp. 135–36.

50. Richard J. Barret and Ronald E. Muller, *Global Reach: The Power of Global Corporations* (New York: Simon and Schuster, 1974), p. 81.

51. Immanuel Wallerstein, *Capitalist World Economy* (Cambridge, U.K.: Cambridge University Press, 1979); Volker Bonschier, Christopher Chase-Dunn, and Richard Robinson, "Cross-National Evidence of the Effects of Foreign Investment and Aid on Economic Growth and Inequality: A Survey of Findings and a Reanalysis," *American Journal of Sociology* 84 (1978), 651–83.

52. Theodore H. Moran, *Multinational Corporations and the Politics of Dependence: Copper in Chile* (Princeton, N.J.: Princeton University Press, 1974), p. 6.

53. See "Payoffs: The Growing Scandal," *Newsweek* (February 23, 1976), pp. 26–33; "The Big Payoff," *Time* (February 23, 1976), pp. 28–36; Gurney Breckenfeld, "Multinationals at Bay," *Saturday Review* (January 24, 1976), pp. 12–22: "How Clean Is Business?" *Newsweek* (September 1, 1975), pp. 50–54.

54. See Barret and Muller, *Global Reach: The Power of the Multinational Corporations,* p. 83.

55. C. Wright Mills, "The Structure of Power in American Society," in Irving Louis Horowitz (ed.), *Power, Politics, and People: The Collected Essays of C. Wright Mills* (New York: Oxford University Press, 1963), p. 27.

56. Thomas R. Dye, *Who's Running America: Institutional Leadership in the*

United States (Englewood Cliffs, N.J.: Prentice-Hall, 1976).

57. Beth Mintz, "The President's Cabinet, 1897–1972," *The Insurgent Sociologist* 5 (1975): 135; Peter J. Freitag, "The Cabinet and Big Business: A Study of Interlocks," *Social Problems* 23 (1975): 148.

58. David Riesman, *The Lonely Crowd* (New Haven, Conn.: Yale University Press, 1969).

59. Arnold M. Rose, *The Power Structure: Political Process in American Society* (New York: Oxford University Press, 1967).

60. Raymond E. Wolfinger and Steven J. Rosenstone, *Who Votes?* (New Haven, Conn.: Yale University Press, 1980).

61. G. William Domhoff, *The Higher Circles: The Governing Class in America* (New York: Vintage, 1971), pp. 309, 313–19.

62. Daniel Yankelovich, "Farewell to President Knows Best," *Foreign Affairs* 57 (1979): 671: Alan Wolfe, *The Limits of Legitimacy* (New York: Free Press, 1979), p. 324; Norman Nie, Sidney Verba, and John R. Petrocik, *The Changing American Voter* (Cambridge, Mass.: Harvard University Press, 1979), p. 36.

63. Leonard Silk and David Vogel, *Ethics and Profits: The Crisis of Confidence in American Business* (New York: Simon and Schuster, 1976), p. 228.

64. Michael H. Crosby, "ITT's Chile Confession: A Definite 'Maybe'," *Business and Society Review* 18 (1976): 66–67.

65. Ralph Nader, *Unsafe at Any Speed,* expanded ed. (New York: Grossman, 1972).

66. See Ted Becker, "Teledemocracy," *The Futurist* (December 1981), pp. 6–9.

Chapter 14

1. Rene Dubos, "Health and Creative Adaptation," *Human Nature* 1 (1978): 74–82; Erdman Palmore and Clark Luikart, "Health and Social Factors Related to Life Satisfaction," *Journal of Health and Social Behavior* 13 (1972): 68–80.

2. "Soaring Hospital Costs," *U.S. News & World Report* (August 22, 1983), p. 39.

3. United Nations, *Demographic Yearbook 1981,* pp. 283–97.

4. Thomas McKeown, *The Role of Medicine: Dream, Mirage, or Nemesis?* (Princeton, N.J.: Princeton University Press, 1979); Thomas McKeown, "The Determinants of Health," *Human Nature* 1 (1978): 60–67.

5. Eliot Freidson, "The Organization of Medical Practice," in Howard E. Freeman, Sol Levine, and Leo G. Raeder (eds.), *Handbook of Medical Sociology* (Englewood Cliffs, N.J.: Prentice-Hall, 1972), p. 344.

6. Ibid., p. 345.

7. Ivan Illich, *Medical Nemesis: The Expropriation of Health* (New York: Random House, 1976), pp. 32–36.

8. Ibid., pp. 40–41.

9. Bureau of the Census, *Statistical Abstract of the United States: 1984,* Table 162, p. 110.

10. Idin W. Anderson, *Health Care: Can There Be Equity?* (New York: Wiley, 1972).

11. Milton I. Roemer, "Nationalized Medicine for America," *Transaction* 8 (1971): 31.

12. "Medical Education in the United States, 1979–80," *Journal of the American Medical Association* 244 (1980): 801, 802–72.

13. Victor R. Fuchs, *Who Shall Live? Health, Economics, and Social Choice* (New York: Basic Books, 1974), p. 69.

14. "Must Doctors' Fees Be So High?" *Changing Times* (March 1981), p. 37.

15. Ibid.

16. "Too Much Surgery?" *Newsweek* (April 10, 1978), pp. 65–67; *New York Times* (January 26, 1976), p. 20.

17. Paul J. Placek and Selma M. Tallel, "One-Sixth of 1980 Births by Cesarian Section," *Public Health Report* (Wash-

ington, D.C.: U.S. Government Printing Office, 1982), p. 183.

18. Department of Health and Human Services, "Non-surgical Procedures in Short-Stay Hospitals" (Washington, D.C.: U.S. Government Printing Office, 1983), pp. 6, 18.

19. Cynthia W. Cooke, M.D., and Susan Dworkin, "Tough Talk About Unnecessary Surgery," *MS.* (October 1981), pp. 42–44; see also Spencer Klaw, *The Greatest American Medicine Show* (Baltimore, Md.: Penguin Books, 1975).

20. Ibid., p. 42.

21. Michael A. Lerner, et al., "New War on Health Costs," *Newsweek* (May 9, 1983), p. 29.

22. Paul Starr, "Medicine Has Overdrawn Its Credit in American Society," *U.S. News & World Report* (September 12, 1983), p. 77.

23. Janice Castro, "Prescription for Profits: Private Hospital Firms Bring Management Skills to the Bedside," *Time* (July 4, 1983), pp. 42–43.

24. See Robert V. Pattison and Hallie M. Katz, "Investor Owned and Not-For-Profit Hospitals," *New England Journal of Medicine* 309 (August 11, 1983): 347–53.

25. Abigail Trafford and Clemens P. Work, "Soaring Health Costs: The Brewing Revolt," *U.S. News & World Report* (August 22, 1983), pp. 39–42; see also Thomas W. Moloney and David E. Rogers, M.D., "Medical Technology— A Different View of the Contentious Debate Over Costs," *New England Journal of Medicine* 301 (1979): 1413–19.

26. Trafford and Work, "Soaring Health Costs," p. 39.

27. Ibid.

28. Ibid.

29. Harris Poll, reported in *The New York Times,* June 12, 1977, p. 55.

30. Department of Health and Human Services, *The Impact of Foreign-Trained Doctors on the Supply of Phy-*

sicians (Washington, D.C.: U.S. Government Printing Office, 1982).

31. Paula Span, "Where Have All the Robots Gone?" *New York Times Magazine* (February 22, 1981), pp. 70–100.

32. See Howard S. Becker, et al., *Boys in White: Culture in Medical School* (Chicago: University of Chicago Press, 1961).

33. Jethro K. Lieberman, *The Litigious Society* (New York: Basic Books, 1981), pp. 66–92.

34. Ferris J. Ritchey, "Medical Rationalization, Cultural Lag, and the Malpractice Crisis," *Human Organization* (Summer 1981), pp. 97–111.

35. Lieberman, *The Litigious Society,* p. 67.

36. Ibid.

37. David Blumenthal and James Fallows, "Health: The Care We Want and Need," *The Washington Monthly* (October 1973), p. 6.

38. Ibid.

39. "Soaring Health Costs," p. 40.

40. Ibid.

41. "Must Doctors' Fees Be So High?" p. 39.

42. A. F. Ehrbar, "A Radical Prescription," *Fortune* (February 1977), pp. 165–72.

43. John Colombotos, Corinne Kirchner, and Michael Millman, "Physicians View National Health Insurance: A National Study," *Medical Care* 13 (May 1975), pp. 369–96.

44. Ibid., Jane Bryant Quinn, "Surgery for Medical Costs," *Newsweek* (April 11, 1983), p. 60.

45. "Soaring Hospital Costs," p. 41.

46. "New War on Health Costs," p. 29.

47. "Soaring Hospital Costs," p. 41.

48. Ibid.; "New War on Health Costs," p. 29; Marvin M. Kristein, Charles B. Arnold, and Ernest L. Wynder, "Health Economics and Preventive Care," *Science* 195 (1977): 457–62.

49. Ibid.

50. Matt Clark, et al., "When Doctors Play

God,'' *Newsweek* (August 31, 1981), p. 49.

51. Ted Gest, ''Abortions in America: ABC's of a Raging Battle,'' *U.S. News & World Report* (January 24, 1983), p. 47.

52. Ibid., p. 48.

53. Michael J. Witkin, *Trends in Patient Care Episodes in Mental Health Facilities, 1955 to 1977* (Rockville, Md.: Department of Health and Human Services, 1980), p. 2.

54. President's Commission on Mental Health, *Report to the President,* Vol. 1 (Washington, D.C.: U.S. Government Printing Office, 1978), p. 8.

55. Ted Gest, ''Criminally Insane: Turned Loose Too Soon?'' *U.S. News & World Report* (June 27, 1983), pp. 52–55.

56. Ibid., p. 54.

57. Robert E. L. Faris and H. Warren Dunham, *Mental Disorders in Urban Areas* (Chicago: University of Chicago Press, 1939).

58. August B. Hollingshead and Frederick C. Redlich, *Social Class and Mental Illness:* A Community Study (New York: Wiley, 1958).

59. Leo Srole, et al., *Mental Health in the Metropolis: The Midtown Manhattan Study,* Books 1 and 2, rev. ed. (New York: Harper and Row, 1978).

60. President's Commission on Mental Health, *Report to the President,* p. 6.

61. See Phyllis Chesler, *Women and Madness* (New York: Avon, 1972).

62. Ibid. See also Pauline B. Bart, ''Depression in Middle-Aged Women,'' in Vivian Gornick and Barbara K. Moran (eds.), *Women in Sexist Society* (New York: Basic Books, 1971), pp. 163–86.

63. R. H. Rosenman, et al., ''Coronary Heart Disease in Western Collaborative Group Study—A Follow-Up Experience of 4½ Years,'' *Journal of Chronic Diseases* 23 (1970): 173.

64. Thomas Scheff, *Being Mentally Ill: A Sociological Theory* (Chicago: Aldine, 1966).

65. Talcott Parson, *The Social System* (New York: Free Press, 1951), pp. 428–73.

66. Erving Goffman, *Asylums: Essays on the Social Situation of Mental Patients and Other Inmates* (Garden City, N.Y.: Doubleday/Anchor, 1961), p. xii.

67. See ''Medicine Dares to Dream of the Impossible,'' *U.S. News & World Report* (May 9, 1983), pp. 116–17.

68. See Rick J. Carlson, *The End of Medicine* (New York: Wiley, 1975).

Chapter 15

1. Conrad H. Waddington, *The Man-Made Future* (New York: St. Martin's Press, 1978), pp. 167–70; see also Jean Gottman, *Megalopolis: The Urbanized Northeastern Seaboard of the United States* (New York: Twentieth Century Fund, 1961).

2. William A. Caldwell (ed.), *How to Save Urban America* (New York: Signet, 1973), pp. 45–56.

3. Caldwell, *How to Save Urban America,* pp. 216–17.

4. Harriet T. Taggart and Kevin W. Smith, ''Redlining: An Assessment of the Evidence of Disinvestment in Metropolitan Boston,'' *Urban Affairs Quarterly* 17 (1981), pp. 9–107.

5. J. John Palen, *The Urban World,* (New York: McGraw-Hill, 1981), p. 263.

6. Joseph P. Fried, ''Arson: A Devastating Big-City Crime,'' *New York Times* (August 14, 1977), p. E4.

7. Morton J. Schussheim, ''Housing in Perspective,'' *Public Interest* (Spring 1979).

8. Jeanne R. Lowe, *Cities in a Race with Time* (New York: Random House, 1967), Chapter 6.

9. Scott Greer, *Urban Renewal and American Cities* (Indianapolis: Bobbs-Merrill, 1965), p. 3.

10. Herbert Gans, *The Urban Villagers,* expanded ed. (New York: Free Press, 1983).

11. Oscar Newman, *Defensible Space* (New York: Macmillan, 1972).

12. ''How to Cure Traffic Jams,'' *U.S.*

News & World Report (June 9, 1969), p. 63.

13. Francis Bello, "The City and the Car," in A. N. Cowings and H. Nagpaul (eds.), *Urban Man and Society* (New York: Knopf, 1957).

14. J. Palen, "The Urban Nexus: Toward the Year 2000," p. 143, in Amos H. Hawley (ed.), *Social Growth* (New York: Free Press, 1979).

15. J. John Palen, *The Urban World* (New York: McGraw-Hill, 1975), p. 315.

16. John Bollens and Henry Schmandt, *The Metropolis*, 3rd ed. (New York: Harper and Row, 1975), pp. 140–41.

17. Bureau of Labor Statistics, U.S. Department of Labor, March 1984.

18. Rushworth M. Kidder, "The Northeast Rebounds," *The Christian Science Monitor* (January 1983), p. 1.

19. Ibid., p. 14.

20. Ibid.

21. Peter Hall, *The World Cities* (New York: McGraw-Hill, 1966), p. 239.

22. Ibid.

23. Palen, *The Urban World*, 2nd ed., pp. 259–60.

24. Jean Gottman, "Urban Centrality and the Interweaving of Quarternary Activities," in Gwen Bell and J. Tyrwhitt (eds.), *Human Identity in the Urban Environment* (Baltimore, Md.: Penguin, 1972), pp. 499–515.

25. Ibid.

26. Theodore J. Lowi, "Machine Politics—Old and New," in J. John Palen (ed.), *City Scenes, Problems and Prospects,* 2nd ed. (Boston: Little, Brown, 1981), pp. 214–17.

27. Geoffry K. Payne, *Urban Housing in the Third World* (Boston: Routledge & Kegan Paul, 1977).

28. Lawrence Susskind, "Public Participation and Consumer Sovereignty in an Era of Cutback Planning," pp. 97–98, in E. W. Hanten, M. J. Kasoff, and F. S. Redburn (eds.), *New Directions for the Mature Metropolis* (Cambridge, Mass.: Schenkman, 1980).

29. See Donald Appleyard, *Liveable Streets* (Berkely, Calif.: University of California Press, 1980).

30. Jane Jacobs, *The Death and Life of Great American Cities* (New York: Vintage, 1961), pp. 150–151.

31. Barbara Basler, "In Belmont Area of South Bronx, Fear and Crime Are Remote Concerns," *New York Times* (February 10, 1981), p. B1.

32. Alfred J. Kahn, *Theory and Practice of Social Planning* (New York: Russell Sage Foundation, 1969).

Chapter 16

1. Rafael Salas, "World Population Growth: Hopeful Signs of a Slowdown," *The Futurist* 12 (October 1978), pp. 276–82.

2. Eric Eckholm, "The Age of Extinction," *The Futurist* 12 (February 1978), pp. 299–300.

3. Betty D. Hawkins, "Cities and the Environmental Crisis," in Melvin Urofsky (ed.), *Perspective on Urban America* (Garden City, N.Y. Doubleday/Anchor Press, 1973), p. 180.

4. "Acid Rains and Poison Snows," *The Futurist* 13 (April 1979), pp. 153–54.

5. Charles B. Nam and Susan O. Gustavus, *Population: The Dynamics of Demographic Change* (Boston: Houghton Mifflin, 1976), p. 225.

6. Robert L. Heilbroner, *The Worldly Philosophers* (New York: Simon and Schuster, 1967), p. 76.

7. Dennis H. Wrong, *Population and Society* (New York: Random House, 1967), p. 102.

8. See Aurelio Peccei, *One Hundred Pages for the Future: Reflections of the President of the Club of Rome* (New York: Pergamon Press, 1981).

9. Mihajlo Mesarovic and Eduard Pestel, *Mankind at the Turning Point: The Second Report to the Club of Rome* (New York: E. P. Dutton, 1974).

10. Dennis L. Meadows, "The Predicament of Mankind," p. 215, in William R. Bursch (ed.), *Readings in Ecology,*

Energy, and Human Society (New York: Harper and Row, 1977).

11. Garret Hardin, "Living on a Lifeboat," in William R. Bursch (ed.), *Readings in Ecology, Energy, and Human Society,* pp. 217–24.

12. Janet Besecker and Phil Elder, "Lifeboat Ethics: A Reply to Hardin," pp. 225–26, in William R. Bursch (ed.), *Readings in Ecology, Energy, and Human Society: Contemporary Perspectives.*

13. Jay A. Weinstein, *Demographic Transition and Social Change* (Morristown, N.J.: General Learning Press, 1976), pp. 57–79.

14. Karen A. Miller and Alex Inkeles, "Modernity and Acceptance of Family Limitation in Four Developing Countries," *Journal of Social Issues* 30, (1974): 167–88.

15. Robert H. Weller and Leon F. Bouvier, *Population: Demography and Policy* (New York: St. Martin's Press, 1981), p. 42.

16. Lester R. Brown, "A Harvest of Neglect: The World's Declining Cropland," *The Futurist* 13 (April 1979), p. 148.

17. Ibid., p. 149.

18. *World Development Forum: Twice Monthly Report of Facts, Trends, and Opinion in International Development* (Washington, D.C.: The Hunger Project, May 31, 1983), p. 3.

19. Ibid., p. 2.

20. William W. Murdoch, *The Poverty of Nations: The Political Economy of Hunger and Population* (Baltimore, Md.: Johns Hopkins Press, 1980), p. 99.

21. The Hunger Project, *World Development Forum* 6 (January 31, 1983), pp. 3–4.

22. Eckholm, "The Age of Extinction," p. 300.

23. Ibid., p. 299.

24. "Acid Rains and Poison Snows," *The Futurist,* p. 153.

25. Frank E. Egler, "Pesticides in Our Ecosystem," in P. Shepard and D. McKinley (eds.), *The Subversive Science* (New York: Houghton Mifflin, 1969), p. 247.

26. Paul Ehrlich and J. P. Holdren, "Hidden Effects of Overpopulation," *The Saturday Review* (August 1, 1970), p. 52.

27. Ibid.

28. Gail Finsterbusch, *Man and Earth: Their Changing Relationship* (Indianapolis: Bobbs-Merrill, 1977), p. 42.

29. Egler, "Pesticides in Our Ecosystem," p. 256.

30. Finsterbusch, *Man and Earth: Their Changing Relationship,* p. 43.

31. G. M. Woodwell, W. M. Malcolm, and R. H. Whittaker, "A-Bombs, Bugbombs and Us," in Shepard and McKinley (eds.), *The Subversive Science,* p. 23.

32. Cy A. Adler, *Ecological Fantasies* (New York: Dell Books, 1973), p. 82.

33. Finsterbusch, *Man and Earth: Their Changing Relationship,* p. 37.

34. "Making the Weather Fit the Crops," *The Futurist* 12 (February 1979), p. 53.

35. Alan Schnaiberg, *The Environment: from Surplus to Scarcity* (New York: Oxford University Press, 1980), p. 34.

36. Arnold W. Reitze, "The Law of Pollution Control," in T. R. Armstrong (ed.), *Why Do We Still Have an Ecology Crisis?* (Englewood Cliffs, N.J.: Prentice-Hall, 1972), p. 76.

37. Hawkins, "Cities and the Environmental Crisis," pp. 168–69.

38. Reitz, "The Law of Pollution Control," p. 176.

39. David P. Rall, "What Needs to Be Done to Save the Environment: An Interview," *U.S. News & World Report* (February 7, 1977), p. 51.

40. Paul R. Ehrlich, *The Population Bomb* (New York: Sierra Club/Ballantine Books, 1971), p. 35.

41. Michael H. Brown, *Laying Waste* (New York: Washington Square Press, 1981), p. 105f.

42. Ibid., p. 108.

43. Michael H. Brown, "New Jersey

Cleans Up Its Pollution Act," *New York Times Magazine* (November 23, 1980), p. 145.

44. William R. Freudenberg and Kenneth M. Keating, "Increasing the Impact of Sociology on Social Impact Assessment," *The American Sociologist* 17 (1982): 71–80.

45. Michael S. Teitelbaum, "Population and Development: Is Consensus Possible?" *Foreign Affairs* (July 1974), pp. 742–60.

46. William R. Catton, Jr. and Riley E. Dunlap, "A New Ecological Paradigm for Post-Exuberant Sociology," *American Behavioral Scientist* 24 (1980): 18.

47. For the most outstanding example, see Herman Kahn, William Brown, and Leon Martel, *The Next 200 Years* (New York: Morrow, 1976).

48. Ehrlich, *The Population Bomb,* p. 140.

49. Stainbrook, "Mental Health and the Environment; Do We Need Nature?" p. 189, in R. A. Tybout (ed.), *Environmental Quality and Society* (Columbus, Ohio: Ohio State University Press, 1975).

50. Stephen Enke, "The Impact of Population Growth on the National Economy," in C. F. Westoff, et al. (eds.), *Toward the End of Growth* (Englewood Cliffs, N.J.: Prentice-Hall, 1973), p. 99.

51. Willis W. Harmon, "The Coming Transformation," *The Futurist* 11 (June 1977), p. 6.

52. Marvin Cetron and Thomas O'Toole, "Careers with a Future," *The Futurist* 16 (June 1982), pp. 11–12.

53. Ehrlich, *The Population Bomb,* p. 141.

54. Nancy Felipe Russo, "The Motherhood Mandate," *Journal of Social Issues* 32 (1976), p. 144.

55. Larry Bumpass and C. F. Westoff, "The 'Perfect Contraceptive' Population," in P. Reining and I. Tinker (eds.), *Population: Dynamics, Ethics, and Policy* (Washington, D.C.: American Association for the Advancement of Science, 1975), pp. 68–72.

56. Duane S. Elgin and Arnold Mitchell, "Voluntary Simplicity: Life Style of the Future?" *The Futurist* 2 (August 1977), p. 202.

57. E. F. Schumacher, *Small Is Beautiful* (New York: Harper and Row, Perennial Library, 1973).

58. Ibid., p. 155.

59. "Small Is Beautiful: Recent Thoughts from E. F. Schumacher," *The Futurist* 11 (April 1977), p. 93.

60. Barry Commoner, "The Economic Meaning of Ecology," in J. H. Skolnick and E. Currie (eds.), *Crisis in American Institutions* (Boston: Little, Brown, 1982), p. 292.

61. Brown, *Laying Waste,* p. 292.

62. Commoner, "The Economic Meaning of Ecology," p. 292.

63. Ibid., p. 296.

64. Margaret Mead, "Preface," in Reining and Tinker, *Population: Dynamics, Ethics and Policy,* pp. v–vi.

65. "An Interview with Bruce Chapman," 1982, p. 52.

66. Robert Bierstedt, "The Quality of Society," in Tybout (ed.), *Environmental Quality and Society,* p. 109.

67. Harmon, "The Coming Transformation," p. 6.

68. *Newsweek* (May 24, 1982), p. 46.

69. Bernard Berelson, "Beyond Family Planning," in Gwenn Bell and Jacqueline Tyrwhitt (eds.), *Human Identity in the Urban Environment* (Baltimore, Md.: Penguin, 1972), pp. 195–209.

70. Lane Jennings, "Counting Our Troubles," a review of Anthony Judge and James Wellesley-Wesley (eds.), *Yearbook of World Problems and Human Potential, The Futurist* 11 (June 1977), pp. 184–85.

71. The Hunger Project, *World Development Forum* (May 31, 1983), p. 4.

Chapter 17

1. See Daniel Bell, *The Coming of Post-Industrial Society* (New York: Basic Books, 1973).

2. Carey W. English, "Why They Call Midwest the 'Rust Bowl,'" *U.S. News*

& World Report (January 17, 1983), pp. 26–27.

3. A. F. Ehrbar, "Grasping the New Unemployment," *Fortune* (May 16, 1983), pp. 106–12.

4. Benjamin M. Cole, "As Business Copes with "White-Collar Bloat,'" *U.S. News & World Report* (May 2, 1983), p. 69.

5. Ibid., pp. 69–70.

6. Ibid., p. 70.

7. *Report of the National Commission on Technology, Automation, and Economic Progress* (Washington, D.C.: U.S. Government Printing Office, 1965).

8. See Alvin Toffler, *The Third Wave* (New York: Morrow, 1980).

9. Ibid., p. 238.

10. "Advances in Automation Prompt Concern over Increased U.S. Unemployment," pp. 14–15.

11. Howard N. Fullerton and John Tschetter, "The 1995 Labor Force: A Second Look," *Monthly Labor Review,* (November 1983), p. 3.

12. Toffler, *The Third Wave,* p. 233.

13. See, for example, "Workers Find 'Flextime' Makes for Flexible Living," *New York Times,* October 15, 1979; "Flexible Work Hours a Success, Study Says," *The New York Times,* November 9, 1977.

14. Charles Silberman and the editors of *Fortune, The Myths of Automation* (New York: Harper & Row, 1966), p. 21.

15. John S. Demott, "After the Mill Shuts Down," *Time* (August 15, 1983), p. 46.

16. Ibid.

17. Alfred Sloate, "When Factories Shut Down," *TransAction* 81 (January 1971), p. 14.

18. Harvey Brenner, *Mental Illness and the Economy* (Cambridge, Mass.: Harvard University Press, 1973).

19. Eleanor Hoover, "Unemployment Rated Major Mental Health Problem," *Los Angeles Times* (September 4, 1975), Pt. I, pp. 1, 22.

20. Ramsay Liem and Paula Rayman, "Health and Social Costs of Unemployment," *American Psychologist* (October 1982), pp. 1116–23.

21. D. D. Braginsky and B. M. Braginsky, "Surplus People: Their Lost Faith in Self and System," *Psychology Today* (August 1975), p. 70.

22. "Opinion Roundup," *Public Opinion* 4 (August/September 1981), pp. 21–40.

23. Special Task Force to the Secretary of Health, Education, and Welfare, *Work in America* (Cambridge, Mass.: MIT Press, 1973), p. 16.

24. "Job Satisfaction Found Waning, Notably Among More Educated," *New York Times* (December 17, 1978), p. 34; see also Anthony F. Chelte, James Wright, and Curt Tansky, "Did Job Satisfaction Really Drop During the 1970s?" *Monthly Labor Review* (November 1982), pp. 33–36.

25. Reported in *Work in America,* p. 13.

26. Eli Chinoy, *Automobile Workers and the American Dream* (Garden City, N.Y.: Doubleday, 1955), p. 21.

27. Harold L. Sheppard and Neil Q. Herrick, *Where Have All the Robots Gone?* (New York: Free Press, 1972).

28. Stanley Parker, *The Future of Work and Leisure* (New York: Praeger, 1971).

29. See Emma Rothschild, "Auto Production in Lordstown," *TransAction* (Winter 1979), pp. 330–42; Ezra Vogel, *Japan as Number One: Lessons for America* (Cambridge, Mass.: Harvard University Press, 1979): William Ouchi, *Theory Z: How American Business Can Meet the Japanese Challenge* (Reading, Mass.: Addison-Wesley, 1981).

30. Studs Terkel, *Working* New York: Random House, 1974).

31. See, for example, Mary Ann Maguire and Alice Kroliczak, "Attitudes of Japanese and American Workers: Convergence or Diversity," *The Sociological Quarterly* (Winter 1973), pp. 107–22.

32. For a good portrait of European workers, see Duncan Gallie, *In Search of the New Working Class* (Cambridge, U.K.: Cambridge University Press, 1980).

33. Robert Blauner, *Alienation and Freedom* (Chicago: University of Chicago Press, 1964), pp. 51–57.

34. Edward S. Greenberg, "Participation in Industrial Decision Making and Work Satisfaction: The Case of Producer Cooperatives," *Social Science Quarterly,* 60 (March 1980), pp. 551–69.

35. Rabi S. Bhagat and Marilyn B. Chassie, "Effects of Changes in Job Characteristics on Some Theory-Specific Attitudinal Outcomes: Results from a Naturally Occuring Quasi-Experiment," *Human Relations* 33 (1980), pp. 297–313.

36. Charles M. Futrell and A. Parasuraman, "Impact of Clarity of Goals and Role Perceptions on Job Satisfaction," *Perceptual and Motor Skills* 52 (1981), pp. 27–32.

37. Daniel Yankelovich, "The New Psychological Contracts at Work," *Psychology Today* (May 1978), p. 46.

38. See Patricia A. Renwick and Edward E. Lawler, "What You Really Want from Your Job," *Psychology Today* (July 1978), p. 79.

39. Clifford J. Mattaz, "Some Determinants of Work Alienation," *The Sociological Quarterly* (Autumn 1981), pp. 515–29.

40. Associated Press, "More Workers Give Bosses Poor Grades," *Bergen Record* (December 15, 1982), p. C23.

41. Abraham Maslow, *Motivation and Personality* (New York: Harper and Row, 1954), pp. 35–47.

42. Frederick Herzberg, *Work and the Nature of Man* (New York: World, 1966).

43. Daniel Zwerdling, *Workplace Democracy* (New York: Harper and Row, 1980).

44. James O'Toole, "Thank God, It's Monday," *Wilson Quarterly* (Winter 1980).

45. "Big Talent Search Among Rank and File," *U.S. News & World Report* (November 30, 1981), pp. 54–55.

46. Ibid., p. 54.

47. See Daniel T. Rodgers, *The Work Ethic in Industrial America, 1850–1920* (Chicago: University of Chicago Press, 1978); Rogene A. Buchholz, "The Work Ethic Reconsidered," *Industrial and Labor Relations Review* 4 (1978): 450–59.

48. This concept is the basis for a functionalist analysis of deviance growing out of the discrepancies between culturally approved goals and means for achieving them in Robert K. Merton, *Social Theory and Social Structure* (New York: Free Press, 1968).

49. See Robert Lekachman, "The Specter of Full Employment," *Harper's* (February 1977), pp. 35–40.

50. Peter L. Berger, "Some General Observations on the Problem of Work," in Peter L. Berger (ed.), *The Human Shape of Work* (New York: Macmillan, 1964), p. 215.

51. Ibid.

52. Lillian B. Rubin, *Worlds of Pain: Life in the Working-Class Family* (New York: Basic Books, 1976), pp. 114–33.

53. Kate Keating, "How Is Work Affecting American Families?" *Better Homes and Gardens* (February 1982), pp. 19–34.

54. See Henry E. Sigerst, *Civilization and Disease* (Chicago: University of Chicago Press, 1962).

55. Bureau of the Census, *Statistical Abstract of the United States, 1984* (Washington, D.C.: U.S. Government Printing Office, 1984), Tables 732–733, pp. 442–443.

56. Michael Mandel, "Labeling Chemicals: What's in a Name?" *Technology Review* (August/September 1981), pp. 76–77.

57. Devra Lee Davis, "Cancer in the Workplace," *Environment* (July/August 1981), p. 29.

58. Mandel, "Labeling Chemicals," p. 76.

59. "A Crack in the Armor," *Environment* (July/August 1981), p. 29.

60. Erik P. Eckholm, *The Picture of Health* (New York: Norton, 1977).

61. Erik P. Eckholm, "Unhealthy Jobs,"

Environment (August/September 1977), p. 34.

62. Jerry DeMuth, "Brown Lung in the Cotton Mill," *America* (March 18, 1978), p. 108.

63. Three particularly helpful writings are Martin Morf, "Eight Scenarios for Work in the Future," *The Futurist* (June 1983), pp. 24–29; Sar A. Levitan and Clifford M. Johnson, "The Future of Work: Does It Belong to Us or the Robots?" *Monthly Labor Review,* (September 1982), pp. 10–14; Herman Kahn, William Brown, and Leon Martel, *The Next 200 Years* (New York: Morrow, 1976).

64. This term was coined by Ivan Illich.

65. These possibilities are envisioned by Toffler, *The Third Wave,* pp. 181–93.

Chapter 1

Opener: Paul Light/Lightwave. Page 12: Ames Room, Reprinted with permission of Science Digest. © The Hearst Corp. 1969. All Rights Reserved. page 15: Charles Gatewood/Image Works. Page 18: Lewis Hine/Library of Congress. Page 20: Ellis Herwig/Stock Boston. Page 26: Harvey Stein. Page 31: Alan Carey/Image Works.

Chapter 2

Opener: Bobbi Carrey/picture Cube. Page 45: Bohdan Hrynewych/Southern Light. Page 52: David Strickler/Picture Cube. Page 57: Cathy Cheney/EKM-Nepenthe. Page 58: Ellis Herwig/Stock Boston. Page 59: Owen Franken/Stock Boston. Page 61: Drawing by Henry Martin. © 1971 The New Yorker Magazine, Inc.

Chapter 3

Opener: Charles Gatewood/Image Works. Page 74: Jerry Howard/Stock Boston. Page 78: Margaret Thompson/Picture Cube. Page 85: Peter Menzel/Stock Boston. Page 96: Owen Franken/Stock Boston. Page 99: Michael Hayman/Stock Boston. Page 103: Mark Antman/Image Works.

Chapter 4

Opener: Frank Siteman/Stock Boston. Page 113: Leonard Speier. Page 117: Barbara Alper/Stock Boston. Page 121: Mario Ruiz/Picture Group. Page 124: Eric Roth/Picture Cube. Page 130: Charles Gatewood/Image Works. Page 133: Marilyn L. Schrut.

Chapter 5

Opener: Owen Franken/Stock Boston. Page 151: Josephus Daniels/Photo Researchers. Page 155: Alan Carey/Image Works. Page 156: AP/Wide World Photos. Page 158: © Richard Tennant. Page 160: Jay Paris/Picture Group. Page 170: Steve Hansen/Stock Boston.

Chapter 6

Opener: Leonard Speier. Page 185: Mark Antman/Image Works. Page 187: Jerry Bernot/Stock Boston. Page 189: Christopher Brown/Stock Boston. Page 195: Daniel Morrison/Picture Cube. Page 200: Jean-Claude LeJeune/EKM-Nepenthe. Page 202: AP/Wide World Photos.

Chapter 7

Opener: Jill Cannefax/EKM-Nepenthe. Page 223: Tom Cheek/Stock Boston. Page 225: Alan Carey/Image Works. Page 231: Jean-Marie Simon/Taurus Photos. Page 236: Peter Menzel/Stock Boston. Page 241: Elizabeth Crews/Stock Boston.

Chapter 8

Opener: Lionel J-M Delevingne/Stock Boston. Page 253: Cary Wolinsky/Stock Boston. Page 257: Elizabeth Hamlin/Stock Boston. Page 256: Frank Siteman/Picture Cube. Page 260: Sharon Fox/Picture Cube. Page 266: Nicholas Sapieha/Stock Boston. Page 274: AP/Wide World Photos.

PHOTO CREDIT LIST

Chapter 9

Opener: Jean-Marie Simon/Taurus Photos. Page 289: Tim Jewett/EKM-Nepenthe. Page 290: Eric Kroll/Taurus Photos. Page 296: Ruth Silverman/Stock Boston. Page 302: George Gardner/Stock Boston. Page 310: Hazel Hankin. Page 314: Alan Carey/Image Works.

Chapter 10

Opener: Leonard Speier. Page 325: Sarah Putnam/Picture Cube. Page 327: Laimute Druskis. Page 329 (top): Steven Stone/Picture Cube. Page 329 (bottom): Courtesy the Bancroft Library, University of California, Berkeley/EKM-Nepenthe. Page 332: Frank Siteman/Taurus Photos. Page 334: Ken Robert Buck/Stock Boston. Page 337: Joan Menschenfreund/Taurus Photos.

Chapter 11

Opener: Peter Menzel/Stock Boston. Page 360: Frank Siteman/Taurus Photos. Page 363: Judith Sedwick/Picture Cube. Page 368: Hazel Hankin. Page 370: Alan Decker/Picture Group. Page 376: Eric Kroll/Taurus Photos. Page 382: Paul Fortin/Picture Group.

Chapter 12

Opener: Janice Fullman/Picture Group. Page 396: Alan Carey/Image Works. Page 398: Arthur Grace/Stock Boston. Page 402: David Powers/Stock Boston. Page 415: Doug Bruce/Picture Group. Page 418: Bohdan Hrynewych/Picture Group. Page 421: Harvey Stein.

Chapter 13

Opener: Leonard Speier. Page 436: Alan Carey/Image Works. Page 438: McDonnell Douglas Corporation. Page 440: Jean-Louis Atlan/Sygma. Page 441: James Holland/Stock Boston. Page 445: Cynthia Benjamins/Picture Group. Page 453: Peter Menzel/Stock Boston.

Chapter 14

Opener: Richard Wood/Picture Cube. Page 464: Paul Fortin/Picture Group. Page 467: Bodhan Hrynewych/Stock Boston. Page 470: David Witbeck/Picture Cube. Page 472: Sherry Suris/Photo Researchers. page 476: Courtesy Health Care Plan of New Jersey, Inc. Page 483: Frank Siteman/Taurus Photos.

Chapter 15

Opener: Mark Antman/Image Works. Page 507: Paul Ockrassa. Page 508: U.S. Department of Housing and Urban Development. Page 510: Eric Kroll/Taurus Photos. Page 512: Ellis Herwig/Stock Boston. Page 513: Dean Abramson/Stock Boston. Page 518: Bob East/Picture Group.

Chapter 16

Opener: Barbara Alper/Stock Boston. Page 538: Mark Antman/Image Works. Page 541: USDA Soil Conservation Service. Page 542: David Austin/Stock Boston. Page 549: Eric Kroll/Taurus Photos. Page 553: Leonard Speier. Page 564: Susan Berkowitz/Taurus Photos.

Chapter 17

Opener: Frank Siteman/Picture Cube. Page 571: Hazel Hankin. Page 574: Eric Kroll/Taurus Photos. Page 584: Lionel Delevingne/Picture Cube. Page 590: J. D. Sloan/Picture Cube. Page 593: Cathy Cheney/EKM-Nepenthe. Page 597: Anestis Diakopoulos/Picture Cube.

AA, 102
Ability grouping, 397-399
Abortion, 477-479
Absolute deprivation, 287-288
Acid rain, 544
Acker, J., 343
Acquired Immune Deficiency Syndrome,
    see AIDS
Activity theory, 240-241
Addiction, 77
AFDC, 311-312
Affirmative Action, 258, 260
Ageism, 218, 220-222
Aging:
  in America:
    demographics of, 216-218
  statistics of, 216
    values about, 218-222
  facts about, 215
  future of, 243-246
  myths about, 222-224
  problems of:
    economic, 227-230
    exploitation, 237-239, 371
    health care, 232-237
    housing, 232
    retirement, 225-227
  sociological perspectives of:
    conflict theory, 242
    individual faults, 239-240
    institutional faults, 240-242
    interaction emphasis, 242-243
  stereotypes of, 222-223
  and value systems, 216
Aid to families with dependent children,
    311-312
AIDS, 119-120
Air pollution, 547-548
Alcohol:
  dangers of, 73-74

effects of, 73
facts about, 71
and social problems, 72-73
use of, 74-75
Alcoholics Anonymous, 102
Alienation:
  definition of, 41
  and human commodity, 59-60
  and powerlessness, 56-57
  and self-estrangement, 57-58
  in work, 582, 591
Altruistic escape, 55
AMA, 465-468, 489-490
American Indians, see Native Americans
American Medical Association,
    465-468
American success syndrome, 588-589
Amphetamines, 76
Anabaptists, 192-193
Anomie:
  conditions of, 50-51
  and cults, new, 54-56
  definition of, 41
  and drugs, 88
  and functionalists, 51
  and loss of community, 49-50
  and secularization, 53-54
  and vagueness, 53
Anslinger, Harry J., 90-91
Antagonistic drugs, 103-104
Anthropocentrism, 552
Appleyard, Donald, 521
Appreciative orientation, 26-27
Appropriate technology, 554-555
Aquifers, 549
Assassination, 193
Assimilation, 277
AT&T, 431
Authoritarian personality, 272-273
Automation, 572-573, 576-577

Banfield, Edward, 301
Bart, 330
Battered wives, 375
Bem, Daryl J., 326
Bem, Sandra L., 326
Bengston, Vern L., 242
Berelson, Bernard, 559
Berger, Peter, 53, 60, 592
Berger, Warren, 174
Bernard, Jessie, 347
Betz, Michael, 305
"Beyond Family Planning," 559
Bioethics, 477-479
Black Americans, 260-261, 268-269
Blaming the victim, 303
Blauner, Robert, 584
Bohannan, Paul, 363
Bonger, Wilem, 165-166
Bradbury, Ray, 63
Brave New World, 558
Brown, Michael, 549
Brownmiller, Susan, 129, 134
Bumpass, Larry, 365, 554
Bumper-rapists, 127
Burnout, 419
Business ethic, 552
Busing, 254-256, 403

Caffeine, 72, 75-76
California Achievement Tests, 399
California Psychological Inventory, 163
Cambridge-Somerville study, 171
Cannon, Susan F., 122
CAT, 399
CETA, 311
Cetron, Marvin, 552-553
Character-flaw fallacy, 21
Chemical dumping, 548-549
Child abuse, 370-371, 375
Children in need of supervision, 160

INDEX

CHINS, 160
Cities:
  background of, 502
  facts about, 501
  future of, 527-529
  housing problems of:
    abandonment, 503-504
    defensible space, 505, 508
    gentrification, 508-509, 511
    public housing, 504-505
    redlining, 503-504
    subsidies, 505
    urban renewal, 504
  policy failures of, 520-522
  political fragmentation in, 519-520
  snowbelt, 514-518
  sociological perspectives of:
    conflict theory, 523-526
    individual faults, 522
    institutional faults, 523
    interaction emphasis, 526
  sunbelt, 513-514
  transportation problems of, 511-512
  and urban America, 502-503
Citizen groups, 452-453
Closed-awareness, 237
Cloward, Richard A., 21, 164-165, 305-306
Cobb, J., 56
Cocaine, 71, 77-78, 80-81
Cohabitation, 359, 361
Coleman, James S., 257, 416
Coleman Report, 257, 401-402
Collaborative planning, 520-521
Commercial-exploitive sex, *see* Pornography
Commodity-self, 58-60
Commoner, Barry, 555-556
Community, 49-50
Compensatory education, 419
Comprehensive Employment and Training Act, 311
Computer-related crime, 156-158
Conflict theory:
  and aging, 242
  and cities, 523-526
  and crime, 165-166
  and drugs, 89-91
  and ecology, 555-556
  and education, 412-413
  and families, 379-380
  and health care, 489-490
  and political power, 449-450
  and population, 555-556
  and poverty, 305-306

  and race relations, 275-276
  and sexism, 343-344
  and sexual expression, 134
  view of, 29-30
  and violence, 204
  and work, 591-592
Conglomerates, 430
Conscription system, 198
Consumer manipulation, 434
Contrast conceptions, 205
Control dilemma, 558-562
Control group, 171
Cook, F. L., 21
Cook, Kenneth H., 8-9, 11
Cost/Benefit Analyses, 17
Cost overruns, 438
Crime:
  computer, 156-158
  and criminal justice system, 167-169
  and deviance, 144-145
  explanations of:
    physical, 162
    psychological, 163
    sociological, 163-166
  facts about, 143
  future of, 174-176
  history of, 145-146
  and juvenile delinquency, 158-162
  and laws, 146-147
  prosecution of, 146-147
  punishment of, 145-146
  reported:
    and existence of crime, 150-152
    index crimes, 148-149
    Uniform Crime Report, 147-148
    victimization reports, 149
  sociological perspectives of:
    conflict theory, 165-166
    individual faults, 163-164
    institutional faults, 164-165
    interaction emphasis, 166
  solutions to, 171-174
  unreported, 150-152
  violent, 186-189
  white-collar, 152-156
Criminal justice system:
  and ethnic groups, 263-264
  police, 167
  prisons, 167-169
  and sexism, 339-341
  solutions for, 172-174
Criminal terrorism, 192
Crisis in the Classroom, 394
Cronbach, Lee J., 398
Cross-impact analysis, 33

Cross-impacts, 33
Crouch, Wayne W., 8-9, 11
Cults, 54-56
Cultural lag, 19-21
Cultural programming, 46-47
Culture of poverty, 301

Data diddling, 156
DDT, 544, 546
Defensible space, 505, 508
Demaris, Ovid, 193
Demographic transition, 536-537
Demography, 589-590
Department of Defense, 437
Dependency ratio, 229
Depressants, 73, 79
Desegregation, 254-256
Detroit Syndrome, 221
Deviance:
  and aging, 239-240
  and cities, 522
  and crime, 144-145, 163-164
  and drugs, 86-88
  and education, 409-410
  and families, 377-378
  and health care, 487
  and political power, 447-448
  and population, 554
  and poverty, 300-303
  primary, 135, 166
  and race relations, 272-275
  secondary, 135, 166
  and sexism, 341-342
  and sexual expression, 112-113, 132, 135
  tertiary, 135
  view of, 23, 26-27
  and violence, 203
  and work, 588-589
Discrimination, 252
Disengagement theory, 241-242
Divorce:
  factors contributing to, 361-362
  impact of:
    on adults, 362-363
    on children, 364-365
  in past, 377-378
  rate of, 361
Doctors, 471-473
DOD, 437
Dole, Vincent, 87
Domhoff, G. William, 447
Dominant Western world view, 552
Douglas, Ann, 326
Drag, *see* Transvestism

Drugs:
  alcohol, 72-75
  amphetamines, 76
  antagonistic, 103-104
  attitudes about, 86
  caffeine, 76-77
  consequences of using:
    accidents, automobile, 94-96
    crime, 93-94
    economic losses, 97-99
    health, 96-97
    sports, professional, 99-100
  control of:
    British approach, 104-105
    corrective efforts, 104
    in past, 100-101
    preventive programs, 101-102
    treatment programs, 102-104
  and cultural factors, 92
  definition of, 72
  depressants, 73, 79
  facts about, 71, 83
  future of, 105-106
  and interest groups, 90-91
  marijuana, 71-72, 79
  narcotics, 83-84
  and norms, societal, 92
  psychoactive, 72
  and social class, 89-90
  sociological perspectives of:
    conflict theory, 89-91
    individual faults, 86-88
    institutional faults, 88-89
    interaction emphasis, 91-93
  subcultures of, 92-93
  tobacco, 71, 84-85
Du Ponts, 429
Durkheim, Emile, 13, 41, 44, 51, 582
Dye, Thomas R., 444

Ecology:
  facts about, 533
  future of, 562-565
  problems of:
    in New Jersey, 550
    persistence of, 550-553
    practices, dangerous, 547-550
    problems of ecosystem, 546-547
    thinking of ecosystem, 544-545
  sociological perspectives of:
    conflict theory, 555-556
    individual faults, 554
    institutional faults, 554-555
    interaction emphasis, 556-558
  and threshold effect, 545

  and trigger effect, 545
Economic power, *see* Political power
Ecosystem, 544. *See also* Ecology
Education:
  bureaucracy in, 394-395
  characteristics of, 392-393
  compensatory, 419
  compulsory, 392-393
  contradictions of, 392-393
  cure for, 411
  decline of, 405-409
  facts about, 391
  future of, 420-422
  history of, 392
  improvement of:
    school districts, 414-418
    teachers, 418-420
  and integration, 400-405
  labeling in, 400-401
  and social class:
    ability grouping, 397-399
    middle-class values, 395-397
  sociological perspectives of:
    conflict theory, 412-413
    individual faults, 407-410
    institutional faults, 410-412
    interaction emphasis, 413-414
  universal, 392
Educational Opportunity Funds, 435
EHAP, 505
Ehrlich, Paul, 545, 552
Eisenhower, Dwight D., 436-437
Elderly, *see* Aging
Elgin, Duane S., 554
Engels, Friedrich, 379
Environmental Protection Agency, 549
EOF, 435
EPA, 549
Equality, ideal of, 212
*Essay on the Principle of Population,
  An,* 534
Ethnic groups, *see* Race relations
Euthanasia, 479
Eutrophication, 548
Experimental group, 171
Experimental Housing Allowance Pro-
  gram, 505
Extended family, 220, 372
Extinction, of species, 542-543
Extrinsic satisfaction, 587

Family:
  contemporary, 358-361
  definition of, 358
  and divorce, 361-365

  extended, 220, 372
  facts about, 357
  future of, 383-385
  help for, 381-383
  nuclear, 221, 372
  single-parent, 365-367
  sociological perspectives of:
    conflict theory, 379-380
    individual faults, 377-378
    institutional faults, 378-379
    interaction emphasis, 380-381
  violence in:
    of children, 370
    of elderly, 371
    factors linked to, 371-372
    incidence of, 367-369
    intervention in, 375-376
    prevention of, 376
    of runaways, 373
    sexual, 373-375
    of spouses, 369-370
Farenheit 451, 63
FCC, 434
FDA, 548
Federal Communications Commission,
  434
Federal Housing Administration, 503,
  505
Federal Housing Authority, 503, 505
Feldberg, Roslyn, 380
Feldman, Roger, 468
Feminine Mystique, The, 358
Feminization of poverty, 292
Fetal alcohol syndrome, 97
Fetal narcotic syndrome, 97
Fetishism, 123
FHA, 503, 505
Finkelor, David, 373-375
Food chains, 544-546
Food and Drug Administration, 548
Freud, Sigmund, 132
Friedan, Betty, 358
Frustration-aggression, 273-274
Functionalists, 28, 51, 56, 342-343
Fundamentalism, 54
Furstenberg, Frank F., 365

Galbraith, John Kenneth, 431
Gans, Herbert, 304-305, 504
Gardner, John W., 452
Gays, *see* Homosexuality
Geller, Daniel, 433
Gelles, Richard J., 367-368, 371-372,
  375
Gender roles, 344

Gentrification, 508-509, 511
Goetting, Ann, 364
Goffman, Erving, 490, 492
Goldberg's study, 328
Gottman, Jean, 517-518
Gould, Stephen Jay, 324
Grade inflation, 408, 409
Greenberg, Edward, 584
Greenhouse effect, 546
Guaranteed annual income, 306
Gurr, Ted R., 194

Hackers, 158
Hall, Peter, 515
Halo effect, 11
Hardin, Garret, 535-536
Harmon, Willis W., 552
Harrington, Michael, 290, 305
Health care:
    bioethics of, 477-479
    for elderly, 232-233
    factors in, 462
    facts about, 461
    future of, 492-494
    mental:
        medical model of, 482-484
        nature of, 482
        problems of, 479-482
        socioeconomic factors of, 484-486
    physical:
        and AMA, 465-568
        changes in, 463
        and doctors, 471-473
        and hospitals, 468-471
        and medical insurance, 473-475
        and medicalization, 463
        and modern medicine, 464-465
        and nurses, 471-473
        and private sector, 475-477
        social organization of, 465
    for poor, 297-298
    sociological perspectives of:
        conflict theory, 489-490
        individual faults, 487
        institutional faults, 487-489
        interaction emphasis, 490-492
Health-Maintenance Organizations,
    476-477
Hearst, Patty, 196
Helplessness, 219
Herman, Judith, 374
Hernnstein, Richard, 398
Heroin, 71, 93
Herrick, Neil Q., 583
Herzberg, Frederick, 587

Heterosexual, 112
Hezbellah, 194
Hidden Persuaders, The, 434
Hierarchy of needs, 587
Hirschi's Social Control Theory, 165
Hispanics, 261, 269
HMOs, 476-477
Holdren, J.P., 545
Homocide, 189-192
Homosexual, 114
Homosexuality:
    in America:
        and gay subculture, 118-120
        relationships in, 118
        treatment of, 115-116
    definitions of, 114
    deviation in, 113-114
    in Europe, Western, 115
    female, 118-119
    in Greece, Ancient, 114-115
    in preliterate societies, 115
    and sex, impersonal, 119-120
Hoover, J. Edgar, 451
Hospices, 237
Hospitals, 468-470
House Committee on Aging, 235
House Un-American Activities Commit-
    tee, 195
Housing:
    for elderly, 232
    for ethnic groups, 261-263
    for poor, 298
    public, 504-505
    subsidies, 505
HUAC, 195
Human rights, 267
Hunger, 541-542
Huxley, Aldous, 558

Ice-age effect, 546
Illegal aliens, 270-271
Impression management, 61-62
Incest, 373-375
Incidence, 16
Index crimes, 148-149
Index of Households touched by crime,
    150
Inkeles, Alex, 537
Institutionalized discrimination, 252
Institutions:
    and aging, 240, 240
    and cities, 523
    and crime, 164-165
    and drugs, 88-89
    and ecology, 554-555

and education, 410-412
examples of, 354
and families, 378-379
and health care, 487-489
and political power, 448-449
and population, 554-555
and poverty, 303-305
and race relations, 275
and sexism, 342-343
and sexual expression, 134
in society, 44-46
view of, 27-29
and violence, 203-204
and work, 589-591
Insurances, medical, 473-475
Interaction:
    and aging, 242-243
    and cities, 526
    and crime, 166
    and drugs, 91-93
    and ecology, 556-558
    and education, 413-414
    and families, 380-381
    and health care, 490-492
    and identities, 60-62
    and political power, 450
    and population, 556-558
    and poverty, 306-307
    and powerlessness, 330, 333
    and race relations, 276-277
    and sexism, 344-346
    and sexual expression, 134-135
    view of, 30-31
    and violence, 204-205
    and work, 592-594
Interaction powerlessness, 330, 333
Interconnectivity, 14
Interlocking directorates, 430
Internalized norms, 9, 11
International Telephone and Telegraph
    Company, 442-443
Interventionist approach, 316-317
Intrinsic satisfaction, 587
IQ tests, 399
IRA, 193
Irish Republican Army, 193
ITT, 442-443

Jacobs, Jane, 521
Jacobson, Lenore, 397
Jencks, Christopher, 395
Jensen, Arthur, 398
Jesuits, 193
Jorgensen, George, 120
Juvenile delinquency:

definition of, 158-160
explanations of:
  physical, 162
  psychological, 163
  sociological, 163-166
history of, 158
medical model of, 161
statistics on, 161-162
and status offenses, 160
violence in, 187-189
Juvenile Justice Code, 158-159

Kahn, Alfred, 521-522
Karp, David A., 62
Katzer, Jeffrey, 8-9, 11
Kelly, Joan, 364-365
Kessler, R. C., 336
Key, Wilson Bryan, 434
Keyes, Ralph, 59
Kidder, Rushworth, 515
Kohen, Janet, 380
Kohlberg, 341
Kropotkin, Alekseevitch, 196
Ku Klux Klan, 184
Kuypers, J. A., 242

Labeling theory:
  and deviance, 30-31
  in education, 399-401
  and poor, 307
  and sexual expression, 135
Ladder, 135
Lasch, Christopher, 59-60, 344
Latent consequences, 32
Law, 146
Laying Waste, 549
Lesbian, 118
Lewis, Oscar, 301
Lifeboat ethic, 535-536
Life expectancy, 216
Life span, 216
Limits to Growth, 535
Lockheed Aircraft, 438, 442

McNamara, Robert, 439
McRae, J. A., 336
Magnet schools, 416
Malpractice, 472-473
Malthus, Thomas R., 534-535
Mankind at the Turning Point, 535
Margolis, D. R., 341
Marijuana, 71-72, 79, 82
Marx, Karl, 449, 582
Maslow, Abraham, 587
Matza, David, 26

MCT, 407, 409
Mead, Margaret, 557
Meadows, Dennis L., 535
Medicaid, 474-475
Medical model, 161-162
Medicare, 474-475
Megalopolis, 502
Mental health
  disorders of, 482
  factors of, socioeconomic, 484-485
  medical model of, 482-484
  problems of, 479-482
Mercy killing, 479
Merton, Robert, 27, 32, 164
Methadone maintenance, 102-103
Metropolis, 511
Mexicans, 261,270-273
Migrant workers, 269-270
Milgram, Stanley, 433
Military-industrial complex, 436-437
Miller, Karen A., 537
Mills, C. Wright, 48, 59, 443-444
Minimum competency test, 407, 409
Minnesota Multiphasic Personality In-
  ventory, 163
Minors in need of supervision, 160
MINS, 160
Mismeasure of Man, The, 324
Mitchell, Arnold, 554
Motherhood mandate, 552-553
Multinational corporations, 440-443

Nader, Ralph, 452
Narcissism, 59-60
Narcotics, 83-84
National Commission on Excellence in
  Education, 405, 407
National Crime Survey, 149
National Education Association, 407
National family policy, 382
National Institute for Occupational Safe-
  ty and Health, 594-595
Native Americans, 264-267
NCS, 149
NEA, 407
Negotiated meanings, 30
Neighborhood Youth Corps, 311
Neo-Malthusian, 535
Neuroses, 482
Newman, Oscar, 505
New woman networks, 348
Nicotine, 84
NIOSH, 594-595
Nonmarital births, 367
Normlessness, 41

Nuclear family, 221, 372
Nurses, 471-473
Nursing homes, 233-237
Nyswander, Marie, 87

Occupation, *see* Work
Occupational ghetto, 336
Occupational identity, 592
Occupational Safety and Health Ad-
  ministrtion, 594-595
Ogburn, William F., 378
Ohlin, Lloyd, 164-165
Oligopoly, 428
Open-awareness, 237
Opiates, 83-84
Organismic analogy, 28
*Origin of the Family, Private Property
  and the State, The,* 379
OSHA, 594-595
O'Toole, Thomas, 552-553
Overmedicalization, 464-465

Packard, David, 439
Packard, Vance, 434
PACs, 435-436
Palen, J. John, 516-517
Parenti, Michael, 429
Parsons, Talcott, 378, 489
Party of God, 194
Passages, 221
Patriarchal unit, 374
Payne, Geoffrey, 520
PDC, 509
Pederasty, 114-115
People's Development Corporation, 509
People's Temple, The, 55-56
Persons in need of supervision, 160
Pesticides, 546
PINS, 160
Piven, Frances Fox, 21, 305-306
Pizzey, Erin, 375
Pluralism, 275
Pluralists, 444
Political action committees, 435-436
Political fragmentation, 519-520
Political power:
  and advertising, 434
  and corporate America:
    conglomerations, 430-431
    evils of, 431-432
    owners of corporations, 429-430
  facts about, 427
  future of, 453-455
  and government-corporate alliances:
    financial benefits, 435-436

military-industrial complex, 436-440
holders of:
  comparison of models, 445, 447
  pluralist model, 444-445
  power elite model, 443-444
and multinational corporations,
    440-443
and people, 451-453
sociological perspectives of:
  conflict theory, 449-450
  individual faults, 447-448
  institutional faults, 448-449
  interaction emphasis, 450
Population:
  in China, 560-561
  and control dilemma, 558-562
  facts about, 533
  future of, 562-565
  pressure of:
    extinction of species, 542-544
    growth, continuing, 538-540
    resource depletion, 540-541
    starvation, 541-542
    trends of, 537
  problem of, 534-537
    persistence of, 550-'553
  and resource depletion, 540-541,
    552-553
  sociological perspectives of:
    conflict theory, 555-556
    individual faults, 554
    institutional faults, 554-555
    interaction emphasis, 556-558
  and unemployment, 575
Pornography, 128-130
Poverty:
  in America, 286
  and elderly, 228
  elimination of, 315-317
  facts about, 285
  feminization of, 292
  future of, 317-319
  impact of, 297-299
  nature of, 286-290
  sociological perspectives of:
    conflict theory, 305-306
    individual faults, 300-303
    institutional faults, 303-305
    interaction emphasis, 306-307
  statistics of:
    and age, 293-296
    and family structure, 291-293
    and locale, 296-297
    in media, 290-291
    and minority status, 291

and welfare:
  for poor, 309-313
  for rich, 313-315
  work of, 308-309
Poverty index changes, 288
Power elite, 443
Powerlessness, 56-57, 330, 333
PPOs, 477
Preferred Provider Organizations, 477
Pregnancy, teenage, 357
Prevalence, 16
Price-fixing, 433
Pronatalism, 551
Propositions, 13
Prostitute, 130-132
Prostitution, 130-132
*Protestant Ethic and the Spirit of
    Capitalism, The,* 570
Proxmire, William, 437
Pruitt-Igoe, 505-507
Psychoactive drug, 72
Psychoses, 482

Quality of life, 40-41
Quality of work life, 587-588
Quasi-theories, 21-22
QWL, 587-588

Race relations:
  and discrimination, institutionalized:
    definition of, 252-253
    in education, 253-257
    in employment, 257-261
    in housing, 261-263
    in legal system, 263-264
  facts about, 251
  future of, 277-279
  problem areas of:
    Black Americans, 268-269
    Hispanics, 269
    illegal aliens, 270-271
    migrant workers, 269-270
    Native Americans, 264-267
  sociological perspectives of:
    conflict theory, 275-276
    individual faults, 271-275
    institutional faults, 275
    interaction emphasis, 276-277
Rape:
  definition of, 124-125
  marital, 126, 373-374
  prevention of, 126-128
  victim of, 125-126
  violence of, 191-192
Reagan, Ronald, 315, 392, 512

Redistricting, 415-416
Redlining, 503-504
Reefer Madness, 91
Regional Plan Association, 503
Regulatory agencies, 451-452
Relative deprivation, 288-290
Renvoize, Jean, 371
Repressive terrorism, 192
Residual norms, 487
Resource depletion, 540-541
Revolutionary terrorism, 192
Revolving door, 439-440
Riesman, David, 444
Rindfuss, Ronald, 364
Robin Hood approach, 316
Rockefeller, John D., 14
Rockefellers, 429
Role distance, 61
Role entrapment, 327
Role overabundance, 47-49
Romig, Dennis A., 171
Rose, Arnold M., 241, 444
Rosenthal, Robert, 397
Rubber-band boundary chart, 10
Rubin, Lillian, 593
Runaways, 373
Ryan, William, 303

Salami, 157
Sanctions, 113
SAT, 405-406
Scapegoating, 274
Scenarios, 33-34
Scheff, Thomas, 487
Scheffler, Richard, 468
Scholastic Aptitude Test, 405-406
School funding, 403-405
Schultz, George, 439
Schur, E., 56
Schutz, Alfred, 276
*Scream Quietly or the Neighbors Will
    Hear,* 375
Scully, 330
Secularization, 53-54
Sedative-hypnotics, 79
Self-estrangement, 57-58
Self-justification, 274-275
Semmelweis, Ignaz, 8-9
Sennet, Richard, 56
Senior citizens, *see* Aging
Serrano v. *Priest,* 404
Sexism:
  in advertising, 344
  areas of change in:
    education, 335-336

employment, 336-339
  legal system, 339-341
biological justification for, 324-325
effects of:
  biological limitations, 328-330
  powerlessness, 330-333
  sexual harassment, 333-335
  women as minority group, 328
facts about, 323
future of, 346-349
and religion, 325-326
and socialization, 325-327
sociological perspectives of:
  conflict theory, 343-344
  individual faults, 341-342
  institutional faults, 342-343
  interaction emphasis, 344-346
Sexual expression:
  conformity in, 112-115
  cross-cultural context of, 112-113
  deviance in, 112-115
  of elderly, 223-224
  facts about, 111
  future of, 135-138
  and homosexuality, *see* Homosexuality
  and pornography, 128-130
  and rape, *see* Rape
  and sexism, 328, 330
  sociological perspectives of:
    conflict theory, 134
    individual faults, 132
    institutional faults, 134
    interaction emphasis, 134-135
  and transsexualism, 120-123
  and transvestism, 123
Sexual harassment, 333
Sexual victimization, 373-375
Sheehy, Gail, 221
Sheppard, Harold L., 583
Shockley, Williams, 398
Silberman, Charles, 394
Silk, Leonard, 447
Silver, Maury, 433
Single-parent families, 365-367
Situationality of sex differences, 345
Skinner, B. F., 410
Skolnick, Jerome, 167
SLA, 196
Smith, Roger, 97
Social breakdown syndrome, 242-243
Social engineering, 412
Socialization, 325-327
Social policy, 24-25
Social problems:
  elements of:

damage, 16-17
  offense, 18-19
  persistence, 14-16
false causes of:
  cultural lags, 19-21
  invisible hand, 22
  quasi-theories, 21-22
future of, 32-34
impediments to defining, 6-7
and individual:
  future of, 62-66
  identities, 60-62
  impact of, 41, 43-49
  quality of life, 40-41
  see also Alienation; Anomie
people affected by, 2
policy nomenclature of, 24-25
and self-expression, 68. *See also*
  Drugs; Sexual expression
and social scientist:
  objectivity of, 11-12
  observation of, 8-11
  theory of, 12
  value judgments of, 7-8
views of, 22-23
  conflict theory, 29-30
  individual faults, 23-27
  institutional faults, 27-29
  interaction emphasis, 30-31
  see also Conflict theory; Deviance;
    Institutions; Interaction
Social promotions, 408
Social scientist:
  judgments of, 7-8
  objectivity of, 11-12
  observation of, 8-11
  theory of, 12
Social Security, 228-230
Society:
  change in, 498
  laws of, 146
  needs of, 354
  problems of, 6-7. *See also* Social
    problems
Software piracy, 158
Something About Amelia, 374
Sowell, Thomas, 260, 398-399
Specialization, 53
SSI, 230, 311
Stanford-Binet Intelligence Test, 399
Status offenses, 160
Stewardess syndrome, 59
Stimulants, 76
Stoddard, Ellwyn R., 154
Straight, 112

Stratification, 18-19
Straus, Murray, 371-372
Subculture of violence, 204
Suicide, 41, 44
Suicide, 13, 42-43, 238
Supplemental Security Income, 230, 311
Survivals, 19
Sutherland, Edwin H., 152-153
Sweatshops, 259
Symbionese Liberation Army, 196
Szasz, Thomas, 490

Teacher's expectations, 397
Technocrats, 431
Teitelbaum, Michael S., 551
Teledemocracy, 454
Telephone sex, 129
Terkel, Studs, 584
Terrorism:
  definition of, 192
  effectiveness of, 194-196
  international, 196-197
  justifications for, 194
  nuclear, 197
  in past, 192-193
  political, 194
  in present, 192-193
  reactions to, societal, 194
  and war, 197-198
Tertiary occupation, 570
  Theory, 13
Thomas, William I., 53
Tobacco, 71, 84, 86
Toffler, Alvin, 62, 394, 417
Tolerance, 76
Tönnies, Ferdinand, 49-50
Total institutions, 490, 492
Transactions, 518
Transformation, 60
Transportation, 511-512
Transsexual, 114
Transsexualism, 120-123
Transvestism, 123
Transvestite, 114
Trend, 16
Trend extrapolation, 33
Trend impact analysis, 33
Trickle-down approach, 315
Trojan horses, 156-157
Turned-out, 130

UCR, 147-148, 187
Unconscious ideology, 553
Unemployment:
  effects of, long-term, 579-581

problems of, 575
statistics of, 575-579
Uniform Crime Report, 147-148, 187
Unions, 258-260
Unsafe at Any Speed, 452
Unwanted fertility hypothesis, 554
Urban centrality, 518
Urban homesteading, 509
Urban renewal, 504
Urban sprawl, 502-503
Urban Villagers, The, 504

VA, 262
Vagueness, 53. *See also* Anomie
Valentine, Charles A., 303
Veteran's Administration, 262
Veto groups, 444
Vigilantism, 184
Violence:
  in America, 184
  criminal, 186-189
  facts about, 183
  in families:
    and child abuse, 370-371
    and elderly, 371
    factors linked to, 371-372
    and incest, 374-375
    incidences of, 367-370
    intervention in, 375-376
    and rape, 373-374
    and runaways, 373
  future of, 205-208
  and homicide, 189-192
  justifications of, 186
  as social problem, 185-186
  sociological perspectives of:
    conflict theory, 204
    individual faults, 203
    institutional faults, 203-204
    interaction emphasis, 204-205

subculture of, 204
and terrorism, *see* Terrorism
and war, *see* War
Violent crime, 186-189
Vogel, David, 447
Voter elite, 444-446
Voucher plans, 416-417

Waller, Willard, 33
Wallerstein, Judith S., 364-365
War:
  in America, 198-199
  nuclear, 199-201
  reasons for, 198
  and terrorism, 197-198
War on Poverty, 286, 302-303
War Production Board, 434
Water pollution, 548-549
WCTU, 89
Wealthfare, 313-315
Weber, Max, 570, 582
Weberian Paradox, 53
Weiss, Robert, 363
Welfare:
  and cash programs, 311-312
  definition of, 309
  effects of, 309-310
  and employment programs, 311
  fraud, 312
  and insurance programs, 310-311
  lifetime, 312-313
  rich, 313-315
  and services programs, 311
  and work, 308-309
Westoff, C. F., 554
Where Have All the Robots Gone?, 583
White-collar crime:
  in codes of profession, 154-155
  concept of, 152-153
  in corporations, 153-154

detection of, 156
and property offenses, 155
prosecution of, 156
Wilson, Charles F., 439
Wirth, Louis, 522
Withdrawal, 77
Women's Christian Temperance Union,
  89
Work:
  background of, 570
  facts about, 569
  future of, 598-599
  hazards in, 595-597
  health in, 594-597
  in Japan, 585
  and job satisfaction:
    attributes of, 586-588
    measuring of, 582-586
  and occupational trends, 570-573
  safety in, 594-597
  sociological perspectives of:
    conflict theory, 591-592
    individual faults, 588-589
    institutional faults, 589-591
    interaction emphasis, 592-594
  and unemployment problems:
    effects of, long-term, 579-581
    statistics of, 575-579
Work ethic, 588
Work in America, 582
Working, 584

Yankelovich, Daniel, 586
*Yearbook of World Problems and Human
  Potential,* 562
Yoels, William C., 62
Zero population growth, 217, 559
Zimbardo, Philip G., 44
Zimmerman, Carl, 377
ZPG, 217, 559